DATE DUE

~~OCT 1 4 2010~~	
~~APR 18 2011~~	
~~APR 3 0 2011~~	
May 23, 11	
June 14, 11	
July 5th, 11	
July 26, 2011	
SEP 2 4 2011	

Probation and Parole

Theory and Practice

Probation and Parole

Theory and Practice

Tenth Edition

Howard Abadinsky
St. John's University

PEARSON
Prentice
Hall

Upper Saddle River, New Jersey
Columbus, Ohio

Library of Congress Cataloging-in-Publication Data
Abadinsky, Howard
  Probation and parole: theory and practice/Howard Abadinsky.— 10th ed.
     p.cm.
  Includes bibliographical references and indexes.
  ISBN-13: 978-0-13-235005-1
  ISBN-10: 0-13-235005-X
  1. Probation—United States. 2. Parole—United States. I. Title.
  HV9278.A2 2009
  364.6'30973—dc22

                                                      2007037864

Editor-in-Chief: Vernon Anthony
Acquisitions Editor: Tim Peyton
Development Editor: Elisa Rogers
Editorial Assistant: Alicia Kelly
Production Coordination: Janet Bolton
Production Editor: Rex Davidson
Production Manager: Pat Tonneman
Design Coordinator: Diane Ernsberger
Cover Designer: Kristina Holmes
Cover Art/Chapter Opener Photo: Patti Sapone/Star Ledger/CORBIS
Director of Marketing: David Gesell
Marketing Manager: Adam Kloza
Senior Marketing Assistant: Alicia Dysert

This book was set in Janson by Aptara, Inc. and was printed and bound by Courier Kendallville, Inc. The cover was printed by Phoenix Color Corp.

Pearson Education Ltd.   Pearson Education Australia Pty, Limited
Pearson Education Singapore, Pte. Ltd.   Pearson Education North Asia Ltd.
Pearson Education Canada, Ltd.   Pearson Educacion de Mexico, S.A. de C.V.
Pearson Education—Japan   Pearson Education Malaysia, Pte. Ltd.

PEARSON
Prentice
Hall

10 9 8 7 6 5 4 3 2 1

ISBN-13: 978-0-13-235005-1
ISBN-10:   0-13-235005-X

For membership information: APPA, P.O. Box 11910, Lexington, KY 40578-1910;
(606) 244-8207; fax (606) 244-8001

Brief Contents

Contents

part 1

Probation

4
The Probation Officer and Juvenile Justice 80

part 2
Parole

5
The American Prison System 134

6

Parole and the Indeterminate Sentence 166

7

Parole Administration and Services 186

part 3
Rehabilitation and Supervision in Probation and Parole

8
Rehabilitation Theory and Practice 220

11

Special Problems and Programs in Probation and Parole 312

12

Intermediate Punishments 350

Preface

The first edition of this book was written while I was a senior parole officer for the New York State Division of Parole. Since that time, new concepts (or sometimes simply buzzwords) have affected both the theory and practice of probation and parole. Some, such as *community-based corrections*, had a brief life, while the *justice model* and *determinate sentencing* had long-lasting effects, creating the need for graduated sanctions and intermediate punishments. More recently, the phrases *restorative justice*, *"broken windows"/community-based supervision*, and *research/evidence-guided supervision* have become popular expressions of the need to respond to political pressures for ensuring greater public safety while conserving tax dollars but without completely abandoning the rehabilitative ideal.

The further hardening of sentiments toward criminals generated "truth- insentencing" (no parole or early release) and "three strikes and you're out" (life imprisonment on third felony conviction) statutes. Political posturing produced such incongruities as mandatory sentences with sanctioning flexibility, as the rush to punish encountered spending curbs and tax shortfalls. The results of "get tough on crime" statutes and the "war on drugs" overburdened our correctional facilities, and sound-bite polemics often replaced careful and thoughtful policy development.

Twenty-first-century probation and parole contain their own incongruities: greater efforts at offender control, often by armed probation and parole officers, intertwined with research-driven supervision with a focus on rehabilitation services. Determinate sentencing of offenders and limited grants of good time have been coupled with meeting offender needs and greater use of flexibility for responding to probation and parole condition violations.

This tenth edition contains 12 chapters organized to further enhance ease of classroom use. To remain at the cutting edge of the field, this edition continues to use materials from juvenile and adult probation and parole agencies throughout the country, providing a state-of-the-art examination of probation and parole practices. (Material whose source is not cited is from the appropriate agency.) In addition, each chapter highlights key terms (which appear in the Glossary) and ends with a list of those key terms as well as relevant Internet sites. As in previous editions, review questions conclude each chapter. The online instructor's resource manual available for this book provides a model curriculum and test questions.

SUPPLEMENTS

The following supplements are available to support this text:

- Companion Website (www.prenhall.com/abadinsky)
- TestGen electronic test manager
- PowerPoints
- Instructor's Manual with Test Bank
- Test Item File for BlackBoard
- Test Item File for WebCT

Instructor
Resource
Center

Register today at www.prenhall.com
to access instructor resources digitally.

To access supplementary materials online, instructors need to request an instructor access code. Go to **www.prenhall.com**, click the **Instructor Resource Center** link, and then click **Register Today** for an instructor access code. Within 48 hours after registering you will receive a confirming e-mail including an instructor access code. Once you have received your code, go to the site and log on for full instructions on downloading the materials you wish to use.

The author would like to thank Tim Peyton and Elisa Rogers at Prentice Hall for their dedication to this project. Also, thanks to production liaison Rex Davidson, production editor Janet Bolton, and Maine Proofreading Services for the copyediting and proofreading.

Finally, thanks to the following for their thoughtful reviews and suggestions: Shannon Barton-Bellessa, Indiana State University; Garry C. Elliott, Reedley College; Altrice Gales, Pitt Community College; Jason Jolicoeur, Longview Community College; and Godpower O. Okereke, Texas A&M University—Texarkana.

Acknowledgments

Note: *New to this edition.

Patricia M. Anderson*
(Wyoming Board of Parole)

Shannon Barton-Bellessa*
Indiana State University

Nancy Beatty
(U.S. Office of Probation and Pretrial
Services)

Robert L. Bingham
(Marion County [IN] Superior Court
Probation Department)

James Birrittella*
(Westchester County [NY] Department of
Probation)

Donald H. Blevins*
(Alameda County [CA] Probation
Department)

Peggy Carr
(Denton County [TX] Adult Probation)

Mary Christensen
(Washington State Department of
Corrections)

Trudy A. Clark
(Nebraska Board of Parole)

Debbie Damiano*
(Humboldt County [CA] Probation
Department)

John D. D'Amico*
(New Jersey State Parole Board)

James E. Dare
(Montgomery County [OH] Court
of Common Pleas, Criminal Justice
Services)

Deb Day*
(Logan County [OH] Family Court)

Garry C. Elliott*
Reedley College

John Evangelista*
(New York City Department of Probation)

John Fitzgerald*
(U.S. Office of Probation and Pretrial
Services)

Kim Frentz
(Volunteers in Prevention, Probation,
and Prisons, Inc.)

Altrice Gales*
Pitt Community College

Al Giacchi*
(Onondaga County [NY] Probation
Department)

Virginia M. Gibbons
(Texas Department of Criminal Justice,
Parole Division)

Scott Hedlund
(Lewis County [WA] Juvenile Court)

Robert Hoffman*
(Vermont Department of Corrections)

Sheila Hudson*
(Allen County [IN] Community
Corrections)

Thomas James*
(New Jersey State Division of Parole)

Sylvia J. Johnson
(Alameda County [CA] Probation
Department)

J. Scott Johnston
(Missouri Board of Probation
and Parole)

Jason Jolicoeur*
Longview Community College

George Kostyrko
(California Youth Authority)

Godpower O. Okereke*
Texas A&M University—Texarkana

Martin J. Krizay
(Yuma County [AZ] Adult Probation
Department)

Ed Ligtenberg*
(South Dakota Board of Pardons
and Paroles)

Marvel J. Maddox
(San Marcos [TX] Community Supervision
and Corrections Department)

Michael Manguso
(Florida Department of Correction)

Kenndall Y. Mayfield
(Harris County [TX] Juvenile Probation
Department)

Richard A. Mertz*
(Franklin County [PA] Adult Probation
Department)

Sheila E. Mitchell*
(Santa Clara [CA] Probation Department)

Jennifer Nunez
(Cook County [IL] Juvenile Court Probation
Department)

Dennis E. Pankratz
(Santa Barbara [CA] Probation
Department)

Rheta Perez*
(Texas Parole Division)

Stan Pflueger*
(Allen County [IN] Community
Corrections)

Walter M. Pulliam, Jr.
(Virginia Community Corrections)

Nina H. Ramsey
(Alameda County [CA] Probation
Department)

Vicki L. Rascona-Saylor
(Somerset County [PA] Probation
Department)

Manuel Real*
(Monterey County [CA] Probation
Department)

Kelly Robbins*
(New Jersey State Division of Parole)

David F. Sanders*
(Pima County [AZ] Adult Probation
Department)

Maurice Scully*
(New Jersey State Division of Parole)

Linda Seidel
(Pima County [AZ] Adult Probation
Department)

Sara Simila
(Ohio Adult Parole Authority)

Glenda Spratt*
(Arkansas Department of Community
Correction)

Mindy Spring*
(Interstate Commission for Adult Offender
Supervision)

Glenn A. Stanley*
(South Dakota Board of Pardons and Paroles)

Mary Ellen Still*
(Dutchess County [NY] Office of Probation
and Community Corrections)

Kayla Sumpton*
(BI Incorporated)

Sherry Tate*
(Pennsylvania Board of Probation
and Parole)

John E. Thorstad
(Lake County [IN] Probation Services)

Raymond B. Wingerd
(San Bernardino County [CA] Probation
Department)

Kathy Welch
(Jefferson County [TX] Juvenile Probation
Department)

Paul J. Werrell
(Lehigh County [PA] Juvenile Probation)

Ron Whitmore
(Tennessee Board of Probation and Parole)

Emily S. Hudgens Wilson*
(Tennessee Board of Probation and Parole)

Sheryl Zuna
(Dutchess County [NY] Probation
Department)

About the Author

Howard Abadinsky is professor of criminal justice at St. John's University. He was an inspector for the Cook County, Illinois, Sheriff's Office for 8 years and a New York State parole officer and senior parole officer for 15 years.
The author holds a B.A. from Queens College of the City University of New York, an M.S.W. from Fordham University, and a Ph.D. from New York University. He is the author of several books, including *Organized Crime*, 8th ed., *Law and Justice*, 6th ed., and *Drug Abuse*, 6th ed.

Dr. Abadinsky encourages communication about his work and can be reached at St. John's University, 8000 Utopia Parkway, Jamaica, NY 11439; abadinsh@stjohns.edu.

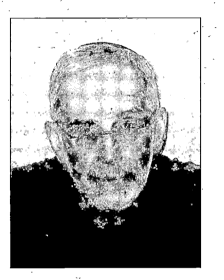

Probation and Parole
Theory and Practice

Probation and Parole in Criminal Justice

It is challenging to try to describe or discuss probation and parole in this country, not only because of the scope and scale of its operations but also because of its structure and organization. The phrases "probation and parole" [and] "community corrections" are used routinely and would imply a single or unified system. Nothing could be further from the truth. Probation and parole agencies are a fragmented, heterogeneous collection of organizations found at the federal, state, county, and municipal levels, housed in the judicial and executive branches.

—*William D. Burrell* (2005: 1)

Chapter Outline

Probation and parole are part of a uniquely American system of criminal justice in which contradictory goals and competing expectations are reconciled in a swirling cauldron of politics. Americans want greater protection from crime while insisting that efforts to afford this protection do not jeopardize treasured constitutional rights. We want a system that deters would-be miscreants and incapacitates those not deterred without imposing significant tax dollar costs (DiIulio 1993). Probation and parole are often made scapegoats for the impossibility of achieving these competing expectations.

THE REALITY OF CRIMINAL JUSTICE

When a probationer or parolee commits a serious crime that generates publicity, questions are raised about why this person was not in prison. Even a single case can result in changes that typically make sound politics but poor practice. For reasons of *justice* (punishment to fit the crime) or *cost* (too expensive to incarcerate all offenders in prison indefinitely), most offenders are not imprisoned, and more than 90 percent of all imprisoned offenders are eventually released. Convicted offenders can be placed on probation, released after completion of their entire sentence, or paroled to supervision in the community. If laws are enacted that limit probation or increase the length of imprisonment by abolishing parole, for example, there must be corresponding increases in prison space to accommodate the results. As any shopper or grocery clerk knows, you can't get 10 pounds into a 5-pound bag.

Key Fact

The cost of imprisonment and, at times, the pressure of overcrowding lead to increased front-door and back-door programs.

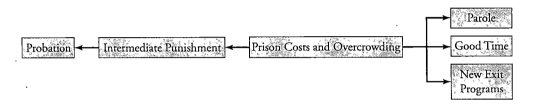

The cost of imprisonment and, at times, the pressure of overcrowding lead to increased **front-door programs** (e.g., probation, intermediate punishments discussed in Chapter 12), **back-door programs** (e.g., parole, early release for good behavior), or additional programs (e.g., "boot camps") that either keep offenders from becoming inmates or let them out early. Thus, although there was a steady decline in the percentage of inmates released by parole boards between 1980 and 2005, the percentage of prisoners being released from prisons to the community increased—despite building more than 200 prisons and hiring more than 100,000 additional prison employees—and more than 4 million adults were already on probation (*Correctional Populations in the United States, 1995:* 1997; Glaze and Bonczar, 2006). Virginia, for example, abolished parole release in 1995 and then number of persons on probation more than doubled ("A Forecast," 2007). Interestingly, a study of inmates released in states that abolished parole revealed that inmates served 7 months less than inmates released in states with parole (Petersilia, 2000b). Between 1995 and 2005, there was symmetry between the number of persons sent to prison and the number placed on probation: The percentage increase in the prison population was identical to the percentage increase in the probation population (Glaze and Bonczar, 2006). In 2006, there were over 4.1 million persons on probation, 1.5 million in prison, 750,000 in jail, and 785,000 on parole (Glaze and Bonczar, 2006).

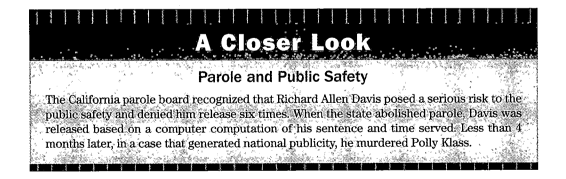

A Closer Look

Parole and Public Safety

The California parole board recognized that Richard Allen Davis posed a serious risk to the public safety and denied him release six times. When the state abolished parole, Davis was released based on a computer computation of his sentence and time served. Less than 4 months later, in a case that generated national publicity, he murdered Polly Klass.

If discretionary release—parole—is not an option (many states have abolished the parole board), then allowing inmates to earn good time at a rate of half or more of their sentence becomes the most viable option. However, so-called **truth-in-sentencing laws** have limited this approach, permitting only small grants of good time—10 or 15 percent. Many states have enacted **"three strikes and you're out" laws**, meaning lifetime imprisonment on a third (or sometimes a second) felony conviction. In California, the "third strike" for one inmate serving a 25-year sentence without parole was theft of three golf clubs from a pro shop; another was sentenced to 50 years for his "third strike," theft of children's videos from a department store (Greenhouse, 2003). As these unreleasable inmates age, they become increasingly expensive wards of the state. In 2003, the Supreme Court upheld the constitutionality of "three strikes" laws (*Ewing v. California*, 538 U.S. 11; *Lockyer v. Andrade*, 538 U.S. 63). In 2004, almost 10 percent of prison inmates were serving life sentences (Butterfield, 2004b).

Key Fact

Truth-in-sentencing and "three strikes and you're out" laws have abolished parole and limited early release.

A Closer Look

Two Strikes and You're In

Georgia's "two strikes" legislation, passed in 1995, mandates that persons convicted for the first time of murder, rape, armed robbery, kidnapping, aggravated sodomy, aggravated sexual battery, or aggravated child molestation serve all their prison sentence without possibility of parole. Persons convicted a second time of any of those seven crimes receive a life sentence.

In the absence of release by a parole board, when probationers or early releasees generate negative publicity, new legislation curtails the use of these schemes, and in an endless cycle, either new prison building and staffing must ensue or additional schemes must be developed to reduce prison populations and achieve a semblance of equilibrium. Getting lost in this often-simplistic approach to crime and criminals is any serious attention to the fate of persons released from prison who are uneducated, unskilled, unemployed, and now hardened by the prison experience. That such persons would resort to crime cannot be surprising, and the wheels of criminal justice continue to spin, generating heat but not light.

Then the reality: In the *New York Times*, Ken Butterfield noted: "After three decades of building ever more prisons and passing tougher sentencing laws, states are suddenly being forced to choose between keeping a lid on taxes or being tough on crime. Lower taxes are winning" (2003: 1, 20). Some states that passed "three strikes" laws, such as Texas and Kentucky, have discovered loopholes allowing them to release inmates early. Those that still have parole boards have asked them to increase releases, whereas those without them are overhauling their sentencing laws.

A Closer Look

Duh?

In New York in 1997, both the mayor of the city and the governor of the state called for the abolition of parole. The mayor cited the case of a man who had been paroled after a manslaughter conviction and charged with shooting a police officer. But the defendant's sentence was 4 years to 12 years, and the 12-year mark had already passed—he would have been free even without parole release. The governor cited the case of a man in Albany accused of killing a young woman; however, that man had been paroled after 5 years of serving a 3.5- to 7-year sentence, so even if he had been kept in prison for 85 percent of his sentence, as the governor proposed, he would have been freed 1 year before the victim was killed (Perez-Peña, 1998).

CRIMINAL JUSTICE IN AMERICA

Criminal justice in America is an outgrowth of a fundamental distrust of government. Authority is divided between central (federal) and state governments, and at each level power is diffused further, shared by three branches—executive, legislative, judicial—in a system referred to as the "separation of powers." In each state, authority is shared by governments at the municipal, county, and state levels. Thus, policing is primarily a function of municipal government, whereas jails are usually run by the county (often by the sheriff). Probation may be a county or state function, whereas prison and (usually) parole systems are the responsibility of state government, although in some states (e.g., Iowa and Oregon), parole and probation supervision is a function of the county or judicial district. There is also a separate federal system of criminal justice (Figure 1.1).

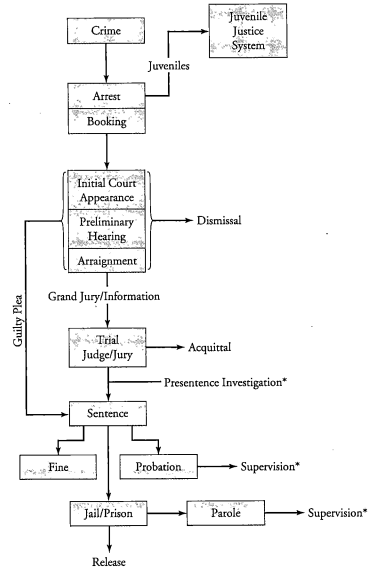

*Points at which probation and parole officers typically enter the system.

FIGURE 1.1 *Probation and Parole in the Criminal Justice System*

As those who work in criminal justice recognize, there is a lack of joint planning and budgeting, or even systematic consultation, among the various agencies responsible for criminal justice. The result is an **unsystematic system.**

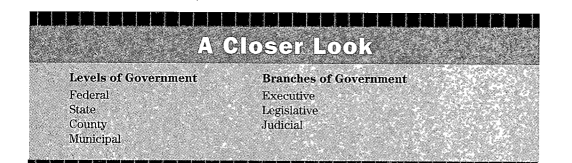

A Closer Look

Levels of Government	Branches of Government
Federal	Executive
State	Legislative
County	Judicial
Municipal	

Although criminal justice agencies, whose members range from police to parole officers, are interdependent, they do not, *in toto*, constitute a system arranged so that its parts result in unity. Although the operations of criminal justice agencies lack any significant level of coordination, each affects the others. A disproportionate share of the criminal justice budget (about 42 percent) goes to the agency that has the most public visibility, the police (plus 6 percent for federal law enforcement). The courts, prosecutors, and public defenders receive about 22 percent; corrections receives about 29 percent. An additional 1 percent is allocated for miscellaneous functions (U.S. Department of Justice statistics). As a result, more persons are brought into the system by the police than the rest of the system can handle adequately. Increasing the number of police officers, and thereby the total number of arrests, places further pressure on the rest of the system of criminal justice.

Because of their large caseloads, judges and prosecutors tend to concentrate on the speedy processing of cases. This, in turn, encourages "bargain justice," which frequently is neither a bargain nor just. When a probation agency is understaffed, judges tend to send marginal cases to prison instead of using probation. Because prisons are underfunded and overcrowded, there is pressure on the parole board to accelerate the release of inmates, thereby overburdening parole supervision, which is also usually understaffed. In more recent years, many states have abolished their parole systems. Although this may have made political sense, it does not respond to the problem of prison overcrowding. As pressure builds on prisons, usually the result of judicial scrutiny and financial considerations, prison officials are forced to release inmates without benefit of the type of analyses a parole board usually provides. Prison overcrowding also places pressure on the judicial system, and more persons are placed on probation as the revolving door of criminal justice continues to spin (Figure 1.1).

Probation and parole are linked to particular segments of the criminal justice system, and criminal justice is tied to a system of laws most frequently invoked against a distinct type of offender. Law reflects the need to protect the person, the property, and the norms of those who have the power to enact laws: The criminal law reflects power relations in society. Thus, the harmful activities of those with power are often not even defined as criminal (e.g., certain antitrust violations) but may instead constitute only a civil wrong (e.g., the savings and loan debacle that cost taxpayers an estimated $100 billion). When the criminal law is invoked, the results may represent distinctions in power; burglary prosecutions, for example, routinely invoke more significant penalties than do business crimes. For crimes committed by large corporations, the sole punishment often consists of warnings, consent decrees, or comparatively small fines. As the title of a book by Jeffrey Reiman (1998) notes, *The Rich Get Richer and the Poor Get Prison.*

A Closer Look

Rich Man, Poor Man, Criminal Man

The United States is the most economically stratified of industrial nations: "For 30 years the gap between the richest Americans and everyone else has been growing so much that the level of inequality is higher than in any other industrialized nation" (Stille, 2001: 15). "The wealthiest 1 percent of American households—with net worth of at least $2.3 million each—owns nearly 40 percent of the nation's wealth. Further down the scale, the top 20 percent of Americans—households worth $180,000 or more—have more than 80 percent of the country's worth, a figure higher than in other industrial nations" (Bradsher, 1995a: C4; Pérez-Peña, 1997). This inequality has continued to increase (Andrews, 2003).

A 1994 report for the Carnegie Foundation by a panel of prominent Americans revealed millions of children deprived of medical care, loving supervision, and intellectual stimulation, the result of parents overwhelmed by poverty. Many are subjected to child abuse and frequently witness random acts of violence (Chira, 1994) which means they are more likely to become juvenile delinquents and adult criminals (Widom, 1996; Widom and Maxfield, 2002). They become the pool from which the criminal justice system draws most of its clients.

WHAT IS A CRIME? WHO IS A CRIMINAL?

Quite simply, a *crime* is any violation of the criminal law, and a *criminal* is a person convicted of a crime. These definitions raise an important question: Is a person who violates the criminal law a "criminal" if he or she is not apprehended or convicted? Consider that most reported crimes do not result in an arrest and conviction. Furthermore, National Crime Victimization Surveys reveal that most crimes are simply not reported to the police. Thus, have probationers or parolees who are not arrested again been rehabilitated, or have they become more successful at avoiding detection? (Or have the police become either corrupt or less adept?)

It is important for the study of probation and parole to consider who actually becomes identified as a criminal, since they are not representative of the U.S. population. Remember that there are corporate offenders who do *not* usually become identified as criminals. A composite sketch of the "average" offender convicted of a crime would reveal that he (more than 90 percent are male) is usually young (more than 40 percent are younger than age 20, and more than 70 percent are younger than age 30), poor, and often from a minority group. Such persons tend to be clustered in particular sections of urban America—areas that are heavily policed—increasing the likelihood of arrest. Persons who have already been arrested become part of the official records of law enforcement agencies, increasing their susceptibility to further arrests, a fact of life with which all probation and parole personnel must deal. However, on average, only about one crime in four is cleared by an arrest. The result is prisons populated and repopulated by the least skillful criminals with multiple convictions.

As we see in later chapters, some offenders are given an opportunity to avoid being put through the criminal process; they are diverted from the criminal justice system by use of some other method. Such programs can easily become another method for providing differential treatment whereby the middle class can avoid the stigma and severity of the criminal process and the poor are made to face the full force and fury of criminal sanctions.

In response to the question of who is a criminal, some observers see the offender as a *victim* of poverty, discrimination, unequal and unjust laws, and law enforcement. In 1902, Clarence Darrow, the famed trial lawyer, noted that "the people who go to jail are almost always poor people" (1975: 29), and most persons on probation and parole come from an underclass. More than a century later, persons convicted of corporate crimes are still often able to avoid the stiff sanctions that typically befall the perpetrators of more conventional crimes, those most likely to be committed by persons from deprived economic circumstances.

EARLY RESPONSES TO CRIME

Early responses to deviant behavior ranged from the payment of fines to trial by combat, banishment, and death by torture. *Lex talionis* (an eye for an eye), a primitive system of vengeance, emerged and was passed down from generation to generation as each family, tribe, or society sought to preserve its own existence without recourse to a written code of laws. About 4,000 years ago, Hammurabi, king of Babylonia, authored a code inscribed on a block of diorite nearly 8 feet high and about 5 feet in circumference. Although in written form, his laws continued the harsh tradition of *lex talionis*—many crimes, including committing theft and harboring a runaway slave, were punishable by death (Harper, 1904).

Later, the Hebrews adopted the concept of an eye for an eye; however, under biblical law this meant financial compensation for the victim of a crime or negligence (there was no compensation for murder, which carried the death penalty), except for the "false witness," in which case "ye shall do unto him, as he had purposed to do unto his brother" (Deuteronomy 19: 19). A perpetrator who was unable to pay compensation was placed in involuntary servitude, a precursor to the concept of probation. The servitude could not last more than 6 years—release had to occur with the sabbatical year—and masters had rehabilitative obligations and responsibilities toward their charges. (Under the Code of Hammurabi, "If the thief has nothing wherewith to pay he shall be put to death" [Harper, 1904: 13].)

The Romans derided the use of restitution for criminal offenses and used the death penalty extensively in ways that have become etched in history. The fall of the Roman Empire resulted in there being little "rule of law" throughout Europe. When law was gradually restored, fines and restitution became important forms of punishment as those in power sought to increase their wealth. Offenders who were unable to pay, however, were often enslaved or subjected to mutilation or death. A parallel issue in contemporary criminal justice, the extensive use of restitution, is discussed in later chapters.

Trial by combat also flourished, in part because of the difficulty of proving criminal allegations. With the spread of Christianity, trial by combat was reserved for private accusations, whereas crimes prosecuted by the crown called for trial by ordeal, an appeal to divine power. A defendant who survived the ordeal (e.g., passing through fire) was ruled innocent. The unsuccessful defendant often received the verdict and punishment simultaneously. Trial by ordeal was eventually replaced with *compurgation* ("wager of law"): The accused was required to gather 12 reputable persons who would swear to the defendant's innocence. Reputable persons, it was believed, would not swear falsely for fear of divine retribution. Compurgation eventually evolved into testimony under oath and trial by jury (Vold and Bernard, 1986). Throughout the Middle Ages in Europe, there was a continuation of the extensive use of torture to gain confessions, and public executions were often accompanied by torture, flaying, or the rack.

Despite biblical admonitions—"You shall not respect persons in judgment; ye shall hear the small and the great alike" (Deuteronomy 1: 17)—for many centuries disparity existed in the manner in which punishment was meted out, with the rich and influential receiving little or no punishment for the same offenses that resulted in torture and death for the less fortunate.

CLASSICALISM

The disparate practices of meting out justice were challenged forcefully in the eighteenth century with the advent of classicalism. **Classicalism** is an outgrowth of the European Enlightenment period of the eighteenth century (sometimes referred to as the

Key Fact

Classicalism views human behavior as based on free will.

"Age of Reason") whose adherents rejected spiritualism and religious explanations for criminal behavior. During this era, philosophers, such as Montesquieu (1689–1755) and Voltaire (1694–1778), spoke out against the French penal code and inhumane and inequitable punishments. Jean Rousseau (1712–1778) and Cesare Beccaria (1738–1794) argued for a radical concept of justice based on equality. At a time when laws and law enforcement were unjust and disparate and punishment was often brutal, they demanded both justice that was based on equality and punishment that was humane and proportionate to the offense. This revolutionary doctrine—equality—influenced the American Revolution, with its declaration that "all men are created equal," and the French Revolution, whose National Assembly enacted a "Declaration of the Rights of Man and Citizen" (1789), which emphasized the equality of all citizens. The roots of this legal and political philosophy can be found in the concept of the social contract and natural rights.

The **social contract** is a mythical state of affairs wherein each person agrees to a pact, the basic stipulation of which is that, all men being created equal, conditions of law are the same for all: "The social contract establishes among the citizens an equality of such character that each binds himself on the same terms as all the others, and is *thus* entitled to enjoy the same rights as all the others" (Rousseau, 1954: 45). According to classical thought, by nature man is free and endowed with natural rights, a philosophical basis for the first 10 amendments to the U.S. Constitution, the Bill of Rights. According to John Locke (1632–1704), all men are by nature free, equal, and independent, and no one can be subjected to the political power of another without his or her own consent. These sentiments were incorporated into the U.S. Declaration of Independence as "all men are created equal" whose "governments are instituted among men, deriving their just powers from the consent of the governed."

The classical notion of the social contract stipulates that because all men are created equal, conditions of law are the same for all. Thus, Rousseau asserts, "One consents to die—if and when one becomes a murderer oneself—in order not to become a murderer's victim" (1954: 48). To be safe from crime, all people have consented to punishment if they resort to crime. This constitutes the greatest good for the greatest number; the social contract is rational and motivated by selfishness (Roshier, 1989).

Contrary to the manner in which law was being enforced, the classical school argued that law should respect neither rank nor station—all men are created equal—and punishment is to be meted out with a perfect uniformity. This premise was given impetus by Beccaria, who, in *An Essay on Crimes and Punishments* (1764; English edition, 1867), states that laws should be drawn precisely and matched to punishment intended to be applied equally to all classes of men. The law, he argued, should stipulate a particular penalty for each specific crime, and judges should mete out identical sentences for each occurrence of the same offense (Maestro, 1973). This makes the administration of justice rational, whereas law is taken, uncritically, as given. Punishment has as its purpose deterrence and must be "the minimum possible in the given circumstances, proportionate to the crime, dictated by the laws" (Maestro, 1973: 33). The prosecution of defendants must be accomplished without resort to torture, common during this period. Not only is torture inhumane, but it is a highly unreliable method of determining guilt. Unlike the position of Rousseau stated earlier, Beccaria opposed capital punishment.

According to the classical position, punishment is justified because offenders who violate the social contract are rational and endowed with **free will**. This concept, which has biblical origins (Deuteronomy 30: 15), holds that every person has the ability to distinguish and choose between right and wrong and between being law-abiding and criminal; in other words, behavior that violates the law is a *rational choice* made by a person with free will—in legal terms, ***mens rea***. The classical school argues, however, that because humans tend toward *hedonism*—that is, they seek pleasure and avoid pain—they must be restrained, by fear of punishment, from pleasurable acts that are unlawful. Accordingly, the purpose of the criminal law is not simply *retribution* but also *deterrence*. In sum, the "individual is responsible for his actions and is equal, no matter what his rank, in the eyes of the law" (Taylor, Walton, and Young, 1973: 2). This approach has an economic perspective in **utilitarianism**—the cost-benefit analysis of behavior. According to Gary Becker (1968: 176), "A person commits an offense if the expected utility to him exceeds the utility he could get by using his time and resources at other activities." Becker argues that "a useful (utilitarian) theory of criminal behavior can dispense with special theories of anomie, psychological inadequacies, or inheritance of special traits [all discussed in Chapter 8] and simply extend the economist's usual analysis of choice" (1968: 40). This approach parallels that of classical economics—capitalism—in which free persons motivated by rational self-interest, based on the principles of the free market, purportedly benefit the entire society.

Two additional requirements—*certainty* and *promptness*—round out the classical position. If law is to serve its deterrent purpose, the would-be violator must be in fear of the consequences. This element of fear requires certainty, whereas promptness, seemingly based on a primitive form of behaviorism (discussed in Chapter 8), is necessary to make a more lasting impression—connecting the deed to the punishment.

The classical approach supported the interests of a rising eighteenth-century commercial class that was demanding legal equality with the privileged noble class as well as protection from the economic-driven predations of the lower class. A contradiction remains between the defense of equality and the emphasis on maintenance of an unequal distribution of wealth and property. Crime could, indeed, be a rational response to severe differentiations in wealth and opportunity. Free will is an oversimplification because one's position in society determines the degree of choice with respect to committing crimes: "A system of classical justice of this order could only operate in a society where property was distributed equally," where each person has an equal stake in the system (Taylor, Walton, and Young, 1973: 6). It is irrational for a society, which in too many instances does not offer a feasible alternative to crime, to insist that criminal behavior is simply a matter of free will; the nature of our prison population for more than 200 years belies this claim. Nevertheless, as noted by Anatole France (1927: 91), "the law [based on classicalism], in its majestic equality, forbids both the poor man and the rich man to sleep under bridges, to beg in the streets, and to steal bread."

In sum, there are eight basic tenets of classicalism (Taylor, Walton, and Young, 1973):

1. Humans are rational.
2. All persons are created equal.
3. All persons have an equal stake in society and thus an equal stake in prevention of crime.
4. Free will endows each person with the power to be law-abiding or criminal.
5. People tend toward hedonism.
6. The purpose of punishment is deterrence.
7. Punishment must be meted out fairly, with absolute equality, and in proportion to the offense.
8. Punishment must be prompt and certain.

Key Fact

Classical theory promotes equality before the law and provides the basis for determinate sentencing.

Classical theory is the basis of our legal system, its pictorial representation appearing on many courthouses and documents in the form of a woman—"Justice"—carrying scales and wearing a blindfold. The classical view provides the basis for definite/determinate sentences, which are discussed in Chapter 6.

NEOCLASSICALISM

According to the classical position, punishment is justified because the offender who violates the social contract is rational, endowed with free will, and therefore responsible for his or her actions no matter what the person's rank. The focus is on laws and the legal system, not on the nature of criminal motivation. In fact, under the U.S. system of justice, an explanation is not a justification unless it reaches the level of a (legal) compulsion, at which point the law does not blame the perpetrator—no *mens rea*. Classicalism provides the basis for a rational legal system that is relatively easy to administer, except for one annoying problem: Implementing a criminal code with perfect equality has proven elusive. This problem became apparent when the French Code of 1791 attempted to implement Beccaria's reforms. Equality and proportionality proved more difficult in practice than in theory, and the French increasingly added to the discretionary powers of judges in the form of neoclassicalism (Roshier, 1989).

Neoclassicalism maintains the basic belief in free will while paving the way for the entry of mitigation (and subsequently aggravation) into criminal justice by considering three areas:

1. Past criminal record
2. Insanity and retardation
3. Age

Punishment can be justified only if crime is freely chosen, intentional, and rational—that is, reasoned behavior. The neoclassicist revisions created an entrée for nonlegal experts—particularly psychiatrists and, later, social workers—into the courts (Taylor, Walton, and Young, 1973). These experts determine the presence of mitigation, and the system is able to continue to maintain a belief in free will. Allowing for the possibility of differences between offenders raises the specter of **determinism**, meaning that to varying degrees, the offender's choices are limited, which is the basic premise of positivism.

POSITIVISM

Key Fact

Positivism attempts to explain the cause of crime and offers a basis for rehabilitating criminals and using the indeterminate sentence.

Positivism, as formulated by Auguste Comte (1798–1857), refers to a method for examining and understanding social behavior. Comte argued that the methods and logical form of the natural sciences—the scientific method—are applicable to the study of man as a social being, producing the field of social sciences. Social phenomena, Comte stated, must be studied and understood by observation, hypothesis, and experimentation in a new discipline that he called *sociology*. Classical theory is based on philosophy and law, whereas the positivist view is based on empiricism in an effort to determine the cause of crime.

The positivist approach to the study of crime became known as *criminology*, a discipline whose early efforts are identified with Cesare Lombroso (1835–1909), a Venetian physician. In his *L'uomo delinquente* (*The Criminal Man*), first published in 1876, Lombroso argued that the criminal is a "primitive throwback" to earlier developmental stages through which noncriminal man had already passed—the influence of **social Darwinism** is obvious (Degler, 1991). Lombroso's research centered on physiological characteristics believed indicative of criminality, although his later work (published in 1911) noted the importance of environmental factors in causing crime (Lombroso, 1968). Instead of the classical emphasis on criminal behavior as rational, positivists tend to see it as a symptom of some form of pathology: biological, psychological, or social. (Positivist theories of crime are reviewed in Chapter 8.)

While Charles Darwin and Herbert Spencer were concerned with a general construct of human evolution and its effect on society, the criminal anthropology initiated by the work of Lombroso employed evolution to explain criminal behavior. Lombroso contributed to the study of crime by using, albeit in a rather imperfect way, the tools of science and shifting the field of inquiry from law and philosophy to empiricism. The positivist view places emphasis not on the crime but on the criminal. It contradicts the

A Closer Look

Social Darwinism

The move toward using science to explain criminality received a major impetus from the work of Charles Darwin (1809–1882). Although his first book (*Origin of Species*, published in 1859) was concerned exclusively with nonhuman organisms, his second (*Descent of Man*, published in 1871) included the idea that humanity was shaped by the forces of natural selection. Darwin's thesis was advanced by the English philosopher Herbert Spencer (1820–1903), who coined the phrase "survival of the fittest," the credo for social Darwinism. Spencer (1961: 305) argued that "there can be no rational apprehension for the truths of Sociology until there has been reached a rational apprehension of the truths of Biology." According to Spencer (1961: 2), biology did not support help for the downtrodden: "As fast as they increase the provision for those who live without labor, so fast do they increase the number who live without labor; and that with an ever-increasing distribution of alms, there comes an ever-increasing outcry for more alms."

Darwin's theory of natural selection supplied the conceptual ammunition for an ideology (later labeled social Darwinism) that allayed the qualms of the rich about not helping the poor by telling them that the latter's sufferings were an inevitable price for societal advancement that could occur only through the struggle for existence ending in the survival of the fittest and the elimination of the unfit (Andreski, 1971). "If the unworthy are helped to increase, by shielding them from that mortality which their unworthiness would naturally entail, the effect is to produce, generation after generation, a greater unworthiness" (Spencer, 1961: 313). Spencer goes on to say, "Fostering the good-for-nothing at the expense of the good is an extreme cruelty. It is a deliberate storing-up of miseries for future generations. There is no greater curse to posterity than that of bequeathing them an increasing population of imbeciles and idlers and criminals" (1961: 314).

Are government policies based on such buzzwords as "self-sufficiency" and "individual responsibility" a twenty-first-century form of social Darwinism?

theory of free will for which positivists have substituted a chain of interrelated causes and, at its most extreme, a deterministic basis for criminal behavior: The criminal could not do otherwise. Because criminal behavior is the result of social and psychological, if not physiological, conditions over which the offender has little or no control, he or she is not culpable (in legal parlance, lacks *mens rea*), so punishment is inappropriate; however, because criminals do represent a threat to society, they must be "treated," "corrected," or "rehabilitated" (or according to early Lombrosians, separated from society, perhaps castrated or executed). In practice, the change in emphasis from punishment to correction did not necessarily result in a less severe response to criminal offenders. Some modern critics contend that rehabilitation opened the door to a host of questionable schemes for dealing with offenders under the guise of "treatment" applied "for their own good." The American Friends Service Committee notes: "Retribution and revenge necessarily imply punishment, but it does not necessarily follow that punishment is eliminated under rehabilitative regimes" (1971: 20). The positivist view provides a basis for the juvenile court discussed in Chapter 4 and the indeterminate sentence discussed in Chapter 6.

The views of the classical and positivist schools are important because they transcend their own time and continue to influence contemporary issues in criminal justice. The question remains: Do we judge the crime or the criminal? This is a central question in the continuing debate over sentencing—definite versus indeterminate—discussed in Chapter 6. Probation and parole, it is often argued, emanate from a positivist response to criminal behavior, a view that is disputed in this book.

A Closer Look

Classical View	Positivist View
Free will	Determinism
Choice	Cause
Punishment/deterrence	Treatment/incarceration

If, as the classical view argues, a person has free will and is rational, he or she will weigh the costs of committing (or not committing) a crime. The threat of sanctions is seen as an effort to tilt the weighing process away from crime. The classical approach would view enhancing education and job skills as increasing choice away from crime. Positivists would view this response as a treatment dealing with the causes of crime.

U.S. System of Criminal Justice

Probation and parole are part of the U.S. system of criminal justice. The next section locates these two services within that system. (See Figure 1.1.)

Entrance into the System

Most crimes are not responded to by the criminal justice system because they have not been discovered or reported to the police; when reported, most crimes are never solved. For the police to arrest a suspect, they must have a level of evidence known as **probable cause**. The Ohio Adult Parole Authority offers the following definition: "Reasonable grounds for suspicion supported by facts and circumstances sufficiently strong in themselves to lead a reasonably cautious person to believe that a person is guilty of a particular crime." Probable cause is also the level of evidence required to initiate a probation or parole violation, and it is significantly less than that necessary to convict a defendant in a criminal trial.

When the police effect an arrest, the subject is transported to a holding facility, usually a police station equipped with cells—a "lockup." As opposed to a jail, a lockup is used on a temporary basis, for 24 to 48 hours. During this time, the suspect will be booked, photographed, and fingerprinted, and the police will request that formal charges be instituted by the prosecutor's office. A fingerprint check reveals whether the suspect has a previous arrest record, is wanted for other charges, or is on probation or parole.

Key Fact

Levels of evidence range from probable cause to beyond a reasonable doubt.

Pretrial Court Appearances

Depending on what time of day the arrest occurred and whether it happened on a weekday, weekend, or court holiday, the suspect may have to spend 24 hours or longer in the lockup before being transported to court. At the first appearance, the primary question concerns bail, and the initial appearance may actually be a bond hearing at which bail is the only issue. If a defendant is under probation or parole supervision, the bail decision is affected; for example, in some jurisdictions, a probation or parole warrant will be filed to preclude release on bail. If the subject is unable to provide bail or a probation/parole warrant is filed as a detainer, he or she will be kept in jail pending further court action. In many jurisdictions, probation or pretrial officers or other specialized court personnel will interview defendants with a view toward assisting the judge in making a bail decision. They may even provide supervision during the pretrial stage (see Pretrial Supervision in Chapter 10).

A Closer Look

Levels of Evidence—High to Low

Beyond a Reasonable Doubt
Guilt in a criminal trial
Finding of delinquency in juvenile court

Clear and Convincing Evidence
Used in extraordinary civil cases, such as commitment and child custody

Preponderance of the Evidence
Most civil cases
Status offense cases in juvenile court
Probation and parole revocation hearings

Probable Cause
Search warrants/arrest warrants
Warrantless arrests
Probation and parole preliminary violation hearings

Pretrial Hearings

At pretrial hearings (sometimes referred to as an initial appearance, preliminary hearing, or arraignment), the official charges are read, the need for counsel considered, and bail set or reviewed (if it has already been set at a bond hearing). Typically, these hearings last only a few minutes. If the case is a misdemeanor, it may be adjudicated at this time, often by a plea of guilty or dismissal of the charges on a motion by the prosecutor. If the charge constitutes a felony, a *probable cause* hearing is held to determine if the arresting officer had sufficient evidence—probable cause—to justify an arrest. This hearing takes the form of a short minitrial during which the prosecutor calls witnesses and the defense may cross-examine and call its own witnesses.

If the judge finds probable cause—evidence sufficient to cause a reasonable person to believe that the suspect committed a crime—the prosecutor files an *information* (details of the charges), which has the effect of bringing the case to trial. In some states, the prosecutor may avoid a probable cause hearing by presenting evidence directly to a *grand jury*—generally, 23 citizens who hear charges in secret. If they vote a *true bill*, the defendant stands indicted and the case proceeds to trial.

Trials or Guilty Pleas

Few cases entering the criminal justice system actually result in a jury trial, an expensive and time-consuming luxury that most participants attempt to keep to a minimum. About 85 to 95 percent of all criminal convictions are the result of a guilty plea, and most guilty pleas are the result of a **plea bargain**, a widely condemned practice for disposing of cases that involves an exchange wherein the defendant agrees to waive his or her constitutional right to a jury trial, providing the prosecutor with a "win" and saving the court a great deal of time and effort; the defendant is rewarded for this behavior by receiving some form of leniency. (The impact of plea bargaining on probation services is discussed in Chapters 2 and 3; its effect on parole is in Chapter 6.) If plea negotiations fail to result in an agreement or if one side or the other refuses to bargain, the case is scheduled for trial. (For an extensive discussion of plea bargaining, see Abadinsky, 2007a.)

The trial is an adversary proceeding in which both sides are represented by legal counsel and whose rules are enforced by a judge. To sustain a criminal charge, the prosecutor must prove the *actus reus* and *mens rea*. **Actus reus** means a wrongful act or deed; it refers to the need to prove that a violation of the criminal law—a crime—actually occurred. The *actus reus* consists of a description of the criminal behavior and evidence that the accused acted accordingly. *Mens rea*, or "guilty mind," is a legal standard that refers to the question of intent: The prosecutor must be able to show that the defendant had a wrongful purpose—willfulness—in carrying out the *actus reus*. The defendant is presumed innocent; therefore, defense counsel need not prove anything but will typically attempt to raise doubts about the evidence or other aspects of the prosecution's case.

Each side can subpoena witnesses to present testimony and can cross-examine adverse witnesses. The defendant can take the stand on his or her own behalf; if the defendant prefers not to testify, he or she can maintain the Fifth Amendment privilege against self-incrimination. Defendants on probation or parole may be reluctant to testify because this would subject them to cross-examination and result in a disclosure of their criminal record to the jury. After lawyers for each side have introduced all their evidence, the judge instructs the jury on the principles of law applicable to the case. Every jury is told (charged by the judge) that the facts pointing to the guilt of the defendant must be established **beyond a reasonable doubt,** as opposed to the **preponderance of the evidence,** which is the standard in all civil and some juvenile cases as well as probation and parole revocation hearings.

The jury now retires to deliberate in private. In most jurisdictions, the jury's decision for guilt or acquittal must be unanimous, or the result is called a *hung jury*. If the jury cannot reach a unanimous verdict, the jurors are discharged; if the prosecutor decides, the case must be tried a second time before a different jury. Except in some relatively rare instances when there are violations of both federal and state laws, the defendant who is acquitted cannot be tried again for the same charges, which would constitute *double jeopardy* (prohibited by the Fifth Amendment). If the jury finds the defendant guilty of one or more of the charges, the case moves to the sentencing stage, and the probation officer enters the case, usually for the first time. (In some jurisdictions, the probation officer is involved in gathering information—the *pre-plea investigation*—for the judge during the plea bargaining stage.)

Key Fact

Plea bargaining affects sentencing and therefore impacts probation and parole.

Sentences

After a verdict or plea of guilty, the judge decides on the sentence, although in some states the sentence is decided by the jury, particularly in cases of murder. The sentencing function reflects societal goals, which may be in conflict:

- *Retribution.* Punishment dimension (*lex talionis,* an eye for an eye, or just deserts) that expresses society's disapproval of criminal behavior.
- *Incapacitation.* Reduces opportunity for further criminal behavior by imprisonment.
- *Deterrence.* Belief that punishment will reduce the likelihood of future criminal behavior either by the particular offender (*individual/specific deterrence*) or by others in society who fear similar punishment (*general deterrence*).
- *Rehabilitation.* Belief that by providing services—social, psychological, educational, or vocational—an offender will be less likely to commit future crimes.
- *Restitution.* Repayment by an offender to the victim or to society in money or services for the harm committed.

Sentencing can be further complicated by concern for (Zawitz, 1988):

- *Proportionality.* Punishment should be commensurate with the seriousness of the crime.
- *Equity.* Similar crimes should receive similar punishment.
- *Social debt.* Severity of punishment should consider the offender's prior criminal record.

These issues are discussed in subsequent chapters.

The trial judge sets a date for a sentencing hearing and in many jurisdictions will order a presentence investigation to be conducted by the probation department. A probation officer will search court records; examine other reports, such as psychiatric and school records; and interview the defendant, spouse, employer, arresting officer, and victim. Information from the presentence investigation will be presented in the form of a written presentence or probation report, which frequently contains the probation officer's sentencing recommendation. After reviewing the report, the judge conducts a sentencing hearing at which both defense and prosecution are allowed to make statements. The judge then imposes a sentence: fine, suspended sentence, probation, incarceration, or any combination thereof. A prison sentence may be definite (classical) or indeterminate (positivist), depending on state law.

A sentence of probation places the defendant, now a convict, under the supervision of a probation officer. A sentence of incarceration results in the defendant being sent to a jail (if convicted of a misdemeanor) for usually not more than 1 year or to a state or federal prison (if convicted of a felony). In most jurisdictions, a parole board can release the defendant (now an inmate) before the expiration of his or her sentence. In other states and the federal system, the inmate can be released early as the result of accumulating time off for good behavior. Parolees and (in many states) persons released for good behavior come under the supervision of a parole officer (the actual title varies from state to state).

Appeals

Although the prosecutor cannot appeal an acquittal (Fifth Amendment), the defendant is free to appeal a guilty verdict in hopes of obtaining a reversal. The defendant can ask an appellate court to review the proceedings that culminated in his or her conviction. In fact, American criminal justice is rather unique for the extensive postconviction review procedures to which a defendant is entitled. A prison inmate may petition the trial court for a new trial or take an appeal to the state's intermediate appellate court; if unsuccessful there, he or she can still appeal to the state court of last resort, and if unsuccessful in state court, he or she can petition the Supreme Court. The prisoner can also attack the conviction *collaterally,* that is, using indirect means, by way of a writ of *habeas corpus,* claiming that his or her constitutional rights were violated in some way by the state court conviction. Having exhausted direct and indirect appeals in state courts, the inmate can move over to the federal courts, claiming again that the conviction was unconstitutional, usually on grounds of lack of due process.

The appellate court cannot act as a trial court, that is, receive new evidence concerning the facts already established at the original trial. It is limited to considering new theories or legal arguments regarding the law applicable to these facts or addressing procedural issues. The appellate court can uphold the verdict, overturn it, or order it reversed and remanded to the trial court for a new trial. The appellate court can also render decisions that affect other cases by setting a precedent or handing down a ruling that governs the actions of criminal justice officials; for example, in *Morrissey v. Brewer* the Supreme Court ruled that parolees are entitled to some basic forms of due process before they can be returned to prison for violation of parole.

Probation and Parole: Why Bother?

Why be concerned with probation or parole? Some simply say, "If you do the crime, do the time." Although later chapters elaborate on this issue, consider the following: There are more than 7 million persons on probation and parole at an average per capita yearly cost of about $1,500. In Tennessee, the daily cost for probation and parole supervision is $2.56 per offender; imprisonment costs $57.33 a day per inmate. The cost of probation supervision in Georgia varies based on the type of supervision being provided: Standard probation supervision costs $1.43 per probationer per day; intensive supervision costs

$3.46. In North Carolina, standard supervision costs $1.96 per probationer per day; intensive, $14.97. There are more than 2 million persons in the nation's jails and prisons, and the annual operating cost of housing a state prison inmate is $25,000–$30,000, although in some states, such as Massachusetts, Minnesota, New York, and Oregon, the cost is closer to $40,000. California spends more than $34,000 a year to house an inmate and about $4,000 to supervise one on parole. The 50 states spend a total of about $30 billion in annual prison operating costs (Stephan, 2004) and the cost of building a new prison is about $250 million (Washington State Institute for Public Policy, 2006).

The cost of imprisonment is typically underestimated because it leaves out many actual expenses such as fringe benefits for employees, which average more than 25 percent of salaries. The cost of building a maximum-security prison averages more than $70,000 per cell. Although a state can float bonds to underwrite the cost of prison building, thereby amortizing the cost (which includes substantial interest) over a long period, operating costs such as staff salaries must be paid immediately out of the state's operating budget—it may be politically easier to build a prison than to staff and operate one.

Key Fact

Incarceration costs 10 to 20 times as much as probation and parole supervision.

Adding to these costs are the problems of acquired immunodeficiency syndrome (AIDS), tuberculosis, hepatitis C, and the increasing number of geriatric offenders, often the result of "get tough" and "three strikes and you're out" (actually *in* for life) legislation. The cost of housing an inmate over the age of 50 with health problems is in excess of $60,000 per year.

Factors of cost, mediated by overcrowded prisons, have led to a dramatic expansion in the use of probation and parole. In 1979, for example, there were 1,086,535 persons on probation; in 1987, there were 2,242,053, an increase of more than 100 percent. By 1990, the number had risen to 2,671,000, and in 2006, there were over 4.1 million persons on probation. In 1979, 218,690 persons were on parole from American prisons; in 1987, there were 362,192, an increase of more than 65 percent. By 1990, that number had risen to 531,000, and in 2006, there were 785,000 on parole (U.S. Bureau of Justice Statistics). In 1994, Congress passed the Violent Crime Control and Law Enforcement Act, which provides prison construction grants. To qualify, however, states must have laws requiring persons convicted of a violent offense to serve at least 85 percent of their prison sentence—and few states have the necessary resources to do so.

Now that this overview of criminal justice is complete, Chapter 2 examines the U.S. court system as well as probation history and administration.

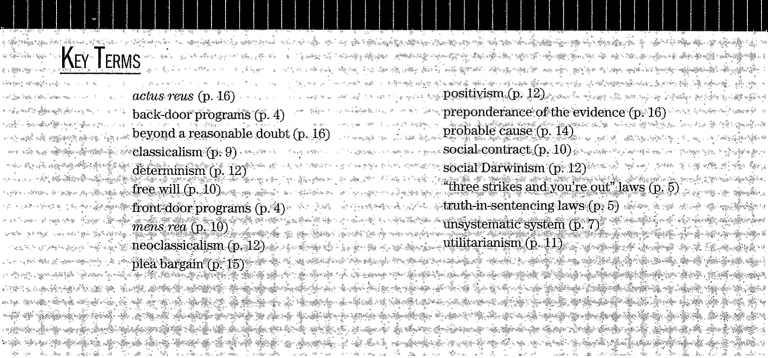

KEY TERMS

actus reus (p. 16)
back-door programs (p. 4)
beyond a reasonable doubt (p. 16)
classicalism (p. 9)
determinism (p. 12)
free will (p. 10)
front-door programs (p. 4)
mens rea (p. 10)
neoclassicalism (p. 12)
plea bargain (p. 15)

positivism (p. 12)
preponderance of the evidence (p. 16)
probable cause (p. 14)
social contract (p. 10)
social Darwinism (p. 12)
"three strikes and you're out" laws (p. 5)
truth-in-sentencing laws (p. 5)
unsystematic system (p. 7)
utilitarianism (p. 11)

INTERNET CONNECTIONS

American Bar Association Criminal Justice links: abanet.org/crimjust/
links.html

Council of State Governments: csg.org

General criminal justice links: lawguru.com/ilawlib/96.htm

Legal Resource Center: crimelynx.com/research.html

National Criminal Justice Reference Service: ncjrs.org

National Institute of Justice: ojp.usdoj.gov/nij

U.S. Department of Justice links: usdoj.gov/02organizations/02_1.html

Vera Institute of Justice: vera.org

REVIEW QUESTIONS

1. What are the contradictory goals and competing expectations in American criminal justice?
2. What are the four levels and three branches of government?
3. How does this division affect criminal justice?
4. How does the criminal law reflect power relations in society?
5. How does classicalism differ from neoclassicalism?
6. How is free will an oversimplification?
7. How can changes in sentencing laws increase the need for front-door and back-door schemes for dealing with offenders?
8. Why can the use of probation be expected to increase when parole is abolished?
9. Why is the system of criminal justice in the United States unsystematic?
10. What are the effects of providing the police with an inordinate percentage of the allocations for criminal justice?
11. How does the definition of *crime* determine who is subjected to probation and parole?
12. How is the enforcement of criminal law a factor in determining who is subjected to probation and parole?
13. What factors increase the possibility of an offender being arrested?
14. What are the major elements of the classical view of law and justice?
15. What distinguishes the positivist view from the classical view with respect to crime and criminal behavior?
16. Under a strictly positivist view of criminal behavior, why is there an absence of culpability or *mens rea*?
17. What are the five societal goals of sentencing?
18. What concerns can complicate sentencing?
19. What is the importance of probation and parole in U.S. criminal justice?
20. How has truth-in-sentencing legislation affected the prison population?
21. What is the effect of "three strikes and you're out" laws on the prison population?
22. How do issues of cost explain the extensive use of probation and parole?

part **1**

Probation

Probation History and Administration

Probation refers to the conditional release of one convicted of a crime into the community during a period of supervision under an assigned probation officer.

—*David N. Falcone* (2005: 207)

Chapter Outline

Probation is the most common sentence in the United States (Petersilia, 1998a). The administration of probation services may be under the auspices of the judiciary or an agency in the executive branch of government; in either event, a probation agency provides three basic services to the courts:

1. *Supervision of adult offenders*
2. *Presentence and pre-plea investigations*
3. *Juvenile services*

Before examining these services and their administration, let us examine how and why probation developed in the United States.

EARLY PROBATION AND JOHN AUGUSTUS

Although probation has antecedents that reach back to biblical times, its American history dates back to the nineteenth century. The concept of probation (from the Latin *probatio*, meaning period of proving) evolved out of the practice of *judicial reprieve*, used in English courts to serve as a temporary suspension of sentence to allow a defendant to appeal to the crown for a pardon. Although originally intended to be only a temporary postponement of punishment, it eventually developed into a *suspended sentence*, whereby punishment was never actually imposed. In the United States, the suspended sentence was used as early as 1830 in Boston and became widespread in U.S. courts, although there was no statutory authorization for such a practice. At first, judges used release on recognizance or bail and simply failed to take further action. By the mid-nineteenth century, however, many courts were using a judicial reprieve to suspend sentences, and this posed a legal question.

"A judge had always had the power to suspend a sentence, if he felt for some reason that the trial had miscarried. But could judges suspend sentences wholesale, after trials that were scrupulously fair, simply to give the defendant a second chance?" (Friedman, 1973: 518). In 1894, this question was litigated in New York, and the court determined that the power to suspend sentence was inherent in criminal courts only when this right had been granted by the legislature. In 1916, the U.S. Supreme Court, in a case (*Ex parte United States*, 242 U.S. 27) that affected only federal courts, ruled that judges did not have the discretionary authority to suspend a sentence. In its decision, however, the Court stated that Congress could authorize the temporary or indefinite suspension of sentence—a predecessor to probation statutes.

The term *probation* was applied by John Augustus to the practice of bailing offenders out of court, followed by a period of supervised living in the community. This pioneer of modern probation was born in Woburn, Massachusetts, and became a successful shoemaker in Boston. In 1852, a "Report of the Labors of John Augustus" was published at the request of his friends, and in it Augustus wrote: "I was in court one morning . . . in which the man was charged with being a common drunkard. He told me that if he could be saved from the House of Correction, he never again would taste intoxicating liquors: I bailed him, by permission of the Court" (1972: 4–5). Thus began the work of the nation's first probation officer, a volunteer who worked without pay.

Augustus's first experience with a drunkard led to an interest in helping others charged with the same offense. He would appear in court and offer to bail a defendant. If the judge agreed, which usually happened, the defendant would become Augustus's charge. The shoemaker would assist the offender in finding work or a residence; Augustus's own house was filled with people he had bailed. When the defendant returned to court, Augustus would report on his progress toward rehabilitation and recommend a disposition of the case, and these recommendations were usually accepted. During the first year of his efforts, Augustus assisted 10 drunkards who, because of his work, received small fines instead of imprisonment. He later helped other types of offenders, young and old, men and women and reported only 10 **absconders** (persons who jumped bail or probation) out of 2,000 cases.

Augustus continued his work for 18 years and generally received support from judges as well as newspapers that reported on his efforts. Prosecutors, however, viewed him as an interloper who kept court calendars crowded by preventing cases from being disposed of quickly. Policemen and court clerks opposed his work because they received a fee for each case disposed of by a commitment to the House of Correction. As a result of his probation work, Augustus neglected his business and eventually experienced financial ruin; he required the help of friends for his support.

Several aspects of the system Augustus used remain basic parts of modern probation. Augustus thoroughly investigated each person he considered helping, including "the previous character of the person, his age and the influences by which in the future he would likely be surrounded" (1972: 34). Augustus not only supervised each defendant but

Key Fact

Modern probation can be traced to the actions of John Augustus in Boston in the decade before the Civil War.

kept a careful case record for each that he submitted to the court. Augustus died in 1859, and until 1878, probation in Massachusetts continued to be the work of volunteers.

EARLY PROBATION STATUTES

After he died in 1859, supporters of John Augustus successfully lobbied the legislature, which in 1878 enacted the first probation statute, authorizing the mayor of Boston to hire a probation officer (PO) who would be supervised by the superintendent of police. For the first time, the position of PO was given official recognition as an arm of the court. The law authorized a PO to investigate cases and recommend probation for "such persons as may reasonably be expected to be reformed without punishment." Probation was made available in Boston to young and old, men and women, felons as well as misdemeanants. In 1880, the legislature granted to all municipalities the authority to employ POs, but few towns and villages did so. In 1891, the power to appoint POs was transferred to the lower courts, and each was required to employ a PO; in 1898, this requirement was also extended to the superior courts. The second state to adopt a probation statute was Vermont, which in 1898 authorized the appointment of a PO by the courts in each county, each officer serving all the courts in a particular county.

Key Fact

In the latter part of the nineteenth century, New England pioneered probation and employed probation officers.

Another New England state, Rhode Island, soon followed Vermont with a probation law that was novel—it placed restrictions on who could be granted probation, excluding persons convicted of treason, murder, robbery, arson, rape, and burglary. This practice violated a basic tenet of positivism: Judge the offender, not just the offense. The restrictive aspects of Rhode Island's probation law, however, were copied by many other states. The Rhode Island probation law, which applied to children and adults, also introduced the concept of a state-administered probation system. A state agency, the Board of Charities and Correction, appointed a state PO and deputies, "at least one of whom should be a woman" (Glueck, 1933: 231).

In 1894, Maryland authorized its courts to suspend a sentence generally or for a specific time, and judges could "make such order to enforce terms as to costs, recognizance for appearance, or matters relating to the residence or conduct of the convicts as may be deemed proper." The courts of Baltimore began using agents of the Prisoner's Aid Society and later appointed salaried POs. In 1897, Missouri enacted a "bench parole law," which authorized courts to suspend sentences under certain conditions. The courts also appointed POs, (mis)named "parole officers," to carry out this probation ("bench parole") work (Glueck, 1933). In 1931, the Alabama legislature passed a law giving the judges power to suspend execution of sentences and place offenders on probation, but this act was declared unconstitutional in 1935. Had it been constitutional, it would have done little more than authorize suspended sentences since in most cases there was no provision for investigation and supervision.

PROBATION AT THE TURN OF THE TWENTIETH CENTURY

The spread of probation was accelerated by the juvenile court movement, which started in the Midwest and developed rapidly (discussed in Chapter 4). In 1899, Illinois enacted the historic Juvenile Court Act, which authorized the world's first juvenile court. The law also provided for the hiring of POs to investigate cases referred by the courts but made no provision for payment of the POs. It was not until 1919 that the Illinois legislature enacted a law providing that counties pay the salaries and expenses of POs. At the end of the first year, there were six POs supported by the Juvenile Court Committee of the Chicago Women's Club; in addition, in each police district a police officer spent part of his time out of uniform performing the duties of a PO (Schultz, 1973: 465).

Key Fact

Probation was spread by the juvenile court movement beginning in Chicago in 1899.

In 1899, Minnesota enacted a law that authorized the appointment of county POs, but the granting of probation was limited to those younger than 18 years of age, but 4 years later, this was changed to 21 years of age. In 1901, New York State enacted a probation law that was initially limited to those under 16 years of age, limited to certain cities, and provided for volunteer POs. In 1903, legislation authorized probation throughout the entire state and included children and adults.

In 1899, Colorado enacted a compulsory education law that enabled the development of a juvenile court using truant officers as POs. By 1925, probation was available for juveniles in every state (Glueck, 1933). In 1873, Michigan instituted a statewide system of juvenile POs they named county agents. Volunteers at first, in 1875 county agents were paid $3 per case for their part-time work; for comparison, an American-born Detroit manufacturing worker at the time earned $457 a year (Hurl and Tucker, 1997). In New York, it was not until 1901 that legislation authorizing the appointment of salaried POs was enacted—until that year they were volunteers (Lindner and Savarese, 1984). In 1908, Suffolk County on Long Island, New York, appointed its first PO: "At the time, there was little appreciation of the value of probation, and the appointment was more in the nature of an experiment. As a part-time position, the PO had no office, and the probationers reported to him at his home, or by mail." The county appointed a full-time PO in 1919, and he was given a small office. Probation for juveniles was authorized in Pennsylvania in 1903 and extended to adults in 1909: Except for the offenses of murder, administering of poison, kidnapping, incest, sodomy, rape, assault with intent to rape, and arson or burglary of an inhabited dwelling, a judge could suspend the sentence and place the offender on probation.

In the early 1900s, federal POs were volunteers. In 1916, the Supreme Court (*Ex parte United States*, 242 U.S. 27) ruled that federal judges did not have the authority to place offenders on probation. In 1925, Congress enacted legislation establishing the Federal Probation System, and in 1929 the first paid U.S. PO was appointed under the Department of Justice. In 1939, probation administration was shifted to the newly created Administrative Office of the United States Courts.

Although Texas enacted the Suspended Sentence Act in 1913 to provide an alternative to incarceration, probation supervision of the convicted offender was not required until 1947. Probation for adults in Alabama did not begin until 1939, when the governor approved an enabling act giving the legislature power to authorize adult probation; before that, it had been held that courts did not have the inherent power to suspend sentences because it was deemed to be an encroachment on the executive power to pardon, commute, and reprieve. By 1956, probation was available for adults in every state (Task Force on Corrections, 1966).

The first directory of POs in the United States, published in 1907, identified 795 POs working mainly in the juvenile courts. Like the first PO in Illinois, many were volunteers, and some who were paid worked only part time. Training for POs was either limited or nonexistent, appointments were often based on considerations of political patronage, and salaries were typically low even when compared with those of unskilled laborers.

Key Fact

Early probation officers were often volunteers or poorly paid employees.

ADMINISTRATION OF PROBATION

Probation in the United States is administered by more than 2,000 separate agencies supervising in excess of 3 million adult offenders on probation for felonies and misdemeanors. In about three-fourths of the states, adult probation is located in the executive branch of state government (where it is typically combined with parole). For example, probation services in Georgia are provided by the Department of Corrections, which also manages all state correctional facilities, while the Board of Pardons and Paroles is responsible for discretionary release. In Pennsylvania, an independent state agency called the Board of Probation and Parole, in addition to its parole responsibilities, supervises probationers sentenced to less than 2 years when directed to do so by the courts; it also oversees county probation agencies. In Michigan, adult felony probation is the responsibility of the Department of Corrections, which also administers parole, whereas adult misdemeanor probation is the responsibility of district (limited jurisdiction) courts' probation departments. In Illinois, probation is a county-level responsibility that is part of the judicial branch, whereas in Iowa, probation (and parole supervision) is the responsibility of the state's judicial districts, each of which encompasses several counties. In New York, each county as well as New York City has a probation department that is part of the executive branch of county/municipal government. In Massachusetts, probation is a state agency employing more than 1,200 probation officers.

More than one-half of the agencies providing juvenile probation services are administered on the local level. Juvenile probation may be provided by a separate juvenile agency or a juvenile or family division of the same agency that administers adult probation, as is seen in Nassau County, New York. Fortunately, the administration of parole, which is discussed in Chapter 7, is much less complex—one agency per state, always in the executive branch. Even with parole, however, there are slight variations: In some states (e.g., Pennsylvania), persons paroled from a local jail come under the supervision of a *county* probation and parole department; in Oregon and Iowa, probation *and* parole supervision are at the county and judicial district levels.

The administration of probation systems can be separated into six categories, and a state may have more than one system in operation:

1. *Juvenile.* Separate probation services for juveniles are administered on a county or municipal level or on a statewide basis.
2. *Municipal.* Independent probation units are administered by the lower courts or the municipality under state laws and guidelines.
3. *County.* Under laws and guidelines established by the state, a county operates its own probation agency.
4. *State.* One agency administers a central probation system providing services throughout the state.
5. *State combined.* Probation and parole services are administered on a statewide basis by one agency.
6. *Federal.* Probation is administered nationally as an arm of the courts, and federal probation officers also supervise parolees.

Many states (about 60 percent) combine probation and parole in one statewide agency. However, in the largest states (e.g., California, Illinois, New York, and Texas), only parole is a state function, whereas probation is administered by the judiciary or executive branch on a county or municipal level. Probation services in the executive branch can be part of state government under the office of the governor, county government under a chief executive officer, or municipal government under a mayor, as in New York City. Probation services may be part of a larger department of corrections, as in Georgia, or part of an independent probation and parole agency, as in Alabama and South Carolina. Probation services as part of the judicial branch of government usually places these services under the judges of the county, as in New Jersey:

> The judges of the County Court in each county, or a majority of them, acting jointly may appoint a *chief probation officer, [and] such men and women probation officers* as may be necessary. Probation officers and *volunteers in probation* shall be appointed with standards fixed by the Supreme Court. All *probation officers* and *volunteers in probation* shall be responsible to and under the supervision of the *Chief Probation Officer* of the county who shall be responsible to and under the supervision of the judge of the county court or, in counties having more than one judge of the county court, the county court judge designated by the Assistant Judge to be responsible for the administration of the *probation department* in the county in accordance with the applicable statutes, rules of the Supreme Court, and directives of the Chief Justice, the Administrative Director of the Courts, and the Assignment Judge of the county.

There are also some variations. For example, Iowa is divided into eight judicial districts, each with a multicounty correctional department operating under a board of directors. The board appoints a director who administers probation, parole, and related services that are funded and monitored by the Iowa Department of Corrections. In

Key Fact

Probation in the United States is administered by more than 2,000 separate agencies on the municipal, county, state, and federal levels in either the judicial or executive branch.

Key Fact

While a majority of states combine probation and parole in one statewide agency, in the largest states they are separate.

Key Fact

Probation may be administered on a municipal, county, or state basis, in either the judicial or executive branch.

Texas, probation services are located in 120 community supervision and corrections departments, organized by the judges of each judicial district and funded by supervision fees and state aid. The Ohio Adult Parole Authority, in addition to parole services, provides probation services to 45 of the state's 88 counties. Although the 31 counties participating in the Minnesota Community Corrections Act (CCA) provide services to persons on probation, supervised release, or parole, the state provides these services to adult offenders in the remaining 56 counties. Juvenile probation and parole services in non-CCA counties are provided by county probation agents or by state agents under contract to the counties. In either case, the state pays up to 50 percent of the agent's salary.

Two basic issues arise in the administration of probation services:

1. Should probation be part of the judicial or executive branch of government?
2. Should probation be under municipal/county or state jurisdiction?

Those who support placement of probation services in the judicial branch state the following advantages (Nelson, Ohmart, and Harlow, 1978):

- Probation is more responsive to the courts, to which it provides services, when administered by the judiciary.
- The relationship of probation staff to the courts creates an automatic feedback mechanism on the effectiveness of various dispositions.
- Courts will have greater awareness of the resources needed by the probation agency.
- Judges will have greater confidence in an agency for which they are responsible, allowing probation staff more discretion than they would allow members of an outside agency.
- If probation is administered on a statewide basis, it is usually incorporated into a department of corrections, and under such circumstances, probation services might be assigned a lower priority than they would have as part of the judicial branch.

Those who oppose the placement of probation in the judiciary note the following disadvantages:

- Judges, trained in law and not administration, are not equipped to administer probation services.
- Under judicial control, services to persons on probation may receive a lower priority than services to the judge (e.g., presentence investigations).
- Probation staff may be assigned duties unrelated to probation.
- The courts are adjudicatory and regulative; they are not service-oriented bodies.

Placement in the executive branch has these features to recommend it:

- All other human services agencies are in the executive branch.
- All other corrections subsystems are located in the executive branch.
- With executive branch placement, program budgeting can be better coordinated, and an increased ability to negotiate fully in the resource allocation process becomes possible.
- A coordinated continuum of services to offenders and better use of probation personnel are facilitated.

E. Kim Nelson and her colleagues conclude:

When compared, these arguments tend to support placing probation in the executive branch. The potential for increased coordination in planning, better utilization of manpower and improved services to offenders cannot be dismissed. A state administered probation system has decided advantages over local administration. A total system planning approach to probation as a subsystem of corrections is needed. Such planning requires state leadership. Furthermore, implementation of planning strategies requires uniformity of standards, reporting, and evaluation as well as resource allocation. (1978: 92)

Mitchell Silverman (1994) points out, however, that state control typically means probation agencies administered by the state executive branch, with centralized administrators who are frequently far removed, both physically and intellectually, from the PO in the field. Often the central administrators have little knowledge and understanding of the important factors that are operating in the local community where the individual PO works. The distance has the potential of creating conflicts of interest when the state-level policy makers demand from the field worker one approach to clients while the local community, in which the PO and client live, demands another. Local administration enhances creativity by providing the capacity to adopt county-specific programs with shorter lines of decision making.

Probation administered by the judiciary (usually) on a county level promotes diversity. Innovative programming can be implemented more easily in a county agency because it has a shorter line of bureaucratic control than a statewide agency. A county agency can more quickly adapt to change, and the successful programs of one agency can be more easily adopted and unsuccessful programs avoided by probation departments in other counties. Those most familiar with the local community—its resources, attitudes, and politics—will be responsible for providing probation services, which can increase public confidence in the services provided by the agency. Although the judiciary is nominally responsible for the administration of probation, the day-to-day operations are in the hands of a professional administrator: the chief probation officer.

Conversely, county-level administration results in a great deal of undesirable variance between agencies. For example, the ratio of POs to clients may differ dramatically from one county to the other—a situation that would not happen with a statewide agency. Because each county sets its own budget, probation staff cannot be shifted from a low-ratio county to a high-ratio county to equalize the services provided. In New Jersey, for example, the State Advisory Board for Probation, in its 1985 report, noted that whereas juvenile supervision caseloads statewide averaged about 80 per officer, in individual counties the range was between 35 and 145. For adult probation caseloads, the state average of 160 ranged from 71 to 284, amounting to a fourfold difference between the extremes.

The New Jersey board found variance with respect to the amount each county expended on probation services and "a great deal of variation in the way work is processed. Thus, the sequence of probation work from county to county is far from uniform." The board noted:

> There is no accepted definition of what comprises quality probation services. Probation supervision, for example, suffers from a lack of definition and structure, making it difficult to determine what is high quality supervision. Finally, there is great variance from county to county in the environment which produces the need for probation services, creating large differences among counties in the work probation services must perform. The extent and seriousness of criminal, social, and economic problems have important implications for staffing, procedures, and resource requirements from county to county.

This finding, of course, can serve as an argument for county control of probation services.

The board, however, raises a question: Does the lack of uniformity in administering probation make justice less equitable statewide? This issue has led states with county-based probation systems to create statewide oversight agencies for better coordination and uniformity of probation services (only Indiana and California operate probation locally without a state oversight agency) (Parent et al., 1994). In Illinois, for example, the Probation Division of the Administrative Office of the Illinois Courts works to "improve the quality and quantity of probation and related court services throughout Illinois, provide more uniformity of organization, structure, and services, and increase the use of probation as a meaningful alternative punishment for nonviolent offenders. As part of these efforts, for example, the division promulgates regulations for the hiring and promotion of all probation personnel throughout the state."

The Texas Community Justice Assistance Division (formerly the Texas Adult Probation Commission) is responsible for establishing statewide standards and providing state aid to those local adult probation departments that choose to participate and are in compliance with the standards. As part of these efforts, the division has supported research and experimental probation programs throughout Texas. The agency has promulgated a "Code of Ethics for Texas Adult Probation Officers" and published standards for all phases of adult probation in Texas. For example, it has a policy on caseload size: "A caseload average within a department should be calculated by dividing the number of cases under direct supervision by the number of officers within the department devoting 80 percent or more of their time to direct case supervision. The average caseload of a probation officer in a department should not exceed 100 cases." Although the standards are not mandatory, the failure of a probation department to maintain them can result in a loss of the considerable funding provided by the state. All New York State probation directors are accountable to their respective chief county officials (executive branch) or, in the case of New York City, the mayor. Although administered locally, supervisory oversight of the administration of probation statewide is the responsibility of the New York State Division of Probation and Correctional Alternatives.

The trend in adult probation services has been toward moving from the judicial to the executive branch—in about 75 percent of the states, probation is in the executive branch. For example, in 1974, probation services in New York City were removed from the jurisdiction of the Judicial Conference of the State of New York and became part of the executive branch of city government, with a director appointed by the mayor.

A Closer Look

New York State Division of Probation and Correctional Alternatives

The New York State Division of Probation and Correctional Alternatives (DPCA) was established in 1985 to exercise general supervision over the operation of local probation agencies and the use of correctional alternative programs throughout the state. DPCA also administers a program of state aid funding for approved local probation services and for municipalities and private nonprofit agencies that have approved alternatives to incarceration service plans. These plans allow localities to maintain inmates in local correctional facilities more efficiently. The agency also funds designated demonstration and other specialized programs.

DPCA's mission is to promote and facilitate probation services and other community corrections programs through funding and oversight. These programs are generally designed to provide a continuum of sanctions, methods of supervision, and approaches to treatment that, when used individually or in combination, provide options to the judiciary and to the state's criminal justice system for the effective handling of offenders and juveniles in the community.

The director adopts and promulgates rules and regulations concerning methods and procedures used in the administration of local probation services and develops standards for the operation of alternatives to incarceration programs. The director also serves as the chairman of the New York State Probation Commission. The commission members, appointed by the governor, provide advice and consultation to the director on all matters relating to probation in the state.

Granting of Probation

Most states have statutory restrictions on who may be granted probation in felony cases. Crimes such as murder, kidnapping, and rape usually preclude a sentence of probation, as do second or third felony convictions. In Texas, a defendant may elect to be sentenced by a jury but can thereby receive probation only if it is proved that he or she "has never before been convicted of a felony in this or any other State." In any event, no person in the Lone Star State is eligible to receive probation for a felony unless assessed a sentence of 10 years or fewer by a judge or jury. In Georgia, a defendant who pleads guilty (or *nolo contendere*, "no contest") and who has never before been convicted of a felony can be placed on probation without the court entering a judgment of guilty. If the person successfully completes the terms of probation, he or she "shall not be considered to have a criminal conviction." In Michigan, those convicted of any crime except treason, criminal sexual conduct in the first degree, robbery while armed, and major controlled substance offenses can be granted probation.

When probation is a statutory alternative, judges differ in their approach to granting it. Although the recommendation of the probation department would be important—it is difficult to envision too many cases in which judges would grant probation against the recommendation of a probation officer—judges may also seek advice from the police and prosecutor. The geographic area where the court is situated may affect the granting of probation. Social and political attitudes in rural and urban jurisdictions can differ and thus affect the process, and when court calendars are crowded, as they are in many urban areas, plea bargaining is more likely to result in probation being granted. The pressing problem of jail and prison overcrowding also exerts influence: One research effort found that in the rural districts studied, many felons are placed on probation as the result of a plea bargain; another study found that in Tennessee this appears to be directly related to the severe prison overcrowding experienced by that state (Champion, 1988a). The judge's feelings toward the particular offense or the offender may also enter into the sentencing decision. The many factors that determine if a defendant is granted probation contribute to the continuing controversy over "differential punishment," a challenge to the classical approach to criminal justice.

However, some factors (to a greater or lesser extent) are considered in all cases relative to the granting of probation: the age and rehabilitation potential of the defendant; the defendant's criminal record, including indications of professional criminality, organized crime, and crimes of violence; the defendant's relationship with his or her family; any evidence of deviant behavior, such as drug abuse or sex offenses; and the attitude of the community toward the particular offense and the particular offender. Other questions may also be considered: Does the defendant's attitude toward the offense indicate genuine remorse? Was probation promised to the defendant to induce him or her to plead guilty? Will being placed on probation enable the defendant to provide the victim with restitution? Will being placed on probation enable the defendant to provide support and care for his or her family?

The sentencing judge must also consider the quality of service provided by a probation agency. Unfortunately, in too many jurisdictions, probation is nothing more than a suspending of sentence because little or no supervision is actually provided. Under such circumstances, a judge who might otherwise be inclined to place an offender on probation may instead impose a sentence of imprisonment. The cost to both the offender and the taxpayer is high—according to most estimates, imprisonment costs from 10 to 13 times as much as probation. In many jurisdictions, a built-in incentive actually exists for sentences of imprisonment, even when probation is a feasible alternative. If probation services are funded by the county and the cost of prisons is always borne by the state, each defendant sent to prison instead of placed on probation represents a savings to county government. A Florida study revealed a pattern of inappropriate sentencing in some counties apparently because they can save money by sending more offenders to state-funded prisons (Sever, 2000). This result can be, at least in part, overcome with a **probation subsidy** through which the state reimburses the county for offenders placed on probation instead of sentenced to a state prison.

The American Bar Association (ABA) presents the advantages of probation over imprisonment (1970: 3–4):

1. The liberty of the individual is maximized by such a sentence; at the same time, the authority of the law is vindicated and the public effectively protected from further violations of the law.
2. The rehabilitation of the offender is promoted affirmatively by continuing normal community contacts.

Key Fact

Granting probation is limited by the seriousness of the offense and prior convictions.

Key Fact

The probation subsidy serves to encourage the granting of probation.

3. The negative and frequently stultifying effects of confinement are avoided, thus removing a factor that often complicates the reintegration of the offender into the community.

4. The financial costs of crime control to the public treasury are greatly reduced by reliance on probation as an important part of the correctional system.

5. Probation minimizes the impact on innocent dependents of the offender.

The ABA sets forth three conditions for a sentence of imprisonment rather than probation (1970: 3–4):

1. When confinement is necessary to protect the public from further criminal activity by the defendant

2. When the offender is in need of correctional treatment that can effectively be provided if he or she is confined

3. When the seriousness of the offense would be unduly depreciated if a sentence of probation were imposed

Figure 2.1 shows the flow of criminal cases from arrest through successful completion of probation.

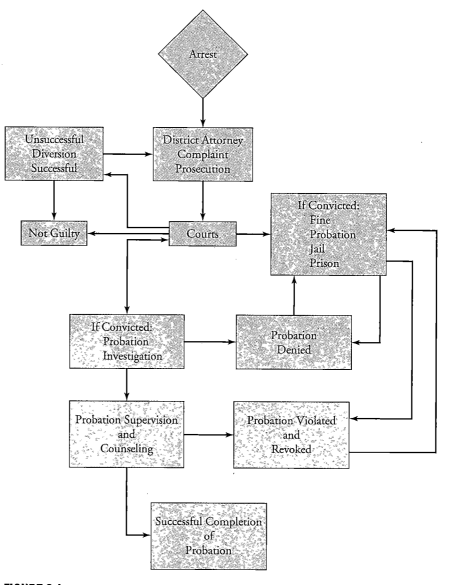

FIGURE 2.1 *Organizational Chart of the San Francisco Adult Probation Process*

CONDITIONS OF PROBATION

Although the Task Force on Corrections (1966: 34) observed more than four decades ago that "differential treatment requires that the rules [of probation] be tailored to the needs of the case and of the individual offender," this suggestion is often not put into practice. Probation agencies require a defendant to sign a standard form usually containing a variety of regulations that may or may not reflect the client's individual needs. There are also special conditions that can be imposed by the judge or the probation department, such as ordering a child molester to avoid places frequented by children.

When conditions of probation are too restrictive or perhaps appear unreasonable or unrealistic, the PO is inclined to overlook their violation. This can result in the PO losing the respect of the probationer, making the supervision process difficult. The ABA (1970: 9) recommends that the conditions of probation be spelled out by the court at the time of sentencing and emphasizes that they should be appropriate for the offender.

The American Probation and Parole Association (APPA) recommends that the only condition that should be imposed on every person sentenced to probation is that the probationer lead a law-abiding life during the period of probation: "No other conditions should be required by statute, but the probation officer in making recommendations [in the PSI report discussed in Chapter 3] should recommend additional conditions to fit the circumstances of each case." In a draft of a position statement, the APPA recommends that conditions "be reasonably related to the avoidance of further criminal behavior and not unduly restrictive of the probationer's liberty or incompatible with his freedom of religion. They should not be so vague or ambiguous as to give no real guidance."

The APPA draft states that conditions may appropriately include, but not be necessarily limited to, matters such as the following:

1. Cooperating with the program of supervision
2. Meeting family responsibilities
3. Maintaining steady employment or engaging or refraining from engaging in a specific employment or occupation (e.g., a drug abuser prohibited from employment in a medical setting)
4. Pursuing prescribed educational or vocational training
5. Undergoing medical or psychiatric treatment
6. Maintaining residence in a prescribed area or in a prescribed facility established for or available to persons on probation
7. Refraining from consorting with certain types of people or frequenting certain types of places
8. Making restitution for the fruits of the crime, or making reparation for losses or damages caused thereby
9. Paying fines, restitution, reparation, or family support
10. Requiring the probationer to submit to search and seizure[1]
11. Requiring the probationer to submit to drug tests (e.g., urine tests) for analysis as directed by the probation officer

Probation regulations in different probation agencies tend to be similar (Figure 2.2). They typically exhort the probationer to live a law-abiding life, work, and support dependents. They require that the offender inform the PO of his or her residence and that permission be secured before leaving the jurisdiction of the court. Some require that the probationer obtain permission before getting married, applying for a motor vehicle license, or contracting any indebtedness. Many probation departments require that the offender

---

[1]Probation (and parole) officers have extraordinary authority to conduct warrantless searches of clients and items as well as places under their control (*Griffin v. Wisconsin*, 483 U.S. 868, 1987).

It is the order of the Bucks County Court of Common Pleas that you shall comply with the following rules and conditions of supervision:

1. I will report to my officer as directed and permit this officer to visit me at my home or place of employment.
2. I will respond promptly to any summons to appear at Court or the Office of the Probation Department. My travel is limited to adjoining counties within Pennsylvania. Any travel beyond those counties, out of state, or overnight travel must be approved by my Probation Officer.
3. I will comply with all federal, state, and local laws. If I am arrested or have contact with law enforcement authorities during supervision, I will notify my officer by the next working day. I will comply with all terms and conditions included in a Protection from Abuse Order.
4. I will report any change of address immediately to my officer.
5. I will make every effort to obtain and hold a legitimate job and support my dependents. I will report promptly to my officer any change in my employment status.
6. I am forbidden to use, possess, or distribute controlled substances and/or dangerous drugs. I will abstain from the excessive use of alcohol.
7. I will voluntarily submit urine, blood, or breath tests as requested.
8. I will not own, use, or possess any type of lethal weapons.
9. I will pay all fines, costs, supervision fees, and restitution in monthly installments as directed by the Probation Officer.
10. I understand that the Adult Probation Department has the authority to search my person, place of residence, or vehicle without a warrant, if there is reasonable cause.
11. I will not enter into any agreement to act as an informant or a special agent of a law enforcement agency without the permission of the Probation Department.
12. I will not physically or verbally threaten, or engage in religious, ethnic, or racial intimidation, toward any Probation Officer.
13. I will abide by the Case Plan, which will be developed by my Probation Officer. I am aware that I will be given the opportunity for input into the plan.
14. I will also comply with the following special conditions imposed by the Court:

I will keep in mind that I am conditionally released and the Court may at any time revoke my probation or county parole for cause. I am aware that should I violate probation or parole, the Bucks County Adult Probation Department has the authority to incarcerate me pending a Violation Hearing. I am further aware that if I am convicted of a new offense during my probation or parole period, I will be brought back before the Court for a Violation Hearing.

FIGURE 2.2 *Bucks County, Pennsylvania Adult Probation Department*

pay a supervision fee, make restitution, or do community service as a condition of probation: In Pennsylvania, for example, probation and parole clients must pay $25 per month unless the fee is waived; in Virginia, clients who are unable to pay the supervision fee may apply for an exemption; they need to prove unreasonable hardship based on insufficient monthly net income. (The issue of fees is discussed in Chapter 11.) Some probation and parole agencies require clients to carry an identification card at all times that reveals their supervision status and contains a telephone number for law enforcement agencies to use.

A Closer Look

Objectives of Probation Supervision

- To provide public protection in keeping with the special duties of a probation officer
- To prepare the probationer for independent law-abiding living
- To provide an opportunity for full participation of the probationer in planning his or her activities in the community
- To identify, use, and create resources in the community to fulfill program needs of probationers
- To provide a system of differential supervision based on the classification and program needs of all probationers
- To conduct a cost-effective supervision program
- To provide restitution or reparation to victims of criminal acts whenever applicable

Source: New York State Code of Criminal Procedure.

LENGTH OF SUPERVISION

The length of probation terms varies from state to state. The ABA recommends that the term should be 2 years for a misdemeanor conviction and 5 years for a felony. Some states, such as Michigan, have followed this recommendation. In Illinois, it is 4 years for the more serious felonies and 30 months for other felonies; for a misdemeanor, it is 1 year. In Texas, "the court may fix the period of probation without regard to the term of punishment assessed, but in no event may the period of probation be greater than 10 years or less than the minimum prescribed for the offense for which the defendant was convicted." In 2007, Texas enacted a law setting the maximum probation sentence for nonaggravated offenses at five years unless the department can show just cause for keeping someone under supervision. In the federal system, termination for a misdemeanor may occur at any time and for a felony after 1 year.

> **Key Fact**
>
> Length of probation supervision may be fixed, such as 5 years for a felony, or be as long as what a sentence of imprisonment would require.

Some states authorize early termination of probation without actually having statutory guidelines as to when it is to be exercised. In most states, however, statutes provide for the termination of probation and the discharge of the offender from supervision before the end of the term. This allows the judge some needed flexibility because it is difficult to determine, at the time of sentencing, how long the term should actually be. In Texas, for example, "at any time, after the defendant has satisfactorily completed one-third of the original probationary period or 2 years of probation, whichever is the lesser, the period of probation may be reduced or terminated by the court." In Illinois, "the court may at any time terminate probation . . . if warranted by the conduct of the offender and the ends of justice." In Oklahoma, probation supervision "shall not normally exceed two years unless it is determined [that] the interests of the public and the probationer would best be served by an extended period of supervision not to exceed the length of the original sentence." In Virginia, probation may be terminated for cases placed on supervision for 2 years or more after serving one-half of the term or 3 years, whichever comes first.

> **Key Fact**
>
> Length of probation supervision may be shortened by the court in response to exemplary probationer performance or high caseloads.

The decision to terminate probation early and discharge the offender from supervision should be based on the offender's exemplary conduct. Unfortunately, the termination decision may not have any direct relationship to the merits of the case but is often a reflection of the need to keep caseloads down to a manageable size. This means that probationers may be discharged even though they are in need of further supervision. (For a discussion of using early termination as a casework tool, see Torres, 1999.)

Probation Supervision in Philadelphia

Once a person has been sentenced to probation, a PO is assigned to conduct an orientation to the rules of supervision and to assess the needs and risks of the offender. The PO then works with the offender to ensure that special conditions stipulated by the judge are met. This department has placed a high priority on the collection of restitution, which is a frequent stipulation imposed by judges. A probation plan is then developed that will aid the offender in completing his or her term successfully.

When necessary, referrals are made to community-based agencies to help clients who require intensive and special treatment for severe drug, alcohol, and mental health problems. These clients may have the option of remaining in a treatment facility if necessary, even when their probation has expired. Offenders who are polydrug abusers or who have obvious psychiatric problems are evaluated by the department's assessment team, composed of psychologists and a psychiatric social worker. A supervision plan is then developed to assist the PO in supervising the case.

If it is found to be appropriate, some clients are referred to a residential drug treatment program at the Philadelphia State Hospital, which provides group and individual counseling to drug abusers and is administered by a staff person from this department. The department also has a special unit that provides group counseling to clients who cannot or will not take advantage of community mental health services. This unit operates under the supervision of a trained psychologist and primarily serves psychiatric and sex offenders. Offenders charged with driving under the influence are supervised by a special unit called the Alcohol Highway Safety Unit, which handles cases that have either pretrial or posttrial status. The unit monitors the offender's attendance in safe-driving school and in the specified treatment facility.

The Victim Services Unit provides appropriate direct and referral services to victims, helps coordinate victim services among providers so that resources can be provided efficiently and effectively, and increases victim input at sentencing and before an inmate's release on parole.

Violation of Probation

As has already been discussed, probationers are required to abide by rules whose violation can result in their being sent to prison. The *New York State Code of Criminal Procedure* states:

> Probation as a sentence or disposition is a means of offering the offender the opportunity for law-abiding adjustment in the community. Although the probationer is not deprived of his liberty, his life situation is circumscribed by the conditions that are intended to ensure protection of the community and adjustment of the probationer through effective supervision. It is the Probation Department's responsibility to see that the conditions of probation are properly enforced and to inform the court of any significant deviation.

There are two types of probation violation:

1. *Technical violation.* When any of the conditions of probation has been violated, a technical violation of probation exists.
2. *New offense violation.* When a violation involves a new crime, it is a nontechnical or new offense violation.

The probation response to a violation is a matter of considerable discretion. For example, in Philadelphia, the Adult Probation Department advises its probation officers: "Minor violations of probation/[county] parole do not necessarily need to be brought to

Agency # DR#: ____________

WARRANT FOR PROBATIONER

STATE OF NEW YORK
COUNTY OF ONONDAGA } SS:

IN THE NAME OF THE PEOPLE OF THE STATE OF NEW YORK:

To any sheriff, constable, marshal, police officer in this State or to any probation officer of this Court
Whereas ____________________
who was convicted in ____________________ Court
on ____________ on the charge of ____________________
____
before Honorable ____________________
and who was placed on probation on said charge, is accused of violating the conditions of his probation. You are hereby commanded, forthwith, to arrest the above-named probationer, ____________________, and bring him before the above-named Court, or if said Court is adjourned, to deliver him to the proper authorities to be kept in custody until lawfully released.

Dated this ________ day of

____

(Seal) Judge

FIGURE 2.3 *Warrant for Probationer*

> ### NOTICE OF ADMINISTRATIVE HEARING FEBRUARY 26, 2006
>
> TO: The Honorable John Downward
>
> FROM: Rebecca Bealmear, Probation Officer
>
> SUBJECT: Michael Nieman
>
> Your Honor:
>
> On February 12, 2006, an Administrative Hearing was held. The hearing was conducted by the probation officer's supervisor, Debra Farmer. The defendant and this officer were present. The problems identified include the following:
>
> - The defendant tested positive for marijuana >150 ng/ml and cocaine = 265 ng/ml on 1/13/06.
> - The defendant failed to follow his monthly payment plan, and is $190.00 behind on his payments toward his $875.00 court-ordered debt.
>
> The solutions presented include the following:
>
> - The defendant is not to test positive for alcohol or controlled substances or fail to appear for any testing.
> - The defendant is to pay $125.00 per month until July, until his monthly payments are caught up.
> - The defendant will follow all his conditions of probation.
>
> The defendant agrees with the above solutions and understands that failure to comply with any or all will result in immediate filing of violation notice.
>
> Respectfully submitted,
>
> *Rebecca Bealmear*
>
> Rebecca Bealmear
> Probation Officer

FIGURE 2.4 *Probation Department, Marion County Superior Court, Adult Services Division Hearing Report*

the attention of the sentencing Judge, but may be handled between the P.O. and the P/P (probationer/parolee) if such violations are not repeated and do not develop into a pattern." Several probation (and parole) agencies provide for a structured, measured response to violations. In Utah, this includes a point system, based on the offender's history and the present violation, that determines the level of the violation—minimum, medium, maximum—and each level provides a choice of responses, such as a reprimand or more restrictive conditions (e.g., curfew, residential drug treatment, incarceration).

In many jurisdictions (e.g., in Allen County, Pennsylvania, and in New York), the PO has the authority to "discuss the alleged violation(s) with the probationer and inform him that repeated or more serious violation(s) will be dealt with by the court." In New York, if the behavior continues but a formal violation of probation is not necessary, "the court shall be informed of the alleged violation(s) and the department's action to date . . . [and] a recommendation may be made to the court requesting that the court require that the probationer appear before it . . . for a judicial reprimand."

To minimize the number of violations filed with the court, POs in Marion County, Indiana, are encouraged to use administrative hearings to address instances where a formal violation of probation is not yet warranted but the probationer is exhibiting some behavior that could lead to a more serious violation. The PO notifies the probationer in writing of the date, time, and reasons for the hearing, which is attended by the probationer, the PO, and the PO's supervisor. A failure to appear results in the filing of a violation of probation request for a warrant (Figure 2.3). At the conclusion, a hearing report, which can include a modification of the conditions of probation, is signed by the participants (Figure 2.4).

Because violations of probation (and parole) are a contributing factor to prison overcrowding, P/P agencies have been using violation of supervision management strategies to avoid incarcerating clients who are in violation of their conditions of supervision. Typically, these strategies involve graduated sanctions ranging from intensive supervision, to a halfway house placement, to a brief period of incarceration (Burke, 2006; Cox and Bantley, 2005).

Key Fact

Probation violation may be nontechnical, for committing a new crime, and/or technical, for violating the rules of probtion.

Some observers are critical of the discretionary powers exercised by probation departments. They maintain that **technical violations** (e.g., changing residence without immediately notifying the PO) are often ignored until it is believed that the probationer has committed a new crime. "Invoking the technical violation thus becomes the result of the probation officer making the adjudication that a crime has been committed. The probationer has a hearing on the technical violation, but is denied a trial on the suspected crime which triggered the technical violation" (Czajkoski, 1973: 13). As we see, it is easier to find a person "guilty" of a violation of probation than it is to prove criminal charges.

The revocation process originates with POs who exercise a "quasi-judicial role" in that they decide whether to seek revocation (Czajkoski, 1973). The PO's attitude toward the probationer and the violation will influence whether revocation action is initiated. Although the actual procedures differ from jurisdiction to jurisdiction, typically the PO confers with his or her superiors; if a violation is considered serious enough, a notice will be filed with the court (Figure 2.5).

The case will then be placed on the court calendar, and the probationer will be given a copy of the alleged violations and directed to appear for a preliminary or **probable**

COURT NOTIFICATION OF A TECHNICAL VIOLATION OF PROBATION

STATE OF NEW JERSEY   SUPERIOR COURT OF NEW JERSEY
-VS-   Bergen County

MICHAEL JOHNSON   Indictment No. S-584-91-01

BEFORE THE HONORABLE

Alfred D. Schiaffo

I, RICHARD L. ALBERA, Chief Probation Officer of the County of Bergen, aforesaid, do hereby charge that MICHAEL JOHNSON late of the Borough of Totowa, County of Passaic was on the 28th day of September, 2005, convicted in the above-entitled Court on a charge of Possession of a Controlled Dangerous Substance (Cocaine) with the Intent to Distribute and that upon said conviction the Court rendered the following judgment:

On December 2, 2005;

COUNT 1–$3000.00 fine and three (3) years probation.

July 20, 2006–Violation of probation: Probation continued with added condition of serving sixty (60) days in Bergen County Jail.

That the said MICHAEL JOHNSON did violate the terms and conditions of said probation in the following respects:

1. Violated Rule No. 2 by failing to report on December 6, 2006; December 13, 2006; December 20, 2006; December 27, 2006; January 17, 2007; January 24, 2007; January 31, 2007; February 28, 2007; or any date subsequent to March 4, 2007, although directed to report on a once-per-week basis.
2. Violated Rule No. 1, by being under the influence of Controlled Dangerous Substance, to wit: Cocaine on November 8, 2006; November 29, 2006; January 3, 2007; January 11, 2007; and February 21, 2007, as witnessed by abnormal results of urinalysis submitted on those dates.

Richard L. Albera
Chief Probation Officer

Dated: March 21, 2007

FIGURE 2.5 *Court Notification of a Technical Violation of Probation*

COMMONWEALTH OF PENNSYLVANIA : IN THE COURT OF COMMON PLEAS
v. : DAUPHIN COUNTY, PENNSYLVANIA
: NO(S):
: CHARGE(S): CD 20 _____

WAIVER OF PREREVOCATION PRELIMINARY HEARING

I hereby waive (give up) my right to have a prerevocation preliminary hearing in the above captioned case. I understand that I have been accused of committing certain violations of my probation/parole as set forth on the notice of alleged violations dated _____

I understand and it has been explained to me that:

_____ 1. I am not required to waive (give up) my right to have a prerevocation preliminary hearing.

_____ 2. The prerevocation preliminary hearing (sometimes called a "Gagnon 1 hearing") is held for the purpose of having a neutral (impartial) hearing officer determine whether there is probable (reasonable) cause to believe that I have committed acts which would constitute a violation of my probation/parole conditions.

_____ 3. At such prerevocation preliminary hearing I would have an opportunity to speak in person, present witnesses and documentary evidence and confront and cross-examine adverse witnesses (unless the hearing officer specifically finds good cause for not allowing confrontation).

_____ 4. At such prerevocation hearing, the hearing officer may also make a determination as to probable cause to detain me pending a revocation hearing to be scheduled before the Dauphin County Court of Common Pleas.

_____ 5. At such prerevocation hearing, I would be able to have the evidence against me disclosed and obtain a written summary of the hearing from the hearing officer.

_____ 6. After having all of the above explained to me, and being given a chance to read this document and ask questions, I was further advised that I could have a lawyer represent me at such prerevocation hearing and that if I could not afford to pay for a lawyer for this hearing that the Court would appoint a lawyer free of cost to me.

Understanding all of the above, I still give up my right to have a prerevocation preliminary hearing.

DATE: _____

_____   _____
                                          PROBATIONER/PAROLEE

_____   _____
WITNESS   PROBATION/PAROLE OFFICER

FIGURE 2.6 *Waiver of Prerevocation Preliminary Hearing, Pennsylvania*

cause hearing. In some jurisdictions, the preliminary hearing is conducted by an official other than a judge. In other jurisdictions such as Texas, "A probationer is not entitled to a preliminary hearing or examining trial to determine whether there is probable cause to proceed to a revocation hearing"; in cases of violation, the case goes directly before a judge for a revocation hearing. (A probable cause hearing is necessary only if the probationer is to be held in custody pending the revocation hearing.) In any event, if a probationer fails to respond to a notice or summons to appear for a hearing, the judge will usually issue a warrant. A probationer may also waive the right to a preliminary hearing (Figure 2.6).

The flowchart in Figure 2.7 indicates the possibilities presented at each stage of the probation revocation process. At the preliminary hearing, the probationer can deny the charges of probation violation or plead guilty to them. If the plea is "guilty," the judge may deal with the case at once; if the probationer denies the charges, the judge will decide if there is sufficient (probable) cause to believe that probation was violated (in order to remand the probationer to custody), and a revocation hearing is scheduled. The judge may remand the probationer to custody pending the hearing or may release him or her on bail or on his or her own recognizance. The probation department will subsequently prepare a violation of probation report (Figure 2.8): "The report shall contain a summary of the probationer's supervision activities to date, and the alleged facts which would be sufficient, if proven, to establish any violation(s) of probation occurred" (*New York State Code of Criminal Procedure*). Rather than a narrow legal document, the violation of probation report contains information about the probationer's behavior under supervision—for example, employment record—and is presented to the judge prior to the revocation hearing.

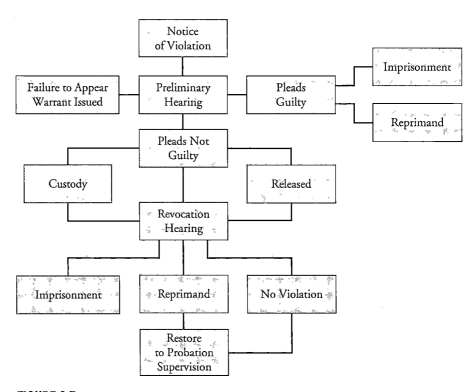

FIGURE 2.7 *Probation Violation Flowchart*

Revocation Hearing

At the **revocation hearing**, the probationer will have an opportunity to testify and present witnesses. An attorney may be present to represent the probationer (according to the provisions outlined in the *Mempa* and *Gagnon* decisions discussed later in this chapter), and in some jurisdictions it is common for the defense attorney and the prosecutor to plea-bargain in probation revocation proceedings as they do when new criminal charges are filed. If the judge finds no violations, the probationer is restored to supervision, but if the judge sustains any of the charges brought by the probation department, the probationer can be reprimanded and restored to supervision, or probation can be revoked and imprisonment ordered. In most cases, the defendant is actually sentenced at the time of conviction, but the imposition of sentence is suspended in favor of probation. Less frequently, the defendant is placed directly on probation without being sentenced. In the latter case, if the violation charge is sustained, the judge can revoke probation and sentence the probationer to a term of imprisonment; the sentence, however, must be in accord with the penalty provided by law for the crime for which the probationer was originally convicted.

Proof of guilt in a criminal trial must be **beyond a reasonable doubt**, but at a probation revocation hearing it need not be greater than by a **preponderance of the evidence**, a lower standard used in civil cases. In a criminal trial, the testimony of an accomplice usually requires **corroboration**—supportive evidence—but no such requirement exists for revocation hearings. Evidence that would not ordinarily be admitted in a criminal trial, such as hearsay testimony, can be entered into evidence at a revocation hearing. When the judge renders a decision on the charges, he or she can consider only the evidence presented at the hearing. When making a decision as to the disposition of a probationer found in violation, the judge can consider many items, such as employment record, relationship to spouse and children, and efforts at drug treatment. The range of options after a finding of "guilty" has been increasing as states seek to avoid the traditional two-dimensional outcomes—prison or continued supervision—that can affect prison overcrowding or (at the other extreme) undermine the supervi-

Key Fact

The probation violation process involves a preliminary (probable cause) hearing and a revocation hearing based on the civil standard of preponderance of the evidence.

SUPERIOR COURT OF CALIFORNIA
COUNTY OF HUMBOLDT

No. CR061950S

THE PEOPLE OF THE STATE OF CALIFORNIA
                                        Plaintiff
                        vs.   **NOTICE OF PROBATION**
                                                                        VIOLATION AND COURT ACTION

Mark Parker
_____

IN CUSTODY   Defendant

TO THE JUDGE OF THE ABOVE-ENTITLED COURT:

On the 9th day of August, 2006, the above-named defendant was granted thirty-six (36) months supervised probation for the crime of violation of Section 646.9(b) of the California Penal Code. Imposition of sentence was suspended.

ALLEGED VIOLATIONS:

Terms of probation violated:

1. Defendant shall obey all laws.
5. Defendant shall comply with the instructions of the probation officer.
12. Defendant shall totally abstain from the use of alcoholic beverages and shall not have in his possession or under his custody or control any alcoholic beverage.
15. Defendant shall not use or have in his possession or under his custody or control any non-prescribed controlled substance.
16. Defendant shall not traffic in controlled substances or associate with any person using or trafficking in controlled substances.
22. Defendant shall enter and successfully complete a residential substance abuse treatment program, at his own expense as directed by the probation officer, and shall not leave without the permission of the probation officer and program director. Defendant shall waive the right to *all* incarceration credits for time served in the treatment program unless he successfully completes *all* phases of the program.

Violated probation as follows:

Defendant was released from HCCF on September 5, 2006, to enter the Salvation Army residential treatment program in San Francisco. Defendant was directed not to leave treatment without the permission of the probation officer.

According to Arcata Police Department case number 06-2785, on September 10, 2006, defendant was arrested on multiple charges including violation of Sections 647(f) and 1203.2 of the California Penal Code, and Section 11377(a) of the California Health and Safety Code.

PERFORMANCE ON PROBATION: Defendant's case was open for supervision on August 23, 2006.

RECOMMENDATION: It is respectfully recommended defendant remain in custody pending an outcome to this matter. Refer for supplemental report.

DATED: September 11, 2006

                                                        BY: _____
                                                             Barbara Robie
                                                             Deputy Probation Officer

READ AND APPROVED BY:

_____
Shaun Brenneman
Supervising Probation Officer

BR/vw

FIGURE 2.8 *Probation Violation Report*

DEFENDANT IN CUSTODY

X You are advised that you should appear before the Court on the 12th day of September, 2006, at 1:20 p.m. Your failure to appear at the time indicated will result in this office seeking a warrant for your arrest.

X COURT ACTION: It is hereby ordered that:

X 1. Defendant's probation is summarily revoked. The said defendant is still subject to the terms of probation pending a revocation of probation hearing in the matter.

___ 2. A bench warrant (with) (without) bail (set at $_____) is issued for defendant herein.

___ 3. Other:

DATED:_____

_____
JUDGE OF THE ABOVE-ENTITLED COURT

SUPERIOR COURT OF CALIFORNIA
COUNTY OF HUMBOLDT

No. CR061950S

THE PEOPLE OF THE STATE OF CALIFORNIA

Plaintiff

vs.

**SUPPLEMENTAL REPORT OF
ADULT PROBATION OFFICER**

Mark Parker
_____
Defendant

CONVICTED OFFENSE: Violation of Section 646.9(b) of the California Penal Code, to wit: Stalking While the Subject of a Restraining Order, a Felony.

VIOLATION OF PROBATION

ATTORNEY: Public Defender
DATE REFERRED: September 13, 2006
REPORT DUE BACK: October 11, 2006
CUSTODY CREDITS:

Pre-sentence Incarceration:
On April 13, 2006, at sentencing for the instant matter, accrued jail time was credited to misdemeanor case numbers CR054067S and CR056230S.

As a Violation:
09-10-06 to 10-11-06   =   31 DAYS

TOTAL ACTUAL DAYS   =   31 DAYS

TO THE HONORABLE COURT:

On August 9, 2006, defendant was granted thirty-six (36) months supervised probation for the crime of violation of Section 646.9(b) of the California Penal Code. Imposition of sentence was suspended.

On September 12, 2006, a Violation of Probation and Court Action was filed. On September 13, 2006, defendant admitted to the violation and the matter was referred to the Probation Department for preparation of supplemental report due at sentencing on October 11, 2006.

PROBATION VIOLATION:

Defendant was released from Humboldt County Correctional Facility on September 5, 2006, to enter the Salvation Army residential treatment program in San Francisco. He was transported by Probation to Arcata for purchase of a bus ticket to San Francisco. He was given written directions to report to treatment that same evening. Defendant was directed not to leave treatment without the permission of the probation officer.

FIGURE 2.8 (continued)

According to Arcata Police Department case number 06-2785, on September 10, 2006, defendant was arrested on multiple charges including violation of Sections 647(f) and 1203.2 of the California Penal Code, and Section 11377(a) of the California Health and Safety Code. Defendant was observed staggering as he attempted to walk down 11th street. When officers approached, defendant was sitting on the sidewalk and yelling. The officer was unable to report what defendant was saying due to severe slurring of his speech. During booking at the Humboldt County Correctional Facility, a Ziplock baggie was found containing suspected methamphetamine.

PERFORMANCE ON PROBATION:

On August 28, 2006, Probation met with defendant at the Humboldt County Correctional Facility (HCCF) to review and sign orders, determine treatment options and develop a case plan. On September 5, 2006, defendant was transported to Arcata to purchase a bus ticket to enter a residential treatment program through Salvation Army in San Francisco. Parker specifically requested this program and obtained entry independent of probation or assistance from HCCF program director Karen Keasey. Defendant apparently chose to stay in Arcata. Less than five days after release, defendant was arrested while intoxicated and had methamphetamine on his person at booking.

STATEMENT OF DEFENDANT:

On September 25, 2005, defendant was interviewed at the Humboldt County Correctional Facility for a statement. Defendant declared plans to submit a written statement to the Court at sentencing. The following is a summary of his statement.

Parker began by stating he had traveled to San Francisco by bus but found the neighborhood to "be too full of druggies." He said, "I didn't know the program was going to be so hard." He then said he returned the next day to Arcata. He later changed his story and claimed he hitchhiked back to Arcata "with whoever would pick me up." Finally, defendant admitted he got off the bus to San Francisco in Rio Dell and never really left the County. "I just didn't want to do the program. I know I need to do a program. I just couldn't bring myself to actually go."

When asked how he spent his time the five days he was in Arcata, Parker relayed, "I knew it was a matter of days before I got arrested. I went to a couple of bars, partied under the 14th Street bridge, got some blotter acid from some friends. I wasn't that drunk when I was arrested, but I was tripping." Defendant claims to not remember much he did during his five days of freedom. He denied calling the victim of his original crime and denied using methamphetamine, despite having some on his person at booking.

"I don't know what should happen now. I'd be willing to go to Crossroads up here, or J Street, HRC, whatever. I think I would do better in Humboldt. I have been sober and happy before."

STATEMENT OF VICTIM:

On September 14, 2006, the victim of the original crime, Janet Kline, left a voice message with the undersigned. She reported defendant had telephoned her house on Friday, September 8th. She advised Probation there was an active restraining order against defendant and stated, "I have a right to know where he is."

On September 19, 2006, Ms. Kline was contacted by telephone to obtain a statement for this report. She declined to make an official statement but did plead for the opportunity to "get on with my life and be left alone."

Ms. Kline was advised of the date and time of sentencing, if she desired to be in Court. It was the impression of this officer, from random comments made, that victim was fearful of retaliation but would not be opposed to defendant's incarceration in a state facility.

CRIMINAL HISTORY:

Parker's arrest history is extensive. From 1980 to 2006, defendant has eighteen misdemeanor convictions and four felony convictions. Defendant has sustained fourteen violations of probation in various cases and has served prison sentences varying in length from 4 years, with 403 days credit for time served, to an 8-month term. He was on probation for two other misdemeanor cases. The following is taken from the PSI report dated July 28, 2006, and penned by Officer Sanders:

"On August 14, 2005, in case number CR054067S, defendant was convicted of violation of Section 415 of the California Penal Code. Defendant was granted three (3) years summary probation. He has violated probation twice in this case. In this case, defendant hit victim in the upper left arm with a closed fist, hard enough to leave a bruise. He also pinched her below the right breast.

"On December 6, 2005, in case number CR056230S, defendant pleaded guilty to violation of Sections 136.1(b) (1) and 422 of the California Penal Code. He was granted three (3) years conditional revocable release and has one sustained violation. In this case, defendant went to victim's residence in violation of a restraining order. He told her he wished to retrieve property he had left in her residence. She agreed but told him he would have to leave after gathering the property. The victim reported once defendant was inside, he said, 'Bitch, you can't make me leave now.' He threatened to kill her if she called law enforcement. She finally called the Sheriff's office one week later, when defendant had still not left."

SUMMARY AND EVALUATION:

Appearing before the Court for sentencing, following a sustained violation of probation, is Mark Parker.

Parker was granted thirty-six (36) months supervised probation for the felonious crime of violation of Section 646.9(b) of the California Penal Code. Imposition of sentence was suspended. Defendant was on two misdemeanor cases involving physical harm to the victim.

Parker put effort into finding and applying for entrance into the Salvation Army residential program in San Francisco. He received acceptance and asked to be released as soon as possible to begin treatment. Parker was given a ride to Arcata, written directions to the treatment facility front door, and written instructions to contact Probation within forty-eight (48) hours of entry to treatment. Defendant signed a case plan that states he will report his whereabouts and comply with Court orders as well as abide by program rules.

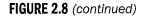

FIGURE 2.8 *(continued)*

Parker departed Arcata by bus September 5, 2006, only to exit the bus in Rio Dell, and he returned to Arcata where he promptly began to "party," using alcohol and acid. He denies use of methamphetamine but was found to be in possession of a "baggie" at booking. Defendant also reported difficulty in remembering his actions while released.

Janet Kline, the victim of two misdemeanor cases and one felony case against defendant, claimed he telephoned her house while released. She declined to make an official statement, but this officer believes victim is afraid of defendant, especially when he is under the influence of drugs and alcohol. She stated, "I just want to get on with my life and be left alone."

As stated in the presentence investigative report, defendant is statutorily ineligible for probation due to his three prior felony convictions. He has a lengthy criminal history including three convictions for driving under the influence, two prior convictions related to his abusive relationship with victim, and felony convictions for domestic violence, burglary and a weapons-related offense. Defendant has not been on any type of supervised probation or parole since 1997.

Parker was given the opportunity to enter a treatment program of his choice and he immediately absconded. He stated he knew he needed treatment but could not bring himself to actually enter treatment. Instead, he became intoxicated, ingested acid and was arrested with possession of methamphetamine.

Defendant asks the Court for another chance. This officer asked defendant if he felt he could comply with probation restrictions and defendant did not answer.

Mark Parker is a threat to victim and to the community. He is a poor candidate for probation and it is recommended he be committed to the Department of Corrections and Rehabilitation for the recommended term of four (4) years.

RECOMMENDATION:

It is respectfully recommended Parker's probation be revoked and defendant be committed to the California Department of Corrections and Rehabilitation for the aggravated term of four (4) years.

In addition, defendant shall pay a restitution Fine of $200.00, pursuant to Section 1202.45 of the California Penal Code.

Finally, defendant is to be advised of a period of parole following his release from state prison.

Respectfully submitted,

DOUGLAS RASINES
CHIEF PROBATION OFFICER

By: _____
Barbara L. Robie
Deputy Probation Officer

READ AND APPROVED BY:

_____
Shaun M. Brenneman
Supervising Probation Officer

DATED: September 28, 2006

BLR/vw

FIGURE 2.8 *(continued)*

sion process. Responses now include short terms in a local jail or halfway house, electronic monitoring, intensive supervision, or some combination thereof (all discussed in Chapters 11 and 12).

Street Time

A defendant is convicted of burglary and sentenced to 3.5 years' imprisonment (written 3-6-0: 3 years, 6 months, 0 days). His sentence is suspended in favor of probation. The probationer spends 1 year (1-0-0) under supervision and then violates the conditions of probation in an important respect. After a revocation hearing, the judge revokes probation and orders the probationer to begin serving the 3-6-0 sentence in prison. Must the offender serve a maximum of 3-6-0 in prison, or is the 1-0-0 year of probation supervision, so-called **street time**, to be subtracted from the 3-6-0 sentence?

The answer to this question varies from state to state. Some states do not recognize the time spent under supervision as time served against the sentence unless the full probationary term is successfully completed; a minority of states provide street time credit for probation violations not involving the commission of a new crime, and others leave it to the discretion of the judge.

LEGAL DECISIONS AFFECTING PROBATION

As the least democratic of our three branches of government, the judiciary—particularly the federal courts and, especially, the U.S. Supreme Court—can decide cases in a manner that may be politically unpopular. It can champion the legal rights of persons who (1) do not represent a significant bloc of votes or a source of campaign funding or (2) cannot generate a great deal of media attention, sympathy, or public support. Thus, in 1966, the Supreme Court rendered the famous *Miranda* decision (*Miranda v. Arizona*, 384 U.S. 436), which mandated that police suspects be informed of certain rights (to remain silent, to have counsel) before any questioning. The following year, in another Arizona case, the Supreme Court rendered the *Gault* decision, which gave important rights to juveniles (discussed in Chapter 4). That same year, the *Mempa* decision gave probationers the right to counsel in certain instances of probation violation. The Court continued to show an interest in persons with a "disadvantaged status"—juveniles, probationers, welfare recipients, prison inmates, the mentally ill, and parolees—in the many cases that are discussed in this section and in Chapters 4, 5, and 7.

Legal decisions that affect probation usually affect parole and vice versa. For example, the *Gagnon* decision to be discussed in this section used the *Morrissey* decision (discussed in Chapter 7), which concerned parole violation, as a precedent. However, for purposes of study, the significant decisions in probation and parole have been divided according to the primary thrust of the case. The basis for these decisions has been the constitutional concern for **due process** contained in the Fourth through Eighth Amendments. The Fourteenth Amendment, which was adopted in 1868 to protect newly freed slaves, applied these amendments to the states: "No state shall make or enforce any law which shall abridge the privileges or immunities of citizens of the United States; nor shall any State deprive any person of life, liberty, or property, without due process of law." However, the courts did not uniformly apply the Fourteenth Amendment to all constitutional guarantees. In 1961, the Supreme Court decided the case of *Mapp v. Ohio* (367 U.S. 643): Evidence (pornographic materials) seized by the police in violation of the Fourth Amendment could not be admitted into evidence in a *state* trial (such evidence was already inadmissible in *federal* trials since 1914). This decision provided a basis for the so-called **exclusionary rule**, which does *not* apply to probation or parole violation proceedings—evidence seized in violation of the Fourth Amendment can generally be used in a probation or parole violation hearing (*Pennsylvania Board of Probation and Parole v. Scott*, 524 U.S. 357, 1998).

Conditions of Probation

In general, the courts can impose any conditions of probation that are reasonably related to the rehabilitation of the offender (e.g., to undergo treatment for drug addiction) or the protection of the community (e.g., to avoid the possession of any weapons). The state has a compelling interest in setting limits on the behavior of probationers; therefore, the Fourth Amendment notwithstanding, probationers have a **diminished expectation of privacy.** Thus, an offender with a history of drug addiction can be required to submit to periodic urinalysis as a condition of probation and a warrantless search by a PO is permitted, although the same search by a police officer might constitute a violation of the Fourth Amendment. Probationers can be required to report in person and to answer all reasonable inquiries by the PO, the Fifth Amendment right to remain silent notwithstanding, although the probationer need not incriminate him- or herself. While a probationer can be compelled to answer questions, answers may not be admitted in criminal proceedings against him or her. If, however, there is no coercion, the probationer must specifically invoke the privilege and remain silent, or incriminating responses to the PO may be used against the probationer (*Minnesota v. Murphy*, 104 S. Ct. 1136, 1984). Probationers can be required to avoid bars or notorious parts of a city (e.g., areas where a great deal of drug trafficking is known to occur).

In 1982, the U.S. Court of Appeals for the Fifth Circuit reviewed a case involving the First Amendment (*Owens v. Kelley*, 681 F.2d 1362). The plaintiff (probationer) claimed that a probation condition requiring him to participate in a program called "Emotional Maturity Instruction" violated his First Amendment freedom of religion because of the religious content of the course. The court stated that a "condition of probation which requires the probationer to adopt religion or to adopt any particular religion would be unconstitutional. . . . It follows that a condition of probation which requires the probationer to submit himself to a course advocating the adoption of religion or a particular religion also transgresses the First Amendment."

Owens also challenged a probation condition that required him to "submit to and cooperate with a lie detector test . . . whenever so directed by the Probation Supervisor [title of probation officers in Georgia] or any other law enforcement officer." The probationer claimed that this condition violated his Fifth Amendment privilege against compelled self-incrimination. The court of appeals rejected this claim: "The condition on its face does not impinge upon Owens' Fifth Amendment rights. The condition does not stipulate that Owens must answer incriminating questions. If any question is asked during [the lie detector] examination which Owens believes requires an incriminating answer he is free to assert his Fifth Amendment privilege, and nothing in the probation condition suggests otherwise."

Probation Violation and the Three Theories of Probation

Traditionally, a person on probation has not been considered a free person, despite the fact that the probationer is not incarcerated. The basis for imposing restrictions (conditions) on a probationer's liberty—and for punishing violations—is contained in three theories:

1. *Conditional privilege.* Probation is an act of mercy by the judge that has not been earned by the defendant. As such, probation can simply be withdrawn if any condition of the privilege is violated.
2. *Contract theory.* Each probationer is required to sign a *contract*—a stipulation agreeing to certain terms in return for conditional liberty. As in any contractual situation, a breach of contract can result in penalties, in this case, revocation of probation.
3. *Custody theory.* Persons placed on probation in lieu of imprisonment are in the legal custody of the court, and therefore quasi-prisoners, with their constitutional rights being abridged accordingly. Under such conditions, the court has the authority to move the convict from a community setting to a prison setting in the event of a violation of the conditions of supervision.

Legal decisions discussed in this chapter have challenged these theories.

Probation Revocation

In 1967, the Supreme Court ruled (*Mempa v. Rhay*, 389 U.S. 128) that under certain conditions a probationer is entitled to be represented by counsel at a revocation hearing. In 1959, Jerry Mempa entered a plea of guilty to the charge of joyriding in a stolen car in the state of Washington. Imposition of sentence was deferred, and Mempa was placed on probation for 2 years on the condition that he spend 30 days in the county jail. About 4 months later, the Spokane County prosecutor moved to have Mempa's probation revoked on the grounds that he had been involved in a burglary while on probation. Mempa, who was 17 years old at the time, was not represented by counsel at his revocation hearing, nor was he asked whether he wanted to have counsel appointed for him.

At the hearing, Mempa was asked if it was true that he had been involved in the alleged burglary, and he answered in the affirmative. A PO testified without cross-examination that according to his information Mempa had been involved in the burglary and had previously denied participation in it. Without asking the probationer if he had any evidence to present or any statement to make, Mempa's probation was revoked, and he was sentenced to 10 years' imprisonment. The judge added that he would recommend to the parole board that Mempa be required to serve only 1 year.

In a companion case considered by the Supreme Court, William Earl Walkling was placed on probation (for burglary), with imposition of sentence deferred. At a subsequent revocation hearing, Walkling informed the court that he had retained an attorney. When the attorney did not arrive on time, the court proceeded with the hearing, at which a PO presented hearsay testimony to the effect that the probationer had committed 14 separate acts of forgery and grand larceny. The court revoked probation and imposed a sentence of 15 years. No record was kept of the proceeding. The *Walkling* case was consolidated with the *Mempa* case by the Supreme Court.

The Supreme Court noted that previously it had held that the right to counsel is not confined merely to representation during a trial, stating that counsel is required at *every* stage of a criminal proceeding when substantial rights of an accused criminal may be affected, and sentencing is one of these critical stages. In *Mempa*, the Court stated that counsel could aid in marshaling facts; introducing evidence of mitigating circumstances; and, in general, assisting the defendant in presenting his or her case with respect to sentence. The Court ruled that some rights could be lost if counsel were not present at a sentencing hearing, and "we decide here that a lawyer must be afforded at this proceeding whether it is labeled a revocation of probation or a deferred sentencing." The importance of the *Mempa* case goes beyond the limited finding made by the Court—it was the first time that the Supreme Court had ruled in favor of the rights of a person on probation.

In the next important probation/parole case (*Morrissey v. Brewer*, 1972), the Supreme Court stipulated that the amount of due process rights to which a person is constitutionally entitled is directly related to the potential loss that can result: **liberty interest**. The greatest amount of potential loss is clearly in a criminal case, where total liberty—and, at times, life itself—may be forfeited. Thus, the criminal process represents the extreme end of the due process continuum: rights to counsel, to remain silent, to a jury trial, and to cross-examine adverse witnesses. Located somewhere at the other extreme would be the due process rights of a student to challenge a course grade. Where are probation and parole located along this due process continuum?

In *Morrissey v. Brewer* (discussed in Chapter 7), the Court ruled that parolees accused of violating the conditions of parole are entitled to certain due process rights, including both a preliminary and a revocation hearing. In 1973, the Court rendered a similar decision in the case of a probation violation, *Gagnon v. Scarpelli* (411 U.S. 778). In 1965, Gerald Scarpelli pleaded guilty to a charge of armed robbery and was sentenced to 15 years' imprisonment, but the sentence was suspended and he was placed on probation for 7 years. The probationer was given permission to reside in Illinois (under the Interstate Compact discussed in Chapter 11), where he was placed under the supervision of the Cook County Adult Probation Department. Shortly afterward, Scarpelli was arrested in a Chicago suburb with a codefendant and charged with burglary. The following month, his probation was revoked, and Scarpelli was incarcerated in the Wisconsin

Key Fact

The controlling case in probation violation, *Gagnon v. Scarpelli*, found that probationers have a liberty interest and are thus entitled to diminished due process rights.

Reformatory to begin serving the 15 years to which he had originally been sentenced; at no time was he afforded a hearing. Scarpelli appealed.

Scarpelli was released on parole in Wisconsin, at which time his appeal reached the U.S. Supreme Court. He claimed that revocation of probation without a hearing and counsel was a denial of due process. The Court ruled that, in legal jargon, Scarpelli had a liberty interest: "Probation revocation, like parole revocation, is not a stage of a criminal prosecution, but does result in a loss of liberty. Accordingly, we hold that a probationer, like a parolee, is entitled to a preliminary and a final revocation hearing under the conditions specified in *Morrissey v. Brewer*, supra." In other words, as noted in a 1982 state of Texas decision (*Rogers v. State*, 640 S.W.2d 248), liberty on probation, although indeterminate, "includes many of the core values of unqualified liberty, such as freedom to be with family and friends, freedom to form other enduring attachments of normal life, freedom to be gainfully employed, and freedom to function as a responsible and self-reliant person."

In *Gagnon*, the Supreme Court held that a probationer is entitled to:

- A notice of the alleged violations
- A preliminary hearing to decide if there is sufficient (probable) cause to believe that probation was violated (to remand the probationer to custody)
- A revocation hearing ("a somewhat more comprehensive hearing prior to the making of the final revocation decision")

At these hearings, the Court ruled, the probationer will have the opportunity to appear and to present witnesses and evidence on his or her own behalf as well as a conditional right to confront adverse witnesses. With respect to the right to counsel, the Court was ambiguous: "We . . . find no justification for a new inflexible constitutional rule with respect to the requirement of counsel. We think, rather, that the decision as to the need for counsel must be made on a case-by-case basis." In practice, however, probationers have been afforded the right to privately engaged or appointed counsel at probation revocation hearings.

Now that we have completed our look at the history, administration, and legal issues surrounding probation supervision, in Chapter 3 we examine the presentence investigation report.

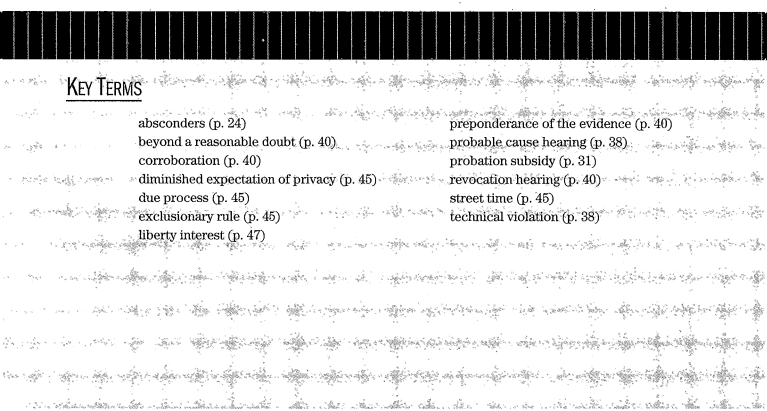

Key Terms

absconders (p. 24)

beyond a reasonable doubt (p. 40)

corroboration (p. 40)

diminished expectation of privacy (p. 45)

due process (p. 45)

exclusionary rule (p. 45)

liberty interest (p. 47)

preponderance of the evidence (p. 40)

probable cause hearing (p. 38)

probation subsidy (p. 31)

revocation hearing (p. 40)

street time (p. 45)

technical violation (p. 38)

Internet Connections

Administrative Office of the U.S. Courts: uscourts.gov

American Probation and Parole Association: appa-net.org

Federal Judicial Center: fjc.gov

Federal Probation and Pretrial Officers Association: fppoa.org

Nation's Court Directory: courts.net

National Center for State Courts: ncsconline.org

Probation agency links: cppca.org/link

State courts links: doc.state.co.us/links.htm

State Justice Institute: statejustice.org

Review Questions

1. What is the difference between a suspended sentence and probation?
2. What activities of John Augustus are part of the services of a modern probation agency?
3. How does placing restrictions on who can be granted probation violate a basic tenet of positivism?
4. What led to the dramatic increase in the use of POs in the United States?
5. What are the six categories into which the administration of probation services can be placed?
6. What are the advantages and disadvantages of placing probation services in the judicial branch of government?
7. What are the advantages and disadvantages of placing probation services in the executive branch of government?
8. How can uniformity be encouraged in states where probation services are administered at the county level?
9. What are the variables that can affect the granting of probation?
10. Why, in some jurisdictions, is there a built-in incentive to sentence a defendant to prison instead of probation?
11. How can the geographic area where the court is situated affect the granting of probation?
12. What is a probation subsidy?
13. Under what conditions is a sentence of imprisonment to be preferred over a sentence of probation?
14. Why would offenders be discharged from probation when their behavior did not justify early termination of supervision?
15. Why is the judiciary in a better position than the other branches of government to guarantee the rights of probationers and parolees (and others)?
16. What are the options available when a probation officer discovers a violation of probation?
17. What three theories have formed the basis for imposing restrictions on a probationer's liberty?
18. What is street time?
19. What have the courts ruled with respect to conditions of probation?
20. What was the issue decided in the case of *Mempa v. Rhay*? What was the real significance of the *Mempa* case?
21. What rights were provided to persons accused of violating probation in the case of *Gagnon v. Scarpelli*?

Sentencing and the Presentence Investigation

The Michigan Supreme Court has indicated that the importance of the presentence investigation [PSI] cannot be overemphasized. PSI is an integral part of the sentencing process, designed to provide the judge with sufficient information to make informed, individualized sentences that are appropriate for the offender and the offense.

—*Thomas H. McTavish* (1997: 8)

Chapter Outline

An investigation before sentencing is the basis for a presentence investigation (PSI) report, sometimes referred to as a probation report or PSI. After the conviction of a defendant and before the sentencing hearing, a judge may (depending on the circumstances and the statutes of the jurisdiction) order a PSI which traditionally has reflected a positivist view interest in the offender (not just the offense). It may be a short-form PSI (usually used in misdemeanor or less serious felony cases) or a long-form PSI (used in most felony cases). This chapter provides examples of these types of PSI reports.

Requiring a Presentence Investigation Report

In some states, the law requires a **presentence investigation (PSI)** report for crimes punishable by more than 1 year of imprisonment; in others, the judge retains the discretion to order a report. In New York and Michigan, for example, a long-form report is required in all felony cases; in misdemeanor cases, the report is discretionary and, when done, is usually in the short form. In Utah, a PSI report is required for all felony and serious misdemeanors, and in Missouri and Nevada, a PSI is mandatory in all felony cases unless the defendant waives the requirement—in which case, at the judge's discretion, a PSI may still be compiled. In Texas, no legal requirement exists that a PSI be prepared in each felony case, so the trial judge has the discretion to order a report or to sentence without one. In Illinois, "a defendant shall not be sentenced for a felony before a written presentence report of investigation is presented to and considered by the court," although this right is frequently waived by the defense counsel because a plea agreement has already been arranged (discussed later).

Purposes of a PSI Report

The PSI report has four basic purposes:

1. The primary purpose is to help the court make an appropriate sentencing decision. The report should help in deciding for or against probation, determining the conditions of probation or deciding among available institutions, and determining the appropriate length of sentence.

2. The PSI serves as the basis for a plan of probation or parole supervision and treatment. The report indicates the problem areas in the defendant's life, his or her capacity for using help, and the opportunities available in the community. During the investigation, the defendant usually begins to relate to the probation department, learning how probation officers (POs) work and gaining some understanding of the nature of the agency.

3. The PSI assists jail and prison personnel in their classification and treatment programs. Institutions are often dependent on the report when the inmate is first received, a time when little is known other than what is contained in commitment documents: conviction and sentence data. The PSI helps institutional staff to understand and classify the offender; it can provide valuable information that will help in planning for the care, custody, and rehabilitation of the inmate. This includes everything from the type of custody required and the care of physical needs to the planning of the various phases of the institutional program.

    Many institutions will have little, if any, background or social, medical, and psychological information other than that provided by the PSI report. This means that the report will have an effect on the way in which an inmate is viewed and approached by institutional personnel because they will take the word of the PO over that of the offender. The ideal report can give focus and initial direction to institutional authorities for treatment and training as well as care and management.

4. If the defendant is sentenced to a correctional institution, the report will eventually serve to furnish parole authorities with information pertinent to release planning and consideration for parole as well as determination of any special conditions of supervision.

In more recent years, an additional dimension—determining the financial condition of defendants—has become important in preparing a PSI report. In the 1984 Criminal Fine Enforcement Act and the 1987 Criminal Fines Improvement Act, Congress cited the need to determine a defendant's ability to pay fines. Financial information is also necessary to assess the defendant's ability to make restitution and to pay any probation

1. Identify the victim of the offense. (Should the victim be deceased, information will be gathered from the surviving spouse, adult children, or closest blood relative.)
2. Itemize economic losses suffered by the victim as a result of the offense.
3. Identify any physical injury suffered by the victim as a result of the offense along with its seriousness and permanence.
4. Describe any change in the victim's personal welfare or familial relationships as a result of the offense.
5. Identify any request for psychological services initiated by the victim or the victim's family as a result of the offense.

FIGURE 3.1 *Victim Impact Statement, Maryland*

supervision fees, which have become rather common. In the federal system, offenders must disclose to POs their assets and liabilities and the sources and amounts of their incomes and expenses. POs must then confirm these amounts by reviewing documentation provided by the offender. "Probation officers carefully review statements from savings and checking accounts including canceled checks, statements from stockbrokers, closing statements and appraisals from real estate transactions, sales and loan agreements on automobiles and other assets, credit card statements, and documentation on other consumer debt. The probation officer examines the supporting documentation to determine if it is consistent with the offender's financial statement" (Berg, 1997: 29).

Some states include a separate **victim impact statement (VIS)** that is attached to the PSI and usually includes a "description of the harm in terms of financial, social, psychological, and physical consequences of the crime." The VIS may also include a statement concerning the victim's feelings about the crime, the offender, and the proposed sentence (Figure 3.1).

The investigating officer in some states may also be required to provide offender information to a victim.

> The probation officer who interviewed victim(s) and witnesses of a felony, as part of the presentence investigation, shall inform them of their right to receive from the Indiana Department of Corrections (IDOC) information regarding when the offender is to be discharged from prison; to be released on parole; is to have a parole release or violation hearing; has escaped; or is going into a temporary release program. The Probation Department shall provide the IDOC with the most recent list of addresses and/or phone numbers of victims no later than five days after receipt of the information from the victim(s). Victims may give the IDOC written notification that they do not wish to receive notification.

In the PSI, the PO attempts in the report to "focus light on the character and personality of the defendant, and to offer insight into his problems and needs, to help understand the world in which he lives, to learn about his relationships with people, and to discover salient factors that underlie the specific offense and conduct in general" and to "suggest alternatives in the rehabilitation process" (Division of Probation, 1974: 48). The report is not expected to show guilt or innocence, only to relate the facts that the PO has been able to gather during the course of the presentence investigation.

Key Fact

PSI reports often include information on offenders' financial status and a victim impact statement.

CONTENT OF A PSI REPORT

PSI reports should be flexible in format, reflecting a difference in the background of different offenders and making the best use of available resources and probation department capabilities. A full report should normally contain the following list of items (American Probation and Parole Association and the Administrative Office of the Illinois Courts):

1. *Legal data.* Arresting officer, victim, original charges filed, and summary of court action as well as complete description of offense and circumstances surrounding it (not limited to aspects developed for the record as part of the determination of guilt).

2. *Defendant statement.* Defendant's version of offense and his or her attitude.

3. *Codefendant(s).* Information about any codefendant(s), including age and court status.

4. *Victim statement.* Statement from victim and description of victim's status, impact on victim, losses suffered by victim, and restitution due to victim.

5. *Prior record.* Full description of offender's prior juvenile and/or criminal record (if any).

6. *Probation/parole.* Offender's prior adjustment and performance on probation, parole, or any other supervised sentence (if any).

7. *Education and employment.* Description of offender's educational background, present employment status, financial status, and capabilities.

8. *Military service.* Description of offender's military record (if applicable)

9. *Social history.* Information on offender's family relationships, marital status, dependents, interests and activities, residence history, and religious affiliations as well as reports from clinics, institutions, and other social agencies with which offender has been involved.

10. *Medical and mental status.* Offender's medical history and (if desirable) psychological or psychiatric report.

11. *Environments.* Information about environments to which offender might return or to which offender could be sent should probation be granted.

12. *Community resources.* Information about special resources available to assist offender, such as treatment centers, residential facilities, vocational training services, special educational facilities, rehabilitation programs of various institutions to which offender might be committed, special programs in probation department, and other similar programs particularly relevant to offender's situation.

13. *Summary and analysis.* List of most significant aspects of report, including specific recommendations as to sentencing (special effort should be made in preparation of PSI reports not to burden the court with irrelevant and unconnected details).

Some jurisdictions have been including **prediction scales** in their PSI reports. These actuarial-type instruments rate the defendant according to criminal history, education and employment record, family and marital history, companions, alcohol and drug problems, emotional and personal attributes, and attitude or orientation (e.g., supportive of crime and unfavorable toward convention). A total score recommends for or against probation and suggests level of supervision.

GATHERING OF INFORMATION FOR A PSI REPORT

Information in the PSI is derived from persons and documents. Obviously, interview skills and the ability to locate, review, and interpret records and reports are crucial in preparing a PSI.

Interviews

Key Fact

Most of the information in a PSI report is gained from interviews.

In probation and parole, much of the necessary information is received directly from people. Thus, report quality is often dependent on the interview skills of probation and parole personnel. In the PSI, a great deal of information is gained by interviewing the defendant: "Interviews shall be directed toward obtaining and clarifying relevant information and making observations of the defendant's/respondent's behavior, attitudes and character" (*New York State Code of Criminal Procedure*, 350.6–3ii). These interviews are conducted in all types of surroundings, from hot and noisy detention pens where dozens of people may be awaiting a court hearing to the relative quiet of the probation office.

A quiet, comfortable setting with a maximum of privacy is obviously the best environment for an interview because a place that lacks privacy or has numerous distractions will adversely affect the productivity of the interview. Sometimes interviews are conducted in the defendant's home, which provides an opportunity to observe the offender's home situation and adds an additional and sometimes vital dimension to the report. New York statutes advise: "Whenever possible, interviews with the defendant/respondent shall be at the probation office; however, visits to the defendant's/respondent's residence may be made when there is an indication that additional information will be obtained that is likely to influence the recommendation or court disposition."

The interview is an anxiety-producing situation for the defendant. Previous experiences in similar situations, such as questioning by the police, may have been unpleasant. The PO tries to lower anxiety by cordially introducing him- or herself and clearly explaining the purpose of the interview and the PSI report. This approach is especially important for the defendant who is not familiar with the criminal justice system in general and the court process in particular.

The PO may try to deal with matters of concern to the defendant. A male defendant may be engaged in a discussion of how his wife and dependents can secure public assistance in the event he is imprisoned. The PO might offer to write a letter of referral for his wife to take with her to the welfare department or other social agency that can provide assistance. Female offenders with children will need help in planning for their care in the event of a sentence of imprisonment. In some way, the officer must show genuine concern and interest in the defendant while being realistic enough to expect many answers and statements that will be self-serving. Because the PO's contact with the defendant is limited, the officer cannot expect to probe deeply into the defendant's personality.

Some defendants will be overtly hostile; others will mask their hostility or anxiety with wisecrack-type answers. The PO must control his or her temper and temperament—he or she is the professional and must never lose sight of that fact during an interview. In questioning, generalized queries (e.g., "What have you been doing?") should be avoided (lest the interviewer be told, "Nothin' much"). Questions should be specific but require an explanation rather than a simple yes or no answer. The PO must avoid putting answers in the defendant's mouth (e.g., "Did you quit that job because it was too difficult?").

When the PSI is complete, the defendant should be reinterviewed to give him or her an opportunity to refute certain information or clarify any aspect of the report that may be in conflict with other parts of the report. In addition to the defendant, the PO may interview the arresting officer, the victim, employers, and significant others in the defendant's environment, such as spouse, parents, siblings, teachers, and clergy. Some recommend interviewing the defense counsel and prosecutor (Storm, 1997).

Records and Reports

The probation officer will be reviewing records and reports in the course of the PSI. The first is the arrest record of the defendant, referred to as a rap sheet. This record will take the form of an arrest sheet(s) of a law enforcement agency, such as the state police. Each rap sheet entry is usually the result of the subject being fingerprinted. The sheet typically contains numerous abbreviations that the PO must decipher if the record is to be useful (e.g., *Att Burg* for attempted burglary or *DUI* for driving under the influence). The arrest sheet does not describe the offense and may not even indicate if it is a felony or misdemeanor; it simply contains the official charge (e.g., *Burg 2*). There is usually no mention of the premises that were burglarized or what (if anything) was taken. In addition, the sheet often omits the disposition of the arrest, so the officer may not be able to determine from the arrest report what happened to a particular case; therefore, it is often necessary to check court records or to contact out-of-state agencies to determine the disposition of a case.

Key Fact

The second greatest source of information in a PSI report is from other reports, particularly the rap sheet containing prior criminal history.

The nature of the defendant's prior record is important. The law usually provides for a harsher sentence if the defendant has one or more prior felony convictions. In addition, the defendant's eligibility for probation and a variety of treatment programs, such as drug rehabilitation, may be affected by a prior criminal record. Also there are the "three strikes and you're out" laws. The PO is especially interested in any information that may influence the sentence that was omitted during the trial, particularly any mitigating or aggravating circumstances, and information that can provide a different perspective on the case. The officer will review any previous PSI reports as well as reports of other correctional agencies that have had contact with the defendant, such as training schools, residential treatment centers, and prison and parole agencies. The PO may also be interested in reviewing the educational records of the defendant. With the increasing number of substance-abusing defendants coming into the criminal justice system, POs must review this dimension of each defendant and explore the appropriateness of a recommendation for substance abuse treatment.

If there are any medical, psychiatric, or psychological reports available, the PO will review and analyze them. To do this review, he or she must understand the nomenclature and the meaning of any tests used by medical and mental health professionals; these professionals often refer to the *Diagnostic and Statistical Manual of Mental Disorders* (referred to simply as DSM), so probation and parole agencies should have copies available for their officers. The PO should make a judgment as to whether a psychiatric or psychological referral should be made during the PSI. Indiscriminate referrals to mental health or court-based clinics waste resources—a crime may be rational, and criminal behavior is not generally symptomatic of an internalized conflict. In cases in which symptoms of mental disorder are apparent and in those situations in which the offender may benefit from an exploration of his or her problems, a referral should be made. If no referral is made and a lack of psychiatric and psychological information exists, the PO should present his or her own observations concerning the defendant's intellectual capacity and personality (e.g., level of social functioning and contact with reality).

If the PO has received conflicting information about the defendant and is unable to reconcile the discrepancies, this difficulty should be pointed out in the report and not left up to the reader to discover (or, more likely, not discover). "The probation officer must also distinguish between facts and the inferences, or opinions, or conclusions based upon those facts" (Storm, 1997: 13).

Of crucial importance in any PSI report are the sections titled "Evaluative Summary and Recommendation" (although in some jurisdictions a recommendation is not provided). In Nevada, statutes require the PSI to contain "a recommendation of a definite term of confinement or an amount of fine or both." Nothing should appear in either of these sections that is not supported by the rest of the report. The summary contains the highlights of the total report and should serve as a reminder to the reader of the information that has already been presented. The recommendation is a carefully thought-out statement, based on the officer's best professional judgment. It contains the alternatives that are available in the case and reflects the individualized attention that each case receives (Carter, 1966). The PO is in a unique position with respect to making a recommendation to the judge: "The officer has had an opportunity to observe the defendant in the community, not only from a legal-judicial, investigative perspective, but also from the viewpoint of a general lifestyle" (Carter, 1966: 41). To present a meaningful recommendation, the PO must have knowledge of the resources and programs that are available. An inexperienced PO may submit a recommendation for a treatment program that is not available either in the community or at a correctional institution.

One issue that the PO must decide is the recommendation for or against a sentence of probation. In many jurisdictions, a conviction for certain crimes or a previous felony conviction precludes a sentence of probation, so the PO must know the statutes of the jurisdiction. The officer must also weigh the potential danger the defendant poses to the community, must evaluate the defendant's rehabilitative potential and ability to conform

Key Fact

Probation officers need to understand terms used by police agencies as well as medical and psychological terminology.

Key Fact

Probation officers often make sentencing recommendations in the PSI, particularly for or against probation.

When a defendant pleads guilty, pleads *nolo contendere* (no contest), or is found guilty after trial, a date is scheduled for sentencing, usually 30 days away. The district attorney refers the case file to the Division of Parole and Probation, at which time an officer is assigned to the case, and he or she begins to research the offender's criminal history and records. Eventually, the defendant completes a preliminary questionnaire and is interviewed by the investigating officer.

Based on the interview and the questionnaire, the officer obtains information regarding the offender's social and environmental background, employment history, education, mental health and substance abuse problems, residential stability, support systems, finances, military experience, future goals, and feelings regarding the offense. The investigator must strive to be a perceptive listener and skilled interviewer who lends a keen ear and is attentive to attitudes, remorse, candor, and a cooperative spirit. It is important to remember that officers interview all types of people, including juveniles, first-time offenders, career criminals, members of organized crime, the mentally disturbed, substance abusers, and white-collar criminals. As one might assume, these people can be hostile, manipulative, and con-wise or they can be pleasant—their crimes notwithstanding.

The investigator must then begin to verify as much information as possible by contacting the victim, the police, and any other relevant persons and agencies. He or she then begins to formulate the report. Using sentencing guidelines that mix classical and positivist elements, the officer determines the probation success probability (positivist) and length of sentence (classical). The report is dictated, typed, proofread, approved, and distributed. The officer's recommendation addresses the risks and needs of the offender, the community, and the victim. The report may recommend special conditions of probation appropriate for the offender and his or her criminal activity. Officers attend sentencing hearings and are called on to answer questions by the judge, district attorney, and defense counsel; recommendations, however, are disclosed only to the judge.

to probation regulations, and must consider whether probation will be construed by the community as too lenient in view of the offense or by the defendant as "getting away with it."

SHORT- AND LONG-FORM PSI REPORTS

There are two basic types of PSI reports: short-form and long-form. The **short-form PSI** is usually less exhaustive and less time-consuming and is typically done in misdemeanor and less serious felony cases. The *New York State Code of Criminal Procedure* states:

> The abbreviated investigation for short-form reports shall consist of the defendant's legal history and primarily current information with respect to: the circumstances attending the commission of the offense, family and social situation, employment and economic status, education and, when available, physical and mental conditions. Such investigation may also include any other matter which the probation department conducting the investigation deems relevant to the recommendation or court disposition and must include any matter directed by the court.

Figure 3.2 is an example of the short form.

In cases of all felonies (or in some locations, only the more serious felonies), judges will order a **long-form PSI**. Figure 3.3 provides an example of a long-form PSI.

Key Fact

PSI reports may be either short- or long-form.

ONONDAGA COUNTY PROBATION DEPARTMENT
PRESENTENCE REPORT

COURT: ONONDAGA COUNTY

JUDGE: HON. J. KEVIN MULROY

PROSECUTOR: JOANNE NAGLE

LEGAL COUNSEL: DONALD D'AMICO

CASE NUMBER: 93-4641

NAME: JAMISON, RALPH

AKA/MAIDEN: N/A

AGE/DOB: 11/27/82

ADDRESS: 173 Briar Place

Tully, New York 13159

PHONE: 315-779-4653

INDICTMENT#: 91-3-19

DOCKET#: 4763

DR#: N/A

COURT CONT. #:

NYSID#: 86543210

FBI#: 428-930-64

OFFENSE DATE: 9/9/06   ARREST DATE: 12/13/06   CONVICTION DATE: 6/24/07

ORIGINAL CHARGES: SEXUAL ABUSE 1ST   FINAL CONVICTION: SEXUAL ABUSE 1ST

CHARGE CODE: 130.65 NYS PENAL LAW

A CLASS "D VIOLENT" FELONY

BY: PLEA: X   VERDICT:

	NAME	DOB	NAME	DOB
CODEFENDANT/CORRESPONDENT:	N/A			

RESTITUTION: N   RELATIONSHIP TO VICTIM: ACQUAINTANCE   VICTIM IMPACT: Sent: X   Received: ___ NA: ___

DISPOSITION DATE: 8/5/07   PLEA BARGAIN: UNKNOWN

FAMILY COURT HISTORY: N   CRIMINAL HISTORY: N   PROBATION/PAROLE/PRETRIAL RELEASE HISTORY: N

INCARCERATIONS/PLACEMENTS: N   PENDING CHARGES: N

SOURCE OF SUPPORT: K TIRES/FT/200/WK   RESIDES WITH/RELATIONSHIP: ERNEST & SHIRLEY PARENTS

EDUCATION: 12TH   CHILDREN: 0   HEALTH/DISABILITY: N   MENTAL HEALTH: Y   SUBSTANCE ABUSE: Y

DISPOSITION: DATE:

CIRCUMSTANCES OF THE OFFENSE

On September 9, 2006, the defendant forced an 8-year-old female, the daughter of his employer's paramour, to touch his penis, then rubbed her vagina with his hand, followed by lying on top of the victim while clothed and "humping her."

DEFENDANT'S STATEMENT

Defendant states that he and the victim were sleeping on her living room floor when he began touching her. He wants to make it clear that he and the child were at least partially clothed. He expressed little remorse, minimizes the serious nature of the offense, and claims that his behavior was an isolated event brought on by depression over problems at home, particularly with his father.

VICTIM IMPACT

The victim's mother states that there is no financial restitution to be made but wants it known that they feel very betrayed by the defendant whom they trusted and considered to be a friend. She says that the child has attended counseling but remains fearful that the defendant will hurt her again. The family wishes to have the defendant receive maximum incarceration for his crime.

MENTAL HEALTH

Defendant has been referred to Child and Family Services for treatment in an adult male sexual perpetrator's group.

SUBSTANCE ABUSE

Defendant admits to drinking a few beers twice a week and says he had consumed three beers on the night of the present offense, although he does not see his use as problematic and does not believe it caused him to commit the crime. Although there is no evidence that the defendant uses illegal drugs, military records show that his association with a civilian drug user led to narcotics and stolen property being found in the defendant's car.

COMMENTARY

This immature and egocentric defendant is lacking in insight and a sense of personal responsibility, making him unlikely to understand and admit the serious nature of his crime unless initially faced with a period of incarceration.

FIGURE 3.2 *Short-Form PSI Report*

RECOMMENDATION

_____ Incarceration	State _____
_____ Probation	Local _____
__x___ Shock Probation	
_____ Conditional Discharge	
_____ Alternative Program	
_____ YO Eligible _____	
Required _____	
_____ Certificate of Relief	
Eligible _____	
_____ Restitution	
__x___ Other (i.e., Fine, Community Service) Order of Protection for Victim and Family	

ATTACHMENT(S)

_____ Prior Presentence Investigation
_____ Juvenile History
__x___ NYSID
_____ Motor Vehicle Abstract
_____ Substance Abuse Evaluation
_____ Psychiatric, Psychological, or Mental Health Information
_____ Victim Impact
__x___ Conditions of Probation
_____ Other_____

DATE/AUTHOR

_____

Linda W. Limpert
Probation Officer

_____

Gayle A. Anderson
Probation Supervisor

FIGURE 3.2 *(continued)*

**IN THE UNITED STATES DISTRICT COURT
FOR THE WESTERN DISTRICT OF NEW YORK**

UNITED STATES OF AMERICA	)
	)
v.	) PRESENTENCE INVESTIGATION REPORT
	)
	) Docket No. CR 05-002-01-KGG
Frank Jones	)

Prepared for: The Honorable Kelly G. Greenblatt
U.S. District Judge

Prepared by: Craig T. Dolan
U.S. Probation Officer
Breaker Bay, New York
(123) 111-1111

Assistant U.S. Attorney **Defense Counsel**
Mr. Robert Kaplan Mr. Arthur Goodfellow
United States Courthouse 737 North 7th Street
Breaker Bay, New York Breaker Bay, New York
(123) 111-1212 (123) 111-1313

Sentence Date: June 5, 2006

Offense: Count One: Tax Evasion (26 U.S.C. § 7201)
5 years/$250,000 fine

Release Status: At liberty on a $50,000 personal recognizance bond with pretrial supervision (No pretrial custody)

FIGURE 3.3 *Long-Form PSI Report,* U.S. v. Frank Jones

Detainers:	None	
Codefendants:	None	

Related Cases:	Nancy Oscar CR 05-002-01	Vincent St. James CR 05-005-01
	Samuel James CR 05-003-01	Donald Goodman CR 05-006-01
	Brian McDonald CR 05-004-01	

Date Report Prepared:	5/15/06	**Date Revised:**	5/25/06

Identifying Data:

Date of Birth:	1/1/50
Age:	56
Race:	White
Sex:	Male
S.S. #:	102-01-0736
FBI #:	743-17-46A
USM #:	51645-217
State ID #:	Not Applicable
PACTS ID #:	1101
Education:	BS degree
Dependents:	Two
Citizenship:	U.S.
Legal Address:	1701 Seagall Lane
	Breaker Bay, NY 14217
Aliases:	None

PART A. THE OFFENSE

Charge(s) and Conviction(s)

1. Frank Jones was named in a three-count indictment filed by a Western District of New York grand jury on November 1, 2005. Counts one through three charge that the defendant attempted to evade income tax due and owed by him and his wife for calendar years 2002, 2003, and 2004, respectively, in violation of 26 U.S.C. § 7201. On November 15, 2005, a superseding information was filed by the United States Attorney's Office in the Western District of New York. The information charges that on October 15, 2004, Jones evaded income tax due and owed by him and his wife for the calendar year 2004 by writing a check to the American Medisearch Organization in the amount of $20,000, for which he received 90 percent back in cash, and by filing a false tax return in which he deducted as a charitable contribution the entire amount of $20,000, in violation of 26 U.S.C. § 7201.

2. On November 21, 2005, Jones appeared before a U.S. Magistrate Judge and pleaded not guilty to all of the charges. He was released after posting bond and was ordered to report to the Pretrial Services Agency. On December 1, 2005, in accordance with the terms of a written plea agreement, the defendant pleaded guilty as charged in the superseding information. The parties entered into a plea agreement per F.R. Crim.P. 11(c)(1)(A), which calls for the dismissal of the original indictment. Jones is scheduled to be sentenced on June 5, 2006.

3. According to his supervising pretrial services officer, Jones made satisfactory adjustment while under pretrial services supervision and reported as directed. Additionally, Jones maintained employment and there were no substance-related issues with the defendant.

The Offense Conduct

4. The American Medisearch Organization is a not-for-profit national corporation that supervises fungus research. Across the country, the American Medisearch Organization derives its funds from 50 charter divisions, which are separately incorporated not-for-profit organizations. The American Medisearch Organization, New York Division, Inc., located in Breaker Bay, New York, is one of the charter divisions employing salaried individuals and volunteers that supports the goals of the American Medisearch Organization and is authorized to use the name of the American Medisearch Organization in fund-raising, educational programming, the issuance of grants in fungus research, and other activities. In late 2004, the New York Medisearch Organization began to raise funds through an annual fall dinner dance, casino night.

5. Nancy Oscar began employment with the New York Medisearch Organization in 1989 as a field services representative. Oscar, who created the dinner dance fund-raising event, was responsible for the fund-raising activities of the Atlantis Medisearch Organization. Three schemes developed from the dinner dance, all of which were aimed at enabling various "contributors" to inflate or falsify the "charitable" donations that could then be reported and, where applicable, deducted on personal, corporate, partnership, or private foundation federal income tax returns. Oscar and other participants collected checks made payable to the American Medisearch Organization and returned 90 percent of the face value of the checks, either in the form of cash or later in the form of chips, which could be converted to cash or to merchandise sold by the vendors at the dinner dance.

FIGURE 3.3 (continued)

6. At least as early as 1999, in connection with the annual dinner dance, Oscar instituted a "check cashing" procedure whereby an individual was permitted to write a check payable to the American Medisearch Organization and send it to Oscar in advance of the affair. However, only 10 percent of the value of the check was retained by the New York Medisearch Organization as a donation to the American Medisearch Organization, and 90 percent of the value of the check was returned to the "contributor" in cash either before or at the dinner dance.

7. At the dinner dance, which was usually held in October or November, guests were permitted to write checks, payable to the American Medisearch Organization, to purchase gambling chips. Ten percent of the value of each check was retained by the New York Medisearch Organization as a donation, but 90 percent was returned to the "contributor" in the form of gambling chips. At the end of the evening all outstanding chips could be redeemed for cash or merchandise. Also at the dance, boutiques sold merchandise and gift certificates at fair market value, which were paid for by checks payable to the American Medisearch Organization, with chips or cash. No portion of the purchase price was a contribution to the organization; however, it did receive a small donation from the vendors.

8. Although the New York Medisearch Organization raised money from other fund-raising events, its major source of income was from the annual dinner dance. Over the years, the number of people attending the dinner dance increased, the amount of advance "check cashing" increased, the amount of checks written for gambling chips increased, and the amount of money the New York Medisearch Organization raised for the American Medisearch Organization increased. In 2001 the organization raised $73,000 and in 2004 the organization raised $360,000.

9. This scheme was in essence a "check cashing" operation, allowing "contributors" to draw checks to the American Medisearch Organization several weeks before the dinner dance affair. Specifically, before each dinner dance, Oscar told the members of the New York Medisearch Organization that if they or their invited guests wished to write a check to the American Medisearch Organization over $3,000, the check would have to be received approximately two weeks before the affair, and 90 percent of the face value would be returned in cash. When the checks were collected in this manner, they were deposited into the New York Medisearch Organization bank account.

10. After the checks cleared the account, Oscar and other employees at her direction would arrange for the bank to ship cash to the dinner dance site. Oscar and some of the officers and members of the New York Medisearch Organization would meet in rooms at the dinner dance site where they took the cash and placed it in envelopes in amounts corresponding to 90 percent of the face value of the checks sent in advance of the dinner dance by the "contributors." Oscar also arranged for additional cash to be available at the dinner dance for those members who chose to redeem their chips for cash. Other "contributors" who did not attend the dinner dance were permitted to cash checks so long as they purchased a ticket for the affair. Those nonattending "contributors" who bought tickets and cashed checks were assigned to a nonexistent "dummy table" that was actually added to the dinner dance guest list.

11. The scheme was able to continue and flourish not only because of the greed of the "contributors" but also due to Oscar's bookkeeping methods. Oscar instructed officers of the organization who were preparing financial reports on the annual dinner to conceal the source of the funds raised through the check-cashing schemes by including those funds in other categories of the financial report, such as gambling receipts.

12. In support of their income tax submissions, "contributors" often attached to their tax returns copies of the fraudulent checks they wrote to the American Medisearch Organization, and during routine audits "contributors" furnished the original copy of the fraudulent check to agents of the Internal Revenue Service and directly or indirectly misrepresented that the full amounts of the checks were charitable contributions to the American Medisearch Organization.

13. Over the years, the number of participants in this scheme substantially increased. According to available records, while the dinner dance attendees increased from approximately 65 in 2000 to approximately 650 in 2004, the government has only sought prosecution of those "contributors" who participated in the various kickback schemes and filed fraudulent tax returns when the total amount of the checks written to the American Medisearch Organization was $30,000 or more over several years or $20,000 in one given year. To date, the government has prosecuted Nancy Oscar, who was the organizer and creator of this scheme. She has recently pleaded guilty to a three-count indictment charging her with mail fraud, income tax evasion, and wire fraud, along with five "contributors," namely, the defendant, Frank Jones, together with Samuel James, Brian McDonald, Vincent St. James, and Donald Goodman. In total, the government expects to obtain indictments for approximately 37 additional "contributors." Although the value of the checks written to the American Medisearch Organization varied from "contributor" to "contributor," the check writers are equally culpable.

14. Frank Jones participated in this false deduction scheme involving the New York division of the American Medisearch Organization and filed fraudulent income tax returns for the years 2002, 2003, and 2004. During each of the years, Jones made contributions of $20,000 but received 90 percent of the contribution (or $18,000) back in cash or in gambling chips, some of which he used to gamble with, but the majority of which he redeemed for cash. However, on each of his individual income tax returns, filed jointly with his wife, Jones deducted the full amount of $20,000 as "charitable contributions," even though he was only entitled to deduct $2,000 in each tax year, which represents the 10 percent retained by the New York Medisearch Organization as a contribution to the American Medisearch Organization.

15. Jones was invited to attend the dinner dance by the former chairman of the board of the Sigma Systems Company, John Adams. In 2002 and 2004 Jones drew personal checks to the American Medisearch Organization for $20,000 each year and attended the dinner dance. At the dance, Jones received $18,000, or 90 percent of his check, back in gambling chips, of which the majority was later redeemed for cash. In 2003 Jones did not attend the dance but learned that he could draw the personal check and still

FIGURE 3.3 (continued)

receive the 90 percent return. As a result, Jones drew the check and gave it to Adams. Several weeks later, Adams gave Jones $18,000 in cash. Jones used the $18,000 he received each year from the New York Medisearch Organization for personal expenditures and did not redeposit any of the funds into his personal bank account.

Victim Impact Statement

16. The Internal Revenue Service is the victim. In each tax year, Frank Jones deducted $20,000 as a charitable contribution from his taxable income when in fact he was only entitled to deduct a total of $2,000 as a charitable contribution during each of the tax years. As a result, Jones underreported his taxable income by $54,000. According to the results of an Internal Revenue Service audit, Jones had outstanding tax liabilities, not including interest and penalties, in the amount of $27,000, which he has paid in full.

Adjustment for Obstruction of Justice

17. The probation officer has no information to suggest that the defendant impeded or obstructed justice.

Adjustment for Acceptance of Responsibility

18. During an interview with Internal Revenue Service agents, and later during an interview with the probation officer, Jones readily admitted his involvement in this offense. Jones explained that he falsely claimed the charitable deductions on his personal tax returns because everyone else who attended the dinner dance was claiming the deductions.

19. Jones added that his involvement in this offense has had an adverse effect on his career and in retrospect he never envisioned the potential impact such wrongdoing would have on his life. He expressed feelings of both embarrassment and regret and assumes full responsibility for his criminal conduct, as supported by his recent tax payment to the Internal Revenue Service in the amount of $27,000. Jones indicates that he will immediately pay the balance of his tax liabilities once the IRS has assessed interest and penaltie

Offense Level Computation

20. The 2005 edition of the *Guidelines Manual* has been used in this case. In accordance with the provisions found in USSG §1B1.3(a)(1), the total amount of evaded taxes has been taken into account in determining the sentencing guideline range.

21. **Base Offense Level:** The guideline for a 26 U.S.C. § 7201 offense is found in USSG. §2T1.1. That section provides that the base offense level for tax offenses is determined in accordance with the tax table found in USSG §2T4.1, which corresponds to the tax loss. In this offense, the total amount of evaded taxes is $27,000. According to USSG §2T4.1(D), the base offense level for tax losses of more than $12,500 but less than $30,000 is twelve.   **12**

22. **Specific Offense Characteristics:** Pursuant to the provision found in USSG §2T1.1(b)(1) since the defendant failed to report or to correctly identify the source of income exceeding $10,000 in any year from criminal activity, the offense level is increased by two levels.   **+2**

23. **Adjustment for Role in the Offense:** None.   **0**

24. **Victim-Related Adjustment:** None.   **0**

25. **Adjustment for Obstruction of Justice:** None.   **0**

26. **Adjusted Offense Level (Subtotal):**   **14**

27. **Adjustment for Acceptance of Responsibility:** The defendant has shown recognition of responsibility for his conduct and a reduction of two levels for acceptance of responsibility is applicable under USSG §3E1.1(a).   **−2**

28. **Total Offense Level:**   **12**

29. **Chapter Four Enhancements:** None.   **0**

30. **Total Offense Level:**   **12**

PART B. THE DEFENDANT'S CRIMINAL HISTORY

Juvenile Adjudications

31. None

Criminal Convictions

32. None

Criminal History Computation

33. A check with the FBI and the local police authorities reveals no prior convictions for Frank Jones. Therefore, Jones has a criminal history score of zero. According to the sentencing table (chapter five, part A), 0 to 1 criminal history points establish a criminal history category of I.

Other Criminal Conduct

34. None

FIGURE 3.3 *(continued)*

Pending Charges

35. None

Other Arrests

36. None

PART C. OFFENDER CHARACTERISTICS

Personal and Family Data

37. Frank Samuel Jones was born on January 1, 1950, in Breaker Bay, New York, to the union of Samuel and Patricia Jones, nee DeAngelo. Jones is an only child and was raised by his parents in the upper river section of Breaker Bay in an upper-middle-class socioeconomic setting. Jones has fond memories of his developmental years, advising that he was reared under Roman Catholic traditions by concerned, loving parents who emphasized hard work, respect, and honesty.

38. The defendant's father was a partner in the New York Tallow Company, a refinery and exporting company which manufactured tallow, the main ingredient in soap. When the defendant was 18 years old, his father became critically ill with tuberculosis and was not expected to recover. Jones withdrew from his daytime studies at college and worked in the father's business. According to the defendant, his father fully recovered approximately three years later and eventually returned to the tallow business, allowing the defendant to pursue other interests.

39. According to the defendant, his father died in 1988 at the age of 68, following a massive heart attack. While reporting a positive relationship with his father, Jones advised us that he felt much closer to his mother, who died of natural causes in 1997 at the age of 80. Prior to her retirement and failing health, the defendant's mother was employed by the Breaker Bay Electric Company as a secretary. According to Jones, after his father's death, he assisted his mother financially and she moved into an apartment in Breaker Bay, closer to the defendant's residence, in view of her declining health. As her health continued to decline, Jones eventually placed his mother in a retirement home where she eventually died.

40. Jones married the former Nancy Lipson Smith on June 17, 1981, in Spring Hill, New York. This union produced two children: Frank, Jr., and Mellisa, ages 13 and 15, respectively, who both attend boarding schools in Central City, New York. According to Mrs. Jones, age 46, the couple were married in 1981. For the past 13 years, the defendant and his family have resided at 1701 Seagull Lane, in a rather reclusive, wooded, upper-class area in Breaker Bay. A home investigation found this 5-bedroom bilevel ranch-style home to be impeccably maintained and tastefully furnished. Prior to the birth of their children, Mrs. Jones was employed by the Breaker Bay school system and later employed by an investment banking firm in Bodega Bay, New York. Mrs. Jones has not been employed outside the home in over 15 years, although in recent years she has participated in charities and other volunteer work.

41. Mrs. Jones describes her marriage in harmonious terms and states that the defendant is a kind, considerate, and devoted husband and father. Jones, for the most part, is a private person and has suffered embarrassment as a result of the publicity in this case. The defendant's wife believes that her husband's actions "were not very well thought out," adding that "he never thinks about the impact his actions may have on his life or family." Mrs. Jones considers the defendant's conduct in this offense as an isolated incident contrary to his otherwise "law-abiding lifestyle." According to Mrs. Jones, her husband has been described by his children as a "workaholic," but he never allows himself to neglect the needs or concerns of his family. Mrs. Jones added that she rarely attended functions such as the one described in this offense and considered her husband's involvement as a business-related activity.

Physical Condition

42. The defendant is 5' 10" tall and weighs 180 pounds. He has brown eyes and slightly greying brown short hair. At our request, the defendant's private physician, John W. Brown, M.D., provided a summary of Jones's overall health, which was described as excellent and free from hospitalizations.

Mental and Emotional Health

43. The defendant states that he has never been seen by a psychiatrist and describes his overall mental and emotional health as good. We have no information to suggest otherwise. Jones was polite and cooperative during the presentence process and presented himself as a professional and soft-spoken businessman voicing normal stress and concerns affiliated with pending legal difficulties.

Substance Abuse

44. Jones states that he rarely drinks alcohol and has never used narcotics. A urine specimen collected by the probation officer tested negative for illicit drug use.

Education and Vocational Skills

45. The defendant graduated from the Breaker Bay Military Academy in 1968 and continued his education at New York University, where he received a bachelor of science degree in marketing on June 12, 1972. Jones advised that he received a master's in business administration (MBA) from New York University in 1973; however, according to university records, Jones enrolled in the MBA program in September 1972 but left the program without completing the requirements in February 1977. Jones maintains that he completed the requirements but "failed to pick up the degree."

FIGURE 3.3 *(continued)*

Employment Record

46. Since March 1992, Jones has been employed by the commodity and securities firm Greater Life Securities, Inc., in Breaker Bay, where he earns approximately $700,000 a year as senior vice president in charge of the commodities division.

47. From December 1984 until March 1992, Jones was a senior vice president and director of the commodities division at Bruger Securities, where he earned $275,000 per year until he resigned. According to Bruger Securities president John Bruger, the defendant was a talented commodities broker who was an asset to the firm. From October 1971 until December 1984, Jones was employed by the Marshall, Jones, and LaBelle securities firm in Breaker Bay as the company's vice president and director of commodities research. Jones earned approximately $65,000 a year and resigned to accept employment with Bruger. In the late 1960s and early 1970s, Jones worked for an economic consulting firm and an economic forecasting firm as a price index analyst. Jones also worked at his father's tallow business for several years, where he was responsible for the purchase of raw materials, such as animal carcasses, used in the production of tallow.

Financial Condition: Ability to Pay

48. A review of the defendant's amended personal income tax returns for 2002 through 2004 (which now reflect the $57,000 in additional income previously reported as charitable deductions) reveals that the defendant earned $616,973 in 2002; $652,751 in 2003; and $704,448 in 2004 in salary and wages from Greater Life Securities. In addition, interest income ranging from $1,231 (2001) to $22,013 (2002) is also shown. In each tax year, Jones appears to have noteworthy long- and short-term capital losses, and in each year he takes the maximum loss allowed ($3,000) on his Schedule D. In addition, Jones reports substantial losses from tax shelters (set up in the form of limited partnerships and trusts), ranging from $91,234 (2002) to $221,008 (2003).

49. Jones submitted a signed joint financial statement and accompanying documentation, which supported the following verified financial profile summarized below:

Assets

Cash

Cash on Hand	$ 5,000
Bank Accounts (4)	206,000
Securities	250,000
Subtotal:	$ 461,000

Unencumbered Assets

2003 Mercedes Benz 450	$ 45,000
2002 BMW	30,000
2002 Nissan Altima	15,000
1968 Camero	20,000
Subtotal:	$ 110,000

Equity in Other Assets

1701 Seagull Lane Breaker Bay, New York (family residence)	$ 580,000 (See Note A)
1471 Vermont Avenue Lake Shore, New York (vacation residence)	$ 150,000 (See Note A)
Subtotal:	$ 730,000
Total Assets:	$ 1,301,000

Unsecured Debts

Credit Cards (3)	$ 13,000
Total Unsecured Debts:	$ 13,000

NET WORTH: $ 1,288,000

Monthly Cash Flow

Income

Defendant's Net Salary	$ 11,038

FIGURE 3.3 *(continued)*

Stocks and Securities		10,000
Interest Income		20,000
Total Income:	$	41,038

Necessary Living Expenses

Property Mortgages	$	1,100
Food		750
Utilities		900
Telephone		300
Credit Cards		300
Life Insurance		800
Car Insurance		1,200
Health Insurance		200
School Tuition		700
Other Expenses		5,000
Total Expenses:	$	11,250
Net Monthly Cash Flow:	$	29,788

Note A: The market value of the family residence is $650,000 and the market value of the vacation home is $160,000, based on sales of comparable homes in the property areas. The outstanding mortgage balance on the family home is $70,000 and the vacation home has a $10,000 mortgage balance.

50. The defendant retained counsel in this offense and states that his attorney's fees have been paid in full. Based on the defendant's financial condition, he has the ability to pay a fine within the guideline range.

PART D. SENTENCING OPTIONS

Custody

51. **Statutory Provisions:** The maximum term of imprisonment for this offense is 5 years pursuant to 26 U.S.C. § 7201.

52. **Guideline Provisions:** Based on an offense level of 12 and a criminal history category of I, the guideline range of imprisonment is 10 to 16 months. Pursuant to USSG §5C1.1(d), if the applicable guideline range is in Zone C of the Sentencing Table, the minimum term may be satisfied by: 1) a sentence of imprisonment; or 2) a sentence of imprisonment that includes a term of supervised release with a condition that substitutes community confinement or home detention according to the schedule in subsection (e), provided that at least one-half of the minimum term is satisfied by imprisonment.

Impact of Plea Agreement

53. Under the plea agreement, Jones has entered a plea to one count of tax evasion, in return for the dismissal of two other tax evasion counts. Pursuant to USSG §3D1.2(a), counts involving the same transaction are grouped together into a single group. Because all of the evaded taxes have been taken into account in determining the sentence guideline range, a conviction on the additional counts would not affect the offense level or any other guideline calculation.

Supervised Release

54. **Statutory Provisions:** If a term of imprisonment is imposed, the court may impose a term of supervised release of not more than three years, pursuant to 18 U.S.C. § 3583(b)(2), since this is a Class D felony.

55. **Guideline Provisions:** The court shall order a term of supervised release to follow imprisonment when a sentence of imprisonment of more than one year is imposed, or when required by statute, pursuant to USSG §5D1.1(a). The court may order a term of supervised release to follow imprisonment in any other case, pursuant to USSG §5D1.1(b). The authorized term of supervised release for this offense is at least two years but not more than three years, pursuant to USSG §5D1.2(a)(2).

Probation

56. **Statutory Provisions:** The defendant is eligible for a term of probation in this offense, pursuant to 18 U.S.C. § 3561(a). The authorized term for a felony is not less than one or more than five years, pursuant to 18 U.S.C. § 3561(c)(1).

57. **Guideline Provisions:** According to USSG §5B1.1, Application Note 2, where the applicable guideline range is in Zone C or D of the Sentencing Table (i.e., the minimum term of imprisonment specified in the applicable guideline range is eight months or more), the guidelines do not authorize a sentence of probation. As the defendant's guideline range falls within Zone C and his minimum sentence is 10 months, he is not eligible for probation.

FIGURE 3.3 *(continued)*

Fine

58. **Statutory Provisions:** The maximum fine for this offense is $250,000, pursuant to 18 U.S.C. § 3571(b)(3).

59. The special assessment of $100 is mandatory, pursuant to 18 U.S.C. § 3013(a)(2)(A).

60. **Guideline Provisions:** According to USSG § 5E1.2(c)(3), the minimum fine for this offense is $3,000 and the maximum fine for this offense is $30,000.

Restitution

61. **Statutory Provisions:** Pursuant to 18 U.S.C. § 3663, restitution may be ordered. In this case, the defendant's outstanding tax obligation has been paid. Interest and penalties are outstanding to the Internal Revenue Service and can be forwarded to the following address:

> Internal Revenue Service
> 111 IRS Tower
> Breaker Bay, NY 11472
> Attention: Mr. Sam Claim

62. **Guideline Provisions:** In accordance with the provisions of USSG §5E1.1, restitution shall be ordered.

PART E. FACTORS THAT MAY WARRANT DEPARTURE

63. The probation officer has no information concerning the offense or the offender that would warrant a departure from the prescribed sentencing guidelines.

PART F. FACTORS THAT MAY WARRANT A SENTENCE OUTSIDE OF THE ADVISORY GUIDELINE SYSTEM

64. No factors have been identified under 18 U.S.C. § 3553(a) that would warrant the court sentencing the defendant outside the advisory guideline range.

Respectfully submitted,

Chief U.S. Probation Officer

by _____
Craig T. Dolan
U.S. Probation Officer

Approved:

_____
Mark T. Clark
Supervising U.S. Probation Officer

SENTENCING RECOMMENDATION
UNITED STATES DISTRICT COURT FOR THE WESTERN DISTRICT OF NEW YORK
UNITED STATES v. FRANK JONES, DKT. # CR 05-002-01-KGG

TOTAL OFFENSE LEVEL: 12
CRIMINAL HISTORY CATEGORY: 1

	Statutory Provisions	Guideline Provisions	Plea Agreement Provisions	Recommended Sentence
CUSTODY:	5 years	10–16 months	None	5 months
PROBATION:	1–5 years	N/A	None	N/A
SUPERVISED RELEASE:	2–3 years	2–3 years	None	2 years, 5 months home confinement
FINE:	$250,000	$3,000–$30,000	None	$30,000
RESTITUTION:	$0	$0	None	$0
SPECIAL ASSESSMENT:	$100	$100	None	$100

FIGURE 3.3 (continued)

Justification

Frank Jones is a successful and respected businessman who appears to be a situational offender, having been motivated by opportunistic greed. While his acceptance of responsibility and remorse are reflected in the guideline calculation, Jones has also paid restitution to the Internal Revenue Service prior to sentencing.

As the guidelines adequately addressed any 18 U.S.C. § 3553(a)(1)-(7) factors, a sentence within the guideline range is recommended. As such, a split sentence of five months in custody followed by five months of home confinement as a condition of supervised release is the recommended sentence in order to reflect the seriousness of the defendant's conduct and to provide just punishment.

The defendant earns a considerable income, has accumulated an impressive financial portfolio of over $1,000,000, and is employed with a reputable commodities firm. Given he has financial acumen, his evasion of the payment of taxes by participation in a fraudulent scheme in the guise of charity merits a sentence reflective of the seriousness of the offense.

In view of Jones's financial profile, a fine of $30,000 is also recommended to be paid immediately in addition to the $100 penalty assessment. Inasmuch as he does not appear to pose a risk to the community or to be in need of correctional treatment, the minimum term of supervised release of two years will be sufficient. Since the defendant will owe interest and penalties to the Internal Revenue Service as soon as they are calculated, it is recommended that collection of these monies be a condition of supervised release. A restriction against incurring any new debts until the criminal sanctions are paid is an additional recommended condition. Disclosure of financial information is also recommended. As this is a felony conviction, Jones must submit to DNA testing.

Voluntary Surrender

Jones has no prior criminal record, has solid ties to the community, and appears to be a good candidate for voluntary surrender.

Recommendation

It is respectfully recommended that sentence in this case be imposed as follows:

Pursuant to the Sentencing Reform Act of 1984, it is the judgment of the court that the defendant, Frank Jones, is hereby committed to the custody of the United States Bureau of Prisons to be imprisoned for a term of 5 months.

Upon release from imprisonment, the defendant shall be placed on supervised release for a term of two years. Within 72 hours of release from the custody of the Bureau of Prisons, the defendant shall report in person to the probation office in the district to which the defendant is released.

While on supervised release, the defendant shall not commit any federal, state, or local crimes, and he shall be prohibited from possessing a firearm or other dangerous device. The defendant shall not possess a controlled substance, and he shall comply with the standard conditions of supervised release as recommended by the United States Sentencing Commission.

In addition, the defendant shall comply with the following special conditions: The defendant shall be placed on home confinement for a period of five months with said placement to commence on a date to be determined by the probation officer. The defendant shall pay any fine that is imposed by this judgment and that remains unpaid at the commencement of the term of supervised release. Further, the defendant shall incur no new debts or open additional lines of credit without the permission of the probation officer unless the fine has been paid in full. The defendant shall provide the probation officer with access to any requested financial information.

Finally, the defendant shall cooperate in the collection of a DNA sample at the direction of the probation officer, pursuant to Public Law 108-405 (Revised DNA Collection Requirements under the Justice for All Act of 2004), if such sample was not collected during imprisonment.

THE COURT FINDS that the defendant has the ability to pay a fine and it is further ordered that the defendant shall pay to the United States a fine of $30,000. This fine, including any interest required by law, shall be paid in full within 30 days. In addition, the defendant is ordered to pay a special assessment in the amount of $100, which shall be due immediately.

Respectfully submitted,

Chief U.S. Probation Officer

by _____
Craig T. Dolan
U.S. Probation Officer

Approved:

_____
Mark T. Clark
Supervising U.S. Probation Officer

FIGURE 3.3 *(continued)*

SENTENCING GUIDELINES AND MANDATORY SENTENCES

By 1994, every state had laws regarding **mandatory sentencing**, the latest being "three (and sometimes two) strikes and you're out" (actually *in* for life—the baseball metaphor accounting for at least some of its popularity). In California, for example, the law requires that persons convicted of a violent crime who have two prior convictions (which need not be violent) must serve a minimum of 25 years. Some states require that the instant offense and the prior felonies be for violent crimes, whereas others permit consideration of juvenile adjudications for violent offenses.

A violent crime does not necessarily mean violent behavior on the part of an offender. For example, in New York residential burglary during the day is a "violent" offense even in the absence of the possession of a weapon or an encounter with an occupant. The same applies to the lookout during a street robbery or a battered woman who severely injures or kills her abuser. Offenders who are convicted of a violent crime in their youth become the subject of mandatory sentencing as adults even when the offense is nonviolent. Ironically, research reveals that violent offenders who are released from prison are much less likely to be convicted of a new offense than nonviolent inmates, particularly drug offenders. This raises questions about the strategy for reducing prison overcrowding by incarcerating only violent offenders.

About 20 states and the federal government use **sentencing guidelines** primarily in an attempt to limit judicial discretion and reduce sentence disparity—a turn toward classicalism. In Minnesota, for example, sentencing guidelines were instituted in 1980 and are changed periodically (Figure 3.4). A judge is provided with a sentencing grid that considers only the severity of the instant offense and the offender's prior criminal history. Departures from mandatory sentences derived from the grid are permitted only under limited circumstances. Probation officers (actually, state parole and probation agents) are responsible for completing the sentencing guidelines worksheet and calculating the presumed sentence; they no longer write PSI reports.

The Federal Sentencing Reform Act of 1984, which became effective in 1987, was designed to reduce sentence disparity and phase out parole release by 1992. The statute also generated a great deal of confusion and litigation—many judges opposed the legislation's sentencing guidelines that removed much judicial discretion. On January 18, 1989, however, the Supreme Court ruled that the 1987 sentencing rules, established by a commission created under the 1984 statute, were constitutional (*Mistretta v. United States*, 488 U.S. 361). This ruling did not end the controversy: Appeals over guidelines interpretation have burdened appellate courts, and judges have been concerned about the lack of consideration given to such factors as age, education, and family ties for rendering sentencing decisions.

The commission established 43 offense levels and assigned each federal offense to one of the levels (e.g., murder scores 43 and blackmail scores 9). Judges must impose sentences according to these levels, adding to or subtracting from them based on factors such as the offender's age, prior record, use of a firearm, or cooperation with the prosecution. "Ordinarily, the judge must choose a sentence from within the guideline range unless the court identifies a factor that the Sentencing Commission failed to consider that should result in a different sentence. However, the judge must in all cases provide the reasons for the sentence. Sentences outside the guideline range are subject to review by the courts of appeals for an abuse of discretion, and all sentences can be reviewed for incorrect application of the relevant guidelines or law" (U.S. Sentencing Commission flier). The guidelines manual is thicker than this book, and hundreds of amendments have been added. Inmates can earn a maximum of 54 days off their sentence per year for good behavior instead of the more typical 1 day for each day served in determinate sentencing jurisdictions. In 2004, the Supreme Court declared unconstitutional a Washington State guidelines scheme based on the federal one, dooming that

Key Fact

Sentencing guidelines serve to limit a judge's sentencing discretion and are supposed to promote sentencing equality.

PRESUMPTIVE SENTENCE LENGTHS IN MONTHS

Italicized numbers within the grid denote the range within which a judge may sentence without the sentence being deemed a departure. Offenders with nonimprisonment felony sentences are subject to jail time according to law.

SEVERITY LEVEL OF CONVICTION OFFENSE (common offenses listed in italics)		CRIMINAL HISTORY SCORE						
		0	**1**	**2**	**3**	**4**	**5**	**6 or more**
Murder, 2nd Degree (intentional murder; drive-by shootings)	XI	306 *261–367*	326 *278–391*	346 *295–415*	366 *312–439*	386 *329–463*	406 *346–480²*	426 *363–480²*
Murder, 3rd Degree Murder, 2nd Degree (unintentional murder)	X	150 *128–180*	165 *141–198*	180 *153–216*	195 *166–234*	210 *179–252*	225 *192–270*	240 *204–288*
Assault, 1st Degree Controlled Substance Crime, 1st Degree	IX	86 *74–103*	98 *84–117*	110 *94–132*	122 *104–146*	134 *114–160*	146 *125–175*	158 *135–189*
Aggravated Robbery, 1st Degree Controlled Substance Crime, 2nd Degree	VIII	48 *41–57*	58 *50–69*	68 *58–81*	78 *67–93*	88 *75–105*	98 *84–117*	108 *92–129*
Felony DWI	VII	36	42	48	54 *46–64*	60 *51–72*	66 *57–79*	72 *62–86*
Assault, 2nd Degree Felon in Possession of a Firearm	VI	21	27	33	39 *34–46*	45 *39–54*	51 *44–61*	57 *49–68*
Residential Burglary Simple Robbery	V	18	23	28	33 *29–39*	38 *33–45*	43 *37–51*	48 *41–57*
Nonresidential Burglary	IV	12¹	15	18	21	24 *21–28*	27 *23–32*	30 *26–36*
Theft Crimes (over $2,500)	III	12¹	13	15	17	19 *17–22*	21 *18–25*	23 *20–27*
Theft Crimes ($2,500 or less) Check Forgery ($200–$2,500)	II	12¹	12¹	13	15	17	19	21 *18–25*
Sale of Simulated Controlled Substance	I	12¹	12¹	12¹	13	15	17	19 *17–22*

☐ Presumptive commitment to state imprisonment. First-degree murder is excluded from the guidelines by law and continues to have a mandatory life sentence.

▨ Presumptive stayed sentence; at the discretion of the judge, up to a year in jail and/or other nonjail sanctions can be imposed as conditions of probation. However, certain offenses in this section of the grid always carry a presumptive commitment to state prison.

¹One year and one day

² M.S. § 244.09 requires the Sentencing Guidelines to provide a range of 15% downward and 20% upward from the presumptive sentence. However, because the statutory maximum sentence for these offenses is no more than 40 years, the range is capped at that number.

FIGURE 3.4 *Minnesota Sentencing Guidelines*

and other similar sentencing systems. The Court found that any factors that increase a criminal sentence, except prior convictions, must be proved beyond a reasonable doubt (Liptak, 2004).

The 1984 law resulted in changes in the content and format of the PSI. Instead of preparing PSI reports focused on a positivist approach to the offender, the PO must now dwell on the details of the offense and the offender's prior criminal history (see Figure 3.4). A federal PO in Philadelphia pointed out that it is imperative "that every detail about offense and offenders be included when these reports are prepared. Otherwise, minor point fluctuations on either offense level or criminal history can make a significant difference of several years in time to be served by convicted offenders" (Marshall, 1989: 10).

In preparing the PSI report, "[T]he probation officer sets out the details of the offense and the defendant's criminal history. The probation officer then applies the sentencing guidelines to those facts" (Adair and Slawsky, 1991: 60). To make a relevant sentencing recommendation, the PO must be familiar with any applicable sentencing guidelines and mandatory sentences in his or her jurisdiction and must study the case to determine whether there are valid grounds for a departure from the guidelines. "The presentence report has become more a legal document than a diagnostic tool, citing facts, statutes, and guidelines, justifying and supporting positions the guidelines treat as relevant in arriving at a sentencing range. The format and presentation of information [are] dominated by facts related to the offender's offense behavior and criminal history, the two primary factors establishing a defendant's sentencing range. Social and personal history information is reported, however, primarily to aid the court in choosing a point within the range, imposing conditions of release, and/or departures" (Denzlinger and Miller, 1991: 51). Sentencing guidelines and mandatory sentencing significantly restrict a judge's sentencing discretion.

Pretrial Services Officers

U.S. pretrial services provide to the court two important services—investigation and supervision—and are the first court representatives that defendants encounter after their arrest. In general, the officer's mission is to investigate defendants charged with a federal crime, recommend in a report to the court whether to release or detain the defendants, and supervise the defendants who are released to the community while they await their day in court. At the core of the day-to-day work of officers is the hallowed principle of criminal law that the defendant is presumed innocent until proven guilty. Officers must balance this presumption with the reality that some persons—if not detained before their trial—are likely to flee or to threaten others. Defendants may pose danger to a person, such as by threatening a victim or a witness, or to the community, such as by engaging in criminal activity. The pretrial services officer's job is to identify persons who are likely to fail to appear or to be arrested if released, to recommend restrictive conditions that would reasonably ensure the defendant's appearance in court and the safety of the community, and to recommend detention when no such conditions exist. If the person does not pose such risk, the officer's mandate is to recommend to the court the least restrictive conditions that will reasonably ensure that the person appears in court and poses no danger.

The officer conducts a pretrial services investigation, gathering and verifying important information about the defendant and the defendant's suitability for pretrial release. In the pretrial services investigation, which forms the basis of the officer's report to the court, the officer interviews the defendant and confirms the defendant's information through other sources. The investigation begins when the officer is first informed that a defendant has been arrested. The arresting or case agent calls the pretrial services office and, ideally, provides information about the defendant (e.g., name, date of birth, Social Security number, charges, circumstances surrounding the arrest, and location). Before

Key Fact

The federal system and other jurisdictions provide for the supervision of pretrial defendants.

interviewing the defendant, the officer runs a criminal history check and also, if possible, speaks to the assistant U.S. attorney about the defendant, the charges, and the government's position as to whether to release or detain the defendant. The purpose of the interview is to find out what the defendant has been doing, where the defendant has been living, and where the defendant has been working (or what the defendant's source of support is). What the officer learns from collateral sources—from other persons, documents, and online research—may verify what the defendant said, contradict it, or provide something more. The officer's research, for instance, may include contacting the defendant's family and associates to confirm background information, employers to verify employment, law enforcement agencies to obtain a criminal history, financial institutions to obtain bank or credit card statements, and the motor vehicle administration to check the defendant's license and registration.

Conducting the investigation in time for the defendant's initial appearance in court can be quite a challenge. Sometimes the pretrial services officer must wait for the arresting agents to make the defendant available or for the U.S. marshals to finish processing the defendant. The defense counsel may be interviewing the defendant or may tell the defendant not to answer the officer's questions. The officer might have to wait for an interpreter or for an interview room. Sometimes verifying information is hard because the defendant gives false information or a false identity or because persons able to verify information are not available. The interview may take place in the U.S. marshal's holding cell, the arresting law enforcement agency's office, the local jail, or the pretrial services office. During the interview, the officer talks to the defendant in private if possible, remains objective while interacting with the defendant, and explains that the information will be used to decide whether the defendant will be released or detained. The officer does not discuss the alleged offense or the defendant's guilt or innocence and does not give legal advice to the defendant or recommend an attorney.

When the investigation is complete, the officer prepares a report that helps the court make an informed release or detention decision. In preparing the pretrial services report, the officer addresses two basic questions: Is the defendant likely to stay out of trouble and come back to court? If not, what conditions should the court impose to increase that likelihood? The officer considers both danger and nonappearance factors before making a recommendation to the court to release or detain the defendant. For example, the offense with which the defendant is charged and the defendant's substance abuse history may present both danger and nonappearance considerations. Factors such as prior arrests and convictions or a history of violent behavior raise danger concerns; factors such as immigration status or ties to family and community may influence nonappearance. If no risk factors are evident, the officer recommends release on personal recognizance, but if risk factors exist, the officer recommends either release with conditions or detention. Release conditions are tailored to the individual defendant but always include the universal condition that the defendant not commit a federal, state, or local crime during the period of release. The officer may recommend (and the court may set) conditions to accomplish any number of goals, including prohibiting possession of weapons, contact with victims, or use of alcohol or drugs; restricting the defendant's freedom of movement or the people with whom the defendant associates; and requiring the defendant to seek or maintain employment, obtain education or training, or surrender a passport. If the defendant is likely to fail to appear, the officer may recommend a financial bond, which the defendant (or the defendant's family) forfeits if the defendant fails to appear in court as directed.

The pretrial services officer supervises offenders in the community to make sure they comply with court-ordered conditions of release. Officers supervise defendants released to the community until they begin to serve their sentence, the charges are dismissed, or they are acquitted. They monitor defendants' compliance with their release conditions; manage risk; provide necessary services as ordered by the court, such as drug treatment; and inform the court and the U.S. attorney if the defendant violates the conditions.

When a case is received for supervision, the officer reviews the information about the defendant, assessing any potential risk that the defendant presents and any supervision issues that may affect the defendant's ability to comply with the release conditions. The officer selects appropriate supervision strategies and develops a supervision plan, which the officer modifies if the defendant's circumstances change. The officer also carries out risk management activities to help ensure the defendant complies with the release conditions: monitoring the defendant through personal contacts and phone calls with the defendant and others, including family members, employers, and treatment providers; meeting with the defendant in the pretrial services office and at the defendant's home and job; helping the defendant find employment; and helping the defendant find medical, legal, or social services.

At the request of the U.S. attorney, the officer investigates whether the defendant is suitable for placement in a pretrial diversion program. Pretrial diversion is an alternative to prosecution that diverts the defendant from prosecution to a program of supervision administered by the pretrial services officer. The U.S. attorney identifies candidates for diversion—persons who have not adopted a criminal lifestyle and who are likely to complete the program successfully. The pretrial services officer investigates the individual, recommends for or against placement, and recommends length of supervision and special conditions. Diversion is voluntary; the person may opt to stand trial instead. If the individual is placed in the program, he or she is supervised by a pretrial services officer, and if the person successfully completes supervision, the government declines prosecution and makes no record of the arrest.

PLEA BARGAINING AND THE PRE-PLEA INVESTIGATION (PPI) REPORT

Most court cases in the United States, criminal and civil, are settled not by trial but by negotiation (or dropping of the action). In the criminal justice system, a negotiated settlement is referred to as a **plea bargain**—an *ad hoc* exchange between a defendant who agrees to plead guilty to a criminal charge and a prosecutor who (explicitly or implicitly) offers leniency in return. Plea bargaining is criticized both for providing criminals with excessive leniency and for coercing defendants to waive their constitutional rights to a trial. Its extensive use can be explained by the time it saves the prosecutor and the defense, as well as the certainty of outcome it offers to both. (For a more detailed discussion of plea bargaining, see Abadinsky, 2007a.)

The extensive use of plea bargaining has reduced the need for a PSI because the plea agreement may actually specify the sentence a defendant will receive. This is particularly true in jurisdictions with determinate sentencing (discussed in Chapter 6) that limit judicial discretion. Under such conditions, a presentence report would not serve any useful purpose at a sentencing hearing. Plea bargaining, however, has resulted in the use of a pretrial/pre-plea investigation (PPI) report (Figure 3.5). If prosecutor and defense counsel negotiate a plea agreement and the judge retains a great deal of discretion over the sentence to be imposed (which is the case in many states—see Chapter 6), the judge may request a pretrial investigation before agreeing to the negotiated plea. In Illinois, for example, for a simple burglary as a first offense, the judge has the discretion to sentence an offender to a term of 3, 4, or 5 years, all the way up to 14 years. In Cook County, which includes the city of Chicago, judges often require a PPI report before confirming a plea agreement; in fact, short-form pretrial reports are more frequent than PSI reports.

The practice of using a PPI report requires the defendant to agree to the investigation (*New York Code of Criminal Procedure*):

> The probation department shall conduct a pre-plea investigation only upon a court order and written authorization by the defendant, his attorney, the prosecuting attorney and the judge ordering the investigation. Such written authori-

STATE OF FLORIDA
DEPARTMENT OF CORRECTIONS
PROBATION AND PAROLE SERVICES
PRE-PLEA RELEASE FORM

Defendant _____   Circuit _____   County _____

Docket No. _____

DEFENDANT'S APPROVAL TO CONDUCT A PRESENTENCE
INVESTIGATION BEFORE CONVICTION OR PLEA

I, _____ defendant, hereby consent to a presentence investigation by the Department of Corrections, Probation and Parole Serivces Office, for the purpose of obtaining information useful to the Court in the event I should hereafter plead guilty, or *nolo contendere*, or be found guilty.

By this consent, I do not admit any guilt or waive any rights and I understand that any report prepared can be shown to the Court before I have been found guilty only if I so agree in writing. Otherwise, I understand that any report prepared will not be shown to anyone unless and until I have been found guilty or entered a plea of guilty or *nolo contendere*.

I have read, or had read to me, the aforegoing consent and fully understand it. No promise has been made to me as to what final disposition will be made of my case.

_____   _____
(Date)   (Signature of Defendant)

_____   _____
(Date)   (Defense Attorney)

DEFENDANT'S CONSENT TO THE COURT'S INSPECTION OF THE PRESENTENCE INVESTIGATION PRIOR TO PLEA OR FINDING OF GUILT

I, _____ defendant, hereby consent to review of my presentence investigation report by a Circuit Judge at any time, including the time prior to entry of a plea of guilty or *nolo contendere* or a finding of guilt.

I have read, or had read to me, the aforegoing consent and fully understand it. No promise has been made to me as to what final disposition of my case will be.

_____   _____
(Date)   (Signature of Defendant)

_____   _____
(Date)   (Defense Attorney)

_____   _____
(Date)   (Prosecuting Attorney)

FIGURE 3.5 *Florida Pre-plea Release Form*

zation shall include statements that no probation department personnel will be called to testify regarding information acquired by the probation department, that information obtained by the probation department may not be used in a subsequent trial, and that this exemption does not apply to defense or prosecution material which may be included in the plea report.

Probation officers in Georgia are instructed: "If the defendant or his/her attorney refuses to sign the authorization, discontinue the investigation and report this fact to the court." In Ohio, a PPI cannot be conducted prior to a finding of guilty unless the defendant, on advice of counsel, has consented to allow the investigation to proceed before adjudication and unless adequate precautions are taken to ensure information disclosed during the PPI does not come to the attention of the prosecution, the court, or the jury prior to adjudication. As in Georgia, refusal of the defendant, his attorney, or both to sign the waiver constitutes an end to the investigation.

Key Fact
Disclosure of PSI information enables the defendant
to contest information that
he or she considers unfair
and to be protected from
the effects of unfounded information, but disclosure
may cause sources of information to dry up.

CONFIDENTIALITY OF THE PSI REPORT

Some controversy exists concerning whether any or all the contents of a PSI report should be disclosed to the defendant or his or her attorney. The basic argument against disclosure is that sources of information must be protected or they will hesitate to provide information. Family members or employers may fear retribution from the defendant if they provide negative information; in addition, law enforcement agencies may be reluctant to provide confidential information if the defendant or the defendant's attorney will be privy to it.

The basic argument in favor of disclosure is to enable the defendant to contest information that he or she considers unfair and to be protected from the effects of unfounded information. Disclosure of the contents of the PSI is more likely to ensure the information presented is more objective and accurate. The American Bar Association rec-ommends that all information that adversely affects the defendant be discussed with the defendant or his or her attorney. The President's Commission on Law Enforcement and Administration of Justice stated that "in the absence of compelling reasons for nondisclo-sure of specific information, the defendant and his counsel should be permitted to exam-ine the entire presentence report" (1972: 356). The National Advisory Commission on Criminal Justice Standards and Goals recommended that the PSI be made available to the defense and the prosecution; the commission rejected the argument that sources of infor-mation will dry up: "(1) [T]hose jurisdictions which have required disclosure have not ex-perienced this phenomenon; and (2) more importantly, if the same evidence were given as testimony at trial, there would be no protection or confidentiality" (1973: 189).

The U.S. Supreme Court has consistently upheld the confidentiality of the PSI re-port. This has been based on the (presumed) neutrality/objectivity of the probation offi-cer—he or she has no interest in punishment; by disposition and training the PO is a helping, not a prosecutorial, agent. Thus, in the 1949 case of *Williams v. New York* (337 U.S. 241), the judge imposed a sentence of death based on information contained in the PSI report. The defendant had been convicted of murder, but the jury recommended life imprisonment. The PSI—to which the jury was not privy—revealed that Williams was a suspect in 30 burglaries. Although he had not been convicted of these crimes, the report indicated that he had confessed to some and had been identified as the perpetrator of others. The judge had referred to parts of the report, indicating that the defendant was a "menace to society."

Williams appealed the death sentence, arguing that the procedure violated due process of law "in that the sentence of death was based upon information supplied by wit-nesses with whom the accused had not been confronted and as to whom he had no oppor-tunity for cross examination or rebuttal." The Supreme Court rejected this argument:

> Under the practice of individualizing punishments, investigational techniques have been given an important role. Probation workers making reports of their investigations have not been trained to prosecute but to aid offenders. Their re-ports have been given high value by conscientious judges who want to sentence persons on the best available information rather than on guesswork and inade-quate information. To deprive sentencing judges of this kind of information would undermine modern procedural policies that have been cautiously adopted throughout the nation after careful consideration and experimenta-tion. We must recognize that most of the information now relied upon by judges to guide them in the intelligent imposition of sentences would be unavailable if information were restricted to that given in open court by witnesses subject to cross-examination. And the modern probation report draws on information concerning every aspect of a defendant's life. The types and extent of this infor-mation make totally impractical if not impossible open court testimony with cross-examination. Such procedure could endlessly delay criminal administra-tion in a retrial of collateral issues.

Williams was executed.

In the federal system, since 1983 the contents of the PSI have been disclosed to the defendant, his or her counsel, and the attorney for the government, and the 1984 Sentencing Reform Act "largely rejected the sentencing philosophy expressed in *Williams*" (Adair and Slawsky, 1991: 58). Under the federal system of sentencing guidelines, the contents of the report determine the parameters for imposing a sentence. As a result, the sentencing hearing has become increasingly hostile. In response to defense attorney objections, the PO "is obligated to review the objections, reinvestigate if necessary, reevaluate decisions made, and discuss the findings with counsel. Any unresolved objections must be summarized for the court in an addendum to the report. On occasion this process consumes more time than the preparation of the presentence report" (Denzlinger and Miller, 1991: 51).

In some jurisdictions, law or custom allows the defendant access to the report, whereas some states give the judge the option of disclosing the contents of the report. In Texas, for example, the statutes require that the entire contents of the report be revealed to the defendant. However, a trend exists toward adopting the position previously used in the federal system. The PSI can be revealed to the defendant or counsel, but the *Rules of Criminal Procedure* exclude the probation officer's recommendation and any "diagnostic opinion [such as a psychiatric report] which might seriously disrupt a program of rehabilitation, sources of information obtained upon a promise of confidentiality, or any other information which, if disclosed, might result in harm, physical or otherwise, to the defendant or other persons."

In Michigan, although the court must permit the prosecutor, the defendant's attorney, and the defendant an opportunity to review the report prior to sentencing, "the court may exempt from disclosure information or a diagnostic opinion which might seriously disrupt a program of rehabilitation or sources of information obtained on a promise of confidentiality. . . . Any information exempted from disclosure by the court must be specifically noted in the PSI and is subject to appellate review." In Ohio, "the Probation Department shall have the report completed no later than ten days prior to sentencing. When the report is completed, it shall be sent to the assigned judge and made available, at the probation department, for review by the defendant's attorney (or by the defendant if he is not represented by an attorney) and the prosecutor. . . . The report made available for review by the attorneys or the defendant shall reflect the fact that information, if any, has been deleted pursuant to [Ohio statutes] and the general categories of the deleted information shall also be noted."

CRITICISM OF THE PSI REPORT

Some critics maintain that many judges do not even read the PSI report, whereas others carefully select passages critical of the defendant to justify their sentences. Judges may discount the report because of the hearsay nature of the information (Blumberg, 1970). One report notes the types of inaccurate or misleading information found in the PSI reports of one state (Dickey, 1979: 33–34):

(1) rumors and suspicions that are reported without any factual explanations; (2) incomplete explanations of events that leave a misleading impression; (3) factual errors relating, usually, to the criminal record of the offender.

Rumors and suspicions are often reported in presentence reports and identified as such. The report that the rumor exists may be accurate. What is objectionable is the fact that the subject of the rumor may cause the reader to give more weight to the rumor than it deserves, if any. If the rumor is without foundation, reference to it is particularly troubling.

It is difficult to assess the impact of rumors, although they sometimes seem to directly affect correctional decisions. For example, one sex offender's presentence report contained the statement that the offender "was rumored to have killed his mother." This was referred to in several parole decisions before it was investigated. Upon inquiry, it was determined to the satisfaction of the parole board that the offender had been confined in another state at the time of his mother's death and had no connection to it.

Some reports do not contain complete information and are therefore misleading. One inmate's PSI contained the statement that he "had been arrested for attempted first degree murder after a bar fight. The charges were later dropped." Investigation showed that the reason the charges were dropped was that the inmate was actually the victim of an attack and not the aggressor. The other person involved was later charged with a crime for the attack. The most frequently recurring factual problem with the reports is related to past offenses. The so-called FBI rap sheet (or yellow sheet) is part of the report. It contains a confounding listing of past offenses that is frequently repetitious (i.e., it reports the same offense more than once), but the repetitions are not identified. Past charges do not always contain their disposition, so the reader is never sure how many offenses there actually were which were dropped and why, what the facts underlying the charges and offenses were, and what the outcome was.

One observer is concerned with the enormous dependence on the PSI that he argues tends to make the PO, rather than the judge, the sentencer (Gaylin, 1974). Numerous studies have indicated a high correlation between the recommendation of the PO and the judge's sentence. For example, research by the American Justice Institute (1981), using samples from representative probation departments throughout the United States, found that recommendations for probation were adopted by the sentencing judge between 66 and 95 percent of the time. A study in Utah revealed that judges followed the recommendation 92 percent of the time (Norman and Wadman, 2000). A study of 1994 sentencing recommendations in Nevada revealed a concurrence rate of 97 percent when probation was recommended and 88 percent when the recommendation was imprisonment. A study in one Iowa judicial district (Campbell, McCoy, and Osigweh, 1990) revealed much less congruity—and in a surprising direction: In many cases, those recommended for incarceration (44 percent) were instead sentenced to probation or some lesser sanction, such as diversion or a fine. The researchers concluded that these decisions were probably the result of a plea bargain and a prosecutor's recommendation for a nonincarceration sentence.

One study examined the relationship between plea bargaining, the PO's recommendation, and the final disposition of the case in a large western county. In this county, after the defendant has accepted a "bargain" in exchange for a plea of guilty, the case is sent to the probation department for a PSI report. The researchers found a high correlation (93 percent) between the recommendation and the sentence (Kingsnorth and Rizzo, 1979); however, the PO may write in the PSI the recommendation that the PO believes will be well received by the judge. One observer suggests that the prosecutor often finds a way of communicating the plea bargain agreement to the probation department, and the latter responds with a conforming recommendation (Czajkoski, 1973). Conversely, in Wisconsin, "the prosecutor is often influenced by the recommendation in the report and the information underlying it. Some prosecutors frequently adopt the report's recommendations as their own recommendation to the court or use it as a benchmark in deciding on their recommendation. Sometimes a plea agreement will include the condition that the prosecutor will adopt the report's recommendation as his own" (Dickey, 1979: 30). In one county, the minutes of the plea bargaining session, including the details of the negotiated agreement, are sent to the probation department before the submission of the presentence report. "Probation officer concurrence with previously negotiated sentence agreements is a consequence, not of case characteristics, but of pressures emanating from the organizational structure of which the probation department is a part, namely the court system itself" (Kingsnorth and Rizzo, 1979: 9). These and other studies serve to remind us that the probation officer is simply one actor in a rather complex setting. How much influence the PO can exert may often depend on procedural or structural variables or perhaps on the officer's force of personality.

In many jurisdictions, the PO is overburdened with PSI reports and does not have the time to do an adequate investigation and prepare a (potentially) useful report. In courts in which the judge usually pays little or no attention to the contents of the report, the PO will not be inclined to pursue the necessary information and prepare well-written reports. Jonas Robitscher, an attorney and psychiatrist, believes that psychiatric reports and evaluations contained in the PSI often make the difference between probation, a short sentence, or a long sentence. However, he goes on to state: "Many of these reports and evaluations contain dynamic formulations about the cause of behavior based on as little as twenty minutes spent with the subject of the report" (1980: 35).

Walter Dickey found a most distressing problem related to the issue of erroneous information in the report:

> Even when an alleged error is challenged at sentencing and a contrary finding made, it does not necessarily follow that the report will be corrected. When a judge makes a finding of fact that is inconsistent with the presentence report, he usually states the finding in the record of the sentencing hearing. . . . Without more, this leaves the report itself uncorrected. The sentencing transcript is not made a part of the report; it is not attached to it. The oral finding does not signal anyone to amend the report or any of the copies of it. Subsequent users of the report, correctional and parole authorities, rely on the uncorrected report. Rarely is the report amended to reflect additional information or findings of fact inconsistent with it at sentencing. (1979: 35)

In Michigan, however, state law requires that "if the court finds that challenged information is inaccurate or irrelevant, that finding will be made part of the court record, and the inaccurate or irrelevant information must be stricken from the report prior to distribution." To improve the reliability of the report, the Massachusetts commissioner of probation provides the following standards:

- The PO should identify the sources of information in the report.
- The PO should make personal contact with informants or sources of information, when practicable, who can substantiate information. The PO should clearly state in the report those instances in which information has not been substantiated.
- The PO should obtain pertinent documentation, such as letters, clinical reports, school reports, and certified statements, when practicable. The PO should indicate when information in the report is supported by such documentation.
- Sources of information should be identified in most instances; however, this does not exclude from a report any relevant information from unnamed sources or informants with whom the PO has had personal contact. If a PO includes such information in an investigative report, the PO shall clearly indicate in the report that the information was obtained from sources or informants not being identified in this report.

Defendants are often dissatisfied with the role of their attorneys in the sentencing process (Dickey, 1979). Federal District Court Judge Irving Cooper (1977: 101) notes: "It is particularly distressing that many attorneys for the defense, who have proven themselves competent as to the facts and law in the case at trial . . . display on sentence hardly more than a faint glimmer as to who their clients really are as human beings." Another author states:

> Another source of the sense of injustice is the belief that lawyers do not provide the court with positive information about the offender to supplement the presentence report which, it is frequently asserted, is incomplete. Sophisticated defendants realize that even the most forceful statements, if they are general, are of little value to their case. They recognize the importance of presenting the court with alternatives to confinement (e.g., job or school plan, place to live) if

probation is sought or a specific statement of plans after release if a short period of confinement is the goal. These defendants are usually dissatisfied because they feel the court is forced to rely on an incomplete report because their lawyers did not provide the additional information. (Dickey, 1979: 36)

In response to this problem, the Legal Aid Society in New York City has used social workers to prepare sentencing memoranda for use by defense counsel at the sentencing hearing. In Buncombe County, North Carolina, I set up a similar effort using senior undergraduate students from Western Carolina University. The students worked for the public defender, providing PSI reports for use by defense counsel. Other profit and nonprofit agencies prepare PSI reports, and privately (for-profit) commissioned PSI reports have proliferated. This trend raises a serious question of equal justice because only those with the necessary financial resources can commission such a report.

In Chapter 4, we turn to the system of juvenile justice, the juvenile court, and the role of the probation officer.

KEY TERMS

long-form PSI (p. 57)

mandatory sentencing (p. 68)

plea bargain (p. 72)

prediction scales (p. 54)

presentence investigation (PSI) report (p. 52)

sentencing guidelines (p. 68)

short-form PSI (p. 57)

victim impact statement (VIS) (p. 53)

INTERNET CONNECTIONS

American Probation and Parole Association: APPA.org

National Association of Pretrial Services: napsa.org

National Criminal Justice Reference Service: ncjrs.org

Probation agency links: cppca.org/link

REVIEW QUESTIONS

1. Why is the presentence report a manifestation of a positivist view?
2. Why does a judge order a PSI?
3. What are the other purposes to which the PSI report can be put?
4. What are the categories of information contained in a PSI report?
5. What are the sources of information for a PSI?
6. What type of questions should the probation officer avoid during PSI interviews? Why?
7. What are the difficulties encountered by the probation officer when trying to decipher/understand the arrest record/rap sheet?
8. Why is the nature of a defendant's prior criminal record important for a probation officer to determine?
9. What variables are considered in making a recommendation for or against a sentence of probation?

10. What is the law and practice with respect to requiring a PSI report?
11. How can plea bargaining influence the PSI?
12. What are the arguments for and against the contents of a PSI report being disclosed to a defendant or defense counsel?
13. What is the basis of the Supreme Court's determination that a PSI report is confidential?
14. What are the various criticisms of the PSI?
15. What has led to the use of the privately commissioned PSI report?
16. Why does the privately commissioned PSI report raise a question of equal justice?

The Probation Officer and Juvenile Justice

The concept of *parens patriae* has largely disappeared from the political and public agenda. The delinquency courtrooms now work more like the criminal system that the juvenile court was supposed to counter.

—*Louise Kiernan* (1997: 12)

Chapter Outline

As opposed to the secondary role of the probation officer (PO) in adult criminal justice, the PO is at the center of juvenile justice. In this chapter, we examine the juvenile court, the history and unique qualities of juvenile justice, the PO's role, and pertinent legal decisions. We will then turn to youngsters in adult criminal court.

HISTORY OF THE JUVENILE COURT

The system of justice used for juveniles in the United States is based on a philosophy radically different from the one on which the adult criminal justice system rests. Before we can examine the services provided by a probation agency to the juvenile court, it is necessary to understand the history and philosophy of this unique institution.

In Europe, from Roman times to the late eighteenth century, children were routinely abandoned by their parents; the classical philosopher Rousseau, for example, boasted of abandoning five of his children to foundling homes (Boswell, 1989). Abandoned children were subjected to extreme levels of deprivation and exploitation. English common law considered children as chattel, and a rather indifferent attitude toward children became characteristic of America, where they became creatures of exploitation. Indeed, the contemporary American concern with the problem of child abuse stands in marked contrast to our earlier history. Child labor remained an important part of economic life into the twentieth century. Children of the poor labored in mines (where their size was an advantage), mills, and factories with unsanitary and unsafe conditions.

The Supreme Court reflected the prevailing belief in *laissez-faire* capitalism and would not intervene—statutes prohibiting children younger than 12 years from employment and those limiting the workday of youngsters older than 12 years to 10 hours were ruled unconstitutional or were routinely disobeyed. Increased immigration, industrialization, and urbanization drastically altered American society. The 10- and 12-hour workday left many children without parental supervision, and family disorganization became widespread. Many children lived in the streets, where they encountered the disorder and rampant vice of the urban environment.

In the early days of colonial America, the family remained the mainstay of social control, "although by 1700 the family's inability to accommodate and discipline its young was becoming more apparent" (Mennel, 1973: xxii). Numerous laws began to appear that threatened parents for failing to properly discipline their children. Furthermore, the British practice of transporting wayward young to America for indenture, which often involved neglect, cruelty, and immorality, left many youngsters without supervision as they fled from these onerous circumstances. By the end of the eighteenth century, society began to realize that a "system of social control would have to be developed apart from the family which would discipline homeless, vagrant, and destitute children—the offspring of the poor" (Mennel, 1973: xxvii). This need led to the rise of **houses of refuge**.

HOUSES OF REFUGE AND ORPHAN ASYLUMS

In 1817, the Society for the Prevention of Pauperism was established in response to the problem of troubled and troublesome children, and in 1824, it was renamed the Society for the Reformation of Juvenile Delinquency. The society conducted campaigns against the "corrupting" influence of taverns and theaters and opposed the use of jails to house children. Their efforts led to the establishment of houses of refuge, also called houses of reformation or reform schools (Krisberg, 1988).

The first house of refuge opened in New York in 1825 and was quickly followed by one in Boston (1826) and another in Philadelphia (1828). These institutions provided housing and care for troublesome children who might otherwise be left in the streets or, if their behavior brought them into serious conflict with the law, sent to jail or prison. The house of refuge was used "not only for the less serious juvenile criminal, but for runaways, disobedient children or vagrants" (Empey, 1979: 25–26). Orphan asylums were used for abandoned or orphaned children, for the children of women without husbands, or for children whose parents were deemed unfit. Both institutions "were established to inculcate children with the values of hard work, orderliness, and subordination and thereby ensure their future good behavior" (Mennel, 1973: 8). To achieve these ends, however, discipline and punishments were often brutal, and the house of refuge in New York experienced group escapes and inmate uprisings.

Although these institutions were operated by private charities, their public charters included the first statutory definitions of juvenile delinquency and provided the basis for state intervention in the lives of children who were neglected or in need of supervision, in addition to those youngsters who had committed crimes (Walker, 1980). In these charters was embodied a "medieval English doctrine of nebulous origin and meaning" (Schlossman, 1977: 8) known as *parens patriae*, originally referring to the feudal duties of the overlord to his vassals and later the legal duties of the monarch toward his or her subjects who were in need of care, particularly children and the mentally incompetent. In its original form, *parens patriae* provided the Crown with authority to administer the estates of landed orphans (Sutton, 1988).

"With the independence of the American colonies and the transplanting of the English common-law system, the state in this country has taken the place of the crown as the *parens patriae* of all minors" (Lou, 1972: 4). This concept gave almost complete authority over children to the state—the Bill of Rights simply did not apply to children (*Ex parte Crouse*, 4 Wharton 9 [1838])—and *parens patriae* became the legal basis for the juvenile court. Although this concept has become identified with the rehabilitation of juvenile delinquents, it originally applied only to dependent children.

Key Fact

Parens patriae provided the legal basis for the juvenile court.

Child-Saving Movement

As immigration, industrialization, and urbanization continued, the fearful image of masses of undisciplined and uneducated children gave rise to the **child-saving movement**. Led by upper-class women of earlier American ancestry, the child savers were influenced by the nativist prejudices of their day as well as by social Darwinism (see Chapter 1). Natural selection resulted in an inferior underclass in need of control but not of aid in the sense of the modern social welfare state. Something had to be done to save these children from an environment that would only lead them into vice and crime and cause them to be the progenitors of the same. Reforming juvenile justice became the task of women who "were generally well-educated, widely-traveled, and had access to political and financial resources" (Platt, 1974: 77). The juvenile court was the result of their efforts, although controversy surrounds the interests and motivations of the child savers.

Key Fact

The child-saving movement provided the impetus for establishing the juvenile court.

Anthony Platt argues that these women, although they "viewed themselves as altruists and humanitarians dedicated to rescuing those who were less fortunately placed in the social order," were actually motivated by boredom and middle- and upper-class social, economic, and political interests (1974: 3). "The child-savers were concerned not with championing the rights of the poor against exploitation by the ruling class but rather integrating the poor into the established social order and protecting 'respectable' citizens from the 'dangerous classes'" of people, who might otherwise be drawn into social revolution, if not criminality (Platt quoted in Empey, 1979: 31). According to Platt, the juvenile court would serve to protect propertied and commercial interests from the predations of lower-class youngsters while ensuring an adequate supply of disciplined and vocationally trained labor. In fact, however, many states had already separated juvenile cases from those of adults without establishing a distinct juvenile court. The movement to establish a juvenile court was part of a larger program of social reform advocated by the Progressives of the late nineteenth and early twentieth centuries. David Rothman (in Empey, 1979: 37) places the issue in perspective: The juvenile court movement "satisfied [both] the most humanitarian of impulses and the most crudely self-interested considerations."

EMERGENCE OF THE JUVENILE COURT

Although juveniles might be sent to a house of refuge, an orphan asylum, or a reformatory—there was confusion over which children should be relegated to which institution—they could be arrested, detained, and tried like any adult accused of a crime. Children older (and sometimes younger) than 14 were routinely prosecuted as adults and punished as adults. Although some modifications of the trial process with respect to juveniles occurred as early as 1869, it was the Illinois Juvenile Court Act of 1899 that established the first law creating a special comprehensive court for juveniles. Consistent with the concept of *parens patriae*, the juvenile court was given jurisdiction over neglected and dependent children in addition to children who were delinquent (e.g., persons younger than 16 years of age who had violated the law):

> For the purposes of this act the words dependent child and neglected child shall mean any child who for any reason is destitute or homeless or abandoned; or has not proper parental care or guardianship; or who habitually begs or receives alms; or who is found living in any house of ill fame or with any vicious or disreputable person; or whose home, by reason of neglect, cruelty or depravity on the part of its parents, guardian or other person in whose care it may be, is an unfit place for such a child.

Nondelinquents in whom the court was interested because of their behavior became known as **status offenders**.

Within 25 years of the Illinois Juvenile Court Act, every state but one had adopted legislation providing for one or all the features of a juvenile court organization (Lenroot and Lundberg, 1925). In Cuyahoga County (Cleveland), the first session of the juvenile court occurred on June 4, 1902, with 20 boys younger than 16 years of age appearing. The initial case involved a 14-year-old boy charged with delinquency for stealing a pair of shoes; he was placed in "care and custody" of one of the three dozen volunteers who served as probation officers. A juvenile court was established in the Territory of Arizona on March 21, 1907; later that year, a probation officer was appointed in Pima County "to make such investigation as may be required by the Court, to be present if practicable when juvenile cases are heard, to furnish such information and assistance as the judge may require, and to take charge of any child, before trial and after trial, as may be directed by the Court." Jefferson County, Texas, appointed its first paid probation officer in 1918, one of the earliest in Texas.

A book originally published in 1927 provides insight into the prevailing concepts of the juvenile court (Lou, 1972: 2):

> These principles upon which the juvenile court acts are radically different from those of the criminal courts. In place of judicial tribunals, restrained by antiquated procedure, saturated in an atmosphere of hostility, trying cases for determining guilt and inflicting punishment according to inflexible rules of law, we have now juvenile courts, in which the relations of the child to his parents or other adults and to the state or society are defined and are adjusted summarily according to the scientific findings about the child and his environments. In place of magistrates, limited by the outgrown custom and compelled to walk in the paths fixed by the law of the realm, we have now socially-minded judges, who hear and adjust cases according not to rigid rules of law but to what the interests of society and the interests of the child or good conscience demand. In the place of juries, prosecutors, and lawyers, trained in the old conception of law and staging dramatically, but often amusingly, legal battles, as the necessary paraphernalia of a criminal court, we have now probation officers, physicians, psychologists, and psychiatrists, who search for the social, physiological, psychological, and mental backgrounds of the child in order to arrive at reasonable and just solutions of individual cases.

Lou's statement clearly embodies the positivist view—or critics might say, positivism run amok—with the child being denied the most basic due process rights. The unstructured and informal system of juvenile justice used in Illinois quickly became the standard as juvenile courts were established throughout the United States. Differences between the adult criminal court and the juvenile court extended even to the terminology used:

Adult Criminal Court	Juvenile Court
Defendant	Respondent
Charges/indictment	Petition
Arraignment	Hearing
Prosecution/trial	Adjudication
Verdict	Finding
Sentence	Disposition
Imprisonment	Commitment
Inmate/prisoner	Resident
Parole	Aftercare

Consistent with the concept of *parens patriae*, the terminology reflects a nonpunitive approach to dealing with troubled and troublesome children (Figure 4.1). Critics often decry the lack of sufficient punishment inflicted in the juvenile court. Such comments indicate a complete misunderstanding of this court, which should *not* punish. Although the concept of *parens patriae* is paternalistic and not inconsistent with the concept of punishment (Weisheit and Alexander, 1988), the use of a punitive approach in juvenile court would make it simply a criminal court for children and, therefore, without grounding as a separate system of justice. Thus, although one could logically argue for abolishing the juvenile court, a juvenile court that imposes punishment has no basis in American history or in logic.

Because of the noncriminal approach, the usual safeguards of due process that were applicable in criminal courts were absent in juvenile court proceedings: rights to counsel, to confront and cross-examine adverse witnesses, and to avoid self-incrimination.

Adoptions: custody hearings, which grant custody to the prospective adoptive parents, and adoption hearings, which grant final adoption

Adjudication: (1) hearing at which the minor enters a plea to one or more allegations of the petition and at which the judge pronounces the child a delinquent minor; (2) contested hearing (trial) at which witnesses testify and evidence is presented at the conclusion of which the judge determines whether or not the child has been found to be a delinquent minor

Advisory: hearing for youth paper-referred to court at which the petition detailing the delinquent allegations is presented, a determination is made whether the minor qualifies for appointed counsel, and a trial review date is selected

Detention: hearing held within 24 hours of the filing of a petition for a detained youth at which counsel is appointed and the court considers whether the minor should be detained or released from custody

Disposition: hearing, analogous to the adult court sentencing, for which the probation officer prepares a comprehensive

report of the adjudicated child's background and at which the judge determines what action(s) the court will take

Restitution: hearing at which the judge determines what restitution to a victim the child must pay to satisfy the conditions of probation

Review: review of the child's adherence to probation conditions to consider revising these conditions or terminating the minor from probation

Revocation: hearing to determine if the minor has violated probation by failure to adhere to the conditions of probation or by committing a delinquent act

Transfer: hearing to determine if the juvenile court should retain jurisdiction for the allegations set forth in the petition or whether the matter should be transferred for prosecution to the adult court

Trial review: hearing at which the child requests that the charges be set for a contested adjudication (trial) or at which he/she admits one or more allegations of the pending petition

FIGURE 4.1 *Guide to the Most Common Hearings Held at the Juvenile Court*

Source: Pima County, Arizona, Juvenile Court.

Because the focus of the juvenile court was on providing help, procedures were often informal (if not vague), and the judge, with the assistance of the probation officer, was given broad powers over young persons. Platt argues that even if we assign benign motives to the child savers, "the programs they enthusiastically supported diminished the civil liberties and privacy of youth. Adolescents were treated as though they were naturally dependent, requiring constant and pervasive supervision. Although the child savers were rhetorically concerned with protecting children from the physical and moral dangers of an increasingly industrialized and urban society, their remedies seemed to aggravate the problem" (1974: 4).

The increasing concern about the extra legal operations of the juvenile court is reflected in the *Gault* decision (details later in this chapter), a 1967 case in which the U.S. Supreme Court ruled in favor of basic due process rights for persons adjudicated in juvenile court.

PROCEDURES IN THE JUVENILE COURT

The juvenile court system differs from state to state and even within states. Jurisdiction over juveniles may be located in a separate juvenile court, in a specialized branch of the superior court, or in various types of courts of limited jurisdiction. It is possible that within one state, jurisdiction may be located in two or more different types of courts. The legal age of a juvenile also varies from state to state, ranging from 14 to 18 years of age. Although juveniles are not routinely fingerprinted or photographed by the police, 47 states allow the police to fingerprint and 44 states allow them to photograph certain juveniles. In Texas, for example, all juveniles with alleged delinquent offenses that are crimes punishable by incarceration for adults are fingerprinted and entered into a statewide central repository; their criminal history record may then be accessed by law enforcement and juvenile justice agencies throughout Texas. A juvenile's name is not usually printed in the newspapers, and the juvenile court has historically been closed to the public. However, about two dozen states now have open hearings in certain cases. In 1997, New York reversed its long-standing policy of keeping family court closed to the public. Although judges still have discretion to close cases, they must have compelling and specific reasons, such as ensuring the privacy of a victim of child sexual abuse (Finder, 1997). Florida also routinely opens family court to the public (Sexton, 1997).

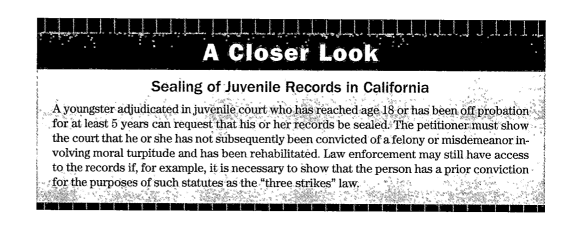

A Closer Look

Sealing of Juvenile Records in California

A youngster adjudicated in juvenile court who has reached age 18 or has been off probation for at least 5 years can request that his or her records be sealed. The petitioner must show the court that he or she has not subsequently been convicted of a felony or misdemeanor involving moral turpitude and has been rehabilitated. Law enforcement may still have access to the records if, for example, it is necessary to show that the person has a prior conviction for the purposes of such statutes as the "three strikes" law.

Although juvenile court records have traditionally been kept confidential, 39 states now permit the release of certain juveniles' names and/or photographs, and more and more juvenile records are becoming available to more agencies and the public. In many states, there are provisions for having a juvenile record sealed—not subject to

STATE OF KANSAS
COURT SERVICES
INFORMATION PERTAINING TO
EXPUNGEMENT OF JUVENILE RECORDS
K. S. A. 38-1610

Any records or files specified in this code concerning a juvenile offender may be expunged upon application to a judge of the court of the county in which the records or files are maintained. The application for expungement may be made by the person who is the juvenile offender or, if a minor, by the person's parent or next friend.

There shall be no expungement of records or files concerning acts committed by a juvenile which, if committed by an adult, would constitute: (1) indecent liberties with a child, (2) aggravated indecent liberties with a child, (3) aggravated criminal sodomy, (4) enticement of a child, (5) indecent solicitation of a child, (6) aggravated indecent solicitation of a child, (7) sexual exploitation of a child, (8) aggravated incest, (9) endangering a child, or (10) abuse of a child, or acts which would constitute an attempt to commit a violation of any of the offenses specified in this paragraph.

After a hearing, the court shall order the expungement of the records and files if the court finds that: (A) the person has reached 21 years of age or that two years have elapsed since the final discharge of the person; (B) since the final discharge of the person, the person has not been convicted of a felony or of a misdemeanor other than a traffic offense or adjudicated a delinquent or miscreant under the Kansas juvenile code or a juvenile offender under the Kansas juvenile offenders code and no proceedings are pending seeking such a conviction or adjudication; and (C) the circumstances and behavior of the petitioner warrant expungement.

Upon entry of an order expunging records or files, the offense shall be treated as if it never occurred, except that the offense may be considered if: (1) the petitioner is a person 16 years of age or over who is charged with a felony or with more than one offense of which one or more is a felony after having been adjudicated in two separate prior juvenile proceedings as having committed an act which would constitute a felony if committed by an adult and the adjudications occurred prior to the date of the commission of the new act charged; (2) upon conviction of a crime or adjudication in a subsequent action under this code the offense may be considered in determining the sentence to be imposed or disposition to be made.

The expungement of a felony adjudication does not relieve a person of complying with any state or federal law relating to the use or possession of firearms.

I have been provided a copy of the above   Consult your attorney for any questions
juvenile offenders code.   regarding expungement of juvenile records.

_____   _____
Offender   Court Services Officer

_____
Date

FIGURE 4.2 *Expungement of Juvenile Records (Kansas)*

examination except by special court order—and in some jurisdictions expunged (Figure 4.2); 18 states, however, prohibit the sealing or expunging of juvenile records (Sickmund, Snyder, and Poe-Yamagata, 1997). Until 1992, the Federal Bureau of Investigation (FBI) collected records only of juveniles tried as adults, but in that year, new regulations gave the FBI's National Crime Information Center (NCIC) authority to receive juvenile court information. Although states do not have to submit juvenile court records to the FBI, the NCIC can instantly transmit to law enforcement agencies and within days to some employers the juvenile court records formerly kept confidential. (For a review of this issue, see *Privacy and Juvenile Justice Records*, 1997.)

The juvenile court typically handles four types of cases:

1. *Delinquency.* Behavior that, if engaged in by an adult, would constitute a crime.
2. *Status offense.* Behavior that, if engaged in by an adult, would not constitute a crime but (in accord with *parens patriae*) provides the basis for governmental intervention, for example, demonstrating chronic truancy, being beyond the control of parents or guardians, or running away.
3. *Neglect or abuse.* Children who are subjected to neglect or abuse by parents or guardians.
4. *Dependency.* Children who do not have parents or guardians available to provide proper care.

As part of a status offense or separately under a special addicted category, juveniles may be subject to juvenile court jurisdiction as a result of addiction to alcohol or other drugs.

Instances of delinquency, a status offense, neglect or abuse, or dependency that come to the attention of the authorities are often handled in a manner that does not involve the formal justice apparatus. School officials or the police, for example, may refer such cases directly to public or private social welfare or child protective agencies. Alternatively, the police may make a station adjustment, so the child is allowed to return home with parents or guardians without further action. Those situations that come to the attention of the juvenile court enter by way of the intake section, which is usually staffed by juvenile probation officers. On the eastern end of New York's Long Island, the Suffolk County Probation Department—which supervises adult offenders—is responsible for juvenile intake services at family court.

Intake

Children are referred to the juvenile court by the police, parents, school officials, or other public or private agency personnel, although law enforcement agencies are the source of more than 80 percent of delinquency referrals and a little less than half of the status offense referrals that reach the petition stage. In some jurisdictions, all cases are received by a PO assigned to the **intake** or complaint unit, while in others, cases that involve criminal complaints are first sent to the prosecutor's office. The first decision to be made at intake is the custodial status of the youngster: Does the respondent's behavior make him or her a danger to him- or herself or to the safety of others? Will the youngster return to court voluntarily? (See Figure 4.3.)

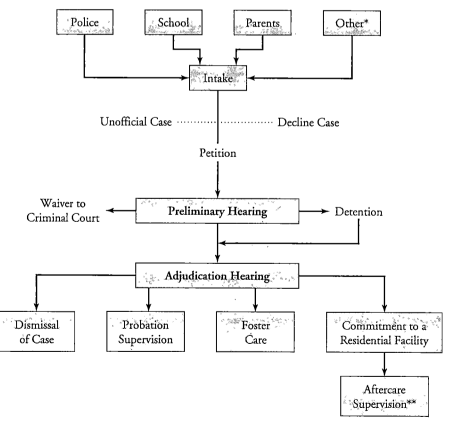

*Public and private agencies.
**Supervision provided by the probation department or a juvenile aftercare (parole) agency.

FIGURE 4.3 *Juvenile Court Process*

A Closer Look

Juvenile Offenders in Texas

It is 1:15 A.M. in Texarkana. James, 15 years of age, and an adult male have been arrested for aggravated robbery. Police are taking the juvenile to the detention center intake unit at the Bowie County Juvenile Probation Department. Harold Harlston, a probation officer on duty, has just been called to the intake office where he must decide if James will be detained or released. In checking the records, Harlston finds that James has a prior arrest for theft, but the initial police report suggests that this time James was influenced to participate in the robbery by the older man.

Harlston awakens James's parents with a phone call. They are quite upset and head for the center. While continuing to interview James, the PO is interrupted by a call alerting him that the police are bringing in a girl involved in a street fight. She is being charged with assault—again. Harlston anticipates a long, busy night.

The girl being brought in is 14 and goes by her street name, "Decca." Streetwise, she has learned to cover her vulnerability with a defiant attitude and abusive vocabulary. She fidgets nervously as she waits for her intake interview. A file check reveals that Decca lives with her mother and several siblings. The father does not live in the home, and the family has a history of court referrals.

Harlston learns that James's parents have just arrived. He tells them their son will be held until his detention hearing, usually occurring within 48 hours. James's parents express their disappointment; they want to take James home tonight. The PO explains the seriousness of the charges and the state law allowing juveniles to be tried in adult court for offenses as serious as aggravated robbery. If James is transferred to adult court, he could be sentenced to prison. The young man is lucky; his parents express their love and pledge to stand by him. Decca is not so fortunate. When her mother is contacted, she tells the PO, "Do whatever you want with her—I'm tired."

The night is young, and Harlston learns the police are bringing in two more youths. Detention center staff prepare for overcrowding by placing temporary cots in the dining area of the 10-bed facility.

Intake in the juvenile court is unique: It permits the court to screen cases not only on jurisdictional and legal grounds but also on social dimensions. The PO interviews the presenting agent, the young person, and the child's parents or guardians. The officer then reviews court files for previous records concerning the child. If the case involves a serious crime or child abuse and has not already been screened by the prosecutor, the PO consults with that office. At this stage, the PO has a dual function: legal and social service.

The **legal function** requires that the PO determine if the juvenile court has jurisdiction and also requires that the child and parents be advised of the right to counsel and the right to remain silent during the intake conference. H. Ted Rubin argues that "defense attorney participation at a[n intake] conference is rare, waivers of rights tend to be finessed, and the norm is for parents to encourage the child to discuss his or her participation in the alleged offense with the intake officer" (1980: 304) (see also Feld, 1988). When defense attorneys are present in juvenile court, tension is inherent in their responsibilities to the client: "a choice between the traditional adversary role (or the procedural model that regulates professional behavior in the criminal court) and the historic treatment or rehabilitative concerns of the family [juvenile] court" (Fabricant, 1983: 41). Barry Feld reports that even when juveniles are represented by counsel, "attorneys may not be capable of or committed to representing their juvenile clients in an effective adversarial manner. Organizational pressures to cooperate, judicial hostility toward adversarial litigants, role ambiguity created by the dual goals of rehabilitation and punishment, reluctance to help juveniles 'beat a case,' or an internalization of a court's treatment philosophy may compromise the role of counsel in juvenile court" (1988: 395). Indeed, he notes that the presence of counsel may actually be disadvantageous to

Key Fact

Juvenile court intake is staffed by POs.

the juvenile—those represented by attorneys tend to receive more severe dispositions. Nevertheless, Feld, a law professor, advocates legislation that mandates counsel and does not permit a waiver of this important constitutional right.

The **social service function** involves an assessment of the child's situation—home, school, physical, and psychological—and can provide the basis for adjusting the case, that is, handling it informally without the filing of a petition. This happens in about half of the cases reaching juvenile court when the situation is not serious, when the matter can best be handled by the family, and when neither the child nor the public is in any danger. When the child is in conflict with parents or school officials, the worker may serve as a mediator.

If the young person and parents agree to informal processing, the juvenile can be placed under supervision of a PO, usually for a period of 90 days (Figure 4.4). Although this may save the young person and his or her parents from the trauma of court action,

---

**IN THE EIGHTH JUDICIAL DISTRICT COURT OF THE STATE OF NEVADA
IN AND FOR THE
COUNTY OF CLARK JUVENILE DIVISION**

INFORMAL SUPERVISION AGREEMENT

In the matter of Michael Nelson
DATE OF BIRTH: July 12, 1991
COMPLAINT: School Vandalism

The minor admits the alleged offense as stated above.

The minor understands that an Informal Supervision period is an attempt by Clark County Juvenile Court Services, the minor, and his parents to resolve the alleged problems without formal judicial action.

The minor does hereby waive the right to a speedy trial and understands that he has the right to legal counsel and the right to remain silent throughout these proceedings and hereby waives these rights.

The minor understands that any information obtained during the supervision period will be admissible in evidence at any adjudicatory hearing and that the minor may withdraw from the Informal Supervision process at any time and demand an adjudicatory hearing.

The minor understands that the Clark County Juvenile Court Services or the District Attorney reserves the right to proceed on any petition heretofore filed against the undersigned and/or to proceed on other petitions for any new offense and may proceed to seek an adjudication on the pending matter in the event the minor fails to cooperate in the attempt at adjustment.

The minor and his parents further understand that the terms of this Informal Supervision Agreement are as follows:

1. That the minor will report in person to Probation Officer John Kerwin at the Clark County Juvenile Court Services, 3401 East Bonanza Road, Las Vegas, Nevada, every Monday, on a weekly basis, until May 30, 2006.

2. That the minor will obey all laws of the city, county, state, and federal governments.

3. That the minor will attend school, unless legally excused, and make every effort to maintain good conduct and an acceptable scholastic record.

4. That the minor will obey the reasonable and proper orders of his parents.

5. That the parents agree to make restitution for the damage caused by the minor to school property.

We agree to the terms and conditions of this Informal Supervision Agreement and waive the rights as stated above.

Signed *Doris Nelson*   Date _____ 2/27/06 _____
    (Parent)

Signed *Kevin Nelson*   Date _____ 2/27/06 _____
    (Parent)

Signed *Michael Nelson*   Date _____ Feb. 27, 2006 _____
    (Minor)

ORDER

Good cause appearing, therefore, the minor is placed under Supervision for a period of 90 days, reviewable (if a petition was filed) on the 30th Day of May, 2006, at the hour of 10:00 A.M.
    Dated this February 28, 2006.

        Michael Harrison
        (Judge or Referee)

FIGURE 4.4 *Informal Probation Agreement*

unofficial handling has its critics. Informal processing requires an explicit or tacit admission of guilt. The substantial advantages that accrue from this admission (the avoidance of court action) also act as an incentive to confess. This approach casts doubt on the voluntariness and truthfulness of admissions of guilt. About 20 percent of delinquency cases brought to the juvenile court result in "unofficial probation."

The period of **informal probation** can be a crucial time in the life of a young person. If successful, the youngster may avoid further juvenile court processing; if unsuccessful, the child will face the labyrinth that is the juvenile court process and the serious consequences that can result. No one is more aware of this than the PO who, using all the skills and resources at his or her command, attempts to assist the youngster and the youngster's parent(s) through the crisis. Counseling, group therapy, tutoring, vocational guidance, psychiatric and psychological treatment, and recreational services, if they are available, will be put to use to help the young person. If the intake worker is professionally trained, he or she may provide the counseling, thus avoiding the time-consuming referral process—a family is most effectively aided at the time of crisis. If informal efforts are unsuccessful, the PO can file a petition that will make the case an official one.

Key Fact

Many cases sent to juvenile court intake are handled by informal probation.

A Closer Look

Juvenile Intake in Texas

In Brazoria County, Texas, each juvenile referral to the department is evaluated by an intake officer, taking into consideration the nature of the offense and the juvenile's referral history. If additional contact with the juvenile is required, the intake officer schedules an interview with the family to assist in the evaluation of the juvenile's school performance, behavior, and family situation. Following the assessment, the intake officer makes a recommendation using state-mandated progressive sanction guidelines and pertinent departmental guidelines. In turn, the assistant district attorney considers the officer's recommendation and directs the course of action taken on any charge.

In Harris County (Houston), law enforcement officers may take a juvenile to one of two intake screening units at the Juvenile Probation Department. Intake screening is responsible for assessing immediate circumstances and deciding where the youth will stay prior to a court hearing. Two 24-hour intake units receive and review incoming cases.

Younger nonviolent offenders may be offered the option of voluntary participation in the Deferred Prosecution Program. This program guides youth through 6 months of intensive counseling and supervision aimed at diverting them from further contact with the juvenile justice system. When a youth is believed to present a threat to the community or to himor herself, the youth will be held in detention awaiting a court hearing.

During the intake process, the PO must determine if the case is to be referred—petitioned—to the court for adjudication. Of the more than 1.5 million delinquency cases received annually by the juvenile court, a little more than half are petitioned, resulting in more than 125,000 status offense cases petitioned annually. The filing of a petition is made through the prosecutor or directly via the clerk of the court, who sets a date for the first of three types of juvenile court hearing.

Preliminary Hearing

Preliminary hearings consider those matters that must be dealt with before the case can proceed further. At the first hearing, the judge (or in some jurisdictions, a referee) informs the parties involved of the charges in the petition and of their rights in the proceeding. If the case involves an abused, neglected, or dependent child, a

guardian *ad litem* is usually appointed to act as an advocate for the child. Depending on the jurisdiction, this person may be an attorney or trained lay advocate, often a volunteer. If appropriate, the hearing may be used to determine whether an alleged delinquent should remain in detention or shelter. If the judge determines, usually with the help of the PO, that the respondent's behavior makes him or her a danger to himself or herself or to the safety of others or that he or she will probably not return to court voluntarily, the judge can order that the child remain in or be remanded to custody.

Detention facilities for juveniles have generally been inadequate. In some jurisdictions, they are merely separate sections of an adult jail. The 1974 Juvenile Justice and Delinquency Prevention Act requires "sight and sound" separation of juveniles held under juvenile court jurisdiction, but the statute does not apply to youth in adult facilities prosecuted as adults in state court. California outlawed the practice of jailing juveniles in 1986, and Utah makes the practice a misdemeanor.

In New York City, the primary detention facility for juveniles, Spofford Juvenile Center in the Bronx, has been plagued with violence and other problems characteristic of adult jails. The facility was closed in 1998, but only briefly. Dramatic increases in young persons awaiting adjudication led the city—which had been holding up to 100 youngsters (some as young as 10 years of age) in a jail barge for adults—to reopen Spofford. The Cook County (Chicago) Juvenile Temporary Detention Center (Audy Home) has been beset with problems, including the assault and gang rape of residents, although there have been some improvements in more recent years (Marx, 1998). This facility houses youngsters 10 to 17 years of age; although it was built to hold 498 children, it often houses as many as 200 more who sleep on cots in the common areas.

> **A Closer Look**
>
> **Kent County (Grand Rapids), Michigan, Juvenile Detention**
>
> The facility, which was opened in 1963, provides secure custodial care for a maximum of 45 youngsters, 12 to 16 years of age, in three living units: two for boys and one coeducational. The 47 staff members are responsible for programmed activities in which the emphasis is on group living through a behavioral management program. A token economy (discussed in Chapter 8) is used, permitting residents to earn points for engaging in positive behavior. These points are necessary for the youth to participate in various recreational activities and to purchase special snacks. Detention facility activities are designed to provide the staff with opportunities to understand the youngsters better and, at the same time, to offer outlets for active, healthy adolescents who are living under controlled conditions.
>
> Individualized instruction is provided at each resident's actual functioning level, and volunteer tutors are available for additional help in reading and math. Students earn credits toward a diploma, and these are transferred to an appropriate school program when the residents leave the facility. Daily use is made of the gymnasium and outdoor athletic fields; in addition, teams from other local juvenile facilities are invited to compete at the facility in various athletic events. Many college, civic, and other community groups provide special activities and seasonal parties for the residents. A day room within each living unit provides an area for a variety of leisure-time activities, such as ping-pong and other table games, and television. A CD player is used for educational and entertaining movies. Adjoining the day rooms are quiet rooms that provide private space for letter writing and reading. A shop stocked with snacks, games, cards, and magazines provides an opportunity for youngsters to spend some of the points they have earned for good behavior. A separate game room with unique activities is also available on a privilege basis. Medical, dental, psychological, and religious services are available for each resident.

The Dauphin County (Harrisburg, Pennsylvania) Juvenile Probation Department uses in-home detention, which provides supervision for juveniles who otherwise would be held in a detention facility. The program has two POs who share a caseload that does not exceed 14 youngsters. The clients are visited once or twice a day at their home, school, or place of employment, and a rigidly enforced curfew is set in cooperation with each youngster's parents. In-home detention is limited to 60 continuous days.

Key Fact

"Sight and sound" separation requires juvenile to be housed separately from adult offenders.

Adjudicatory Hearing

The **adjudicatory hearing** ("trial") is for the purpose of deciding ("adjudging") whether the child should be made a ward of the juvenile court because he or she is delinquent, abused, neglected, or dependent or is a status offender. If appropriate, the child (respondent) makes a plea, either an admission or denial of the allegations contained in the **petition**. The plea process has been the subject of criticism because "much of the country either has not addressed it at all or has not fully developed standards regarding the guilty plea process in juvenile court" (Sanborn, 1992: 142). Thus, pleas are being rendered by juveniles who are incapable of fully understanding the process or to whom the process has not been adequately explained, bringing into question intelligence, voluntariness, and accuracy. This is particularly troubling in view of the move toward a more punitive response in juvenile court (discussed later in this chapter).

If a denial is made, evidence must be presented to prove "beyond a reasonable doubt" that a delinquent act occurred; in the case of a status offender, it must be proved with a simple "preponderance of evidence" that the child is in need of court supervision. If the allegations are sustained, the judge makes a finding of fact (that the child is delinquent, abused, neglected, or otherwise in need of supervision), sets a date for a dispositional hearing, and orders a social investigation or predisposition report.

PREDISPOSITION REPORTS

The goal of the juvenile court is to provide services. To do so on the basis of the best available information, the judge orders a predisposition investigation. The PO who conducts the investigation will present his or her findings in a **predisposition report** that includes the sociocultural and psychodynamic factors that influenced the juvenile's behavior, providing a social history that is used by the judge to determine a disposition for the case. Because the judge's decision will often be influenced by the contents of the report, it must be factual and objective—a professional statement about the child's family, social and educational history, and any previous involvement with public or private agencies. It also indicates the physical and mental health of the child, as reported by a court psychologist or psychiatrist. The report will typically include the following:

- Review of court records
- Review of school records
- Review of police records
- Interviews with the respondent
- Interviews with family members
- Interviews with teachers and school officials
- Interviews with employers, youth workers, and clergy (whenever appropriate)
- Interviews with complainant, police officer, or witnesses
- Results of any psychological or psychiatric examinations
- Recommendation (including available treatment alternatives)

POs must present their findings with supportive statements as to the actual situation found in the investigation. Other than a recommendation, suppositions or opinions are to be avoided. Sometimes the recommendation of the PO is not included in the report but is transmitted orally to the judge. The completed report should enable the judge to make the best disposition available based on the individual merits of the case and the service needs of the young person (Figure 4.5). One problem encountered at the disposition stage is the paucity of available alternatives for helping a youngster, which can be exacerbated by an (inexperienced) PO who recommends treatment that is simply not available. A youngster will often be placed on probation because of a lack of feasible alternatives.

Key Fact

An adjudicatory hearing in juvenile court parallels a criminal trial without a jury.

Key Fact

A predisposition report is similar to a presentence report.

PROBATION OFFICER'S REPORT OF PRELIMINARY INQUIRY AND/OR
PREDISPOSITIONAL REPORT

STATE OF INDIANA

Marshall County Superior Court

In the Matter of: ___John Smith___

A child alleged to be a Delinquent Child

Date Completed: ___9/25/06___

Assigned P.O.: ___Eirnie Grabbits___   Report Prepared By: ___Ernie Grabbits___

JUVENILE INFORMATION

Case No.(s): ___86C01-9309-JD-665___

Legal Name: ___John Smith___

Alias(es)/Nickname(s): ___None___

Custodial Person(s) or Agency: ___Mike and Sue Smith, parents___

Street Address: ___1800, North Wonder Valley___

City: ___Bowling Green___   State: ___Indiana___   Zip: ___47112___

Telephone: ___(219) 555-1203___   Social Security No.: ___305 -77-7777___

DOB: ___5/22/89___   POB: ___Bowling Green, Indiana___

Age: ___17___ Race: ___W___ Gender: ___M___ Ht.: ___5' 7"___ Wt.: ___145___ Eyes: ___Br___ Hair: ___Br___

ID Marks: ___None___

Driver's Lic. No.: ___N/A___   State of Issue: _____ Status: _____

JUVENILE'S LEGAL INVOLVEMENT

___Chg(s) pending   ___Detainer(s)   _X_Inf. Adj.   ___Probation   ___Res. Plcmnts.   ___IDOC

___DFCS Ward   ___Violations   ___Parole   ___Waived   ___Adult Status   _X_Other Contacts

DELINQUENT ACT(S) INFORMATION

Alleged Offense: ___Shoplifting___   Date Committed: ___8/22/06___

I.C.: ___35-43-4-3___ Class (if committed by an adult): _A_   Felony/(Misdemeanor)(Circle One)

Alleged Offense: ___Criminal Mischief___   Date Committed: ___9/4/06___

I.C.: ___35-43-1-2___ Class (if committed by an adult): _A_   Felony/(Misdemeanor)(Circle One)

Alleged Offense: ___Vehicle Theft: Poss. Stolen Property___   Date Committed: 9/18/06: 9/24/06

I.C.: ___33-4-2.5: 35-43-4-2___ Class (if committed by an adult): _D_   (Felony)/Misdemeanor (Circle One)

Referring Agency: ___Marshall County Sheriff___

Custody Status: ___Electronic Home Detention___

Co-Offender(s)/Status: ___Alfred Doe - pending disposition___

Case No.(s): ___86C01-9309-JD-666___

PRIOR LEGAL HISTORY

Date of Referral	Charge(s).	Case No.	Disposition (Date/Type)
9/22/02	Curfew	N/A	9/29/05 - Warned and Released
4/2/03	Incorrigible	86C01-9304-JS-078	4/27/06 - Informal Adjustment

FIGURE 4.5 *Predisposition Report, Indiana*

EDUCATION, EMPLOYMENT, HEALTH

School: ___Bowling Green High School___ Grade/Status: ___11th/withdrew/compl.___

Special Educational Classification: ____Yes _X_ No Special Educational Placement: ___Yes X No

Mental Health Referrals: _X_ Yes ____ No

Physical Problems: ____ Yes _X_ No If the answer is yes to any of the questions in this
section, an explanation is required in the "additional
Alcohol/Drug Use: ____ Yes _X_ No information" section.

Gang Involvement: ____ Yes _X_ No

Employer: ___Sam's Amoco Filling Station, 111 Elm Street, Bowling Green, IN___

Position: ___Attendant___ Hours: ___16 hrs/week___ $6.25 /hr.

FAMILY INFORMATION

Father's Name: ___Mike Smith___ SSN (if available): _____

Address: ___1800 North Wonder Valley, Bowling Green, Indiana 47112___

Employment: ___Disabled___ Hours: ___N/A___

Home Telephone: ___(812) 555-1203___ Work Telephone: ___N/A___

Mother's Name: ___Sue Hemmingway Smith___ SSN (if available): _____

Address: ___Same___

Employment: ___Administrator for Nurses, Vernon Hospital___ Hours: ___9am-4pm weekdays___

Home Telephone: ___(812) 555-1203___ Work Telephone: ___(812) 555-3340___

Guardian: _____

Address: _____

Employment: _____ Hours: _____

Home Telephone: _____ Work Telephone: _____

Significant Other(s): ___Alice Smith___ Relationship: ___Grandmother___

Address: ___1955 North Wonder Valley, Bowling Green, Indiana 47112___

Employment: ___Retired___ Hours: _____

Home Telephone: ___(812) 555-6789___ Work Telephone: _____

NAME	REL.	AGE	ADDRESS	LEGAL HISTORY
Melissa Ann Smith	S	12	Same as youth	None

ADDITIONAL INFORMATION

Youth attended one appointment at the Marshall County Mental Health Center for a prior referral. Reports indicate that the parents were not willing to participate as needed. Youth indicates a desire to take the GED test and then enter the military. However, due to his age, he would need permission from the court to take the test.

EVALUATION/SUMMARY

John has two prior referrals to this court for status offenses. At this time, it appears that youth is remorseful about his actions. Parents appear to provide adequate supervision but, based on past behaviors, may not follow recommendations from the court without continued court involvement.

FIGURE 4.5 *(continued)*

RECOMMENDATIONS

Preliminary Inquiry:

_____ Dismissal   _____ Referral to Other Agency

_____ Informal Adjustment   _____ Warning and Release

_X_ File Petition   _____ Other _____

Reason for recommendation: _____ Seriousness of offense _____

_____

Custody Recommendation:

_X_ Release to Parent   _____ Release to Guardian   _____ Informal Home Detention

_____ Formal Home Detention   _X_ Electronic Surveillance   _____ Shelter Care

_____ Juvenile Center   _____ Not in Custody   _____ Other _____

Comments: _____ Father is home at all times to provide supervision as he is disabled. _____

_____

Predispositional Report:

If juvenile admits to charge, recommendations for disposition (Complete if applicable):

_____ Probation recommends the case be set for disposition in order to complete a predispositional report. _____

_____

JOHN SMITH
86C01-9309-JD-665

I. COURT INFORMATION

Marshall County Superior Court   Judge Bill Newark, Jr.
Probation Officer: Ernie Grabbits   Prosecutor: Samuel Loven
Address: 99 Public Square, Bowling Green, IN 47112
Telephone: (812) 555-1446
Defense Attorney: George D. Clar   C.A.S.A./G.A.L.: None

II. SOURCES OF INFORMATION

Mother—Sue Smith

Father—Mike Smith

School Records—Bowling Green High School

Bowling Green City Police Records

Marshall County Sheriff's Department Records

Marshall County Prosecutor's Records

Marshall County Probation Department Records

Indiana State Police Investigation Records

III. PRESENT OFFENSE

A. Official Version

See Bowling Green City Police case summary of events and the Petition for Delinquency, both attached herein.

B. Juvenile's Version

The juvenile made the following statement:

"We (Alfred Doe and I) got the Cadillac on Labor Day weekend. We had been talking about getting it and so I got the keys to it and Alfred drove it from the lot. We took it out into the country near where Alfred lived. We stored it out there in a barn and then Alfred lost the keys to it. We took the car to possibly sell it later. On Thursday, September 16, Alfred came down to the gas station where I worked

FIGURE 4.5 *(continued)*

and talked with me. I was real upset because my parents had just gotten on me about my grades and they were going to ground me, beginning the weekend. I discussed with Alfred about running away and starting a new life. On Friday morning, September 17, Alfred gave me his Subaru wagon. We had devised a plan in which he would tell the authorities that I had taken the vehicle after lending him the keys to get something out of the vehicle. I told him I would go to Muncie and spend time there with my friend, Josh Blanton."

"After driving up there, I learned that my friend was coming back to Bowling Green for the weekend so I drove back here too. I stayed in the wagon, near Alfred's house, that night. Alfred happened to see the wagon the next morning and came by to see if I was in it. He told me that he would pick me up that evening and take me to town. It was about 5:00 P.M. when he came by and got me. We left the wagon in the barn where the Cadillac was and went to town. During that evening we decided to get another vehicle since they would be looking for the wagon. We drove by the high school bus compound and I remembered that they usually left the keys in the vans in the compound. Alfred held up the fence while I crawled under it. The first van I checked did not have a key in it but the second van did. I turned the van around, hitting the white van in its side. I then gunned the van and ran through the gate of the compound. We drove the van out into the country and left it in the barn where the other two vehicles were parked."

"We then returned to town and went by the compound again. Alfred decided to take a vehicle this time so I let him out and he went and got another van. He drove that one out and he went and got another van. He drove that one out into the country and to the barn. We both slept that night in the vehicles and the next day I took one of the vans and went back to Muncie in it."

"During the week, I stayed in the van and Josh helped me out with food and clothing. He and I wrote to Alfred and told him to go to my house and get the key to the video store that Josh had made during the summer. We told him to sneak into my house, get the key and go to the video store and get money." (That letter was intercepted by Alfred's parents on the Friday John was arrested in Muncie.)

"Then on Friday, September 24th, I got picked up for shoplifting some clothes. I told the Muncie Police about the theft of the vans and the Cadillac and they called Marshall Police and reported the incident. Then that evening the Sheriff's Deputy and a State Policeman came to Muncie and got me and brought me back to Bowling Green. I was placed in detention at the Regional Detention Center and held until Tuesday morning when I was released to my parents under house arrest."

IV. PRIOR LEGAL HISTORY

A. Juvenile History

09/22/05 Marshall Co., IN	Curfew Warned & Released	09/29/05	Verified
04/02/06 86C01-9304-JS-078 Marshall Co., IN	Incorrigible Informal Adjustment	04/27/06	Verified
09/24/06 Muncie, IN	Shoplifting Released to custody of Sheriff Dept in Marshall Co., IN	09/24/06	Verified
08/22/06 86C01-9309-JD-665 Marshall Co., IN	Possession of Stolen Property	Pending in This Disposition	Verified
09/04/06 86C01-9309-JD-665 Marshall Co., IN	Theft of Vehicle	Pending in This Disposition	Verified
09/18-19/06 86C01-9309-JD-665 Marshall Co., IN	Theft of 2 Vehicles	Pending in This Disposition	Verified

B. Previous Supervision and/or Placements

John had been warned and released by the Marshall County Probation Officer for his curfew violation in 2005. Then in the spring of 2006, John was placed on 3-month Informal Adjustment for the crime of Incorrigible. During that period of time he was to report to the probation department on a regular basis (once per month), complete counseling and pay fees associated with such programs. He reported on four occasions but did not complete the required counseling.

FIGURE 4.5 *(continued)*

Following his arrest in Muncie on this delinquency and upon his return to Bowling Green, he was placed in secure detention at the Clark County Regional Detention Center for a period of 3 days. He was released to the custody of his parents following the detention hearing. The court placed John on home detention with electronic monitoring. John has complied completely with the electronic monitoring program.

C. Adult History

None

D. Summary

This juvenile has been before the Probation Department in the past. He was picked up one night at the local Hardees' Restaurant at 2:30 A.M. The probation officer was contacted and his parents were notified. The parents indicated that they had a minor disagreement earlier in the evening and were not aware that he had left the home. His parents indicated that they were willing to deal with the problem and did not need probation's intervention. The juvenile was warned about this behavior and released to his parents.

Then in early Spring of 2006, the probation department was contacted because of his rebellious behavior at home. He was placed on Informal Adjustment for 3 months and required to attend counseling with his parents.

The juvenile is presently before the court on charges of Shoplifting in Muncie, IN and Possession of Stolen Property, three counts of Auto Theft and Criminal Mischief in Marshall County, IN.

When the juvenile was arrested in Muncie, IN, and charged with shoplifting, he confessed to having with him a van that had been stolen from the Bowling Green High School Bus Compound the previous weekend. He also confessed to having assisted in the theft of two other vehicles and the damage to the bus compound.

The juvenile was held in detention pending full investigation of the incidents in Muncie and Marshall, IN.

E. Parental Response

Mr. Smith stated that "Every time I hear this story, I just get mad. Me and Mr. Doe have volunteered to pay the fees and restitution for damages to the vehicles. I do have one hard feeling and that is if they had just leveled with us, some of it could have been prevented. I feel John has a chance to make something with his life if he gets in the service. But if he sits around for half a year or so, he will get himself into something else. He took the GED, after the Judge signed an order allowing him to take it, and he has taken the test to get into the military. He also goes to New Albany on Saturday to take his SAT. According to his military test, there is indication he will be placed in the environmental section which is a good field if he applies himself. As far as the Court system, I thought it would move faster than it did. I'm trying to do what is best for the boy and that is what you would do if it was your boy. I don't condone what they have done.There is no reason for it. He has never been short of money, he had a good job, paying good money, and now he has thrown his life away."

V. VICTIM IMPACT INFORMATION

The Bowling Green Community School System, Mr. James Dobson, the owner of the Cadillac, and their respective insurance companies, wish to be reimbursed for their damages per claims filed with the probation department.Those claims are attached in this report. The total amount of restitution requested is $6,324.16.

VI. FAMILY BACKGROUND

A. Maternal History

Name: Sue Hemmingway Smith   Phone#: 555-1203
Address: 1800 North Wonder Valley, Bowling Green, IN 47112
Birth date: 9-18-60   Age: 46   SS#: 645-90-1234
Source of Information: Mr. Mike Smith and John Smith

Sue Hemmingway Smith was raised in Marshall County, having moved here with her parents at a very early age. She attended Bowling Green High School and Indiana University. She married Mike Smith and they adopted John when he was 3 years old, thinking they could not have children. Two years later she gave birth to a girl, Melissa Ann.

Sue was a Spanish teacher at Bowling Green High School for approximately 10 years. She also ran a day care center for about 4 to 5 years before becoming the Administrator for Nurses in North Vernon, IN, which she has done for the past 7 years. She is reported to be in good health, uses no drugs or alcohol, and has never been arrested for any criminal offense. She is a member of the Indiana University Alumni Association and is involved in the Indiana Nurses Organization.

John reports that the relationship between him and his mother is fine but that they fight a lot. He states the reason they fight is because John does not do what his mother expects of him and she "gets on him." These are not physical fights but are usually arguments that go on and on.

FIGURE 4.5 *(continued)*

B. Paternal History
Name: Mike Smith   Phone#: 555-1203
Address: 1800 North Wonder Valley, Bowling Green, IN 47112
Birth date: 10-14-59   Age: 47   SS#: 671-48-1959
Source of Information: Mr. Mike Smith and John Smith

Mike is a native of Marshall County. After graduation from Bowling Green High School, he was married briefly to Beverly Johnson. This marriage ended in divorce after 2 years due to incompatibility. The relationship produced one child, a son, who is now married and lives in Louisville, KY. There is still contact between Mike and his son when they get the time.

Mike enlisted in the United States Army. He was involved in the Vietnam conflict, advancing to Sergeant, prior to being wounded in action. He lost one leg and severely hurt the other. He was in Walter Reed Army Hospital and Veteran's Hospital for about a year and then was discharged from the Army in 1977 with honors and full disability.

After returning from the Army, he married Sue Hemmingway. After trying to have children for 2 years, they adopted John when he was 3 years old. Two years after adopting him, they had a daughter, Melissa Ann. According to Mr. Smith, ever since Melissa has been born, there has been a strain between John and his mother. There has always been this resentment as to why she adopted a child when she learned she could have one herself.

Mike stated that John is the type of kid that will not listen, saying "He has to push you to the limit before he will do anything." Mike continued, "John goes ahead and does his thing and then he gets caught; he gets on your nerves." This has been his pattern over the years according to Mr. Smith. "I've been overprotective of him. I tried to keep him from trouble and I believe I stood too tight to him, yet I believe if I had not, he would have been in trouble long before now."

Mike enjoys restoring vehicles, although he had farmed for a while after returning from Veteran's Hospital. He farmed approximately 70 acres, raising cattle and hay. The pain in his leg got to the point that he could not take the pressure any longer. They sold the farm and moved into town. Mike reports that his health is good, except for "what goes with age." He uses no drugs or alcohol, except an occasional social drink, and has never been arrested except for minor traffic offenses. He was active in the Veteran's Organization and Random Rider's Car Club but has slowed down his involvement in these activities in the past few years.

C. Step-Parent(s) History
None

D. Parental Finances
Both of John's parents receive a substantial income. His mother, Sue, is Administrator of Nurses, making $65,895 per year. She receives medical and dental care from the hospital and has very few bills outside the normal grocery and home cleaning supplies.

Mike Smith is receiving total disability compensation and benefits from the Army. He receives approximately $29,000 per year, including stipends for the children. His medical fees are covered by the Veteran's Hospital, and he has privileges at Ft. Knox and other military facilities. They reinvested the money made from the sale of their farm into their new house. Their home is modestly decorated and they have no extraordinary bills or debts. He enjoys customizing vehicles and takes on the task of remodeling several during the year. This also gives him additional income.

E. Siblings
Mike Smith states that his daughter, Melissa Ann, was born on May 1, 1994, just 2 years after they had adopted John. They had thought that they could not have children at the time they adopted John. Melissa Ann is now 12 years old and is in the 8th grade at Bowling Green Junior High. She has had a difficult time with her brother's involvement with the court. Being from a small community, everyone knows about the incident John is involved in and Melissa Ann has received a great deal of teasing. She is an excellent student but missed nearly a week of school, due to other children teasing her after her brother was returned home from detention.

Her relationship with her brother has been strained during this period of time. It is reported that they were quite close prior to his criminal involvement. It is also reported that John was jealous of her because of her relationship with her mother. John has sensed that he really wasn't wanted after Melissa Ann was born. This feeling has been unfounded by this writer, although Mrs. Smith seems to be quite strict with John.

F. Family Relationships
John was adopted when he was 3 years old. Two years later, a girl was born to Sue & Mike Smith. This addition has caused a great deal of strain on the family. They feel that the bonding of John never occurred and he has always been a problem child.

They state that they love him and feel very close to him, but there are indications these are just "surface feelings" and are not sincere. Both adopted grandparents live in the Bowling Green area and are involved in John's life. These relatives have supported John, although like John's parents, they, too, are not happy about what he did. For leisure-time activities, the family typically watches TV or goes boating

FIGURE 4.5 *(continued)*

if the weather permits. John usually worked on Friday and Saturday nights, so there was little time to spend on other things. The parenting style of the family was having expectations of John, rules for him to follow, and consistent discipline. John had worked most afternoons after school at a local gas station.

Mr. Smith states that John has been very manageable except for a few frustrating periods. There have never been any major upheavals, family violence, or abuse. The family had talked to this officer in the past regarding the curfew violation and was also brought before this officer on the Informal Adjustment. At no time did John indicate that his problems at home were getting to the point he would commit a crime to get out of the home. This writer feels that part of John's problem was seeking attention from his mother. He has felt that she was not as close to him as she has been with her daughter.

Since this delinquency involved an offense against the school, John was to be suspended for the remainder of the semester. However, rather than seeing him be suspended, the parents withdrew John and convinced the Court to give them special permission for John to take his GED. John and his family want him to enlist in the Army and leave the Bowling Green area. He has taken the military entrance exam, passing it with a high score.

G. Home and Neighborhood

The Smith family live just on the edge of the Bowling Green city limits in a newly developed area. They have a very nice three-bedroom brick ranch-style home. They have lived in this area for the past 6 years. Prior to this location they lived in a country setting approximately 3 miles outside of Bowling Green. The children have their own rooms and the home is kept very neat and organized. The home is attractive and well-kept.

The family has high expectations of John. He is required to comply with chores, curfew and appropriate peer relationships. It is reported that although John has only a few chores, he has to be "ridden" by his parents to get them done. Generally, John's parents have shown an attitude of trust, support, acceptance and understanding. They have had their normal conflicts with John, but nothing "out of the ordinary."

It is reported by some community members that John's parents have been too strict on John, putting unnecessary pressure on him and grounding him over things that were not major or did not need such action.

There have been several occasions when his parents have caught him sneaking out of the home or doing some things they did not agree with. However, these problems have been generally handled at home, without requesting court intervention. The parents stated to this officer that they were embarrassed that they could not handle their child.

John has been described by Mr. James Dobson, his employer, as a trustworthy person. Mr. Dobson was in absolute shock when he learned that John had been involved in stealing the Cadillac from his gas station lot. John's parents feel that one of the good things John had in his favor was his job.

The parents' main method of discipline with John was grounding him. Although John feels that he was grounded unnecessarily at times, his parents feel their actions were justifiable and fair.

Mrs. Smith is perceived as the dominant parent with regard to discipline. John stated to this officer, "When she gets on your ass, she just doesn't get off. She just keeps at it until you either do what she says or get grounded. She is persistent." John feels that, for the most part, his mother's discipline has been consistent and appropriate.

H. Other Agency Involvement

John's family has never needed or utilized public assistance of any kind. According to John, his parents have always been good providers. Although John and his family have been referred to the local community mental health center for personal and family counseling services, they have not attended.

VII. JUVENILE'S BACKGROUND

A. School History

John has been a student at Bowling Green Community Schools since beginning his school career. He had completed the 10th grade and was enrolled in the 11th grade at Bowling Green High School when the current delinquency occurred. He had a cumulative GPA of 2.929 his freshman year and a 2.696 with 29.5 credits by the end of his sophomore year. Attendance has been good, and there were no recorded incidents of behavior problems or other disruptions at school.

B. Employment History

John has worked for the local Amoco filling station for the past year. John would usually work after school each day for a couple of hours and a few hours on weekends. He earned $6.25 an hour. During this time, his employer, Mr. James Dobson, came to know him as a person he could trust and have confidence in. To say the least, Mr. Dobson was shocked when he learned that John participated in stealing the Cadillac from his filling station lot.

FIGURE 4.5 *(continued)*

Mr. Dobson has agreed that, should the Court place John on probation, he would be willing to continue employing John. Mr. Dobson would also see that John uses his earnings to pay toward the restitution owed.

C. Juvenile's Financial Information

John worked at his gas station job approximately 16 hours per week, earning $6.25 per hour. John owns a small Sony stereo "rack" system, which he purchased last year for $500. John has no other income or valuable personal property.

D. Religious Orientation

The Smith family is a member of the Southside Christian Church. John and his family attend church once or twice per month. He feels that attending church gives him an opportunity to think and reflect on his actions.

E. Social Orientation

John did not have a large peer group with whom to associate. He primarily "hung out" with just a few individuals. Most of these were within his own age and grade level. One of John's few hobbies was playing golf, but he had ceased doing much of this in the last year or so. His statement was that he had to work all the time, so he had very little time for other things. John also stated that he was in the French Club last school year but dropped out of it this year.

John has also been active in the local bowling league, where he has an average score of 198. He bowls each Saturday morning in a league at the local bowling center.

F. Physical Health

John is reported to be in excellent health. He has seldom missed school and has had no major illnesses.

G. Mental Health

Earlier this year, John was required to seek counseling with his family at the Marshall County Community Mental Health Center after he was placed on Informal Adjustment for Incorrigibility. The parents went to only one session but felt that there was nothing the counselor could do for them or John. They did not return for further appointments. The parents believed that "it was just up to (the family) to get John going in the right path."

A preliminary evaluation and discharge summary are attached herein. The counselor, Don Straight, MSW, indicated that the parents appeared somewhat frustrated with John's behavior. However, they did not seem willing to engage in the necessary counseling to overcome their, or John's, problems.

John takes no medication and has never had any suicidal tendencies as far as his parents know.

H. Substance Use/Abuse

John stated that he had consumed alcohol (beer) on only one occasion at the age of 13, on an experimental basis, but has not made a practice of it. He stated that, to his knowledge, he has never taken any illegal drugs. He does not smoke and has never experimented with marijuana. (This officer gave him a urine screen when he was arrested and it was returned as negative in all areas of the test.)

VIII. EVALUATION/SUMMARY

The court has before it a 17-year-old white male who has had two previous encounters with the probation department in the last year. Both of those encounters were status offenses. He is now before the court at this time on charges of Shoplifting, Theft of Vehicles (three counts), Criminal Mischief and Possession of Stolen Property.

John Smith reportedly has had a normal childhood after having been adopted at the age of 3. He has made average grades in school during his formative years. According to various friends outside the family structure, his parents have seemingly provided appropriate discipline for him. At other times, however, they have grounded him for no apparent reason, other than that he did not do something exactly as they wished.

Currently at the age of 17, he has his learner's permit but not his driver's license. This is due to his parents "making deals" with him in response to his inappropriate behaviors. On one occasion, he was given the choice to either report to probation or tear up his learner's permit. He chose to tear up his learner's permit.

John's recent school grades have been a big issue with the parents, and especially with his mother. Notably, John and his mother had a bad argument concerning his 6-week grades the evening prior to him leaving his home.

In looking at John's overall delinquent behavior, even though it has been brief, there are a number of facts and circumstances that should be chronologized and addressed.

1. Sometime in mid-August, John hid a key in his bedroom at home. This key was to the Video West Establishment, a key which his friend Josh Blanton had illegally duplicated while he was working there. This key would eventually be used to enter the business during the upcoming Christmas vacation. Josh had stated that the owner kept large sums of money there during the holidays.

FIGURE 4.5 *(continued)*

2. John then participated in stealing a 2005 Cadillac from the Sam's Amoco filling station on Saturday, September 4th or Sunday, September 5, 2006. John not only worked here but had been entrusted with the business and was looked upon by the owner as a trusted employee. During the weeks following the theft, John worked at the station each afternoon and weekend, continuing to work side by side with the unsuspecting and trusting owner.

3. On Thursday, September 16, 2006, John and Alfred Doe discussed a plan in which John would run away from home. On Friday, September 17, 2006, John took Alfred's 1999 red Subaru four-door station wagon. He drove this vehicle to Muncie, IN, to see his friend, Josh Blanton. Learning that Josh would be coming home for the weekend, John returned to Bowling Green in the Subaru.

4. During the evening and early morning of September 18th and 19th, John and Alfred Doe stole two vans from the Bowling Green Community School Bus Compound. Extensive damage was done to the compound gate and fence, including damage to three vans. One of the vans, which was not taken, was damaged when it was hit by one of the two stolen vans.The two stolen vans were taken to the country and hidden. John took one of them to Muncie, IN, on Sunday, September 20, 2006.

5. John was soon arrested for shoplifting in Muncie on Friday, September 25, 2006. He confessed the theft of the vans and told the police about the Cadillac and Subaru, which were stored in the barn near Alfred's house.

6. John was then placed in detention over the weekend. On Monday, September 28th, he was released to the custody of his parents and placed on house arrest with electronic monitoring pending his initial hearing.

7. An order was issued by the Court on September 27th allowing John to complete a course of study and all necessary testing so that he may complete his GED.

8. John took his GED exam and scored between the 86th and 99th percentile.

In consideration of the foregoing facts and events, this officer belives that John acted in an extremely irresponsible, careless, reckless and destructive manner. His consideration of the feelings and property of others was, at a point, non-existent. However, in the past couple of months, John has shown a revived sense of responsibility and remorse for his actions. The parents, as well, have shown more of a willingness to do whatever is necessary to bring the family, and John, back "on track." With this in mind, this officer feels that John may now be able to overcome his more recent delinquent behaviors and begin acting like a young adult. John is honestly embarrassed by his actions; he has already asked for forgiveness from the victims, and he requests the Court's understanding and leniency.

It is this officer's impression that with proper supervision, family intervention through counseling, and John's acceptance of responsibility through payment of restitution to the victims, John may indeed have an opportunity to become a productive and responsible adult.

IX. RECOMMENDATION

It is this officer's recommendation that the Court commit John Smith to the Indiana Boys' School until age 21. The Court should suspend this commitment and place John on formal probation until age 21, or until earlier release by the Court upon successful completion of the terms of probation. In addition to all of the regular rules of juvenile probation, the Court should order the following special conditions:

1. The juvenile shall complete 150 hours of community service as arranged by the Probation Department.

2. He shall write a letter of apology to each of the victims, as approved by the Probation Department.

3. The juvenile shall pay restitution to the victims in an amount to be determined by the Court. Should the juvenile's cohort in this matter, Alfred Doe, be placed on probation in the near future, John's responsibility for payment of the restitution may be reduced accordingly.

4. The juvenile shall not have regular contact with his cohort, Alfred Doe.

5. In accordance with the parental participation order, John and his parents should be required to attend and complete counseling through the Marshall County Community Mental Health Center. The parents will be responsible for all costs associated with this requirement.

6. The juvenile should also be ordered to pay the normal $25 monthly probation user fee.

Respectfully submitted,

Ernie J Grabbits

Ernie Grabbits
Probation Officer
Marshall County Circuit/Superior Courts

FIGURE 4.5 *(continued)*

A Closer Look

Disposition Hearing

William Price and his mother sat uneasily before the judge. The allegations of the amended petition had been sustained on the basis of a full admission. The judge was looking through the PO's report for information on which to base his disposition. His eye was drawn to the psychologist's report attached to the court report. The courtroom was silent, all eyes on the judge.

In the report, William was described as "fairly handsome" and "athletically built." The judge glanced up and looked directly at the boy. William turned his eyes away. The judge decided that the boy might be called handsome despite his "waterfall" haircut and a slight case of acne, but he was certainly not sufficiently robust to be dubbed "athletic."

The psychologist's report indicated that William might or might not be aggressive to girls in the future. "That's not much help," the judge thought. "It could apply to most young men. Chances are the boy feels worse about the situation than the girl. At least he *looks* remorseful."

"William, do you realize you could have seriously injured that girl?"

"I didn't mean to hurt her. I thought it was what she wanted."

"That was a dangerous supposition, young man. I hope you realize by now that any use of violence in any circumstances can have the most serious consequences. Society doesn't regard such things lightly."

"Yes, sir."

"Besides the offense with the girl, you also ran away from the officer who was trying to arrest you."

"I'm sorry about that. I guess I lost my head."

"Are you in the habit of losing your head?"

"No, sir. I just wasn't thinking."

"William," the judge said sternly, "I have serious doubts about allowing you to remain in the community. How do I know you won't lose your head again and really hurt someone the next time?"

"I promise, Judge. I won't do anything foolish again."

The judge turned to Mrs. Price and said sympathetically, "I know it has been very difficult for you to raise William by yourself. It would be a pity for all that effort to go to waste."

Tears welled up in Mrs. Price's eyes. "Yes, Your Honor. Please let William come home. I know he'll be good. And I've changed my job now so I can be with him more," she said in a trembling voice. William's eyes were focused on his mother while she talked. The judge noted that concern for her was mirrored in his face.

"How has Bill been doing since he came home from Juvenile Hall, Mrs. Price?"

"Just like always, Judge. He's a good boy."

"William," the judge said, "what would you do with yourself if I allowed you to remain in your home?"

"Go to school."

"I see you are a year behind in your school grade. Do you plan to finish high school?"

"Yes, sir." William's face noticeably brightened.

"And then what do you plan to do?"

"I guess I'll go in the service."

The judge looked at the PO. "Mr. Clarke, I'm going to follow your recommendation and make William a ward of the court and place him on probation. If he stays out of trouble during the next year, I want him brought back to court so we can terminate his case. By my calculation, he could be off probation about 9 or 10 months before he graduates. This should be long enough so that his record will not hinder him from entering the service."

The judge turned back to William. "I hope you've learned a lesson from this, son. If you stay out of trouble, you should have a good opportunity to make something of yourself. The burden is on you. Don't spoil your chances for a career and for a decent life for yourself and your mother."

"Thank you, Judge," Mrs. Price said. "William is a good boy. I don't think he'll make any more trouble for anyone." She and her son left the room, the boy with his arm around her shoulders.

Source: Based on Cohen, 1975.

A Closer Look

Juvenile Cases in Florida

A youth younger than 18 adjudicated for a crime is referred to the Florida Department of Juvenile Justice. The department has a Chief Probation Officer/Circuit Manager in each of the 20 judicial circuits throughout the state. The Chief Probation Officer/Circuit Manager supervises juvenile probation and community corrections efforts in that circuit. The department provides a recommendation to the state attorney (prosecutor) and the court regarding appropriate sanctions and services for the juvenile. The recommendation is based on interviews and information from the arresting law enforcement officer, the victim, the juvenile and his or her family, and other sources (e.g., school).

When making a recommendation, the department has several options that allow the juvenile to remain in his or her home community. One is diversion, which uses programs that are alternatives to the formal juvenile justice system. It is for juveniles who have just started offending and have been charged only with minor crimes.

Another is court-ordered juvenile probation. If a juvenile is placed on probation, he or she must complete court-ordered sanctions and services. For example, the juvenile may be ordered to work at a local community center, or the juvenile may be ordered to pay money to the victim if the victim was harmed or suffered losses as a result of the crime. The juvenile may also be ordered to abide by a curfew or attend substance abuse or mental health counseling. Each juvenile is assigned a Juvenile Probation Officer, who monitors compliance and helps the juvenile link up with services.

If the juvenile offender does not comply with probation, is charged with a serious crime, or has a significant history of offenses, he or she may be ordered to live in a Department of Juvenile Justice residential facility for a period of time. After the juvenile offender is discharged from the facility, he or she is placed on conditional release supervision (much like parole in the adult criminal justice system). Conditional release supervision, similar to probation supervision, is designed to provide monitoring and services to those juveniles who are transitioning back to the community after being in a residential juvenile justice facility. Juveniles have court-ordered sanctions and services that they must complete.

Juveniles on probation or conditional release may be ordered by the court (or referred by the department) to attend a day treatment program while they are being supervised. Day treatment programs provide additional monitoring of juveniles and typically offer an alternative educational setting. They also provide additional services, such as anger management classes, social skills building, and substance abuse education.

Disposition Hearing

Traditionally, the disposition stage of the juvenile court process has been based on the concept of *parens patriae*. Distinctions between dispositions were based on the needs of the children and not necessarily the behaviors that brought the cases to the attention of the juvenile court—dispositions were based not on justice but on rehabilitation. Although the Supreme Court ruled that the juvenile court must adhere to due process, its *raison d'être* as a separate court continued to be as a vehicle for providing social services to children in need. In many jurisdictions, however, the line between the adult criminal court and the juvenile court has become blurred as the latter moves toward a **justice model**—what the youngster deserves—rather than a **social services model**—what the youngster needs. (The justice model for adults is discussed in Chapter 6.) The state of Washington provides an example of this trend.

In 1977, Washington State abrogated the doctrine of *parens patriae* and in its place adopted a new philosophy based on a justice model (Schram et al., 1981):

- Make juvenile offenders accountable for their criminal behavior.
- Provide punishment commensurate with age, crime, and criminal history.

Key Fact

A disposition refers to a sentence in juvenile court.

Nowhere is the rehabilitation of the juvenile offender mentioned as a purpose or intent in the law.

As part of this approach, the Washington Division of Juvenile Rehabilitation promulgated "Juvenile Disposition Sentencing Standards" to guide juvenile court judges in making uniform dispositions based not on the needs of the child but on the delinquent behavior—a classical approach. This, of course, reduces the role of the PO in juvenile court. Colorado, Idaho, and New York have mandatory minimum periods of incarceration for juveniles—a clear distortion of the purposes of the juvenile court. In Washington and other states that have adopted a hard line on juvenile offenders, statutes enable reconsideration of severe sentences for a variety of mitigating circumstances, including "manifest injustice." In fact, write Patricia Harris and Lisa Graff (1988), the "hard line against juveniles" is often less than meets the eye: Few of the harsher statutory provisions are mandatory. The state of Washington also relinquished juvenile court jurisdiction over status offenders. Barry Feld (1992: 59) refers to jurisdictional modifications that have narrowed "the scope of juvenile courts at the 'hard' end through the removal of serious juvenile offenders and at the 'soft' end through the removal of noncriminal status offenders."

> **Key Fact**
>
> The distinction between the adult criminal court and the juvenile court has become less clear as the latter moves toward a justice model.

Contraction of Juvenile Court Jurisdiction

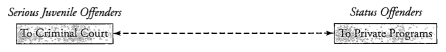

Serious Juvenile Offenders   *Status Offenders*

To Criminal Court ◀------------------------------▶ To Private Programs

STATUS OFFENDERS

As the juvenile court has moved closer to the adult criminal court in both application of legal principles and use of punishment, there has been a corresponding shift away from exercising jurisdiction over status offenders. Official intervention by the legal system in the lives of children who have not been accused of criminal behavior—status offenders—has long been a center of controversy. In 1976 this writer argued: "The juvenile court's continued use of coercion and the stigma it creates are grounds for serious concern. The 'bottom line' of juvenile court authority is the policeman, ready to use his revolver, club and handcuffs to carry out the court's orders. A society that considers preventive detention repulsive has, in some strange way, learned to tolerate the threat or the actual use of force against persons who have not been found guilty of a crime" (p. 458).

Those who support continued jurisdiction of the juvenile court over status offenders (sometimes referred to as "minors in need of supervision," MINS; "children in need of supervision," CHINS; or "persons in need of supervision," PINS) argue that status offenders are not essentially different from those youngsters committing delinquent acts—they are children in need of services and without the intervention of the juvenile court, these services would not be forthcoming.

> **Key Fact**
>
> Status offenders are subject to juvenile court jurisdiction for behavior that would not be of court interest if they were adults (e.g., truancy).

Opponents argue that juvenile court intervention does not help youngsters because the services are often inadequate and intervention intensifies existing problems by stigmatizing children. In other words, a juvenile may not be able to discern the subtle differences between the juvenile court and the criminal court—differences that are becoming vague (as in the justice model). Thus, the child, as well as the child's parents, friends, and community, may react to juvenile court intervention as if the child were facing charges in criminal court.

Edwin Schur warns that the "labeling" that results can set in motion "a complex process of response and counter-response with an initial act of rule-violation and developing into elaborated delinquent self-conceptions and a full-fledged delinquent career" (1973: 30). However, one research effort found that "the majority of those whose first referral was a status offense did not become more serious delinquents. If anything, they became something considerably less than serious delinquents" (Sheldon, Horvath, and

A Closer Look

CHINS in Clark County (Las Vegas), Nevada

The most common status offenses involve those youngsters who are unmanageable, runaways, or truants. Clark County responds by using community-based shelter care, counseling, and a network of community resources. Families in need of immediate assistance may come to the Admissions/Intake Division at Juvenile Court, which operates on a 24-hour basis, and meet with an intake officer who is experienced in crisis management. The officer will conduct an intake interview to evaluate the family situation and needs and then determine if alternative counseling or short-term emergency shelter care services are appropriate without further juvenile court intervention. If appropriate, services may be directly provided by the juvenile court (e.g., information/referral, extended evaluation, psychological consultation, or 90-day probation supervision).

Diagnostic Interviews

The intake officer will consult with law enforcement and school officials and gather as much information as possible to thoroughly assess the family's situation. After completing the assessment, the officer develops a plan of action that requires continued parental involvement; the intent is to promote family unity. The officer will also explore parental rights and responsibilities regarding CHINS. Clark County Juvenile Services recognizes that CHINS behaviors are difficult for everyone to deal with and that at times parents become extremely frustrated with their children and look to the court for quick and easy solutions, which are not available. Helping CHINS to grow up and behave better takes time, work, and patience. Court programs can be effective only if the parents and concerned others agree to address the problem.

Community Service Referrals

The community offers many excellent resources for families in need, and intake officers are aware of the various services of both public and private agencies. When a family's needs can best be met through a referral to one of them, such a plan of action is preferable. These agencies may divert CHINS from the court and into the most appropriate setting available within the community. Through such brokering, families may access the services they need.

Emergency Shelter Care

Some children are temporarily out of control. When the parent-child relationship has deteriorated to a point at which temporary separation is necessary, the intake officer can arrange for the child to be placed in an emergency shelter care facility and refer the family to the probation division for continued supervision under a Family Services Agreement. The county has contracts with five emergency shelter care homes, and CHINS are referred to these facilities rather than being confined in the court's secure detention center for delinquents.

Family Services Agreement

Some children continue to exhibit more severe and more chronic CHINS behavior despite previous service attempts. For these CHINS, the probation department has an ongoing supervision program. The Family Services Agreement is an informal voluntary contract between the family and the juvenile court that spells out mutual responsibilities and service expectations. Basically, it provides for 3 months of supervision by a PO and outlines what can be expected of the child, parents, and the court. Participation in individual or family counseling is usually indicated, and if the child is temporarily removed from the home and placed in shelter care, the agreement specifies the conditions for length of stay, reunification efforts, and financial obligations. Children are expected to obey reasonable and proper orders of their parents, attend school regularly, and participate in a treatment plan tailored to their individual needs. The PO monitors these expectations, coordinates interagency efforts, and participates in direct counseling with the child.

Mental Health Services

Psychological screenings and referrals for psychiatric services can be made in those instances in which a severely emotionally disturbed child comes to the court's attention as a CHINS referral.

Tracy, 1989: 214). Another study (Brown et al., 1991) also contradicted the labeling argument: Youngsters adjudicated in juvenile court on their first referral were less likely to have criminal records as adults than those whose referrals were delayed until further misbehavior occurred.

Status offense (MINS, CHINS, PINS) petitions are most often filed on behalf of the children's parents, ostensibly because the youngsters are beyond their control. The child's behavior is often merely a symptom of a wider problem. Children frequently become status offenders by running away from pathological family situations or alcoholic and/or abusing parents. Girls are often subjected to juvenile court for sexual behavior that goes unnoticed when committed by boys (Chesney-Lind, 1997). Children who are found to be status offenders are usually warned or placed on probation in their initial encounter with the court. Probation can include placement in a shelter, group home, or foster care. If a youngster fails to cooperate with the treatment program, he or she can be returned to court for further disposition, which can lead to placement in a secure facility, such as a training school. The Juvenile Justice and Delinquency Prevention Act of 1974 requires the deinstitutionalization of status offenders, which sometimes required litigation to accomplish. "Slippage has occurred and researchers have documented wholesale replacement of juvenile court institutionalization of status offenders with 'voluntary' mental health commitments in some states" (Swanger, 1988: 211). In 1998, Georgia reached an agreement with the U.S. Department of Justice to stop incarcerating an estimated 8,000 status offenders annually (Butterfield, 1998b).

JUVENILE COURT JUDGES

Central to implementing the helping philosophy of the juvenile court is the juvenile court judge. However, the position presents an anomaly—although most judicial posts require only a knowledge of law and legal procedure, the juvenile court judge, in addition, needs a working knowledge of several disciplines: sociology, psychology, and social work. If persons with such backgrounds were readily available, the relatively low prestige of the juvenile court would make their recruitment difficult. In most states the juvenile court is located at the bottom of the judicial organizational chart, and the position of juvenile court judge is often seen as the entry level for a future appointment to a more prestigious court. (Exceptions would include Illinois and Arizona, where the juvenile court is a division of the superior court.)

In response to these difficulties, states provide training for juvenile court judges, often by or in conjunction with the National Council of Juvenile Court Judges. The council sponsors a national college located on the campus of the University of Nevada at Reno. The college trains judges and holds periodic sessions throughout the year on topics designed to help juvenile court judges keep abreast of the laws and behavior approaches related to the problems of delinquency, neglect, and child abuse. Other topics include drug and alcohol abuse, juvenile institutions and their alternatives, and waiver of cases to the criminal court. Some jurisdictions use *referees* or *masters*, specialized attorneys who represent the judge and who are empowered to hold certain juvenile court hearings.

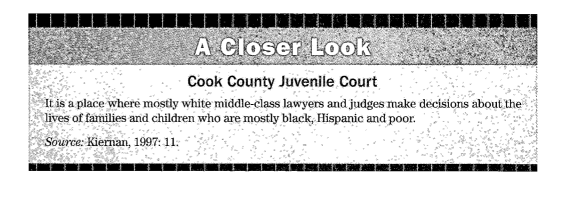

A Closer Look

Cook County Juvenile Court

It is a place where mostly white middle-class lawyers and judges make decisions about the lives of families and children who are mostly black, Hispanic and poor.

Source: Kiernan, 1997: 11.

LEGAL DECISIONS

As noted in this chapter, the juvenile court operated for many decades without attention or adherence to due process requirements or scrutiny by the judicial branch of government. This era of juvenile court history ended during the latter half of the 1960s, an era marked by the judicial activism of the Supreme Court with respect to issues involving civil liberties. Because of the central role of the PO in the court, juvenile cases decided by the Supreme Court affected probation services.

In 1966, the Supreme Court reviewed the operations of the juvenile court in *Kent v. United States* (383 U.S. 541). While on probation, Morris Kent, 16 years of age, was convicted in criminal court of raping a woman in her Washington, D.C., apartment and sentenced to a prison term of 30 to 90 years. In juvenile court, he would have faced a maximum term of incarceration until 21 years of age. In accord with existing federal statutes, the case had first been referred to the juvenile court, where over the objections of defense counsel, jurisdiction was waived to the criminal court. On appeal, in a 5–4 decision, the Supreme Court ruled that before a juvenile can be tried in criminal court, he or she is entitled to a waiver hearing with counsel, and if jurisdiction is waived, the judge must state the reasons.

Kent is significant for changing the Supreme Court's hands-off policy that had been in existence since the juvenile court was established in 1899. In its decision, the Court expressed concern over the lack of due process in the juvenile court:

> Although there can be no doubt of the original laudable purpose of juvenile courts, studies and critiques in more recent years raise serious questions as to whether actual performance measures well enough against theoretical purpose to make tolerable the immunity of the process from the reach of constitutional guarantees applicable to adults. There is much evidence that some juvenile courts, including that of the District of Columbia, lack the personnel, facilities, and techniques to perform adequately as representatives of the state in a *parens patriae* capacity, at least with respect to children charged with law violation. There is evidence, in fact, that there may be grounds for concern that the child receives the worst of both worlds, that he gets neither the protections accorded to adults nor the solicitous care and regenerative treatment postulated for children.

The following year, the Supreme Court addressed the issue of due process in the juvenile court (*In re Gault*, 387 U.S. 1, 1967). Gerald Gault, age 15, had been arrested by the police on the complaint of a female neighbor that he and his friend had made lewd and indecent remarks over the telephone. Gerald's parents were not notified of their son's arrest and did not receive a copy of the juvenile court petition charging him with delinquency. Furthermore, Gerald was not advised of his right to remain silent or his right to counsel. The complainant was not present at the hearing, nor did the judge speak with her on any occasion. Instead, Gerald's mother and two POs appeared before the juvenile court judge in his chambers. No one was sworn, nor was a transcript made of the proceeding.

At a second hearing, a conflict occurred concerning what had transpired at the first hearing. For the second time, the complainant was not present; the judge ruled that her presence was not necessary. Gerald was declared to be a juvenile delinquent and committed to a state training school for a maximum of 6 years, until he turned 21. Had Gerald been an adult (older than 18 years of age), the maximum sentence would have been a fine of not more than $50 or imprisonment for not more than 60 days. Because no appeal in juvenile court cases was permitted under Arizona law, Gerald's parents filed a petition of *habeas corpus* (a legal challenge to custody), which, although it was dismissed by the state courts, was granted (*certiorari*) a hearing by the U.S. Supreme Court.

In its decision, the Supreme Court acknowledged the helping—*noncriminal*—philosophy on which the juvenile court is based. But the decision also revealed a sense of outrage over what had transpired in the case of Gerald Gault: "Under our Constitution, the condition of being a boy does not justify a kangaroo court." The justices stated that even a child cannot be denied reasonable standards of due process and that he or she is entitled to:

- Written notice of the charges
- Right to counsel
- Protection against self-incrimination
- Right to confront and cross-examine witnesses
- Right to have written transcripts and appellate review

Because of the noncriminal nature of the juvenile court, instead of the proof beyond a reasonable doubt standard used in criminal trials, the level of evidence for a finding of delinquency was typically that used in a civil proceeding: preponderance of the evidence. In 1970, in the case of *In re Winship* (397 U.S. 358), the Supreme Court noted: "The reasonable-doubt standard plays a vital role in the American scheme of criminal procedure. It is a prime instrument for reducing the risk of conviction resting on factual error." Accordingly, the Court ruled that "the constitutional safeguard of proof beyond a reasonable doubt is as much required during the adjudicatory stage of a delinquency proceeding as are those constitutional safeguards applied in *Gault*."

The right to an impartial jury in criminal trials is guaranteed by the Sixth Amendment, but the Supreme Court decided against granting this right in juvenile proceedings. In the 1971 decision of *McKeiver v. Pennsylvania* (403 U.S. 528), the Court ruled that a juvenile court proceeding is not a criminal prosecution within the meaning of the Sixth Amendment. Accordingly, the Court held that the "imposition of the jury trial on the juvenile court system would not strengthen greatly, if at all, the fact-finding function." Nevertheless, more than 15 states permit the use of juries in juvenile court.

In 1975, the Supreme Court was faced with the question of double jeopardy—which is prohibited by the Fifth Amendment—with respect to the juvenile court. *Breed v. Jones* (421 U.S. 519) concerned a 17-year-old who was the subject of a juvenile court petition alleging armed robbery. After taking testimony from two prosecution witnesses and the respondent, the juvenile court judge sustained the petition. At a subsequent disposition hearing, the judge ruled that the respondent was not "amenable to the care, treatment and training program available through the facilities of the juvenile court" and ordered that Breed be prosecuted as an adult. The youngster was subsequently found guilty of armed robbery in criminal (superior) court, which led the Supreme Court to rule: "We hold that the prosecution of respondent in Superior Court, after an adjudicatory proceeding in Juvenile Court, violated that Double Jeopardy Clause of the Fifth Amendment, as applied to the States through the Fourteenth Amendment."

In 1984, the Supreme Court (*Schall v. Martin*, 467 U.S. 253), in a strong affirmation of the concept of *parens patriae*, upheld the constitutionality of the preventive detention of juveniles. *Schall* involved a New York statute that authorizes the detention of juveniles arrested for an offense when there is "serious risk" that, before trial, the juvenile may commit an act that, if committed by an adult, would constitute a crime. In this case Gregory Martin, 14 years of age, along with two others, was accused of hitting a youth with a loaded gun and stealing his jacket and sneakers; when arrested, Martin was in possession of the gun. The Court found that juveniles, unlike adults, "are always in some form of custody," that is, "by definition, [they] are not assumed to have the capacity to take care of themselves [but] are assumed to be subject to the control of their parents, and if parental control falters, the State must play its part as *parens patriae*." The Court stipulated that the detention cannot be for purposes of punishment and must be strictly limited in time; the Court found that the maximum detention under the New York statute, 17 days for serious crimes and 6 days for less serious crimes, was proper.

According to Barry Feld (2003), providing greater due process rights to juveniles has had unintended consequences because it legitimated the imposition of more punitive sentences. He notes further that once juveniles are given adult-like protections, judges more readily depart from the pure rehabilitative model, which had formed the basis of the juvenile court.

DISPOSITIONS

Juveniles are sometimes released to the custody of their parents for placement in private boarding schools, military academies, and other private facilities, a disposition most often limited to children from at least middle-income status. Dale Mann notes: "One obvious effect is to guarantee that public institutions for juvenile offenders serve an underclass population" (1976: 12). Jerome Miller (1992: 5) states that a "two-tiered system of residential care has grown up across the country with a dramatic surge in short-term hospitalization in private psychiatric hospitals for recalcitrant, disobedient, or drug-abusing suburban adolescents." He notes that the effect "is to spare these youngsters the correctional diagnosis and the labels which undermine hope—'psychopath,' 'sociopath,' 'unsocialized aggressive.' Such terms apply only to the children of the poor and the racial minorities who populate our youth correctional institutions."

Female offenders often receive harsher treatment in juvenile court because of the lack of alternative programs for them (Female Offender Resource Center, 1979: 13):

> Although a sentencing judge may be willing to consider a variety of dispositional alternatives, he or she is often faced with only one program possibility—the state training school or reformatory. [In addition,] once institutionalized, girls are afforded fewer services and program opportunities than boys. Boys, on the other hand, suffer from disadvantages which result from confinement in larger institutions which are filled to capacity. . . . Some people in the juvenile justice system justify the differences in programs and services available in girls' institutions by arguing that it is cost effective to spend the limited funds that do exist on boys who commit more serious crimes and who outnumber girls in the system nearly four to one.

There is no indication this situation is changing.

In many states, although a judge can order an adjudicated youth committed to the department having responsibility for institutional care, the judge cannot determine the type of institution to which the youth be confined. In Idaho, for example, youth in the Department of Juvenile Corrections custody go through an observation and assessment process to determine the best placement; a judge may not specify secure confinement or make any recommendations for placement of adjudicated youth.

Basic to dispositions in the juvenile court is the concept of the **least restrictive alternative**, meaning that a disposition should not be more restrictive than that which will adequately serve the needs of the child. The following review of dispositions generally follows this principle, progressing from the less to the more restrictive: probation supervision, day treatment, group home, residential treatment center, training school, and youth authority; also covered are issues associated with aftercare.

Key Fact

Juvenile court dispositions are governed by the least restrictive alternative.

Probation Supervision

Probation supervision is used in about 20 percent of the adjudicated delinquency cases. This disposition is appropriate for children who are not seriously delinquent and not in obvious need of intensive services available only in a residential setting. Youngsters with severe behavior problems may be placed on probation, however, not because it is necessarily the most appropriate response but because probation is the only readily available response.

As a condition of probation, juveniles are usually required to obey their parents or guardians, attend school regularly, be home at an early hour in the evening, and avoid disreputable companions or other persons on probation (Figure 4.6). The PO supervising the youngster works toward modifying some of the juvenile's attitudes to help the child relate to society in a law-abiding, prosocial manner (Figure 4.7). At the root of

Key Fact

Most juvenile cases result in probation.

RULES OF PROBATION
LOGAN COUNTY FAMILY COURT
Bellefontaine, Ohio
Judge Michael L. Brady and Judge C. Douglas Chamberlain

Name: _____   Date: _____

Offense: _____   Case #: _____

At a hearing held in Juvenile Court you were found delinquent/unruly and placed on probation. You are expected to abide by the following rules:

_____ 1. I shall report to my Probation Officer as directed by him/her. If I am unable to make the assigned time, I will notify the Probation Department. I will follow all instructions of any Court Officer.

_____ 2. I will comply with all STATE, LOCAL LAWS, RULES, AND REGULATIONS.

_____ 3. I will not purchase, possess, own, use or have under my control any firearms, deadly weapons, ammunition, or dangerous ordnance.

_____ 4. I will attend school every day, maintain passing grades, follow all school rules, and treat and address school staff members with respect at all times.

_____ 5. I will conform to the discipline of my parents. I will abide by all house rules. Parents must know my whereabouts at all times and with whom I am associating.

_____ 6. I will not use or engage in the sale of any alcoholic beverage, drug or narcotic or possess any drug paraphernalia, unless use is prescribed by a licensed physician. I will submit to random urinalysis testing. I understand the cost of this test shall be my responsibility and my parents, unless otherwise ordered by the Court. Further, I will not use or possess tobacco products.

_____ 7. Curfew: Sun.-Thurs. _____ Fri.-Sat. _____. Exceptions to these curfew hours are when I am accompanied by my parent or with permission from my P.O. I may leave Logan County if I am with my parents; otherwise I must have prior approval. I will not leave the state of Ohio without prior approval from my P.O.

_____ 8. I will not engage in conduct detrimental to the health, morals, or well-being of myself or others.

_____ 9. I understand that pursuant to Section 2151.411(C)(2)(b) of the Ohio Revised Code, authorized P.O.s engaged within the scope of their supervisory duties or responsibilities may conduct searches during the period of probation if they have reasonable grounds to believe I have not been abiding by the law or otherwise not complying with the conditions of my probation and the search may extend to a motor vehicle, another item of tangible or intangible person, property, or a place of residence or other real property in which a notified parent, guardian, or custodian has a right, title, or interest and that parent, guardian, or custodian expressly or impliedly permits the child to use or occupy or possess.

_____ 10. I will not socialize with other individuals on probation unless otherwise authorized by my P.O.

_____ 11. I shall report any arrest, citation, or any other contact with law enforcement to my P.O.

_____ 12. I will keep my P.O. informed regarding: change in residence, telephone number, employment, school, or use of a vehicle.

_____ Additional rules:

I have read and understand the foregoing rules of probation and will abide by them, realizing if I violate the rules, I may be subject to arrest, prosecution, and/or further appearances in Court.

_____
Juvenile

I/we have read the foregoing rules of probation and agree to help my/our son/daughter abide by them, realizing that if I/we permit my/our son/daughter to violate the rules, I/we may be subject to prosecution for Contributing to the Delinquency of a Minor, or Acting in a Way Tending to Cause the Delinquency of a Minor.

I/we understand it is the parent's responsibility to pay the probation fee as assessed.

I/we also acknowledge that pursuant to O.R.C. Section 3321.38 entitled Failure to Send Child to School, I/we shall make sure that the child under my/our care attends school as provided by law and remains a pupil in school during the term prescribed by law. Failure to do so shall result in a complaint being filed against me/us and an appearance before the Juvenile Court on said charge.

_____   _____
Parent/Guardian   Parent/Guardian

_____ P.O., Logan County Juvenile Court

FIGURE 4.6 *Rules of Probation, Logan County Family Court*

MONTHLY LOG

Name Harold Bent   Month April 2006

4-1-06
Home
visit   With youth and mother. Youth is home due to suspension from Jackson High School for fighting until next Thursday (4-9-06). PO counseled youth in alternate ways of handling conflict.

Later:
School
visit   With principal of Jackson High School, Mr. Jones. He advised youth was found with a small quantity of drugs as well. PO left a school report to be completed and mailed and telephoned youth officer to request copy of arrest report.

4-7-06
Report
rec'd: PO received arrest report on incident at school, which indicates he was station adjusted for battery and possession of a marijuana cigarette.

Later:
TX   Called mother at home to advise of the problem as noted in police report and to notify that a VOP will be filed for 4-16-06 on Cal. #52.

4-16-06
Ct. Hrg.   Case on Cal. #52 for VOP for battery and possession of marijuana. Present were youth, mother and undersigned.

DISP: Denial entered, cont. for trial to 5-26-06.

Later: PO discussed possible drug problem with youth and mother. Both were urged to contact Treatment Alternatives to initiate an intake interview for drug abuse counseling.

4-19-06
TX   Call to Treatment Alternatives to complete referral. Intake wkr. Judy Watson verified Mrs. Jones called to set up appointment for intake on 4-26 and will obtain a release so the social inv. can be requested.

4-27-06
Att. home
visit   PO made unscheduled visit to home. No one responded to bell. Left card in door.

FIGURE 4.7 *Juvenile Probation Officer Monthly Log*

Source: Cook County, Juvenile Probation Department, Illinois.

antisocial behavior in many juveniles is a difficulty in relating to authority and authority figures. Parents, school officials, and others who have represented authority to the young person have caused him or her to develop a negative, even hostile, attitude toward authority in general, which leads to rebellion at home and at school or against society in general. The PO must help the young person revise his or her ideas about people in authority by providing a role model as a healthy authority figure or by helping the young person develop healthy attitudes toward others who can provide a desirable role model. These persons may be teachers, athletic coaches, or perhaps a recreation leader in the community.

The probation officer must be able to accept the young person and be able to demonstrate an attitude of respect and concern. At the same time, the PO must be honest and firm with the youngster, setting realistic limits for him or her—something parents are often unable (or unwilling) to do. Misbehavior or antisocial activities cannot be accepted, but the client must be.

In the course of the helping process, the PO will involve the family and meet with the young person on a regular basis. The PO will also work with school officials, sometimes acting as an advocate for the child to secure a public school placement, which is often a difficult task. The youngster has usually exhibited disruptive behavior

Lehigh County School-Based Probation Program

In the central Pennsylvania county of Lehigh, juvenile POs are stationed in the high schools where, in addition to monitoring probationers attending school, they visit classrooms to talk to students and faculty about the juvenile justice system. The program seeks to improve attendance and grades, avoid suspensions, and decrease the need for institutional placement. The POs are available to deal with clients involved in school violations. The officers also make home visits and involve family members in the students' programs. The POs coordinate reentry conferences for students returning to school after suspension to help increase their chances of a positive reintegration.

Juvenile Probation Supervision, Amarillo, Texas

Barry Gilbert will visit schools this morning to check on 8 youths on his intensive supervision caseload at the Randall County Juvenile Probation Department. He meets with Amarillo High School administrators to check out 4 probationers and is glad to learn their attendance and behavior are good. The PO heads for Fannin Middle School and finds 2 other youths on his caseload are also doing well. As he is leaving, police officers checking a report of a gun on campus ask if he has time to help interview a suspect who is currently on probation. Gilbert values the cooperation his agency receives from the police department and is glad to assist.

Once he completes the investigative interview, the PO visits two other schools, grabs a quick lunch, and returns to his office where he prepares paperwork for residential placement of 2 children on intensive supervision. It takes time to complete the 30-page application required for out-of-home placement of children in Texas. Gilbert seeks drug treatment for one child and a suitable residential placement for the other.

The PO makes curfew checks on 24 of the 32 youngsters on his caseload. In the next few hours, he will make 18 face-to-face meetings with probationers who never know when he will drop by. Gilbert, a former youth pastor and police officer, makes sure they know that intensive supervision is serious business for youngsters in trouble.

Orange County, California, Juvenile Court Work Program

The Juvenile Court Work Program was established about 30 years ago to provide a meaningful alternative to incarceration for certain juvenile offenders. The young men and women in the program are an average age of 15 to 16 years old, but they could be as young as 11 or as old as 21. In lieu of serving an institutional commitment in juvenile hall or a juvenile camp, these young men and women literally work off their debt to society on weekends. Typically, a juvenile will serve 20 eight-hour days (10 weekends) on a work crew of 10 to 12 young people. Accommodations are made for school sports events and weekend jobs. Juveniles who fail to complete the work program are returned to juvenile court for further sanctions—generally serving a commitment in a juvenile institution. Municipalities, school districts, and other government agencies pay to have these crews service their property. The money raised helps to offset program costs.

Rules are strict. Youth are not permitted to arrive at work under the influence of alcohol or illegal drugs. On any weekend day, 20 to 23 work program crews can be found spread throughout Orange County. The crews might be weeding riverbeds as part of wetlands restoration, clearing brush from hillsides adjacent to public schools to remove hazards, or picking up debris and trash from city and county beaches and parks.

at school, so officials are understandably resistant to his or her return. If necessary, the officer will seek placement in a foster home for the client (and in some circumstances, adoption).

Many orders of probation require restitution or community service. The term *restitution* refers to the compensation provided by an offender to his or her victim; it can involve financial payments or a service alternative. An increasing interest in restitution as a condition of probation has been spurred by an increasing concern for the victims of crime. The service alternative is often imposed on youngsters who are unable to provide financial restitution, although it rarely means direct service to the victim; instead, the juvenile is usually involved in unpaid work for a nonprofit community agency, such as the Salvation Army or the Red Cross.

If the youngster violates any of the conditions of probation, the PO prepares a violation of probation report and the youngster can then be subjected to a motion to revoke probation in favor of a more restrictive setting, such as an institutional placement (Figure 4.8).

Day Treatment

Community-based day treatment programs are cost-effective because they avoid the need to provide the total care environment of residential programs. **Project RISE** (Reentry into Successful Education) provides an example. Located in Pima County,

---

IN THE CIRCUIT COURT OF
JACKSON COUNTY, MISSOURI
JUVENILE DIVISION

IN THE INTEREST OF
James Matthews
M/DOB: 7/12/89
PETITION NO. JV87-10010
LIFE NO. 11326

MOTION TO REVOKE PROBATION

COMES NOW the Juvenile Probation Officer and moves the Court to enter an order revoking the above-named juvenile's probation and, in support thereof, states to the Court:

1. On the 2nd day of November, 2004, the Court committed the above-named juvenile to the custody of the Juvenile Officer at McCune and suspended execution of said commitment and placed the juvenile in the custody of his mother, subject to rules of probation.

2. The juvenile has violated the following term of his probation: To obey all laws and ordinances.

3. The juvenile violated the aforesaid term of probation in that:

    On or about November 22, 2005, in Jackson County, Missouri, the juvenile knowingly altered and defaced a motor vehicle, a 2005 Nissan 300ZX automobile, without the consent of the owner thereof, in violation of Section 569.080 (Tampering, First Degree-Class C Felony), for which the juvenile would be criminally responsible if tried as an adult,

    WHEREFORE, the Juvenile Officer prays the Court revoke the juvenile's probation and enter a dispositional order in the best interests of the juvenile.

Forestal Lawton

Forestal Lawton
Juvenile Officer

FIGURE 4.8 *Motion to Revoke Probation*

A Closer Look

Restitution in Utah

The statewide Utah Juvenile Court operates a structured juvenile restitution program. In most cases, youth make restitution directly in the form of financial payments. Others may be ordered to participate in community service programs to earn money to make restitution payments. Under state law, the Utah Juvenile Court may order youth to repair, replace, or make restitution for victims' property and other losses. POs are authorized to develop restitution or community service plans, even in cases in which youth are not formally brought before the court by petition. In such cases, consent agreements are signed by youth and parents, and restitution is often paid directly to the victims.

The court may withhold a substantial portion of fines paid by juveniles to underwrite a work restitution fund. The fund allows juveniles otherwise unable to pay restitution to work in community service projects in the private or public sector to earn money to compensate their victims. The juvenile's earnings are paid directly from the fund to the victims.

A Closer Look

Dauphin County, Pennsylvania, Adolescent Foster Home Care Program

Established in 1980, the Adolescent Foster Home Care (AFHC) program, in cooperation with County Social Services and Youth Agency, recruits, screens, and trains foster parents and provides specialized services to both dependent and delinquent youth. The AFHC program provides carefully screened delinquent youth with experiences in family living that are essential to positive and constructive growth and development.

A delinquent youth is referred to the AFHC program by the active PO, either an intake officer or line officer. The foster home care specialist PO reviews all available information concerning the youth and the natural family. He or she interviews the youth and the natural family to explain the program and to determine the appropriateness of the referral. If the foster home care specialist deems the child to be amenable to treatment in foster home care (rather than in some other modality of treatment), he or she schedules a placement planning conference with the child and youth agency to identify a prospective foster family.

A weekend preplacement visit for the prospective foster family and foster youth is arranged and implemented by the foster home care specialist. In this way, both the adolescent and the foster family have the opportunity to express any concerns they may have regarding the proposed placement. If foster family members do not believe they can meet the needs of a particular youth, they may disapprove the placement in their home. After a successful preplacement visit with the foster family, the youth is scheduled for a juvenile court dispositional hearing. The assigned PO recommends to the juvenile court judge that the youth be placed in the custody of the Dauphin County Social Services for Children and Youth Agency for placement in the AFHC program. The youngster is also placed on strict probation under the supervision of the Juvenile Probation Office. The foster home specialist supervises all delinquent youth in foster home care. In most cases, the youth is also placed on suspended commitment to an appropriate juvenile facility where the youth will go if he or she fails to comply with the terms of the AFHC program. Only the juvenile court judge can commit juveniles to the program.

When the goals of the Family and Placement Service Plan have been achieved and the foster home care specialist believes the child can be successfully reunited with the natural family (or meet an alternative placement goal), he or she will recommend to the juvenile court judge that the youth be released from the program. If the youth returns to the natural or surrogate home, he or she remains under probation supervision for approximately 3 months to ensure continued successful community adjustment and to allow the foster home care specialist to provide continued support services to the reunited family unit.

Arizona (which includes the city of Tucson), RISE is a community-based noncustodial response to troubled youth. Over the years, the Pima County Juvenile Court has found that there is a strong correlation between a child's school problems and delinquent behavior. All too often, school officials and the juvenile court would work in isolation. In 1982, a project at Howenstine School was begun to combine the treatment of the dual problems of delinquency and school failure. This program was a joint venture between the Tucson Unified School District and the Pima County Juvenile Court. Teachers, teacher aides, probation officers, and probation aides work side by side with a few juveniles to provide maximum supervision and a favorable environment for learning. The success of the Howenstine program was responsible for the Sunnyside School District inaugurating a similar program in 1983. Both programs are now known as Project RISE, a full-time day program for about 40 youngsters which combines the best of the educational and juvenile justice systems from which the project receives its clients. The goals of the program are to reduce serious delinquent activity, improve school attendance, decrease school behavioral problems, raise the child's reading level by 2 years, and inculcate positive social values and survival skills in the youth. To accomplish these goals, Project RISE is housed in facilities separate from the mainstream high schools. Students are either transported to school or issued city bus passes. The staff-to-child ratio is extremely low, ensuring intensive daily supervision in an innovative learning environment.

Key Fact

Day treatment offers a range of services to those on juvenile probation.

As children progress, their success is rewarded within the context of a behavior modification system (behavior modification is discussed in Chapter 8). In this manner, undesirable activities and habits are eliminated, and healthy, socially acceptable behaviors are reinforced. The child's self-image is bolstered by repeated successes in interpersonal and academic tasks. Emphasis is placed on frequent organized outings to broaden the child's growing socialization.

Group Home

Residential treatment can be classified according to the degree of custodial care provided, and at the lower end of this scale is the group home. The group home may be privately operated under contract with the state (or other level of government), or it can be operated by the state. Generally, anywhere from 6 to 15 youngsters live in the home at any one time. The typical home has several bedrooms and baths, as well as a large living room, dining area, and basement recreation area. The interior of the home approximates that of a large single-family dwelling. Group homes are usually located in residential areas that are in proximity to public transportation, public schools, and recreation facilities.

The group home is for youngsters with one or more of these issues:

- They are in unresolvable conflict with their parents but are not seriously disturbed or psychotic.
- They have inadequate homes and need to develop skills for independent living.
- They need to deal with community social adjustment problems in a therapeutic family environment.
- They need to deal with individual adjustment problems and to learn about themselves in relation to others.
- They need to develop self-confidence through successful experiences.

Each resident has daily chores, such as doing dishes, making beds, or mowing the lawn. Houseparents, usually a married couple with graduate degrees in a therapeutic discipline such as social work or psychology, perform surrogate parent roles by preparing or overseeing the preparation of meals, enforcing a curfew, and helping with homework, as well as doing other tasks usually handled by parents in healthy families. Youngsters attend local schools on a full-time basis, or they have a schedule that incorporates both school and employment.

There are group counseling sessions conducted by group workers geared to help the residents understand and overcome problems that have led to the placement and to define goals consistent with their individual abilities. Individual counseling programs are provided for those youngsters who need help in preparing for independent living and improving their family relationships. Day-by-day counseling and conflict resolution are handled by the houseparents.

The most difficult aspects of the group home are relationships with the surrounding community—vigorous neighborhood resistance typically exists to placing such a facility in the immediate area. Although both professionals and laypersons generally agree that the group home concept is an excellent one for many youngsters coming to the attention of the juvenile court, this has not translated into widespread acceptance of the reality. Group homes, not only for troubled youngsters but also for persons with mental retardation and other disabilities, have been vigorously and all too often successfully resisted by local residents (Holloway, 1995).

This problem became so severe that in 1989 the U.S. Department of Justice brought suit against a Chicago suburb (Chicago Heights) because the municipality refused to permit the building of a group home for 15 adults with mental retardation (Johnson, 1989a). A similar suit was brought by United Cerebral Palsy against a group of Southeast Dade County (Florida) homeowners who were attempting to thwart the opening of group homes for persons with disabilities (Hartman, 1994). The 1988 Federal Fair Housing Act, which bars discrimination against persons with disabilities, has been interpreted by the courts as outlawing local zoning laws that deny housing to persons with mental retardation, the mentally ill, and drug addicts. In 1995, the Supreme Court ruled that this statute prohibits municipalities from using single-family zoning to bar group homes. In this case, the city of Edmonds, Washington, had attempted to prevent a national organization, Oxford House, from operating a group home for recovering substance abusers (*City of Edmonds v. Oxford House*, 514 U.S. 725). Although we may accept the moral imperative and recognize the value of helping the unfortunate, too often it is a concern for real estate values that prevails. *L'hypocrisie est un hommage que le vice rend à la vertu.*

Residential Treatment Center

The term **residential treatment center (RTC)** is being used to identify private and public institutions that provide residential care for youngsters, with or without intervention of the juvenile court and devoid of coercive elements associated with correctional facilities (e.g., locks, bars, and barbed-wire/razor fences). Generally, the RTC provides a wide variety of enriched services, and the private RTC receives a great deal of public funding. Despite the fact that almost all receive tax money, the private RTC retains the privilege of screening its residents, a luxury not afforded public institutions. One study found, however, that in southern California considerable competition exists for residents between private facilities, and juveniles admitted to private institutions do not significantly differ from those sent to public facilities (Shichor and Bartollas, 1990). Private centers can also mix adjudicated delinquents, status offenders, and voluntary clients in a manner that would not be permissible in a public institution, although the mixing of delinquent and nondelinquent children runs contrary to the prevailing wisdom in the field (Curran, 1988).

Training School

During the early 1990s, serious juvenile crime rates increased 60 percent, making juvenile crime a national issue. While rates decreased after 1994, by the latter 1990s they were still well above mid-1980s levels. In 1997, juveniles were responsible for 14 percent of all murder and aggravated assault arrests, 37 percent of burglary arrests, and 24 percent of

A Closer Look

Camp Wilmont Sweeney

The Alameda County, California, Probation Department operates an unlocked facility for delinquent youth ranging in age from 15 to 18. Residents first enter the 60-bed transitional unit and after an orientation period move to one of four dormitories that house a total of 90 youth. During their last 3 months, residents who have demonstrated a high level of responsibility and positive change can return to the transitional unit to provide positive role models for new entrants.

The 7 deputy POs who act as case managers, along with 25 group counselors and 3 psychologists, service the youth while in residence. The treatment approach uses a "normative model" emphasizing the importance of norms (social agreements) that help people to bond. Residents are challenged to build a network of prosocial relationships that will support them as they return to the community. Techniques used include "town hall meetings," guided group interaction (see the next section), and peer-led committees focused on specific tasks. Services available include drug and alcohol treatment, conflict mediation training, and gang violence prevention. Residents can earn their high school diploma and are offered classes in computer repair. Athletics, religious services, field trips, and cultural appreciation events round out the program.

By accomplishing individual case objectives that he developed with his treatment team—an on-site psychologist, his PO, a group counselor, a peer mentor, his parent(s) or guardians—and making positive contributions to the camp community, a resident can earn his graduation from the facility, usually within 6 months to 1 year.

weapons arrests. States responded by adjudicating more children as delinquent, sending more delinquents to correctional facilities, and increasing the number of children tried and imprisoned as adults. By the turn of the twenty-first century, juvenile arrests began to decline; in California, for example, arrests per 100,000 juveniles went from 6,550 in 1994 to 4,228 in 2003, with a corresponding decline in the rate of juvenile incarceration (Turner and Fain, 2005). At the same time, states moved away from placing juvenile delinquents under the adult corrections agency and toward separate juvenile corrections agencies or joint juvenile corrections and child protection agencies.

The **training school** is a public institution that accepts all youngsters committed by the courts. Each training school is usually set up to handle particular categories of juveniles who may be assigned on the basis of age, aggressiveness, or delinquent history. This is done to avoid mixing older children with younger ones, adjudicated delinquents with status offenders, or more disturbed youngsters with those with less serious problems. The training school usually provides a level of security not available in other types of juvenile institutions (although less than that offered in a correctional facility). Juveniles are committed to training schools based on four criteria:

Key Fact

Training schools are secure public institutions housing juvenile delinquents.

1. A finding of fact occurs indicating that the child has committed an offense that would be punishable by imprisonment if committed by an adult.
2. The parents are unable to control their child or provide for his or her social, emotional, and educational needs.
3. No other child welfare service is sufficient.
4. The child needs the services available at the training school.

The establishment of the Lyman School for Boys in Massachusetts, which opened in 1847 for 400 boys, began an era of providing separate facilities for juvenile offenders. These pre–juvenile court facilities—training or reform schools—were patterned after adult prisons. They were regimented with large impersonal dormitories, and each provided some basic medical and dental treatment and limited educational and vocational training. Although the juvenile court "forced a breach in the wall of the criminal justice system," notes Jerome Miller (1992: 8), it did not fully resolve the question of whether to treat or punish, and this dilemma "was complicated by the existence of reform schools, which had been around for most of the century before the juvenile court was invented. Their presence ensured that juvenile offenders would receive the worst the system could offer—punishment labeled as treatment."

Over the years, there has been an increased emphasis on vocational training, remedial education, and rehabilitation through the use of social workers, teachers, psychiatrists, psychologists, and recreation workers. Like a prison or hospital, a training school operates 168 hours per week; this fact, combined with the level of security and services provided, makes the training school an expensive institution in which annual costs can easily run in excess of $30,000 per resident. In Idaho, for example, the estimated annual cost per resident in a Department of Juvenile Corrections facility ranges from $36,000 to $48,000.

One training school, the Warwick School for Boys, is located 55 miles from New York City and is one of the training schools operated by the New York State Office of Children and Family Services. The school is a pleasant-looking institution with 700 acres of lawns and trees; it houses about 170 residents in several dormitories. Some individual rooms are also assigned on a "merit" basis. The residents are adjudicated delinquents who have committed offenses ranging from petty larceny to serious felonies, all before they turned 16. The school has about 180 staff members, and there are no walls or gates around the school—security is maintained through the use of supervised activities and a high staff-to-resident ratio. The daily schedule calls for 2 hours of compulsory academic instruction and 2 hours of physical education, with additional services for those who require more help. Both individual and group counseling are provided, as is vocational training in such areas as mechanical drawing, woodworking, electricity, and painting.

The Giddings State School of the Texas Youth Commission is a maximum-security facility for more than 300 juveniles, mostly boys (96 percent); more than 25 percent have committed murder. Located in a rural community about 50 miles northeast of Austin, a high fence surrounds the campus of one-story buildings. Only the lockup rooms—for rule violators—provide a prison-like aura. An accredited high school and extensive vocational training (for automobile repair, welding, and building trades), as well as a gym, indoor pool, game room, and television rooms in the dorms, are available; sports teams and arts and crafts instruction are some of the other extracurricular activities. Residents sleep in large open rooms arranged barracks style. The training school provides specialized treatment, for violent sex offenders and those chemically dependent, and "capital offender treatment." Treatment includes guided group interaction: Members live, eat, and attend class together; problems are dealt with in a group process. Medical, psychiatric, and psychological services are all provided at the facility.

Youth Authority

Some states (e.g., California and Ohio) have a state agency responsible for receiving cases from both juvenile and criminal courts. Typically, youngsters adjudicated delinquent in juvenile court, persons prosecuted and convicted under youthful or young offender statutes in criminal court, and juveniles prosecuted in criminal court under mandatory or optional waiver provisions are remanded to a **youth authority** for a period of confinement and aftercare (parole) supervision.

California Youth Authority.   The California Youth Authority (CYA) was created in 1941 and began providing institutional care and parole supervision for juvenile and young adult offenders in 1943. It is the largest youthful offender agency in the United States, with more than 10,000 young men and women in institutions and camps and approximately 6,000 more on parole.

After a youngster is committed by the court and accepted by the authority, he or she is transferred to a reception center and clinic for about 4 weeks for evaluation and testing before making an appearance before the seven-member Youthful Offender Pa-

A Closer Look

Los Angeles County Residential Treatment Program

The Los Angeles County Probation Department Residential Treatment Program is divided into two age groupings: senior (16 to 18 years of age) and junior (13 to 15 years of age). One junior camp and two senior camps are secure (fenced); the remaining ones are open (not fenced) camps. The security camps are used to maintain minors who represent a significant escape risk—essentially impulsive youngsters with a low degree of self-control. In these camps, emphasis is placed on developing self-control.

The system is composed of 15 institutions, 14 of which are located in mountain settings. An intake facility with 60 beds is maintained at San Fernando Valley Juvenile Hall. Almost all boys ordered to camp are screened here for medical or psychiatric problems, and academic levels are established before the minors are assigned to a camp. Girls are processed directly from the juvenile hall in which they are detained. Deputy probation officers in all camps provide ongoing individual and group counseling to all camp wards. Treatment programs are individual, and the length of stay for each minor is dependent on individual progress in the camp setting.

The principal objective of junior camps is to evaluate academic skills and achievement. These youngsters spend the bulk of the program day in school, and work is limited to in-camp maintenance and culinary assistance. The focus in senior camps is oriented more toward instilling work ethic disciplines. Senior youngsters ordinarily spend half of each day in school and half in parks and recreation work crews. A juvenile alternative work services program has been implemented whereby work crews are provided to public agencies on a contract basis. Extensive vocational training in such areas as welding, foundry work, and automobile repair is available at one of the camps.

role Board. Community assessment reports are generated by CYA parole agents after visiting the ward's family and contacting appropriate local agencies. These reports add information about the ward's family and community relationships to information gathered by the clinic staff from the ward, probation reports, and any psychological or educational testing done at the clinic. All this information is compiled into a document called a clinic study and presented to the Youthful Offender Parole Board. The board uses this report in making decisions about the youngster. Once the ward appears before the board and decisions about length of stay and program are made, the youngster is transferred to his or her institution.

The Youth Authority's offender population is housed in 11 institutions, 4 rural youth conservation camps, and 2 institution-based camps; 2 institutions are used primarily as reception centers. Female offenders are housed at Ventura Youth Correctional Facility, where there also is an intake center for them. A youth is assigned to a facility based on age, maturity, delinquent sophistication, educational/vocational needs, security needs, and behavior. Although in most cases wards are placed in an institution or conservation camp for a period of time and then released on parole, a few are placed on parole immediately after diagnostic studies. Under certain circumstances, a youngster committed from a criminal court may be assigned to an institution of the Department of Corrections. Commitments from both criminal and juvenile courts may also be assigned to an institution of the Department of Mental Health.

While in a CYA institution, younger residents attend school all day, while older ones might be in school part-time and in vocational training part-time. Many are assigned jobs within the institution; for example, they work on the grounds or in food preparation. All wards are assigned a counselor, and some are placed in psychiatric or psychological treatment. The CYA has special programs for drug and alcohol abusers, sex offenders, and the seriously mentally ill, but because of limited resources, not everyone needing specialized treatment can be assigned to these programs.

When the ward is considered ready for parole by the Youthful Offender Parole Board, the parole agent makes all the necessary arrangements for his or her return to the community. The agent contacts family members, law enforcement, and other agencies and assesses the need for special conditions of parole that the youngster must follow. The agent then completes the reentry report, which includes a preliminary parole plan describing employment, training, and education and establishes goals to be achieved during the first 30 to 90 days. For the first 90 days on parole, intensive reentry services are provided: The parole agent has frequent contact with the youngster and his or her family and provides needed brokerage with community agencies. The level and intensity of supervision gradually diminish as the ward becomes increasingly self-sufficient. The decision to reduce the level of supervision uses a classification system that determines the level of control necessary based on the youngster's potential risk score and his or her need for supportive services.

Parole staff work out of 16 parole offices. There also are two residential intensive drug treatment programs for parolees who have evidenced drug and alcohol problems but who have committed no new criminal act. The department is using electronic monitoring as an enhancement to parole supervision. In selected cases, this occurs at the time of release on parole; in other cases, it may be applied as a control or sanction when a technical parole violation occurs.

Like many states, California has significant problems with institutional care for young offenders. A study commissioned by the state found deplorable conditions in CYA institutions, with poorly maintained and antiquated facilities producing more than 4,000 serious assaults annually and dozens of attempted (and some successful) suicides (Broder, 2004).

Ohio Department of Youth Services.   The Ohio Department of Youth Services (DYS) provides a secure environment, education, vocational guidance, and other developmental programs for young people 12 to 18 years of age who have been charged with felony-level offenses and committed to the department by one of the state's 88 county juvenile courts. Serious felonies require a minimum commitment of 1 to 3 years; less serious felonies, 6 months. A judge may order early release at any time during the minimum commitment period, and in all commitments, a youth may be held until he or she turns 21.

The department's philosophy emphasizes care that is aimed at ultimate reintegration of troubled youth into the community. Planning for this reintegration begins at the time of commitment to DYS, when he or she is first assigned to the diagnostic reception center for 3 weeks of testing and planning. There are also special classes to prepare the youth for effective group living in an institutional setting and to heighten awareness of the harm done to victims. A team consisting of DYS staff and the ward, as well as his or her family, establishes a plan of development when the youth is committed to DYS. Obtainable goals, including educational goals, are set to help the youth develop self-control and discipline. The DYS Youth Recovery Program focuses on helping youth become free from chemical dependency, developing skills to avoid further contact with the juvenile justice system, and eliminating vocational handicaps as a result of being chemically dependent.

A reception center, eight institutions with capacities ranging from 120 to 200, three residential treatment centers whose capacities do not exceed 42, three private facilities with a capacity of 20 to 30 residents, a central medical facility, and eight regional offices are within the jurisdiction of the DYS. Youth assignments to DYS institutions are made on the basis of age, felony level of offense committed, and proximity of the DYS institution to the youth's home. Some youngsters are placed in private facilities under contract with the DYS. The average daily institutional population is about 2,000—at a per diem cost of more than $120—with another 2,700 in the aftercare program where they are supervised by DYS parole officers operating out of regional offices located in every major metropolitan center in the state.

Included in the array of institutions is the Indian River School, located near Akron, which houses about 200 of the most serious felony offenders and residents from other institutions who are security risks and/or have exhibited assaultive behavior. Indian

River has eight units with 24 rooms, a school, a library, a modern gymnasium, and a 6-acre athletic field, all surrounded by a 14-foot chain-link fence; windows are barred, and there are electronic metal doors on all dormitories and exits, as well as closed-circuit televisions for continuous surveillance.

Each DYS institution has a fully accredited school that all youth are required to attend. Educational opportunities are available for all residents, including those with learning disabilities and special needs. Some institutions offer college-level courses in conjunction with local universities. Vocational programs in several of the DYS institutional high schools offer youth a variety of possible career paths to choose from once they are reintegrated into their communities. These programs include automobile mechanics, graphic arts, building maintenance, small engine repair, cosmetology, and barbering. A variety of recreational activities and extracurricular activities are available at each institution. At one location, youth have a chance to be on the award-winning DYS drill team or in the break-dancing group, which gives public performances throughout the year at schools and community events. Youth at DYS make positive contributions to the community by doing volunteer work in litter control programs and by working with elderly citizens.

Aftercare and Parole

Aftercare is the planned release of a juvenile from a residential placement (group home, residential treatment center, training school, correctional institution) to supportive services in the community. Each year, about 100,000 juvenile offenders are released from residential facilities (Griffin, 2005). The juvenile may be supervised by a juvenile probation officer (as is the case with Glen Mills in Pennsylvania), a youth agency parole officer/agent (as in California and Ohio), or another aftercare worker. Aftercare services are usually provided by the same state agency that administers the juvenile training schools (Hurst and Torbet, 1993). For example, this author worked for the New York State Department of Social Welfare, which used to operate the state training schools. My job title was youth parole worker, and I was responsible for supervising juveniles released from the boys' training schools. In 1978, New York enacted the Juvenile Offender Law, which mandates that youngsters 13 to 19 years of age who commit certain felonies be prosecuted in adult criminal court. If convicted, the youngster can serve a term in a secure facility of the Office of Children and Family Services (OCFS). During that term, the juvenile becomes subject to the jurisdiction of the New York State Board of Parole for a release decision—parole— and eventual community supervision by a parole officer. Thus, the same agency that supervises adult felons in New York, the Division of Parole, also supervises juveniles convicted of certain violent felonies. In the state of Washington, parole counselors from the Juvenile Rehabilitation Administration (JRA) supervise those released from JRA institutions for a period of no more than 24 weeks (except for certain sex offenders).

A Closer Look

Court-Controlled Reentry

Advocates of court-controlled aftercare/reentry services argue that there are natural advantages: knowledge and familiarity with local conditions, enhanced capacity to monitor and respond to a juvenile's everyday behavior, and historical position of leadership in their communities (Griffin, 2005).

Key Fact

Juvenile aftercare or parole may be provided by different agencies, including probation departments.

Similarly, in Minnesota, parole agents of the Department of Corrections supervise juveniles who have been sentenced to a correctional facility. In Michigan, youngsters 12 to 19 years of age who have been adjudicated delinquent or found to be in need of supervision (status offenders) by the juvenile division of a probate court can be committed to the Department of Social Services for placement in their own home or a foster home, group home, youth camp, diagnostic center, halfway house, residential treatment center, or state training school. In Michigan, status offenders are often committed to the Department of Social Services when the particular juvenile court has insufficient resources available for the youngster. The department offers secure juvenile residential treatment facilities, which may be used as the last resort for the most seriously delinquent youth. Delinquent wards remain under state authority until they are discharged by the Youth Parole and Review Board (YPRB) or reach age 19. The Colorado Juvenile Parole Board is responsible for release decisions concerning juvenile delinquents who have been committed to the Department of Institutions. It grants, denies, revokes, suspends, or modifies conditions of parole to youth offenders who have been adjudicated as delinquent. When considering a youngster for aftercare, a release board will consider the case record, which in some jurisdictions includes a report and recommendation from a juvenile probation officer (Figure 4.9).

A Closer Look

Utah Youth Parole Authority

Youngsters committed to any secure facility in the state come under the jurisdiction of the Youth Parole Authority, whose 10 members are appointed by the governor for terms of 4 years; they serve part-time. The authority initially establishes a length of stay guideline for each committed youth and reviews his or her progress to determine when parole to the community is appropriate. The authority also conducts violation of parole hearings.

Aftercare supervision is similar (if not identical) to probation supervision and, as noted earlier, is sometimes provided by a juvenile probation agency. The first responsibility of the aftercare worker is to plan for the release and placement of the young person. Placement plans include where the juvenile will live, whether he or she is to work or attend a school or training program (or both), and what arrangements for supportive services may be needed by the client that are available in the community. The young person released/paroled from a training school may be returned to his or her own home, if this is desirable, or be placed in an alternative setting such as foster care, a group home, or a halfway house. (Halfway houses are discussed in Chapter 11.) The aftercare worker usually investigates placement alternatives and finalizes a program plan that is submitted to training school officials and those responsible for the release decision.

Once back in the community, the young person will be supervised by an aftercare worker, probation officer, or parole officer and will be required to abide by a set of rules identical to probation rules, the violation of which can cause a return to a "secure setting." The worker will make regular visits to the youngster's residence, school, or place of employment and will involve family and school officials in an effort to facilitate the young person's reintegration and rehabilitation. Unfortunately, juvenile aftercare has typically been underfunded, despite its obvious importance.

REQUEST FOR CONDITIONAL RELEASE/AFTERCARE

NAME: Michael DeWitt

BIRTH DATE: July 12, 1991

ADDRESS: 1900 West Briar Place

ENROLLMENT: June 6, 2007

DATE OF REPORT: November 28, 2007

I. REASON FOR PLACEMENT

Michael was committed to the McCune School for Boys on June 6, 2007, by Judge Harrison for Sexual Abuse.

II. ADDITIONAL REFERRALS

There have been no additional referrals.

III. ADJUSTMENT DURING PRESENT PERIOD OF SUPERVISION

While at McCune, Michael has made substantial advancement. Upon entrance into the program he was unable to work with his peers. Michael was often the target of harassment from other residents. He had told a story about his being offered chili to eat from resident Timothy Mordell working in the cafeteria. Michael asked if the meat in it was human flesh, and the incident became the source of ridicule during the remainder of his stay at McCune.

Over the past 6 months, Michael learned how to deal more appropriately with the harassment. He was also able to overcome racial problems that he had experienced since entering McCune. He has learned to deal with his prejudice in a fashion that permitted friendships to be established interracially.

He did so well in the McCune School that he was selected for Resident of the Week on three occasions. His grades reflect this:

English	B+	Math	A
Science	A	Social Studies	A
Physical Ed	A	Citizenship	A
Vocational Preparation	A		

There were no problems in the community, and Michael spent almost all of his furlough time with his parents. On one occasion, his mother brought Michael back to McCune early because they saw and spoke with an individual who was associated with the victim. The resident and his mother were fearful that this individual would accuse Michael of some indiscretion, so he wanted to check back in at McCune. No complaints were received.

The only medical problem was the result of Michael striking a glass hallway window and putting his hand through it on the weekend of June 26, 2007, following a verbal altercation with another resident. Michael was taken to the hospital where he received both stitches and a medical furlough.

IV. FAMILY SITUATION AND RELATIONSHIPS

Michael is an only child and lives at the above address with his parents, Charles and Barbara DeWitt; his relationship with his parents has improved significantly while being at McCune. Barbara DeWitt has attended virtually every Family Group Therapy session. As a result, mother and child have moderated their interactions; previously, they were characterized by emotional exaggeration. Michael earned all but two possible home visits.

V. DIAGNOSIS AND PLAN OF TREATMENT

Michael has completed all four of the phases of the program. He has made great strides in the areas of authority, peer interaction, school and family relationships. Possible problems in the future will involve his reputation for sexual acting out, although this has not yet been the case. He has been on furlough and attended Newtown High School.

VI. SPECIFIC RECOMMENDATION

Michael has successfully completed his 3-week furlough period. McCune staff, as well as his family, feel Michael is ready to return home. It is, therefore, recommended that Michael DeWitt be placed on Conditional Release and receive the services of an Aftercare Worker.

Carol Spalding

Carol Spalding

Juvenile Probation Officer

FIGURE 4.9 *Request for Conditional Release/Aftercare*

A Closer Look

Juvenile Reentry/Aftercare Authority

Court Control

The laws of only 4 states—Alabama, Idaho, Iowa, and Pennsylvania—provide for reentry supervision by probation officers working as agents of the courts.

Shared Control

In 17 states, postrelease supervision is a joint responsibility:

- In Mississippi, Nevada, North Carolina, Ohio, Tennessee, and Virginia, state agents provide the supervision, but local courts hear allegations of parole violations and determine whether they merit the offender's return to the commitment institution.
- In Georgia, Kansas, Minnesota, New York, Virginia, and Wisconsin, the state handles juvenile reentry in some counties, while local courts and probation departments take responsibility in others. In some of these states, such as Kansas and Virginia, juvenile courts also hear and resolve allegations of parole violations, even for state-supervised juveniles.
- In Arkansas, Florida, Indiana, Ohio, and West Virginia, while the state commitment agency generally oversees juvenile parole, the local committing court has the power to inject itself into the reentry process by placing a committed juvenile on postrelease probation—either at the time of the original disposition or at the time of release.

Corrections Control

In the remaining 29 states plus the District of Columbia, supervision of juveniles following release from state commitments is entirely the responsibility of the agency that oversees the state's commitment institutions.

Source: Griffin, 2005.

ADMINISTRATION OF JUVENILE SERVICES

The administration of juvenile services is complex, with different levels and branches of government sharing responsibility. Juvenile probation is administered by the juvenile court in most states, although a few have a statewide executive branch agency administering juvenile probation. State institutions for delinquent juveniles are always in the executive branch; however, states vary the type of executive department in which they choose to place the responsibility for juvenile corrections: the social service department (e.g., Michigan), the corrections department (e.g., Illinois), or separate departments for either family and children's services or youth services (e.g., Idaho Department of Juvenile Corrections). The 168 juvenile probation agencies in Texas are monitored by the Texas Juvenile Probation Commission (TJPC), which sets standards and provides technical assistance to guarantee uniformity of services. The TJPC also monitors juvenile facilities through audits and unannounced visits to ensure health and safety conditions are in compliance. States without a specialized youth authority/commission typically have their juvenile facilities under the auspices of the same department that is responsible for incarcerating adults. In Illinois, for example, the Juvenile Division of the Department of Corrections receives delinquents adjudicated in juvenile court and those youngsters tried as adults in criminal court. (From 1954 to 1970, these were responsibilities of the Illinois Youth Commission, which was subsequently abolished.) The Juvenile Division provides secure custody and rehabilitation programs to about 1,500 youths, 13 to 21 years of age, in six centers statewide that range from minimum to maximum security. Annual cost per resident is between $25,000 and $40,000. (By way of comparison, average annual costs in the state of Washington are more than $45,000.)

JUVENILES IN CRIMINAL COURT

During the 1990s, legislation in nearly every state transformed the juvenile justice system. "Most notably, the jurisdiction of the juvenile courts over serious crimes, older juveniles, and repeat offenders has been cut back in State after State. The pool of cases eligible for criminal court handling has been vastly expanded" (Torbet et al., 2000: 1).

Transfer to Criminal Court

About 20,000 juvenile cases a year are transferred to criminal court (Figure 4.10), with juvenile court judges accounting for about half of the transfers. Most (but not all) states require transfer hearings before a waiver of jurisdiction to criminal court. "Although the

---

STATE OF INDIANA
COUNTY OF GRANT JUVENILE DIVISION

IN THE MATTER OF
Michael Silver; DOB: 8/14/92

A CHILD ALLEGED TO BE DELINQUENT
PROSECUTOR'S MOTION FOR WAIVER OF JUVENILE JURISDICTION

The State of Indiana, by the undersigned Deputy Prosecuting Attorney, hereby alleges and represents to the Court as follows:

1. That said child, Michael Silver, was born on the 14th day of August in the year 1992 and was fourteen (14) years of age or older, and under eighteen (18) years of age, at the time of the charged offense.

2. That said child is subject to the jurisdiction of the Juvenile Court herein by virtue of a Petition Alleging Delinquency having been filed on the 4th day of March in the year 2007.

3. That the act charged would be an offense if committed by an adult, to wit: ATTEMPTED MURDER.

4. That said offense charged is:

   (x) heinous or of an aggravated character;

   (x) an act against person;

   (x) part of a repetitive pattern of offenses (even though less serious in nature) in that the child has heretofore been arrested and/or adjudicated for: UNLAWFUL POSSESSION OF A FIREARM.

5. That there is probable cause to believe that said child committed the offense charged herein, and that said child is beyond re-habilitation under the juvenile justice system, and that it is in the best interest of the safety and welfare of the community that said child be required to stand trial as an adult, and that a waiver of juvenile jurisdiction is sought under the provisions of I.C. 31-6-2-4(b).

   WHEREFORE, your petitioner requests that a hearing be set by the Court to determine whether juvenile jurisdiction should be waived herein, and that after said hearing that the Court waive juvenile jurisdiction over the offense charged herein to the Criminal Court of Grant County, a Court that would have jurisdiction over the offense charged if that act were committed by an adult, and said waiver to be for the offense charged, and any lesser included offenses.
   Dated this 6th day of April, 2007.

   John L. Jamisen
   John L. Jamisen
   Deputy Prosecuting Attorney

FIGURE 4.10 *Waiver of Jurisdiction*
Source: Grant County, Indiana, Juvenile Division.

term 'transfer' refers to three general mechanisms, only one (judicial waiver) actually involves the transfer of a juvenile from the juvenile court to the adult criminal court. Cases that follow the other two paths may never pass through the juvenile court system" (*OJJDP Research 2000*, 2001: 9). Every jurisdiction in the United States has one or more of these three basic mechanisms (five states use them all):

1. *Statutory exclusion.* Statutory provisions exclude certain crimes from the jurisdiction of the juvenile court. Some states exclude only the most serious offenses against persons, such as murder, rape, or robbery with a firearm. In addition to the most serious crimes against persons, some states exclude traffic, boating, fish and game, and other minor violations, which typically do not involve incarceration. This approach is a purely classical one used in more than 30 states (Steiner and Wright, 2006).

2. *Judicial waiver.* Almost all states authorize juvenile court judges to "waive" (transfer) their jurisdiction over certain juvenile offenders, usually on a motion by the prosecutor (Puzzanchera, 2001). This discretion is limited by statutory criteria regarding such factors as age, type of offense, prior record, amenability to treatment, and dangerousness: "[L]egislative exclusion uses the seriousness of the offense to control decisions about adult status, whereas judicial waiver relies upon clinical assessments of amenability to treatment or dangerousness to decide child versus adult status" (Feld, 1992: 66).

Key Fact

Juveniles may be transferred to criminal court by statutory exclusion, judicial waiver, or prosecutorial discretion.

3. *Prosecutorial discretion.* In about 15 states, prosecutors can charge juveniles in either juvenile or adult courts. This discretionary power may be limited by statutory criteria regarding age and type of offense (Steiner and Wright, 2006).

"In most instances when a transfer request is denied, the case is then scheduled for an adjudicatory hearing in juvenile court" (Butts et al., 1996: 13).

The state of Florida, in a dramatic move toward a justice model, enacted legislation in 1981 that provides prosecutors with almost unlimited discretion—"when the public interest requires it"—to transfer 16- and 17-year-olds to criminal court. A study of transfer practices in Florida revealed that the direct transfer provisions have seldom been used for the serious and chronic offenders for whom transfer is arguably justified. In fact, the study found that relatively few cases are subjected to direct transfer provisions and that "many of those who are transferred seem inappropriate" (Bishop, Frazier, and Henretta, 1989: 195). In 1978, New York enacted the Juvenile Offender Law, considered at the time to be among the toughest in the country—children as young as 13 can be tried in criminal court. In practice, however, most juvenile cases sent to criminal court have resulted in dismissal or probation. In his study of a sample of juvenile offenders transferred to criminal court in New York and New Jersey, Aaron Kupchik (2006) found that after controlling for severity of offense there was little difference in the sentences imposed.

There is research indicating a lack of significant differences in sentence outcome for youngsters adjudicated in juvenile court and those tried in criminal court, controlling for the severity of the offense. The juvenile court is not as lenient as its critics would have it; furthermore, minors are likely to be looked at differently by prosecutors, probation officers, and judges in the criminal courts. They are younger than most defendants, and even jurors may view a young person in criminal court differently. In the cases examined, there were more findings of "not guilty" in the criminal court than in the juvenile court. "The labeling process may be different in the two courts. While a minor may be looked upon as a hardened criminal in the juvenile court, (s)he may be viewed as a mere innocent youngster in criminal court" (Sagatun, McCollum, and Edwards, 1985: 87).

In part, these outcomes may be the result of the types of cases being transferred to criminal court. A study in Cook County (Chicago), for example, revealed that 66 percent of the 393 youngsters transferred to adult court in 1999 had been charged with nonviolent drug offenses, and 61 percent had no previous prior juvenile convictions at all ("Youth Justice, Separate and Unequal," 2000). In another study, more than 90 percent of

A Closer Look

Getting Tough Works—For Politicians

"Commit an adult crime; do adult time." It rhymes and it sounds good in a political speech. Unfortunately, just because something rhymes does not necessarily make it good policy (Klein, 1998). If the rationale for enacting legislation to require youth to be prosecuted as adults because of specific offenses is to deter them from further criminal activity, the legislation is ineffective, as demonstrated by the recent recidivism research in Florida. If, however, the intent of the legislation is to provide the illusion that politicians are concerned about juvenile crime and that they are taking action to deal with the problem, then the recent spate of legislation is a success (Merlo, Benekos, and Cook, 1997).

A Closer Look

Imprisoning Juveniles

"[W]hen [the juvenile offender] is released back into the community in his twenties—under-educated, unsocialized, unemployable, and at the peak of his physical power—he will be the very model of the very person we wished most to avoid" (Dighton, 1997: 12). In 1994, voters in Oregon passed Measure 11, which requires youngsters 15 to 17 charged with certain serious crimes to be tried in adult court. If convicted, they must be imprisoned—they cannot receive probation—and are not eligible for early release for good behavior or parole.

the judicial waiver or prosecutorial discretion cases tried in adult court resulted in guilty verdicts, with fines or probation imposed on half the convicted juveniles. In one jurisdiction, "property offenders with a long history of property offenses tend to receive a substantially lighter sentence in adult court than they would have received when moving up the ladder in juvenile court. Conversely, personal and aggravated personal offenders with few prior offenses received significantly more punitive treatment in adult court than did comparable offenders in juvenile court" (Barnes and Franz, 1989: 133). And a study of juveniles sentenced in criminal court in Pennsylvania found that, compared to other young adult offenders (ages 18 to 24), being a juvenile exerts "a significant influence on courtroom decision-making, resulting in a substantial juvenile penalty" (Kurlychek and Johnson 2004; 506): Juveniles received more severe sentences than their adult counterparts.

Blended Sentence

A more recent approach to juvenile dispositions is highlighted by legislation that took effect in Minnesota in 1995, creating a new sentencing category for the serious juvenile offender: the **blended sentence**. These offenders are tried as juveniles but given full due process protections, including the right to a jury trial. If convicted, they are given an adult sentence, which is applied *only* in the event they do not satisfactorily complete the juvenile court disposition (Stevenson et al., 1996). In some states (e.g., California and Florida), the case is tried in criminal court, which has the authority to impose a juvenile or adult sanction; in other states, the case is adjudicated in either juvenile or criminal court, but the sentencing judge can impose a sanction involving the juvenile or adult correctional system (Torbet et al., 1996).

A youth tried in adult criminal court, depending on the state, may be sent to an institution operated by the same agency with responsibility for adults—a department of correction—or to a specialized agency that provides institutionalization for juveniles and young adults. For example, the Illinois Department of Corrections has a Juvenile Division that receives delinquents and juvenile offenders who have not reached their twenty-first birthday; at age 21, they may be transferred to an adult facility. In California, a judge has the option to sentence offenders 16 to 20 years of age to state prison but order them housed in a California Youth Authority (discussed earlier) facility until their twenty-fifth birthday or expiration of their sentence, whichever occurs first. Offenders under 16 years of age in New York are sent to a facility operated by the Office of Children and Family Services (discussed previously), whereas those who have reached their sixteenth birthday are sent to a reformatory operated by the Department of Correctional Services.

Both conventional wisdom and research have revealed that juvenile offenders in adult facilities present a significant management problem for institutional officials. One study, for example, found that compared with other young inmates, "imprisoned juvenile offenders exhibited significant adjustment problems in the institutional environment" (McShane and Williams, 1989: 266). Juvenile correctional facilities are often quite inadequate. In 1998, in an agreement with the U.S. Department of Justice, the state of Georgia promised to reform "egregious," "abusive," and "grossly substandard" conditions in its juvenile prisons. Similar agreements or court orders have impacted juvenile prisons in Kentucky and Louisiana (Butterfield, 1998b, 1998c). Relatively few facilities exist for the most violent adolescents; as a result, youths are often released after less than 1 year of confinement (Treaster, 1994b). Tens of thousands of offenders younger than the age of 18 are now confined in adult correctional facilities. In response to the problem of mixing adolescents with adult offenders, prison officials in many states are attempting to segregate this population: "At the core of their response is the realization that teenagers in adult prisons are vulnerable to sexual assault and physical assault and that being around older inmates can turn youthful offenders into hardened criminals" (Rimer, 2001: 13). At the other end of the problem, youthful offenders can be hard to control and a threat to older inmates.

In Part Two, we will move our discussion to adult prisons and parole.

KEY TERMS

adjudicatory hearing (p. 94)
aftercare (p. 123)
blended sentence (p. 129)
child-saving movement (p. 83)
guardian *ad litem* (p. 92)
houses of refuge (p. 82)
informal probation (p. 91)
intake (p. 88)
justice model (p. 105)
least restrictive alternative (p. 111)
legal function (p. 89)

parens patriae (p. 83)
petition (p. 94)
predisposition report (p. 94)
Project RISE (p. 115)
residential treatment center (RTC) (p. 118)
social service function (p. 90)
social services model (p. 105)
status offenders (p. 84)
training school (p. 119)
youth authority (p. 120)

INTERNET CONNECTIONS

American Bar Association Juvenile Justice Center: abanet.org/crimjust/ juvjus/home.html

Council of Juvenile Correctional Administrators: cjca.net

National Center for Juvenile Justice: ncjj.org

National Council of Juvenile and Family Court Judges: ncjfcj.org

National Institute of Corrections: nicic.org

Office of Juvenile Justice and Delinquency Prevention: ojjdp.ncjrs.org

REVIEW QUESTIONS

1. During the twentieth century, what was the attitude toward children in America?
2. How does the juvenile court differ from the criminal court?
3. What is the traditional philosophy of the system of justice used for juveniles in the United States?
4. What were houses of refuge?
5. Who are the child savers? Why are they controversial, and what did their efforts accomplish?
6. How does the terminology used in the juvenile court reflect its philosophy?
7. Why should the juvenile court not punish children?
8. What led to the establishment of the juvenile court?
9. What is the justice model in juvenile court?
10. Why does the juvenile court represent a manifestation of positivist theory?
11. How does the concept of *parens patriae* conflict with due process?
12. What are the four different types of cases that may come under the jurisdiction of a juvenile court?
13. What is the purpose of a preliminary hearing in juvenile court?
14. What is informal probation in juvenile court?
15. What is the purpose of an adjudicatory hearing in juvenile court?
16. What is contained in a predisposition report, and what is its purpose?
17. What are the responsibilities of a juvenile court intake officer?
18. Why is it particularly difficult to be a judge in juvenile court?
19. Why are the juvenile services provided to girls usually inferior to those provided to boys?
20. What is a blended sentence?
21. What is a "waiver" of juvenile court jurisdiction?
22. What are the different ways of transferring a juvenile to criminal court?
23. What did the Supreme Court rule in the case of *Kent v. United States*?
24. What rights did the *Gault* decision provide respondents accused of delinquency in juvenile court?
25. According to the *Winship* decision, what is the standard of proof required in a delinquency proceeding?
26. What did the *McKeiver* decision rule with respect to jury trials in juvenile court?
27. What was the issue in *Breed v. Jones,* and what did the court rule?

28. What are the unintended consequences of providing youngsters greater due process rights in juvenile court?
29. What is meant by the phrase "the least restrictive alternative"?
30. What is a group home?
31. What are the advantages of community-based day treatment?
32. What is the difference between a training school and a residential treatment center?
33. What are the purposes of juvenile aftercare?
34. What is a youth authority?
35. What agencies provide juvenile aftercare services?
36. What are the sentencing options for youth convicted in criminal court?
37. What are the problems associated with placing youngsters in correctional institutions as if they were adults?

Parole

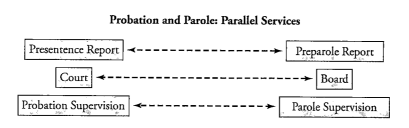

Probation and Parole: Parallel Services

The American Prison System

The degree of civilization in a society is revealed by entering its prisons.

—*Dostoyevsky*, The House of the Dead

Chapter Outline

Compared with citizens of other industrialized nations, Americans tend to be more religious and entrepreneurial. We have more millionaires, we are the world leader in Nobel Prizes, and we send more people to universities—and prisons—than any other Western nation (Murphy, 2001). To understand the development of parole and its current state, we need to appreciate the crisis in American prisons and the history of the American prison system.

AMERICA'S PRISON CRISIS

Whom will we find upon entering America's prisons? About 1.5 million persons[1] (and jails hold another 750,000): About 93 percent are male; almost half are black, and about 20 percent are Hispanic; more than 60 percent are younger than 30 years of age; about 70 percent have not completed high school, and about 40 percent are unable to read; more than 20 percent are incarcerated for a drug offense, and most inmates have a history of substance abuse; about one-half grew up primarily in one-parent households; and many have been victims of neglect and/or child abuse. A federal study (Widom and Maxfield, 2001: 1) revealed that "being abused or neglected as a child increased the likelihood of arrest as a juvenile by 59 percent, as an adult by 28 percent, and for a violent crime by nearly 30 percent." About one-half of prison inmates were unemployed or employed only part-time at the time of their arrest. A majority are parents of a child younger than the age of 18. *In America's prisons are persons who are poorer, darker, younger, and less educated than the rest of the population.*

Key Fact

The United States leads the Western world in the percentage of residents who are incarcerated.

It should come as no surprise that America leads the industrial world in the percentage of its citizens who are incarcerated while having the widest gap between rich and poor (Bradsher, 1995b; Myers, 1995). The rate of incarceration for the United States is about 740 per 100,000 adults, compared to less than 100 per 100,000 for most Western European countries and less than 40 per 100,000 for Japan (U.S. Department of Justice figures).[2]

What will we find upon entering America's correctional institutions? A system not capable of managing such a large population in a manner that meets constitutional standards. In 2003, state prisons were operating at between 1 percent and 17 percent above capacity (Harrison and Beck, 2003). Despite a significant decline in the crime rate since 1992, by 2000 the incarceration rate (jails and prisons) was 702 per 100,000 persons, more than double the 1985 rate of 313 (Beck 2000a, 2000b; Beck and Karberg, 2001); today that figure is 740. While there were 592 state and federal prisons in 1974, that number grew to 1,023 by 2000. In 1923, there were only 61 (Butterfield, 2004a). State prisons now house more than 1.2 million inmates, about 115 percent above their design capacity, while the federal prison system is operating at 134 percent over capacity. Jails house an additional 750,000 prisoners.

In Oklahoma, which rates fourth in the percentage of its residents who are incarcerated (above Alabama and below Louisiana, Texas, and Mississippi), whenever the prison population exceeds 95 percent of capacity, inmates who have served at least 15 percent of their sentence and are within 1 year of their parole consideration date can be released. Legislation to accomplish this release was necessary because of the severity of overcrowding—previously the state was simply releasing inmates without benefit of parole supervision. In Florida, if the prison population reaches 98 percent for a period of 7 consecutive days, the Department of Corrections has authority to release certain inmates who meet established criteria. In Connecticut, the prison population went from 3,600 in 1980 to more than 19,000 in 2005; a state law mandates the immediate release of 10 percent of the prison population if the number of male prisoners exceeds 110 percent of capacity for 30 consecutive days. In Texas in 2000, the legislature balked at a $500 million bond proposal for building three new maximum-security units to deal with chronic overcrowding and pushed the parole board to liberalize its guidelines and release more inmates—and it worked. The Texas inmate population in July 2001 was 146,855, down from a peak of 153,500 in July 2000, but it is now about 170,000. In 2004, Arkansas officials released almost 700 inmates to ease overcrowding and adhere to a court-ordered maximum—another 800 were being housed in local and county jails awaiting transfer to state prisons ("Arkansas: Early Release for 630 Inmates," 2004). Security problems

---

[1] In 1985, the number was less than a half-million persons.
[2] "From the 1960s to the early 1970s, the prison population was slowly but steadily shrinking by about one percent a year. While the U.S. incarceration rate historically has been higher than that of other Western countries, it was not until the 1970s and 1980s that it began to radically exceed them" (Gottschalk, 2006: 4).

generated by overcrowding are exacerbated by America's antiquated prisons. In Illinois, for example, the "newest" maximum-security prison was opened in 1920.

Along with many other states and the federal government, Illinois opened a super-max prison—built at a cost of $73 million, with operating expenses for each of the 500 inmates averaging about $35,000 per year—because the overcrowded state prisons "had become so violent and so overrun by gangs . . . that prison staff were no longer safe" (Eig, 1998: 62). Reflecting a return to the Pennsylvania system (discussed later), supermax inmates spend 23 hours per day in a solitary 7-foot-by-14-foot concrete cell equipped with a sink, toilet, desk, stool, and sleep platform. The steel door's bottom and sides contain strips to muffle sounds so that inmates cannot communicate with one another. Once a day they leave their cells for 1 hour of solitary exercise. There are more than 30 of these prisons in operation, and they contain more than 20,000 inmates (Kluger, 2007).

A Closer Look

Prison Overcrowding in California

By 2007, California's prison population was at an all-time high: More than 173,000 inmates were in a system designed for 100,000 and were subjected to double bunking; more than 16,000 inmates were housed in prison gyms and day rooms throughout the various 33 correctional institutions. Conditions are so bad that the state has been unable to fill 4,000 correctional officer vacancies. A federal judge ordered the state to ease the overcrowding, and in 2007 Governor Arnold Schwarzenegger declared a state of emergency and created a commission to review California's sentencing system. Later that year, the legislature approved the largest single prison construction program in the nation's history—$8.3 billion dollars—and agreed to send 8,000 inmates to other states (Steinhauer, 2007).

A tremendous increase in the number of prison facilities and the expansion of existing facilities during the last few years—in excess of 30,000 beds—have not had a significant impact. At any one time, 35,000 inmates are being housed in local jails because of a lack of state prison space, and many jails are also under court order to reduce overcrowding. For a decade, spending on prisons has been the fastest-growing or second-fastest-growing part of state budgets (competing with education). The bills have arrived for those tough crime laws.

The economic realities of imprisonment began to loom large as declining state revenues intertwined with a critical shortage of corrections officers. In response, many systems are hiring officers as young as 18—the only viable alternative to substantially increasing salaries (and thus the cost of imprisonment). In some states, the problem of a shortage of corrections officers is so serious that it has contributed to prison breaks or attacks on staff (Belluck, 2001). With the second-largest prison system in the country, Texas houses more than 152,000 inmates with a budget of $8 billion. The state has been unable to hire and retain experienced corrections officers sufficient to provide an adequate level of protection for staff, inmates, and the public and has a shortage of about 2,600 officers and a 25 percent annual turnover rate. Many officers have not received the required in-service training. This was highlighted in 2001 when seven inmates escaped from a maximum-security prison and subsequently killed a police officer during a robbery. How did we reach this crisis? The historical review in this chapter and Chapter 6 is designed to help answer this question.

Key Fact

Spending on prisons has been the fastest- or second-fastest-growing part of state budgets, yet prisons continue to be overcrowded.

ORIGINS OF THE AMERICAN SYSTEM OF PRISONS

The American colonies inherited the English approach to crime and punishment. The English system of laws into the eighteenth century impresses one with the extent to which the death penalty was used, often for seemingly minor offenses: "Thus it is believed that Henry VIII [1491–1547] executed 72,000 thieves and vagabonds during his reign"; under George III (1738–1820), as many as 220 offenses were punishable by death (Hall, 1952: 116). By 1780, 350 capital crimes existed, most of which were for property offenses (Lilly and Ball, 1987).[3] At the same time, England established institutional approaches to the elderly and the infirm, vagrants, beggars, homeless children, and certain criminals: gaols, bridewells, and houses of correction (Hirsch, 1992).

Local jails emerged throughout the American colonies, usually under management of a sheriff. These poorly constructed institutions, David Rothman (1971: 56) notes, "were not only unlikely places for intimidating the criminal, but even ill-suited for confining him." Escapes were frequent. In Massachusetts, under Puritan rule, fines and corporal punishment—stocks, pillory, lashes, and dunking—prevailed, while capital punishment was relatively rare (Hirsch, 1992).

Dramatically different conditions in England and the colonies resulted in differing needs, which affected the response to criminals. In England, land was scarce and an excess labor supply had the potential for political and social unrest. "As a matter of policy," notes Bradley Chapin, "it must have seemed that no great harm was done if the hangman thinned the horde of vagrant Englishmen. In the colonies, the need for labor urged the use of penalties that might bring redemption" (1983: 9). Consequently, beginning with William Penn in 1682, the use of capital punishment in the American colonies was severely restricted and virtually banned for property crimes (Melossi and Pavarini, 1981).

In Pennsylvania, however, Quakers were in an economic quandary: British law was so severe that colonial juries would often find defendants not guilty rather than subject them to the extreme punishments in place for property offenses. "In this way, criminals had escaped all discipline, and the community had allowed, even encouraged, them to persist in their ways" (Rothman, 1971: 60). It was Quaker property that was often at risk in Philadelphia, where their Calvinist urgings—honesty, thrift, and hard work—resulted in economic success as a rising commercial class. (For the relationship between Calvinism and economic success, see Weber, 1958.) The use of imprisonment provided a way to mete out punishment in a manner that was proportionate to the severity of the offense, a classical concept. This appealed to both the humanitarian and economic concerns of the Quakers, who rejected the Calvinist belief in the immutability of human character in favor of redemption (Hirsch, 1992).

Three intertwined developments led to the establishment of the American system of prisons: religious doctrine, the American Revolution, and classicalism. Thorsten Sellin states, "[C]redit for the gradual substitution of imprisonment for corporal and capital punishments must go to the [classical] philosophers of the 18th century" (1967: 19). After the Revolution, repugnance for things British inspired Americans to discard corporal punishment in favor of imprisonment, a process that was complete at about the time of the Civil War. The type of imprisonment that resulted had its origins in quasi-Calvinist socioreligious doctrine, which can be seen in the life of John Howard (1726–1790), who coined the term **penitentiary** as a place to do penance, and the work of Quaker reformers in Philadelphia and New York (Teeters, 1970).

Prison history in the United States can be arranged in terms of five overlapping eras:

1. Pennsylvania—circa 1790
2. New York/Auburn—circa 1820
3. Big House—circa 1930
4. Corrections—circa 1945
5. Just deserts—circa 1975

These will be covered in the following sections.

---

[3]In practice, however, there was extensive use of pardons and the dismissal of indictments for technical reasons (Kelman, 1987).

Pennsylvania System

Walnut Street and Other Early Prisons

The first prison in the United States was authorized by the Connecticut legislature in 1773, and that same year the colony converted an abandoned copper mine into a prison for serious offenders (Durham, 1989c). Newgate (not to be confused with a New York prison by the same name) consisted of a wooden lodging house for communal habitation built about 20 feet below the surface. The first keeper, a retired military officer, lived across the road, and a lack of security personnel presented a problem. Within 3 weeks of receiving its first prisoner, the prisoner managed to escape, and escapes continued to plague Newgate. As opposed to early prisons established elsewhere, no reformative or rehabilitative agenda existed, and it was expected that the prison would be self-supporting. In the early days of the prison, miners were hired to provide inmate instruction, but mining failed to achieve a profit. Other trades were initiated but also failed to achieve any level of economic success. The Revolutionary War and a rash of violent incidents led to the closing of Newgate in 1782; it reopened in 1790 as a Connecticut state prison (Durham, 1989c).

By 1762, Quaker reformers in Philadelphia were successful in having the list of capital offenses limited and in substituting fines and imprisonment for torture and execution for many offenses; in 1786, the Pennsylvania legislature enacted penal reform to replace capital punishment for certain crimes. The law called for convicted felons who were lodged in the Walnut Street Jail to be subjected to hard labor "publicly and disgracefully imposed . . . in streets of cities and towns, and upon the highways of the open country and other public works" (Atherton, 1987: 1). With shaved heads and bizarre dress and with heavy metal balls and chains riveted to their ankles, the convicts working in the streets drew the ridicule and abuse of passing crowds—the work was both onerous and humiliating. However, Paul Takagi (1975) states that convicts working in the city streets drew large crowds of sympathetic people, including friends and relatives of the prisoners. They made contact and, at times, received liquor and other goods. In any event, at the urging of Benjamin Rush, the Philadelphia Society for Alleviating the Miseries of the Public Prisons (later renamed the Philadelphia Prison Society and then the Pennsylvania Prison Society) was formed at the home of Benjamin Franklin in 1787. In 1789, the society succeeded in having the 1786 law repealed.

John Howard, the son of a Calvinist merchant, was born in England in 1726. His interest in penal reform led him to publish *The State of the Prisons* a year after the American Declaration of Independence. Because of his strong religious commitment, Howard influenced other religiously endowed reformers, the Quakers of the Philadelphia Society for Alleviating the Miseries of the Public Prisons, with whom he was in contact. As a result, in 1790 a law was enacted creating a penitentiary in a portion of the Walnut Street Jail, and the jail became a state prison based on a Calvinist model of hard labor, isolation, and religious study (Atherton, 1987).[4]

At Walnut Street, most inmates were confined in separate cells and released to work in a courtyard during the day at a variety of tasks—handicrafts, such as weaving and shoemaking, and routine labor, such as beating hemp and sawing logwood—all in total silence. The "hardened and atrocious offenders," persons who formerly would have been whipped, mutilated, or executed, were confined in isolation and almost total darkness with nothing but a Bible: "The old Quakers, sensitive as they were to the inflicting of bodily pain, seem to have been unable to form in their minds an image of the fearful mental torture of solitude in idleness" (Wines, 1975: 152). These convicts were blindfolded on arrival and remained in their cells until released; they never saw another inmate. Inspectors from the Prison Society provided oversight at Walnut Street and had the authority to hire and fire penitentiary officials.

Key Fact

The Pennsylvania system featured solitary confinement to prevent fraternization between prisoners and to promote penitence.

---

[4]Takagi (1975) states that it was the Episcopalians of the Philadelphia Society who argued for hard labor, while the Quakers stressed solitary confinement.

Solitary confinement was seen as a way of preventing fraternization between prisoners, behavior that would only lead to the spread of evil inclinations among inmates. In 1833, two European observers reported, "If it is true that in establishments of this nature, all evil originates from the intercourse of the prisoners among themselves, we are obliged to acknowledge that nowhere is this vice avoided with greater safety than at Philadelphia, where the prisoners find themselves utterly unable to communicate with each other; and it is incontestable that this perfect isolation secures the prison from all fatal contamination" (Beaumont and de Tocqueville, 1964: 57).

John Howard and the Quakers shared a common religious lifestyle that led them to favor imprisonment as a form of purgatory, "a forced withdrawal from the distractions of the senses into silent and solitary confrontation with the self." It was out of solitude and silence that the convict "would begin to hear the inner voice of conscience and feel the transforming of God's love" (Ignatieff, 1978: 58).[5]

News of the "success" of Walnut Street attracted many persons from other states and countries. One of these visitors was a Quaker from New York, Thomas Eddy (1758–1827), who had been imprisoned briefly as a Tory during the Revolutionary War. A successful businessman, he was able to devote himself to philanthropy. Eddy was influenced by what he saw in Philadelphia—orderly and humane management, and claims of success in making the streets of Philadelphia safer—and as a result of his efforts, New York constructed its first penitentiary in Greenwich Village, a then-rural part of what is now lower Manhattan. Newgate was named after the famous British prison, and Eddy became its first agent. Consistent with the prevailing belief of prison reformers, Eddy maintained that the goal of deterrence required inflicting pain on criminal offenders (Lewis, 1965). However, he discarded the idea that it was necessary to keep inmates in solitary all day; instead, convicts slept in congregate rooms measuring 12 feet by 18 feet and housing eight inmates. Fourteen cells for solitary confinement were used as punishment for violating prison rules. Eddy encouraged religious worship, established a night school, and approved of provisions in the law that prohibited corporal punishment at Newgate. Despite improvements in treatment at the prison, in 1802 a bloody riot and mass escape attempt required calling in the military. In response to these developments, Eddy recommended that future penitentiaries use single cells for all inmates at night and shops where they could work in strict silence during the day. His suggestions were incorporated into a new prison that was built in Auburn, New York.

Eddy either was removed because of political considerations (Lewis, 1965) or resigned in protest when, in 1803, the state turned the prison industries over to a private contractor (McKelvey, 1972). In either event, difficulties increased at Newgate, and a return to flogging was legislated in 1819 (Lewis, 1965). Although it was built to house less than 450 prisoners, by 1821 the population had reached 817 and was kept in check only by a liberal use of "good time" laws and pardons ("Newgate," 1998). In 1828, the penitentiary was abandoned in favor of a newly completed prison at Ossining: Sing Sing.

Key Fact

The demise of early prisons, Newgate and Walnut Street, was due to overcrowding.

In Philadelphia, overcrowding caused the demise of Walnut Street. Industry and isolation became unworkable in the congested prison, discipline lapsed, and riots ensued (McKelvey, 1972). "While the original inspectors were still active in the oversight of the prison, thus preventing rampant corruption of guards and overseers," there was little they could do to prevent the decline of conditions at the institution. "The funds needed to create a system of solitary confinement were simply greater than had been anticipated" (Dumm, 1987: 105).

After Walnut Street

The Pennsylvania Prison Society succeeded in having prisons built in Pittsburgh (Western State Penitentiary opened in 1826) and in the Cherry Hill section of Philadelphia (Eastern State Penitentiary opened in 1829). These institutions featured massive stone walls, 30 feet high and 12 feet thick, around a building that branched out from a central rotunda like the spokes of a wheel—architecture influenced by the panopticon penitentiary, a circular

---

[5]The traditional form of Quaker worship is based on silent meditation, a turning inward to hear one's inner voice.

design advanced by the British classical philosopher Jeremy Bentham (1748–1832). The design has a guardhouse at the center and prevented prisoner contact; inmates remained in their 12-by-7-feet-wide, 16-feet-high cells and work area, except for 1 hour of exercise in a yard also designed to prevent inmate contact. Prisoners could not see one another, even at Sunday religious services, because pews were designed as individual cubicles.

The **Pennsylvania system** "isolated each prisoner for the entire period of his confinement. According to its blueprint, convicts were to eat, work, and sleep in individual cells. They were to leave the institution as ignorant of the identity of other convicts as on the day they entered" (Rothman, 1971: 82). In addition,

> The guiding principles were punishment and reformation through penitence: The convicted prisoner was to be kept totally separated from other prisoners, but not from human contact. The avenue to reform was through repentance— the true and deep recognition of one's "sins" and acceptance of God's leadership in one's life. It was obvious that prisoners left totally alone would be unable to follow this path; for this, guidance was needed, good examples, people who could help the convict accept responsibility for his/her crimes and embark on the difficult path of repentance and redemption. (Atherton, 1987: 7)

Guidance and role models were provided by four groups of people: prison staff, chaplains, officials of the Prison Society, and the Board of Inspectors.

The penitentiary reached its apex during the 1830s; facilities proliferated, and "visitors traveled great distances to view American prisons in action" (Hirsch, 1992: 112). It was during this period that the French philosopher/politician Alexis de Tocqueville (1805–1859), most noted for his *Democracy in America* (1835), traveled to the United States to study its penitentiary system. Although he came away with a generally favorable view, economics would soon lead to the demise of the penitentiary, which had been adopted by only two other states, New Jersey and Rhode Island.[6] Stateville, in Illinois, which opened in 1925, has one unit based on the panopticon design—it is the only one currently in operation in the United States.

The Pennsylvania system proved expensive—the cost of constructing an institution for solitary confinement was staggering, and little profitable exploitation of inmate labor under such conditions could occur (McKelvey, 1972). Eastern Penitentiary was built to house 250 inmates at a cost of $780,000, an enormous sum in those days (Dobrzynski, 1997). At the beginning of the nineteenth century, an increasing need for labor existed: New legislation made slave trading more difficult, new territories were settled, and rapid industrialization with a corresponding increase in wages occurred. Prisons with solitary confinement deprived the market of needed labor (Melossi and Pavarini, 1981). As a result, most states patterned their prisons after the next great milestone in American prison history, an institution suggested by Thomas Eddy which became the world's most frequently copied prison. Even New Jersey and Rhode Island abandoned the Pennsylvania model. Beginning in the 1850s, the isolation of prisoners at Eastern State Penitentiary was breaking down, and inmates began sharing cells: "In 1913 the system, which had become so diluted as to be unrecognizable, was officially abolished and from then on, it became just another Auburn-type prison" (Teeters, 1970: 11).[7]

Key Fact

Issues of cost led to the demise of the Pennsylvania system.

Auburn/New York System

Auburn, New York, present day population about 28,000, is 30 miles west of Syracuse. The prison at Auburn opened in 1819 and as designed by its first agent, featured a center comprised tiers of cell blocks (each cell measured 7 by 3.5 feet and was 7 feet high) surrounded by a vacant area (the yard), with a high wall encircling the entire institution:

---

[6]Outside the United States, however, the Pennsylvania system proved popular, and hundreds of prisons were built on this model.

[7]Eastern Penitentiary's last 28 prisoners were moved to modern quarters in 1970. It is now a national historic site and tourist attraction (Dobrzynski, 1997).

[The cells were] designed for separation by night only; the convicts were employed during the day in large workshops, in which, under the superintendency of Elam Lynds [1784–1855], formerly a captain in the army, the rule of absolute silence was enforced with unflinching sternness. Captain Lynds said that he regarded flogging as the most effective, and at the same time the most humane, of all punishments, since it did no injury to the prisoner's health and in no wise impaired his physical strength; he did not believe that a large prison could be governed without it. (Wines, 1975: 154)

Instead of replacing corporal punishment with imprisonment, as was advocated by the religious reformers, the practice of flogging became widespread in the penitentiary system—criminals were punished with imprisonment, and prisoners were punished with flogging and other forms of corporal punishment. No written regulations governed the use of the whip; guards were simply authorized to impose flogging—up to 39 lashes (the number has biblical roots)—when "absolutely necessary."

The **Auburn system** divided its inmates into three classes: The most difficult inmates were placed in solitary, a less dangerous group spent part of the day in solitude and worked the rest of the time in groups, and the "least guilty" worked together throughout the day and were separated only at night when they returned to their individual cells. As in Walnut Street, solitary confinement played havoc on the psyche—inmates jumped off tiers, cut their veins, and smashed their heads against walls. Solitary confinement in Auburn was discontinued, except as punishment for violations of prison rules (Lewis, 1965).

New Yorkers believed that the complete isolation of prisoners from arrival to release was inhumane, unnatural, and cruel. Far from reforming men, they believed such absolute solitude resulted in insanity and despair. In addition, there was the issue, perhaps more pressing, of expense to the state. Inmates restricted to their cells 24 hours per day contributed nothing to the cost of their own confinement, so the state had to provide all food, clothing, supplies, and materials to its prisoners. "If the prisoners were to learn the advantages and satisfactions of hard work and thrift, New York authorities believed, there could be no better way than to be compelled to work together in harmony. If such a system also offered the potential for inmates to grow and harvest their own vegetables, raise and butcher their own meat, make their own clothes, and manufacture other items for use or sale by the state, such a boon to the state's budget could not be reasonably ignored" (New York State Special Commission on Attica [Attica Commission], 1972: 8).

Under the system developed by Lynds, an army captain in the War of 1812 who became warden when William Brittin died in 1822, prisoners worked in small, strictly supervised units in workshops or outdoors during the daytime and returned to individual cells at night. They dressed in grotesque and ridiculous-looking black-and-white-striped uniforms and caps; they marched in complete silence, worked in complete silence, and ate in complete silence: "A breach of this rule was punished by flogging. Discipline was extremely strict in all other respects. Inmates were required to keep their eyes downcast when walking" (Erikkson, 1976: 50).

Auburn developed the infamous lockstep shuffle. Inmates stood in line, with the right foot slightly behind the left, and outstretched the right arm, with the hand on the right shoulder of the man in front; they moved together in a shuffle, sliding the left foot forward, then bringing the right foot to its position just behind the left, then the left again, and then the right. Heads had to be turned toward the "keeper" so lip movements could be detected (keepers also tiptoed shoeless up and down cell blocks to detect whispers). Citizens were encouraged to visit the prison, where for a small fee they could view the inmates, an act that was designed to cause further degradation. Prisoners were known only by number, and as in Pennsylvania, their reading matter was limited to a Bible ("Auburn Correctional Facility," 1998). Beaumont and de Tocqueville report on their visit to Auburn: "Nothing is heard in the whole prison but the steps of those who march, or the sounds proceeding from the workshops. But when the day is finished, and the prisoners have retired to their cells, the silence within these vast

Key Fact

The Auburn/New York system successfully exploited inmate labor.

walls, which contain so many prisoners, is like that of death. We have often trod during night those monotonous and dumb galleries, where a lamp is always burning; we felt as if we traversed catacombs; there were a thousand living beings, and yet it was a desert solitude" (1964: 65).

The administrators of Auburn believed their most important task was the breaking of an inmate's spirit to drive him into a state of submission. Some had differences of opinion about what to do after the "breaking" process. One school of thought stressed deterrence as its goal and was determined to derive as much economic benefit from inmate labor as possible. In fact, in the early years, Auburn actually made a net profit for the state. Another school of thought held that rehabilitation was the ultimate goal and that, after breaking, inmates should be helped through education and religion so that they could return to society better persons (Lewis, 1965).

The Auburn system consisted of an unrelenting routine of silence, hard labor, moderate meals, and solitary evenings in individual cells 6 days per week: "Their labor is not interrupted until the hour of taking food. There is not a single instant given to recreation" (Beaumont and de Tocqueville, 1964: 65). On Sundays, when there was no work, inmates attended church—in silence—where they were addressed by the prison chaplain, who stressed the American virtues of simple faith and hard work (Attica Commission, 1972). A Sunday school was established and those not participating were locked in their cells and forced to stand until lights out ("Auburn Correctional Facility," 1998).

The Auburn-style prison became the prototype for American prisons; it was cheaper to construct than those of Pennsylvania and allowed for a factory system that could make profitable use of inmate labor. The concept of reformation gradually declined; by the end of the nineteenth century, rehabilitation had virtually disappeared—prisons were viewed simply as places to keep criminals incarcerated as cheaply as possible. This view was reflected even in the name of the warden's first assistant, the "principal keeper" (Attica Commission, 1972). Prisons became bleak and silent factories with labor pools of broken people disciplined with summary floggings.[8]

Convict Labor

Imprisonment has its roots in penal servitude: "The prisons operated on the Auburn plan, in particular, were, most of them, notorious for the maltreatment of prisoners and for the excessive labor required of them in an attempt to meet the demand of legislators that prisons be self-supporting and even show a profit if possible" (Sellin, 1967: 21). The use of convict labor often made American prisons not only self-supporting institutions but also profit-making enterprises throughout the nineteenth and well into the twentieth century. Auburn Penitentiary balanced its books in 1829 and produced a profit of $1,800 in 1831; Sing Sing netted $29,000 in 1835 (Melossi and Pavarini, 1981). In Alabama, prison labor netted the state profits of almost $1 million annually, and just one prison industry manufacturing shirts in Florida netted that state almost $150,000 annually (Gillin, 1931). Minnesota's Stillwater Prison netted $25,000 annually as late as 1930 and served as a model for other northern prisons (Hagerty, 1934). In 1964, the Arkansas state penitentiary showed a net profit of nearly $500,000; it also gave rise to the scandalous conditions uncovered at the Tucker Prison Farm, which were portrayed in the motion picture *Brubaker*. However, prison industries also prevented the forced idleness that plagues many contemporary correctional institutions and helped maintain discipline.

Three systems were used to exploit convict labor:

1. *Contract system.* Under the **contract system**, convict labor was sold to private entrepreneurs who provided the necessary machinery, tools, raw materials, and (in some cases) supervisory staff. In many cases, the prison was built as a factory with walls around it: "As late as 1919 a committee of the American Prison Association re-

---

[8]Although flogging was outlawed at Auburn in 1847, it was replaced by other gruesome punishments ("Auburn Correctional Facility," 1998).

ported, after a national survey, that "most prisons worked their prisoners in a manner reminiscent of the early forms of penal servitude and that reformation was an empty word" (Sellin, 1967: 21).

2. *Lease system.* The prisoners under the **lease system** were leased out to private business interests for a fixed fee. This system was used extensively in agriculture and mining, particularly in the South. In Florida, for example, in 1877 the state "transferred the control and custody of prisoners to private contractors who could now employ them anywhere in the State. Prisoners were leased to individuals and corporations and set to work in phosphate mines and in turpentine camps in forests" (Sellin, 1967: 22). In North Carolina, as early as 1875, private employers could lease inmates as laborers; under the lease, businesses had complete responsibility for the inmates. Many worked in rock quarries and built railways. In 1901, the system was changed to provide for contract inmate labor. Inmates worked for private employers, but prison officials retained responsibility for the inmates' custody. A system of mobile camps developed that moved from worksite to worksite. In the post–Civil War South, this system exploited emancipated blacks, who provided a readily available source of cheap labor (Hallet, 2004). In some respects, this was worse than slavery: "The private contractors had no incentive to invest in the well-being of the leased inmates. After all [unlike with a slave], if a convict died, the state supplied another one for the same bargain price" (Gottschalk, 2006: 49).

3. *State use system.* Under the **state use system**, prison inmates produce goods for use or sale by state agencies, for example, office furniture and license plates. Other than that necessary for prison maintenance, this work is the most frequent form of prison labor in use today. In Texas, the agricultural division grows or raises most of the food consumed by staff and inmates, and the sale of its surpluses raises several million dollars annually (Silverman, 2001).

By 1874, the contract system was used in 20 state prisons, the lease system in 6, and a mixed system in 7 (Mohler, 1925). For wardens of the convict labor era, the ability to turn a profit was the determining factor in whether he kept his job: "The nineteenth century's most famous wardens first gained recognition because of their fiscal success" (Durham, 1989a: 127). Wardens unable to run self-sufficient institutions were replaced by legislators forced to appropriate funds to maintain the prison.

During the latter part of the nineteenth and into the twentieth century, numerous scandals involved the use of inmate labor. The growing labor union movement in the United States saw inmate labor undermining employee leverage for increased wages and improvements in working conditions. At times, inmate labor was leased out to break strikes. The National Anti-Contract Association, a manufacturers' group whose members—small businessmen—suffered from having to compete with goods produced by cheap convict labor, campaigned against the contract system. These activities resulted in laws curbing convict labor in several industrial states: Massachusetts, New York, and Pennsylvania. The federal government enacted legislation in 1887 that forbid the contracting of any federal prisoners (McKelvey, 1977).

In the states of the Confederacy, the lease system continued to be widespread into the twentieth century when, as a major reform of the Progressive era, southern states slowly began to abolish the practice, the last to do so being Alabama in 1928 (Gottschalk, 2006; Sellin, 1967). In its place, states turned to the chain gang and prison farms. Shackled together, inmates toiled on roads and built levees and railroads. Penal farms increased profits by diversifying into light industry and further reduced costs by employing inmate guards, trustees who were armed and received early release for their service. Texas continued to use (unarmed) inmate guards until a Supreme Court decision (*Ruiz v. Estelle*, 503 F.Supp. 1265, 1980) put an end to the practice.

The contract system remained widespread until the Great Depression and the passage of the Hawes-Cooper Act in 1929 and the Ashurst-Sumners Act in 1935. These federal statutes eventually curtailed interstate commerce in goods produced with convict

Key Fact

The Great Depression beginning in 1929 put an end to the contract system.

labor, and their constitutionality was upheld by the Supreme Court in 1936 (*Whitfield v. Ohio*, 297 U.S. 439).

The curtailing of convict labor had two long-ranging effects:

1. It increased the cost of imprisonment and thus encouraged the development of parole (whose history will be reviewed in Chapter 6).
2. It forced prison officials to find other ways to deal with prison idleness, so many prisons initiated programs to train and educate their inmates.

A Closer Look

Modern Prison Industries

In 1979, Congress enacted the Prison Industry Enhancement Act, which removed the blanket federal restrictions on the sale of prisoner-made goods in interstate commerce. Instead, the amendment sets forth minimum conditions under which such sales can occur, including consultation with labor unions, the need to avoid any impact on local industries, and a requirement that inmates be paid the prevailing local wage for work of a similar nature. The law also permits the establishment of pilot projects using prison labor by private enterprise. The Comprehensive Crime Control Act of 1984 further expanded the scope of prison industries, and by 1987, 38 such projects employed more than 1,000 inmates (Auerbach et al., 1988). In 1997, when more than 18,000 inmates were employed, criticism from manufacturers began to increase. The American Furniture Manufacturers Association, for example, endorsed legislation that would curtail the advantages enjoyed by Federal Prison Industries, a division of the Federal Bureau of Prisons, which, among other products, produces furniture ("Manufacturers Complain of Prison Work Programs," 1997). For years, small businesses have lobbied in Congress against a policy that requires federal agencies to purchase goods from Federal Prison Industries (Hoover, 2001). Nevertheless, by 2000, there were 80,000 inmates employed by government or private companies. Private-sector employment programs are operating in 36 states and employing 3,500 inmates, while the federal government employs more than 20,000 in a program that has become a $546 million business (Hoover, 2001; Leonhardt, 2000).

In response to prison overcrowding and prison construction costs, some states now utilize inmate labor to help build correctional facilities. These states are typically those in which organized labor is relatively weak, such as South Carolina where inmates have been constructing new correctional facilities and expanding and renovating existing facilities. Inmates are volunteers from medium- and minimum-security institutions who are paid $0.35 an hour and become eligible for salary increases and bonuses. They also receive additional days off their sentences depending on their level of skill, which serves as an incentive to improve their skills through available training programs. Unsatisfactory performance or rule violations result in their being dropped from the program. In other states, inmates are not paid but receive time off their sentences while learning employment skills. Inmate worker turnover and the need to take counts of inmates several times a day reduce the efficiency of these construction projects. An audit of inmate construction projects revealed that they took twice as long to complete but that labor costs were 50 percent less than for private contracting.

California uses more than 3,000 inmates in its Conservation Camp Program. In 38 conservation camps run by the Department of Corrections in cooperation with the Department of Forestry and Fire Protection, inmates fight fires that periodically threaten the state's forests. They also clear streams, plant trees, and do flood control work and other community service projects. The inmates are carefully screened volunteers; those with histories of violent crimes, sex offenses, arson, or escape are excluded. In North Carolina and about a dozen other states, inmate volunteers staff tourist information services. From behind prison walls and barbed wire, female inmates answer telephone inquiries from people who call the toll-free tourist information number.

BIG HOUSE ERA

"The move from 'hard labor' to 'hard time,' begun in the Depression and completed by war's end, forced prison administrators to overhaul their management practices. Always authoritarian, prison wardens had to rely much more on pure regimentation, epitomized by the Big House of the 1930s and 1940s" (Weiss, 2001: 262). Architecturally, the **Big House** is an Auburn-style prison: one- or two-inmate cells clustered in cell blocks on tiers surrounded by a high stone wall with guard towers, often holding in excess of 2,000 inmates. Unlike Auburn, however, silence, hard labor, the lockstep shuffle, and official use of corporal punishment were absent. The cells had toilets and sinks, were ventilated and heated, and had more space than the typical Auburn cell. In the Big House, inmates were frequently permitted to furnish and decorate their own cells. The better-equipped institutions had recreational facilities, baseball diamonds, and basketball and handball courts. Many prisoners were black, but in most Big Houses outside the South, the inmates were mostly white. A great deal of idleness and an absence of rehabilitative programming were problems (Irwin, 1980).

Scholarly studies of the prison environment, such as the one by Donald Clemmer (1958) during the 1930s, reported a phenomenon that became known as prisonization and the existence of an inmate subculture. **Prisonization** refers to the process by which an inmate is socialized into the prison environment. Although they may arrive with varied backgrounds, prisoners share a common suspicion and fear of other inmates and guards, so they tend to align themselves into cliques that serve to counter, if not subvert, the power of prison officials. These cliques form the basis of the **inmate subculture** that emerged in the less rigid environment of the Big House. This subculture developed and enforced its own rules. Several contemporary scholars argue, however, that the subculture found in the Big House by earlier researchers did not develop in prison but was actually brought into the prison by inmates who shared a common subcultural orientation. In either event, the guards faced a terrifying problem.

Big House guards on duty during one shift were vastly outnumbered by often idle inmates who were organized into cliques and formed a distinct subculture in opposition to the prison administration. Although prison officials could rely on help from outside forces, such as the state police and National Guard, sufficient coercive force was not immediately available for them to be routinely in effective control of the institution. Corporal punishment was no longer (officially) permitted, and loss of "good time" (time off for good behavior) or use of solitary confinement often proved ineffective in controlling behavior in the volatile atmosphere of a prison. As a result, guards developed effective informal control strategies involving personal agreements and corrupt favoritism (Irwin 1980): Personal agreements between guards and inmates were implicit or tacit exchange relationships in which inmates would refrain from rule-violating behavior in return for favors or special consideration from guards; corrupt favoritism involved guards who granted special privileges to key prisoners who served as inmate leaders in return for their support in maintaining order. Inmate leaders maintained order in two ways:

1. By keeping their own violations within acceptable limits and supporting the prevailing prison norm, which required inmates to "do your own time" (e.g., mind your own business and don't make no waves), and thereby encouraging conformity
2. By threatening or actually using violence against other prisoners who disrupted the prison routine and thereby endangered the privileged inmates' special arrangements with the guards

Prison officials tolerated and sometimes encouraged these activities and the convict organization because they promoted a high degree of order within the prison. In effect, the inmates ran the prison and officials rarely needed to intervene. There was little emphasis on rehabilitation (Austin and Irwin, 2001).

We have moved from Walnut Street and the Pennsylvania system to Auburn and the Big House. The next stop is in California, where a new model of penology, based on positivism, emerged.

Key Fact

In the Big House type of prison, control was achieved by corrupt relationships between inmate leaders and guards.

CORRECTIONS ERA

Toward the end of World War II, a penological revolution occurred in California, where former prosecutor Earl Warren (1891–1974) had been elected governor in the wake of a prison scandal. Under Warren's leadership, California reorganized its prison system according to the positivist ideal of individual reformation. The system was organized not for punishment but for around rehabilitation. California would apply the methods of the behavioral sciences to *correct* criminal behavior.

To operationalize the new approach to penology, California implemented an extreme version of the indeterminate sentence: Judges would remand a criminal with an

Key Fact

California organized the corrections model around rehabilitation.

A Closer Look

Prison Security Levels

There are four types of prisons for adults, and within each there are different custodial levels, depending on perceived risk presented by the inmate.

Super-maximum-security prisons are comprised of cells with sliding cell doors that are remotely operated from a secure control station. Inmates remain in their 6-by-12-foot cells 23 hours per day; during the other hour, they may be allowed to shower and exercise in the cell block or in an exterior cage. All inmate movement is strictly controlled with the use of physical restraints and correctional officer escort. The perimeter barrier is designed with a double fence with armed watch towers and/or armed roving patrols.

Maximum-close-security prisons are comprised of single cells and divided into cell blocks, which may be in one building or multiple buildings. Cell doors are usually controlled remotely from a secure control station. Each cell is equipped with its own combination plumbing fixture, which includes a sink and toilet. The perimeter barrier is designed with a double fence, armed watchtowers, and/or armed roving patrols. Inmate movement is restricted and supervised by correctional staff, and inmates are allowed out of their cells to work or attend various programs and recreation inside the facility. About 30 percent of all prisons are super-maximum or maximum. More than one-third of inmates are confined in maximum-security facilities.

Medium-security prisons are comprised of single cells (as in maximum-security institutions) that house 2 inmates each or secure dormitories that provide housing for up to 50 inmates each. Each dormitory contains a group toilet and shower area as well as sinks. Dormitory inmates sleep in a military-style double bunk and have an adjacent metal locker for storage of uniforms, undergarments, shoes, and so on. Each dormitory is locked at night, with a correctional officer providing direct supervision of the inmates and sleeping area. There is less supervision and control over the internal movement of inmates than in a maximum-security prison, although the facility usually has a double-perimeter fence with armed watchtowers or armed roving patrols. Most inmate work and self-improvement programs are within the prison, although selected medium-custody inmates work outside the prison under supervision of armed corrections officers. Each medium-security prison typically has a single-cell unit for the punishment of inmates who violate prison rules. A little more than 40 percent of all prisons are medium security.

Minimum-security prisons house inmates in nonsecure dormitory-style rooms divided into cubicles and routinely patrolled by corrections officers. Like the medium-security dorm, it has its own group toilet and shower area adjacent to the sleeping quarters, which contain double bunks and lockers.

Some facilities may be surrounded by a fence and guard tower; others have a single-perimeter fence that is inspected on a regular basis, but they have no armed watchtowers or roving patrols. There is less supervision and control over inmates in the dormitories and less supervision of inmate movement within the prison than at a medium-security facility. Minimum-custody inmates at minimum-security prisons usually participate in community-based work, and all inmates may participate in prerelease transition programs. About 30 percent of all prisons are low or minimum security.

indefinite sentence to the California Adult (or Youth) Authority, which would determine his or her treatment needs through a process of classification and assign the convict-client to an appropriate facility—not a prison but a correctional institution. A convict would remain "under treatment"—incarcerated—until the Adult (or Youth) Authority determined that the client had been rehabilitated, at which time he or she would be paroled to a community-based treatment program, that is, supervision by a parole agent.

Prisons no longer existed in California; they became "correctional institutions." Guards became "correction officers," and wardens became "superintendents." New institutions—medium- and minimum-security correctional facilities—were built. Adult Authority clients could be moved from maximum- to medium- to minimum-security facilities and then to parole, or if their behavior required, they could be moved from parole supervision back into the institution for further "treatment in a secure setting."

Correctional Institutions: Divisions, Rebellions, and Riots

Into these correctional institutions came the *treaters*. New superintendents often had extensive education in the behavioral sciences, and their institutions employed teachers, social workers, psychologists, and psychiatrists to implement a rehabilitative regimen. Slowly but steadily, the California system was copied, at least in part, by all the other states and the federal system—prisons virtually disappeared from the United States. Parole and the indeterminate sentence became intertwined with the idea of corrections and a medical model approach to dealing with criminal behavior. (Both subjects are discussed in Chapter 6.)

Despite the corrections revolution, prison officials remained preoccupied with management and security issues; most of the allocations for correctional institutions were for administration and security, leaving about 5 percent for items that could reasonably be labeled "rehabilitative." Providing such services has always been problematic. Correctional salaries are relatively low, and most prisons are located in rural areas, where land is relatively cheap and the prison provides important economic benefits to local residents,[9] but these areas are not particularly attractive to urban graduates trained in therapeutic disciplines.[10] Inadequate funding results in vocational training that is out-of-date and often of little use to inmates seeking employment based on skills developed in the correctional institution.

A Closer Look

Offender Employment

For some inmates, institutionalization is a traumatic hell for which suicide or attempts to escape are strong considerations. For others, prison is a welcome relief from the stresses of using drugs and living on the streets. But for all, prison creates a deep hunger for everything that cannot be had and a thirst for self-respect and dignity. If upon release from prison, a person is not prepared to secure work and be self-supporting, his or her return to prison is almost inevitable. For without viable work, self-respect cannot be restored and life is without dignity.

Source: Krienert and Fleisher, 2004: ix.

---

[9]A 1,200-bed prison requires about 200 construction workers and about 500 permanent positions.
[10]There is research indicating that prisons do not actually provide significant economic benefits to rural communities (King, Mauer, and Huling, 2004).

The problems encountered by the corrections approach were compounded by differences between corrections officers and the treaters. Older members of prison staff, particularly those responsible for prison security, were often resistant to the changes brought in by the treaters, which could be expected based on an examination of their differing backgrounds. Corrections officers were typically rural, white, Protestant, and socially and politically conservative, with (at best) a high school education; they tended to be poorly trained. The treaters tended to be reform-minded urban college graduates, many of whom were Catholics and Jews—and women.

A Closer Look

Benefits of Imprisonment

Prisons in impoverished rural areas have become a cornerstone of economic development (Kilborn, 2001; Schlosser, 1998). In Connecticut and New York, for example, "Republican lawmakers representing rural constituencies that benefit economically from new prisons have opposed relaxing the tough mandatory minimum sentences for drug offenses" (Wren, 1998: 23) (see also "Full-Employment Prisons," 2001). Despite the fact that they cannot vote, the Census Bureau counts inmates where they are incarcerated, not where they resided, increasing the electoral clout of prison communities. Because federal benefits to counties are based on population, counting inmates increases allocations for which inmates are not eligible (Butterfield, 2004a). In 2007, the governor's attempt to close some prisons in New York met with vigorous opposition from the union representing corrections officers and rural lawmakers.

Furthermore, the rhetoric did not match the reality. By the 1960s, the "correctional" expectations of prisons were not being fulfilled: "The spending of years in confined quarters, perhaps as small as eight by ten feet, in a setting dominated by a toilet and a possibly criminally-aggressive cellmate, can hardly be considered conducive to encourage socially acceptable behavior upon release" (Hahn, 1976: 6). The prison is what Erving Goffman refers to as a **total institution**: "a place of residence and work where a large number of like-situated individuals, cut off from the wider society for an appreciable period of time, together lead an enclosed, formally administered round of life" (1961: xiii). As such, these institutions have a tendency to mold persons into compliant and often shapeless forms to maintain discipline and a sound working order, or for less utilitarian reasons. The prison provides a dreary uniformity that leaves little room for self-assertion and decision making—the requisites for living in the free community. This corrections approach met with financial problems (i.e., reluctance to spend tax dollars on inmates), and prisoners soured on rehabilitative programs that raised unrealistic expectations. "After prisoners were convinced that treatment programs did not work (by the appearance of persons who had participated fully in treatment programs streaming back to prison with new crimes or violations of parole), hope shaded to cynicism and then turned to bitterness" (Irwin, 1980: 63).

During the 1950s, prisoners were usually divided to the point of impotence: "The prisonization process, which had aligned the great majority of inmates against their keepers, had also divided them from one another, making effective collaboration extremely difficult. Only a rumor of an excessively brutal incident or a report of revolts elsewhere could arouse a sense of community sufficient to support a riotous outbreak" (McKelvey, 1977: 323). However, there were such outbreaks during the 1950s in California, Louisiana, Massachusetts, Michigan, Missouri, New Jersey, Ohio, Pennsylvania, and Washington.

Into this environment came thousands of new African American and Latino inmates. During the 1950s, the number of blacks and Latinos committed annually to adult federal and state prisons increased from 17,200 to 28,500 (McKelvey, 1977), and this figure continued to grow during the 1960s and 1970s. Although the predominantly white inmates of the Big House could relate to their keepers, the young urban blacks and Hispanics found no such comfort. In 1954, the Supreme Court handed down its decision in *Brown v. Board of Education of Topeka, Kansas* (347 U.S. 483), which helped set off the civil rights revolution in the United States.

Rising black consciousness occurring in the wider community took on more radical dimensions inside the prison. The Black Muslims emerged as a major separatist organization and confronted prison officials with demands based on religious freedom. The antiwar movement and activities of radical groups, such as the Black Panthers and Students for a Democratic Society, stirred and politicized inmates, black and white. These inmates confronted correctional officials with demands often couched in Marxist terminology.

The traditional relationship between inmates and correctional officers, *rapprochement* based on private agreements or corrupt favoritism, started to come apart. Inmates became increasingly militant in their refusal to cooperate with their keepers, and correction officials responded in the best tradition of the Big House—with repression that touched off violence in institutions throughout the United States, including riots at California's San Quentin in 1967 and Philadelphia's Holmesburg Prison in 1970. In 1968, correctional officers and police killed 6 inmates and wounded 68 others in quelling a riot at North Carolina's Central Prison. Correctional institutions simmered throughout the 1960s into 1971, when in September the focus of attention shifted to a small upstate New York town where the last of the Auburn-style prisons was built. The events at Attica would prove to be a turning point in corrections and the history of parole.

Key Fact

The racial makeup of prisons changed dramatically during the 1960s, and radical political movements on the outside began to impact correctional institutions.

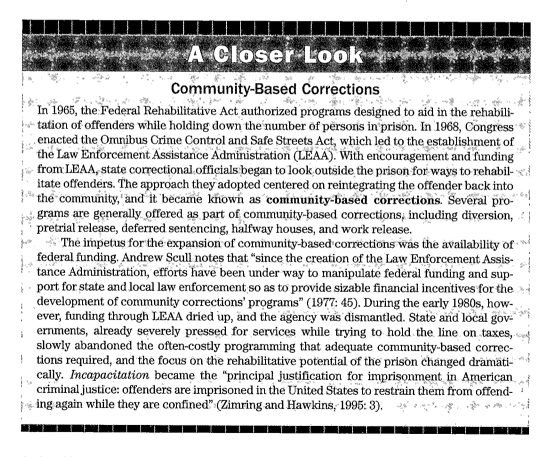

A Closer Look

Community-Based Corrections

In 1965, the Federal Rehabilitative Act authorized programs designed to aid in the rehabilitation of offenders while holding down the number of persons in prison. In 1968, Congress enacted the Omnibus Crime Control and Safe Streets Act, which led to the establishment of the Law Enforcement Assistance Administration (LEAA). With encouragement and funding from LEAA, state correctional officials began to look outside the prison for ways to rehabilitate offenders. The approach they adopted centered on reintegrating the offender back into the community, and it became known as **community-based corrections**. Several programs are generally offered as part of community-based corrections, including diversion, pretrial release, deferred sentencing, halfway houses, and work release.

The impetus for the expansion of community-based corrections was the availability of federal funding. Andrew Scull notes that "since the creation of the Law Enforcement Assistance Administration, efforts have been under way to manipulate federal funding and support for state and local law enforcement so as to provide sizable financial incentives for the development of community corrections' programs" (1977: 45). During the early 1980s, however, funding through LEAA dried up, and the agency was dismantled. State and local governments, already severely pressed for services while trying to hold the line on taxes, slowly abandoned the often-costly programming that adequate community-based corrections required, and the focus on the rehabilitative potential of the prison changed dramatically. *Incapacitation* became the "principal justification for imprisonment in American criminal justice: offenders are imprisoned in the United States to restrain them from offending again while they are confined" (Zimring and Hawkins, 1995: 3).

Attica Uprising

The state prison at Attica, a town 30 miles east of Buffalo that in 1971 had a population of fewer than 3,000, was completed in 1931. It boasted of being the most secure, escape-proof prison ever built; at the time, it was also the most expensive prison ever built. Attica was a response to an outbreak of prison riots throughout the United States in the late 1920s. In 1929, Clinton Prison in Dannemora, New York, experienced a riot protesting overcrowded conditions; three inmates were killed. In that year, the prison at Auburn experienced a riot in July during which four inmates escaped and two others were killed; several guards were seriously injured and two were shot. In December, another riot ensued. Inmates with firearms took the warden, six guards, and a foreman hostage, and the principal keeper was shot and killed. The prison was retaken after eight prisoners were killed and seven employees injured. Three inmates were later executed for their role in the riot ("Auburn Correctional Facility," 1998).

Typical of prisons in New York and elsewhere, Attica was placed in a rural area where residents would accept the institution as a basis for employment and other economic benefits. On July 8, 1970, Attica (as well as the other maximum-security prisons in New York) received a name change. There were no more prisons in New York; in their places stood six maximum-security "correctional facilities." The prison wardens became "institutional superintendents," the former principal keepers became "deputy superintendents," and the old-line prison guards/keepers awakened that morning to find themselves suddenly "corrections officers." "No one's job or essential duties changed, only his title" (Attica Commission, 1972: 18).

Fourteen months later, Attica Correctional Facility had more than 2,000 inmates who were locked in their cells for 12 to 16 hours per day being "rehabilitated" and who spent the remainder of the day with little to occupy their time. No gymnasium was available, and recreational opportunities were limited. Showers were available for most inmates—once a week. Meaningful rehabilitation programs were almost totally absent.

Most inmates were African Americans and Hispanics from the downstate New York area or upstate cities such as Buffalo, Syracuse, and Rochester. All but one (he was Puerto Rican) of the fewer than 400 corrections officers were non-Hispanic whites drawn primarily from the communities surrounding Attica. Although the superintendent had a master's degree in correctional administration, corrections officers who began their jobs between World War II and the late 1950s received no formal training. Those who started after that were given 2 weeks of training. They were expected to enforce the dozens of petty rules typical of correctional institutions and to relate in a meaningful way to inmates with whom they had little in common.

Attica had a large number of Black Muslims (members of the Nation of Islam) who had difficulty with a prison diet that was heavy with pork. Muslims also objected to the lack of ministers. Correctional officials would not allow the ministers, many of whom had prison records, into Attica. Black Muslims spent their recreation time in the yard engaging in worship and highly disciplined physical exercise. The correctional staff, which never understood the Black Muslims, was quite fearful of this group, who exhibited military-type discipline and remained aloof from both staff and other inmates.

As was typical of large correctional institutions, in Attica "popular conceptions of homosexual advances and assaults in prison were not exaggerated" (Attica Commission, 1972: 78). Corrections officers were unable to protect inmates who were forced to resort to forms of self-protection, such as carrying a "shiv" (homemade knife), in violation of prison rules: "The irony was not lost on the inmates. They perceived themselves surrounded by high walls and gates, and tightly regimented by a myriad of written and unwritten rules; but when they needed protection, they often had to resort to the same skills that had brought many of them to Attica in the first place" (Attica Commission, 1972: 79).

During the summer of 1971, a number of peaceful protests by inmates over conditions at Attica occurred. Leaders of previously antagonistic inmate groups, such as the Young Lords (a Puerto Rican group) and the Black Panthers and Black Muslims, gained greater political awareness, submerged their differences, and joined with white inmates in a peaceful effort to effect changes at Attica. "Inmates had petitioned state

Key Fact

The inmate uprising at Attica in 1971 led to a concerted attack on the corrections model and the indeterminate sentence.

correction officials to ease chronic overcrowding and censorship rules, and to improve conditions that limited them to one shower a week and one roll of toilet paper a month" (Haberman, 2000: 23). The new solidarity among inmates frightened officials. The superintendent responded by attempting to transfer the leaders as troublemakers but was prevented from doing so by the new Commissioner of the Department of Correctional Services Russell G. Oswald, who had been chairman of the New York State Board of Parole. Oswald met with inmate representatives at the prison but was called away on a personal emergency—his wife was seriously ill—before any agreement could be arranged.

On September 8, 1971, when a corrections officer attempted to discipline two inmates who appeared to be sparring, a confrontation ensued. The incident passed without any action on the part of the outnumbered staff. That evening officers appeared and took the inmates from their cells. A noisy protest ensued during the evening, and it was renewed when inmates gathered for breakfast on the morning of September 9. A melee broke out, corrections officers were taken hostage, and a riot quickly developed. Prison officials had no plan, nor had they been trained to deal with such an emergency. As a result, within 20 minutes inmates secured control of the four main cell blocks and seized 40 hostages. Corrections officers were beaten and 1 died later as a result of his wounds. The Black Muslims, who had not taken part in the initial uprising, moved to protect the hostages who were used as a basis for negotiations. An inmate committee for that purpose was formed.

When he arrived at Attica, Commissioner Oswald found the police were not prepared to retake the prison immediately. By the time sufficient forces had gathered, negotiations were already underway and Oswald chose to continue them in an effort to avoid more bloodshed. At the request of the inmate committee, several outside observers, including reporters, lawyers, and politicians, were permitted to enter Attica. Although the negotiations were quite disorganized, Oswald agreed to most of the inmate demands for improved conditions at Attica. The negotiations broke down, however, over the issue of complete amnesty because one of the injured officers had died after the negotiations began. Governor Rockefeller ordered that the prison be retaken.

On the morning of September 13, in a poorly planned and uncoordinated 9-minute assault, heavily armed state police and corrections officers retook the prison. More than 2,000 rounds of ammunition were fired; 2 hostages were seriously injured by the inmates, and 10 hostages and 29 inmates were killed by state troopers and corrections officers (Wicker, 1975). In 1989, the New York State Court of Claims awarded $1.3 million to 7 inmates who, although they had not participated in the uprising, had been injured at Attica by state police gunfire (Kolbert, 1989). In 1997, the first of 1,281 plaintiffs in the Attica litigation was awarded $4 million. Paroled in 1973, the former inmate, who has worked as a paralegal investigator for more than 20 years, had been tortured by corrections officers in the aftermath of the uprising (McFadden, 1997); in 1999, his $4 million award was overturned by a federal appeals court. In 2000, New York agreed to pay $8 million to 1,280 inmates (or their survivors) who claimed they were tortured, beaten, and denied medical treatment in the aftermath of the Attica rebellion—$6,500 to $125,000 each. The state also agreed to pay the inmates' lawyers up to $4 million in legal fees and costs. In the agreement, the state admitted no wrongdoing (Chen, 2000).

A number of official investigations occurred in the aftermath of the rebellion at Attica. In particular, rehabilitation, the parole board, and indeterminate sentencing received severe criticism. As Cullen and Gilbert point out, "Americans in the first half of the 1970s were faced with the prospect of an intractable crime rate and confronted with the reality—powerfully symbolized by Attica—that their prisons were both inhumane and grossly ineffective. In this context, a culprit was needed to take the blame, and a candidate was readily found. Rehabilitation would take the rap" (1982: 6). A new prison era would now emerge—just deserts.

JUST DESERTS ERA

Did the events at Attica result in any lasting changes? At Attica, Islam is now a recognized religion, inmates are allowed to stay in the exercise yard into the evening, and prisoners who can afford them are allowed television sets in their cells. Observers of the current state of our prisons, however, would be hard-pressed to document any positive changes of substance. Reflecting the move into the era of **just deserts**, a distinct political turn to the right has increased the number of prison commitments and lengthened the terms of imprisonment in many states that now have no parole system with which to deal with overcrowding. This has been exacerbated by politicians scrambling on board the "tough on crime" bandwagon with policies that, although they fail to deal with public protection, pander to constituent emotions. Some have focused on making prison life more difficult by prohibiting television, exercise equipment, and other recreational material that aid prison officials in maintaining discipline and control. In some states, legislation bars certain amenities—air conditioning, for example—that inmates do not have. In 1998, Congress enacted laws prohibiting federal prisons from showing movies rated R, NC-17, or X; the legislation also prohibits instruction in boxing, wrestling, weightlifting, judo, karate, or kickboxing.

John Irwin and James Austin (1994: 82, 111) state:

> Now prison administrators and other policy makers have completely abandoned the goal of reducing prisoners' isolation from outside society. They build prisons in the remotest regions of the state with only security in mind and further reduce contact with outside organizations and individuals through their custody-oriented policies. These practices, along with greatly diminished rehabilitative resources, are producing prisoners who have deteriorated in prison and return to the outside much less equipped to live a conventional life than they were when they entered. . . . We should be concerned by the fact that the prison systems are spewing out such damaged human material, most of whom will disappear into our social trash heap, politely labeled the "homeless" or the underclass, or, worse, will violently lash out, perhaps murdering or raping someone, and then be taken back to the dungeon.

A Closer Look

How to Fight Crime

In 1994, Congress removed prison inmates from eligibility for Pell grants, a federal program to help low-income students pay for college. Pell grants were the basis for most prison-based college programs, and many states followed the federal lead, removing prison inmates from their own college aid programs (Fried, 2006).

During an era when crime has been declining, the prison population has increased dramatically while across the country there has been a trend toward returning to the old Pennsylvania system, now referred to as the **super (or maxi) max prison**. These modern institutions are characterized by solitary confinement and minimal human contact. Cells, which inmates rarely leave, are self-contained units with showers; food and other services, such as law books from the library, are brought to the cells, and religious services are via closed-circuit television. The cost of imprisonment is roughly double that of a typical maximum-security prison (Anderson, 1998). In California, more than 1,200 inmates every year go from isolation to the street: Locked in their cells for 23 hours at a time and fed all their meals through a slot in the door—the next day they are on a bus heading home (Schlosser, 1998).

A Closer Look

Overview of 24 Hours in Prison, North Carolina Department of Correction

In *close-security prisons*, inmate movement from one area of the prison to another is restricted. Armed correctional officers man security towers to stop escape attempts. At 3:30 A.M., the first inmates are awakened—kitchen workers who get up to prepare the morning meal. These inmates live and work together. Correctional officers escort them to the kitchen as a group.

All inmates are awakened at 6 A.M. for the formal inmate count. Correctional staff count and recount inmates over and over throughout the day. Around 7 A.M., breakfast begins. All inmate workers report to their jobs at 7:30 A.M. Second-shift inmate workers may use the gyms, recreation yard, and canteens. Inmates work in the kitchen, license tag plant, or laundry or perform maintenance or janitorial tasks during the day. Around 3 P.M., the inmate usually checks his mail and spends some time in the recreation yard prior to returning to the dining hall for the evening meal at 4 P.M. After the evening meal, the inmate will have access to the gym, auditorium, or recreation yard. Depending on the day of the week, he may be involved in some organized recreational activities. On Wednesdays, Fridays, Saturdays, and Sundays, there is noncontact visitation with individuals who are on the inmate's approved visitors list. The visits are usually from an hour to an hour and a half in duration. At approximately 6:30 P.M., inmates may attend classes in the school or take part in other activities such as Alcoholics Anonymous or Narcotics Anonymous. At 8:30 P.M., another formal count is conducted. At 9 P.M., inmates return to their housing area and are allowed to watch television; play checkers, chess, or cards; or write letters. At 11 P.M., the inmate is locked in his cell, and the lights are dimmed for the night.

The routine in *medium-security prisons* is similar, except inmates are housed in dormitories and some inmates leave the prison under armed guard to work on road squads cutting brush or working the fields at the state prison farm.

Minimum-security prisons prepare inmates for return to the community. Although those entering minimum custody are assigned to jobs and remain at the prison, inmates in later phases leave the prison for work assignments. In the final stage of minimum custody, inmates may take part in work-release jobs and family visits.

PRISONS FOR PROFIT

Although prisons have proved to be a costly liability for state governments since the Great Depression, some localities and private entrepreneurs view them as a source of potential income. For example, the farming community of Appleton, Minnesota, with a population of about 1,500, built a 472-bed medium-security prison at a cost of $28.5 million. The town issued prison bonds in anticipation of the economics of imprisonment. Although the state has an overcrowded prison system, Minnesota does not have money available to make use of the Appleton facility (Terry, 1993). In 1993, however, after a national search, an agreement was reached with Puerto Rico to house 170 of the commonwealth's inmates at Appleton. Colorado's Fremont County, population 40,000, according to local souvenir T-shirts is the "Corrections Capital of the World." The claim is not an exaggeration: Its 13 prisons are the economic lifeblood of the county (Brooke, 1997).

One of the more recent responses to the problem of an increasing prison population has been the "privatization" of corrections: "Confinement service or facility management contracts are another way of expanding corrections capacity—without imposing any burden for facility construction on the government" (Mullen, 1985: 4).

Private firms have been able to establish and operationalize facilities more quickly than public agencies, which are constrained by a variety of political and bureaucratic requirements, because **private prisons** can be built without the need for public approval. By the end of 2000, there were about 185 privately operated prisons (Austin and Coventry, 2001).

According to Charles Logan, competition between public and private prisons will provide long-needed improvements in incarceration:

> Competition does not just contain costs; it advances other goals as well. When it is possible for a commercial company to take business away from a competitor (including the state) by showing that it can do a better job, then that company becomes a self-motivated watchdog over other companies (and over the state). Such a company will have an interest in critically evaluating the quality of its competitors' services and an interest in improving its own. (1990: 75)

In the case of prisons, the existence of competition, even potential competition, will make the public less tolerant of facilities that are crowded, costly, dirty, dangerous, inhumane, ineffective, and prone to lawsuits. Indeed, the fact that these conditions have existed for so long in monopolistic state prisons is a big part of what makes private prisons seem attractive.

The private facility has long been accepted in the area of juvenile care, whereas with adults this facility is more controversial. Several dozen of these facilities exist; most (but not all) are equipped to handle only minimum-security inmates and are thus more closely related to halfway houses (discussed in Chapter 11) than traditional prisons. The largest customer of the private facility has been the U.S. Immigration and Naturalization Service (INS), which has contracted out the detention of illegal aliens to the Corrections Corporation of America, Inc. (CCA), based in Nashville. In 1985, the CCA proposed a takeover of the entire correctional system in Tennessee, but that bid was rejected by the state legislature. CCA has been criticized for making profits by understaffing its institutions and employing guards with little or no experience to handle high-security prisoners. This has led to an extraordinary number of escapes and violence (Yeoman, 2000). Another INS prison contractor, Esmor Correctional Services, was the subject of a scathing report that found poorly trained guards preying on immigrant detainees, a situation that resulted in a violent uprising (Dunn, 1995). The firm has successfully bid on numerous corrections projects by submitting low bids and cutting costs (Sullivan and Purdy, 1995).

Entry of the private sector into what has traditionally been thought of as a public responsibility is controversial; for example, it has been opposed by the National Sheriffs' Association, although state correction commissioners have tended to be more supportive. Supporters of the idea contend that private operators can maintain or exceed the level of services provided by public agencies at less cost. They are not bound by the bureaucracy or the mandated salaries and retirement benefits of government agencies whose employees are often unionized—about 70 percent of prison operating costs are related to employees' salaries and benefits (Austin and Irwin, 2001).

Opponents question the propriety of handing over to private entrepreneurs so basic a public responsibility as punishment. Opposition has been vigorous on the part of organized labor, particularly by the American Federation of State, County, and Municipal Employees which represents many prison workers.

Although minimum-security facilities have generated less concern, the question of turning over medium- and maximum-security prisoners to a private firm has troubled observers who point out that in such institutions the constant threat of the use of force, including deadly physical force, exists. The privately employed security officers are typically trained at the same state academies that train public correctional officers and enjoy the same peace officer powers. Whether private employees should be entrusted by government with such authority is an unanswered legal question. In at least one case, a guard for a private prison operating under contract with the INS accidentally discharged a shotgun, killing one inmate and wounding another (*Medina v. O'Neil*, 589

Key Fact

The popularity of private prisons has waned as their cost approaches that of public prisons.

F.Supp. 1028 S.D. Tex. 1984). At the other end of the spectrum of possibilities, in 1990 the leader of a multimillion-dollar drug ring used a .25-caliber handgun to overpower his guards and escape with two other inmates from a jail being run by the Wackenhut Corporation under contract with Bexar County, Texas. In 1997, the Supreme Court ruled (*Richardson et al. v. McKnight*, 521 U.S. 399) that "employees of companies that run prisons under contract with a state or local government are not entitled to the [qualified] immunity from prisoner lawsuits that shields prison guards who are on the public payroll" (Greenhouse, 1997: 12). Qualified immunity (as opposed to the absolute immunity enjoyed by judicial officials) is a powerful shield, making it extremely difficult to successfully sue a public official.

Some opponents contend that to keep jail and prison space at a maximum level, private corrections corporations would seek to make Americans even more fearful of crime, through advertising and political campaigns. Other issues include the following: What will happen in the event of a strike by the private employees of a private prison? What if the firm decides to go out of business or enters into bankruptcy? One of the most basic of many legal issues involves the power of government to delegate its authority to private entrepreneurs to provide as basic a service as imprisonment. "A private entity," notes Ira Robbins, "exercises governmental power when it deprives a person of life, liberty, or property at the behest of government" (1988: 36–37). Because a private prison might have an economic interest in imposing a punishment that denies privileges (thereby decreasing prison costs) or denying good-time credits (which keeps the inmate incarcerated; from which the firm may benefit financially), the prison would not typically be permitted control over such actions. Arguments for contracting out prison services would also appear to justify similar contracting for police services—or possibly probation and parole. In any event, James Austin and Gary Coventry (2001: ix) found that private prisons "offer only modest cost savings, which are basically a result of moderate reductions in staffing patterns, fringe benefits, and other labor-related costs." They typically perform at the same level as public institutions (Austin and Irwin, 2001).

In more recent years, some of the worst conditions in juvenile facilities have been found among the growing number of privately operated prisons (Butterfield, 1998d). At one such facility in Florida, guards staged gladiator matches in which 13- and 14-year-olds beat each other before fellow inmates. Some juveniles were held beyond their release dates to increase company income (Jackson and Grumman, 1999). In 2000, Louisiana agreed to end its use of private facilities for juvenile offenders in the wake of lawsuits that disclosed numerous abuses, including the denial of food, clothing, and medical care to inmates, who were also routinely beaten (Butterfield, 2000a: 12). "Gone are the heady days of the mid-1990s, when private prisons were portrayed as an inexpensive panacea that would provide economical beds for state governments and deliver fat profits to investors." Stock prices have plummeted as criticism and problems have mounted. James Austin and Garry Coventry (2003) report that although private prisons have dramatically increased over the past two decades, inroads were limited to certain geographic areas, in particular the South and (to a lesser extent) the West, and are tapering off. Absence of such facilities in the Midwest and Northeast, they argue, is related to the power of labor unions, which have successfully resisted attempts to privatize. Nevertheless, in 2003, privately operated facilities housed about 94,000 inmates (Harrison and Beck, 2003).

Although there are unresolved policy questions (e.g., Should the power to deprive people of their liberty be delegated to private firms? Should power to use coercive force, including deadly force, be delegated to private firms?), issues of cost and efficiency have largely been determined. There is little (if any) evidence that private prisons are cheaper to operate: "There is nothing that is much different between the public and private prison. . . . Private prisons have no unique management system, innovative architectural design, or high tech innovations. The same people that were wardens in public prisons are now governing the private system" (Austin and Coventry, 2003: 6).

INFECTIOUS DISEASES IN PRISONS

Adding to the numerous safety and health problems endemic to prisons are those presented by several infectious diseases, in particular, HIV/AIDS, tuberculosis (TB), and hepatitis C. AIDS and its precursor, human immunodeficiency virus (HIV), were first identified in the United States in 1981. Today about one in six AIDS patients has spent time in an American prison or jail. Intravenous drug users and male homosexuals have been identified as primary groups at risk for the disease, and prisons house many intravenous drug users and inmates who resort to homosexual practices in the absence of available female partners. AIDS also spreads in prison through rape, a rather widespread problem officials appear unwilling or unable to curtail (Lewin, 2001a). Inmates frequently sport prison tattoos, and the sharing of primitive tattoo needles is also a source of infection. The number of HIV positive state and federal inmates has stabilized at about 25,000 persons, but only 22 states test all inmates. The rate of confirmed AIDS cases is three times that of the general population (Maruschak, 2006).

A Closer Look

Death Sentence for Auto Theft

In 1993, Michael B. began serving a 7-year sentence for auto theft in the Menard Correctional Center, a maximum-security prison in Illinois. After the first few times he was raped, he got an HIV test, but the married 24-year-old tested negative. However, the assaults did not stop. Michael B. was turned into a sex slave and traded by gang members for cigarettes and drugs. According to a lawsuit he filed later, he was raped by 10 men in the showers, by his cellmate while in "protective custody," and on dozens of other occasions. In March 1994, he was again tested for HIV; this time, he was positive.

Source: Weed, 2001.

Additional dangers arrived at the prison gate with increases in TB, a bigger killer worldwide than AIDS. "TB is not usually a highly contagious disease but given the right conditions . . . the probability of transmission increases significantly" (Wilcock, Hammett, and Parent, 1995: 2). According to Hammett et al. (1994: xi), "Prisons and jails, like other congregate facilities, are high-risk settings for the spread of tuberculosis infection. Living conditions are invariably crowded, and many buildings have antiquated systems with poor ventilation and air circulation. Inmates are already more susceptible to TB infection and TB disease because of factors associated with their high-risk lifestyles and inadequate access to health care services, as well as increased prevalence of HIV/AIDS among them. Finally, the appearance of multidrug resistant tuberculosis raises the threat of an often untreatable disease spreading in a closely confined population." Approximately 12,000 inmates with TB are released each year (Butterfield, 2003b).

TB infection is spread through the air in tiny droplets containing the bacterium exhaled by persons with active TB disease, primarily when they cough or sneeze. TB commonly affects the lungs but may attack other parts of the body (Hammett et al., 1994). Inmates weakened by AIDS are at particular risk for new drug-resistant strains of TB, but all inmates and prison personnel are at risk from this contagious disease. TB can be contracted by an otherwise healthy individual because the disease is spread by coughing in an environment without adequate ventilation: "Not only do inmate populations contain concentrations of persons at risk for both TB and HIV, but the facilities themselves are high-risk settings for TB transmission because of crowded conditions and poor ventilation" (Crawford, 1994: 31). The Centers for Disease Control has guidelines for isolating persons with active TB; however, in a prison setting, these are expensive to implement, and most prisons have inadequate methods for dealing with TB.

Hepatitis C, an often-fatal liver disease, is spread primarily through contact with human blood and sexual contact and is prevalent among intravenous drug users. An estimated 4 million Americans have the disease. About 1.5 million inmates with the disease are released each year (Butterfield, 2003b). Carriers often have no symptoms, and the disease can progress undetected for years, silently destroying the liver. Although most state prisons do not require hepatitis C testing for inmates—it is expensive—the number of those with the disease has been estimated by health officials to be about 20 percent of the prison population. Treatment requires the use of drugs at a per-patient cost of about $10,000 to $20,000 per year; advanced cases can be cured only with a liver transplant. In 2001, New York was treating 95 infected inmates at a cost of $6 million per year. There is great concern in the medical community that hepatitis C will spread as infected inmates are released into the community, and there is also concern about the safety of prison workers (Rhode, 2001).

Key Fact

Prisons are breeding grounds for a number of serious diseases: HIV/AIDS, hepatitis C, and TB.

A Closer Look

Dark Side of America

Drug-resistant strains of tuberculosis, easily transmitted in tight spaces, have become a common problem. Illegal drugs ferried in by prison employees—and used by inmates who share needles—have made prison a high-risk setting for HIV infection and most recently liver-destroying hepatitis C. . . . By failing to confront public health problems in prison, the country could be setting itself up for new epidemics down the line.

Source: New York Times editorial, May 17, 2004, p. 20.

DRUG-ABUSING, MENTALLY ILL, AND GERIATRIC INMATES

Prison officials are also acknowledging the difficulties created by widespread use of drugs in their institutions: "Drug use has become a major problem with a variety of ramifications, including threats to prison order, violence among inmates, and corruption of guards and other employees" (Malcolm, 1989c: 1). This problem is apparently widespread (Purdy, 1995). In Pennsylvania, for example, in a 6-year period, 11 inmates died of drug overdoses (Associated Press, 1995). The dramatic increase in convicted drug offenders has been a driving force behind prison overcrowding and the smuggling of drugs into correctional institutions. In Illinois, drug offenders have been the fastest-growing segment of the prison population for several years; in New York, the number of inmates serving time for drug-related offenses has surpassed those imprisoned for any other type of crime.

Key Fact

Despite their level of security, prisons often suffer from drug use problems.

Beginning in the 1960s, states began closing their institutions for treating the mentally ill. According to the plan, instead of expensive residential care, patients would be treated more economically with antipsychotic drugs at mental health clinics in their communities. However, the clinics failed to materialize, and the mentally ill often live in the streets or are incarcerated. Because the authorities—police and judges—have nowhere else to send them, mentally ill persons are being sent to institutions of last resort: jails and prisons. Thus, in addition to all the other problems facing our correctional institutions, they are being used to make up for the inadequacies of our mental health system (Butterfield, 1998a).

As noted in Chapter 1, increasing numbers of elderly inmates—the result of longer sentences and "three strikes" legislation—are adding extra burdens to the prison system. Because of lifestyle deficiencies, the average inmate is physiologically 10 years older than men who have never been incarcerated. Thus, 50 years is "senior inmate" status whose cost of incarceration is approximately three times that of a younger man (Harrison, 2006).

Inmates over 50 have higher rates of incontinence, sensory impairment, impaired flexibility, respiratory illness, cardiovascular disease, and cancer. They suffer from chronic ailments associated with aging: arthritis, high blood pressure, ulcers, prostate problems, heart disease, cognitive impairment, reduced vision and hearing, muscle mass loss, incontinence, and dietary intolerance. Inmates who are denied an opportunity for parole will die in prison—but before they do, they will require medical treatment as well as special facilities and provisions to accommodate those who need wheelchairs, walkers, and colostomy bags; require help bathing; and have special dietary needs. Those suffering from Alzheimer's disease will be totally unable to care for themselves in prison.

Key Fact

Prisons are often home to the mentally ill, for whom there is a paucity of services.

Key Fact

With more "lifers" in prison, the geriatric population will increase, along with the cost of incarcerating elderly inmates.

A Closer Look

Louisiana State Penitentiary, Angola, 2001

[A]n old toothless man, Eugene Scott, whom the other inmates call Shippy because his head is as big as a boat, is dribbling in his wheelchair; a stroke has stripped him of his ability to speak. Another, fighting emphysema, is hooked to an oxygen tank; still another, blind from glaucoma, rolls about in bed.

Source: Stolberg, 2001: 20.

PRISON VIOLENCE

Prison violence is widespread: Assaults on employees increased from fewer than 1,700 per year in 1988 to more than 13,000 in 1994 (Porter, 1995). In 1985, dozens of inmates were murdered by other inmates in Texas prisons. A particularly grisly prison outbreak occurred at the New Mexico State Penitentiary, which was built in 1957 to house 850 inmates. On February 1, 1980, the prison had nearly 1,000 inmates and was badly understaffed; only 18 corrections officers were on duty when prisoners took over the institution. Although the prison was quickly retaken by police and the National Guard, inmates had systematically slaughtered 33 of their fellow prisoners—many of whom were tortured to death.

A Closer Look

Sexual Violence

He was forced to have oral sex with one inmate. A second demanded anal intercourse. When he refused, the inmate tore off his pants, shoved a pillow over his head so he could not scream, and raped him. It was quite painful. For the next 4 hours, several dozen inmates dragged him from cell to cell, raping him. The next night, he was gang raped again (Marx, 1994a).

In Texas, a 23-year-old inmate was attacked by a group of some 20 inmates within a week of entering prison. The inmates demanded sex and money, but the victim refused. He was beaten for almost 2 hours and died of head injuries a few days later ("Rape Crisis in U.S. Prisons," 2001).

Overcrowding was seen as a major reason for the 1989 2-day prison riot at the Correctional Institution at Camp Hill, Pennsylvania, a facility built to house 1,826 that had 2,607 inmates; more than 118 persons were injured, and half of the facility's 31 buildings were destroyed. At the Southern Ohio Correctional Facility at Lucasville, overcrowding was a modest 120 percent of capacity—the lowest for all the state's prisons. Nevertheless, in 1993, led by a Muslim faction aligned with members of the white Aryan

A Closer Look

Prison Gangs

Mexican Mafia

Found in at least nine state prison systems and reputed to be the most powerful of the prison-organized groups, the Mexican Mafia (also known as "la M"—pronounced emee) is comprised primarily of Mexican American convicts and ex-convicts from the barrios of East Los Angeles. Like many other prison gangs as well as their street counterparts, the Mexican Mafia has a blood-in-blood-out credo: Murder or the drawing of blood is a prerequisite for membership, and those seeking to resign will be killed.

Its origins are traced to the Deuel Vocational Institute in Tracy, California, where in 1957, 20 young Mexican Americans from the Maravilla area of East Los Angeles formed the Mexican Mafia as a self-protection group. They soon began to control such illicit activities as homosexual prostitution, gambling, and narcotics. Attempts by the Department of Corrections to diminish gang power by transferring members to other institutions only helped to spread their influence. Vigorous recruiting occurs among the most violent Mexican American inmates, particularly those housed in adjustment centers for the most dangerous and incorrigible. In 1967, Mexican Mafia reliance on wholesale violence increased, and in that year members attacked the first Mexican American outside their group. This attack on an inmate from rural northern California led to the formation of a second Mexican American gang, La Nuestra Familia, with whom the Mexican Mafia has been feuding since 1968.

By the mid-1960s, the Mexican Mafia had assumed control over prison heroin trafficking and numerous other inmate activities. In 1966, it started to move its operations outside the prison and is reputedly attempting to organize Hispanic gangs into a confederation to confront black Los Angeles gangs for control of the drug trade (Mydans, 1995). The gang asserts control over drug trafficking by Hispanic street gangs and collects "street taxes" in exchange for the privilege of staying in business and protection against encroachment by other gangs. In 1998, 12 members of la M were convicted in a federal court in California for directing a terror campaign from their prison cells to control drug trafficking by street gangs (Associated Press, 1998).

Aryan Brotherhood

Founded in 1964 by white inmates at San Quentin and primarily made up of members of outlaw motorcycle clubs (in opposition to the Black Guerilla Family), the Aryan Brotherhood soon became infamous for their level of violence, extraordinary even by prison standards. By 1975, the gang had spread into most of California's prisons, with members sporting a green shamrock on their hands. Once dismissed as a fringe white supremacist gang, its members have now taken control of large parts of America's maximum-security prisons in California, Illinois, Texas, and Kansas. Also known as A.B. and the Brand, the Aryan Brotherhood established a hierarchical structure and asserted control over various prison rackets including gambling—debtors pay up by having a relative or friend send an untraceable money order to a designated member on the outside. In an effort to thwart their power, prison officials have transferred many identified members to supermax prisons. While the leadership is serving life sentences, released members maintain gang ties and represent a community threat (Grann, 2004). In 2006, three A.B. leaders received life terms for what prosecutors called decades of terrorizing some of the nation's most dangerous prisons.

Brotherhood, inmates rioted, seized 18 staff members as hostages, killed 1 corrections officer and 9 inmates, and injured 48 inmates and several corrections officers (one lost an eye) before surrendering. Prison overcrowding has been compounded by the perennial problem of prison discipline, and violence has been exacerbated both by court orders limiting the authority of correctional officials and by the phenomenon of prison gangs.

Prison Gangs

Some gangs developed in prison, often as mutual protection groups; others were brought into the institution by convicted gang members. In either case, the contemporary prison has provided fertile soil for the proliferation and growth of these often-dangerous entities. In most instances, gangs are organized along racial or ethnic lines. Instead of the politicized groups of the 1960s, an array of gangs with exotic-sounding names has appeared. So extensive is gang membership that a U.S. court of appeals in Illinois concluded that 90 percent of Pontiac Correctional Center's inmates are gang members and that they were running much of prison life (Crawford, 1988). The gangs have increased the potential for violence, with members using the power of their gang affiliations for various extortion practices. Inmates without the protection of a gang are vulnerable and often easy prey for the violence-prone gang members. Attempts by correctional officials to dissipate the power of the gangs by transferring their leadership to other institutions have often served only to spread the phenomenon. The gangs often transcend the prison, with members active inside and outside the institution, which has obvious implications for parole officers.

Key Fact

Prisons continue to be plagued by violence, which is exacerbated by the prison gang phenomenon.

Gang members engage in extortion as well as drug and weapons trafficking: "Many prison gangs have a 'blood-in-blood-out' policy, meaning that an inmate may become a member only after killing or assaulting another prisoner or staffer and that his blood will be spilled before he is allowed to quit the gang. Members released from prison remain in the gang, often providing support and enforcement for the organization outside" (President's Commission on Organized Crime [PCOC], 1986: 75). The U.S. Department of Justice has identified more than 100 different prison gangs with greatly varying structures, the largest being the Aryan Brotherhood, Black Guerrilla Family, La Nuestra Familia, Mexican Mafia, and Texas Syndicate.

PRISONS AND THE COURTS

Throughout most of our history, the courts have been unwilling to intervene in matters pertaining to prisons "out of concern for federalism and separation of powers and a fear that judicial review of administrative decisions would undermine prison security and discipline" (Jacobs, 1980: 433). Once the requirements of due process had been met, leading to conviction and sentencing, the judiciary had taken a hands-off policy. Prisons are difficult to manage, and this difficulty made judges reluctant to impose their legal standards in place of the expertise of prison administrators. In 1961, however, the Black Muslims began to litigate their First Amendment claims in New York, California, and the District of Columbia. These cases served to "open the floodgates" of prison litigation (Cripe, 1997). Once the courts became involved in prisons, they had no easy way to withdraw.

Key Fact

The courts ended their hands-off policy during the 1960s by providing inmates with some limited rights.

In 1968, 14 years after segregation in public schools was declared unconstitutional, the U.S. Supreme Court ruled that the racial segregation of prisoners violated the Fourth Amendment (*Lee v. Washington*, 390 U.S. 333). The following year, the Court ruled that prison officials must permit prisoners ("jailhouse lawyers") to assist their fellow inmates with legal questions (*Johnson v. Avery*, 393 U.S. 483). In 1971, the Court expanded this right by requiring prison officials to provide legal materials, law books, legal forms, and so on for inmates (*Younger v. Gilmore*, 404 U.S. 15). In 1974, the Court extended its previous decisions by requiring correctional officials to provide either adequate law libraries or adequate legal assistance (*Bounds v. Smith*, 430 U.S. 817); that same year, the Court limited the power of prison officials to censor inmate letters (*Procunier v. Martinez*, 417 U.S. 817). In 1989, however, the Court (*Thornburgh v. Abbott*, 104 L.Ed.2d 459) limited the *Procunier* decision to *outgoing* mail and held that incoming items can quickly circulate throughout the institution and be a source of disorder. Accordingly, the Court gave prison officials greater flexibility in censoring publications that inmates may receive: "In the volatile prison environment, it is essential that prison officials be given discretion to prevent such disorder."

In 1974, the Supreme Court ruled that prisoners are entitled to minimal due process protections whenever disciplinary action threatens their "liberty" by imposing solitary confinement and loss of privileges of good time (*Wolff v. McDonnell*, 418 U.S. 817): "[T]hough his rights may be diminished by the needs and exigencies of the institutional environment, a prisoner is not wholly stripped of constitutional protections when he is imprisoned for a crime. There is no iron curtain drawn between the Constitution and the prisons of this country." In 1977, however, the Court apparently decided to draw a line between the prison and the Constitution: It rejected the notion that prisoners had the right under the First Amendment to organize an inmate union (*Jones v. North Carolina Prisoners' Union*, 433 U.S. 119). In 1978, the Court ruled that solitary confinement in a harsh setting for more than 30 days constitutes cruel and unusual punishment (*Hutto v. Finney*, 437 U.S. 678).

A great deal of litigation has arisen over prison conditions, particularly with respect to overcrowding. Federal and state courts in many jurisdictions have ordered prison officials to reduce inmate populations and to take other corrective steps to bring their institutions in line with constitutional requirements. In 1979 (*Bell v. Wolfish*, 441 U.S. 520) and 1981 (*Rhodes v. Chapman*, 452 U.S. 337), however, the Supreme Court overturned lower court decisions that found overcrowding per se to be unconstitutional. The Court ruled that the Constitution does not require inmates to be housed in single cells; double bunking is permitted even for those prisoners in jail awaiting trial who are legally still innocent. In *Chapman*, the Court ruled that prison conditions were constitutional as long as the totality of the conditions does not "involve the wanton and unnecessary infliction of pain." The 1994 federal Crime Bill prohibits federal judges from finding that prison or jail overcrowding is unconstitutional "in general terms." Instead, the statute requires a plaintiff to prove that the overcrowding causes the infliction of cruel and unusual punishment—a violation of the Eighth Amendment—*on that particular inmate*.

Key Fact

Much of the successful litigation against prisons has been based on the Eighth Amendment and the problem of overcrowding.

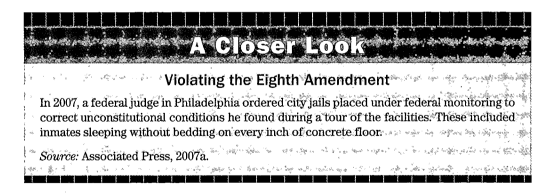

Violating the Eighth Amendment

In 2007, a federal judge in Philadelphia ordered city jails placed under federal monitoring to correct unconstitutional conditions he found during a tour of the facilities. These included inmates sleeping without bedding on every inch of concrete floor.

Source: Associated Press, 2007a.

In 1983 (*Hudson v. Palmer*, 468 U.S. 517), the Supreme Court ruled that the Fourth Amendment's protection against unreasonable search and seizure does not apply to prison cells. In a 5–4 decision, the Court held: "The recognition of privacy rights for prisoners in their individual cells simply cannot be reconciled with the concept of incarceration and the needs and objectives of penal institutions." In *Hudson*, the Court overturned a U.S. court of appeals decision that had upheld the right of a convicted bank robber in Virginia to sue prison officials for the destruction of his property resulting from a search of his cell by correction officers. In 1994, the Court ruled unanimously that prison officials can be found liable for failing to protect inmates from the violence of other inmates; the successful litigant, an inmate at the federal prison at Terre Haute, Indiana, alleged that the beatings and rapes he suffered were the result of official indifference (*Farmer v. Brennan*, 62 L.W. 4446). In a 1995 decision (*Sandin v. Conner*, 115 S. Ct. 2293), a 5–4 majority made it substantially more difficult for prisoners to challenge prison officials, stating a prisoner can challenge only when officials' actions impose "atypical and significant hardship on the inmate." Prison officials should have, the Court ruled, the flexibility "in fine-tuning of the ordinary incidents of prison life." The case involved an inmate in Hawaii who had not been allowed to call witnesses at a disciplinary hearing that imposed solitary confinement for 30 days—he lacked a "liberty interest" (an issue that was discussed in Chapter 2 and is examined again in Chapter 7). The federal Prison Litigation Reform Act of 1996 "has, for all practical purposes, removed the federal courts from involvement in correctional issues except in the most flagrant violations of the Constitution" (Breed, 1998: 15): Before an inmate can file a civil rights action in federal court, the inmate must exhaust all available administrative remedies and show physical injury to receive damages for mental or emotional injury suffered while in custody.

Chapter 6 examines the development of parole and the indeterminate sentence and looks at the impact of the just deserts model on both.

KEY TERMS

Auburn system (p. 142)
Big House (p. 146)
community-based corrections (p. 150)
contract system (p. 143)
inmate subculture (p. 146)
just deserts (p. 153)
lease system (p. 144)

penitentiary (p. 138)
Pennsylvania system (p. 141)
prisonization (p. 146)
private prisons (p. 155)
state use system (p. 144)
super (or maxi) max prison (p. 153)
total institution (p. 149)

INTERNET CONNECTIONS

American Correctional Association: aca.org
American Jail Association (AJA): corrections.com/aja/index.html
Corrections industries links: corrections.com/industries
Corrections links: corrections.com/links/viewlinks
National Institute of Corrections: nicic.org
Official Home of Corrections: corrections.com

REVIEW QUESTIONS

1. How does the prison population differ from the rest of the population in the United States?
2. How did different conditions in England and the colonies result in different responses to criminals?
3. What are the five eras of prison history?
4. Why were colonial juries often unwilling to find defendants guilty?
5. What were the three intertwined developments that led to the establishment of the American system of prisons?
6. What was the Quaker approach to punishment?
7. What led to the demise of the Walnut Street Jail?
8. What are the characteristics of the Pennsylvania system?
9. Why did most states pattern themselves after the Auburn system rather than the Pennsylvania system?
10. What are the characteristics of the Auburn system?
11. What are the three categories of convict labor?
12. What factors led to the demise of most forms of convict labor?
13. What were the long-range effects of the curtailing of convict labor?
14. What is meant by a Big House prison?
15. What are prisonization and inmate subcultures?
16. How did guards maintain control of a Big House despite being vastly outnumbered by inmates?
17. What types of jobs currently use inmate labor?
18. What led to the reemergence of positivism in penology after World War II?
19. What were the factors that led to the prison disturbances of the 1960s and early 1970s?
20. What has made the problem of prison discipline more difficult today than in the period of the Big House?
21. Why was the riot at Attica a turning point in American prison history? What model emerged out of Attica?
22. What is community-based corrections?
23. What led to the popularity of community-based corrections?
24. What are the programs traditionally included in community-based corrections?
25. What led to the demise of community-based corrections?
26. Why was the corrections approach difficult (if not impossible) to implement in prisons?
27. Why are AIDS, hepatitis C, and TB particularly problematic in prisons?
28. Why were the courts reluctant to consider inmate lawsuits protesting prison conditions?
29. According to Supreme Court rulings, what rights are inmates entitled to?
30. What are the pros and cons of using private prisons?

Parole and the Indeterminate Sentence

Society has always struggled with how best to help inmates re-integrate once released, but the current situation is unprecedented. The number of returning offenders dwarfs anything in America's history. The needs of offenders appear more serious, the parole system retains few rehabilitation programs, and the housing and employment barriers offenders face upon return are even more daunting.

—Joan Petersilia (2005: 66)

Chapter Outline

Parole, from the French parol *referring to "word of honor,"
was a means of releasing prisoners of war who promised
not to resume arms in a current conflict. Modern parole, "a
period of conditional supervised release following a prison
term," has several antecedents (Glaze 2003: 5).*

ANTECEDENTS TO PAROLE

Transportation of Laborers to America

In colonial America early in the seventeenth century, a shortage of labor led to the transporting of children—the indentured poor and delinquents—as well as pardoned criminals from England. In the beginning, no specific conditions were imposed on those who received these pardons. However, after several of those pardoned evaded transportation or returned to England before the expiration of their term, certain restrictions had to be imposed. Around 1655, the form of pardons was amended to include specific conditions and provide for the nullification of the pardon if the recipient failed to abide by the conditions imposed.

During the early days of laborer transportation, the government paid a fee to contractors for each prisoner transported. Subsequently, this arrangement was changed, and the contractor was given what was called "property in service"—custody of the prisoner until the expiration of his full term. Once prisoners were delivered to the contractor, the government took no further interest in their welfare or behavior unless they violated the conditions of the pardon by returning to England prior to the expiration of their sentences.

When the pardoned felons arrived in the colonies, their services were sold to the highest bidder. The contractor then transferred the property-in-service agreement to the new master, and the felon was no longer referred to as a criminal but became an **indentured servant**. These indentures bear a similarity to the procedure now followed by parole boards. Like the criminal *qua* indentured servant, a prisoner released on parole agrees in writing to accept certain conditions; a release form is signed by the prisoner and the parole board, and some of the conditions imposed today on parolees are similar to those included on the indenture agreement (New York State Division of Parole, 1953). The termination of the Revolutionary War ended transportation of laborers to America (from then to 1879, England sent her convicts to Australia) (Hughes, 1987).

Maconochie and Norfolk Island

Torsten Erikkson refers to 1840 as the year in which "one of the most remarkable experiments in the history of penology was initiated" (1976: 81). In that year, Alexander Maconochie (1787–1860), a former naval officer, became superintendent of the remote British penal colony on Norfolk Island, about 930 miles northeast of Sidney, Australia, which was reserved for convicts who had committed crimes while in Australian or Tasmanian prisons. Maconochie set out a philosophy of punishment based on reforming the individual criminal: The convict was to be punished for the past and trained for the future. Because the amount of time needed to instill self-discipline and train a criminal could not be estimated in advance of sentencing, Maconochie advocated sentences that were open ended, what is known today as an **indeterminate sentence**. He set up a system of marks to be earned by each inmate based on good behavior; a sentence could not be terminated until a certain number of marks had been achieved. Norfolk housed the most dangerous felons, and riots occurred both before Maconochie arrived and after he left the island. His system, however, brought tranquility to the colony. Convicts passed through three stages on the way to release, each with an increasing amount of personal liberty; misbehavior moved an offender back to an earlier stage. Although Maconochie's experiment at Norfolk was successful from the standpoint of penology, he was opposed by authorities back in Australia who viewed him as "coddling criminals" while incurring extra costs on the government. Maconochie was relieved of his position in 1844 and returned to England, where in 1849 he became governor of a new prison; 2 years later, criticism of his approach as too lenient again led to his dismissal. Maconochie then embarked on a campaign for penal reform as a writer and speaker, and one of those he influenced was Walter Crofton.

Crofton and the Irish System

In 1853, Parliament enacted the Penal Servitude Act, which enabled prisoners to be released—paroled—on a **ticket of leave** and supervised by the police. That same year, Sir Walter Crofton (1815–1897) was commissioned to investigate conditions in Irish prisons and in 1854 became director of the Irish prison system. Crofton was familiar with the work of Alexander Maconochie, and their views on the reformation of criminals were similar. The **Irish system** that Crofton established was based on Maconochie's work at Norfolk Island and consisted of four stages:

1. The first stage involved solitary confinement for 9 months; during the first 3 months, the inmate was on reduced rations and was allowed no labor whatsoever. It was reasoned that after 3 months of forced idleness, even the laziest prisoner would long for something to do. He would then be given full rations, instructed in useful skills, and exposed to religious influences.
2. The convict was placed in a special prison to work with other inmates in the second stage, during which time he could earn marks to qualify for a transfer to the third stage.
3. This third stage involved transportation to an open institution where the convict, by evidencing signs of reformation, could earn release on a ticket of leave.
4. In the fourth stage, ticket-of-leave men were conditionally released and, in rural districts, supervised by the police; those residing in Dublin, however, were supervised by a civilian employee who had the title of inspector of released prisoners. He worked cooperatively with the police, but his responsibility was to secure employment for ticket-of-leave men. He required them to report at stated intervals, visited their homes every 2 weeks, and verified their employment—he was the forerunner of a modern parole officer.

Parole Developments in the United States

A modified version of the Irish system was adopted in England, and Crofton's work was widely publicized in the United States. American supporters of the Irish system, however, did not believe that adoption of the ticket of leave would ever be accepted in the United States. Their attitude was apparently based on the belief that it would be un-American to place any person under the supervision of the police, and they did not believe that any other form of supervision would be effective. A letter written by Crofton in 1874, in reply to an inquiry sent to him by the secretary of the New York Prison Association, stressed that the police of Ireland were permitted to delegate competent persons in the community to act as custodians for ticket-of-leave men, and he suggested a similar system for the United States (New York State Division of Parole, 1953). These principles were first implemented in the Elmira Reformatory.

Elmira Reformatory

In 1869, a **reformatory** was authorized for Elmira, New York, to receive male offenders between the ages of 16 and 30. The following year, the first convention of the American Prison Association met in Cincinnati. A paper based on the Irish system, dealing with the idea of an indeterminate sentence and the possibilities of a system of parole, was presented by the noted Michigan penologist Zebulon R. Brockway. The prison reformers meeting in Cincinnati urged New York to adopt Brockway's proposal at Elmira. When the Elmira Reformatory opened in 1876, Brockway was appointed superintendent. Instead of the nineteenth-century penology of silence, obedience, and labor, Elmira's goal would be reform of the convict ("Elmira," 1998).

Key Fact

Zebulon R. Brockway was influenced by the Irish system, and his efforts led to the establishment of Elmira Reformatory in 1876 and the use of an indeterminate sentence.

Brockway drafted a statute directing that young first offenders be sent to Elmira under an indeterminate sentence not to exceed the maximum term that was already in place for nonreformatory offenders. The actual release date was set by the board of managers based on institutional behavior: "After the inmate accumulated a certain number of marks based on institutional conduct and progress in academic or vocational training, and if the investigation of his assurance of employment was positive, he could be released" (New York State Division of Parole, 1984: 6). An entire building was set up as a trade school; by 1894, there was instruction in 34 trades ("Elmira," 1998). This system at Elmira "was designed to instill youthful offenders with the habits of order, discipline, and self-control and to mold obedient citizen-workers" (Pisciotta, 1994: 7–8). According to Brockway (1926: 111), this was a difficult task because the inmates "constitute a living antisocial human mass not easily resolved and brought into accord with the orderly life of a good community."

The Reverend Frederick Wines, a colleague of Brockway, described the principles on which the Elmira system was based (a clear manifestation of positivism):

> Criminals can be reformed; that reformation is the right of the convict and the duty of the State; that every prisoner must be individualized and given special treatment adapted to develop him to the point in which he is weak—physical, intellectual, or moral culture, in combination, but in varying proportions, according to the diagnosis of each case; that time must be given for the reformatory process to take effect, before allowing him to be sent away, uncured; that his cure is always facilitated by his cooperation, and often impossible without it. (1975: 230)

This cooperation was fostered by corporal punishment and the use of inmate classifications, according to which privileges were dispensed. Behavior judged to be "reformative" was rewarded by reclassification, which meant increased privileges, eventually leading to release on parole.

Brockway, reflecting the popularity of social Darwinism (discussed in Chapter 1) in his day, believed that his charges "belong to the grade of humanity that is inferior. The whole inmate population may be divided in this connection into two grades of inferiority—those whose defectiveness is apparent and others whose mental and moral defects are concealed under good (and sometimes quite brilliant) capabilities in given directions" (1926: 110). Despite its reform pretensions, Elmira had many problems:

> [It] was overcrowded, understaffed, and grossly mismanaged. Key treatment programs did not fulfill their stated goals and objectives. Violence, escapes, smuggling, theft, homosexuality, revolts, arson, and other forms of inmate resistance were serious problems. Inmates suffered extraordinarily harsh punishments—including severe whippings and months of solitary confinement in dark, cold dungeons—and deliberate psychological torture. Elmira was, quite simply, a brutal prison. (Pisciotta, 1994: 33–34)

Investigations led to charges against Brockway, but he succeeded in remaining superintendent until his retirement in 1900 ("Elmira," 1998).

On being admitted to Elmira, each inmate was placed in the second grade (of classification); 6 months of good conduct meant promotion to the first grade, but misbehavior could result in being placed in the third grade, from which the inmate would have to work his way back up. Continued good behavior in the first grade resulted in release—America's first parole system. Paroled inmates remained under the jurisdiction of reformatory authorities for an additional 6 months, during which the parolee was required to report on the first day of every month to his appointed guardian (from which parole officers evolved) as well as provide an account of his situation and conduct. Some believed that a longer period under supervision would be discouraging to the average parolee: "Inmates were released conditionally, subject to return if the Board believed there was actual or potential reversion to criminal behavior" (New York State Division of Parole, 1984: 6). However, no real attention was given to the training of prisoners for their future adjustment in the community, and both prison administrators and inmates soon accepted the idea that whether the inmate was reformed or unreformed, allowance of time for good behavior was automatic and release at the earliest possible date was a right rather than a privilege. After release, supervision was either nonexistent or totally inadequate, a deficiency also found in other states using parole release, such as Minnesota and Illinois (Pisciotta, 1992).

Key Fact

Elmira Reformatory provided a model for the modern boot camp–style prison.

Early Use of the Indeterminate Sentence and Parole

The Elmira system—which included military-style uniforms, marching, and discipline—was copied by reformatories in other states, such as the Massachusetts Reformatory at Concord, the Minnesota State Reformatory at St. Cloud, and the Illinois State Reformatory at Pontiac, and made applicable to all or part of the prison population in Pennsylvania and Michigan (Pisciotta, 1992; Wines, 1975). In 1893, Nebraska granted the governor the power to parole any inmates who had served the minimum time for the crimes for which they were convicted and, in 1911, established a three-member parole board. Alabama enacted a parole law in 1897, while Ohio and California had parole release statutes in place before the turn of the twentieth century (Zevitz and Takata, 1988). In 1907, New York extended indeterminate sentencing and parole release to all first offenders, except those convicted of murder. On the heels of prison riots in 1930, New York established a full-time three-member parole board, transferring release decisions from the Department of Corrections, and created the Division of Parole to supervise parolees (Dressler, 1951). Georgia enacted legislation in 1908 that gave the Prison Commission authority to implement a system of "parole or conditional pardons;" however, there were no parole officers to provide supervision, so offenders were placed under supervision of an employer or sponsor. By 1940, the state employed six parole officers.

In 1911, Minnesota enacted indeterminate sentencing for all felony offenders who could be kept under the jurisdiction of the Board of Control until they reached their maximum sentence. In 1913, Massachusetts established the Commonwealth Board of Parole; before that, the commissioner of prisons and many correctional institutions conducted independent discharge or conditional release programs. In 1907, Montana authorized parole release by the Board of Prison Commissioners; Tennessee enacted indeterminate sentencing and parole in 1929. By 1939, only four states (Florida, Mississippi, South Carolina, and Virginia) did not have provisions for parole. Florida used the governor's authority to pardon inmates in an effort to keep down the cost of imprisonment—the governor and his cabinet often presided over 200 pardon applications in a day—but in 1941, the Florida Parole Commission was established. South Carolina began to use parole that same year, and Virginia established a parole system in 1942. By 1944, all 48 states had enacted parole legislation. Although most states had a mechanism in place for parole release prior to 1929, the impetus for the expansion of the use of parole was the Great Depression, as the following statistics for parole release indicate (Cahalan, 1986):

    1923: 21,632
    1926: 19,917
    1930: 29,509
    1936: 37,794

The Great Depression, which began in 1929 and ended with the onset of World War II, resulted in many unemployed workers and (as noted in Chapter 5) led to legislation that effectively abolished the economic exploitation of convict labor. This abolishment was accompanied by prison overcrowding, the prohibitive cost of prison construction, and an outbreak of prison riots. A 1931 report by the National Commission on Law Observance and Law Enforcement described the overcrowding of America's prisons as "incredible"; Michigan, for example, had 78.6 percent more inmates than its original capacity; California, 62.2 percent; Ohio, 54.1 percent; and Oklahoma, 56.7 percent. In

Key Fact

Most states had a mechanism in place for parole release prior to 1929, but the impetus for the expansion of parole was the Great Depression.

1923, 81,959 inmates were in prison (74 per 100,000 population); in 1930, 120,496 (98 per 100,000 population); and in 1940, the eve of World War II, 165,585 (125 per 100,000 population) (Cahalan, 1986). *Pressing economic conditions, not the press of prison reform, led to the popularity of parole release.*

By 1935, more than 60,000 persons were on parole in the United States, although only six states had what was described as "suitable" parole systems (Prison Association of New York, 1936). For example, although Texas had a system of parole release—actually conditional pardons—as early as 1905, there were no parole officers until 1937, when volunteer parole supervisors were authorized; they were the only form of supervision until well after World War II.

Before the Depression, parole systems stressed employment—criminals were idlers who needed the discipline of work—and depended on employers to monitor parolees. This was weakened by widespread unemployment during the Depression and, at the same time, the pressure to release more persons on parole (Simon, 1993: 70). With World War II, industrial production increased, unemployment decreased, and parolees became eligible (for the first time since 1833) for military service. Before the war ended, every state had a parole system in place.

POSITIVISM AND THE MEDICAL MODEL OF CORRECTIONS

Despite its ravaging consequences, war can provide the impetus for many long-lasting social and scientific advances: With total mobilization, widespread unemployment ends, and improvements in manufacturing, communication, transportation, and medicine occur. During World War II, the United States experienced such important developments as the jet plane and the rocket, streptomycin, radar, sonar, and atomic energy. The war also provided psychologists with funds and an environment for extensive research and experimentation (Herman, 1995). By the end of the war, the horizons of science appeared to be unlimited, and the influence of positivism reemerged in penology.

Medical Model of Corrections

Key Fact

The medical model views criminals as "sick" and in need of rehabilitation.

This great faith in science was occurring during a period of concern over the apparent rise in crime as measured by the *Uniform Crime Report*. The war had kept the wheels of industry spinning; unemployment did not exist. Suddenly, wartime production had ceased, and millions of young men who had been trained to kill and destroy (and who had done little else for several years) were returning from overseas. The vast allocation of societal resources in wartime had proved successful in the area of science, so perhaps a corresponding commitment of resources could prove successful in dealing with the problem of crime: a (scientific) "war on crime," based on the **medical model.**

The positive approach to crime and criminals seeks to explain and respond to criminal behavior in a manner not dependent on (classical) issues of law, philosophy, or theology. Instead, criminal behavior is to be examined using the principles and methods of science, much as physical illness is subjected to examination by the physician: "This new approach to criminal behavior stressed deviance as pathology. The criminal was not seen as 'bad' but as 'mad,' and he was to be given the benefit of the medical approach to madness. He should be helped to understand his unconscious motivation and to go through a process of psychoanalytic change" (Robitscher, 1980: 44). According to one author, "In its simplest (perhaps oversimplified) terms, the medical model as applied to corrections assumed the offender to be 'sick' (physically, mentally, and/or socially); his offense to be a manifestation or symptom of his illness, a cry for help" (MacNamara, 1977: 439). The medical metaphor extended to the postconviction process:

- Examination = presentence investigation report
- Diagnosis = classification
- Treatment = correctional program

According to the medical model as applied to corrections, the effects of a treatment program are subjected to review by the parole board, which determines if the offender is sufficiently rehabilitated to be discharged from the correctional institution. A positive response means that treatment will continue on an outpatient basis in the form of parole supervision. The American Friends Service Committee (AFSC) sums up the rationale for this approach: "It rejects inherited concepts of criminal punishment as the payment of a debt owed to society, a debt proportioned to the magnitude of the offender's wrong. Instead it would save the offender through constructive measures of reformation, [and] protect society by keeping the offender locked up until the reformation is accomplished" (1971: 37).

The medical model is based on two questionable assumptions:

1. Criminals are "sick" and can thus benefit from treatment/therapy.
2. The behavioral sciences can provide the necessary treatment/therapeutic methods.

Although a paucity of systematic research supported this approach to criminal behavior, the medical model of corrections was adopted in most states—in theory, if not practice. William Parker argues that the theory never actually matched the practice: "The theory of rehabilitation has made some changes in the prison: terminology has changed, there are more programs, sweeping floors is now work therapy. The theory of rehabilitation has merely been imposed upon the theories of punishment and control" (1975: 26).

Criticisms of the Medical Model

From its inception in California in 1944 under Governor Earl Warren, the medical model approach continued without serious opposition into the 1970s. Any opposition came primarily from the right of the political spectrum, as exemplified by the attacks of FBI Director John Edgar Hoover, who saw parole as "coddling" criminals, releasing them before they completed their sentences. During the 1970s, however, the attack on the medical model of corrections shifted to the political left.

In 1971, the Quaker-sponsored AFSC published the first comprehensive attack on the indeterminate sentence and parole. The AFSC noted that the indeterminate sentence and parole rested on the view that crime is a result of individual pathology and that it can best be "cured" by treating *individual* criminals. Such an approach, the AFSC noted, downgrades environmental factors, such as poverty, discrimination, and lack of employment opportunities. Furthermore, the committee argued, even if the medical model approach is valid, the achievement level of the behavioral sciences does not offer a scientific basis for treatment.

Key Fact

The medical model approach to criminals began in California and spread across the United States.

The work of the AFSC had only limited impact and no practical effect until 1974. In that year, sociologist Robert Martinson published a review of correctional treatment efforts titled "What Works?" to which he answered: Virtually nothing! "What Works?" (1974) was actually a synopsis of the research findings of Martinson, Douglas Lipton, and Judith Wilks; the complete work was published the following year. The three researchers surveyed 231 studies of correctional programs up until 1968, about which Martinson (1974: 25) concluded: "With few and isolated exceptions, the rehabilitative efforts that have been reported so far have had no appreciable effect on recidivism." Although the Martinson summary is more critical than the larger report, both lent credence to the arguments of the AFSC. In a review of the Lipton, Martinson, and Wilks (1975) research, a panel of the National Research Council concluded that it was "reasonably accurate and fair in the appraisal of the rehabilitation literature"; in fact, the panel concluded, Lipton et al. "were, if anything, more likely to accept evidence in favor of rehabilitation than was justified" (Sechrest, White, and Brown, 1979: 31).

According to Paul Gendreau and Robert Ross, the research examined by Martinson was dated; furthermore, substantial literature since 1968 (Martinson's cutoff date) demonstrated that "successful rehabilitation of offenders had been accomplished, and continued to be accomplished quite well" (1987: 350). In fact, "between 1973 and 1980 reductions in recidivism, sometimes as substantial as 80 percent, had been achieved in a considerable number of well-controlled studies. Effective programs were conducted in a variety of community and (to a lesser degree) institutional settings, involving predelinquents, hardcore adolescent offenders, and recidivistic adult offenders, including heroin addicts" (1987: 350–351). These results were not short-lived: "Follow-up periods of at least two years were not uncommon, and several studies reported longer follow-ups" (1987: 351). The debate over correctional treatment effectiveness continued (e.g., Andrews et al., 1990; Lab and Cullen, 1990), with rigorous analysis indicating positive outcomes in a variety of studies.

Alternative Models of Corrections

Whatever the merits, criticism of the indeterminate sentence, the medical model of corrections, and the use of parole increased. David Fogel presented a **justice model** in which he criticized the unbridled discretion exercised by correctional officials, particularly parole boards, under the guise of "treatment":

> It is evident that correctional administrators have for too long operated with practical immunity in the backwashes of administrative law. They have been unmindful that the process of justice more strictly observed by the visible police and courts in relation to rights due the accused before and through adjudication must not stop when the convicted person is sentenced. The justice perspective demands accountability from all processors, even the "pure of heart." (1975: 192)

Instead of the often-hidden discretion exercised by parole boards, Fogel recommended both a return to flat time/determinate sentences, with procedural rules in law limiting sentencing discretion, and the elimination of parole boards and parole agencies. Furthermore, Fogel argued, whatever "treatment" is offered in a prison should be voluntary and should in no way affect the release date of an inmate.

Andrew von Hirsch (1976) offered the concept of **just deserts**, according to which the punishment is to be commensurate with the seriousness of the crime—a return to the classical approach. "A specific penalty level must apply in all instances of lawbreaking which involves a given degree of harmfulness and culpability" (von Hirsch and Hanrahan, 1978: 4). Indeterminacy and parole would be replaced with a specific penalty for a specific offense.

The Twentieth Century Fund Task Force on Sentencing offered the **presumptive sentence**: Each category of crime would have a presumptive sentence "that should generally be imposed on typical first offenders who have committed the crime in the typical fashion" (1976: 20, italics deleted). For succeeding convictions or other aggravating circumstances, the judge could increase the presumptive sentence by a specific (albeit limited) percentage; mitigating circumstances could similarly reduce the presumptive sentence.

In sum, the basic thrust of these criticisms and proposals was to limit judicial discretion, eliminate the indeterminate sentence, and abolish the parole board. Here was an issue on which both the political left and right could agree—but for different reasons. Alfred Blumenstein notes:

> In the mid-1970s a striking consensus of the political left and the political right emerged in opposition to the indeterminate sentence. The political left was concerned over the excess of discretion in decisions about an individual's liberty and the excessive disparity that appeared in sentences in presumably similar cases. The political right appeared to be far more concerned about "leniency" than about disparity. They viewed the parole boards as excessively ready to release prisoners early and expressed shock that prisoners were back on the street on parole well before the maximum sentence. (1984: 130, edited)

Franklin Zimring and Gordon Hawkins (1995: 9) point out that this coalescing of otherwise divergent views "is a pretty reliable indication that some of the participants in the policy debate do not have a clear understanding of the practical implications of their stance."

Good Politics Can Generate Bad Policy

The parole board is always vulnerable to criticism, and parole release often proves a tempting target for demagogic attack. After all, no one supports the release of a prison inmate who subsequently commits a heinous crime—the value of predictive hindsight. The issue, of course, is not if an inmate should be released but what mechanism will be used to make the release decision. Prisons are overcrowded, and virtually all inmates will eventually be released, facts usually overlooked in the focus on a particular crime or parolee. Nevertheless, governors in many states would rather advocate abolishing parole than have to defend such a politically vulnerable system.

As sentiments toward crime and criminals hardened, political changes generated by (often pandering) politicians led to "tough on crime" statutes that have further clogged our correctional facilities. "Sound-bite policy" replaced careful and thoughtful policy development. In Michigan, for example, the governor proposed abolishing parole and establishing a determinate sentencing system. He called this system **truth in sentencing**, which has now become a popular metaphor for eliminating release discretion but which offers no method for controlling the prison population. He also proposed eliminating **good time** (reduction of time served as a reward for no violations of prison rules) for violent criminals and making "the threat of additional punishment [sic] the best incentive for inmates to behave in prison." These proposals must be viewed against the realities of Michigan's prison population, which has increased 220 percent since 1985, a year when the state was automatically releasing inmates as new commitments were received. Michigan parole supervises about 13,000 offenders per year (probation supervises another 55,000), and by 2007, the prison system was packed with about 52,000 inmates—an all-time record occurring at a time of fiscal crisis. The federal government took the lead in promoting truth in sentencing, and in 1994 Congress passed the Truth-in Sentencing Incentive Grants law. To qualify for the prison-building grants, states have to require people convicted of violent crimes to serve at least 85 percent of their sentences.

In at least nine states, prosecutors were active in leading the fight to abolish the indeterminate sentence and parole. "Clearly, parole was an easy target for those looking

Release of Inmates

"Because states sharply curtailed education, job training and other rehabilitation programs inside prisons, the newly released inmates are far less likely than their counterparts two decades ago to find jobs, maintain stable family lives or stay out of trouble that leads to more prison. Many states have unintentionally contributed to these problems by abolishing early release for good behavior, removing the incentive for inmates to improve their conduct" (Butterfield, 2000b: 1).

Approximately 97 percent of those in prison will eventually be released. In 2004, of the approximately 650,000 persons released from prison and the 7 million released from jail, 3 out of 4 have substance abuse problems, but only 13 percent have received formal treatment prior to release. More than half have children under age 18. Despite research that correctional education and vocational training reduce recidivism (MacKenzie, 2006), 2 out of 3 released inmates lack a high school diploma and only 1 out of 3 received any vocational training while incarcerated; at least 1 out of 3 reports some physical or mental disability (Re-Entry Policy Council, 2005).

Key Fact

Determinate and truth-in-sentencing laws have severely restricted discretionary/parole release.

for political opportunities," notes Barbara Krauth, and "the emotional appeal of an attack on the system that released criminals to the streets may have benefited some political careers more than it actually addressed any of the complex problems of criminal justice" (1987: 52). By 1980, eight states had already adopted some form of determinate sentencing, including (in 1977) the pioneering state of California; the federal government and several other states have abolished the indeterminate sentence and parole release since that time, although a few (e.g., Colorado and Connecticut) have reintroduced the indeterminate sentence and parole supervision.[1]

Most states that have retained some discretionary parole release restrict eligibility. In Georgia, for example, persons convicted of such serious crimes as rape and armed robbery must serve their entire sentence; in New York, violent offenders must serve six-sevenths of the sentence, after which they are subject to 5 years of parole supervision. In New Jersey, persons convicted of first- or second-degree violent crimes or burglary must serve 85 percent of their sentence, after which they remain under parole supervision for 5 years (first-degree crimes) or 3 years (second-degree crimes). There is also mandatory parole supervision for life for those convicted of certain violent or sex crimes.

The federal Sentencing Reform Act of 1984, which abolished the indeterminate sentence, was designed to reduce sentence disparity and phase out parole release by 1992. However, the discretion lost by judges has been assumed by prosecutors, resulting in longer prison terms and an increasingly overcrowded federal prison system, and federal judges have been vociferous in their criticism of their lack of discretion in rendering sentencing decisions (Urbina, 2003).

As the next section indicates, this scenario has often been repeated in state systems. In states that have retained the indeterminate sentence, to be eligible for parole, an inmate prisoner must demonstrate that he or she has a job, or is likely to be able to secure employment, and a satisfactory residence. In the absence of discretionary release by a parole-board there is little if any pressure on prisoners to prepare for post-release life (Visher and Travis, 2003).

INDETERMINATE VERSUS DETERMINATE SENTENCING

Key Fact

Indeterminate sentencing usually involves a minimum and a maximum, with the actual date of release determined by a parole board or the result of the accumulation of good time.

Under indeterminate sentencing, originally established as part of the Elmira system, a judge imposes a prison term that has both a minimum and a maximum length.[2] For example, a defendant convicted of a class 3 felony could receive a sentence with a minimum of 3 years (written 3-0-0) and a maximum of 9 years (written 9-0-0); the actual release of the inmate (between 3-0-0/9-0-0) is determined by a parole board. In some states, such as New Jersey, the judge sets a maximum and an inmate becomes eligible for parole release after serving one-third of the sentence. A provision is usually made for good-time credit, time deducted from the maximum sentence because of good institutional behavior (typically about a third of the sentence, although in Iowa it is 50 percent). For example, an inmate with a maximum sentence of 9-0-0 could accumulate up to 3-0-0 years of good time, thus being released after 6-0-0 years without the intervention of the parole board. In Wyoming, good time can reduce the minimum by one-third and the maximum by 25 percent. In some states, so-called truth-in-sentencing legislation has abolished parole and reduced or eliminated the use of good time, leaving prison officials without an effective mechanism to discipline inmates (see Proctor, 2000 for a discussion of this issue).

Under a system of indeterminate sentencing, persons convicted for the same class of offense could receive different sentences. For example, a first-degree robbery may carry a

---

[1]Actually, Connecticut uses a determinate sentence, but persons convicted of nonviolent offenses are eligible for parole release after serving half their sentence. Certain violent offenders or those who, regardless of the instant offense, possess a criminal history that includes certain violent offenses are required to serve 85 percent of their sentence prior to being considered for parole.

[2]In 1995, New York enacted legislation permitting judges to sentence select second felony offenders convicted of nonviolent crimes directly to parole supervision.

minimum sentence range of 2-0-0 to 6-0-0 and a maximum sentence range of 8-4-0 to 25-0-0. Even those who receive the same sentence, for example, 3-0-0 to 9-0-0, can be released (paroled) at different times: 3-0-0, or 4-0-0, or 5-0-0, all the way up to 9-0-0 (minus good time). Criticism of the indeterminate sentence has involved this differential treatment of persons convicted of similar crimes, which is contrary to the classical approach to criminal behavior: "Critics of the indeterminate sentence argued that the treatment model has never realized its lofty objectives in practice and that, given the nature of the correctional system, these goals never will be realized. Furthermore, they maintained that the indeterminate sentence has created a situation of gross sentencing disparity that no longer can be justified by referring to treatment goals" (Goodstein and Hepburn, 1985: 17).

In response to criticism of indeterminate sentencing and parole boards, a variety of so-called flat, definite, or **determinate sentence** schemes have been adopted. Although each requires the setting of a *specific* sentence—no minimum and maximum— these sentencing models differ according to the amount of discretion left to the judge:

- *Definite sentence/no discretion.* The legislature provides for a specific sentence for each level of offense. For example, all crimes that constitute a class 2 felony would require the judge to impose a specific sentence—no deviations permitted. If a class 2 felony was punishable by imprisonment for 7 years, all judges would be required to sentence all defendants convicted of a class 2 felony to 7-0-0.

- *Definite sentence/wide discretion.* The legislature provides for a range of sentences for each level of offense. For example, a class 2 felony would be punishable with a sentence between 3-0-0 and 7-0-0. Under this system, the judge retains discretion to sentence a class 2 offender to 3-0-0 or 4-0-0, all the way up to 7-0-0. The sentence imposed is definite—for a specific number of years—but the judge's discretion is wide.

- *Presumptive sentence/narrow discretion.* The legislature limits discretion to a narrow range of sentences for each level of offense; for each level, a presumed sentence exists from which the judge cannot deviate, except if aggravating or mitigating circumstances apply, and then in only a limited manner. For example, if a defendant is convicted of a class 2 felony, the judge could be required to set a sentence of 5-0-0. On a showing of aggravation by the prosecutor, however, the judge could increase the presumptive sentence to 6-0-0; on a showing of mitigation by the defense, the judge could decrease the presumptive sentence to 4-0-0. In some states (e.g., Minnesota), the presumed sentence is increased by a fixed amount based on the severity of any prior convictions (see Figure 3.4 in Chapter 3).

- *Presumptive sentence/wide discretion.* As in the presumptive sentence with narrow discretion, the legislature provides three possible terms for each class of felony. However, although each class has a presumptive sentence, the judge may decrease (for mitigation) or increase (for aggravation) by significantly fixed amounts; for example, a presumptive sentence of 12 years could be decreased to 6 years or increased to 16 years.

In 2007, the U.S. Supreme Court (*Cunningham v. California*, No. 05-6551) found the presumptive system used in California unconstitutional insofar as it allowed the judge to use a fact-finding process to decide which of three sentences to impose; fact finding, the Court noted, is reserved for juries.

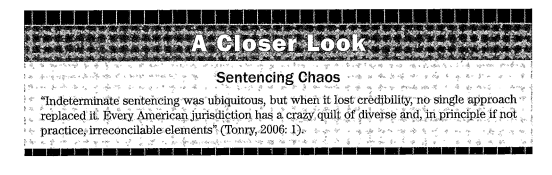

A Closer Look

Sentencing Chaos

"Indeterminate sentencing was ubiquitous, but when it lost credibility, no single approach replaced it. Every American jurisdiction has a crazy quilt of diverse and, in principle if not in practice, irreconcilable elements" (Tonry, 2006: 1).

Determinate sentencing systems usually include a provision for good time, ranging from 15 to 50 percent off the sentence, to promote prison discipline. A defendant sentenced to a determinate sentence of 5-0-0 in a system using 50 percent good time would be released (presuming good behavior) after 2-6-0. In practice, good time is deducted in advance, when the offender is first received at the institution; misbehavior results in time being added. In some states, an inmate may be entitled to additional time off the sentence for exemplary performance: "meritorious good time" or "industrial good time." These grants of additional time off (which can be used to circumvent truth-in-sentencing laws) are usually the result of prison overcrowding in states without parole release but may also be used to reduce sentence minimums so that inmates can more quickly qualify for parole release. More than half of inmate releases are the result of good-time provisions (Glaze, 2003).

Florida, which abolished the indeterminate sentence and parole release in 1983, would start with Basic Gain Time, in which one-third is taken off the sentence when the inmate is received at a correctional institution. On the first day of each month, an inmate would receive an additional 20 days off (Incentive Good Time) as a reward for class attendance, satisfactory work performance, and general good behavior. One-shot Meritorious Gain Time could remove up to 60 days for exemplary performance. As a result of critical overcrowding, in 1987 the legislature provided for Provisional Release Credit, an additional 60 days per month whenever the prison system is more than 97.5 percent of capacity. As a result of these schemes, the average Florida inmate served a little more than one-third of his or her sentence (Malcolm, 1989a). In response, the legislature put its "get tough" mode in full gear and—ignoring the pressing problem of prison overcrowding—enacted mandatory minimum sentences for a host of offenses (Bales and Dees, 1992), which exacerbated overcrowding and required new schemes for early release.

The wheels of Florida justice continued to spin. In 1993, Florida became one of the first states to repeal mandatory sentences for several crimes, particularly possession of small amounts of drugs. The following year, as a result of increased prison construction and a reduction in the number of felony cases receiving prison sentences—the expanded use of probation—Florida achieved compliance with court-ordered reductions in prison population, and the governor ordered a cutback in the amount of good time granted to inmates who had been serving about 45 percent of their sentences. Florida's experience reveals the often poor fit between theory and practice when it comes to getting tough on criminals.

More than half of prison releases are the result not of discretionary parole board decision making but of good time (mandatory release) provisions. In most states, these mandatory releasees are placed under the supervision of a parole officer and thus are often referred to as "parolees." Ohio mandates postrelease supervision for serious offenders; for others, it is discretionary. In making the determination whether to impose discretionary postrelease control, the Ohio Parole Board considers the prisoner's criminal history, any juvenile court delinquency adjudication, the record of the prisoner's conduct while imprisoned, and any recommendations from the Office of Victim Services. If the current sentence involves harm and/or threat of harm, the offender will be placed on postrelease control and actively supervised by a parole officer. Violators of postrelease control may be subject to progressively restrictive sanctions. More serious violators can be returned to prison for up to nine months per violation, with the cumulative prison term for all violations not exceeding one-half of the original sentence served in prison. In California, determinate sentencing limits parole supervision to four years and the time that parole violators can be returned to prison is no more than one year.

In the absence of discretionary release, the incentive for adequate funding of offender supervision is often absent—no one (the governor or parole board) can be held accountable for the serious misconduct of mandatory releases. In Illinois, for example, a budget crisis in 1987 led to the layoff of 98 of the state's 159 parole agents, but most were reinstated at the beginning of 1989 (and 29 new agents added) because of a substantial increase in parole violations as well as new arrests among releasees. No delinquency action was being taken against releasees because parole agents were not available, so violations had dropped from 35 percent to 20 percent. By 1995, however, the number of agents was down to 69, and they were "supervising" about 30,000 offenders. The governor responded to criticism by recommending that offenders be released without any supervision. In the state of Washington, parole release and supervision were abolished in 1984; subsequently the public reacted adversely to serious offenders being released without community supervision, and in 1988 supervision was restored.

In place of parole, several states have substituted *split sentencing*, which reverses the normal sequence of probation, prison, and parole. The offender is sentenced to a term of imprisonment and upon completion is released to probation supervision. In Maine, the first state to abandon parole release (and parole supervision), postrelease supervision was reestablished by Maine's judges in the form of split sentences—"judicial parole"—whereby offenders are sentenced to imprisonment followed by a period of probation supervision (Anspach and Monsen, 1989). In Virginia, which abolished parole release in 1995, inmates can earn a maximum of 4.5 days for each 30 days served. About 80 percent of inmates have what is called *supervised probation* following incarceration: The name of the game has changed, but the game continues.

Key Fact

In the absence of discretionary release, the incentive for adequate funding of offender supervision is often absent, as is offender interest in prison rehabilitation programs.

A Closer Look

Abolishing Parole

- "When a board has no ability to *select* those who will be granted release, they are forced to supervise a population not of their own choosing. . . . It is impossible to assure cooperation of offenders when they know they must be released regardless of their willingness to agree to certain conditions. And we have seen, in states such as Illinois, that when the parole board loses its discretion over release, it tends to lose its visibility and power in the system. Field supervision tends to be underdeveloped and, eventually, underfunded and understaffed" (American Probation and Parole Association, 1995: 14).

- Although nearly 600 of the 1,700 inmates housed at the Big Muddy River Correctional Center in Illinois are sex offenders, empty beds remain in the sex offender unit, which houses up to 200 inmates. The program administrator notes why—a simple lack of motivation. Illinois does not have parole, and in the absence of discretionary release, sex offenders apparently have no incentive to enter treatment (Monti, 1997).[3]

Determinate Sentencing, Prosecutorial Discretion, and Disparate Justice

Although in theory the determinate or definite sentence was supposed to reduce any unwarranted variation in sentencing and the amount of time served in prison, the practice has been otherwise. No state, for example, has adopted a determinate sentence with no

---

[3]Research into the Sex Offender Treatment Program of the Alaska Department of Corrections revealed that inmates "who were in treatment longer tended to last longer in the community without a re-offense. Those who completed all stages of treatment through the advanced stage had a zero re-offense rate for sexual re-offenses. This included Sexual Assault offenders (rapists) who generally tend to re-offend more quickly and at a higher rate" (Mander et al., 1996: 2).

discretion, whereas several have adopted schemes with wide discretion. Thus, in Illinois, a defendant convicted of selling drugs as a first offense can receive a *determinate* sentence of anywhere from 4-0-0 all the way up to 30-0-0.

The issue of prosecutorial discretion presents the most obvious deficiency in the proposals set out by Fogel, von Hirsch, and others. This discretion is typically exercised privately, outside the scrutiny of official review, and affects sentencing more often and more significantly than does judicial discretion. Although a judge acting under a definite system with narrow discretion or a presumptive system with narrow discretion must apply a specific sentence for a particular class of crime (in the absence of mitigation or aggravation), the prosecutor, using charging powers, determines the particular class of crime to charge and whether to move for aggravation or oppose a motion for mitigation.

Key Fact

Determinate sentencing may shift discretion from the judge and parole board to the prosecutor.

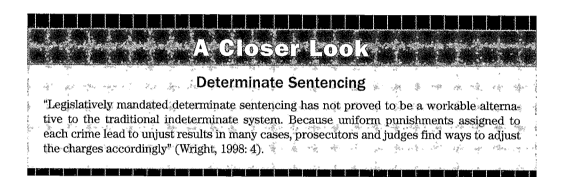

A Closer Look

Determinate Sentencing

"Legislatively mandated determinate sentencing has not proved to be a workable alternative to the traditional indeterminate system. Because uniform punishments assigned to each crime lead to unjust results in many cases, prosecutors and judges find ways to adjust the charges accordingly" (Wright, 1998: 4).

In return for cooperation—a plea of guilty—the prosecutor can reduce the class of crime for which the offender will be charged and may also agree not to move for aggravation or accept mitigation offered by defense counsel. By manipulating the charging decision, the prosecutor (not the judge) can often determine the actual sentence. Thus, determinate sentencing can increase the ability of a prosecutor to **plea bargain**. In many instances, determinate sentencing merely shifts discretion away from judges and parole boards and toward the prosecution end of criminal justice; in other words, release decisions are being made at the front end rather than the back end of the system. Because the defendant's primary interest is in how much time he or she must actually serve, new laws limiting good time (under so-called truth-in-sentencing provisions) are now added to the plea bargaining equation.

Furthermore, the abolition of parole boards, a practical accomplishment of determinate sentencing schemes, ignores the role of the board in reducing the sentence disparity that the classicalists decry. Because the parole board reviews the sentences of all state prisoners, it is in a position to act as a panel for mediating disparate sentences for similar criminal behavior. In Nebraska, for example, the board of parole "serves as an 'equalizer.' Within the framework of the law, it attempts to produce equity and uniformity in the sentencing structure caused by the inherent disparity which understandably results from having ninety-three prosecuting offices and multiple judicial districts." The Georgia Board of Pardons and Paroles states that "the board's unique central position and authority allow it to reduce sentencing disparity. Excessive harshness is more readily reduced, but excessive leniency in the form of a too-light confinement sentence may be corrected partially by parole denial." Figure 6.1 provides a hypothetical example of the parole board as a sentencing review panel. "All parole boards, either implicitly or explicitly, serve the vital function of equalizing justice between judges, courts, and counties. Board members removed from the heat of trial are familiar with case practices in all jurisdictions and are able to apply a common statewide standard of justice. Left to their own devices, the . . . judges, district attorneys, defense counsel, juries, community temperament and the sophistication of defendants [produce] some very strange and disparate results" (Holt, 1995: 20).

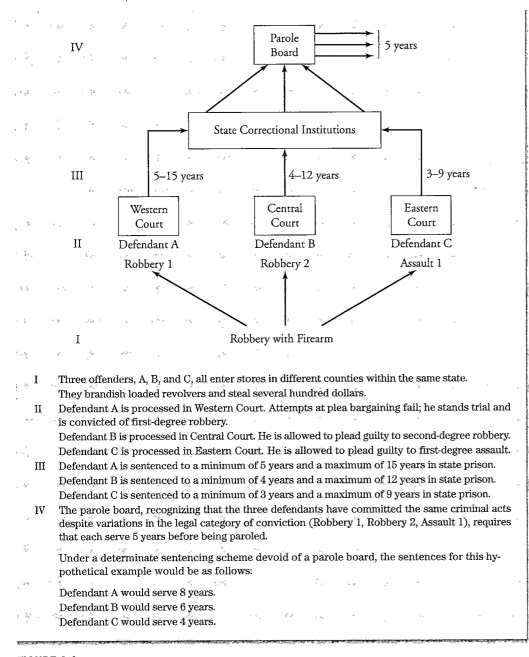

I Three offenders, A, B, and C, all enter stores in different counties within the same state. They brandish loaded revolvers and steal several hundred dollars.

II Defendant A is processed in Western Court. Attempts at plea bargaining fail; he stands trial and is convicted of first-degree robbery.

Defendant B is processed in Central Court. He is allowed to plead guilty to second-degree robbery.

Defendant C is processed in Eastern Court. He is allowed to plead guilty to first-degree assault.

III Defendant A is sentenced to a minimum of 5 years and a maximum of 15 years in state prison. Defendant B is sentenced to a minimum of 4 years and a maximum of 12 years in state prison. Defendant C is sentenced to a minimum of 3 years and a maximum of 9 years in state prison.

IV The parole board, recognizing that the three defendants have committed the same criminal acts despite variations in the legal category of conviction (Robbery 1, Robbery 2, Assault 1), requires that each serve 5 years before being paroled.

Under a determinate sentencing scheme devoid of a parole board, the sentences for this hypothetical example would be as follows:

Defendant A would serve 8 years.
Defendant B would serve 6 years.
Defendant C would serve 4 years.

FIGURE 6.1 *Parole Board as Sentencing Review Panel*

THE "WHY?" OF PAROLE

Some (AFSC, 1971; Fogel, 1975; MacNamara, 1977) presume that parole is based on a medical model or some humanitarian effort gone astray, but the history of prisons and parole in the United States underscores the fact that parole release has been used (and possibly abused) as a mechanism for maintaining prison discipline and reducing prison overcrowding. The parole board evolved out of the power of governors to issue pardons to selected convicts; before the creation of parole boards, governors often used their pardoning powers to relieve prison overcrowding. In the middle of the nineteenth century, pardons accounted for more than 40 percent of the releases from U.S. prisons (Hibbert, 1968). In Ohio, for example, whenever the state prison exceeded a certain number of inmates, the governor granted pardons to make room for new prisoners. In

1867, Nevada created a pardon board with the power to release inmates through commutation, and in 1909, the board's authority was expanded to include the parole of prisoners who were required to report to the governor's private secretary at least once per month. In 1898, Virginia passed an act permitting prisoners who had served half their sentence to file a petition with the governor, who (upon the recommendation of the board of penitentiary directors) could grant a conditional pardon. The act was later amended—the word *parole* was substituted for pardon, and release authority was transferred from the governor to the penitentiary directors. As late as 1938, parole was simply a conditional pardon in many states.

In Florida, the pardon board often presided over as many as 200 pardon applications per day until the Parole and Probation Commission was established in 1941. In Utah, the Board of Pardons continues to have parole responsibilities, and the Alabama Board of Pardons and Paroles, established in 1939, has final authority on all pardons. The Vermont Parole Board was created in 1968; until that time, release from prison was by conditional pardon granted by the governor.

Blumenstein (1984: 131) points out that "one of the functions the parole agencies carried out during the period of indeterminate sentencing was serving as a 'safety valve' for crowded prisons. As prison populations began to approach or exceed the prison capacity, the parole board could simply lower the threshold of the degree of rehabilitation that warranted release." The clear use of parole as a safety valve for prison population control is highlighted by the Texas experience. Faced with overcrowding during the 1980s, Texas simply increased parole releases: "In 1983, about 40 percent of inmates were released on parole after their first hearing. By the end of the decade, this had increased to nearly 80 percent" (Kelly and Ekland-Olson, 1991: 604). In 1980, with 15,257 prison admissions, the parole board released 5,660 inmates; in 1991, when prison admissions reached more than 37,000, the parole board released more than 31,000 inmates—an increase of more than 400 percent (Bodapati, Marquardt, and Cuvelier, 1993). A similar situation occurred in Georgia where, in 1980, 14,000 inmates were in prison; a decade later there were 44,000 prisoners, and county jails were backing up with prisoners sentenced to state prison. A class-action lawsuit—which state officials believed they would lose—was initiated. In response, the parole board accelerated the parole release of thousands of inmates (for which the board was labeled "soft on crime"). Nationally, increases in the prison population result in even greater increases in the parolee population: In 1983, there were 437,248 prisoners and 251,708 parolees (58 percent); in 1988, there were 627,402 prisoners and 407,977 parolees (65 percent) (National Institute of Justice data).

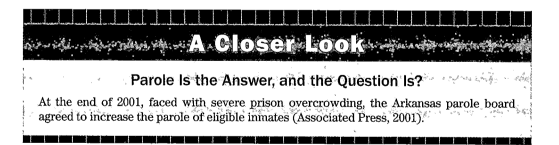

A Closer Look

Parole Is the Answer, and the Question Is?

At the end of 2001, faced with severe prison overcrowding, the Arkansas parole board agreed to increase the parole of eligible inmates (Associated Press, 2001).

In many states using determinate sentencing, the same release function is being carried out by prison officials using good-time or "special release" provisions. However, prison officials lack the information, time, or expertise to make rational release decisions—a reason why parole boards developed. Those who see parole as simply a rehabilitative device have bought the *rhetoric* but not the *reality*—parole is more realistically understood as "risk management." Corrections officials in several states that have abolished the indeterminate sentence have (by necessity caused by overcrowding) become *de facto* parole boards. In Delaware, which abolished parole release (but not the parole board) in 1989, the Department of Correction may apply to the parole board for a modification of the inmate's sentence. The board then holds a hearing for the purpose of providing a recommendation to the sentencing judge. In Florida, as the result of overcrowding (and a federal lawsuit), the parole board was reconstituted as the Control Release Authority to act under the state's determinate sentencing laws in essentially the same capacity as it had under indeterminate sentencing; again "a change in name but not the game."

A Closer Look

New Jersey

Parole is seen as a method for encouraging inmates to avoid institutional disciplinary infractions and to participate in institutional programs while incarcerated. "In addition to helping the department of corrections maintain order and security in the prisons, parole provides a powerful incentive for the inmate to develop pro-social personal goals and strengths and to become motivated for law-abiding behavior" (*State Parole Board Annual Report 2005*, 2006: 3).

David Greenberg and Drew Humphries (1980) argue that the forces of the political right co-opted the issues of sentencing reform and abolition of parole and were successful in implementing changes that are increasing the length of time served by offenders, now without the possibility of parole release, in a prison atmosphere devoid of any rehabilitative component. Illinois provides an example: The state went from indeterminate to determinate sentencing in 1978, and since that time "tough on crime" legislation has significantly increased the penalties for criminal behavior without any available modification via the parole board. In a strong defense of the medical/rehabilitative model, Francis Cullen and Karen Gilbert (1982: xxix) state: "Whatever its failings, criminal justice rehabilitation has thus persisted as a rationale for caring for offender needs and not for making the wayward suffer. Without its humanizing influence, the history of American corrections would be even bleaker than is now the case."

	Corrections Model (Positivism)	Justice Model (Classicalism)
Cause of crime	Psychological/sociological factors over which the offender has little or no control	Rational choice made by the offender operating with free will
Sentence	Indeterminate/parole	Determinate/definite
Sentencing goal	Rehabilitation	Punishment/deterrence
Discretion	High	Low with stress on equality of punishment commensurate with the offense

FIGURE 6.2 *Corrections Model versus Justice Model*

Key Fact

Most inmates will eventually be released—the question is, who will make the release decision?

A relevant question is now at issue: Do we entrust the decrease of prison populations, reduction of sentencing disparity, and risk management of criminal offenders to judges, prison officials, or parole boards? A review of the history that led to the establishment of parole in the first instance argues for this discretion to be the responsibility of a professional parole board.

Now that the review of the history of prisons and parole is complete, Chapter 7 examines the services provided by a parole agency.

KEY TERMS

determinate sentence (p. 177)

good time (p. 175)

indentured servant (p. 168)

indeterminate sentence (p. 168)

Irish system (p. 169)

just deserts (p. 174)

justice model (p. 174)

medical model (p. 172)

plea bargain (p. 180)

presumptive sentence (p. 174)

reformatory (p. 169)

ticket of leave (p. 169)

truth in sentencing (p. 175)

INTERNET CONNECTIONS

American Probation and Parole Association: www.appa-net.org

Corrections news/topics: corrections.com

Parole boards: crimelynx.com

Parole boards and departments of correction: www.crime-guide4all.com

Probation and parole links: www.talkjustice.com/links.asp?453053932; www.co.pinellas.fl.us/bcc/juscoord/eprobation.htm

REVIEW QUESTIONS

1. What are the similarities between the property-in-service/indentured servant agreement and the procedure followed by parole boards?
2. What is the connection between the system employed by Alexander Maconochie at Norfolk Island and the indeterminate sentence?
3. What was the Irish system established by Walter Crofton?
4. What are the characteristics of the Elmira system?
5. Why did events in 1929 lead to the expansion of parole in the United States?
6. What are the characteristics of the penological revolution that occurred at the end of World War II?
7. What is meant by the medical model approach to criminal behavior?
8. What are the questionable assumptions on which the medical model approach to corrections is based? Why are they questionable?

9. What is the difference between an indeterminate and a determinate sentence?

10. What did Robert Martinson's 1974 review of correctional treatment efforts in his article "What Works?" conclude?

11. What were the criticisms that led some states to abandon the indeterminate sentence and parole?

12. What is the basis of criticism of the indeterminate sentence by those on the right of the political spectrum?

13. What is the basis of criticism of the indeterminate sentence by those on the left of the political spectrum?

14. How do the four types of determinate (or definite) sentences differ?

15. What is meant by good time, and how does it affect inmates?

16. What is meant by truth-in-sentencing laws?

17. What is the relationship between determinate sentencing and plea bargaining?

18. What has developed in light of prison overcrowding and the absence of parole release in some states?

19. Why is parole an easy political target?

20. What are the arguments in favor of maintaining parole release?

Parole Administration and Services

The truth is that most released prisoners do not go to a job and stay clean. This is not because they planned to return to crime; rather, it is because they are stigmatized, prisonized, ill-prepared social cripples, and their experiences on the outside disorganize, discourage, and eventually derail them.

—*John Irwin* (2005: 172).

Chapter Outline

Administration of Parole Services

Conditional Release

Parole Boards

Guidelines for Parole Boards

Parole Services

Conditions of Parole

Length of Supervision

Violation of Parole/Conditional Release

Executive Clemency

Legal Decisions Affecting Parole

A parole agency can provide three basic services: parole release, parole supervision, and executive clemency. For administrative purposes, these can be classified into three categories:

1. *Institutional services*
2. *Field services*
3. *Executive clemency*

In several states that have abolished parole release (e.g., California), parole officers/agents continue to supervise offenders released from prison (not by a parole board, but) on "good time." The administration of parole is less complex than that of probation because parole services are usually administered centrally on a statewide basis. Some local jurisdictions (e.g., Los Angeles County) have their own city/county parole from jails with supervision pro-vided by probation officers. In Iowa, probation and parole supervision is the responsibility of a judicial district. In 1998, Oregon moved probation and parole supervision from being a function of the state to a function of individ-ual counties, and Oregon counties hired most of the state's former probation and parole officers.

ADMINISTRATION OF PAROLE SERVICES

There are two basic models for administering parole:

1. *Independent model.* In the **independent model**, a parole board is responsible for making release and revocation determinations *and* for supervising persons released on parole (and good time); it is independent of any other state agency. This model is used in Connecticut and New York.

2. *Consolidated model.* In the **consolidated model**, the parole board is an autonomous panel within a department that also administers correctional institutions. The board makes release and revocation decisions, but supervision of persons released on parole (and good time) is under the direction of the commissioner of corrections. This model is used in Colorado, Rhode Island, and most other states that have parole boards.

In both models, probation services are sometimes combined with parole services in a single statewide agency. For example, Alabama, North Dakota, Vermont, and Wyoming use a consolidated model in which probation services are part of a department of corrections. In Pennsylvania, the courts have the statutory alternative of referring presentence investigations and the supervision of probationers and (county jail) parolees to the Board of Probation and Parole, an independent state agency, rather than the county probation department. In Nevada, probation and parole supervision is the responsibility of the Division of Parole and Probation headed by a chief appointed by the governor and located within the Division of Motor Vehicles and Public Safety. In Alabama, while the Board of Pardons and Parole determines which prisoners serving in the jails and prisons of the state will be paroled, the Jefferson County Parole Board exercises jurisdiction over jailed inmates in that county.

The Task Force on Corrections (1966) summarized arguments for the independent model:

- The parole board is in the best position to promote the idea of parole and to generate public support and acceptance. Because the board is often held accountable (by the public, news media, public officials) for parole failures, it should be responsible for supervising parolees.

- The parole board in direct control of administering parole services can more effectively evaluate and adjust the system.

- Supervision by the parole board and its officers properly divorces parole release and parolees from the correctional institution.

- An independent parole board in charge of its own services is in the best position to present its own budget request to the legislature.

The Task Force on Corrections (1966) also summarized arguments for including both parole services and institutions in a single department of corrections:

- The correctional process is a continuum; all staff, institutional and parole, should be under a single administration rather than be divided, with both resultant competition for public funds and friction between policies.

- A consolidated correctional department has the advantage of consistent administration, including staff selection and supervision.

- Parole boards are ineffective in performing administrative functions. Their major focus should be on case decisions, not on day-to-day field operations.

- Community-based programs partway between institutions and parole, such as work release, can best be handled by a single centralized administration.

Critics contend that the independent model tends to be indifferent or insensitive to institutional programs and that the parole board in this model places undue stress on variables outside the institution. Conversely, critics of the consolidated model argue that the parole board will be under pressure to stress institutional factors in making parole decisions, although these are of dubious value in making a parole prognosis.

CONDITIONAL RELEASE

Conditional release (sometimes referred to as "mandatory release") is the term used to describe inmates released on good time. In such cases, either the parole board has denied them parole release or the state does not have a parole board. Inmates in most states are eligible for good time, that is, they can accumulate days, months, and years off their maximum sentence by avoiding institutional infractions and/or participating in prison programs. Georgia is an exception to the near unanimous use of good time.

In addition, some states have meritorious good time for exemplary behavior and emergency good-time provisions to reduce the prison population in cases of severe overcrowding. In states using indeterminate sentences and parole boards, good time can usually be accumulated at the rate of 10 days per month—one-third off the maximum sentence. In some of these states, good time may also be subtracted from the minimum sentence, making the inmate eligible for parole before the minimum sentence has actually been served. In Texas, inmates classified as "Trusties" earn 30 days for each 30 days served and may earn up to an additional 15 days of good conduct time per month for completing vocational or educational programs while in prison. The Texas Parole Board may block good-time releases "when it determines that an offender's good conduct does not accurately reflect the potential for rehabilitation and that the offender's release would endanger the public." In Maryland, good time is granted at the monthly rate of 5 days for displaying good behavior; 5 days for performing industrial, agricultural, and administrative tasks; and an additional 5 days for making satisfactory progress in vocational and educational training. In Wyoming, in addition to being eligible for 10 days of good time per month, inmates can receive an additional 15 days of "special good time" for exemplary behavior.

In states using determinate sentencing, good time usually amounts to 1 day off for every day served. Those with truth-in-sentencing laws have reduced this to 15 percent of the sentence (although in cases of severe prison overcrowding, it can be increased by any number of schemes). In New York, where determinate sentencing is now the rule for most offenders, they must serve at least six-sevenths of the sentence (unless prison overcrowding demands otherwise) after which they must begin serving a period of court-imposed postrelease supervision of one and a half to five years.

Most states in which (discretionary) parole release has been abolished have retained supervision requirements for offenders released on good time. In California, for example, all persons serving nonlife terms are released to community supervision that cannot exceed three years.

In some of these states, decisions regarding good time and revocation of conditional release are the responsibility of a variety of boards: In California, it is the Board of Prison Terms; in Illinois, it is the Prisoner Review Board; and in Missouri, the Board of Probation and Parole was placed in the Department of Corrections and Human Services, where it deals with questions of good time and supervision revocation. In Minnesota, where the parole board has been abolished, supervision of conditional releasees is the responsibility of the commissioner of corrections, who delegates this authority to the executive director of adult release. The Florida Conditional Release Program requires postprison supervision for inmates who are sentenced for certain violent crimes and have served a prior felony commitment or who are sentenced as a habitual offender, violent habitual offender, violent career criminal, or sexual predator.

Key Fact

Conditional release is based on accumulation of good time and is devoid of (parole board) discretion.

Conditional release supervision by correctional probation officers is for a period of time equal to the gain time that they received in prison. These offenders are subject to conditions of supervision set by the Florida Parole Commission, and this supervision can be revoked and the releasee returned to prison if the commission determines that a violation of supervision has occurred.

These (nonparole) boards are also responsible for making parole decisions for persons imprisoned under indeterminate sentencing statutes that have since been repealed and for persons serving "life sentences." Some also serve as a pardons board, considering requests for the granting of executive clemency. In California, as in most states, the Department of Corrections is responsible "for deducting good time credit from the sentence and for establishing procedures to deny good time credit." If good time is denied to an inmate, the person can appeal through department appeals procedures. A final department appeal can be submitted for review to the Board of Prison Terms, which conducts a hearing on the matter. In Illinois, the Prisoner Review Board has broader responsibilities:

> [P]anels of at least 3 members [the board has 10 members] hear and decide cases brought by the Department of Corrections against prisoners in custody of the Department for alleged violation of Department rules with respect to good conduct credits . . . in which the Department seeks to revoke good conduct credits, if the amount of time at issue exceeds 30 days or when, during any 12-month period, the cumulative amount of credit revoked exceeds 30 days. However, the Board is not empowered to review the Department's decision with respect to the loss of 30 days of good conduct credit for any prisoner or to increase any penalty beyond the length requested by the Department. . . . Upon recommendation of the Department the Board restores good conduct credit previously revoked.

PAROLE BOARDS

Parole Board Members

As in most states, the 7 members of the Wyoming Parole Board are appointed by the governor for 6-year terms. In Georgia, the 5 members of the Board of Pardons and Paroles are appointed by the governor and serve 7-year terms. In New Jersey, the board consists of a chairperson, 12 associate members assigned to panels to review adult and young offender cases, 2 associates assigned to a panel to review juvenile offender cases, and 3 alternate members. The 3 members of the Utah Board of Pardons are appointed by the Board of Corrections for 6-year terms; in South Dakota, the Board of Pardons and Paroles has 9 members who serve terms of 4 years: 3 appointed by the governor, 3 by the attorney general, and 3 by the state supreme court. The Texas Board of Pardons and Paroles has 18 members appointed by the governor for 5-year terms. The 5 members of the Alaska Board of Parole are appointed by the governor for 5-year terms. In Connecticut, the chairperson and 2 vice chairpersons serve full-time for 4-year terms; the other 12 members serve part-time for 4-year terms. The Iowa Board of Parole consists of 5 members; the chairperson and vice chairperson serve full-time, while the 3 other members are on a per diem basis. The New York State Board of Parole has 19 members; its chairperson serves as Director of the Division of Parole, and its officers supervise released offenders.

Parole boards have been criticized because members may lack relevant background or education. Specific professional qualifications are required for board members in only a few states. Maryland requires "at least a B.A. or B.S. degree in one of the social or behavioral sciences or related fields . . . [and] at least three (3) years experience in a responsible criminal justice or juvenile justice position, or equivalent experience in a relevant profession such as law or clinical practice." In Vermont, the governor "shall appoint as members

A Closer Look

Parole in Michigan

The Michigan Parole Board consists of 10 full-time non–civil service employees appointed by the Director of the Department of Corrections. The parole board gains jurisdiction of a case when a prisoner serving a nonlife sentence has served his or her minimum sentence, less any good time or disciplinary credits the prisoner may have earned. (In most cases the minimum sentence is set by the judge, the maximum by statute.)

The parole board is divided into three-member panels. The decision whether to grant or deny parole is made by majority vote of a parole board panel. (All cases involving a life sentence must be decided by a majority vote of the full parole board.) If the panel denies parole, a date is selected for the next parole board review.

Parole board members conduct prisoner interviews throughout facilities in Michigan. Each facility visit is for 3 to 4 days, and a typical interview lasts 15 to 20 minutes. During the interview, the parole board questions the prisoner about the nature of the offense and whether the prisoner accepts appropriate responsibility for his or her prior criminal record, as well as his or her behavior and adjustment while in prison, participation in programming, and mental health and substance abuse history.

The factors considered by the parole board in making parole decisions include the parole guidelines score. The parole guidelines score, mandatory for all prisoners eligible to be considered for parole, is a numerical scoring system designed to assist in applying objective criteria to any decision made by the parole board. Information used to calculate the parole guidelines score is the prisoner's current offense, prior criminal record, institutional conduct and program performance, age, mental status, and statistical risk. Michigan law and departmental policy allow parole to be granted without interview if the prisoner's parole guidelines score falls in the high guidelines, provided the prisoner is not serving time for a crime involving a sex offense or a death.

persons who have knowledge of and experience in correctional treatment, crime prevention or related fields, and shall give consideration, as far as practicable, to geographic representation to reduce necessary travel to the various parole interview centers of the state." In Iowa, the board must contain one minority group member, one attorney knowledgeable in correctional procedures and issues, and one person with a master's degree in social work or a counseling-related discipline who is knowledgeable in corrections. Pennsylvania requires members of the Board of Probation and Parole to have at least 6 years of professional experience in parole, probation, social work or related areas (including 1 year in a supervisory or administrative capacity) and a bachelor's degree.

The role of patronage politics in the selection of parole board members is similar to that of many other responsible government positions, although the relatively low salary and extensive travel requirements tend to make parole board membership less attractive to those with other opportunities for political appointments.

Parole Board Hearings

Typically, from one to three parole board members briefly interview an inmate who is eligible for parole, and they usually hold release hearings in the state's prisons. In Maryland, these hearings are open to the media as well as victims or their designees; in Iowa, the board uses a two-way fiber-optic system for interviews conducted from the board's conference room. The members of the board panel will have available a case folder prepared by an institutional parole officer (or correctional staff person) containing information about each inmate: the presentence investigation report; institutional reports relative to education, training, treatment, physical and psychological examinations, and misconduct; and a release plan in the event that parole is granted.

Key Fact

In some states, a panel of parole board members will interview eligible inmates; in others, inmates are interviewed by a parole examiner who reports to the board with a recommendation.

Parole in Texas

Several months before an offender's parole eligibility review date, the inmate is interviewed by an institutional parole officer. The parole officer prepares a case summary that includes the facts of the offender's offense; other relevant information such as assaultive behavior or the use of narcotics; personal history; assignments, adjustment, and disciplinary record while in prison; physical and mental condition; and a summary of positive and negative factors.

As the offender's parole eligibility review date approaches, the offender's case is reviewed by a parole board panel. The offender may be interviewed by one of the members of this panel before the panel votes. For most offenders, the panel will consist of 3 members of the board, and 2 of the 3 panelists must vote for parole before it can be granted. A few categories of offenders may be paroled only with a two-thirds majority vote of the entire 18-member board.

Parole panel members look at the circumstances and seriousness of the offense; any prior prison commitments; relevant input from victims, family members, and trial officials; the prisoner's adjustment and attitude in prison; the offender's release plan; and factors such as alcohol or drug use, violent or assaultive behavior, deviant sexual behavior, use of a weapon in an offense, institutional adjustment, and emotional stability. Based on the entirety of the available information, the parole panel then determines whether the offender deserves the privilege of parole.

In some states, this aspect of parole release is handled by parole examiners who interview the inmate and report back to the board with a recommendation; some states do not conduct hearings or interviews—decisions are made on the basis of written reports. In New Jersey, a parole examiner considers each inmate for release at an interview session held between 4 and 6 months before parole eligibility. If parole is recommended by the examiner, the case is reviewed by a panel of parole board members. If they accept the recommendation, a parole release date is set. If the examiner recommends against parole or if the parole panel denies parole, a panel hearing at which the inmate appears is arranged. In Colorado, the manner in which the parole hearing is conducted depends on the seriousness of the inmate's offense. For violent crimes or for inmates with a history of violence, two board members may conduct an initial hearing and submit their recommendation to the seven-member board (four affirmative votes are required for parole release). A single board member may hear nonviolent cases, which can be face to face or by telephone; if the decision is to grant parole, an additional board member must agree (West-Smith, Pogrebin, and Poole, 2000).

According to David Stanley, the parole hearing is of dubious value: "It is a traumatic experience for the inmate, and parole board members are subjected to the rigors of holding hearings far away from home, with hours spent in travel and in prisons" (1976: 42). Furthermore, Stanley reports, hearings "are of little use in finding out whether the inmate is likely to succeed on parole." He argues that a strong case can be made for abolishing parole hearings:

> [I]n cases where the information in the file and the board's own precedents plainly show that parole must surely be granted or denied, the hearing is a charade. And in those cases where the outcome is not so obvious it is a proceeding in which the inmate is at a great disadvantage and in which he has reason to say anything that will help his chances for parole. The atmosphere at such a hearing is full of tension and latent hostility. Under these circumstances the hearing is an ineffective way to elicit information, evaluate character traits, and give advice, all of which parole boards try to do. (1976: 43)

One way to deal with some of these issues is to permit the inmate to have representation at the hearing. The National Advisory Commission on Criminal Justice Standards

---

A Closer Look

Presumptive Parole in New Jersey

An inmate *shall* be released on parole at the time of parole eligibility unless it is demonstrated by a preponderance of the evidence that the inmate has failed to cooperate in his or her own rehabilitation or that there is a reasonable expectation that the inmate will violate conditions of parole if released on parole.

---

and Goals believes representation helps promote a feeling of fairness and can enable an inmate to communicate better and thus participate more fully in the hearing, stating that "representation can also contribute to opening the correctional system, particularly the parole process, to public scrutiny" (1973: 403). The commission makes note of the fact that representation at parole hearings may be considered "annoying" to parole officials—there is fear that the hearing may take the form of an adversary proceeding—but adds that "these inconveniences seem a small price for the prospective gains" (1973: 403). The Hawaii Paroling Authority not only permits representation at its release hearings but offers inmates the right to appointed counsel if they cannot afford to hire an attorney; however, this is unusual, and most jurisdictions do not permit representation at parole hearings. In Maryland, for example, it is noted that "relatives or other interested and responsible individuals may request a conference with the Commission, submit letters, or other pertinent data relative to an inmate's parole consideration at any time prior to the hearing. They may not appear at parole hearings." In Pennsylvania, "As the interview is not an adversarial process, the Board does not permit counsel representation at these interviews." In 1979, the U.S. Supreme Court (*Greenholtz v. Inmates*, 442 U.S. 1) ruled that the Constitution does not require that an inmate be given the opportunity to participate in parole board hearings (or to be informed of the reasons for denial of parole). However, Stanley (1976: 43) concludes that, given the present parole system, hearings are necessary as an expression of our national tradition and culture: "A man has his day in court before he is convicted and sentenced. In all sorts of situations we feel outraged if a person is not even confronted with the evidence before something adverse is done to him. In the hearing the prisoner is at least given a chance to state his case, correct erroneous statements, and impress the board with his determination (real or alleged) to reform."

Key Fact

At parole release hearings, inmates are typically not permitted to be represented by counsel.

Victim Participation

Most states permit victims or their next of kin to appear before the parole board, and others permit written statements to be considered at the parole hearing. In Nevada, for example, state law "provides that victims of crimes may attend meetings of the Nevada Board of Parole Commissioners. The Parole Board will provide notice of pending parole hearings if the victim of crime provides the board with a current address and requests such notice." In Alabama, "Victims of violent crimes and families of children who have been abused are notified prior to an inmate's being considered for parole by the Board. The Victim's right to be present at the Parole Hearing and to express their concerns in person and in writing to the Board is provided by law." In New Jersey, at the time of sentencing, the prosecutor notifies any victim injured as a result of a crime in the first or second degree, or the nearest relative of a murder victim, of the opportunity to present a statement to be considered during a parole hearing or to give in-person testimony before the board concerning the victim's harm; the board notifies victims or relatives who have contacted the board requesting an opportunity to submit a statement or to provide testimony. In Connecticut, victims are notified of pending hearings and advised of their right to appear and testify. In Iowa, victims can use the state's two-way fiber-optic communications system to address the board from a site near their residence. New Jersey requires the county prosecutor to

Key Fact

Parole boards typically provide for input by victims through either a personal appearance or the submission of a statement.

notify any victim injured as a result of a crime of the first or second degree, or the nearest relative of a murder victim, of the opportunity to present a statement to be included with the parole reports considered at the parole hearing or to testify to the parole board concerning harm at the time of the parole hearing. Many states include a victim impact statement (VIS) as part of the documentation considered by the parole board. While most parole boards invite victims to attend the parole hearing, there are less hearings and victim's rights are thereby less meaningful (Travis and Petersillia, 2001).

A Closer Look

Victim Services

The Massachusetts Victims Services Unit provides a wide array of support services to victims who have been certified to receive information regarding offenders by the Criminal History Systems Board. The unit's staff acts as the parole board's representative in addressing and advancing victim/witness issues by collecting victim/witness input for board consideration, providing timely notifications of parole hearing dates and hearing results, providing information about parole and criminal offender record information, assisting citizens in completing impact statements, directing referrals to other criminal justice or social services agencies for collateral assistance, and heightening the community's level of awareness regarding victim/witness issues through both the media and direct contact.

In Pennsylvania, the Office of Victim Assistance is charged with keeping victims apprised of the status of the inmate and assists in preparing oral or written testimony by registered victims before the parole board. Staff will also refer victims for community services and provide training for correctional, probation, and parole staff on victim issues.

Guidelines for Parole Boards

Parole boards usually consider the crime, the length of time served, and the inmate's age, prior criminal history, use of alcohol or drugs, and institutional record. Some parole boards may request a recommendation from the prosecutor. All will certainly consider opposition to an inmate's parole from the police and the news media. A study of parole decisions in Massachusetts (Luther, 1995) found that the election of a "law and order" governor caused the board (whose membership remained almost unchanged) to decrease parole release rates, particularly for high-security inmates for whom they were virtually eliminated. The widespread use of parole guidelines has reduced the importance of general criteria.

Parole Board Countervailing Pressures

| Prison Overcrowding | - - - - - - - ►/◄ - - - - - - - | Political (Public/Media) Reaction |

As criticism of parole and parole boards began to mount in the 1970s, the U.S. Board of Parole engaged a group of researchers to develop a model for improved decision making. In particular, the board was interested in a means of reducing disparity and making the decision-making process intelligible (and defensible) to both inmates and the public. The researchers derived a set of variables that they saw as fairly representative of those used by board members in making decisions—the most salient being the seriousness of the offense and the parole prognosis. They also conducted a 2-year study of 2,500 federal parolees and uncovered a variety of "success factors," which they reduced to seven variables. The combined variables for severity of offense and parole prognosis were arranged in the form of a grid (Figure 7.1) to determine the actual length of imprisonment. For example, an adult

PAROLE SUCCESS LIKELIHOOD FACTORS

NAME	NUMBER	INSTITUTION	DATE

These guidelines indicate the customary range of time to be served for various combinations of offense and offender characteristics. It is emphasized that mitigating or aggravating factors may warrant decisions outside the guidelines, and in appropriate circumstances, the Board will exercise its discretion as provided by law. The basic guideline presupposes good institutional adjustment and program progress. Deviation from the normal conduct expected of all inmates could result in decisions outside the guidelines.

If the convicted person is serving sentences for multiple offenses, the most serious offense will determine the crime severity level. "Attempted" offenses will be rated one grade below the principal offense.

Convicted persons will appear for parole consideration when they have met the requirements of Nevada law.

The establishment of these standards is not intended to create any right or interest in liberty, nor to create any reasonable expectation of parole, nor to establish any basis for a course of action against the State, its political subdivisions, agencies, boards, commissions, departments, officers or employees. The release or continuation on parole is an act of grace of the State.

1. Age at first commitment:
   18 or older .... = 2
   17 or younger .... = 0

2. Prior convictions (F & M):
   None .... = 3
   One .... = 2
   Two/three .... = 1
   Four or more .... = 0

3. Incarcerations since age 17
   prior to instant offense:
   None .... = 2
   One .... = 1
   Two or more .... = 0

4. Parole/probation failure:
   No failure .... = 1
   Otherwise .... = 0

5. No use, possession or attempt
   to obtain heroin, cocaine, opiates,
   amphetamines .... = 2
   History of drug abuse .... = 0

6. Current offense did not involve
   burglary or forgery, credit card or
   bad checks .... = 1
   Otherwise .... = 0

7. Fully employed or full-time
   school for 6 months in year
   preceding offense .... = 1
   Otherwise .... = 0

8. Injury to/death of victim:
   Yes .... = 0
   Otherwise .... = 2

9. Use of weapon:
   Yes .... = 0
   Otherwise .... = 2

10. Not previously convicted of
    similar offense .... = 1
    Otherwise .... = 0

11. Prison programming:
    Has addressed educational/voca-
    tional deficiencies .... = 1
    Has sought and participated in
    counseling on substance abuse,
    alcohol or psychological programs .... = 1
    No history of prison problems .... = 1
    All .... = 3

Parole Success Likelihood Score

GUIDELINES—RECOMMENDED MONTHS TO SERVE

Read across from your Crime Severity Level and down from your Parole Success Likelihood Score to find your guidelines-recommended months to serve. For Crime Severity Level I through V, the grid reflects a shift in months to serve based on the court-imposed sentence length. If your sentence is less than 25 percent of the statutory maximum penalty, the lesser figure is used. If your sentence exceeds 75 percent of the statutory maximum penalty, the greater figure is used. For all other sentence lengths, the median figure is used. For Crime Severity Levels VI or VII, the guidelines recommendation will be one-third of the court-imposed sentence length or the grid recommendation, whichever is greater. The Board, using its discretion in your case, may depart from the guidelines recommendation.

FIGURE 7.1 *Parole Success Likelihood Factors, Nevada*

| PAROLE SUCCESS LIKELIHOOD SCORE | | | |
Crime Severity Level	Excellent 15–20	Good 10–14	Average 6–9	Poor 0–5
I	4	6	8	14-16-18
II	12	14	16-18-20	18-20-22
III	20-22-24	22-24-26	24-26-28	26-28-30
IV	28-30-32	30-32-34	32-34-36	34-36-38
V	36-38-40	38-40-42	40-42-44	42-44-46
VI	48	54	60	66
VII	60	66	72	78
VIII	90	102	114	126
IX	138	150	162	174

Crime Severity Level: ....

Parole Success Likelihood Score: ....

Guidelines-Recommended Months: ....

FIGURE 7.1 *(continued)*

offender convicted of forgery under $1,000, "Category Two," and whose parole prognosis is "good" would normally be released on parole after serving between 8 and 12 months; an offender convicted of multiple robberies, "Category Six," whose parole prognosis is "poor" would normally serve between 78 and 100 months before being paroled.

Parole board guidelines typically go well beyond the *medical/rehabilitative model*, on which the indeterminate sentence is often presumed to be based. Indeed, satisfactory progress in those institutional programs that are "rehabilitative" may not even affect the parole decision. Good institutional behavior is *expected*, not rewarded, although poor behavior can be punished with denial of parole (Krajick, 1978). In fact, the institutional adjustment of an offender has never been an accurate guide for predicting postinstitutional behavior (Dolan, Lunden, and Barberet, 1987); some evidence exists that certain offenders (e.g., substance abusers and professional criminals) most often perform well in prison but tend to recidivate.

In effect, the use of guidelines whose primary focus is *just deserts* is a form of deferred sentencing. Some critics claim that no justification exists for deferring sentence (the term of imprisonment) and that it creates problems by adding to the offender's uncertainty. Others argue that the parole board is relatively free of the "heat" that certain crimes and criminals can generate. The board does not typically operate with the same high visibility of a court; unlike a sentencing judge, the parole board is not normally under the gaze of the community and news media. These observers stress that the parole board, using guidelines, is better equipped to make a rational decision commensurate with just deserts than is a sentencing judge. The possibility of parole release also serves as an incentive for inmates to control their behavior and take advantage of rehabilitative programming.

Guidelines used by state parole boards consider the seriousness of the present offense and prior criminal history; most also consider rehabilitative items and parole prognosis. For example, the Georgia Board of Pardons and Paroles, in a mix of the classical and positive views, states: "Justice demands that punishment should be tailored to fit both the offense and the offender." A board hearing examiner identifies an inmate's crime severity level from a table of offenses ranked in seven levels from lowest to highest in severity (the higher the severity, the longer the inmate will be recommended to serve time). Then the hearing examiner calculates the inmate's parole success likelihood by adding weighted factors with proven predictive value from the inmate's criminal and social history. A history of factors such as prior imprisonment, parole or probation failure, heroin use or possession, and joblessness would increase the risk of paroling the inmate and cause him or her to be recommended for longer confinement. The parole board may go beyond the guideline range in the event of mitigating or aggravating circumstances, but the detailed reason for such decisions must be provided to the inmate in writing.

Key Fact

Parole guidelines consider the seriousness of the offense and prior criminal history, and most also consider parole prognosis.

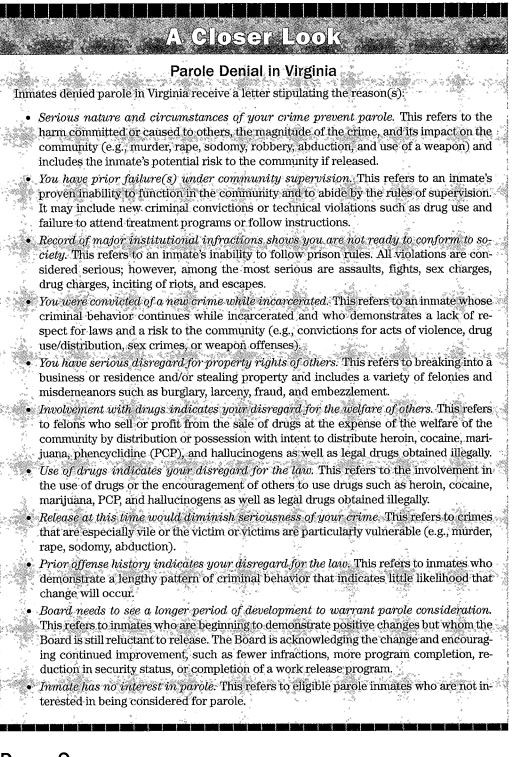

A Closer Look

Parole Denial in Virginia

Inmates denied parole in Virginia receive a letter stipulating the reason(s):

- *Serious nature and circumstances of your crime prevent parole.* This refers to the harm committed or caused to others, the magnitude of the crime, and its impact on the community (e.g., murder, rape, sodomy, robbery, abduction, and use of a weapon) and includes the inmate's potential risk to the community if released.
- *You have prior failure(s) under community supervision.* This refers to an inmate's proven inability to function in the community and to abide by the rules of supervision. It may include new criminal convictions or technical violations such as drug use and failure to attend treatment programs or follow instructions.
- *Record of major institutional infractions shows you are not ready to conform to society.* This refers to an inmate's inability to follow prison rules. All violations are considered serious; however, among the most serious are assaults, fights, sex charges, drug charges, inciting of riots, and escapes.
- *You were convicted of a new crime while incarcerated.* This refers to an inmate whose criminal behavior continues while incarcerated and who demonstrates a lack of respect for laws and a risk to the community (e.g., convictions for acts of violence, drug use/distribution, sex crimes, or weapon offenses).
- *You have serious disregard for property rights of others.* This refers to breaking into a business or residence and/or stealing property and includes a variety of felonies and misdemeanors such as burglary, larceny, fraud, and embezzlement.
- *Involvement with drugs indicates your disregard for the welfare of others.* This refers to felons who sell or profit from the sale of drugs at the expense of the welfare of the community by distribution or possession with intent to distribute heroin, cocaine, marijuana, phencyclidine (PCP), and hallucinogens as well as legal drugs obtained illegally.
- *Use of drugs indicates your disregard for the law.* This refers to the involvement in the use of drugs or the encouragement of others to use drugs such as heroin, cocaine, marijuana, PCP, and hallucinogens as well as legal drugs obtained illegally.
- *Release at this time would diminish seriousness of your crime.* This refers to crimes that are especially vile or the victim or victims are particularly vulnerable (e.g., murder, rape, sodomy, abduction).
- *Prior offense history indicates your disregard for the law.* This refers to inmates who demonstrate a lengthy pattern of criminal behavior that indicates little likelihood that change will occur.
- *Board needs to see a longer period of development to warrant parole consideration.* This refers to inmates who are beginning to demonstrate positive changes but whom the Board is still reluctant to release. The Board is acknowledging the change and encouraging continued improvement, such as fewer infractions, more program completion, reduction in security status, or completion of a work release program.
- *Inmate has no interest in parole.* This refers to eligible parole inmates who are not interested in being considered for parole.

PAROLE SERVICES

Institutional Staff

The primary responsibility of institutional parole staff is to prepare reports on inmates for the parole board. The staff also help inmates secure furloughs, work release, or halfway house placement and may assist with personal problems ranging from matters relating to spouse and children to questions of a technical or legal nature.

A Closer Look

Institutional Parole Officer, Connecticut

In correctional institutions, the parole officer performs case management and counseling activities for an assigned group of inmates; meets with and interviews inmates who are eligible for parole consideration; reviews Department of Correction files and retrieves data relevant to offense and sentencing information; verifies parole eligibility and discharge dates; obtains information and verifies inmates' involvement in rehabilitative programs; provides inmates with information regarding parole process; conducts administrative reviews of cases and makes disposition recommendations to Board of Parole in accordance with agency criteria; coordinates attendance of victim and inmate families at Board of Parole hearings; ensures completeness of inmates' files; attends Board of Parole hearings and serves as administrative hearing officer; presents case documentation to Board members; answers questions from Board members regarding case files; takes notes at Board hearings, records official minutes, and processes disposition of Board hearings; and processes violation of parole cases.

Under ideal conditions, when an offender is first received at an institution, he or she is interviewed by a member of the parole staff. The results of the interview, the psychiatric and psychological tests, and the information in the presentence report are then used to help plan an institutional program for the inmate. The parole staff periodically update the material with additional information. Staff members discuss release plans with inmates and request the field staff to visit and interview family members and prospective employers. When an inmate is ready to meet the parole board, the staff provide a report on the inmate that includes an evaluation of changes made since the offender was first received at the prison. The report may also contain a completed parole guidelines form and a recommendation if requested by the board.

Institutional parole staff may also hold group meetings with new inmates to orient them about parole; these group sessions are then followed by individual interviews. At preparole group sessions, parole staff attempt to lower anxiety about meeting the board or hearing examiners. When an inmate has been granted parole or becomes eligible for conditional release, he or she will meet with a parole staff member for a final discussion of the release program and rules of supervision before leaving the prison.

In some jurisdictions, institutional parole staff are responsible for notifying victims and local law enforcement agencies of the impending release of certain offenders. (Some states require that when an offender is released, the police in the area where the parolee is to reside or where the crime occurred be notified. In some instances, the parolee must register in person with the local law enforcement agency.) The institutional parole staff must determine the probable disposition of any warrants that have been lodged against an inmate. When appropriate, the staff arrange for an out-of-state program under the Interstate Compact (discussed in Chapter 11). In some states, the nonparole institutional staff perform the same or similar functions as institutional parole officers; these persons sometimes have the title of *correctional counselor*.

Field Staff

Field services staff usually operate out of district offices located throughout the state. The New York State Division of Parole, for example, has field staff assigned to the supervision of parolees and conditional releasees in about 20 field area offices throughout the state. They conduct field investigations requested by institutional staff relative to parole release programs as well as supervise parolees and conditional releasees. Parole field staff may also be involved in a variety of special programs, such as work release and furloughs. In New York

Key Fact

The primary responsibility of institutional parole staff is to prepare reports on inmates for the parole board.

A Closer Look

Institutional Parole Services in New Jersey

Members of the institutional parole staff are housed in 14 major institutions, providing services to all state penal and correctional facilities and training schools. They conduct personal interviews with inmates, provide counseling on specific matters to resolve problems, and help develop suitable preparole plans. Staff members afford every inmate prerelease classes and assist each inmate in obtaining necessary clothing and transportation from the institutions to a residence; they also provide institutional services to county correctional institutions and to various community release/residential centers. The increase in the use of home visits and furloughs as well as the number of state prisoners in county correctional facilities has added considerably to the workload of institutional parole office staff.

Street Readiness Program in Nevada

The Street Readiness Program of the Department of Probation and Parole works with inmates about to be released into the community on parole and those committed for 120-day evaluations who are returning to court for sentencing. These inmates become students for several hours a day over a period of 3 weeks, normally just before their release. The curriculum consists of classroom lecture, discussions, activities, and homework. Subjects include parole orientation, goals, decision-making skills, substance abuse, domestic relations, financial responsibility, citizenship, employment skills, sex education, law, insurance, human relations, and driver training. Established in 1981, the program is almost totally dependent on community volunteers.

"some Field Officers are assigned to correctional facilities to supervise Temporary Release participants—inmates permitted by the Department of Correctional Services to work, attend school, provide community service, and reestablish family ties (furloughs)."

Field Services in California. The overall objective of the Parole and Community Services Division is to reduce the frequency and severity of criminal behavior and to facilitate the community adjustment of adult offenders, fully recognizing their individual and changing circumstances and actions, through a program structure of appropriate prerelease, supervision, and support management functions. Supervision, surveillance, and services delivery are the responsibilities of parole field staff throughout the state. The primary means by which a parole agent fulfills these responsibilities is through contacts with parolees and persons involved with the parolees. Parole staff will cooperate and collaborate with criminal justice and human services agencies that may be involved with the parolees. Following are some duties and obligations of the parole agent:

- Obtain information about parolee activities and needs.
- Intervene in parolee behavior that violates the conditions of parole or that may jeopardize the safety of the public or the parolee.
- Provide supportive services to assist the parolee in the transition between imprisonment and discharge.
- Share information about the parolee with law enforcement personnel and the personnel of other agencies who have a demonstrated or compelling need to know.

Field Services in Pennsylvania. The immediate goal of parole supervision is the protection of society, which can best be accomplished by reintegrating the offender into the community as a responsible and productive citizen. Specifically, this goal means helping the parolee obtain and hold a meaningful job; resolving any adjustment problems within the family and the community; meeting education, mental health, or other normative needs, when relevant; and becoming part of the community through participation in

1. **Reports.** You must report to your supervising officer within 24 hours after your release. In the event that falls over a weekend, you are required to report on the next workday. Thereafter, you must report as instructed by your supervising officer. All written and oral statements made by you to your supervising officer must be truthful.

2. **Employment/Education.** You must maintain approved employment or be enrolled in an approved education program unless otherwise directed. You must obtain permission from your supervising officer before quitting your employment or education program. If you lose your job or are terminated from your education program, you must notify your supervising officer within 48 hours.

3. **Residence and Travel.** You must obtain prior approval from your supervising officer to change your place of residence, stay away from your approved residence overnight, or leave your assigned county.

4. **Laws.** You must obey all federal and state laws, local ordinances, and court orders. You are required to pay all court-ordered fines, fees, and restitution. You must report any arrest, citation, or summons to your supervising officer within 48 hours.

5. **Weapons.** You must not own, possess, use, pawn, sell, or have under your control any firearm (or imitation) or other dangerous weapon or be in the company of any person possessing such weapons. You must not possess any ammunition.

6. **Alcohol/Controlled Substances.** You will avoid the excessive use of alcohol, or abstain completely if directed, and will stay out of bars, taverns, clubs, and liquor stores. You must not sell, deliver, possess, or use controlled substances except as prescribed by a physician. You will submit yourself to random testing for the use of intoxicants and/or controlled substances.

7. **Association.** You must not associate with convicted felons, persons who are engaged in criminal activity, or other persons with whom your supervising officer instructs you not to associate. (Association with convicted felons at work, in counseling programs, in church, or in other locations and circumstances specifically approved by the Post Prison Transfer Board or your supervising officer is not prohibited.)

8. **Supervision Fees.** You must pay a monthly supervision fee unless granted an exemption. Community service work in lieu of supervision fees may be required.

9. **Cooperation.** You must, at all times, cooperate with your supervising officer and the Post Prison Transfer Board. You must submit yourself to any rehabilitative, medical, or counseling program that the Post Prison Transfer Board or your supervising officer deems appropriate.

10. **Search and Seizure.** You must submit your person, place of residence, and motor vehicles to search and seizure at any time, day or night, with or without a search warrant, whenever requested to do so by any Department of Community Corrections officer.

11. **Waiver of Extradition.** Your acceptance of conditional release constitutes an agreement to waive extradition to the State of Arkansas from any jurisdiction in or outside the United States where you may be found, and you also agree that you will not contest any effort by any jurisdiction to return you to the State of Arkansas to answer a charge of violation of any of the conditions of your release.

12. **Special Conditions.** _____

FIGURE 7.2 *Arkansas Conditions of Release*

activities and organizations that reflect the person's interests and capabilities. This involves working not only with the person under supervision but also with the various community agencies and resources that have the capability of assisting in solution of problems of parolees.

One of the tools of the supervision staff is "Conditions Governing Parole/Reparole" established by the board to be used as a structuring force in the life of the parolee. These conditions define what course of behavior is acceptable if the client wants to complete the period of parole supervision successfully. Although several common conditions are to be adhered to, the board recognizes the needs of the individual offender and has provided for one or more special conditions to be imposed as needed.

CONDITIONS OF PAROLE

Every conditionally released or paroled prisoner is required to sign an agreement to abide by certain regulations. This aspect of parole has its origins in the ticket of leave, and as noted in Chapter 6, modern parole conditions resemble ticket-of-leave regulations. Parole conditions are similar throughout most jurisdictions and are also similar or identical to probation regulations. Conditions of parole can generally be divided into two parts: *standard conditions*, which are applicable to all parolees/conditional releasees and which typically involve restrictions on travel, association with other offenders, drug and alcohol use, employment, and residence; and *special conditions*, which are tailored to the individual requirements of a particular offender (Figure 7.2). For example, persons with a history of sex offenses against children will be prohibited from areas where children typically congregate, such as playgrounds; persons with a history of alcohol abuse may be prohibited from using alcohol or being in facilities such as bars where alcohol is consumed. In more recent years, some parole agencies have been requiring parolees to pay supervision fees. In Texas, parolees are required to pay a standard monthly fee of $10 plus $5 for the victim's fund; those convicted of certain offenses must pay an additional $8 to the fund. In New York, parolees are required by law to pay a supervision fee of $30 per month.

Length of Supervision

The length of time an offender must spend on parole/conditional release supervision is governed by the length of the sentence and the laws of the state where he or she was convicted. In Oregon, a conditional releasee "is subject to a period of supervision similar to parole, not to exceed six months or the maximum date, whichever comes first." In Indiana, persons are to be discharged no later than 1 year after conditional release, whereas in Illinois, the length of supervision for a conditional releasee varies from 1 to 3 years, depending on the class of crime for which the offender was convicted. In California, for persons sentenced under a life sentence, the maximum period (including time under parole supervision and time under revocation status) cannot exceed 7 years; for persons sentenced under a nonlife sentence, the maximum period (including time under supervision and time under revocation status) cannot exceed 4 years. In Ohio, those convicted of serious felonies must be under supervision for 3 to 5 years. For less serious felonies, supervision up to 3 years is discretionary with the parole board, which may reduce the term. In Missouri, after the releasee has 3 years of successful supervision, the parole board may discharge an offender from parole or conditional release.

In most states, a parolee/releasee can be discharged before the expiration of a sentence or a mandated period of supervision. In California, based on satisfactory performance, a nonlife releasee can be discharged from supervision after 1 year and a lifer after 3 years. In Kentucky, a parolee can request a final discharge from parole after the expiration of 24 months, but those serving a life sentence must wait 5 years. The Hawaii Paroling Authority can issue a discharge whenever "the parolee has demonstrated for a sustained period of time that the parolee is unlikely to commit another crime and the parolee's discharge is compatible with public safety," and in any event, parolees under supervision for at least 5 years "shall be brought before the Paroling Authority for purposes of consideration for final discharge." In Alaska, the board may discharge a parolee after he or she has successfully completed 2 years of supervision; in Oklahoma, active supervision of parolees will not normally exceed 3 years. In Alabama, however, "early termination in parole cases may be accomplished only by means of a Pardon, which will be considered after a subject has served five years under supervision." The same board that is responsible for parole in Alabama, the Board of Pardons and Paroles, has the power to grant pardons. In Vermont, "although the Board may terminate parole supervision at any time, it will normally consider termination only after successful completion of one half of the maximum parole term."

Violation of Parole/Conditional Release

Probation violation is linked to the judicial system, whereas parole violation is an administrative function typically devoid of court involvement. Although some variation exists with respect to the procedures used, Figure 7.3 presents a general overview of the system and indicates the possibilities available at each stage of the process.

There are two types of parole violation:

1. *Technical violation.* A **technical violation** occurs when any of the conditions of parole have been violated.
2. *New offense violation.* A **new offense violation** involves an arrest and prosecution for the commission of a new crime.

Key Fact

Parole conditions are similar throughout most jurisdictions and are also similar or identical to probation regulations. Conditions can generally be grouped into standard conditions and special conditions.

Key Fact

In most states, a parolee can be discharged before the expiration of a sentence or a mandated period of supervision.

Key Fact

There are two types of parole violation: technical and new offense.

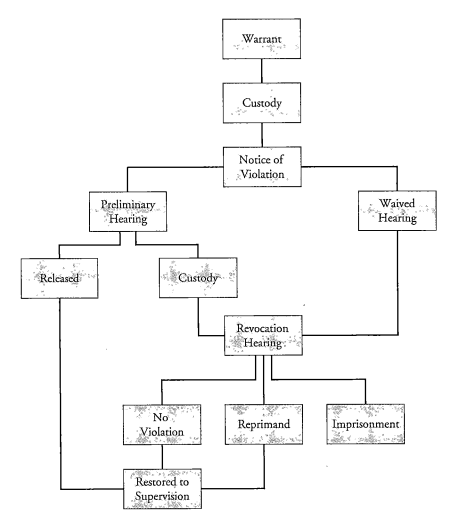

FIGURE 7.3 *Parole Violation Flowchart*

In practice, new offense violations often involve technical violations. A new offense violation (e.g., an arrest for robbery that involves a firearm) also constitutes a technical violation of the conditions prohibiting possession of firearms.

In either event, the violation process begins when a parole officer (PO), who may also be called a probation and parole officer, parole agent, correctional program officer, or probation/parole supervisor, becomes aware of a violation. The PO can usually take steps short of a formal violation of parole. The Alaska Division of Community Corrections advises POs that "if the violation is a conditions violation, it does not require any notification to the Parole Board. You, as the Parole Officer, can verbally make the parolee aware of the violation and issue a verbal warning." The Alaska parole officer can also issue a written reprimand and "hold these charges in abeyance should there be any future violations," or the officer can impose more restrictive conditions, but the parolee must agree: "If the parolee does not agree to the new condition, a preliminary hearing must be held within 15 days of the imposition of the condition."

In most agencies, after discussing the situation with a supervisor, a decision is made as to whether there is **probable cause** (evidence needed to determine that a violation has probably occurred) relative to the issuance of a warrant. This stage has the greatest amount of variance among agencies. In Pennsylvania, parole agents can use an "order to detain for 48 hours" in lieu of a warrant when circumstances require it. A similar situation obtains in New York, where field parole officers carry a 24-hour detainer-warrant. Thus, in Pennsylvania and New York, a parole agent/officer who becomes aware of a serious violation of parole while in the field can summarily take the violator into custody and receive telephone authorization for the use of the order to detain or a 24-hour detainer-warrant. (These temporary detainers must be replaced by a warrant: in Pennsylvania, within 48 hours; in New York, within 24 hours.) When I was a PO in New York, it was not unusual to unexpectedly encounter parolees who were in serious violation of the conditions of their release: those heavily involved in abusing heroin (and engaging in criminal acts to support the habit); those prohibited from the use of alcohol (because of the dangerous nature of their behavior while under the influence) in an intoxicated state; or child sex offenders found in the company of children. I could take such persons into custody immediately and use the telephone for detainer-warrant authorization. (In the opinion of this writer, agencies that do not provide their officers with this authority endanger public safety. This point is discussed further in Chapter 9.)

In jurisdictions that are rather conservative about issuing violation warrants, the process may be time-consuming and involve a written request to the board of parole. In Oregon, in lieu of a summary arrest, the parole officer may issue a citation requiring the parolee/releasee to appear for a violation hearing. This citation is authorized when the person has violated a condition of supervision, but the nature of the violation does not jeopardize the safety of the general public, and the person, if left undetained, is not likely to flee. In Iowa

> A parole officer having probable cause to believe that any person released on parole has violated the conditions of parole may arrest such person, or the parole officer may make a complaint before a magistrate, charging such violation, and if it appears from such complaint . . . that there is probable cause to believe that such person has violated the terms of parole, the magistrate shall issue a warrant for the arrest of such person. In either event, the violator must be taken before a magistrate for consideration of release on bail—"bail is discretionary with the magistrate and is not a matter of right" in Iowa.

Most jurisdictions do not permit a parole violator to be released on bail.

In Wisconsin, in lieu of an arrest or warrant issuance, a parole agent's immediate supervisor can order the alleged violator to appear for a case review: "The focus of case review is threefold: to determine whether there is probable cause to believe there was a violation of the rules or conditions of probation or parole, to determine whether, if there is probable cause, it makes correctional sense to revoke, and to determine whether the client should remain in custody during revocation proceedings." Although this case review has many of the characteristics of a preliminary hearing (to be discussed shortly), the review is both more broadly focused—it can consider issues relating to supervision adjustment—and less formal: "It is hoped by making the proceedings less formal and adversary, the client, the client's attorney, the agent and the agent's supervisor can frankly discuss the issues in an atmosphere that focuses attention on the most important issues." As noted in Chapter 12, because parole violators are a contributing factor to prison overcrowding, agencies have been using graduated sanctions ranging from intensive supervision, a halfway house placement, or a brief period of incarceration, in place of revocation and imprisonment.

Preliminary Hearing

If a parolee/conditional releasee has been arrested pursuant to a violation warrant or if the offender is in custody for a new offense and a violation warrant has been filed as a detainer, the PO will provide him or her with a notice of a **preliminary hearing** and a list of the alleged violations. The purpose of the preliminary hearing is to determine if probable cause exists to establish that the offender has committed one or more acts that constitute a violation of the conditions of release.

This hearing is required if the offender is to be detained on a warrant pending a revocation hearing; furthermore, the hearing is required within 15 days of the time the warrant was executed by arrest or was filed. If no warrant has been issued—the subject is not being held in custody by parole authorities—but the offender has been summoned

Parole Violations in Georgia

When a parolee has reportedly violated a condition of release, a board warrant may be issued for his or her arrest. If the alleged violation is absconding from parole supervision or if the parolee is otherwise not available to the board for a hearing, a temporary revocation order may be issued. This order suspends the running of the sentence from the date of the order.

A parolee arrested on a board warrant for allegedly violating a parole condition is afforded a preliminary hearing within a reasonable time at or near the place of the alleged violation before a board hearing officer not directly involved in the case. The purpose of the preliminary hearing is to determine whether there is probable cause to believe the parolee violated a parole condition and whether he or she should be held under arrest pending the board's decision on revocation.

A preliminary hearing is not required if the parolee is not under arrest on a board warrant, has absconded from supervision, has signed a waiver of preliminary hearing, has admitted any alleged violation to any board representative in the presence of a third party who is not a board employee, or has been convicted of any new crime in a Georgia court, a court of another state, or a federal court.

The parolee is given written notice of the preliminary hearing, allowing reasonable time to prepare his or her case. The parolee may retain counsel to represent him or her at the preliminary hearing, may present witnesses and documentary evidence in his or her own behalf, and may cross-examine adverse witnesses unless the hearing officer determines that a witness would be subjected to risk of harm if his or her identity were disclosed. The parolee is invited to make statements and answer questions but is not required to do so.

The hearing officer may issue subpoenas to compel the attendance of witnesses resident within the county of the alleged violation and may also issue subpoenas for the production of documents or other written evidence at the hearing. After the preliminary hearing, the hearing officer submits to the board a written report on the testimony, on the findings, and on any decision to release the parolee on personal recognizance. The board then ratifies or overrules the hearing officer's findings, including any decision to release, and decides whether to hold a final hearing.

A parolee charged with violating a parole condition is afforded a final hearing within a reasonable time before the board. The purpose of the final hearing is to determine whether the parolee has violated a parole condition and whether the violation warrants parole revocation. The parolee is given written notice of the final hearing, allowing reasonable time to prepare his or her case. At the final hearing, the parolee has the same rights a parolee has at a preliminary hearing (as specified previously). The board may subpoena witnesses from throughout Georgia to appear at the final hearing and may issue subpoenas for the production of documents or other written evidence at the hearing; after the final hearing, the board decides by majority vote whether to continue or revoke parole. A final hearing is not required if the parolee, free on personal recognizance, fails to appear for a final hearing—the board may summarily revoke his or her parole—and is not required if the parolee has admitted the violation and signed a waiver of final hearing. A final hearing is not permitted and revocation is mandatory by law if the parolee is sentenced by a federal court or a Georgia state or superior court to a term of imprisonment, including one reduced to time served, for any felony crime or for a state misdemeanor involving physical injury to another, which the parolee committed during his or her parole term.

to appear for a revocation hearing, a preliminary hearing is not necessary. (About a half-dozen states do not use a preliminary hearing.) The offender may also waive the right to a preliminary hearing.

At the preliminary hearing, the parolee/conditional releasee will have an opportunity to challenge the alleged violations and (a limited right) to confront and cross-examine adverse witnesses, including the PO, and to present evidence on his or her own behalf (Figure 7.4). The offender can be represented by legal counsel, although

NEW JERSEY
STATE PAROLE BOARD
DISTRICT OFFICE # 9

NOTICE OF PROBABLE CAUSE HEARING

To: <u>ROBERT BROWN</u>   Inst#: <u>EC 72456</u>   Date: <u>6/22/06</u>

   <u>c/o Essex County Jail</u>

   <u>Newark, NJ 07105</u>   DOB: <u>9/24/1980</u>

---

1. You are advised that you will be given a Probable Cause Hearing on the date and at the time indicated on the reverse side of this letter. The purpose of the hearing is to determine whether there is probable cause to believe that you have committed a violation of parole. (See reverse side of this letter.)

2. You are asked to indicate on the attached form whether you wish to have a hearing, wish to waive the hearing, or wish a postponement, and to list your representative, witness, letters and any other documents, if any. Please return the form in the enclosed stamped, addressed envelope promptly.

3. You are hereby notified of the following rights to which you are entitled relative to the hearing:

   A.   The right to representation by an attorney or such other qualified person as you may retain. Further, if you are indigent and financial circumstances prohibit your retaining private counsel, you may request an investigation to determine if you are eligible for representation by a court-appointed attorney.

   B.   The right to appear and speak on your own behalf, to be aided by an interpreter if such aid is determined to be necessary by the Hearing Officer.

   C.   The right to remain silent.

   D.   The right to present witnesses to testify on your behalf as to matters relevant to the alleged violation(s) of parole.

   E.   The right to confront and cross-examine adverse witnesses, unless the Hearing Officer determines that such witnesses would be subjected to risk or harm.

   F.   The right to present documentary evidence and any other relevant material or information.

   G.   The right to waive such hearing.

   H.   The right to request postponement of such hearing.

4. Upon completion of the hearing, the Hearing Officer will immediately advise you verbally of those violations (if any) sustained and will complete a written Notice of Probable Cause Decision Report, and a copy will be forwarded to you within one week. The Hearing Officer will determine whether there is probable cause to hold you for a final decision by the Parole Board on revocation of your parole. Should the Hearing Officer find probable cause, then this determination will be sufficient to continue your detention and return you to a state correctional institution pending a final decision by the Parole Board. If charges are pending, your return to an institution may be deferred pending disposition of those charges or approval from the county prosecutor's office to return you to a state correctional institution prior to disposition of the charges.

George Green
District Parole Supervisor

cc: DO# <u>9</u>
Warrant Authorized By: <u>Sgt. R. Miller</u>
Senior Parole Officer: <u>Howard Marcus</u>
State Parole Board
ORU
Counsel

Date Paroled: <u>5/1/06</u>   Parole Max Date: <u>8/20/06</u>
Commitment Offense(s): <u>VOP Possession of CDS</u>
Sentence(s): <u>364 days</u>   Released from: <u>Essex County Jail</u>

A.   You have been charged with the following violation(s) of the terms, conditions, and limitations of your parole at the time, date, and places indicated and under the circumstances described, with specific documents and witnesses listed in parentheses, as evidence for each violations:

FIGURE 7.4 *Notice of New Jersey Probable Cause Hearing*

B. A Probable Cause Hearing will be held for you on _7/14/06_

at _____

to determine if there is probable cause to believe that you have committed these violations.

C. Indicate on the attached form letter whether or not you wish to have a Probable Cause Hearing and return it to the address indicated not less than three days before the date set for your hearing.

D. You may also request a five-day adjournment on the attached form letter.

E. You should list on the attached form letter the names of person(s) you plan to call as your witnesses and indicate what they will say at the hearing. You are responsible for arranging for your witnesses to be present at the hearing. You should also list and summarize on the attached letter the letters, affidavits, documents and other evidence you will use at the hearing.

F. Although a Parole Officer may have already discussed with you the issue of representation, you are also asked to indicate on the attached form your decision on this matter.

VIOLATIONS

General Conditions:
#2 You failed to report as instructed as evidenced by your failure to report to parole on 5/23/06 or any date thereafter.
(Reference made to Special Report dated 6/15/06 and chronological entries dated 5/18/06, 5/23/06, 5/26/06, 5/31/06, 6/2/06 and 6/7/06).

Special Condition:
You failed to submit to random urine monitoring as evidenced by your failure to report to parole on 5/23/06 or any date thereafter, thus, making yourself unavailable for urine monitoring. (Reference made to Special Report dated 6/15/06 and chronological entries dated 5/23/06, 5/31/06 and 6/7/06).

You failed to refrain from the use and possession of CDS, as evidenced by your use and possession of cocaine and heroin on or about 5/17/06. (Reference is made to Special Report dated 6/15/06, Admission of Use Form dated 5/18/06 and chronological entry dated 5/18/06).

You failed to comply until successful discharge with outpatient counseling, as evidenced by your failure to enroll in Kintock for OPDC. (Reference is made to Special Report dated 6/15/06 and chronological entries dated 5/12/06, 5/18/06 and 5/24/06).

FIGURE 7.4 (continued)

A Closer Look

Probable Cause, Wyoming

Probable cause is defined as the state of facts that would lead a person of ordinary caution or prudence to believe and conscientiously entertain a strong suspicion of an individual's violation of the terms of parole or conditional release. It is a determination that the allegations of the violations are not frivolous but present a substantial and easily recognizable question that is worthy of consideration by the parole board.

Key Fact

A preliminary parole violation hearing is to determine if there is probable cause to detain a parolee for a revocation hearing.

the state is not constitutionally required to provide an attorney (see Figure 7.4). As opposed to the rules of evidence in the criminal process, hearsay is admissible at preliminary hearings (although hearsay is not used alone to determine probable cause). The hearing officer who presides is usually an attorney regularly employed for this purpose by the agency; however, any agency employee who is not directly involved in the case may fulfill this role. As a senior (supervisory) PO in New York, for example, I served as a hearing officer when personnel normally fulfilling this function were unavailable. Because this hearing is a relatively minimal and informal inquiry, the hearing officer need not hear all the allegations for a finding of probable cause.

If the hearing officer determines that evidence sufficient to make a finding of probable cause has not been presented, the parolee/conditional releasee will be restored to supervision. If probable cause is found, the offender will be held in custody pending a revocation hearing (Figure 7.5). Before the revocation hearing, the PO will prepare a parole violation report for use at the hearing (Figure 7.6).

STATE OF NEVADA BOARD OF PAROLE

SUMMARY OF PRELIMINARY INQUIRY HEARING

RE: Blackstone, John L.
   File No. L82-001
   Criminal Case No. 28001

The above-named subject appeared for a Preliminary Inquiry on July 19, 2006, at the hour of 2:20 P.M. at the Carson City Jail.

RIGHTS VERIFIED

Hearing Officer Sally Gomez inquired of defendant Blackstone if he had received copies of the Violation Report dated July 6, 2006, and the "Notice of Preliminary Inquiry Hearing" form listing his rights per the *Morrissey* and *Scarpelli* decisions. Blackstone replied that he had both documents and had read them. He also indicated that he fully understood the charges and his rights during the violation process as explained in the form. It is noted that Blackstone retained as private counsel for this hearing Michael Smith, Esq., of Carson City. Blackstone says he is satisfied with counsel and the time for preparing the defense case. With the indication that Mr. Blackstone fully understands his rights in this matter, we will proceed with the hearing.

VIOLATION CASE

Parole and Probation Officer James Richards read in part the Violation Report dated July 6, 2006, which indicates that Mr. Blackstone is charged with violation of Rule 9 of the Parole Agreement, WEAPONS. It was read that Blackstone was found in possession of a snub-nose .38 pistol by Police Sergeant John Brown in the After Hours Bar, 111 N. Carson Street, City of Carson, Nevada, at about 11:00 P.M. on July 4, 2006. Blackstone had shown the weapon to another customer of the bar, a Mr. William Mundy, allegedly stating to Mundy: "Sucker, I'm going to blow you apart if you keep bugging me tonight." Mundy left the bar and phoned the police to complain of the threat from Blackstone. Sgt. Brown arrived at the bar with several officers and asked Blackstone about the alleged weapon. Blackstone admitted to having an unloaded revolver in his coat pocket, and Sgt. Brown removed same without incident. Blackstone was then placed under arrest for "assault" and an "ex-felon in possession of a firearm." He was transported to the Carson County Jail and booked. Parole Officer Richards placed a Hold for Parole Violation Investigation on Blackstone the following day, July 5, 2006, at about 10:00 A.M.

Officer Richards called William Mundy as his first witness. Mundy told how Blackstone had come into the bar and sat next to him at the counter. Mundy tried to engage Blackstone in some friendly conversation, but Blackstone told him to "shut up and to quit bugging him" or he'd "blow his body apart," showing Mundy a small pistol taken from his coat pocket. Mundy says that he immediately left the bar and called the police, complaining of the incident and asking that the police arrest Blackstone. Mundy identified John L. Blackstone as the person who threatened him in the After Hours Bar on July 4, 2006. Mundy was dismissed after the defense had no questions of him.

Officer Richards called his second witness, Sgt. John Brown of the Carson City Police Department, to testify in this case. Brown related that he was dispatched to the After Hours Bar at about 10:55 P.M. on July 4, 2006, to investigate a citizen's complaint of a man with a gun making threats in the bar to shoot him. On arrival, Brown said he was met by Mr. Mundy at the entrance of the bar and that Mundy pointed Mr. Blackstone out for him in the crowded bar. The officer approached Blackstone and asked him if he was carrying a weapon in his coat pocket; Brown said that Blackstone informed him that he had an unloaded pistol in his right-hand coat pocket. Sgt. Brown then removed the weapon from Blackstone's right coat pocket and found that it was empty of shells. Sgt. Brown directed Blackstone to step outside the bar with him. Sgt. Brown advised Blackstone that he was being placed under arrest for "simple assault" on the complaint of Mr. William Mundy and that he would have to come to the jail for booking but could post bail that evening. Blackstone went along to the jail without incident.

On arrival at the jail, the head jailer told Sgt. Brown that Mr. Blackstone was a parolee and should also be booked for the felony charge of "ex-felon with a firearm." Thus, he was so booked. Sgt. Brown was dismissed after the defense offered no cross-examination.

Officer Richards rested his prosecution case, noting that Blackstone has one felony charge of "Felon in Possession of Firearm" pending in Carson Justice Court. A preliminary hearing has been set for July 30, 2006, on the case. The weapon was not present at this hearing but listed as in the evidence locker of the Carson City Police.

DEFENSE CASE

Attorney for the accused Blackstone stated that he would decline to present any evidence or statements at this time regarding the possession of the weapon as the case was a felony charge awaiting disposition in Justice Court. However, attorney Smith did offer a defense witness, Gary Jones, to tell of the alleged threats in the bar. Jones was called into the hearing room and related he was sitting near the counter at a small table next to John Blackstone and Mundy at about 10:30 on July 4, 2006. Mundy, Jones explained, was "pretty drunk" and kept slapping Blackstone on the back, calling him "pal" and "buddy," and so on. Blackstone told Mundy to leave him alone and Mundy got mad and left the bar in a "huff," Jones testified. A short time later, Jones testified, police officers took Blackstone out of the bar and that is the last time he saw Blackstone until today. Attorney Smith suggested that Blackstone did not threaten Mundy in the manner alleged by Mundy. Hearing Officer Gomez asked Jones if he saw Blackstone take anything out of his coat pocket and show it to Mundy. Jones replied, "no." Richards asked Jones if he could have missed seeing Blackstone show Mundy the gun and say he was going to "blow him apart." Jones was hesitant but said he was pretty sure; because of the back slapping, he was watching the incident pretty closely, wondering what Mundy was going to do next.

FIGURE 7.5 *Summary of a Nevada Preliminary Hearing*

Attorney Smith closed the defense, advising Blackstone not to make any statements to the hearing officer until the Justice Court case was held.

FINDINGS

Having considered the evidence presented in this case by both the charging officer and the defendant, this hearing officer finds that probable cause exists to continue detention on the charge of violation of parole rule #9, WEAPONS. The hearing officer has determined that probable cause exists to continue detention pending your formal revocation hearing before the Board of Parole. You are duly notified that at the formal revocation hearing the Board of Parole has the discretion to review and act on all charges that were presented at this preliminary inquiry. With no further evidence to be heard, this hearing will be closed at 3:40 P.M., July 19, 2006.

Respectfully submitted,

Sally Gomez

Hearing Officer

FIGURE 7.5 *(continued)*

STATE BOARD OF PARDONS AND PAROLES
Montgomery, Alabama

REPORT OF PAROLE VIOLATION
Date: **1/5/07**
Field Office: **Montgomery**

Name of Parolee   **John Doe**   No. **123,456**

Pace, Sex, & Age **BM - 30**   County of Conviction **Montgomery**

Offense   **Theft of Property 1st Degree**   Sentence   **2 years penitentiary**

Date Convicted   **4/10/05**   Date of Parole   **2/17/06**

Date Sentence Expires   **4/10/07**

RESTITUTION

Amount Paid $ **249.00**

Balance $ **101.00**

If declared Delinquent, subject can be located at the following place: **Dan Jones, State Probation Office, Room 334, County Courthouse,** Montgomery, Alabama 36104

CHARGE NO. 1

VIOLATION OF CONDITION NO. 7
NEW OFFENSE— BURGLARY III

LEGAL FACTS:
Subject was arrested on 12/24/06, by the Montgomery Police Department for the offense of Burglary 3rd degree; bond was set at $2,000.00. A preliminary hearing was held 1/5/07, and the case was bound to the Grand Jury. Indictment was returned, arraignment held and case set for trial 2/17/07. A Parole Officer's Authorization of Arrest was issued 12/25/06.

DETAILS:
Police reports reflect that at 2 A.M., on 12/24/06, Officer M. D. Jones with the Montgomery Police Department, while on routine patrol, observed a black male subject exit Ace Hardware, 4240 Ames Road, Montgomery, Alabama, by way of a back window, in possession of a box. The subject fled on foot but was caught by Officer Jones about three hundred feet from the building. The person was identified as John Doe. He had in his possession property identified as having come from Ace Hardware by the manager, A. L. Pope. It was determined that the hardware store had been entered by forcing open an air conditioning vent at the rear of the store.

FIGURE 7.6 *Alabama Parole Violation Report*

CHARGE NO. 2
VIOLATION OF CONDITION NO. 3
FAILURE TO REPORT

LEGAL FACTS:

A Parole Violator's warrant was issued and given to the Sheriff's Office on 12/25/06, to prevent the subject's release pending Board action.

DETAILS:

According to the records of the supervising officer, on 12/17/06, subject was instructed by Officer Dan Jones regarding parole conditions and specifically that he must report to the Parole Office each month by the 3rd. He stated he understood all parole conditions.

Subject failed to report or have any contact with the parole officer for the months of October, November, and December 2006.

On 9/19/06, he reported for the month of September. He stated he forgot to report by the 3rd. He was reprimanded and encouraged to report in accordance with instructions.

On 10/10/06, I visited his residence. He was not present. His mother, Mae Doe, said she had not seen him in three days. I asked that she have him report. On 10/15/06, I wrote subject a letter to report and received no response. On 10/25/06, I visited his home; his mother said he received my letter. He was not present. I requested she attempt to have him report and advised of consequences if he failed.

On 11/5/06, a letter was written to subject reminding and instructing that he make contact with his parole officer. On 11/19/06, I called his residence and spoke with his 17-year-old sister, Sue Doe, and requested she tell him to report. On 11/30/06, I visited his father, Joe Doe, at their residence and requested he have subject report.

On 12/6/06, I visited subject's residence and talked with his parents. They stated he had been told to report, but he refused. On 12/10/06, I wrote him a letter instructing that he report within 7 days or I would file a Report of Parole Violation, which would likely cause him to be arrested as a parole violator. He failed to contact the Officer thereafter.

RECOMMENDATION:

I recommend revocation.

Signed and dated at Montgomery, Alabama, this 5th day of January, 2007

Dan Jones
Dan Jones
Alabama Probation and Parole Officer

DJ/lm

FIGURE 7.6 *(continued)*

Revocation Hearing

A **revocation hearing** is similar to and takes place within 90 days of a preliminary hearing, except that it is comprehensive and the violator is entitled to counsel. In New York, violators have an absolute right to counsel and an attorney will be provided if the parolee cannot afford to hire one. The purpose of the revocation hearing is to determine if the violation of parole/conditional release is serious enough to revoke supervision and return the offender to prison or if some less drastic response is sufficient. In Oregon, certain violators are sent to prison for a time-limited term—6 months—but under rather austere conditions:

> [They are] housed in a medium-security facility and for the first 30 days are allowed out of their individual cells (which have no windows) only three times a week for showers, and for one hour three times a week to exercise in a small concrete structure. After 30 days, they are placed in a two-person cell and given slightly more amenities. After the second 30-day period, they spend the next four months in a dormitory with somewhat increased privileges and amenities. (Parent et al., 1994: 20)

In addition to considering the allegations of parole violation, the revocation hearing will consider information about the offender's adjustment to supervision with respect to making

Key Fact

A revocation hearing is similar to a preliminary hearing but more comprehensive. The accused violator is entitled to counsel, and the purpose is to determine if the violation of parole is serious enough to return the offender to prison.

timely reports, maintaining employment/education, supporting dependents, and other critical elements of the supervision process. In most jurisdictions, the revocation hearing is presided over by one or more members of the parole board; in other states, it is the responsibility of hearing officers who make recommendations to the parole board for or against revocation. In Iowa, revocation hearings are conducted via two-way fiber-optic communications from the board's conference room; if the board votes against revocation, the offender is restored to supervision. In New York, revocation hearings are held before administrative law judges appointed by the parole board, and they have the power to render final decisions.

A Closer Look

Violation Centers in Pennsylvania

Pennsylvania has reduced the number of parolees returned to prison for technical violations, particularly substance abuse violators in need of treatment, by establishing a Violation Center in each of the state's parole regions. Located within secure portions of community corrections centers, each can accommodate between 25 and 75 offenders for a period of 90 days.

Street Time

Key Fact

Street time practices vary, but in general parole violators have it deducted from the time they owe.

If parole/conditional release is revoked, the question arises as to just how much time the parolee must serve in prison. This can vary from jurisdiction to jurisdiction. In California, parolees returned to prison for a technical violation can be confined for only 1 year. In New York, a parolee receives credit for the time spent under supervision (street time) before the violation, so an inmate who is paroled after serving 2 years of a 4-year sentence is required to be on parole for 2 years, the remainder of the sentence. If, after 1 year, the parolee violates parole and is returned to prison, he or she will have to serve only the 1 year remaining on the sentence. However, in a state that does not give credit for street time, this same parolee would be required to serve 2 years in prison; the 1 year of satisfactory time on parole would not be credited against the 4-year sentence in the event of a parole violation that results in being returned to prison.

EXECUTIVE CLEMENCY

Key Fact

Executive clemency consists of the reprieve, the commutation, and the pardon.

All states and the federal government (Article II, Section 2, of the Constitution) have provisions for **executive clemency** (a reprieve, commutation, or pardon). In 31 states and the federal government, the chief executive holds the final clemency power, and in most of these states, the parole board or a clemency board appointed by the governor investigates clemency applications at the request of the governor. In some states, clemency authority is vested entirely in a special board, usually a board of pardons and paroles. In North Dakota, there is a pardon advisory board made up of the attorney general, two members of the parole board, and two gubernatorial appointees, but the Board of Pardons in Pennsylvania is completely separate from the parole board. Some states conduct formal hearings, and the governor generally must report annually to the legislature on all clemencies granted (National Governors' Association, 1988).

Reprieve

A **reprieve** is a *temporary* suspension of the execution of sentence. As noted in Chapter 2, probation developed (in part) out of the judicial reprieve. Its use today is limited and usually concerns cases in which capital punishment has been ordered. In such cases a governor or the president of the United States can grant a reprieve—a stay of execution—to provide more time for legal action or other deliberations.

In Georgia, the Board of Pardons and Paroles may grant a reprieve lasting a few hours or a few days to an inmate so he or she may visit a critically ill member of the family or attend the funeral of an immediate member of the family. A reprieve may also be granted in Georgia when it is shown that an inmate is suffering from a definable illness for which necessary treatment is available only outside the state prison system. An inmate granted a reprieve will have the reprieve period credited to the sentence if he or she does not violate any of the conditions of the reprieve.

Commutation

A **commutation** is a modification of sentence to the benefit of an offender. Commutation has been used when an inmate provided some assistance to the prison staff, sometimes during prison riots. Commutation may also be granted to inmates with a severe illness, such as cancer. The laws governing commutation differ from state to state. In New York, an inmate sentenced to more than 1 year who has served at least one-half of the minimum period of imprisonment and who is not otherwise eligible for release or parole may have his or her sentence commuted by the governor. In Georgia, the Board of Pardons and Paroles will consider commuting a sentence when it receives substantial evidence that the sentence is excessive, illegal, unconstitutional, or void; evidence that justice would be served by a commutation; and evidence that commutation would be in the best interests of society and the inmate. The board may also consider commutation of sentences of death after all other legal remedies have been exhausted; a person whose death sentence has been commuted by the board cannot be pardoned or paroled before serving 25 years. In Maryland, correctional personnel identify candidates who meet criteria established by the governor's office for commutation, and their names are submitted to the parole board for a recommendation to the governor.

Pardon

Following the American Revolution, it was necessary to find a new basis for the pardoning power to replace the English theory that it resided in the king as the fountainhead of justice and mercy. This new basis was found in the theory that the power to issue a **pardon** was a sovereign power, inherent in the state but not necessarily inherent in the chief executive or in any branch of government. Because the people were the ultimate sovereign, the power resided in them, and they could provide for its exercise through any agency of government they deemed proper.

Although historically the executive would seem the most natural agency with which to entrust this power, the attitude of the American people after the Revolution did not lead to this conclusion. The struggle with the mother country had left them suspicious of the chief executive. This conflict was natural enough because the royal governor was not usually sympathetic to the colonists (the champion of the people was usually the lower house of the legislature). Not surprisingly, the early constitutions that replaced the colonial charters tended to place restrictions on the governor's power in many respects, including the power to pardon: Only five states left this power with the governor alone; six, including the newly admitted state of Vermont, provided that the governor could pardon only with consent of the executive council; Georgia deprived the governor of the pardoning power entirely, giving him only power to reprieve until the meeting of the assembly, which could then make such disposition of the matter as it saw fit; and Connecticut and Rhode Island continued to function under their colonial charters, by which the pardoning power was exercised by the general assembly.

By the time the federal Constitution was written, however, opinion had begun to swing back toward placing greater power in the hands of the governor. The framers of the Constitution gave the pardoning power to the president without any limitations as to its exercise or supervision by any other official or agency, and President George Washington was the first to exercise this power in 1795 (when he granted amnesty to participants in the so-called Whiskey Rebellion). The executive councils that several states had set up as a means of preventing too much power from being vested in one person began to lose favor about the same time, and several states began abolishing them, giving the power to the governor. Toward the end of the nineteenth century, an overwhelming movement occurred to give the governor some assistance in this task by providing an advisory pardon officer or pardon board. Some states set up pardon boards not merely to advise the governor but to actually exercise pardoning power, although the governor was a member, if not the controlling member, of the board (U.S. Attorney General, 1939).

As noted in Chapter 6, the pardon has been used historically in the United States as a form of "parole." As the indeterminate sentence came into use, pardon boards, originally established to advise the governor with respect to release, began to act independently, developing into parole boards. Despite widespread use of parole, however, the power of pardon has continued. In Utah, for example, the Board of Pardons, an independent state agency, has rather extraordinary powers. This three-member body serves as a board of parole, deciding when and under what conditions persons convicted and serving sentences should be released from imprisonment; in addition, the board can commute sentences of death, reduce terms of imprisonment, and completely terminate an offender's sentence, regardless of whether he or she is an inmate or on parole. The board also has absolute pardoning authority for the state and can forgive the sentence and restore civil rights, although this power is rarely exercised.

In Utah, executive clemency is usually limited to deciding on the granting of relief from disabilities, a limited pardon that restores certain civil and political rights, such as the right to apply to vote (the local board of registrars makes final decisions) and to hold certain licenses. To be considered for such a pardon, a person discharged from prison without parole must wait 2 years, parolees wait 5 years under supervision or 2 years after discharge, and probationers wait 2 years after discharge from supervision. The pardon report, which is prepared by state probation and parole officers, is exhaustive and allows the board to determine whether the applicant has become a law-abiding person and a useful citizen in the community.

In California, the Board of Prison Terms investigates all pardon petitions from persons who have been free of criminal conduct for 9.5 years since discharge from probation, parole, or custody. In Maryland, a pardon requires at least 5 years of exemplary crime-free behavior following release from incarceration and after expiration of any parole supervision. Pardon requests are received by the parole board, which investigates and makes a recommendation to the governor. A governor's pardon restores citizenship rights to the person who has demonstrated a high standard of constructive behavior following conviction for an offense. Pardon applications are considered only after an offender has been discharged from probation or parole for at least 10 years and has not engaged in further criminal conduct. The 10-year rule may be waived in truly exceptional circumstances if the applicant can demonstrate an earlier need for the pardon.

The basis for a pardon may vary in different states, but the pardon is not used extensively anywhere. In New York, the only basis for a pardon is new evidence indicating that the person did not commit the offense for which he or she was convicted. In Florida, a pardon is a declaration of record that a person is relieved from the legal consequences of a particular conviction; as in New York, a pardon will be granted only to a person who proves his or her innocence of the crime for which convicted. Florida also has a *first-offender pardon*, which carries no implication of innocence and may be granted to an actual first offender. This pardon restores civil and political rights and removes legal disabilities resulting from the conviction. A *10-year pardon* works the same way and may be granted offenders who have had no further convictions for 10 years after completing his or her sentence.

In Georgia, a pardon is a declaration of record by the board that a person is relieved from the legal consequences of a particular conviction; it restores civil and political rights and removes all legal disabilities resulting from the conviction. A pardon may be

Key Fact

Most chief executives have the power of executive clemency whose exercise usually involves a recommendation from the parole board.

granted in two instances: First, a pardon may be granted when a person proves his or her innocence of the crime for which he or she was convicted under Georgia law; second, a pardon that does not imply innocence may be granted to an applicant who has completed his or her full sentence obligation, including any probated sentence and paying any fine, and who has thereafter completed 5 years without any criminal involvement (the 5-year waiting period may be waived if it is shown to be detrimental to the applicant's livelihood by delaying his or her qualifying for employment in a chosen profession).

The president of the United States typically grants hundreds of pardons: President Gerald Ford pardoned former President Richard Nixon in 1974, Jimmy Carter issued 566 pardons during his 4 years as president, and Ronald Reagan granted 406 during his 8 years as president (Moore, 1989). In 1992, as he was leaving office, President George Bush pardoned 6 persons alleged to have been involved in the Iran-Contra episode; he granted a total of 71 pardons during his 4 years in office. Bill Clinton pardoned 77 inmates during his 8 years as president, but with only hours before he was to leave office, in a controversial action, he pardoned 140 persons.

In Texas, executive clemency is the power of the governor to grant a full or conditional pardon, a full pardon based on innocence, a commutation of sentence, a remission of a fine or forfeiture resulting from a criminal conviction, an emergency medical reprieve, or a 30-day reprieve of execution. In accordance with the Texas Constitution, the governor may grant executive clemency only on the recommendation of the Board of Pardons and Paroles. The board is limited to recommending clemency and to setting minimal eligibility requirements for clemency applicants.

A full pardon restores certain citizenship rights forfeited by law as the result of a criminal conviction, such as the right to vote, the right to serve on a jury, and the right to hold public office. In Texas and many other states, voting rights are automatically restored when one discharges a felony sentence, even without a pardon. A full pardon will remove barriers to some (but not all) types of employment and professional licensing— licenses are granted at the discretion of the state licensing boards of each profession. A pardon will not restore eligibility to become a licensed peace officer in Texas.

LEGAL DECISIONS AFFECTING PAROLE

As already noted, legal decisions that affect probation also affect parole. Thus, the decision rendered in *Gagnon v. Scarpelli* (discussed in Chapter 2) relating to probation violation used precedents established in the *Morrissey v. Brewer* decision (discussed later in the section on parole revocation), which relates to parole violation. The three theories of parole violation are also similar (if not identical) to the three theories of probation violation.

Parole Release and Parole Hearings

In 1970, the U.S. Court of Appeals for the Second District considered the case of *Menechino v. Oswald* (430 F.2d 403). Joseph Menechino (a "jailhouse lawyer") was serving a 20-year to life sentence in New York for murder in the second degree. He was paroled in 1963 and returned to prison as a parole violator 16 months later. Subsequently, he appeared before the board of parole and admitted consorting with persons having criminal records and giving misleading information to his PO.

Then, 2 years later, Menechino appeared before the board for a release hearing and parole was denied. He brought a court action claiming that his rights were violated by the absence of legal counsel at both his revocation and parole release hearings. The court ruled:

- A parole proceeding is nonadversarial in nature because both parties, the board and the inmate, have the same concern—rehabilitation.
- Parole release hearings are not fact-finding determinations because the board makes a determination based on numerous tangible and intangible factors.

- The inmate has "no present private interest" to be protected (he has no **liberty interest**) because he is already imprisoned—he has nothing to lose—and this "interest" is required before due process is applicable.

The court further stated that "it is questionable whether a board of parole is even required to hold a hearing on the question of whether a prisoner should be released on parole." Relative to the question of parole revocation, however, the court advised that a minimum of procedural due process should be provided because at this stage a parolee has a present private interest in the possible loss of conditional freedom.

Although Menechino's case before the federal court was initiated regarding parole release, it set forth important legal arguments relative to parole revocation. The opinions of the three judges who heard the case clearly indicate that if Menechino had initiated an action concerning his parole revocation, he would have won the case on a 2–1 basis. This fact was duly noted by the New York State Court of Appeals in the second *Menechino* case, discussed later.

In 1979, the U.S. Supreme Court reversed a court of appeals decision in a class action brought by inmates of the Nebraska Penal and Correctional Complex in *Greenholtz v. Inmates of Nebraska Penal and Correctional Complex* (442 U.S. 1, 1979). The inmates claimed that they had been unconstitutionally denied parole release by the board of parole, but the Court established in its decision that:

- A convicted inmate has no constitutional right to be released before the expiration of his or her lawful sentence.
- Although a state may establish a parole release system, it has no constitutional obligation to do so. According to Nebraska law, at least once a year initial parole hearings must be held for every inmate, regardless of parole eligibility. At the initial hearing, the board examines the inmate's total record and provides an informal hearing during which the inmate can present statements and documents in support of a claim for release.
- If the board determines from the record and hearing that the inmate is a likely candidate for release, a final hearing is scheduled. However, the Nebraska law provides that the board "shall order an inmate's release unless in the final hearing, the board concludes that inmate's release should be deferred for at least one of four specified reasons." This procedure is a somewhat unusual, possibly peculiar to the state of Nebraska. Rolando del Carmen points out that this amounts to a "state-law created liberty interest," an expectation of being granted parole release (1985: 50). As noted earlier, whenever this liberty interest exists, some minimum due process is required.

Del Carmen and Paul Louis conclude that "an inmate does not have a constitutional right to be released on parole, nor does he or she enjoy any constitutional right in the parole release process. In more succinct language, the parole board can do just about anything it pleases [with respect to release], and whatever it says and does prevails because it enjoys immense discretion" (1988: 20). Although parole boards are not constitutionally required to provide reasons for denying release, the use of parole guidelines often provides inmates with such documentation.

Parole Violation and the Three Theories of Parole

Traditionally, a person on parole has not been considered a free person, despite the fact that he or she has been released from imprisonment. The basis for imposing restrictions on a parolee's freedom is contained in three theories:

1. *Grace theory.* Parole is a conditional privilege, a gift from the board of parole. If any of the conditions of this privilege are violated, parole can be revoked.
2. *Contract theory.* Every parolee and most conditional releasees are required to agree to certain terms and conditions in return for conditional freedom. A violation of the conditions is a breach of contract, which can result in penalties—a return to prison.

3. *Custody theory.* The parolee is in the legal custody of the prison or parole authorities, and as a result of this quasi-prisoner status, his or her constitutional rights are automatically limited and abridged. The *Menechino* and *Morrissey* decisions challenged these theories.

Until the 1970s, parole agencies operated without any interference from the judiciary, but this policy changed when the New York Court of Appeals handed down a decision in *Menechino v. Warden,* which granted parolees the right to counsel and the right to call their own witnesses at parole revocation hearings for the first time. Although the decision applied only to New York, it indicated the direction in which the courts would rule in future decisions and provided a precedent for the U.S. Supreme Court.

The 4–3 decision required that an attorney be present at a parole revocation hearing and also permitted a parolee to call witnesses who would speak on his or her behalf. The New York court recognized that it was entering an uncharted area of law. The issue the court was called on to resolve was stated succinctly at the beginning of the majority opinion: "whether parolees are constitutionally entitled, under the Federal and State Constitutions, to the assistance of counsel in parole revocation hearings." *Menechino* cited other legal decisions, such as *Mempa v. Rhay* and *In re Gault* (see Chapters 2 and 3). Although probationers, juveniles, and welfare recipients had already obtained limited due process protections at hearings that might cause the loss of freedom or financial distress, these protections had not yet been extended to parolees.

Morrissey v. Brewer (408 U.S. 471, 1972) marked the beginning of the U.S. Supreme Court's involvement with parole revocation procedures. Until June 1972, the Court had not ruled in this area. The issue in this case was whether the due process clause of the Fourteenth Amendment required that a state afford a person the opportunity to be heard before revoking parole.

Morrissey was charged with the false drawing of checks in 1967 in Iowa. After pleading guilty, he was sentenced to 7 years in prison but was paroled from the Iowa State Penitentiary in June 1968, only 7 months later. Morrissey, at the direction of his PO, was arrested in his hometown as a parole violator and held in a local jail. One week after review of the PO's written report, the Iowa Board of Parole revoked Morrissey's parole, and he was returned to prison. He had received no hearing before the revocation decision.

Morrissey violated the conditions of his parole by buying a car under an assumed name and operating it without the permission of his PO; he also gave false information to the police and an insurance company concerning his address after a minor traffic accident. Besides these violations, Morrissey also obtained credit under an assumed name and failed to report his residence to his PO. According to the parole report, Morrissey could not explain adequately any of these technical violations of parole regulations.

Also considered in the *Morrissey* case was the petition of Booher, a convicted forger who had been returned to prison in Iowa by the Board of Parole without a hearing. Booher had admitted the technical violations of parole charges to his PO when taken into custody.

The Supreme Court considered all arguments that sought to keep the judiciary out of parole matters, and it rejected the "privilege" concept of parole as no longer feasible. The Court pointed out that parole is an established variation of imprisonment of convicted criminals—it occurs with too much regularity to be simply a "privilege": "It is hardly useful any longer to try to deal with this problem in terms of whether the parolee's liberty is a 'right' or a 'privilege.' By whatever name the liberty is valuable and must be seen within the protection of the Fourteenth Amendment. Its termination calls for some orderly process however informal."

The Court pointed out that parole revocation does not occur in just a few isolated cases—it has been estimated that 35 to 40 percent of all parolees are subjected to revocation and return to prison. The Court went on to state that, with the numbers involved, protection of parolees' rights was necessary. The Court did note, however, limitations on a parolee's rights:

> We begin with the proposition that the revocation of parole is not part of the criminal prosecution and thus the full panoply of rights due to the defendant

Key Fact

Parole revocation, as governed by the decision in *Morrissey v. Brewer,* requires minimal due process for parolees who have a liberty interest.

in such a proceeding does not apply to parole revocation. Supervision is not directly by the court but by an administrative agency which sometimes is an arm of the court and sometimes of the executive. Revocation deprives an individual not of absolute liberty to which every citizen is entitled but only the conditional liberty properly dependent on observance of special parole restrictions.

Also found in the decision is the New York State Court of Appeals response to the problem raised by the *Menechino* case. The Supreme Court held: "Society thus has an interest in not having parole revoked because of erroneous information or because of an erroneous evaluation of the need to revoke parole, given the breach of parole regulations. See Parole ex rel *Menechino v. Warden*."

In *Morrissey*, the Supreme Court viewed parole revocation as a two-stage process: (1) the arrest of the parolee and a preliminary hearing, and (2) the revocation hearing. Because a significant time lapse usually occurred between the arrest and revocation hearing, the Court established an interim process for all parole violators, a hearing before the final or revocation hearing: "Such an inquiry should be seen in the nature of a preliminary hearing to determine whether there is probable cause or reasonable grounds to believe that the arrested parolee had committed acts which would constitute a violation of parole conditions."

The Court specified that the hearing officer conducting this preliminary hearing need not be a member of the parole board, only someone who is not involved in the case; that the parolee should be given notice of the hearing; and that the purpose is to determine whether there is probable cause to believe that the parolee has violated a condition of parole. On the request of the parolee, persons who have given adverse information on which parole violation is based are to be made available for questioning in the parolee's presence. Based on this information presented before the hearing officer, a determination should be made if a reason exists to warrant the parolee's continued detention (pending a revocation hearing).

The Court stated that "no interest would be served by formalism in this process; informality will not lessen the utility of this inquiry in redressing the risk of error." This author served as an auxiliary hearing officer, conducting preliminary hearings in New York held at local correctional facilities. All persons were placed under oath, and a legal reporter recorded all testimony verbatim. The PO alleging the violation "prosecuted" the case, although in significant cases a legal advocate was provided by the Division of Parole for that purpose. Following all the testimony, I would write down my decision in summary form: The violation of parole charges considered and sustained were listed. A copy was given to the parolee. If none of the charges were sustained, the parole officer would be directed to arrange for the parolee's release from custody.

In reference to the revocation hearing, the Court stated: "The parolee must have an opportunity to be heard and to show if he can that he did not violate the conditions or if he did, that circumstances in mitigation suggest the violation does not warrant revocation. The revocation hearing must be tendered within a reasonable time after the parolee is taken into custody. A lapse of two months as the state suggests occurs in some cases would not appear to be unreasonable."

The Court also suggested minimum requirements of due process for the revocation hearing:

> Our task is limited to deciding the minimum requirements of due process. They include (1) written notice of the claimed violation of parole; (2) disclosures to the parolee of evidence against him; (3) opportunity to be heard in person and to present witnesses and documentary evidence; (4) the right to confront and cross-examine adverse witnesses (unless the hearing officer specifically finds good cause for not allowing confrontation); (5) "neutral and detached" hearing body such as a traditional parole board, members of which need not be judicial officers or lawyers; and (6) a written statement by the fact finders as to the evidence relied on and reasons for revoking parole.

The Supreme Court left open the question of counsel: "We do not reach or decide the question whether the parolee is entitled to the assistance of retained or to appointed counsel if he is indigent." In practice, parole boards have permitted parolees to be represented by counsel, although they usually do not provide such assistance.

Parole Board Liability

In a unanimous decision (*Martinez v. California*, 444 U.S. 277, 1980), the Supreme Court affirmed the constitutionality of statutory provisions that provide parole officials with immunity from tort claims. In this instance, Thomas, a parolee convicted of attempted rape, tortured and murdered 15-year-old Mary Martinez 5 months after his parole release from prison. Thomas had been labeled as not amenable to treatment, and the sentencing court recommended that he not be paroled. Nevertheless, after serving 5 years of a 1- to 200-year sentence, Thomas was paroled. The deceased girl's parents argued that in releasing Thomas, parole authorities subjected their daughter to deprivation of her life without due process of law.

Key Fact

Parole board members do not have the total immunity enjoyed by judges.

Justice Stevens, delivering the opinion for the Court, stated that "we cannot accept the contention that this statute deprives Thomas' (a paroled offender) victim of her life without due process of law because it condoned a parole decision that led indirectly to her death. The statute neither authorized nor immunized the deliberate killing of any human being. This statute merely provides a defense to potential state tort law liability. At most, the availability of such a defense may have encouraged members of the parole board to take somewhat greater risks of recidivism in exercising their authority to release prisoners than they otherwise might. But the basic risk that repeat offenses may occur is always present in any parole system." But because parole boards act only in a *quasi*-judicial capacity, they do not enjoy the total immunity conferred on judges. Justice Stevens pointed out that in this decision: "We need not and do not decide that a parole official could never be deemed to 'deprive' someone of life by action taken in connection with a prisoner on parole."

Now that the examination of the historical, administrative, and legal aspects of probation and parole is complete, Chapter 8 turns to rehabilitation theory and practice in probation and parole.

KEY TERMS

commutation (p. 211)
conditional release (p. 189)
consolidated model (p. 188)
executive clemency (p. 210)
independent model (p. 188)
liberty interest (p. 214)
new offense violation (p. 201)

pardon (p. 211)
parole board guidelines (p. 196)
preliminary hearing (p. 203)
probable cause (p. 202)
reprieve (p. 210)
revocation hearing (p. 209)
technical violation (p. 201)

Internet Connections

American Probation and Parole Association: www.appa-net.org;
www.talkjustice.com/links.asp?453053932
National Institute of Corrections: nicic.org
Parole board links: crimelynx.com

Review Questions

1. Distinguish the independent model of parole administration from the consolidated model.
2. What are the advantages and disadvantages of the independent model?
3. What are the advantages and disadvantages of the consolidated model?
4. How does conditional release differ from parole release?
5. Why is the administration of parole less complex than that of probation?
6. What are the three basic services provided by a parole agency?
7. What is conditional release, and how does it differ from parole?
8. Why have parole release hearings been criticized?
9. Why do most parole boards deny inmates the right to legal representation at parole release hearings?
10. What are the two most important factors considered when making a parole release decision?
11. What led to the development of parole release guidelines?
12. How do parole board guidelines take into account both classical and positivist school views?
13. How are parole release guidelines used?
14. Why can the parole board be in a better position than the sentencing judge to render a decision based on just deserts?
15. What is the primary responsibility of institutional parole staff? What other services might they provide?
16. What is the purpose of a preliminary parole violation hearing?
17. Provide examples of special rules of parole.
18. How is the length of parole/conditional release supervision determined?
19. How does a technical violation differ from a new offense violation?
20. How does a final or revocation parole hearing differ from a preliminary hearing?
21. What rights does an alleged violator have at a violation of parole hearing?
22. With respect to parole release, what has the Supreme Court ruled?
23. What did the Supreme Court rule in the 1972 case of *Morrissey v. Brewer*?
24. What are the different types of executive clemency?
25. What has the Supreme Court ruled with respect to parole board liability?

part 3

Rehabilitation and Supervision in Probation and Parole

Rehabilitation Theory and Practice

Research has consistently identified certain dynamic correlates of criminal behavior (also known as criminogenic needs) such as antisocial attitudes, antisocial peers, antisocial personality, poor familial relationships, and low educational or vocational achievement.

—*Christopher Lowenkamp et al.* (2006: 3–4)

Chapter Outline

Probation and parole (P/P) have traditionally been viewed as having two primary goals—protection of the community and rehabilitation of the offender. Of course, the two are not incompatible: Rehabilitation of the offender improves community safety.

Some modes of rehabilitation[1] are more easily applied than others to P/P practice. Some methods require more training than most P/P officers have received, and their use may require an expenditure of time that is not realistic in most P/P agencies. In practice, P/P officers use a variety of techniques, tailoring them to different clients. Effective supervision is based on sound theoretical principles, yet rehabilitative services tend to be atheoretical (Russell, Latessa, and Travis, 2005). P/P officers often use techniques without understanding the theoretical basis or even recognizing it as part of a particular mode of rehabilitation—"flying by the seat of the pants" is often characteristic of P/P. Nevertheless, most P/P officers, even when they do not provide extensive direct rehabilitative services, refer clients to programs for such problems as substance abuse, pedophilia, unemployment, mental illness. Knowledge of various modalities, therefore, is important in P/P. Therapeutic rehabilitation, no matter the discipline, requires both theoretical knowledge and sound principles applied to specific cases. Being knowledgeable about both theory and therapy enables the P/P officer to make appropriate referrals, understand treatment reports, and better relate to rehabilitation professionals.

---

[1] Some might object to the use of the term *rehabilitation* because it refers to a restoration of previous functioning. In fact, many P/P clients have never had a satisfactory level of social functioning. The word *habilitation*, however, has an unfamiliar ring to it, so rehabilition will refer to both a restoration of previous functioning *and* habilitation.

What Is Theory?

A **theory** is part of an explanation—a statement about the relationship between two classes of phenomena that permits us to better understand our environment, that helps to explain events by organizing them in the world so they can be placed in perspective. A theory also explains the causes of past events and predicts when, where, and how future events will occur. "A theory consists of a set of assumptions; concepts regarding events, situations, individuals, and groups; and propositions that describe the interrelationships among the various assumptions and concepts" (Binder and Geis, 1983: 3).

Theories are abstract, a necessary dimension if they are to be applied to more than one specific set of circumstances, facts, or observations. We cannot determine the cause of particular criminal behavior based on a satisfactory explanation for a single case; however, if enough individual cases fit into the same explanation, we can develop a theory and test it against future cases of criminal behavior. The ability to predict is a measure of a theory's validity. Validity requires testing, and any theory that cannot be tested—and, therefore, disproved—is not (according to scientific principles) a theory. A purported cause of crime that does not permit testing, therefore, has more in common with theology than criminology—it lacks scientific merit.

A Closer Look

Nature versus Nurture

Whenever a theory of crime is offered, two essential elements must be considered. First, theories of crime can be distinguished by how the authors or supporters conceive of the nature of human behavior. Prominent in any discussion of human behavior is the *nature versus nurture* controversy. Both sides address the same question: What is the dominant force shaping human behavior? Supporters of the *nature* position answer that behavior can be explained primarily by genetic, biological, or other properties inherent in the individual. In short, human behavior is largely inherited. Conversely, proponents of the *nurture* position look to the social environment for the causal factors, that is, human behavior is largely the product of social interaction.

There are three basic theoretical models for rehabilitation in P/P:

1. Psychoanalytic theory
2. Reality therapy
3. Behavior/learning theory

These and other therapies and theories will be covered in the following sections.

Psychoanalytic Theory and Stages of Development

Psychoanalytic theory refers to a body of work fathered by Sigmund Freud (1856–1939). Over the years the theory has undergone change, although Freud's basic contribution, his exposition of the importance of phenomena of the **unconscious** in human behavior, remains: Personality is strongly influenced by determinants in the unconscious that develop early in life. Simply put, this concept argues that the most important determinants of our behavior are not available to our conscious thought (Cloninger, 2004). These determinants evolve during the stages of psychological development.

Freud postulated unconscious processes in the stages of psychological development that, although not directly observable, were inferred from case studies with patients. He divided mental phenomena into three groups:

1. *Conscious*. Contents of a person's thoughts at any given time.
2. *Preconscious*. Thoughts and memories that can easily be called into conscious awareness.
3. *Unconscious*. Repressed feelings and experiences that can be made conscious only with great difficulty.

"The unconscious is essentially dynamic and capable of profoundly affecting conscious ideational or emotional life without the individual's being aware of this influence" (Healy, Bronner, and Bowers, 1930: 24). Unconscious feelings and experiences are related to normal stages of psychosexual development through which each person passes on the way to adulthood (psychosexual maturity). Memories of these stages of psychosexual development are repressed and, therefore, unconscious—not part of conscious or preconscious memory—yet they drive behavior and serve as a source of anxiety and guilt, the basis for psychoneurosis and psychosis. The stages overlap, and transition from one to the other is gradual, the time spans being approximate:

1. *Oral stage*. During the **oral stage** (birth to 18 months), the mouth, lips, and tongue are the predominant organs of pleasure for the infant. In the normal infant, the source of pleasure becomes associated with the touch and warmth of the parent, who gratifies oral needs. When this is lacking, deviant behavior, particularly drug and alcohol abuse, is to be expected in the adult. Drugs and alcohol serve as a substitute for maternal attachment; in adults, drug abuse is seen as a regression to an unfulfilled oral stage. The infant actually enters the world a "criminal," that is, unsocialized and devoid of self-control.
2. *Anal stage*. In the **anal stage** (18 months to 3 years), the anus becomes the most important site of erotic interest and gratification. Pleasure is closely connected to the retention and expulsion of feces as well as the bodily processes involved and the feces themselves. During this stage, the only partially socialized child acts out rather destructive urges, breaking toys or even injuring living organisms such as insects or small animals. A great deal of psychopathology in the adult, including violent behavior and sociopathological personality disorders, is traced to disruptions during this stage.
3. *Genital stage*. Erotic interest becomes associated with the genitals during the **genital stage** (3 to 5 years) and in normal persons is maintained by them thereafter. During this period of life, the child experiences *Oedipus* (in boys) and *Electra* (in girls) *wishes* in the form of fantasies of incest with the parent of the opposite sex. The healthy child must relinquish the dependent paternal/maternal attachment and deal with the feelings of sadness that result. Sexual problems, such as pedophilia, are linked to this stage when the adult remains fixated on a parent and is not attracted to adults of the opposite sex. Drug and alcohol abuse are also traced to failures during this stage of development (see Abadinsky, 2008).
4. *Latent stage*. A lessening of interest in sexual organs, as well as an expanded relationship with playmates of the same sex and age, occurs during the latent stage (5 years to adolescence).
5. *Adolescence-adulthood stage*. A reawakening of genital interest and awareness occurs at the adolescence-adulthood stage (13 years to death). The incestuous wish is repressed and emerges in terms of mature (adult) sexuality.

When a person is passing through the first three stages of psychosexual development, the mind simultaneously undergoes the development of three psychic phenomena:

1. *Id*. The **id** is a mass of powerful drives that seeks discharge or gratification—it is asocial, devoid of values and logical processes. Constituting wishes, urges, and psychic

tensions, according to Freud (1933: 104), the id is "a cauldron of seething excitement," seeking pleasure and avoiding pain. The id is the driving force of the personality, and from birth until about 7 months of age, it is the total psychic apparatus.

2. *Ego.* Through contact with the reality around them and the influence of training, infants modify their expressions of id drives. This development of the **ego** is pragmatic and permits them to obtain maximum gratification with a minimum of difficulty in the form of restrictions that their environment places on them—learning from experience. Without the ego to act as a restraining influence, the id would destroy the person through its blind striving to gratify instincts in complete disregard for reality. As a result of disturbances in psychosexual development, a person may remain at the ego level of development: "The child remains asocial or behaves as if he had become social without having made actual adjustment to the demands of society" (Aichhorn, 1963: 4). Feelings of rage and aggression associated with the anal stage lurk in the background awaiting an opportunity to break through to satisfaction.

3. *Superego.* Often viewed as a conscience-type mechanism, the **superego** exercises a criticizing power, a sense of morality over the ego: "It represents the whole demands of morality, and we see all at once that our moral sense of guilt is the expression of tension between the ego [which strives to discharge id drives] and the super-ego" (Freud, 1933: 88). A healthy superego is the result of an identification with the parent(s)—the superego is an internalized parent—that is accomplished during the genital stage of psychosexual development. In Freud's words, "The role which the super-ego undertakes later in life is at first played by external power, by parental authority" (1933: 89). Another author states, "The super-ego then supports the ego in controlling the instinctive [id] impulses" (Smart, 1970: 45).

A delicate balance is maintained by unconscious forces as a person experiences various sociocultural and biological aspects of existence. When the balance is upset, the psyche passes from the normal to the psychoneurotic or the psychotic (mental illness). The fact that a thin line exists between the normal and the neurotic and between the neurotic and the psychotic is basic to psychoanalytic theory. In fact, only a difference of degree separates the "normal" and the "abnormal": The degree to which there is a malfunctioning in psychic apparatus is the degree to which a person is "abnormal" or "sick," that is, socially dysfunctional.

CRIME AND THE SUPEREGO

Crime Causation

"[The] psychoanalytic theory of crime causation does not make the usual distinction between behavior as such and criminal action" (Falk, 1966: 1). The distinction is a legal one, that is, crime is behavior defined by a society as illegal (discussed in Chapter 1). Antisocial behavior is seen as a neurotic manifestation whose origin can be traced back to early stages of development: "There is no fundamental difference between the neurotic criminal and all those socially harmless representatives of the group of neurotic characters; the difference lies merely in the external fact that the neurotic lawbreaker chooses a form of acting out his impulses which is socially harmful or simply illegal" (Alexander and Staub, 1956: 106).

According to August Aichhorn (1963: 221), "the superego takes its form and content from identifications which result from the child's effort to emulate the parent. It is evolved not only because the parent loves the child, but also because the child fears the parent's demands." However, Freud (1933: 92) states that "the superego does not attain to full strength and development if the overcoming of the Oedipus [in males] complex has not been completely successful."

The superego keeps primitive (oral and anal) id impulses from being acted on. Persons with an **antisocial personality disorder**, with a poorly developed superego (e.g., psychopaths or sociopaths), are restrained only by the ego, which alone cannot exercise adequate control over id impulses. Such persons suffer little or no guilt as a result of engaging in socially harmful behavior. They are characterized by a combination of antisocial behavior and emotional detachment (Black, 1999).

At the other extreme are persons whose superego (internal parental voice) is destructive. Their superego is overwhelming and cannot distinguish between *thinking about* and *doing* bad deeds. Unresolved conflicts of earlier development and id impulses that are normally repressed or dealt with through other secondary processes (such as reaction formation or sublimation) create a severe sense of (unconscious) guilt. This guilt is experienced (at the unconscious level) as a compulsive need to be punished. To alleviate this (unconscious) guilt, the actor is impelled toward committing acts for which punishment is virtually certain. Delinquents of this type are the victims of their own morality (Aichhorn, 1963). Persons employed in the criminal justice system often see cases in which the crime committed was so poorly planned and executed that it would appear that the perpetrator *wished* to be caught.

A Closer Look

No Willie Sutton!

- Richard G. entered the Bay Bank in Haverhill, Massachusetts, went up to a counter, and wrote on a deposit slip: "This is a holdup. Give me all the money." He left the bank with $5,201. With red dye from an explosive device used to mark stolen bills streaming from his bag, Richard G. mounted an old two-speed bicycle. He was caught within minutes, covered with red dye, sneezing, and coughing. The note he had handed the teller was discovered to contain his name and home address (Associated Press, April 18, 1992).

- Lee W. entered a Connecticut bank and presented a withdrawal slip to the teller on which he had written: "The money." He was quickly arrested by police, who found $3,000 on him—Lee had written his name on the withdrawal slip *twice*.

The FBI catches between 40 and 50 bank robbers per year who write their note demanding money on the back of a deposit slip for their own checking accounts (Martin, 1995).

In sum, criminal behavior is related to the superego function, which is a result of an actor's relationship to parents (or parental figures) during early developmental years. Parental deprivation through absence, lack of affection, or inconsistent discipline stifles the proper development of the superego. Parental influence is thus weakened by deprivation during childhood development, so in adulthood the actor is unable to adequately control aggressive, hostile, or antisocial urges. Overly rigid or punitive parents, conversely, can lead to the creation of a superego that is rigid and punitive, for which the actor seeks punishment as a way of alleviating unconscious "guilt."

A P/P officer must be able to distinguish those offenders with an inadequate superego from those with a punitive one. With the latter, attempts to deter criminal behavior through the application of threats may actually have an opposite effect; with the former, the P/P officer may need to act in a parental role to replace a poorly developed superego.

Psychoanalytic Treatment

Psychic disorders are treated by psychoanalysis or one of its variants, such as psychotherapy. According to Freud, psychoanalysis "aims at encouraging the patient to give up the repressions belonging to his or her early life and to replace them with more psychically mature reactions. To achieve this goal, a psychoanalyst attempts to get the patient "to recollect certain experiences and the emotions called up by them which he has at the moment forgotten" (Reiff, 1963: 274). To the psychoanalyst, present symptoms are tied to repressed material of early life—the primary stages of psychosexual development. The symptoms will disappear when the repressed material is exposed under psychoanalytic treatment.

Today, most psychoanalytically oriented therapists practice a variety of approaches (such as ego psychology whose focus is more immediate) rather than classical Freudian analysis (Nietzel et al., 2003), and psychoanalysis is not used in P/P because it requires highly trained and thus expensive practitioners, treatment takes many years, and it needs a level of verbal ability in patients beyond that of most persons on P/P. In fact, psychoanalytically oriented therapists may underestimate how difficult it is to verbalize experience, even for otherwise verbal patients (Omer and London, 1988). Instead of psychoanalysis, psychoanalytic theory has traditionally been applied in P/P through the use of social casework.

Key Fact

In P/P, psychoanalytic theory has traditionally been applied through the use of social casework.

Social Casework

Social work has its roots in charity work and **social casework**—the supplying of concrete services to persons in need—solving problems rather than changing personalities. Mary Richmond (1917), whose colleagues included many physicians, presented the practice of social work as including (nonpsychoanalytic) psychological and sociological aspects of a person's behavior. She also set the groundwork for what is sometimes referred to as the **medical model** of therapy, dealing with nonphysiological problems through the method of study, diagnosis, and treatment.

In the years following World War I, social work was characterized by practice based primarily on the psychoanalytic perspective and the medical model (Miley, O'Melia, and DuBois, 2004). During the 1930s, some American physicians began to use psychoanalytic treatment, and social workers adopted this "talking cure"—one that did not require medical training—to their own practice (Specht, 1990). Psychoanalytic theory was still central to social work education when this writer received his master's of social work degree in 1970.

Key Fact

Social casework focuses on problems that block or minimize the effectiveness of an individual to carry out expected social roles.

Social casework is one of the basic specialties of social work, "an art in which knowledge of the science of human relations and skills in relationship are used to mobilize capacities in the individual and resources in the community appropriate for better adjustment between the client and all or any part of his total environment" (Bowers, 1950: 127). Social casework "can be defined essentially as the development of a relationship between worker and client, within a problem-solving context, and coordinated with the appropriate use of community resources" (Brennan et al., 1986: 342). The purpose of social casework is "the solution of problems that block or minimize the effectiveness of the individual in various roles" (Skidmore, Thackeray, and Farley, 1988: 64).

As Freudian thought had its impact on social work, caseworkers began examining the client's feelings and attitudes to understand and "cope with some of the unreasonable forces that held him in their grip" (Perlman, 1971: 76). The client's behavior is conceived as purposeful and determined, but some of the determinants are unconscious. Casework was thus expanded to include work with psychological and social or environmental stress and adopted the open listening style of relationship—even the notion of relationship is grounded in Freudian thought (Payne, 1997). It is the therapeutic relationship that serves as a medium for facilitating change: The caseworker helps clients to maintain constructive reality-based relationships, solve problems, and achieve adequate and satisfying independent social functioning within the client's existing personality structure (Torgerson, 1962). To accomplish this task, social workers use encouragement and moral support, persuasion and suggestion, training and advice, comfort and reassurance, together with reeducation and some sort of guidance (Casius, 1954).

Although social casework borrowed much of its theory from Freud, it avoided the psychoanalytical goal of trying to effect personality changes. Instead, a more immediate and pragmatic version of the Freudian model was adopted, helping people "perform in their appropriate social roles by providing information and knowledge, social support, social skills, and opportunity" (Specht, 1990: 354). Twenty-first-century social casework, while recognizing the influence of early development, social environments, and traumatic events, generally focuses on immediate concerns and addresses maladaptive behaviors and adverse conditions that perpetuate problems in current functioning (Borden, 2000). Whereas the medical model searches the past to detect problems in the present, contemporary social work—while not discounting the importance of the developmental past—explores the present for client strengths and resources that can promote effective social functioning (Miley, O'Melia, and DuBois, 2004).

The importance of social casework in P/P practice (sometimes called *forensic* social work) goes beyond theory and into the skills and training that schools of social work provide. These include "an extension and refinement of information on how to interview, how to obtain facts about the client's background, how to identify and distinguish surface from underlying problems, what community resources exist, and how to refer" (Wilensky and Lebeaux, 1958: 288–89). "The knowledge base developed for social casework is eclectic, interdisciplinary, tentative at best, complex and often subjective" (Johnson and Yanca, 2007: 42). The newer approaches borrow from ego psychology, emphasizing coping and social functioning. Instead of the medical model terms *study, diagnosis,* and *treatment,* modern social casework adopted the terms *assessment, planning,* and *action* (Johnson and Yanca, 2007):

- *Assessment.* Collection and analysis of relevant information on which to base a plan.
- *Planning.* Thoughts about and organization of facts into a meaningful goal-oriented explanation for action.
- *Action.* Implementation of the plan.

> **Key Fact**
>
> Psychoanalysis searches the past to detect problems in the present, while social casework explores the present for client strengths and resources that can promote effective social functioning

Assessment

Assessment determines the nature of the client's current situation, resulting in a written report (variously called a psychosocial study, intake report, or social history, among other nomenclature). The assessment involves gathering information from documents and through interviews with persons familiar with the offender as well as the client him- or herself. It provides the "here and now" and how it got that way. More complex and significant than data collection, assessment incorporates the tasks of deciding which data to seek and how to organize it (Bisman, 2000). Assessment includes identifying strengths and resources that exist within the client and his or her environment (Johnson and Yanca, 2007). "When assessment is complete, the social worker should be able to describe the problem or situation accurately and identify what needs to be changed to improve the client's situation" (Sheafor, Horejsi, and Horejsi, 2000: 301).

During this phase, client interviews provide the basis for a relationship. To accomplish this, the worker must be what Gordon Hamilton calls "a person of genuine warmth" (1967: 28). Using face-to-face interviews, the worker conveys acceptance and understanding. Walter Friedlander notes that "caseworkers communicate their respect for and acceptance of the client as a person whose decisions about his own living situation are almost always his own to make" (1958: 22). The caseworker seeks to understand the client's press and stress: "People are affected by *press* from the environment and by *stress* from conflicts within themselves" (Payne, 1997: 80).

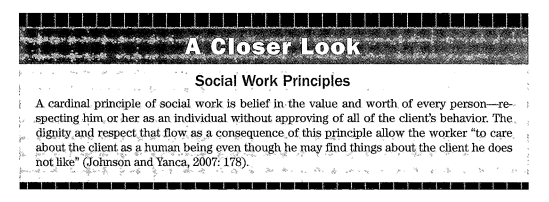

Social Work Principles

A cardinal principle of social work is belief in the value and worth of every person—respecting him or her as an individual without approving of all of the client's behavior. The dignity and respect that flow as a consequence of this principle allow the worker "to care about the client as a human being even though he may find things about the client he does not like" (Johnson and Yanca, 2007: 178).

Caseworkers know that the way they communicate will have an effect on clients' perceptions of them and the worker-client relationship. Therefore, they must be cognizant of the way they greet clients; the way they use tone of voice, facial expressions, and posture; and the way they express themselves verbally. In P/P practice, workers who exude authority, who are curt, and who emphasize the enforcement aspect of their position will encounter difficulties in establishing a sound casework relationship.

Caseworkers engage clients in the helping process and make certain judgments about clients' motivation—how much they want to change and how willing they are to contribute to bringing about change. Workers recognize that a client brings attitudes and preconceptions about being on probation or parole. The P/P client is fearful, or at least realistically on guard, because he or she recognizes the power of the P/P officer.

An anxious client will be resistant to a caseworker's efforts, and in the mandated setting that is P/P practice, a P/P officer can easily raise a client's anxiety level, thus increasing resistance, including "evasive, angry, and uncooperative behaviors" (Hutchinson, 1987: 591). Psychoanalytic theory also posits resistance that is unconscious. P/P clients frequently have a negative impression of all authority figures, a perception usually based on experiences with parents, school officials, police officers, court officials, training schools, or prisons. In addition, a client may have a low self-image, a severe superego, or a chronically high anxiety level. The result will be resistance. The worker must not become defensive about client resistance or take negative behavior personally.

To lessen resistance, workers may discuss the client's feelings about being on P/P, allowing him or her to vent some feelings and anxiety. This approach will also enable workers to clarify any misconceptions that clients have about P/P supervision. Elizabeth Hutchinson (1987: 592) suggests "letting it all hang out": "It is essential for the social worker to make early acknowledgement of client reluctance toward the mandated transactions and to validate such reluctance as understandable. This makes the issue explicit rather than latent and assures the client of the acceptability of his or her feelings as well as the genuineness of the social worker."

The client's motivation can also be influenced by the psychoanalytical concept of **transference**: He or she may view the worker as a friendly parent or as an authoritarian and demanding mother or father. The worker can be influenced by *countertransference* because he or she may view the client as a childlike figure; if the worker is a great deal younger than the client, the former may view the latter as a parent or older sibling.

The caseworker prepares a psychosocial study of the client. In non-P/P agencies, workers often stress the importance of early childhood development and experiences with a view toward applying a psychoanalytic explanation to the client's behavior. This practice is not usual in P/P settings, where "the unique constellation of social, psychological, and biological determinants of the client's current stressful situation" is more relevant and appropriate to analyze (Friedlander, 1958: 47). In P/P practice, the primary focus of assessment is on the present or the recent past.

The P/P officer seeks information that will provide an indication of the client's view of his or her present situation, is concerned with the client's plans for improving the situation, and weighs the sincerity and intensity of the latter's commitment to change. During the assessment phase, "particular attention needs to be given to assessing client strengths [because this] builds hopefulness and uncovers possibilities for dealing with the problem" (Sheafor, Horejsi, and Horejsi, 2000: 304). When the caseworker interprets the situation as needing to fix something that is wrong, it gives him or her the status of "expert" with the expectation that the worker will bring about change rather than the client: "The real work must be done by the client; otherwise it either does not get done or the change is temporary" (Johnson and Yanca, 2007: 61). The caseworker reviews the client's relationship with his or her family and evaluates the impact of the client's current situation. While engaged in study, the worker must also be aware of the cultural, racial, and ethnic factors that influence a client.

In P/P, material from the unconscious is not sought, but with clients who are mentally ill, material that in the better-functioning person is normally repressed may be brought to the fore. In such situations, the worker must direct his or her efforts toward keeping the client in touch with reality and should usually avoid exploring the normally repressed material.

Planning

The planning phase converts the assessment content into a goal statement that describes the desired results (Johnson and Yanca, 2007). Helen Perlman (1957: 168–69) suggests what this phase of casework involves:

- Nature of the problem and goals sought by the client
- Nature of the person who bears the problem (his or her social and psychological situation and functioning) and who needs help with the problem
- Nature and purpose of the agency and kind of help it can offer or make available

In discussing the origin of the client's malfunctioning, Perlman refers to "this history of his development as a problem-encountering, problem-solving human being" and notes that this can provide the worker with an understanding of the client's present difficulties and the probable extent of his or her ability to cope with them (1957: 176). For a plan to be complete, psychological testing or a psychiatric evaluation may be necessary. The results of a clinical examination will indicate if the client is in need of any special therapy (e.g., whether he or she is psychotic). In many instances a psychological or psychiatric report will not be available, so the P/P worker must make the determination if an evaluation will be of enough help in planning to justify the expense.

"[The evaluation] plan considers both process and outcomes by specifying intermediate objectives as well as end goals" (Johnson, 1998: 294). Anticipating difficulties that may be encountered, the plan needs to be flexible to be effective. In P/P, the plan provides a basis for holding the offender accountable for his or her efforts toward achieving a productive and law-abiding lifestyle.

Action

The action phase involves activity designed to bring about change in a systematic way (Johnson and Yanca, 2007). During this stage, the relationship between worker and client enables the P/P officer to use his or her influence. It is a basic concept in social work that the client has a right to **self-determination**: The worker has no right to impose his or her goals. Obviously, the authority inherent in the P/P officer's role necessarily limits self-determination; for example, the P/P officer may be bound by statute or agency regulation to make decisions about the client's living situation. Dale Hardman (1960: 250) states that "authority conflict is a major causative factor in delinquency," a proposition that is widely accepted in correctional social work, so helping the offender come to grips with the reality of authority is a basic goal of P/P rehabilitation. The client's relationship with a P/P worker is often the only positive experience he or she has ever had in dealing with an authority figure. "Many clients' involvement with the law expresses a need for control they cannot themselves provide. If used with respect and care, the authority of the court can be invoked by the forensic social worker to strengthen the client's weak motive to get treatment and to improve impulse control" (Brennan et al., 1986: 345).

Social caseworkers in other than correctional settings must also deal with the reality of their authority. They require clients to keep appointments, provide personal information, and pay fees—usually under the threat (implied or expressed) of denying the client the help or service the client is asking for. Workers in child welfare agencies may even be required to remove children from their parents or guardians in neglect or child abuse cases. In addition, because of the impact of an agency setting or the phenomenon of transference, the caseworker is always an authority figure. The concept and the use of authority and the limits placed on self-determination by reality are not alien to the practice of social casework, but "unwilling clients often do not see the need for service, do not believe help is possible, or have difficulty in developing a relationship with the worker" (Johnson and Yanca, 2007: 160).

Key Fact

Social casework adopted three terms for the process of helping: assessment, planning, and action.

The plan for intervention in social casework will use procedures that, it is hoped, will move the client toward the goal of enhancing the ability to function within the realities placed on him or her by society in general, and the client's present probation/parole status in particular. Three basic techniques are involved: change in the environment, ego support, and clarification.

Change in the Environment.   Effecting a change in the environment may involve obtaining needed resources if these are available from the agency or locating other agencies that can provide them. In using this technique, the worker may assume a mediator or advocate role when the client is unable to secure a service that he or she needs and to which he or she is entitled. In P/P practice, this role is common; as advocates, P/P officers act as intermediaries between clients and agencies and may function as spokespersons for clients needing to deal with the bureaucratic maze of governmental agencies (Miley, O'Melia, and DuBois, 2004). The technique is used by the juvenile P/P officer who is seeking placement for a youngster in a foster home, group home, or residential treatment center and by the aftercare worker who is trying to place a juvenile back in public school after a stay at a juvenile institution. The P/P worker may have to intervene on behalf of clients who require financial assistance from the welfare department or may help a client to secure a civil service position or a necessary license/certificate to enter a particular trade or profession.

The P/P worker may help his or her client by talking to an employer or school official while helping the client to modify behavior relative to problems encountered at work or school. Many P/P clients have had few positive work or school experiences, and their difficulty with authority extends to employers and teachers. By using role playing, reflection, and suggestion, the worker tries to modify the client's behavior, at least to the degree required for continued employment or schooling.

While being of direct assistance when necessary, the P/P officer should promote independence on the part of the client. The worker realizes that he or she is not continually available, and treatment is rarely indefinite. *The worker should not do anything for the client that the client is capable of doing for him- or herself.*

Ego Support.   The use of ego support entails attempts by the worker to sustain the client through expressions of interest, sympathy, and confidence. The worker, through the use of his or her relationship with the client, promotes or discourages behavior according to whether the behavior is consistent with the goals of rehabilitation. The P/P worker also encourages the client to vent and deals with any anxiety that may inhibit functioning.

Central to the casework process is the relationship between the client and P/P worker. The worker imparts a feeling of confidence in the client's ability to deal with problems, makes suggestions about the client's contemplated actions, and indicates approval or suggests alternatives relative to steps that the client has already taken. The officer may, at the very least, provide a willing and sympathetic ear to a troubled and lonely client—it is not unusual for the P/P worker to be the only person available to an offender to whom he or she can relate and talk. When the relationship is a good one, the client cannot help but view the worker as a friend.

The officer is also supportive of the client's family, parents, or spouse. In P/P practice, home visits are a usual part of the responsibilities. During the home visit, the worker has an opportunity to observe the client's environment directly, and this first-hand information adds another dimension to the worker's knowledge of the client.

The knowledge that a client lives in substandard housing or in a high-delinquency area is easy for the worker to incorporate into his or her working methodology, but the concept is an intellectual one. A home visit provides direct information about the smell of urine in the hall, roaches, broken fixtures, and substandard bathroom facilities as well as housing that is hot in the summer and cold in the winter; a home visit also enables the worker to experience the presence of drug addicts huddling in a hallway, waiting for their connection. The worker is able to see, hear, and smell the environment in which a client is forced to live and thus understand the hostility and frustration that fill the life of many P/P clients almost from the time they are born.

By working directly with parents or a spouse, in addition to working with the client, the P/P officer broadens his or her delivery of help to the client. The worker can make referrals for the client's children when special aid is necessary—indeed, he or she can intervene on behalf of the client in the role of mediator/advocate to get services for any family member. The P/P officer can assist with marital problems (marital discord is an acute problem in many parole cases when a client has been incarcerated for many years). The worker may try to deal with the problem directly or may provide a referral to a specialized agency for the client and spouse. For example, it is not unusual for a distraught wife to call the P/P officer to complain about her husband. Sometimes she is merely seeking some way of venting her feelings; at other times, the situation may be more serious (e.g., she may have been subjected to physical abuse).

When a client is living with parents, the worker strives to involve them in the rehabilitation effort, which is often difficult. The client may be the perennial black sheep in a large family or may come from a family that also has other members on probation, in prison, or on parole. This may dissipate the family's energy and resources and directly affect their ability to help the client.

Clarification.   According to Florence Hollis (1950), clarification is sometimes called counseling because it usually accompanies other forms of rehabilitation in casework practice. Clarification includes providing information that will help a client to see what steps he or she should take in various situations. The worker, for example, may help the client weigh the issues and alternatives to provide a better picture on which to base a decision. Hollis notes that the client "may also be helped to become more aware of his own feelings, desires and attitudes" (1950: 418–19).

The client is encouraged to explain what is bothering him or her. If the problem is external, verbalizing it may be relatively easy; if the difficulty is internally caused, however, it may go deep and provoke anxiety. This difficulty will cause resistance, and the P/P officer will need great skill to secure enough information about the problem to be able to be of assistance. In response to the information, the worker may provide a direct interpretation to the client; more often, the P/P officer will ask questions and make suggestions designed to help the client to think out the problem more clearly and to deal with it in a realistic manner.

LEARNING THEORY AND BEHAVIOR MODIFICATION

To understand learning theory and behavior modification, one may place the various modes of rehabilitation related to P/P practice on a continuum represented by a straight horizontal line. Acceptance of psychoanalytic theory is on the extreme left of this line and rejection on the extreme right. Social casework would be at the left of center; reality therapy (discussed later) is toward the right of center, while behavior modification is firmly on the extreme right of this imaginary line.

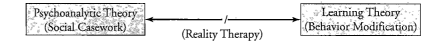

Psychoanalytic Theory
(Social Casework)   /   Learning Theory
                     (Reality Therapy)   (Behavior Modification)

Key Fact

Behavior modification proceeds on the theory that all forms of behavior are the result of learning responses to certain stimuli—behavior is strengthened by its consequences.

Behavior modification, the application of **learning theory** (the theory that all behavior is shaped by its consequences) which emanated from the science laboratory and experimental psychology, rejects psychoanalytic theory as an unscientific basis for an even more unscientific mode of rehabilitation. B. F. Skinner (1904–1990), America's foremost behaviorist, argued that analytically oriented therapists "rely too much on inferences they make about what is supposedly going on inside their patients, and too little on direct observation of what they do" (Goleman, 1987: 18). "If a client's aggressive behavior has been rewarded, at least part of the time, no further explanation in terms of internal needs is necessary; the client has simply learned to behave aggressively" (Nietzel et al., 2003: 47).

Behaviorists take pride in displaying and subjecting their methods and results to rigorous scientific analysis. Behavior modification proceeds on the theory that all forms of behavior are the result of learning responses to certain stimuli. "Disturbed" behavior, for example, is a matter of learning responses that are inappropriate (London, 1964). The behaviorist contends—and has been able to prove—that animal behavior, human and otherwise, can be modified through the proper application of behaviorist principles.

Behavior is "*strengthened* by its consequences, and for that reason the consequences themselves are called 'reinforcers'" (Skinner, 1972: 40). When some aspect of (animal or human) behavior is followed by a reward, this action is a **reinforcer**, and it makes it more likely that the action will be repeated. "Reinforcers are types of consequences that strengthen a behavior" (Baldwin and Baldwin, 1998: 42). The reward is called **positive reinforcement**. If the probability of a behavior goes up after the *removal* of a stimulus, then **negative reinforcement** has occurred: "A negative reinforcer strengthens any behavior that reduces or terminates it" (Skinner, 1972: 47). For example, the negative reinforcement that occurs when a heroin addict fails to ingest enough heroin—withdrawal symptoms—strengthens drug-seeking behavior; as opposed to negative reinforcement, *punishment* (e.g., imprisonment) suppresses the frequency of an operant—heroin use. "Punishment either takes away something an organism wants or gives it something it does not want" (Hergenhahn and Olson, 1999: 289). While punishment is frequently used interchangeably with negative reinforcement, the two are quite different: "Punishment occurs when the introduction of a stimulus decreases the frequency of the behavior" (Oltmanns and Emery, 2004: 35).

Key Fact

Operant conditioning involves positive and negative reinforcement.

Thus, according to Skinner (1972), punished behavior such as crime is likely to reappear after the punitive contingencies are withdrawn. These applications form the basis for **operant conditioning**, conditioning that follows positive and negative reinforcers.

Antisocial behavior is merely the result of learning directly from others (e.g., peers) or the failure to learn how to discriminate between competing norms, both lawful and unlawful, because of inappropriate reinforcement. When conforming behavior is not adequately reinforced, an actor can more easily be influenced by competing, albeit antisocial, sources of positive reinforcement (e.g., money and excitement from criminal behavior). To be effective for learning, however, reinforcement must follow rather closely the behavior that is to be influenced: "Generally, operant conditioning is most likely to occur when reinforcers and punishers follow immediately after an operant" (Baldwin and Baldwin, 1998: 89). Offenders have problematic reinforcement contingencies and often engage in behavior that provides an immediate payoff but has negative long-term consequences. If criminal behavior is almost always rewarding, significant but intermittent punishment is unlikely to suppress it.

The behaviorist stresses client analysis to discover the variables that are reinforcing and then attempts to discover the situational demands and emotions that are related to the patient's behavior. The analysis deals with the day-to-day functioning of the subject in order to discern the cause (independent variables) of the maladaptive behavior (dependent variables). The therapist attempts to elicit specific descriptions of actual events that constitute a problem—functional analysis—so that he or she can evaluate which components of the situation are amenable to change by behavioral techniques (Nietzel et al., 2003). Whenever possible, the specific description is based on direct observations or interviews with the client and/or significant others (e.g., parents or spouse) and a review of any relevant records. Maladaptive behavior is analyzed in terms of intensity and frequency and is often presented in the form of graphs.

The therapist teaches the client to conduct his or her own functional analysis for subsequent self-produced modification of the environmental contingencies that are reinforcing the maladaptive behavior. The functional analysis can be combined with self-monitoring techniques. A highly motivated client maintains a daily log of the specific problem—for example, lack of temper control—and records the number of times that he or she exhibits the specific manifestations of a lack of temper control. Although this technique can be combined with other forms of therapy, alone it seems to have the power to modify behavior because it increases awareness and makes the response sequence less automatic. This may provide the opportunity for the person to suppress the response or engage in some incompatible behavior. Additionally, self-monitoring may encourage the person to reward or punish him- or herself depending on whether appropriate gains have been made. Investigators have shown that self-reinforcing statements, such as "I am doing well," are important in maintaining a behavior. "A recording system which facilitates this process undoubtedly will be effective in helping people to change their own behavior as well" (Bootzin, 1975: 11).

Cognitive Behavioral Therapy

The need for timely reinforcement makes operant conditioning difficult to apply in P/P practice. For example, stimulants (such as cocaine) and depressants (such as heroin) are powerful reinforcers—they provide instant gratification to those who find their use pleasant; competing with this reality in many cases is difficult and often impossible. Albert Bandura points out, however, that in humans, "outcomes resulting from actions need not necessarily occur instantly," because as opposed to lower animals, people "can cognitively bridge delays between behavior and subsequent reinforcers without impairing the efficacy of incentive operations" (1974: 862).

The cognitive position, which has become dominant in psychology—and which has been found to reduce recidivism (Lipsey, Chapman, Landenberger, 2001; Pearson et al., 2002; Wilson, Bouffard, and MacKenzie, 2005)— maintains that it is necessary to look to thoughts, memory, language, and beliefs. The emphasis is on inner rather than environmental determinants of behavior (Hollin, 1990). Bandura (1974) argues that to ignore the influence of covert reinforcement in the regulation of behavior is to deny a uniquely human capacity. According to the cognitive view, a human being is an active participant in his or her operant conditioning processes—the individual determines what is and what is not reinforcing. For example, to become a drug abuser, one must *learn* that ingesting certain chemicals is desirable (Abadinsky, 2008); in other words, human behavior is complex and reinforcement often abstract. Humans have a unique capacity to use abstractions, or symbols, that can serve as important reinforcers, such as the medals and trophies dear to any amateur athlete. Behavior can be learned vicariously through observation without obvious reinforcement (Nietzel et al., 2003).

The cognitive behavioral approach to criminal offenders has a focus on coping and problem-solving skills. The offender is suffering from faulty thinking patterns and lacks that level of social competence necessary to cope adequately with a variety of situational demands. "Their behavior may be guided by dysfunctional assumptions about how one should behave, for example, 'you have to punish people for messing with you or they won't respect you,' 'you have to rebel against authority or they will break you'" (Lipsey, Chapman, Landenberger, 2001: 145). Cognitive behavior therapy (CBT) is designed to correct dysfunctional and criminogenic thinking patterns.

A Closer Look

Cognitive-Behavior Therapy

"CBT attempts to change negative behaviors by attacking, as it were, from both ends. Clients are not only taught more positive behaviors to replace their old ways of getting through life, they are also shown how to be more attuned to the thought processes that led them to choose negative actions in the past" (Morris Thigpen in Foreword to Milkman and Wanberg, 2007: vii).

Since people can monitor and change their cognitive activity—"think crime"—and resulting behavior—"do crime"—the therapeutic process begins with an assessment of positive and negative aspects of their behavior. The assessment includes a focus on the social, physical, and emotional environments in which the behavior occurs. After the assessment, the role of the therapist is to enable the person to deal with cues that trigger problem behavior in a manner that avoids resorting to illegal activity, with the patient's own report of the negative aspects (e.g., arrest, incarceration) serving as a motivator for adopting more positive coping strategies (Donovan, 1988). Negative reinforcement in the form of avoidance strategies serves to prevent the occurrence of influences that trigger criminal behavior.

Self-reinforcement in humans may take on many tangible or symbolic dimensions. In reality therapy (discussed in a later section in this chapter), praise and encouragement are dispensed by the therapist; in correctional settings, the positive reinforcements are often privileges dispensed through secondary reinforcers or *tokens*.

Token Economy

Operant conditioning has been used in prisons (and other total institutions) where reinforcing variables can be controlled to a degree not possible elsewhere. In the controlled setting of the total institution, the application of behavior modification is often referred to as the *token economy*. The use of tokens has important advantages:

> First, they can be given immediately after a desirable behavior occurs and cashed in at a later time for a backup reinforcer. Thus, they can be used to "bridge" long delays between the target response and the backup reinforcer, which is especially important when delivery of the backup reinforcer immediately after the behavior is impractical or impossible. Second, tokens make it easier to administer consistent and effective reinforcers when dealing with a group of individuals. (Martin and Pear, 1992: 305)

In some correctional programs, inmates are issued punch cards with numbers every morning. As they move through the various prison activities during the day, points are earned and punched out on the cards by corrections officers trained in behavior modification techniques. Points can be earned for a variety of "good" behavior (e.g., bed making, vocational and educational performance), and the points accumulated on the punch cards are convertible into access to certain privileges (e.g., the television room, cigarettes, movies, snacks). Such programs can often reduce the need for standard forms of coercion typically used in correctional institutions.

The token economy has limited application:

> One obvious disadvantage related to TE [token economy] is that rather close control over environmental contingencies is required. The status of the S [subject] whose behavior is to be modified is that of a "captive." In the absence of environmental control, it is not possible to introduce critical contingencies. If control is present initially, but is then lost for whatever reason, the removal of the contingencies allows the altered behavior to revert in the direction of its original baseline rate. In an effort to maintain behavior when the subject has lost his status as a captive, operant conditioners have attempted to gradually alter the manipulated contingencies in respect to the behavior being modified so that the changed behavior itself would tend to result in natural intrinsic reinforcement. [The difficulty is that delinquents/criminals] tend to be highly resistant to the usual types of natural or intrinsic reinforcement that appear to function so effectively for other "normal" populations. (Stampfl, 1970: 105)

Other Behavior Modification Systems

Operant conditioning can also use **aversive therapy**, which involves the avoidance of punishment in a controlled situation in which the therapist specifies in advance an unpleasant event that will occur if the subject performs an undesirable behavior. According to a report by the American Psychiatric Association (APA) (1974: 25), "the most effective way to eliminate inappropriate behavior appears to be to punish it while at the same time reinforcing the desired behavior." This method of rehabilitation is obviously controversial, and many behaviorists disapprove of the use of punishment on both ethical and treatment grounds—its effects do not seem to last as long as results conditioned by positive reinforcement. According to Skinner, "What's wrong with punishments is that they work immediately, but give no long term results. The responses to punishment are either the urge to escape, to counterattack or a stubborn apathy. These are the bad effects you get in prisons or schools, or wherever punishments are used" (quoted by Goleman, 1987: 18).

Some have told horror stories about the use of aversive therapy, which was portrayed in the Stanley Kubrick movie *A Clockwork Orange*. In real life, California prisoners were injected with Anectine (succinylcholine), a muscle relaxant that causes brief paralysis but leaves the subject conscious. The prisoners were unable to move or breathe voluntarily, a sensation that simulates the onset of death; at the same time, the therapist would tell the subjects that they must change their behavior. Some observers state that this program was not an example of aversive conditioning but rather merely punishment.

Drug antagonists can serve a similar function by rendering the use of alcohol or other substances ineffective (lack of positive reinforcement) or extremely unpleasant (negative reinforcement or punishment). Disulfiram (Antabuse), metronidazole, or chlorpropamide can serve this purpose for alcohol abusers. Antabuse—the best known of these substances—disrupts the metabolism of alcohol in the liver, producing a severe reaction that includes stomach and head pain, nausea, and vomiting. One substance has the appearance and smell of cocaine and even produces a numbing effect but is not psychoactive; it is used in conjunction with an aversive chemical, one that induces vomiting, for example. In voluntary patients, electric shocks may be self-administered whenever a craving for the chemical arises. Alternatively, verbal aversion techniques may be used when a patient is asked to imagine strongly aversive stimuli (usually vomiting) in association with imaginal drug-related cues, scenes, or behaviors. Similar procedures can be used with sex offenders such as pedophiles by associating erotic feelings toward children with a negative consequence.

Other behavioral therapies use biofeedback and relaxation training, and sometimes assertiveness training, to prepare drug abusers to cope better with the stress and anxiety that are believed linked to drug use. Researchers have found that certain environmental cues can serve as triggers to activate drug cravings (Dole, 1980). When desensitization is used, "patients are usually first relaxed, then given repeated exposure to a graded hierarchy of anxiety-producing stimuli (real or imaginal)" to provide a form of immunity (Childress, McLellan, and O'Brien, 1985: 957).

Unlike other forms of treatment, behavior modification does not require the acquiescence of its subjects to be successful. In fact, behavior modification may at times be more successful when used without the knowledge of those whose behaviors are being subjected to it.

As in psychoanalytic theory, learning theory does not distinguish between behavior as such and criminal behavior; both are seen as based on the same principles of learning. In expounding the behaviorist position on crime, C. Ray Jeffrey (1971: 177) states that "there are no criminals, only environmental circumstances which result in criminal behavior. Given the proper environmental structure, anyone will be a criminal or a noncriminal." In both theories—psychoanalytical and learning—the person defined as a criminal is not in control of his or her behavior—a denial of *free will*—which raises serious legal issues with respect to holding persons accountable for their actions. This concept is known in law as *mens rea*.

Behaviorists analyze symptoms in terms of observable behavior components. The therapist keeps a record of frequency counts on a particular behavioral component; for example, a parent will be asked to record the number of outbursts exhibited by a youngster within a given period. The therapist then makes a functional analysis designed to determine the circumstances under which the undesirable behavior seems to occur as well as the elements within the environment that may be supporting (and thus encouraging) the behavior. In this example, the parent may be told to ignore the outbursts, no matter what the intensity, while providing positive reinforcers for positive behavior. The results of this approach will be measured against the original baseline of frequency counts. The empirical nature of the behaviorist approach has significant appeal; however, human behavior is driven by subjective meanings that may be known only to the actor.

Positive reinforcement, the timely application of rewards, is more easily accomplished in an institutional setting, where the environment can be controlled and manipulated to reinforce certain behaviors, than in the community, where most P/P rehabilitation occurs. This accounts for the paucity of articles on the use of behavior modification in P/P in professional journals. In one published report (Thorne, Tharp, and Wetzel, 1967), probation officers were trained in behavior techniques, and they, in turn, gained the cooperation of parents whose youngsters were on probation. The officers explained the behavior techniques to be used and taught the parents how to apply them. Behavior was monitored by the parents, and charts were used to record frequency counts. Positive reinforcers were given for desired behavior, such as attendance at school, scholastic work, and satisfactory behavior, and were withheld when the child misbehaved. The rewards were specific and related directly to the positive behavior. For example, a girl on probation was given telephone privileges and permitted weekend dates, contingent on her attendance at school all day. In this case the attendance teacher would give a note to the child at the end of the school day attesting to her attendance. When the child gave her mother the note, she earned the privilege of receiving and making calls that day. If she received four notes, she earned a weekend date; five notes earned two weekend dates.

In another case, rewards included both tangible and intangible items. For example, for studying 30 minutes a day, the youngster was both praised and given permission to ride his bicycle. Money, access to television, and other rewards were used as reinforcers for specific behavior on a specified basis. This form of treatment is often referred to as *behavioral contracting*: "an agreement in which the performance of predetermined responsibilities or duties results in receipt of privileges or rewards" (O'Leary and Wilson, 1975: 480). It has been used predominantly with children because (in noninstitutional settings) they can be subjected to greater environmental controls than adults. In another published study on

Key Fact

Learning theory does not distinguish between behavior as such and criminal behavior because both are based on the same principles of learning.

Key Fact

Positive reinforcement, the timely application of rewards, is difficult to apply where the environment cannot be controlled and manipulated to reinforce certain behaviors.

contingency management with adult drug offenders on probation, probation officers used reduction in probation time as a reinforcer (Polakow and Docktor, 1974).

REALITY THERAPY

Reality therapy (RT) was developed as a mode of rehabilitation by William Glasser, a psychiatrist. It is probably the easiest of the three modes of rehabilitation to describe, and simplicity has been a major reason for its popularity in P/P practice. Glasser's book *Reality Therapy* (originally published in 1965), which contains only 166 pages, describes RT as a method "that leads all patients toward reality, toward grappling successfully with the tangible aspects of the real world" (1975: 6). As opposed to RT, "conventional therapy goals do not include client responsibility or personal actions as primary" (Bersani, 1989: 177). RT attempts to teach people a better way of fulfilling their needs and taking responsibility for themselves and their behavior—reality therapy stresses accountability.

Although Glasser accepts the developmental theories of psychoanalytic theory, he rejects them as a useful basis for rehabilitation: "It is wishful thinking to believe that a man will give up a phobia once he understands either its origins or the current representation of its origin in the transference relationship" (1975: 53). Glasser believes that conventional treatment depends far too much on the ability of the patient to change his attitude and ultimately his behavior through gaining insight into his unconscious conflicts and inadequacies (1975: 51). The reality therapist denies the claims of psychoanalytic theorists that cure depends on the recovery of traumatic early memories that have been repressed. The ability of psychoanalysis to cure persons, states Melitta Schmideberg (1975), a psychiatrist whose mother (Melanie Klein) was eminent in the field of psychoanalysis, has never been clinically substantiated. "The goal of reality therapy [in contrast to psychoanalytical approaches] is neither insight about underlying causes of problems nor resolution of unconscious conflicts. Rather, the desired outcome is a change in behavior resulting in need satisfaction and greater happiness" (Wubbolding, 2000: 10).

Various mental problems, Glasser argues, are merely symptomatic illnesses that have no presently known medical cause and that act as companions for the lonely people who *choose* them. The behaviors or symptoms are actually chosen by the person from a lifetime of experiences residing in the subconscious. In place of conventional treatment, the reality therapist proposes first substituting the term *irresponsible* for mental health labels (e.g., neurotic, personality disorder, and psychotic). A "healthy" person is called *responsible*, and the task of the therapist is to help an irresponsible person to become responsible. Furthermore, notes Schmideberg, the psychoanalytic approach of "dwelling on the past encourages the patient to forget his present problems, which is a relief at times, but often—undesirably—the patient feels that after having produced so many interesting memories, he is now entitled to rest on his laurels and make no effort to change his attitude or plans for the future" (1975: 29). This diverts attention from the client's current problem(s), which is a reality that should be dealt with directly.

Glasser argues that conventional treatment does not deal with whether a client's behavior is right or wrong in terms of morality or law but "contends that once the patient is able to resolve his conflicts and get over his mental illness, he will be able to behave correctly" (1975: 56). Societal realities, however, particularly in P/P practice, require direct interventions with a client, with the therapist not accepting "wrong" behavior.

"Reality therapy is based upon the theory that all of us are born with at least two built-in psychological needs: (1) the need to belong and be loved and (2) the need for gaining self-worth and recognition" (Glasser, 1980: 48). According to Glasser, people with serious behavior problems lack the proper involvement with someone; and lacking this involvement, they are unable to satisfy their needs. Therefore, to be a helping person, the therapist must enable the client to gain involvement, first with the worker and then with others. The traditional therapist maintains a professional objectivity or distance, whereas the reality therapist strives for strong feelings between worker and client. This

Key Fact

Simplicity has been a major reason for the popularity of reality therapy in P/P practice.

type of relationship is necessary if the therapist is to have an impact on the client's behavior. The therapist, although always accepting of the client, firmly rejects irresponsible behavior and can then teach the client better ways of behaving.

To accomplish this reeducation, the P/P worker must know about the client's reality—the way he or she lives and his or her environment, aspirations, and *total reality*. Reality is always influenced by culture, ethnic and racial group, economic class, and intelligence. The worker must be willing to listen open-mindedly and learn about the client (Schmideberg, 1975). While observing, the counselor develops a relationship with the client, a relationship that can lead to responsible behavior. Alluding to the fact that RT does not always work, Glasser states that the fault is with the therapist who is unable to become involved in a meaningful way with the client; however, mandated correctional clients may avoid counseling because of their difficulties with intimacy (Harris and Watkins, 1987). For many people, it feels safer to reject someone trying to help them than to risk accepting that help, only to be disappointed. Such clients try to create physical and emotional distance in relationships. Paradoxically, a warm and empathetic counselor often is met with barriers to bonding in the therapeutic relationship, and too much pursuit of the client to bring about intimacy only intensifies the client's anxiety.

Glasser expresses a great deal of support for the work of P/P officers, although he cautions persons in corrections, as well as other fields, against the use of punishment: "For many delinquents," he notes, "punishment serves as a source of involvement. They receive attention through delinquent behavior, if only that of the police, court, probation counselor, and prison [workers]. . . . A failing person rationalizes the punishment as a reason for the anger that caused him to be hostile" (1976: 95).

Like behavior modification, RT is symptom oriented. The P/P client is in treatment because he or she has caused society to take action as a result of his or her behavior. If the P/P worker can remove the symptoms and make the client responsible, that will satisfy society and relieve the client of anxiety caused by fear of being incarcerated.

Schmideberg (1975: 24) states that for a delinquent symptom to disappear, it is usually necessary for the person to accomplish three interrelated tasks:

1. Face it fully with all of its implications and consequences.
2. Decide to stop it and consider the factors that precipitate it.
3. Make a definite effort to stop it.

She maintains that a general and nondirective method is not likely to change symptoms that the client may find satisfying (e.g., drugs to the addict, excitement and money to the robber, or forced sex to the rapist). Reality therapists "ask clients to do more than merely describe their behavior, their wants, their perceptions, their level of commitment, or their plans. They ask clients to make judgments about them," as if they were looking in a mirror (Wubbolding, 2000: 111). RT requires that clients evaluate their actions.

Richard Rachin (1974) states that the reality therapist seeks to help the client act responsibly. As opposed to someone taking the more distant approach of social casework, the reality therapist becomes emotionally involved—warm, tough, interested, and a sensitive human being who genuinely gives a damn and demonstrates it. RT is concerned only with behavior that can be tried and tested on a reality basis; only with the problems of the present. And the reality therapist is not interested in uncovering underlying motivations or drives; rather, he concentrates on helping the person act in a manner that will help him or her meet his or her needs responsibly. While the reality therapist praises responsible behavior and provides recognition for positive accomplishment, he or she offers no crying towel. Sympathy can indicate that the worker lacks confidence in the client's ability to act responsibly.

Glasser developed RT while he was a psychiatrist at the Ventura School, an institution for the treatment of older adolescent girls who had been unsuccessful on probation. Because this technique evolved within the field of corrections and the realities of dealing with delinquent behavior, many have accepted and applied RT to P/P rehabilitation. RT flows easily from the P/P officer's need to hold the offender accountable for his or her behavior. Some maintain that the value emphasis in RT coincides with the paternalistic and perhaps authoritarian attitudes of some P/P officers. Carl Bersani states that "Glasser's writings do not provide a systematic methodology for clearly separating the moral standards of the counselor from that of the client" (1989: 188). Although Glasser does not deal with theory and RT is practice oriented, the theoretical underpinnings are close to those in behavior modification. Instead of manipulating the environment or using tangible reinforcers, the therapist develops a close relationship with the client and uses praise or concern as positive and negative reinforcers. For this method to be carried out effectively, the counselor needs to be a genuinely warm and sympathetic person who can easily relate to persons who have often committed very unpleasant acts and whose personalities may leave a great deal to be desired—no easy task. Thus, although training someone in the use of RT may be relatively easy, success requires qualities of personality that are not part of the basic qualifications for becoming a P/P officer.

In more recent books, Glasser (1998, 2000) notes that his earlier work did not present a theoretical foundation for RT, and he offers **choice theory**, which replaces "the term responsibility with the more explicit idea that we choose all our behavior because we can't be anything but responsible for all that we choose to do" (2000: 227). He argues that people *choose* problematic behavior as their best effort to deal with a present unsatisfying relationship or, worse, no relationships at all. According to choice theory, "[All] significant conscious behaviors that have anything to do directly with satisfying basic needs [love/belonging, freedom, fun, power, and survival] are chosen" (Glasser, 1998: 71). Therefore, "you are either the beneficiary of your own good choices or the victim of your own bad choices" (1998: 77). To the person whose behavior is destructive or inimical to his or her interests, Glasser states: "You are choosing what you are doing, but you are capable of choosing something better" (1998: 77).

But RT remains practice-based, not theory-based, "to teach clients how to act and think more effectively so they can better satisfy their needs," with the objective of guiding people in the direction of actually doing something about their problems (Glasser, 2000: 67).

GROUP WORK

Group work provides a therapeutic milieu wherein individuals agree to help one another; in contrast with the therapist in casework, the group is the agency of help. According to Allan Brown, the basic operating premise of social group work is that "groups of people with similar needs can be a source of mutual support, mutual aid and problem solving" (1986: 10). Offenders discover in the group that they are not alone with their problems and that others share similar difficulties (Morgan and Winterowd, 2002). In the group, "every member is a potential helper" (1986: 11). Helen Northern states that one of the advantages of the use of groups "is that stimulation toward improvement arises from a network of interpersonal influences in which all members participate" (1969: 52). The theory underlying the use of the group is that the impact provided by peer interaction is more powerful than worker-client reactions within the one-to-one situation of social casework. Furthermore, groups "help members realize that they are not alone with their problems" (Toseland and Rivas, 1998: 17). They can instill hope and impart information through a shared interaction, and their members promote the learning of basic social skills. The group serves a cathartic function: Members can experience and express feelings in a safe and confidential environment (Gladding, 1999). Truth and conflicts are brought to the surface and participants are guided to examine and grapple with all of the positions and options involved" (Drumm, 2006: 20).

> **Key Fact**
>
> The basic premise of social group work is that people with similar needs can be a source of mutual support, mutual aid, and problem solving.

In P/P, groups consist of members who share a common status, in this case a legally determined status. Groups in P/P may also be organized on the basis of age or around a common problem, such as substance abuse. The group is a mutual aid society in which members are given an opportunity to share experiences and assist each other with problems in a safe, controlled environment. The group helps to confirm for each member the fact that others share similar problems—"they are in the same boat"—thus reducing the sense of isolation. With the help of the therapist, members are able to share a sense of purpose and develop a commitment to helping each other through patterns of group interaction: "As members offer solutions to common problems, make supportive comments, and share in the skill development of fellow members by participating in group exercises, they become committed to helping each other" (Shaffer and Galinsky, 1987: 26).

The group can reduce the anxiety of having to report alone to a P/P officer; collaboration tends to offset the more direct authority of the one-to-one situation and to lower the impact of sociocultural differences between client and P/P worker. As Gisela Konopka (1983: 93) points out, "In a group members support each other; they are not alone in the face of authority." In a group, she notes, the offender is surrounded by equals; he or she is not a client, but a *member*, an arrangement that permits "feelings of identification that are impossible to achieve on an individual basis with even the most accepting social caseworker" (1983: 97). Group work also requires a level of skill and training that is not widely available in social work in general and P/P practice in particular. In P/P, the groups are typically open-ended because members enter and leave— complete their sentence or violate supervision—at various intervals.

A variety of approaches to group work may be applied in correctional settings, often depending on the theoretical stance of the agency or worker, and include gestalt therapy, transactional analysis, and psychoanalytic group therapy, all of which are rooted in psychoanalytic theory, and guided group interaction, which is based on sociological small-group theory and behavior modification. Sex offenders may more easily manipulate treatment providers in a one-to-one casework approach, so cognitive-behavioral treatment is often delivered through group work (Stalans, 2004).

A popular group approach in P/P entails the application of cognitive behavior theory and is known as **cognitive skills training (CST)**; some call it *problem-solving therapy (PST)*. This approach views criminal behavior not as the symptom of some disease but as the result of a combination of social and economic situations and behavioral factors, the result of inadequate socialization. Basic to this approach is a belief that conventional prosocial thinking and behavior can be taught, that offenders can learn to anticipate the consequences of their actions and consider alternate courses of action. Thus, a low social intelligence involves offenders who have deficits in the ability to envision the consequences of their behavior and are unable to use means-ends reasoning to achieve their goals. Operating at the ego level of development, they are unable to place themselves in someone else's position or understand another's behavior. The CST approach is based on a belief that "individuals can be taught to be better problem-solving thinkers" (Husband and Platt, 1993: 34).

According to Husband and Platt, "[CST] emphasizes the importance of problem-solving skills that can be applied to a variety of problem situations. These include skills such as awareness of interpersonal problems, defining problems, causal thinking, consequential or alternative thinking, means-ends thinking, and perspective-taking" (1993: 33). Training is designed to modify impulsive, egocentric, illogical, and rigid thinking and to teach offenders to think—consider the consequences—before acting. The sessions can be conducted by P/P officers who receive relevant training. Generally, 40 two-hour sessions with audiovisual presentations, role playing, behavior rehearsal, and reasoning exercises are offered. With 6 to 10 offenders, the therapist—called a *coach*—leads the group in problem solving, anger management, negotiation skills, value enhancement, critical reasoning, creative thinking, planning, and decision making. A focus is placed on enabling offenders to think in terms of options/alternatives to gain greater control over their own lives. Exercises ask offenders to respond to dilemmas, target skills, apply the skills and techniques, and then return to the group to discuss the experience.

Some problems in implementing CST include the use of groups that require a specific starting and completion date, which is complicated by offenders being placed on supervision and completing supervision at different times. Also, P/P officers may not be comfortable in the role of a coach and may resist training. Research into a program in New York City (Greenlight Reentry) that used the CST approach with prerelease inmates and parolees found no benefits (Wilson and Davis, 2006). However, observers question the manner in which the program was implemented (Marlowe, 2006; Rhine, Mawhorr, and Parks, 2006).

A Closer Look

Moral Reconation Therapy (MRT)

Used by P/P agencies ranging from Arkansas to the state of Washington, moral reconation therapy (MRT) is a program designed to promote positive lifestyle changes—*reconation* refers to a redirecting of decision making to higher standards of moral reasoning. This group approach is led by a facilitator trained in MRT, its philosophy and its method. Participants are chosen based both on a perceived willingness to change current lifestyles and on a shared problem such as substance abuse or sex offenses. There are reading and homework assignments. Group members are asked to briefly look at their past to gain insight into choices they have made and the specific motivations behind these choices; then they take an in-depth look at what makes up their life situation and how they are spending their time. Participants are encouraged to set goals and break these down into achievable steps.

Psychological theories and methods of rehabilitation have been examined; the next section looks at some sociological theories that have application to P/P practice.

SOCIOLOGICAL THEORY

Psychological theory attempts to identify causes of criminal behavior within the individual actor and to treat the causes accordingly. Sociological theory places crime in a social context, adding to our understanding of individual offenders. The following sections briefly review sociological theories relevant to P/P practice.

Anomie

The concept of **anomie**, derived from the Greek meaning "lack of law," was developed by the French sociologist Emile Durkheim (1858–1917) to explain variations in suicide rates. In 1938, Robert Merton "Americanized" the concept of anomie, which became part of what are often called **strain theories**. Merton argues that no other society is as close to the United States in considering economic success as an absolute value. Furthermore, he says, in the United States, "the pressure of prestige-bearing success tends to eliminate the effective social constraint over the means employed to this end. The 'end-justifies-the-means' doctrine becomes a guiding tenet for action when the cultural structure unduly exalts the end and the social organization unduly limits possible recourse to approved means" (Merton, 1938: 681). "The desire to make money without regard to the means in which one sets about doing it is symptomatic of the malintegration at the heart of American society" (Taylor, Walton, and Young, 1973: 93).

According to Merton, anomie results when people are confronted by the contradiction between goals and means—strain. "[They] become estranged from a society that promises them in principle what they are denied in reality [economic opportunity]," so despite numerous success stories—the poor boy from humble origins who becomes rich and famous—"we know that in this same society that proclaims the right, and even the duty, of lofty aspirations for all, men do not have equal access to the opportunity structure" (Merton, 1964: 218). This point is particularly true of the most disadvantaged segments of our population who become the clients of our probation, prison, and parole systems.

How do persons respond to the anomic condition? Most simply scale down their aspirations and conform to conventional social norms. Some rebel, rejecting the conventional

Key Fact

Anomie results when people are confronted by the contradiction between goals and means and resort to retreatism and criminal innovation.

social structure and seek, instead, to establish a "new social order" by utilizing political action or by establishing alternative lifestyles. Two responses, retreatism and innovation, are of particular interest for P/P practice.

Retreatism means that all attempts to reach conventional social goals are abandoned in favor of a deviant adaptation—a "retreat" to alcohol and drug abuse. Time and energy are now expended to reach an attainable goal: getting "high."

Innovation is a term used by Merton to describe the adoption of illegitimate means to gain success. Societal goals of success have been incorporated and accepted, but the person finds access to legitimate means for becoming successful limited—and anomie results. Crime is viewed as a basically utilitarian adaptation to the anomic situation. Thus, with the innovation response, the ends justify the means; with retreatism, the ends ("getting high") are sufficiently reduced to make the means readily accessible.

Merton assumes a consensus and commitment to "American values"—an attitude fixated on moneymaking pervades our society. This assumption does not account for nonutilitarian deviance or the class-linked dynamics of criminal behavior. More recent versions of strain theory have expanded the goals of American youth to include such short-term variables as popularity with the opposite sex, good school grades, and athletic achievements. This enlargement would explain conditions of strain experienced by middle-class youth because these goals are not necessarily class linked. For adults, the failure to achieve expected goals causes strain that in some persons leads to anger, resentment, and rage—emotional states that can lead to criminal behavior (Agnew, 1992). Robert Agnew (1992) suggests that social justice or equity might be at the root of strain; in this case, a sense of being dealt with unfairly—adversity is blamed on others—and not simply an inability to reach goals, results in strain.

What does the theory of anomie offer the P/P officer and the real problems of his or her practice? One consideration has to do with aspirations. Offenders often have unrealistic goals: Their aspirations surpass their ability. In such cases, if anomie is to be avoided, the P/P officer must help the client to make a realistic assessment of the situation and then to assist him or her with achieving goals that are both constructive and reality based. Each client should be encouraged to achieve to the limits of his or her ability. The officer also has a responsibility to see that the client's goals are not blocked by such barriers as discrimination; in such instances, the P/P officer must make use of the various agencies that are responsible for enforcing equal opportunity laws.

Differential Association

As proposed by Edwin Sutherland (1883–1950), **differential association** explains how criminal behavior is transmitted (not how it originates). According to Sutherland (1973), criminal behavior is learned, and the principal part of learning criminal behavior occurs within intimate groups based on the degree of intensity, frequency, and duration of the association. The person learns, in addition to the techniques of committing crime, the drives, attitudes, and rationalizations that add up to a favorable precondition to criminal behavior. Most criminal and noncriminal behaviors have the same goal—securing economic and personal status—but differential association accounts for the difference in selecting criminal or noncriminal methods for achieving the goal.

The process of learning criminal behavior by association with criminal and anticriminal patterns involves all the mechanisms that are involved in any other learning (Boy Scouts and gangsters learn behavior in the same manner).

In sum, criminal behavior results from the strength or intensity of criminal associations and is the result of an accumulative learning process. A pictorial portrayal of differential association can easily be conceived in terms of a balanced scale that starts out level: On each side are the various accumulated weights of criminal and noncriminal associations, and at some theoretical point, criminal activity will tip the scale with an excess of criminal associations over noncriminal or prosocial ones.

What import does this theory have for P/P practice? As noted earlier in the discussion of P/P regulations (see Chapters 2, 4, and 7), they usually contain prohibitions against certain associations. A person on P/P is usually cautioned against associating with others similarly situated, a recommendation that can easily be seen as a practical attempt to respond to the theory of differential association. In addition, the P/P officer can provide exposure to prosocial associations, an exposure whose influence conceivably can help to balance our theoretical scale. The officer can assist the client by encouraging him or her and helping him or her to secure association with community, charitable, religious, athletic, fraternal, and other such organizations.

Delinquent Subcultures

"Subcultures are patterns of values, norms, and behavior which have become traditional among certain groups. These groups may be of many types, including occupational and ethnic groups, social classes, occupants of 'closed institutions' [e.g., prisons, mental hospitals] and various age grades [and are] important frames of reference through which individuals and groups see the world and interpret it" (Short, 1968: 11).

Key Fact

Delinquent subcultures serve to promote antisocial values.

Albert Cohen (1965: 86) argues that certain lower-class subcultures negate middle-class values, and this negation is a severe handicap. Certain cultural characteristics are necessary to achieve success in our society, and the upbringing of a middle-class child is more likely to develop these characteristics, such as ability to postpone gratification, skills for achievement, industry and thrift, control of physical aggression, and cultivation of manners and politeness. Certainly, most P/P clients lack many of these requisites for adjustment to the wider society.

James Short (1968: 16) concludes that the subcultural delinquent gang discourages expression of conventional values because "values which are given active support within the context of gang interaction, for example, toughness and sexual prowess, are not conducive to conventional types of achievement." According to Walter Miller (1958), the delinquent is adhering to forms of behavior as they are defined within his or her community. The **delinquent subculture** is different, the focal concern being *trouble*, which often involves fighting or sexual adventures while drinking; troublesome behavior for women frequently means sexual involvement with disadvantageous consequences. Miller contends that any desire to avoid troublesome behavior is based less on a commitment to legal or larger social norms than on a desire to avoid the possible legal and other undesirable consequences of the action. This position would justify the threat of a P/P violation as a valuable tool for P/P officers. Although trouble-producing behavior is a source of status, non-trouble-producing behavior is required to avoid legal and other complications. This source of conflict for the lower-class youngster may be resolved in a legitimate manner by becoming part of an organization with high levels of discipline, such as the military or the police.

Another focal concern is *toughness*, traced by Miller (1958: 9) to the significant proportion of lower-class boys reared in female-dominated households and the resulting concern over homosexuality, which "runs like a persistent thread through lower-class culture." Miller refers to some of the sentiments commonly expressed in lower-class culture: "No one's going to push me around," and "I'm gonna tell him to take the job and shove it." He states that expressions of autonomy often contrast with actual patterns of behavior and that many lower-class persons actually desire a highly restrictive social environment (ranging from prison to the armed forces) with strong external controls over their behavior. Miller contends that for the lower-class person, "being controlled is equated with being cared for" (1958: 13). Thus, the P/P officer will find clients resentful of controls yet acting in such a manner as to ensure recommitment after a short period of relative freedom. The P/P officer must strive to moderate these extremes for the benefit of the client.

Elijah Anderson (1994: 82) describes a street subculture in African American communities with a "set of informal rules governing interpersonal public behavior, including violence. The rules prescribe both a proper comportment and a proper way to respond if challenged." At the center of this subcultural arrangement is preoccupation with the need for respect, being treated "right," with proper deference. The participant in this street subculture is obsessed with the possibility of being "dissed"—sensitive to slights that middle-class persons would regard as petty. Status is associated with showing "nerve," a willingness to "mess" with others' property coupled with a cavalier attitude toward death. "Generally people outside the ghetto have other ways of gaining status and regard and thus do not feel so dependent on such physical displays" (Anderson, 1994: 89).

The code of the streets is actually a cultural adaptation to a lack of faith in criminal justice and the frustrations of chronic poverty. "The police are most often seen as representing the dominant white society and not caring to protect inner-city residents," and the subcultural adaptation to this dilemma requires "taking care of yourself" (Anderson, 1994: 82). Frustrations associated with chronic poverty create the short-fuse phenomenon: Verbal and physical abuse become routine. Indeed, research (e.g., Lemmon, 2006) confirms the connection between childhood maltreatment and the severity of delinquency, particularly violent offending. Children "learn that to solve any kind of interpersonal problem one must quickly resort to hitting or other violent behavior" (Anderson, 1994: 83). Furthermore, inner-city children are frequently subjected to neglect and must learn to fend for themselves, further hardening the street code adaptations.

Neutralization

Gresham Sykes and David Matza (1957) refer to a social psychological mechanism—**neutralization**—which permits a delinquent to accept the social norms of the wider society and, at the same time, violate these norms. Sykes and Matza maintain that the delinquent actually retains his or her belief in the legitimacy of official middle-class norms: "The juvenile delinquent frequently recognizes both the legitimacy of the dominant social order and its moral rightness" (1957: 664). They argue that "if there existed in fact a delinquent subculture such that the delinquent viewed his illegal behavior as morally correct, we could reasonably suppose that he would exhibit no feelings of guilt or shame at detection or confinement. Instead, the major reaction would tend in the direction of indignation or a sense of martyrdom." However, the authors note, many delinquents do, indeed, experience a sense of guilt, "and its outward expression is not to be dismissed as a purely manipulative gesture to appease those in authority" (1957: 664–65).

Sykes and Matza (1957: 666) postulate that "the delinquent does not necessarily regard those who abide by the legal rules as wrong or immoral." Furthermore, many delinquents are probably not totally immune from the demands for conformity made by the dominant social order. Therefore, "the juvenile delinquent would appear to be at least partially committed to the dominant social order in that he frequently exhibits guilt or shame when he violates its proscriptions, accords approval to certain conforming figures, and distinguishes between appropriate and inappropriate targets for his deviance" (Sykes and Matza, 1957: 666). They conclude that "the delinquent represents not a radical opposition to law-abiding society but something like an apologetic failure, often more sinned against than sinning in his own eyes" (1957: 667).

By using various techniques of neutralization, delinquents are able to avoid guilt feelings for their actions. They contend that rules are merely qualified guidelines limited to time, place, and person conditions. This line of reasoning is in accord with the legal code that requires *mens rea*, criminal intent, to be present for penal sanctions to be imposed. Delinquents justify their actions in a form that, although not valid to the larger society, is valid for them. Sykes and Matza (1957) present five types of neutralization:

1. *Denial of responsibility.* Rationalization that delinquency was not their fault (e.g., they were simply victims of circumstances).
2. *Denial of injury.* Premise that nobody got hurt (e.g., just a prank was involved, or the insurance company will cover the damage).
3. *Denial of the victim.* Belief that the victim deserved to be hurt.

4. *Condemnation of the condemners.* Focus on the weakness and motives of those in authority or judgment (e.g., police, school officials, and judges are corrupt or hate kids).

5. *Appeal to higher loyalties.* Conviction of the necessity of their action for friends, family, neighborhood, and so on.

These sentiments, or variants of them, are often encountered by P/P officers in the course of presentence investigations or P/P supervision. Sykes and Matza caution against dismissing them as merely postaction rationalizations because they indicate a genuine commitment to societal norms and a basis for rehabilitation.

Differential or Limited Opportunity

Richard Cloward and Lloyd Ohlin (1960) attempt to integrate anomie with differential association to explain how delinquent subcultures arise, develop various law-violating ways of life, and persist or change over time. They distinguish among three types of delinquent subcultures that are a result of anomie and differential association:

1. *Criminal subculture.* Gang activities devoted to utilitarian criminal pursuits (e.g., racketeering).
2. *Conflict subculture.* Gang activities devoted to violence and destructive acting out as a way of gaining status.
3. *Retreatist subculture.* Activities in which drug abuse is the primary focus.

Each of these subcultural adaptations arises out of a different set of social circumstances or opportunities. Cloward and Ohlin state that the dilemma of many lower-class people is that they are unable to locate alternative avenues to success or goals: "Delinquent subcultures, we believe, represent specialized modes of adaptation to this problem of adjustment" (1960: 107). The criminal and conflict subcultures provide illegal avenues, while the retreatist "anticipates defeat and now seeks to escape from the burden of the future" (1960: 107). Criminal behavior is not viewed as an individual endeavor but as part of a collective adaptation. Cloward and Ohlin note that "many lower-class adolescents experience desperation born of the certainty that their position in the economic structure is relatively fixed and immutable—a desperation made all the more poignant by their exposure to a cultural ideology in which failure to orient oneself upward is regarded as a moral defect and failure to become mobile as proof of it" (1960: 106–107).

> **Key Fact**
>
> Differential opportunity explains that illegitimate means of success are not equally distributed throughout society, so most criminals are double failures.

The turn toward alternative means of success is to be understood in terms of this social-psychological phenomenon. However, Cloward and Ohlin also point out that illegitimate means of success, like legitimate means, are not equally distributed throughout society: "Having decided that he 'can't make it legitimately,' he cannot simply choose among an array of illegitimate means, all equally available to him" (1960: 145). Thus, for the average lower-class adolescent, a career in professional or **organized crime** (Abadinsky, 1983, 2007b; Sutherland, 1972) can be as difficult to attain as any lucrative career in the legitimate sphere of society.

This difficulty warns the P/P officer of the need to be able to differentiate persons involved in "professional" and "organized" criminality from the more frequent offender who has only limited skills and contacts. Professional and organized criminals are usually not good candidates for the rehabilitative efforts of P/P agencies because such persons are not likely to give up criminal skills and status, which were achieved only after a considerable expenditure of time and effort, for a more conventional and law-abiding lifestyle. In these cases, the investigative and control (not the therapeutic) skills of the P/P officer must be used.

Social Control Theory

If, as control theorists generally assume, most persons are sufficiently motivated by the potential rewards to commit criminal acts, why do only a few engage in criminal behavior? According to **social control theory**, "delinquent acts result when an individual's bond to society is weak or broken" (Hirschi, 1969: 16). The strength of this bond is determined by internal and external restraints; in other words, internal and external restraints determine if we move in the direction of crime or law-abiding behavior.

Internal restraints include what psychoanalytic theory refers to as the superego; they provide a sense of guilt. As noted earlier, dysfunction during early stages of childhood development or parental influences that are not normative can result in an adult who is devoid of prosocial internal constraints; some refer to this as psychopathology or sociopathology, or they apply the diagnostic term *antisocial personality disorder*[2] (Black, 1999). (Some evidence also ties antisocial personality disorder to a central nervous system defect.) Whether they are thought of in terms of psychology or sociology, internal constraints are linked to the influence of the family (Hirschi, 1969), an influence that can be supported or weakened by the presence or absence of significant external restraints, such as the P/P officer.

External restraints include social disapproval linked to public shame or social ostracism and fear of punishment. People are typically deterred from criminal behavior by the possibility of being caught and the punishment that can result, ranging from public shame to imprisonment (and in extreme cases, capital punishment). The strength of official deterrence—force of law—is measured according to two dimensions: risk and reward. Risk involves the ability of the criminal justice system to detect, apprehend, and convict the offender, and the amount of risk is weighed against the potential rewards. Both risk and reward, however, are relative to one's socioeconomic situation: The less one has to lose, the greater is the willingness to engage in risk; the greater the reward, the greater is the willingness to engage in risk. This theory explains why persons in deprived economic circumstances would be more willing to engage in certain criminal behavior. However, the potential rewards and a perception of relatively low risk may also explain why persons in more advantaged economic circumstances would engage in remunerative criminal behavior, such as corporate crime.

Instead of conforming to conventional norms, some persons, through differential association, organize their behavior according to the norms of a delinquent or criminal group with which they identify or to which they belong. This affiliation is most likely to occur in environments characterized by relative social disorganization, where familial and communal controls are ineffective in exerting a conforming influence. The increasing number of children living below the poverty level intertwined with a collapse of many inner-city families is creating "America's new orphans" (Gross, 1992). Data clearly associates poverty with juvenile crime (Snyder and Sickmund, 2006). Conforming prosocial behavior may be dependent on the ability of the P/P officer to carefully monitor the client combined with a realistic threat of punishment. From the casework dimension, the P/P officer may offer the client an opportunity to repair weak or broken bonds and thereby move the client in the direction of conventional behavior.

Drift

Does the juvenile delinquent move on to become an adult criminal, or does the youngster mature and become a law-abiding member of society? This process of gradually maturing and becoming law-abiding is referred to as **drift**. David Matza (1964: 59) views the delinquent's lifestyle as not fully committed: "He drifts between criminal and conventional action." Matza denies the portrayal of a juvenile delinquent as a person committed to an oppositional culture; instead, the delinquent reveals a basic ambivalence toward his or her behavior. Matza believes that juveniles are less alienated than

---

[2]Diagnostic categories are found in the *Diagnostic and Statistical Manual* (DSM) published by the American Psychiatric Association.

others in society, and that most of the time delinquents behave in a noncriminal manner: "The image of the delinquent I wish to convey is one of drift; an actor neither compelled nor committed to deeds nor freely choosing them; neither different in any single fundamental sense from the law abiding, nor the same; conforming to certain traditions in American life while partially unreceptive to other more conventional traditions" (1964: 28).

Although Matza does not contradict the idea of a delinquent subculture, he finds that the subculture is not a binding force on its members: "Loyalty is a basic issue in the subculture of delinquency partially because its adherents are so regularly disloyal. They regularly abandon the company at the age of remission for more conventional pursuits" (1964: 28). The "age of remission" is a time when adolescent antisocial behavior is abandoned in favor of adult prosocial or conventional behavior. The crime-prone years for young men are roughly ages 15 to 25, with remission occurring after age 25. Matza's theory has important policy implications: Justice system intervention can stigmatize—label—a juvenile, thereby blocking entry into a conventional lifestyle as he or she matures into adulthood.

> **Key Fact**
>
> Participants in delinquent subcultures typically exit with the onset of adulthood, unless justice system intervention is an impediment.

Labeling

A stigma, sometimes referred to in terms of **labeling** (also called *societal reaction theory*), is the concern of a sociological perspective known as *symbolic interactionism*:

> Symbolic interactionists suggest that categories which individuals use to render the world meaningful, and even the experience of self, are structured by socially acquired definitions. They argue that individuals, in reaction to group rewards and sanctions, gradually internalize group expectations. These internalized social definitions allow people to evaluate their own behavior from the standpoint of the group and in doing so provide a lens through which to view oneself as a social object. (Quadagno and Antonio, 1975: 33)

The focus is not on the behavior of any social actor (person) but on the way that behavior or actor is viewed by others (e.g., society). The societal reaction labels—stigmatizes—the actor, which results in a damaged self-image, a deviant identity, and a host of negative social expectations. Think about the societal reaction to the terms *mentally ill, ex-convict,* and *parolee.* Furthermore, some argue, the damaged self-image and its ramifications can result in a self-fulfilling prophesy. Edwin Schur (1973: 124) notes that "once an individual has been branded as a wrongdoer, it becomes extremely difficult for him to shed that new identity." The ex-convict finds it difficult to secure employment, increasing the attraction of further criminal activity. According to Edwin Lemert, the labeled deviant reorganizes his or her behavior in accordance with the societal reaction and "begins to employ his deviant behavior, or role based on it, as a means of defense, attack, or adjustment to the overt and covert problems created by the consequent societal reaction to him" (1951: 76). Lemert has termed this process *secondary deviation,* which is evidenced by deviants seeking to associate with others like themselves. The negative influence of the delinquent label is viewed as so detrimental to future conduct that Schur (1973) argues for *radical nonintervention:* The focus should be on avoiding the movement of adolescents into the official agencies of social control.

> **Key Fact**
>
> Labeling results in a damaged self-image, a deviant identity, and a host of negative social expectations.

The P/P officer is constantly faced with the dynamics of labeling as clients encounter difficulty in returning to school, securing employment, obtaining housing, and making friends because of the stigma (label) inherent in the terms *delinquent, criminal, probationer,* and *parolee.* The label results in a negative self-image, whereby the offender's view of him- or herself is that of an inferior and unworthy person. In such a condition, he or she may seek the companionship of others similarly situated and may engage in further antisocial activities in an effort to strike back at the society that is responsible for the labeling.

> ## A Closer Look
>
> ### Value of a Bad Reputation
>
> In fact, far from stigmatizing, prison evidently confers status in some neighborhoods. Jerome Skolnick . . . found that for drug dealers in California, imprisonment confers a certain elevated "home boy" status, especially for gang members for whom prison and prison gangs can be an alternative site of loyalty. And according to the California Youth Authority, inmates steal state-issued prison clothing for the same reason. Wearing it when they return to the community lets everyone know they have done "hard time" (Petersilia, 1995: 23).

Conflict Theory

Conflict theory takes its fundamental philosophy primarily from the work of Max Weber and Karl Marx. Conflict theorists are concerned with differences in power relationships. More recent conflict theorists, usually of a Marxist bent, are an outgrowth of the sociopolitical—civil rights, anti–Vietnam War, counterculture—movements of the 1960s and early 1970s. They conceive of society as better characterized by conflict than by consensus; what passes for crime and criminal justice actually represent the interests of powerful classes. Otherwise, they argue, how could a burglary netting a few dollars be classified as a felony, whereas corporate officials who pad defense contracts with millions of dollars in overcharges or who flagrantly violate the safety and restraint of trade laws avoid incarceration or even the labeling that accompanies the processing of conventional (i.e., poor) delinquents/criminals? As noted in Chapter 5, in every generation a specific class of persons always inhabits our prisons—the poor.

The conflict approach eschews theory that treats criminal behavior as a manifestation of individual pathology; instead, crime is seen as a phenomenon generated by the social arrangements of a capitalist system. Capitalism leads to a class system of severely differentiated wealth and power: Inequities in wealth and power (in life chances) cause alienation; an alienated segment of the underclass (those whose interests are not furthered by capitalism) reacts in ways defined as criminal. The legal apparatus, including a monopoly over sanctions and the use of force, serves to control the alienated population and helps to perpetuate domination by the ruling class. The criminal justice system is simply a mechanism through which the self-interests of the ruling classes are protected by functionaries in their employ. Their rule is given legitimacy by an ideology of democracy, free enterprise, and property rights whose benefits accrue primarily to those who already have wealth and power. As Karl Marx pointed out, the ideas of the ruling class are always the ruling ideas.

Within this approach, criminal behavior is sometimes romanticized as "rebellion" and criminals as some type of "primitive rebel," although most conventional crime is committed by the underclass against the underclass. During the 1960s and early 1970s, some offenders on probation or parole or prison inmates espoused conflict theory—a reflection of a politically active era. Conflict theory sensitizes the P/P officer to some of the basic inequities in our society, certainly as they are reflected in criminal justice. Although dealing with system inequities is beyond the role of the P/P officer, he or she does have an advocate role, which is discussed in Chapter 9.

Key Fact

The conflict approach denies that criminal behavior is a manifestation of individual pathology but is instead generated by the unequal social arrangements of a capitalist system.

Key Terms

anal stage (p. 223)

anomie (p. 241)

antisocial personality disorder (p. 225)

aversive therapy (p. 235)

behavior modification (p. 232)

choice theory (p. 239)

cognitive skills training (CST) (p. 240)

conflict theory (p. 248)

delinquent subculture (p. 243)

differential association (p. 242)

drift (p. 246)

ego (p. 224)

genital stage (p. 223)

group work (p. 239)

id (p. 223)

innovation (p. 242)

labeling (p. 247)

learning theory (p. 232)

medical model (p. 226)

negative reinforcement (p. 232)

neutralization (p. 244)

operant conditioning (p. 232)

oral stage (p. 223)

organized crime (p. 245)

positive reinforcement (p. 232)

psychoanalytic theory (p. 222)

reality therapy (RT) (p. 237)

reinforcer (p.232)

retreatism (p. 242)

self-determination (p. 229)

social casework (p. 226)

social control theory (p. 246)

strain theories (p. 241)

superego (p. 224)

theory (p. 222)

transference (p. 228)

unconscious (p. 222)

Internet Connections

Academy of Criminal Justice Sciences: acjs.org

American Psychological Association: apa.org

American Society of Criminology: asc41.com

Glasser Institute on Reality Therapy: wglasser.com

National Association of Social Workers: naswdc.org

Reality therapy links: socc.ie/~wgii/address.htm

Review Questions

1. What is a theory?
2. What is the importance of psychoanalytic theory in probation and parole (P/P)?
3. According to psychoanalytic theory, what is the importance of unconscious feelings and experiences?
4. According to psychoanalytic theory, what are the causes of behavior defined as criminal?
5. How can the superego cause criminal behavior?
6. What type of criminal behavior in the adult is related to the anal stage of development?

7. What is the relationship between social casework and the medical model?

8. What should the caseworker accomplish during the study/assessment phase of the rehabilitation process?

9. What is meant by ego support in the social casework process?

10. What is the basis of changing behavior in reality therapy (RT)?

11. Why has RT been attractive to P/P agencies?

12. According to behavior modification and learning theory, what is the cause of criminal behavior?

13. What are the techniques for changing behavior according to learning theory?

14. Why is it difficult to apply behavior modification techniques to P/P practice?

15. What are the advantages of social group work over the more traditional one-to-one approach to counseling in P/P?

16. What is cognitive skills training (CST)?

17. What is the difference between psychological and sociological explanations of criminal behavior?

18. How does Robert Merton use the concept of anomie to explain certain types of criminal behavior in the United States?

19. How should P/P officers deal with anomie among their clients?

20. Which P/P rules are responses to differential association?

21. According to the theory of differential association, what determines if a person becomes a criminal?

22. According to Richard Cloward and Lloyd Ohlin (proponents of differential opportunity), what are the three types of delinquent subcultures that are the result of anomie and differential association?

23. According to control theory, what determines if persons engage in criminal behavior?

24. What are the characteristics that Albert Cohen states are necessary to achieve success in our society (characteristics that lower-class youth do not possess)?

25. What are the techniques of neutralization?

26. What are the negative results of labeling?

27. What is the conflict view of criminal behavior?

28. How does labeling impact P/P work?

Probation and Parole Officers

A well-rounded officer can lead a counseling group in the morning and conduct surveillance in the field and make an arrest if warranted in the afternoon.

—*Robert L. Thornton* (2003: 15)

Chapter Outline

This chapter examines the roles, responsibilities, and qualifications of the approximately 75,000 probation and parole (P/P) officers in the United States as well as the use of volunteers. The first section outlines the varied tasks of P/P officers.

TASKS OF PROBATION/PAROLE OFFICERS

Most P/P officers spend their working time writing reports, visiting and interviewing clients, making referrals, and talking to persons in and out of the criminal justice system. These tasks can be divided into 10 parts (based on Strong, 1981):

1. *Information manager.* The primary focus is the collection, classification, and analysis of data about the individual case and the community.

2. *Evaluator.* The main objectives involve assessing personal or community problems, weighing alternatives and priorities, and making decisions for action.

3. *Enabler.* The primary focus is to provide support and to facilitate change in the behavior patterns, habits, and perceptions of individual clients. The key assumption is that problems may be alleviated or crises may be prevented by modifying, adding, or extinguishing discrete bits of behavior; increasing insights; or changing values and perceptions.

4. *Educator.* Instruction is used in the sense of an objective rather than a method. The primary objectives are to convey and impart information and knowledge and to develop various kinds of skills. A great deal of social casework is simple instruction.

5. *Broker.* The primary objective is to steer (refer) clients to existing services that can be of benefit to them. The focus is on enabling or helping people to use the system and to negotiate its pathways. A further objective is to link elements of the service system with one another. The essential benefit of this objective is the physical hookup of the person with the source of help and the physical connection of elements of the service system with one another.

6. *Advocate.* The main focus is to fight for the rights and dignity of people in need of help. The key assumption is that there will be instances when practices, regulations, and general conditions will prevent individuals from receiving services, using resources, or obtaining help. This position includes the notion of advocating changes in laws, rules, and regulations on behalf of a whole class of persons or a segment of society. Advocacy aims at removing obstacles or barriers that prevent people from exercising their rights, receiving benefits, and using the resources they need. When I was a parole officer in New York, because of Department of Motor Vehicles regulations, parolees with legitimate employment needs had difficulty obtaining a motor vehicle license. Advocacy on the part of the Parole Officers Association was effective in changing these regulations and removing the unnecessary obstacles.

7. *Mediator.* The primary objective is to mediate between people and resource systems and among resource systems. The key assumption is that problems do not exist within people or within resource systems but rather in the interactions between people and resource systems and among systems. As opposed to the advocate, the mediator stance is one of neutrality.

8. *Community planner.* The main objectives involve participating in and assisting neighborhood planning groups, agencies, community agents, or governments in the development of community programs to ensure client needs are represented and met to the greatest extent feasible.

9. *Agent of detection.* The primary focus involves identifying when a client is at risk or when the community is at risk from the client. The first step for the officer is to identify the individuals who are experiencing difficulty (they are in crisis) or who are in danger of becoming a risk to the community. A second step is to identify conditions in the community itself that may be contributing to personal problems of the client and that might raise his or her assigned risk level (such as lack of jobs or job training, or the influx of easily available controlled substances). A third step is to determine when the community is at risk from the offender and what is needed to protect the community.

10. *Enforcer.* The main objective requires the use of authority to revoke supervision because of changes in the status quo, which involves heightened community or individual risk outside the control of the officer.

The degree to which one task will be favored over another is dependent on the model of the particular agency that employs the P/P officer.

Probation/Parole Officers: Roles and Agency Models

What role will the P/P officer assume toward the client? The literature (e.g., Allen, Carlson, and Parks, 1979; Klockars, 1972) reveals three basic roles:

1. *Law enforcement.* The P/P officer's primary concern is the protection of the community through control of the P/P client.
2. *Rehabilitation.* The P/P officer's primary concern is the improved welfare of the P/P client.
3. *Blend.* The P/P officer's primary concern is to effect a combination of law enforcement and treatment when dealing with a P/P client.

These roles, however, are deficient when discussed outside these agency contexts or models:

- *Control model.* Control of the P/P client's activities is the primary focus of the **control model**. Unannounced home and employment visits, checks for drug use, and a close working relationship with law enforcement agencies are the standard practice.
- *Social services model.* The primary focus of the **social services model** is on client needs, including employment, housing, and counseling that provide social and psychological support. These agencies often have contracts with private service providers.
- *Combined model.* The **combined model** requires P/P officers to provide social services while attending to control functions.

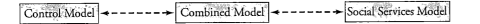

Most P/P agencies would be located somewhere in the middle of this continuum, with probation agencies typically found on the right of the combined model and parole agencies on the left. Although it would not be unusual to find many social services model agencies, particularly in probation, the *control* model would not be found anywhere in its pure form, although specific programs—such as electronic monitoring and intensive supervision (discussed in Chapter 12)—may be based on a control model. The P/P officer with a law enforcement focus is more likely to be found in—indeed, would be appropriate for—the control or combined model agency. The P/P officer with an emphasis on rehabilitation would be most likely found in the social services model agency. The issue, then, is not what role the P/P officer will assume with respect to clients but rather whether the role is compatible with the agency model. In the combined model, some use can be made of P/P officer role variation (I prefer the term *style*). Supervisors can assign cases on the basis of matching the officer's style with the salient characteristics of the offender; for example, an officer with a more authoritarian style would be matched with "heavy" (i.e., professional or career) criminals. An officer with a gentler style would be appropriate for certain situational offenders or perhaps youthful clients.

In a combined model agency, officers integrate their control or community protection role with their social services role while maintaining flexibility to stress one over the other in an individualized response to each case. For example, a young offender under supervision for joyriding in a stolen car will receive a different response than an experienced offender who is associated with organized criminal activity. In P/P treatment, officers adapt those methods that are useful to their practice while sacrificing the rest (sometimes cynically) on the altar of reality. Support for combining the social services and the control functions comes from Elizabeth Hutchinson (1987), who argues that social workers should avoid sending out other people to carry out coercive actions.

Georgia Parole Officers (POs). Charged with the task of protecting Georgia's citizens by assisting with the reintegration of the inmate back into the community and returning to prison those who fail, an officer is, on the one hand, a counselor and mentor and, on the other hand, a law enforcement officer and a prosecutor. In the course of 1 day, a PO may participate in the arrest of a parole violator, help another get a job, counsel a family dispute, interview an inmate or his family, assist in obtaining treatment for a substance abuser, testify at a parole revocation hearing, and make an assortment of contacts with parolees, their families, and their employers. Every day, POs travel Georgia's city streets and rural back roads, in many cases areas that are potentially dangerous, to monitor parolee compliance with the conditions of parole and to help them break with their criminal past. Being a PO means being accessible around the clock, with after-hours calls from parolees, anxious families, and law enforcement always a possibility. As certified peace officers, they are frequently called on to assist in emergency situations, such as floods and tornadoes. Still, many POs find the time to volunteer for community projects, school programs, church activities, and an assortment of other events that they know will positively impact the quality of their hometown life. Georgia's POs work every day to intervene with and to successfully bring about change in others who had until that point been unable to abide by the rules of society.

Multnomah County (Portland, Oregon) Probation/Parole Officers. The Multnomah County Department of Community Justice promotes public safety and strives to reduce recidivism among juvenile delinquents and adult offenders through a balance of supervision, services, and sanctions. Officers provide counseling, case management, and supervision of adult clients on formal P/P. They identify individual needs of clients; assess clients' immediate functional and dysfunctional patterns; work with community agencies to develop and implement individual and family treatment plans; and counsel clients on how to comply with their P/P conditions, legal obligations, and other requirements of the court. P/P officers counsel clients on the consequences of noncompliance, develop time frames to assist clients in meeting goals and court-ordered conditions, and monitor clients' compliance through reviewing provider agency reports and by making unannounced visits to clients' residence or place of employment. They develop individual supervision plans to enhance clients' compliance with probation or parole conditions; they conduct searches and seize evidence as authorized; and they may arrest, detain, search, handcuff, and transport clients. They must maintain a chronological record of all contacts and an ongoing evaluation of clients' progress. P/P officers also prepare presentence and postsentence investigation reports for the court.

Probation/Parole Officers as Agents of Rehabilitation

Chapter 8 reviewed a variety of approaches to rehabilitation, the implication being that P/P officers can operationalize these approaches with their clients. Requirements for P/P officer positions (discussed later in this chapter) are usually a bachelor's degree, which is hardly adequate to provide the background (let alone the skills) for carrying out a sophisticated rehabilitation role. Shelle Dietrich (1979: 15) points out that "the probation officer usually has not received extensive specialized training for the function of change agent; that is, the function of being competent to facilitate another person's changing his behavior, attitude, affect, or personality style." Generally, the P/P officer is not educated or trained to be a treatment agent: "It is an unrealistic expectation of probation [and parole] officers to expect themselves to be competent in an area for which they have not received adequate training" (Dietrich, 1979: 15).

In a review of the literature purporting to advise P/P officers whose background is otherwise deficient on how to become effective change agents, Dietrich (1979: 16–19) found it simplistic and at times potentially harmful to the client. Thus, she argues, professional intrusion is often advocated in areas for which the P/P officer lacks training. Cynically, she proposes, "Why not go ahead and prescribe medications, prepare legal documents, or write an insurance plan for the probationer?" (1979: 17). Dietrich cautions: "And what about the probationer? Certainly, his position in relation to the probation officer is a vulnerable one. Shouldn't the probationer be protected from being the involuntary patient of an unlicensed and untrained person, even if the person's intentions are the most purely humanistic?" (1979: 18).

Dietrich raises two other related issues:

1. Is the therapeutic enterprise possible in a P/P setting?
2. Given a positive response to this question, is it realistic to expect the delivery of treatment in P/P where caseloads usually average between 80 and 100?

She argues that even if the P/P officer "were optimally skillful in such therapeutic endeavors," without the full promise of confidentiality (impossible in a P/P setting), full and open discussion—the basis for a therapeutic relationship—is not possible (1979: 18). Dietrich is using a rather narrow definition of *therapy*, however, and within that definition she is correct in saying that therapy is not possible in a P/P setting. This author believes that therapy is more usefully defined here as the purposeful use of self to improve the social and psychological functioning of a client; defined in that way, therapy is possible within the confidentiality limitations of a P/P agency. Therapy, however, is *not* possible given the lack of adequate education and training and the (usually) excessive caseloads encountered in P/P practice. Accordingly, some propose that treatment should take the form of the P/P officer acting as broker or advocate.

Key Fact

The P/P officer is expected to be an agent of rehabilitation, although preparation for this role may be limited (if not deficient).

PROBATION/PAROLE OFFICERS AS BROKERS AND ADVOCATES

The provision of necessary services in P/P practice often requires that the P/P officer act as a **broker** and/or an **advocate**. Private and public agencies may view the P/P client as undesirable or even undeserving, and welfare, mental health, and educational agencies may see the client as threatening. Their responses to a client's needs may lead to a client's frustration, and a frustrated client who reacts in a manner that does indeed appear threatening—frustration control is often a problem with P/P clientele—becomes a self-fulfilling prophecy.

Eric Carlson and Evalyn Parks see the *brokerage* approach in P/P as almost diametrically opposed to the treatment approach because the P/P officer "is not concerned primarily with understanding or changing the behavior of the probationer, but rather with assessing the concrete needs of the individual and arranging for the probationers to receive services that directly address these needs" (1979: 120).

Carlson and Parks expand on the brokerage approach:

[There] is significantly less emphasis placed on the development of a close, one-to-one relationship between the probation officer and the probationer. The probation officer functions primarily as a manager or broker of resources and social services that are already available from other agencies. It is the task of the probation officer to assess the service needs of the probationer, locate the social service agency which addresses those needs as its primary function, to refer the probationer to the appropriate agency, and to follow up referrals to make sure that the probationer actually received the services. [Thus] under the brokerage approach, it can be said that the probation officer's relationship with community service agencies is more important than his relationship with an individual probationer. The brokerage approach does share with the casework approach the importance of the probationer's participation in developing his own probation plan. (1979: 120–21)

They note that "the essential tasks of the brokerage orientation to probation are the management of available community resources and the use of those services to meet the needs of probation clients" (1979: 123).

Accordingly, little emphasis is placed on the quality of the relationship between the P/P officer and the client; rather, emphasis is placed on the close working relationship between the P/P officer and the staff members of community social services agencies. Counseling and guidance are considered inappropriate activities for the officer; no attempt is made to change the behavior of the probationer. The primary function of the P/P officer as a broker or advocate is to assess the concrete needs of each client and make appropriate referrals to existing community services. Should the needed service not be available in the community, the officer is responsible for encouraging the development of that service.

Key Fact

The broker/advocate role links clients to needed services, with little concern for the relationship between officer and client.

Probation/Parole Officers as Law Enforcement Agents

The most controversial role of a P/P officer is that of enforcer. The P/P officer as law enforcement agent is related to the control model of supervision in much the same way as the rehabilitation or broker/advocate role is related to the social services model. For a discussion of the law enforcement role of P/P officers to be meaningful, one must consider this position within the context of an agency model; however, many critics of a law enforcement role for P/P officers render unequivocal statements without any discussion of the model. Thus, without any attention to an agency model, the American Correctional Association (1981: 36), in its *Standards for Adult Probation and Parole Field Services*, states: "Probation/parole officers do not routinely carry weapons in the performance of their duties."

A more productive approach is to identify the agency model and then decide if it is compatible with a law enforcement role. Paul Keve (1979: 432) states that agencies "suffer sharp internal problems" when agency policy seems to require surveillance and arrest activities while the agency prohibits officers from carrying firearms. For example, a community corrections (parole) officer in the state of Washington "conducts searches and arrests; detains serious violators after proper approval; serves parole subpoenas; transports arrested offenders to jail"—but can carry a firearm while on duty only if he or she or immediate family members have been threatened. Montgomery County (Ohio) Community Control (probation) Officers and Solano County (California) POs are expected to make arrests and conduct searches and seizures but are prohibited from carrying firearms or other weapons or chemical agents in the performance of their duties. A more rational approach was taken by the Texas Adult Probation Commission, which voiced its opposition to *both* arrest powers and the carrying of firearms by POs (now called community supervision officers).[1] In Virginia, although they are authorized to carry firearms, P/P officers are directed to have law enforcement personnel make arrests and conduct searches.

A Closer Look

More Dangerous . . .

"Probation and parole work can be dangerous. . . . Many officers believe, with good reason, that their work has become even riskier. Offenders sentenced to probation and released on parole commit more serious crimes than in the past, and more offenders have serious drug abuse histories and show less hesitation in using violence" (Finn and Kuck, 2001: 1).

---

[1] In 1998, Texas P/P officers were given permission to carry concealed firearms, which is the right of any civilian in Texas who has completed the required training. For a discussion of this issue, see Lopez (2007).

In 1975, I surveyed 53 adult parole agencies in the United States (the 50 states, the District of Columbia, Puerto Rico, and the U.S. Division of Probation, which also supervised parolees). The survey revealed that parole agencies differ greatly with respect to officers carrying firearms and arresting violators. A few years later, Keve (1979) conducted a similar survey of top administrators in P/P in the United States and found that a little more than half of the jurisdictions prohibited the carrying of a firearm. In 1986, the Oklahoma Department of Corrections surveyed all 50 states with respect to the carrying of firearms by P/P officers: "The study indicated that about 48 percent of all P/P agencies allowed their officers to carry a firearm on the job. Only 24 percent of the jurisdictions polled said their officers routinely carried a weapon" (Jones and Robinson, 1989: 90).

A Closer Look

Probation and Parole Models

"There seems little doubt that probation and parole work has moved away from a general embracing of offender assistance [social services] models into a solid marriage with control, compliance, and punishment models of community supervision" (Castellano, 1997: 22).

In more recent years, as more and more P/P agencies move toward a control model of supervision, arrest powers and the carrying of firearms by P/P officers have become increasingly common—for several compelling reasons. Many agencies are confronted by P/P personnel who feel endangered by having to enter high-crime areas, particularly during evening hours, to visit serious offenders at home. In Winnebago County, Illinois, "the concern of officer safety became apparent because of escalating violence in the community which brought in discretion and common sense in terms of when and when not to accomplish certain field contacts. This also resulted in the development of specific home visit procedural guidelines and availability of pepper spray and a radio." Maryland P/P officers may also opt to carry pepper spray (but not firearms). P/P officers in jurisdictions that require fieldwork but do not permit the carrying of firearms are apparently being exposed to increasing levels of danger. A study in Minnesota, for example, found that about 20 percent of P/P officers had been physically assaulted (4 percent one or more times in the past year); 43 percent reported being physically or verbally threatened one or more times during the past year (Arola and Lawrence, 1998). A study in Pennsylvania highlights the danger of P/P work: "Victimization of Pennsylvania P/P workers is extensive and pervasive" (Parsonage and Bushey, 1989: 24). William Parsonage (1990) expresses concern over similar findings in other states. In many agencies, officers are demanding protective training and the right to carry firearms, and Parsonage (1990: 35) reports that "during the past few years, an increasing number of agencies have authorized the carrying of firearms under various circumstances." In Minnesota, however, "the majority of probation officers seem to agree that the authority for carrying firearms and making arrests is best left with police officers" (Arola and Lawrence, 1998: 10). Since 1998, there has been a dramatic change in the number of probation officers authorized to carry firearms in New York State. In 2003, the New York City Department of Probation began arming its almost 900 officers, and in at least five New York counties, carrying a firearm is required for new POs.

Hazards of Parole Supervision

The very nature of supervising offenders subjects P/P officers to potentially hazardous events on a routine basis. Fortunately, not every officer has had a bad or harrowing experience, but many have. On one occasion, New York State Parole Officer Tom Brancato was strangled almost to the point of unconsciousness in a remote wooded area where he stopped to see his parolee at work. This surprise attack occurred after Officer Brancato had asked the parolee to have a seat in his car. As soon as they were seated, the parolee reached over, grabbed Officer Brancato by the throat, and began choking him. Wedged between the bucket seats of his Volkswagen, the officer's right arm and gun were pinned beneath him. After considerable effort, he managed to get his gun with his left hand and stick the barrel in the parolee's ear. Case closed.

In many jurisdictions, particularly in high-crime urban areas, the police/sheriff is either unwilling or unable to provide sufficient warrant enforcement services. In 1999, for example, California had 2.5 million unserved warrants (Associated Press, 1999) and in 2007, New York had more than 250,000 (Mahoney, 2007). If the P/P agency does not enforce its own warrants, they often go unattended; the potential danger to the public is obvious as hundreds (or in larger jurisdictions, thousands) of warrants go unenforced. Warrants turned over to outside agencies are occasionally used to force P/P violators into becoming informants, and P/P agencies usually have rules against using clients as informants.

Absconders

Absconding from supervision is a perennial problem in P/P: Offenders stop reporting and their whereabouts are unknown. The failure to expeditiously locate and arrest these persons presents a danger to the community and encourages other probationers/parolees to follow their example. The New York State Division of Parole has always placed a high priority on this problem and has a unit in place to track down absconders. Field POs have 45 days to follow all readily available leads in locating and arresting their absconders, at which time the case is turned over to the six-person Absconder Search Unit (ASU). Because ASU officers have no caseloads to supervise, they can spend time conducting surveillances of known residences or hangouts in addition to using other fugitive apprehension techniques.

In practice, P/P agency policy with respect to firearms falls into one of three categories:

1. *Officers are not permitted to carry firearms based on either state law or agency policy.* District of Columbia court services (probation) officers, Hawaii and Tennessee parole officers, and Kansas, Maryland, Minnesota, Nebraska, Rhode Island, Vermont, and Wyoming P/P agents/officers are not permitted to carry firearms.

2. *Officers are by statute peace/law enforcement officers, but the agency either restricts or discourages the carrying of weapons.* Although they are peace officers, POs of the Alameda County (California) Probation Department are prohibited from carrying firearms. The San Francisco Adult Probation Depart-

ment prohibits the routine carrying of firearms but permits certain officers to carry weapons (e.g., those assigned to the gang violence suppression program). Arrest authority and the carrying of firearms by POs in Illinois are at the option of the circuit court of each county. Cook County (Illinois) POs are prohibited from carrying firearms, except those assigned to special units such as intensive supervision. The Adult Probation Department of Allen County, Indiana, states that although its personnel are allowed by statute to carry firearms and arrest probationers, the court discourages the carrying of a firearm. In Marion County (Indiana), a special unit of POs has been certified as special deputies with the county sheriff and is responsible for serving warrants and conducting high-risk field investigations. The Montgomery County (Ohio) Adult Probation Department allows officers to carry firearms only on special assignments, such as transportation of a probation violator, or in emergency situations, such as the escape of a dangerous offender or a "highly threatening office disturbance." Bucks County (Pennsylvania) POs are designated peace officers but are prohibited by agency policy from carrying firearms. Washington permits community corrections officers to carry firearms only as a result of a threat while on duty and then only for a maximum of 90 days.

3. *Officers are by statute peace/law enforcement officers, and the agency permits or requires all qualified personnel to carry firearms.* Employment as a P/P officer in Alabama, Arkansas, Delaware, Idaho, Nevada, and North Dakota and as a parole officer in New Jersey and New York requires firearms qualification and carrying of weapons while on duty. Firearms training is mandatory for California (adult and youth) parole agents, Colorado community parole officers, Connecticut correctional rehabilitation services (parole) officers, Maine probation officers, North Carolina P/P officers, North Dakota field (P/P) officers, Oklahoma P/P officers, South Dakota parole agents, and Westchester County (New York) probation officers; they are all authorized or required to carry department-issued weapons while on duty. Illinois, Kentucky, Massachusetts, Michigan, Missouri,[2] Montana, and Pennsylvania P/P officers/agents are permitted to carry firearms provided they have met applicable training and proficiency standards. Probation officers in Dauphin County and Franklin County, Pennsylvania; Bibb County, Georgia; Suffolk County, Nassau County, and Onondaga County, New York; Pima County, Arizona; and Humboldt County and San Bernardino County, California; as well as Florida correctional probation officers, Iowa and New Mexico P/P officers, Virginia probation officers, and West Virginia probation (but not parole) officers who have qualified in the handling of weapons may carry a firearm. Probation officers for the Georgia Department of Corrections who complete firearms training and receive permission from the deputy commissioner may carry firearms.

Key Fact

The carrying of firearms by P/P officers varies by agency and can be grouped into three categories: prohibited, limited/discouraged, permitted/required.

In some jurisdictions, P/P personnel secure firearms authorization by being deputized by a cooperative sheriff's office. And many states now have "shall issue" statutes requiring that civilians who meet relevant criteria, such as no criminal history, be issued a permit to carry a concealed handgun. A gray area on this issue may exist, exemplified by the policy of the Federal Probation and Pretrial Services Division. Although federal probation and pretrial services officers are not permitted to carry firearms routinely, an officer who has presented sufficient reasons why carrying a firearm is necessary in general or for a specific assignment can be granted authority. The actual degree to which firearms authority is granted varies considerably from district to district. In Idaho, although P/P officers are weapons-trained peace officers, they do not routinely carry weapons; however, the district manager can give permission to carry a weapon. In Iowa, each of the state's eight judicial districts is free to decide if its P/P officers will carry firearms.

---

[2]Missouri P/P officers who take required training are allowed to carry firearms, but the agency prohibits them from making arrests.

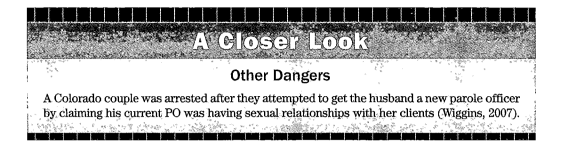

Other Dangers

A Colorado couple was arrested after they attempted to get the husband a new parole officer by claiming his current PO was having sexual relationships with her clients (Wiggins, 2007).

Should P/P Officers Make Arrests and Carry Firearms?

In 1975, while still a parole officer, I answered with a resounding "yes." More than three decades later, I find myself still in agreement with the legendary New York parole chief David Dressler (1951: 152), who wrote: "I am convinced a parole system worth its salt *has* to make its own arrests." Departments that fail to provide the maximum amount of community protection possible within a P/P setting are in danger of having their services shifted or contracted out to public or private social services agencies. The privatization of prisons, presentence investigation reports (in certain instances), and supervision of misdemeanants should serve as a warning to the self-interests of P/P personnel.[3]

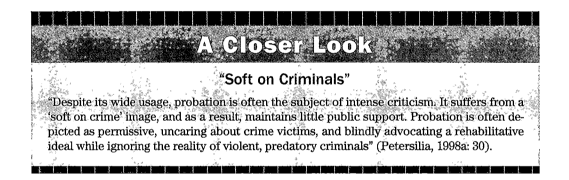

"Soft on Criminals"

"Despite its wide usage, probation is often the subject of intense criticism. It suffers from a 'soft on crime' image, and as a result, maintains little public support. Probation is often depicted as permissive, uncaring about crime victims, and blindly advocating a rehabilitative ideal while ignoring the reality of violent, predatory criminals" (Petersilia, 1998a: 30).

Key Fact

Controversy continues over whether or not P/P officers should be responsible for arresting P/P violators or if this should be left to the police.

Although many (typically nonpractitioner) observers bemoan the existence of a role conflict in P/P or an incompatibility between control and treatment, this author never experienced such conflicts in practice, nor did his colleagues in New York. Indeed, given the nature of P/P clientele, sound treatment demands the use of appropriate methods of control—offenders under supervision often engage in behavior that is self-destructive and dangerous to the community. As a trained social worker, I found that the application of casework principles was enhanced by the legal powers inherent in P/P settings. Indeed, if role conflict is inherent in P/P practice, as Todd Clear and Edward Latessa (1989: 2) note, such is the nature of many professional positions, but "among other professions, role conflict is seldom seen as a justification for eviscerating the profession of a few less salient tasks; rather, it is felt that the 'true' professional finds a way of integrating various role expectations, balancing them and weighing the appropriateness of various expressions of the roles."

Misunderstanding of the control/enforcement role vis-à-vis the social services role is highlighted by Norval Morris and Michael Tonry, who argue that "there is no way in which effective, regular, but unpredictable urine testing to ensure that the convicted offender is drug free can be made other than as a police-type function" (1990: 185). As a social worker, I disagree: Preventing drug abuse—the purpose of drug testing—is to the client's advantage; testing enhances the ego function of the offender, strengthening

---

[3]Utah, for example, has enacted a Private Probation Provider Licensing Act.

resolve to avoid harmful substances. Indeed, the client can demur when under pressure from drug-using associates: "Can't man; got to report to my PO and he'll check me out." This approach is sound social work.

As a private citizen with a working knowledge of P/P, I have certain concerns about personal safety—that of my family, friends, and neighbors. From this (I believe typical) layperson's perspective, I evaluate a P/P agency by providing some examples. During the course of an office or home visit, a P/P officer may discover that a client is using heroin or cocaine. If the offender is unemployed, the drug habit is probably financed by criminal activities, so the client is a clear and present danger to him- or herself and to the community. A P/P agency whose officers cannot immediately (and safely) arrest such a person is not providing an adequate level of client service or community protection. P/P agencies also supervise offenders who have been involved in sex offenses against children, vehicular homicide as a result of intoxication, burglary, and armed robbery. A P/P agency whose officers have no responsibility to enforce prohibitions, through investigation and arrest, against frequenting play areas, drinking and driving, and carrying tools for forced entry or who cannot investigate money sources or a lifestyle that cannot be supported by the offender's employment status is not providing the minimum acceptable level of community safety.

A Closer Look

Parolees, Firearms, and Public Safety

In 1996, parole officers on a routine evening home inspection in Denver found that their client was not at home, but his sister permitted the officers to check the premises. Inside his closet, the officers found a pistol. As they were removing the weapon, the parolee arrived and was met by the officers in front of the house. Informed that he was to be taken into custody, the parolee bolted and ran behind the house with the officers in pursuit. Suddenly, he halted, drew a handgun, and aimed at the officers, who fatally shot the parolee.

Furthermore, the adult (and frequently the juvenile) P/P client is often a serious law violator who has proved to be a potential danger to the community. Many have been involved in crimes of violence, and the public and elected officials expect that probationers and parolees, if they are to remain in the community, will be under the scrutiny of P/P authorities. This scrutiny is why the law of most jurisdictions empowers P/P agencies with law enforcement responsibilities. However, the question is often raised whether the P/P officer should be the law enforcer or merely the treatment agent or broker.

A Closer Look

Firearms and Self-Defense

In 1993, in a change of policy, the Florida legislature authorized correctional probation officers (CPOs) to carry firearms. Subsequently, a CPO made a routine field visit to a client's home. Unknown to the officer, the client had expressed his intention to kill the CPO in retaliation for the arrest of the offender's brother for technical violations (the brother was returned to prison). After the officer completed his visit and was driving away from the home, he was shot twice and lost control of his car, which struck a tree. The offender continued to advance toward the car, but the officer was able to draw his weapon and return fire, striking the offender three times and saving his own life (Papy, 1997).

Do arrest powers and the carrying of a firearm interfere with the P/P officer's ability to form a casework relationship with which to provide treatment? I am of the opinion that they do not. Indeed, because of P/P officers' relationships with their clients, in delinquency situations they are able to effect an arrest without the tension and hostility that often accompany arrests made by other law enforcement officers (who have no relationship with the client). In fact, whether the P/P officer actually makes the arrest, the client knows that the P/P officer initiated the warrant action. In Maricopa County, Arizona, probation officers may initiate arrests only when police officers are present, so if an offender who is to be taken into custody reports to the probation office, the probationer must be *deceived* into waiting until the police arrive. This is both poor law enforcement and poor social work.

In my many years of parole work, I often posed the following question to clients: "I know that you are determined not to get into trouble, so this is a hypothetical question. If you violate parole, would you prefer the police, or would you rather that I came to arrest you?" Typically, stories about being badly treated by the police ensued before they generally responded, "If I gotta go back, you come, please." In Massachusetts, when it was decided that unarmed POs from the Dorchester Division of the District Court would make unannounced home visits at night, they required police escorts—poor social work practice on at least two levels: First, it draws attention to the client, violating confidentiality; second, it conveys a (perhaps unintended) message that the client is too dangerous to visit without a police escort, which may actually enhance the prestige of a gang-involved youth. Nevertheless, the "Massachusetts model" has been extended to Boston and other jurisdictions, such as Alameda County, California, where it is part of a program of "community probation." Although that county's probation officers "shall be active in the enforcement of probation conditions" and wear body armor and are equipped with handcuffs, the department prohibits POs from carrying firearms. "Project Spotlight," housed at Sam Houston State University in Huntsville, Texas, promotes police officer–probation officer teams to provide intensive supervision and surveillance, including evening, early morning, and weekend visits to the homes and communities of probationers. In Washington, D.C., the P/P status of clients is flagrantly displayed by community supervision officers and uniformed police officers who use marked police vehicles to conduct accountability tours—joint visits to offenders in the community—throughout the city. In some jurisdictions, such as Redmond, Washington, and Ogden City, Utah, police officers are authorized to make parolee home visits. For more than a decade, the writer made evening, early morning, and weekend visits to parolees in New York, as did his colleagues, without unduly displaying his parole status or needing to be escorted by police officers.

In Wyoming, unarmed P/P agents are encouraged to conduct home visits in teams only after a "pre-plan and prepare" has been developed. Agents conducting solo home visits call or radio their location to a "contact person" who they advise of the estimated length of time to be spent at the residence. "Agents are to make the initial call prior to entering the residence and a second call once exiting the residence." (I am refraining from any comment on this approach, but readers can probably guess what it would be.)

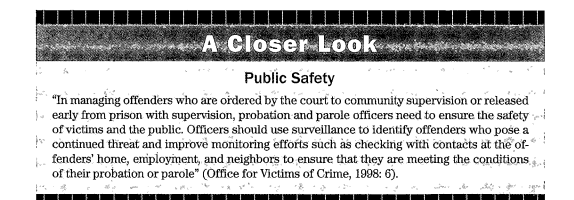

A Closer Look

Public Safety

"In managing offenders who are ordered by the court to community supervision or released early from prison with supervision, probation and parole officers need to ensure the safety of victims and the public. Officers should use surveillance to identify offenders who pose a continued threat and improve monitoring efforts such as checking with contacts at the offenders' home, employment, and neighbors to ensure that they are meeting the conditions of their probation or parole" (Office for Victims of Crime, 1998: 6).

P/P clients are potentially dangerous and usually reside in high-crime neighborhoods, which is reason enough to be armed. This facet of parole work was dramatically revealed while I was a parole officer in New York. My colleague, 32-year-old Donald Sutherland, attempted to arrest a parole violator on the street and was shot to death. The parolee was subdued at the scene by other parole officers. After being convicted of murder, the parolee escaped from prison and eluded law officers for several weeks (on one occasion after an exchange of gunfire). He was finally killed after refusing to surrender to a combined force of city and state police and parole officers.

A Closer Look

In the Field

Georgia Parole Officer Joje Wilson-Gibbs turns into East Lake Meadows, a housing project just inside Atlanta city limits, and notes that the surroundings are particularly lively for so early an hour. Throughout the warren of circling streets sprawl barrack-like apartments, several tattooed with graffiti and one encircled by a flower garden. A gray-bearded old man crouches in the corner of his stoop; two carloads of young men pass while slowly inspecting the sedate blue sedan driven by the parole officer.

Wilson-Gibbs is checking on her parolee, but it's not him she fears. Like most parole officers, the unpredictability of the environment most concerns her. Next to her on the seat is a bulky purse, on which is perched a can of pepper spray and in which is concealed a .38-caliber revolver. "I don't want to use my gun in a real-life situation," she says. "I don't want to use pepper spray, either, but I feel better knowing I'm trained and can react with these weapons if I'm in a life-threatening situation. All sorts of things add up to a sense of security for me—including having good tires on a reliable car that won't leave you stranded."

Although carrying a firearm does not guarantee safety, a person with a firearm may discourage attacks by carrying him- or herself more confidently than others who might be selected for victimization. Knowing that P/P officers are routinely carrying firearms has a deterrent value. Indeed, many *unarmed* P/P officers (perhaps unknowingly) gain a degree of safety because they are perceived as police officers or are believed to be armed.

Related to this issue is a peculiar prohibition: Some agencies that permit the carrying of firearms on duty forbid P/P officers from carrying a firearm while off duty. In North Dakota, for example, field officers (title of P/P officers) "will not routinely carry firearms while off duty." Virginia P/P officers, while they are authorized to carry weapons on duty, are told "the weapon will not be carried while in an off duty status." In Cook County, Illinois, probation officers assigned to intensive supervision must be armed while in the field, but the "officer shall not carry a firearm during off-duty hours, except when traveling [not more than 1.5 hours] to and from work." A similar prohibition exists for Illinois parole agents. This policy appears to be based on a lack of trust and a fear that weapons would be used off duty in an inappropriate manner by the very officers employed and trained by the agency. The policy is bad for morale and public safety and is unsound P/P practice. If a P/P officer is trained in law enforcement and firearms, he or she should have the same privilege of carrying a weapon off duty as do almost all other peace officers. P/P officers may encounter their clients during off-duty hours, as did this author many times during his career as a parole officer, and a hostile (perhaps ex-) client can be dangerous under such circumstances. P/P personnel must not be intimidated, or their effectiveness will be undermined, yet the nature of their clientele and the revocation powers of P/P officers make them vulnerable to intimidation. The ability to carry a weapon at all times reduces feelings of vulnerability and, therefore, the potential for intimidation. A community that provides P/P officers with weapons authority is that much safer by having in its midst trained and armed personnel sworn to enforce the law (see box titled "Oklahoma P/P Officers").

A Closer Look

Oklahoma P/P Officers

Two Oklahoma P/P officers were interviewing a client in his apartment when someone entered and directed their attention to a man standing nearby who was arguing with a woman—he was holding an assault rifle. The officers approached from behind, drew their weapons, identified themselves, and ordered the man to drop his weapon. The man glanced back at the officers, who continued to shout for him to drop his weapon. He suddenly moved his hand to the weapon, turned, and pointed it at the officers, one of whom fired a fatal shot into the man's chest (Thornton, 2003).

Probation and Parole Officers' Powers of Search and Seizure

"Over the past two decades there has been a dramatic shift in the sympathy displayed by courts regarding the rights of prisoners and those under supervision in the criminal justice system" (Jermstad, 2002: 17). This is highlighted by the interpretation of the Fourth Amendment's protection against unreasonable searches and seizures as applied to probationers and parolees. Persons on probation and parole sign rules of supervision that routinely permit a warrantless search of their property and person. In 1987, the Court held (*Griffin v. Wisconsin*, 107 S. Ct. 3164) that the special needs attendant to supervising probationers justified a warrantless search based on "reasonable grounds," that is, evidence less than the search warrant standard of "probable cause."

In 1998, in another 5–4 decision, the Supreme Court ruled that evidence seized by parole officers without a search warrant, which would be barred at a criminal trial by the exclusionary rule, could be used at a parole violation hearing. In this case (*Pennsylvania Board of Probation and Parole v. Scott*, 524 U.S. 357, 1998), Keith Scott had been serving a 10- to 20-year sentence for third-degree murder when he signed a parole agreement that stipulated: "I expressly consent to the search of my person, property and residence, without a warrant by agents of the Pennsylvania Board of Probation and Parole. Any items in [*sic*] the possession of which constitutes a violation of parole/reparole shall be subject to seizure, and may be used as evidence in the parole revocation process." After receiving information that Scott had violated his parole by possessing firearms, consuming alcohol, and assaulting a coworker, parole officers obtained an arrest warrant and arrested him at a diner. They then went to his residence where they commenced a search without asking for or receiving permission from Scott's mother, who owned the residence; they found five firearms in Scott's room. The Pennsylvania Supreme Court held that Scott's Fourth Amendment protection was not waived by his signing of the parole agreement; furthermore, the court ruled that the exclusionary rule applies to parole violation hearings. The U.S. Supreme Court, in overruling the Pennsylvania court, stated:

> In most cases the State is willing to extend parole only because it is able to condition it on compliance with certain requirements. The State thus has an "overwhelming interest" in ensuring that a parolee complies with those requirements and is returned to prison if he fails to do so. The exclusion of evidence establishing a parole violation hampers the State's ability to ensure compliance with these conditions by permitting the parolee to avoid the consequences of his noncompliance.

Key Fact

As a condition of P/P, offenders authorize searches on less than probable cause, and the courts have supported this authority.

The Court noted that the usually adversarial relationship between a criminal suspect and police is not a characteristic of the parole officer/parolee relationship: "Their relationship is more supervisory than adversarial."

In 2001, this time in a unanimous decision (*United States v. Knights*, 122 S. Ct. 587), the Supreme Court expanded the *Scott* decision, ruling that a probationer's residence can be subjected to a warrantless search based on "reasonable suspicion." This does not violate the Fourth Amendment, the Court ruled, even when the search (in this case by sheriff's officers) is for "investigatory" rather than probation purposes. A California court's sentencing order (rules of probation) "included the condition that Knights [the probationer] submit to search at any time, with or without a search or arrest warrant or reasonable cause, by any probation or law enforcement officer." Knights was "unambiguously informed of the search condition"; thus, his "reasonable expectation of privacy was significantly diminished." This condition, the Court stated, furthers the two primary goals of probation: rehabilitating the client and protecting society from future criminal violations. The Court concluded that "the very assumption of probation is that the probationer is more likely than others to violate the law," so the state "may justifiably focus on probationers in a way that it does not on the ordinary citizen." Jermstad states, "It is clear from the context and tone of this opinion that the Supreme Court's overall expectation of probation was to be much more oriented toward law enforcement than serving the needs of probationers" (2002: 15).

In 2006, the Court ruled 6–3 (*Samson v. California*, No. 04-9728) that the Fourth Amendment does not prohibit a police officer from conducting a suspicionless search of a parolee. The Court noted that "parolees, who are on the 'continuum' of state-imposed punishments, have fewer expectations of privacy than probationers, because parole is more akin to imprisonment than probation is." And California requires every prisoner eligible for release on state parole to agree in writing to be subject to search or seizure by a parole officer or other peace officer with or without a search warrant and with or without cause. In the above case, the search resulted in finding methamphetamine.

SELECTION OF PROBATION/PAROLE OFFICERS

Selection System

The selection of P/P officers is typically done by a process similar to that used to select most public employees. One of three systems—the merit system, the appointment system, or a combined system—is generally employed:

1. *Merit system.* Under the **merit system**, applicants who meet the minimum qualifications for the position are required to pass a competitive written examination. Persons who score at or above the minimum passing grade are placed on a ranked list; from this list, candidates are selected, generally in the order of their rank. In some systems, applicants are graded on the basis of their education and employment background. The merit system was developed to remove public employment from political patronage. Critics argue, however, that a written examination cannot determine who will be a good P/P officer.

2. *Appointment system.* Under the **appointment system**, applicants who meet minimum requirements are hired on the basis of an evaluation by the agency. Applicants do not take a written examination, although they are usually interviewed by agency representatives. This system provides agency officials with the greatest amount of flexibility; it also has a history of being used for political purposes.

3. *Combined system.* The **combined system** involves elements of both the merit and appointment systems. Applicants are first screened through a qualifying examination. Those who receive a passing grade are placed on a list from which candidates are selected, usually after an interview with agency representatives.

Key Fact

P/P officers are hired through one of three methods: merit, appointment, combined.

A Closer Look

Requirements and Training for Georgia Parole Officers

Georgia's parole officers are among the most highly qualified and best-trained community supervision professionals in the country. All are required to have an undergraduate degree and must pass a complete background check, which includes a psychological test, to determine their job competency. Some come to the agency directly from college, whereas others come from backgrounds as diverse as law enforcement, social work, education, and private enterprise.

Soon after they are hired, all the officers attend the agency's Basic Training Program, a 6-week package of instruction at the Georgia Police Training Center in Forsyth. The course of instruction prepares them for the many roles they will fill as they go about their daily duties. Included are classes and hands-on training in report writing, interpersonal communications, cultural diversity, arrest procedures, lifesaving techniques, and firearms training and certification. On graduation, the new parole officers have the critical knowledge to return to their respective offices and begin their work. Every year the officers return for more training in the form of 40 hours of agency-mandated in-service training.

A Closer Look

Standards for New Jersey Parole Officers

- Knowledge of the economic, social, emotional, and other problems of paroled persons and of the reactions to be expected of such persons
- Ability to read, interpret, and apply information on the laws of New Jersey relevant to probation, parole, the operation of law enforcement agencies, and the courts
- Ability to read and interpret information on the theory of modern social casework, penology, sociology, and criminology
- Ability to function as a peace officer for the detection, apprehension, arrest, and conviction of offenders
- Ability to recognize and evaluate potentially dangerous situations involving parolees and to exercise caution and independent judgment in the handling of these circumstances
- Ability to assist with the work involved in supervising persons on parole who may be of varied ethnic and social backgrounds, who may possess varied levels of intellectual comprehension and English ability, and who may be antagonistic and/or emotionally disturbed
- Ability to visit and speak with businesspersons, employers, judges, clergy, police officers, school officials, and representatives of health, welfare, civic, and business organizations to enlist their cooperation in plans for the rehabilitation of parolees and, as required, to collect information for future action
- Ability to conduct interviews of prospective parolees and investigations of parole violations
- Ability to set appropriate payment schedules to collect court-imposed revenue obligations concomitant with the capability to pay, to coordinate the efforts necessary to collect payments in default, and to maintain records thereon
- Ability to plan and work constructively with parolees in the areas of improved family life, steady employment, and wholesome personal and neighborhood associates
- Ability to be proficient in the care, use, and security of firearms and other restraint/defense equipment
- Ability to apprehend and arrest parole violators

- Ability to investigate and evaluate the living conditions of parolees
- Ability to prepare correspondence; clear, sound, accurate, and informative case histories; summaries; and other reports concerning parole matters containing findings, conclusions, and recommendations
- Ability to maintain essential records and files

Personal Qualities

The characteristics generally considered desirable for P/P officers can be divided into four categories:

1. *Basic knowledge.* A P/P officer should have a working understanding of psychology, sociology, criminal statutes, police operations, and court and correctional systems. In some jurisdictions, particularly federal probation, an increase in the number of white-collar offenders referred for a presentence investigation or under supervision requires officers with knowledge of the Internet, securities, accounting, and banking.
2. *Individual characteristics.* A P/P officer needs the ability to relate to all offenders and to deal with their sometimes subtle or overt hostility, to exercise authority in an appropriate manner, to work well with other staff members, to organize work properly, and to prepare written reports in a coherent and timely manner.
3. *P/P agency.* The P/P officer must be willing to accept the responsibilities engendered by working for a public agency that handles offenders and to enforce its rules and adhere to its regulations.
4. *Other agencies.* The P/P officer has to be able to deal effectively with many kinds of agencies and persons, usually divided into criminal justice (police, prosecutors, judges, and correctional officials) and social services (treatment, welfare, employment, and educational agencies). These agencies often have varying attitudes toward offenders that must be handled appropriately.

A Closer Look

Qualifications for Probation/Parole Officers

The American Correctional Association sets the following standard for entry-level P/P field positions: "An entry-level probation or parole officer possesses a minimum of a bachelor's degree or has completed a career development program that includes work-related experience, training, or college credits providing a level of achievement equivalent to a bachelor's degree." Virtually all P/P agencies require at least a bachelor's degree, usually in a relevant major: sociology, criminal justice, psychology, or social work. Some require graduate education in a relevant field or counseling experience; some agencies permit relevant experience to substitute for up to 2 years of the educational requirement.

VOLUNTEERS IN PROBATION/PAROLE WORK

Probation in the United States originated with **volunteers**. The tradition was reactivated in 1959 by Keith J. Leenhouts, judge of the Royal Oak, Michigan, municipal court. In that city, the municipal (misdemeanor) court probation department was staffed entirely by volunteers. Through the efforts of Judge Leenhouts, a national organization, Volunteers in Prevention, Probation, and Prisons, Inc. (VIP), was formed. VIP merged with the National Council on Crime and Delinquency in 1972; in 1983, it reverted to independent status.

Carlson and Parks (1979: 237) present four volunteer service models:

1. *One-to-one model.* On a one-to-one basis, volunteers seek to obtain the trust and confidence of P/P clients and help them to maintain their existence, clarify their role in society, and plan for the future.

2. *Supervision model.* Working as a case aide to a P/P officer, the volunteer provides services to several clients at the direction of the officer.

3. *Professional model.* The volunteer is a professional or semiprofessional in his or her field (e.g., teacher or mechanic) who provides specialized services to several clients, such as literacy help or automotive skills training. In Florida, for example, the Department of Corrections has volunteer financial planning specialists available to assist probationers in maintaining a realistic family budget.

4. *Administrative model.* The volunteer assists with P/P administrative functions and interacts only indirectly with clients.

The primary approach of Judge Leenhouts and VIP is mentoring the juvenile and misdemeanor court clients. This venue is seen as critical because the "vast majority of all crimes and offenses are tried in these courts . . . [and] it is estimated that as many as 80 percent of all felonies are committed by persons who first are convicted of a misdemeanor or juvenile offense" (Reeves, 2003: v). Therefore, according to Bob Reeves, "there is no better place to identify and divert a (usually) young apprehended offender from a life punctuated with habitual criminal activity" (2003: v). Mentors typically work with youths sentenced to probation, spending time that features recreation and education.

Some P/P agencies and staff members are critical of the use of volunteers. They may view the efforts of volunteers as interference with their prerogatives or may be concerned about sharing information with volunteers because of the confidential aspect of P/P practice. Chris Eskridge and Eric Carlson (1979) report that in some agencies the regular P/P workers see volunteers as a threat to their jobs. Some P/P officers resent the fact that volunteers are able to play the "good guy," while they have control and enforcement functions. Some complain of volunteers acting as advocates for the offender in opposition to regular P/P work.

Because volunteers are not paid, they need to derive some satisfaction from their efforts. Satisfaction results when a level of success exists, and to be successful, volunteers require adequate training and supervision. In other words, the successful use of volunteers is not "cost free"; staff is required for the training, coordination, and supervision of volunteers. If additional staff are not to be employed for these tasks, the agency has to take away from the working time of regular P/P agency personnel. Eskridge and Carlson (1979) report that lack of success in volunteer programs is a function of management operations rather than the volunteer concept. Faulty management includes the inability to assign volunteers expeditiously, inadequate volunteer training, poor supervision or support for volunteers, and lack of communication between volunteers and officers.

Volunteer Programs

Brockton (Massachusetts) Volunteer Probation Officer Program. For 20 years, Brockton's district court has operated the state's largest continuing volunteer program. With its own director and board of directors—probation officers, past volunteers, and community representatives—the program uses about 600 volunteer probation officers (VPOs) who have completed formal training. The program focuses on repeat offenders ages 17 to 25. Each VPO is matched with three clients to whom they provide a mentoring relationship. The VPO does not substitute for the probation officer, who maintains overall responsibility for supervision, but functions more in the role of older sibling, friend, or even parent surrogate. Several volunteers have been recruited from the ranks of successful probationers. The VPO is in contact with each client at least an hour per week for a year (or less if the client has completed the court's sentence). VPOs report on their activity through weekly contact sheets and attend monthly VPO meetings.

Los Angeles County Reserve Deputy Probation Officer Program. Reserve deputy probation officers are deputized volunteers who complete a 75-hour (minimum) training course and a subsequent 6-month on-the-job training period; for specialized assignments, they may be required to complete additional training. The reserve probation officers work on weekdays, weekends, or evenings for a minimum of 20 hours per month. Under the direct supervision of regular officers, they provide support services and aid in the investigation and supervision of juveniles and adults. Other counties in California, such as San Diego, also use reserve deputy probation officers.

New Jersey Volunteers in Parole Program. As a component of the New Jersey Bureau of Parole, the Volunteers in Parole Program is designed to provide help through a pool of individuals from the community. These individuals are qualified and willing to assist bureau personnel in serving the varied needs of its many diverse clients. The following volunteer categories reflect the service needs of the Bureau of Parole while showing the scope of ways in which volunteers provide valuable assistance:

- *Parole officer aide.* He or she helps the parole officer with various investigations and assists as officer of the day for routine office interviews; however, involvement with law enforcement activities is prohibited.
- *Professional aide.* He or she is a member of a profession offering specific services on an as-needed basis.
- *Administrative aide.* He or she works in a district office in an administrative or clerical capacity.
- *Student intern.* He or she assumes the same role as the parole officer aide while a student from one of the various colleges and universities that provide internships within the bureau as part of a cooperative arrangement.

Juvenile Court of Jackson County (Missouri). In Kansas City, Missouri, the juvenile court of Jackson County has a victim assistance program staffed by volunteers. The program assists victims by empowering them with knowledge of the juvenile court process and being with them at the court hearing. Below are some of the services provided by these volunteers:

- Visiting victims in cases of delinquency, and preparing an impact statement that informs the court of a victim's losses and attitude toward the offense and the offender
- Providing referrals for victims requiring crisis counseling, repair of property, emergency funding, and other vital services
- Informing victims of the ability to file a civil action to recover losses
- Assisting victims in filling out victim compensation claims
- Assisting victims in recovering their property from police departments where it is being held as evidence
- Providing victims/witnesses with transportation to court when necessary
- Preparing letters for victims/witnesses to employers relative to any loss of work time
- Meeting with victims/witnesses before their court appearance, and staying with them until the hearing is complete
- Providing mediation of restitution payments if the court decides that the victim should meet with the offender and the victim agrees to do so
- Providing information to the public on the juvenile court process

Volunteers are used by the Delaware Department of Correction and the Missouri Board of Probation and Parole on a one-to-one basis. Both agencies use volunteers to increase the services available to P/P clients. In Missouri they are provided with training in reality therapy (discussed in Chapter 8) and are expected to influence behavior by setting an example while being patient listeners. The volunteer helps the client to develop and carry out realistic plans, provides advice and encouragement, and may offer concrete assistance by helping the client secure employment.

South Carolina Department of Probation, Parole, and Pardon Services. South Carolina offers a variety of volunteer opportunities:

- *Job developers.* These volunteers help offenders find employment and learn new job skills. They aid the offender's job search and provide pointers on interviews, demeanor, and job conflicts. They also make referrals to employment agencies and develop a job bank for offenders.
- *Community sponsors.* These sponsors are matched with offenders to develop a relationship of guidance, support, and motivation. They assist offenders with obtaining support and rehabilitative services. Through recreation, conversation, and other activities, the volunteer provides a positive role model.
- *Court assistants.* These volunteers aid the department with such tasks as processing offenders placed on probation, investigating and collecting information, reviewing information with offenders, and monitoring other court activity.
- *Agent/team assistants.* These assistants help P/P agents by monitoring and meeting the needs of offenders, which includes maintaining contacts with service and referral agencies, law enforcement agencies, court offices, family members, and employers.

Sixth Judicial District (Iowa) Department of Correctional Services. The department provides two types of opportunities for volunteers and college student interns:

1. *Caseworkers.* These volunteers assist offenders who are ordered to provide community service work. They interview and place offenders, communicate with placement agencies, and provide client follow-up.
2. *Probation/parole trainees.* These volunteers receive a complete and professional hands-on training experience in case management. They monitor offenders for rule compliance, provide service referrals, and complete client reassessments.

Hennepin County (Minnesota) Community Corrections Volunteer Program. Adult Field Services (Probation) has several volunteer/intern opportunities available. A minimum time commitment of 4 hours per week for 6 to 12 months is required, and all positions work directly or indirectly with probation staff. Qualifications range from little work experience plus a high school diploma to extensive work experience and college- or graduate-level work. Below are some of the volunteer positions along with their responsibilities:

- *Probation officer's assistant.* This assistant helps probation staff with their caseloads, which may mean working one-on-one with a high-needs client or handling a caseload of 30 to 70 clients. All work is done under the direct supervision of a probation officer.
- *Support staff assistant.* This person assists a lead clerical support staff worker with processing P/P paperwork. It may include computer and telephone work.
- *Domestic special services.* This volunteer monitors defendants who have successfully completed the counseling/therapy component of their probation. Computer skills are very helpful.
- *Case monitor, restitution.* Someone who is a case monitor contributes to the restoration of wholeness for crime victims through collection of court-ordered restitution.
- *Drug court.* This volunteer works alongside drug court staff. He or she may also escort defendants through the court process, prepare and organize documents, and enter and retrieve information on the computer.

Missouri Board of Probation and Parole.   Volunteers may serve as P/P aides who assist officers in the supervision of adults; this can include both offender and collateral contacts. They can opt for serving as reparation board members who assist in the implementation of restorative justice programs (discussed in Chapter 10).

There are also volunteer positions available with juvenile probation:

- *Mentor.* A mentor develops a long-term stable relationship with a juvenile probationer (a 1-year commitment).
- *Probation officer assistant.* This assistant works in close cooperation with the assigned probation officer, providing supervision, maintaining case records, and being available for court appearances with the juvenile.
- *Sole sanction restitution.* This volunteer monitors a large number of cases with court-ordered consequences to ensure court orders are followed and restitution payments are made.
- *Victim services case manager.* This volunteer manager contacts victims to answer questions regarding victims' rights in the court process and to verify losses.

A Closer Look

Pennsylvania Citizen Advisory Committees

In Pennsylvania, the Board of Probation and Parole promotes public involvement through volunteer Citizen Advisory Committees comprising 7 to 15 members in each of the board's 10 districts. Committee volunteers are assisted by the District Director, who serves as an ex-officio member and is charged with promoting good communications between the board and the public, employment opportunities for offenders, and contacts with community service agencies to provide needed services to offenders. Each committee meets at least four times a year; twice a year there is a statewide meeting of chairpersons and one other committee member from each of the 10 district committees that the parole board chairman and other parole staff attend. The agenda includes reporting on the work of the board, reviewing pending legislation, discussing new programs and initiatives, and sharing each district committee's work.

> **Key Fact**
>
> Volunteers in P/P can fill various roles, from clerical duties to direct services.

LEGAL LIABILITY OF PROBATION/PAROLE OFFICERS

P/P officers have generally been successful in avoiding **legal liability** for actions performed in the course of their duties. Although state agencies are generally exempt from liability for their governmental activities unless waived, immunity ordinarily is unavailable to individual state officers who can thus be sued. P/P officials can be sued as individuals. Immunity for probation officers is often dependent on the agencies for which they work and the nature of the functions they perform, but in general they merely have qualified immunity (as opposed to the absolute immunity enjoyed by judges). Probation officers who are employees of the court and who work under court supervision, while they do not enjoy the same absolute immunity of judges, are vested with judicial immunity for some acts, such as preparing and submitting a presentence report in a criminal case, because they are performing a quasi-judicial function (del Carmen et al., 2001).

P/P officers may be vulnerable to civil liability for such wrongs as negligence and failure to warn. **Negligence**, the most common form of tort action, refers to a failure to exercise that degree of care which a person of ordinary prudence would exercise under similar circumstances or conduct that creates an undue risk of harm to others. There are four elements in a negligence action: (1) A legal duty is owed to the plaintiff, (2) there is a violation of that duty by an act or omission to act, which constitutes a breach

> **Key Fact**
>
> Although P/P officials may be sued as individuals, generally they have been successful in avoiding legal liability for actions performed in the course of their duties.

of that duty, and (3) that act or omission was the proximate cause (4) for the injury or damage suffered by the plaintiff.

Although no definitive Supreme Court decision exists concerning the liability of parole officers for a **failure to warn** in the supervision process, state and federal cases have established liability for crimes committed by parolees under their supervision within a narrow set of circumstances. Case law has established a duty to warn third persons when there is a "special relationship" between certain types of professionals and a person under their care. This duty to warn arises because of the professional's training and expertise, which place the professional in a good position to predict that the person presents a reasonably foreseeable risk of harm to a particular third person. This "special relationship" could be seen in the relationship between a P/P officer and an offender under the officer's supervision. The P/P officer, in some situations, could be in a position to predict that the offender presents a reasonably foreseeable risk of harm to a particular third person.

A leading federal case in the area of the failure to warn is *Reiser v. District of Columbia* (563 F.2d 462, 1977), which ruled that because of the special relationship between a parole officer and parolee with a history of brutal violence against women, appropriate warnings to employers and other persons foreseeably at risk were required. In this case, the parolee used his position as an apartment building custodian to gain access to a woman's apartment, where he murdered her. The court held the agency liable.

The common element in these circumstances, notes del Carmen and Louis, is the rather unclear concept of a "special duty" on the part of the P/P officer:

> For this "special duty" to be relevant, there must be a *reasonably foreseeable risk* which exists when the circumstances of the relationship between the parolee and a third party suggest that the parolee may engage in criminal or antisocial conduct related to his or her past conduct. This, in turn, results from a combination of three factors: (a) the parolee's job; (b) his or her prior criminal background and conduct; and (c) the type of crime for which he or she was convicted. For example, it is reasonably foreseeable that a parolee convicted of child sexual assault would commit a similar act if employed in a childcare center, but not if employed as a janitor on a college campus. (1988: 37; emphasis in original)

Now that we have completed our examination of the tasks and work roles of P/P officers, agency models, and volunteers in P/P, in Chapter 10 we review and analyze the supervision process.

KEY TERMS

advocate (p. 257)

appointment system (p. 267)

broker (p. 257)

combined model (p. 255)

combined system (p. 267)

control model (p. 255)

failure to warn (p. 274)

legal liability (p. 273)

merit system (p. 267)

negligence (p. 273)

social services model (p. 255)

volunteers (p. 269)

INTERNET CONNECTIONS

American Probation and Parole Association: www.appa-net.org

Criminal justice links: faculty.ncwc.edu/toconnor

Probation agency links: cppca.org/10_links.shtml

Volunteers in Prevention, Probation, and Prisons: vipmentoring.org

REVIEW QUESTIONS

1. What are the various tasks of the P/P officer?
2. What are the three basic P/P agency models?
3. What are the three basic role typologies that may be assumed by P/P officers?
4. What is meant by the broker/advocate role of the P/P officer?
5. What agency model is compatible with a law enforcement role? Why?
6. Why have arrest powers and the carrying of firearms by P/P officers become increasingly common?
7. What are the arguments for and against a law enforcement role and the carrying of firearms by P/P officers?
8. What are the three basic categories with respect to agency policy regarding P/P officers making arrests and carrying firearms?
9. What has the Supreme Court ruled with respect to the search of the residences of probationers and parolees?
10. What are the three systems used to select P/P officers? What are their advantages and disadvantages?
11. What are the various roles that volunteers may play in P/P?
12. What are the advantages and disadvantages of using volunteers in P/P?
13. What have the courts ruled with respect to the liability of P/P officers?

Probation and Parole Supervision

Embracing the rehabilitative model requires a significant role redefinition and organizational change for probation and parole. An entire generation of staff has grown up in the field without exposure to treatment and rehabilitation.

—*William D. Burrell* (2005: 5)

Chapter Outline

Although probation and parole (P/P) supervision across agencies may differ in the details, there are commonly shared concerns: that the offender will recidivate (particularly when the nature of the recidivism generates media coverage) and that personnel resources are insufficient to meet the service needs of clients and the safety concern of the community. In this chapter, we begin our examination of the supervision process with a method for dealing with the problem of insufficient resources—classification.

CLASSIFICATION IN PROBATION AND PAROLE

Prisons have traditionally classified inmates on the basis of the security needs of the institution and the physical limitations or handicaps (if any) of the prisoner. With the advent of the corrections model, **classification** was expanded to include items relevant to rehabilitation programs offered by the correctional department in its various facilities. The de-emphasis of the corrections model has, correspondingly, lessened the importance of institutional classification (at least for rehabilitation). However, classification has become widespread in P/P, primarily for caseload management.

During the 1970s, P/P administrators came to the realization that their resources would never be sufficient to even approach the service needs of their clientele and that the typical P/P officer approximated agency objectives (protection of the community and rehabilitation of the offender) through the use of an unofficial and unarticulated classification system:

> Because not all offenders require the same level of supervision or exhibit the same problems, most experienced P/P agents utilize an intuitive system of classifying offenders into differential treatment or surveillance modes, usually based on their judgments of client needs and their perception of the client's potential for continued unlawful behavior. It seems reasonable to assume that without this type of caseload management, successes would diminish and failures increase. . . . [But] this untested, highly individualized approach does not provide information necessary to rationally deploy staff and other resources. (Baird, Heinz, and Bemus, 1982: 36)

Enter the risk/needs assessment.

Risk/Needs Assessment

During the late 1970s and early 1980s, the use of formal classification in P/P expanded greatly. This movement was led by the state of Wisconsin, which in 1975 received funding from the Law Enforcement Assistance Administration (LEAA) for a Case Classification/Staff Deployment Project. After 4 years, the **risk/needs assessment** was designed, implemented, and evaluated statewide.

The system developed in Wisconsin was adopted by the National Institute of Corrections and, subsequently, by many other P/P jurisdictions. The basic strengths of the risk/needs assessment system are its completeness, simplicity, and utility to management—indeed, classification for supervision is basically a management tool. Although variations exist between jurisdictions, all risk/needs classification schemes quantify variables along two dimensions:

Key Fact

The risk/needs classification system used in P/P is for caseload management.

1. Degree to which the offender presents a *risk* of recidivism (commitment of a new offense)
2. Degree to which the offender has *needs* and requires assistance from the P/P agency

Taken together, these two dimensions allow for a prognostication that has implications for the level of supervision required and thus for caseload management and deployment of personnel.

The system tested in Wisconsin demonstrated its effectiveness in predicting success or failure in completing P/P terms. In a sample of 8,250 clients, the percentage of individuals who were rated low risk and whose probation or parole was later revoked was 3 percent; of the cases rated high risk, 37 percent were revoked. Other jurisdictions have also tested the system. The Los Angeles Probation Department found that the risk scale (in comparison with intuitive judgments by probation officers) did well in predicting which cases would be successful and which would not; the needs scale, however, was found to have almost no predictive value (Program Services Office,

1983). In Massachusetts, when using a variation of the Wisconsin instrument, half the clients classified as "maximum" risk were subsequently recidivists compared with 36 percent of those classified as "moderate" and 17 percent of those classified as "minimum." It was noted that the predictive ability of the assessment could be improved by using four levels of supervision/risk: intensive, maximum, moderate, and minimum (Brown, 1984). A test of the Wisconsin Juvenile Probation and Aftercare Risk instrument revealed that this basis was not suitable for predicting recidivism (Ashford and LeCroy, 1988). Another study revealed that training in its use "appeared to increase officers' receptivity to less drastic means than revocation (and eventual incarceration) for addressing misconduct in offenders" (Harris, Gingerich, and Whittaker, 2004: 267).

The instrument used by the Pennsylvania Board of Probation and Parole is typical of most jurisdictions (Figure 10.1). The P/P officer places a number in a box that corresponds with the case record or the officer's assessment for each of the 11 risk assessment variables, adds up the score, and records that in a box labeled "Total." He or she then proceeds to do the same for the 13 needs assessment variables. Afterward, the two final scores are compared; whichever is higher (risk or needs) determines the level of supervision—reduced, regular, close, and intensive. (In some jurisdictions, only three levels of supervision exist: minimum, medium, and maximum.) Some flexibility is possible because the procedures provide for an override: "If, after completing the Initial Client Assessment or Client Reassessment, there is a compelling reason to raise or lower the client's grade of supervision, the agent may recommend such a change to his/her supervisor for review and approval/disapproval." Typically, after a case is classified along the risk/needs dimension, it is assigned to a P/P officer according to a predetermined workload distribution.

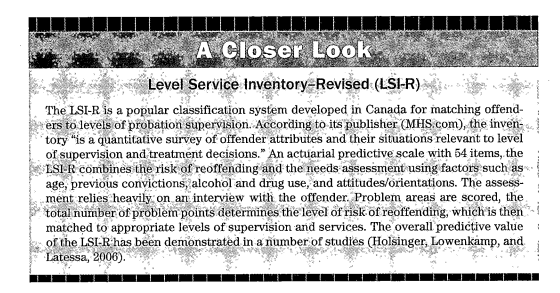

A Closer Look

Level Service Inventory–Revised (LSI-R)

The LSI-R is a popular classification system developed in Canada for matching offenders to levels of probation supervision. According to its publisher (MHS.com), the inventory "is a quantitative survey of offender attributes and their situations relevant to level of supervision and treatment decisions." An actuarial predictive scale with 54 items, the LSI-R combines the risk of reoffending and the needs assessment using factors such as age, previous convictions, alcohol and drug use, and attitudes/orientations. The assessment relies heavily on an interview with the offender. Problem areas are scored, the total number of problem points determines the level of risk of reoffending, which is then matched to appropriate levels of supervision and services. The overall predictive value of the LSI-R has been demonstrated in a number of studies (Holsinger, Lowenkamp, and Latessa, 2006).

Classification Levels and Workload Distribution in Texas.   The Department of Criminal Justice probation guidelines require assignment of cases to probation officers in "such a manner as to promote public protection through offender supervision and the attainment of a 100 point workload" for each officer using the following weights:

Level I   = 4.00
Level II = 2.50
Level III = 1.33
Level IV = 1.00

INITIAL CLIENT ASSESSMENT

CLIENT NAME (Last, First, Middle Initial)	PAROLE NO.	AGENT NAME	OFFICE	DATE

RISK ASSESSMENT

1. **Age at First Conviction: (or juvenile adjudication)**
   24 or older 0
   20–23 2
   19 or Younger .... .4 ☐

2. **Number of Prior Probation/Parole Revocations:** (adult or juvenile)
   None 0
   One or more .... .4 ☐

3. **Number of Prior Felony Convictions: (or juvenile adjudications)**
   None 0
   One 2
   Two or more .... .4 ☐

4. **Convictions or Juvenile Adjudications for:**
   (Select applicable and add for score. Do not exceed a total of 5. Include current offense.)
   Burglary, theft, auto theft, or robbery 2
   Worthless checks or forgery .... .3 ☐

5. **Number of Prior Periods of Probation/Parole Supervision: (Adult or Juvenile)**
   None 0
   One or more .... .4 ☐

6. **Conviction or Juvenile Adjudication for Assaultive Offense within Last Five Years:** (An offense which involves the use of a weapon, physical force or the threat of force.)
   Yes .... .15
   No .... .0 ☐

7. **Number of Address Changes in Last 12 Months:** (Prior to incarceration for parolees)
   None 0
   One 2
   Two or more .... .3 ☐

8. **Percentage of Time Employed in Last 12 Months:** (Prior to incarceration for parolees)
   60% or more 0
   40%–50% 1
   Under 40% 2
   Not applicable .... .0 ☐

9. **Alcohol Usage Problems: (Prior to incarceration for parolees)**
   No interference with functioning 0
   Occasional abuse: some disruption of functioning 2
   Frequent abuse; serious disruption; needs treatment .... .4 ☐

10. **Other Drug Usage Problems: (Prior to incarceration for parolees)**
    No interference with functioning 0
    Occasional abuse: some disruption of functioning 1
    Frequent abuse; serious disruption; needs treatment .... .2 ☐

11. **Attitude:**
    Motivated to change; receptive to assistance 0
    Dependent or unwilling to accept responsibility 3
    Rationalizes behavior; negative; not motivated to change .... .5 ☐

    TOTAL ☐

INITIAL ASSESSMENT SCALES

Risk Scale		Needs Scale
0–5	Reduced Supervision	.... –8–10
6–18	Regular Supervision	 1–10
19–30	Close Supervision	 11–25
31 & above	Intensive Supervision	.... 26 & above

SCORING AND OVERRIDE

Score Based/ .... Intensive ...... ☐ Regular .... ☐
Supervision Level
           Close .... ☐ Reduced .... ☐
Score Override .... No .... ☐ Yes .... ☐
FINAL GRADE .... Intensive ...... ☐ Regular .... ☐
OF SUPERVISION
Override Explanation: Close .... ☐ Reduced .... ☐

NEEDS ASSESSMENT

1. **Academic/Vocation Skills**
   High school or above skill level .... –1
   Adequate skills; able to handle everyday requirements 0
   Low skill level causing minor adjustment problems .... +2
   Minimal skill level causing serious adjustment problems .... +4 ☐

2. **Employment**
   Satisfactory employment for one year or longer .... –1
   Secure employment; no difficulties reported; or homemaker, student or retired 0
   Unsatisfactory employment; or unemployed but has adequate job skills .... +3
   Unemployed and virtually unemployable; needs training ...+6 ☐

3. **Financial Management**
   Long-standing pattern of self-sufficiency; e.g., good credit rating .... –1
   No current difficulties 0
   Situational or minor difficulties .... +3
   Severe difficulties; may include garnishment, bad checks or bankruptcy .... +5 ☐

4. **Marital/Family Relationships**
   Relationships and support exceptionally strong .... –1
   Relatively stable relationships .... 0 ☐
   Some disorganization or stress but potential for improvement ....+3 ☐
   Major disorganization or stress .... +5 ☐

5. **Companions**
   Good support and influence .... –1
   No adverse relationships 0
   Associations with occasionally negative results .... +2
   Associations almost completely negative .... +4 ☐

6. **Emotional Stability**
   Exceptionally well adjusted; accepts responsibility for actions .... –2
   No symptoms of emotional instability; appropriate emotional responses 0
   Symptoms limit but do not prohibit adequate functioning; e.g., excessive anxiety .... +4
   Symptoms prohibit adequate functioning; e.g., lashes out or retreats into self .... +7 ☐

7. **Alcohol Usage**
   No interference with functioning 0
   Occasional abuse; some disruption of functioning .... +3
   Frequent abuse; serious disruption; needs treatment .... +6 ☐

8. **Other Drug Usage**
   No interference with functioning 0
   Occasional substance abuse; some disruption of functioning ...+3
   Frequent substance abuse; serious disruption; needs treatment .... +5 ☐

9. **Mental Ability**
   Able to function independently 0
   Some need for assistance; potential for adequate adjustment; mild retardation .... +3
   Deficiencies severely limit independent functioning; moderate retardaton .... +6 ☐

10. **Health**
    Sound physical health; seldom ill 0
    Handicap or illness interferes with functioning on a recurring basis .... +1
    Serious handicap or chronic illness; needs frequent medical care .... +2 ☐

11. **Sexual Behavior**
    No apparent dysfunction 0
    Real or perceived situational or minor problems .... +3 ☐
    Real or perceived chronic or severe problems .... +5

12. **Recreation/Hobby**
    Constructive 0
    Some constructive activities .... +1
    No constructive leisure-time activities or hobbies .... +2 ☐

13. **Agent's Impression of Client's Needs**
    Minimum .... –1
    Low 0
    Medium .... +3 ☐
    Maximum .... +5

    TOTAL ☐

FIGURE 10.1 *Initial Client Assessment, Pennsylvania*

Level I.   This classification is calculated as 4 workload points and extends the most restrictive nonresidential supervision to these offenders:

- They have a documented pattern of serious noncompliance while supervised at a less restrictive level.
- They have a motion to revoke filed against them for a law violation.
- They match the jurisdiction's profile of offenders historically committed to prison/jail.
- They have regressed from a less restrictive level of supervision.

Level II.   This classification is calculated as 2.5 workload points and extends a heightened level of supervision to these offenders:

- They are a demonstrable risk based on these issues:
    1. Shock community supervision
    2. Supervision in lieu of revocation
    3. Direct sentence
- They have progressed from a more restrictive level of supervision, including residential supervision.
- They have regressed from a less restrictive level of supervision.
- They have documented special risks or needs that are included in the profile of offenders historically committed to prison/jail.

Level III.   This classification is calculated as 1.33 workload points and extends a moderate level of supervision to these offenders:

- They have regressed from a less restrictive level of supervision.
- They have progressed from a more restrictive level of supervision, including residential supervision.
- They demonstrate a documented necessity for a moderate level of supervision.

Level IV.   This classification is calculated as 1 workload point and extends a minimum level of supervision to these offenders:

- They have progressed from a more restrictive level of supervision.
- They present the least risk to the community.
- They are considered to be initial or interim community supervision placements but have not been classified.

Supervision Levels in Georgia.   The P/P officer interviews a new client, and with the help of the presentence report, institutional reports (for parolees), and other relevant documents, he or she fills out a risk/needs instrument similar to the one used in Pennsylvania (see Figure 10.1). A total is derived from the scoring of information on the instrument and is plugged into a particular level of supervision; typically, a reassessment is performed every 6 months. Because clients with a higher level of supervision require a greater expenditure of P/P officer time, equity is determined based not simply on **caseload** (the total number of clients supervised) but on **workload** (the anticipated amount of time each case will demand). This quantification allows for the easy use of computers, which can determine the need for more P/P officers in a particular jurisdiction (or if additional officers are not economically feasible, a corresponding reduction in the amount of supervisory time devoted to each case).

Each case is placed in one of six levels of supervision:

1. *Administrative.* No standard of supervision required for this classification (but probationers who have absconded, who are serving a prison sentence on a new offense and have not been revoked on the present offense, and who are receiving no direct supervision per court approval should be classified as administrative).

2. *Minimum (nondirect supervision).* Mailed-in change of address or employment; monthly payment of fine, restitution, and court costs; and monthly telephone contact with probationer.

3. *Minimum (direct supervision).* Monthly telephone contact and quarterly face-to-face contact.

4. *Medium.* Monthly telephone contact, quarterly face-to-face contact, and one field contact or collateral contact quarterly

5. *High.* Two monthly face-to-face contacts, monthly field contact, and monthly collateral contact.

6. *Maximum.* Four monthly face-to-face contacts, two monthly field contacts, and two monthly collateral contacts.

The use of the minimum or administrative supervision classification for active cases is troubling since these offenders will not be given an opportunity to develop a personal relationship with a P/P officer: "Clearly, processes of interpersonal change based on offender identification with the change agent and the internalization of new values will not transpire" (Castellano, 1997: 24).

A Closer Look

Nebraska Supervision Levels

- *Intensive.* Parolees must meet face-to-face with their parole officers at least once per week. They must also submit a monthly report and any required documentation as directed by their parole agreement once per month. They are required to submit a urine specimen each month.

- *Maximum.* Parolees must meet face-to-face with their parole officers at least once per month. They must submit a monthly report and any required documentation as directed by their parole agreement.

- *Medium.* Parolees must meet face-to-face with their parole officers at least once per month. They must submit a monthly report and any required documentation as directed by their parole agreement.

- *Minimum.* Parolees must meet face-to-face with their parole officers at least once every 90 days. They must submit a monthly report and any required documentation as directed by their parole agreement each month.

- *Conditional.* Parolees must meet face-to-face with their parole officers at least twice per year. They must also submit a monthly report and required documentation as directed by their parole agreement. See Figure 10.2 for an example of a monthly report.

SUPERVISION PROCESS IN PROBATION AND PAROLE

Key Fact

While parolees are generally more serious offenders than probationers, the supervision process is similar, and in many agencies officers supervise both.

The supervision process in probation and parole, which are handled by the same agency in many states, is similar, if not identical. However, parolees (by definition) have been imprisoned, and imprisonment generally reflects the severity of the offense and the criminal history of the offender. Therefore, parolees are generally considered a greater danger to the community than are probationers. Furthermore, given the lack of adequate educational and training resources in prison, most parolees leave the institution without the literacy and job skills necessary for employment.

Parolees differ from probationers as a result of their prison experiences. The changeover from prison life to community living requires a major readjustment. In

SEND OR DELIVER TO: FILE #: _____ PO: _____

Siskiyou County Probation Department
805 Juvenile Lane
Yreka, CA 96097
Phone: (530) 841-4180 FAX: (530) 841-4188

DATE: _____

NOTE: This form is due on the FIRST day of each month. All lines MUST be filled in completely. Just writing "same" is not acceptable.
Check if this is a new address _____

Name: _____

Address: _____

Street Number City State Zip Code

Mailing Address: _____

Street Number City State Zip Code
I live with: _____ Phone No.: _____
Employer: _____

Street Number City State Zip Code

Job Title _____ Work Location _____
Take-Home Pay/Monthly $ _____
Unemployed Since _____ Unemployment/Monthly $ _____
Other Family Income: AFDC, SSI, SSP, Other Amount $ _____
Family Vehicle(s): Year _____ Model _____ Color _____
License No. _____
Year _____ Model _____ Color _____ License No. _____
Purchases Over $200.00 This Month

NOTE: Fill Out the Following Items If They Are a Term of Your Probation:

Have you been arrested, cited, or contacted by law enforcement since the last report? Yes ___ No ___

If yes, please explain _____
I have paid $ _____ on my fine/restitution on _____ (date)
I have paid $ _____ supervision fee on _____ (date)
I have completed _____ hours of community service this month.
I have attended NA/AA _____ times this month on (dates) _____

My counselor is _____

NOTE: Please List Any Changes of Your Probation Status from Last Month: ____

I have obeyed all the terms of my Probation Yes ___ No ___
I declare that the above information is true to the best of my knowledge.

Signature _____

FIGURE 10.2 *Monthly Report Form–Adult*

prison, the offenders' lives are rigidly controlled: They are told when to sleep, when to eat, when to work, and when to have recreation. When they are released into the community, they must adjust to managing their own lives. This may be compounded by police harassment, particularly in smaller communities. Social agencies often do not recognize parolees' needs and somehow believe that they should be receiving assistance from the parole agency (based on Elliot Studt in Law Enforcement Assistance Administration, 1973). Unfortunately, most parole (and probation) agencies are extremely limited in their ability to deliver tangible services. This fact, coupled with the usual lack of employable skills, often makes parolees a burden on their families, worsening what

A Closer Look

Female Offenders

"The correctional system has historically been male-dominated. Not only [is] the structure of prison settings, the rules, the operating procedures, and the treatment programs largely based on the needs of males, but research studying the effectiveness of programs is also based on male subjects. Correctional systems frequently can assign male inmates to programs based on the individual rehabilitative or treatment needs of the offender, the severity of the crime the offender committed, and/or the security risk of the offender. Female offenders are not offered these same considerations" (Shearer, 2003: 46). Because they are less likely to be considered high risk—to have committed personal rather than property or "victimless" offenses—they are less likely to receive needed attention and may even be viewed as burdensome or inconvenient because of their high level of needs. "Women offenders often suffer from trauma and victimization, and officers may feel uncomfortable with or incapable of dealing with these issues and unsure of their ability to secure appropriate resources in the community" (Sydney, 2006b: 37).

Female offenders are usually poor, lack education and employment skills and are single mothers of at least two children: "They enter the criminal justice system with a host of unique medical, psychological, and financial problems" (Chesney-Lind, 1997: 170). In Georgia, for example, 99 percent of female parolees are mothers with more than two children. For women who have primary childcare responsibilities, participating in community service, attending treatment sessions, or even reporting to their probation/parole officer requires making childcare arrangements (Sydney, 2006b). While female offenders often have extensive social services needs, the limited resources of parole agencies are being focused, instead, on controlling the behavior and movement of parolees (Schram, et al., 2006).

"Women offenders are disproportionately low income women of color who are undereducated and unskilled, with sporadic employment histories" (Bloom, Owen, and Covington, 2003: 2). Females represent about 24 percent of the probation population and 13 percent of parolees, and most are single mothers with minor children. "The majority of women in the correctional system are mothers, and a major consideration for these women is reunification with their children" (Bloom, Owen, and Covington, 2003: 16). Thus, "engaging the family, particularly her children, in the recovery process can promote successful outcomes for a woman" (Bloom and McDiarmid, 2001: 11).

"Although relationships with others (family, friends, partners) are often the impetus to criminal involvement, these relationships may also support offenders' success in community corrections" (Sydney, 2006b: 34). However, P/P conditions prohibit associating with other offenders and female offenders will likely have significant others with a criminal history. Thus, this prohibition may have to be adjusted in specific cases.

may have been an already difficult family situation. This is particularly the case with female offenders.

Parolees have told this author that even so minor an experience as taking a bus ride can be traumatic to a newly released offender—several stated they were not aware of the required fare and exact change and had a feeling that everyone on the bus, especially the driver, recognized that they had just been released from prison. Being in prison also isolated them from normal social contacts with members of the opposite sex. They were self-conscious and often believed that because of the way they looked at women everyone would realize that they had been in prison. Parolees must "unlearn" prison habits and acquire new patterns of behavior if readjustment is to be accomplished quickly. Parolees are often subjected to social rejection because of their status and usually lack the necessary connections and economic resources that are effective in dealing with crisis situations.

Case Assignment

The supervision process begins when the offender is placed on the caseload/workload of a P/P officer. This aspect of supervision, case assignment, can be accomplished in a variety of ways, depending on the practice used by the particular agency and the scope of its jurisdiction. In agencies that have statewide jurisdiction (such as most parole agencies), district/area offices are located throughout the state and each office covers a specific geographic area. County probation agencies, depending on the size of the county, may also have (sub)offices scattered throughout the jurisdiction. Some P/P agencies are offering services through neighborhood centers, a decentralization that parallels community policing efforts in many communities, or P/P officers may work out of police substations. Offenders on probation or parole are directed to report to the office responsible for the area in which they (intend to) reside. At the P/P office, they will be assigned to a caseload either on a totally random basis or according to the specific area in which they plan to reside. Caseloads incorporating geographic considerations are advantageous insofar as they limit the travel time involved in supervising the offender; each officer also gains greater familiarity with his or her territory and the social and law enforcement agencies therein (not to mention places to eat and clean washrooms), which can enhance the supervision process. In more rural areas, where travel will be extensive, caseloads will be smaller than in urban areas, where offenders are usually clustered in certain areas of the city. In the caseload assignment process, the agency typically attempts to achieve parity by keeping the size of caseloads roughly equal. In Beaumont County, Texas, juveniles on probation are placed on caseloads according to their home schools, which allows one officer to see all of his or her clients by making one stop and fosters ongoing relationships with school personnel.

Offenders are assigned to **specialized caseloads** by virtue of a salient characteristic, such as a history of drug abuse or mental illness (discussed in Chapter 11). Another model uses classification schemes (discussed previously); quantitative weights are assigned to each case based on the level of supervision indicated by each case (e.g., risk/needs classification), and workloads are balanced by maintaining ongoing comparative statistics for P/P officers assigned to field supervision. Although this approach is the most rational one for achieving parity in supervision, it is also the most difficult to operationalize, particularly for an agency that has statewide responsibilities.

Key Fact

An offender may be assigned to a caseload or workload based on his or her residence and/or a salient characteristic, such as a substance abuse problem.

Initial Interview

The initial interview in P/P practice is considered a crucial time in the supervision process. The first meeting between the client and the P/P officer usually occurs in the P/P office and is a time of apprehension and anxiety: The officer "represents a power that can, and does, limit his freedom" because the offender is in the office *involuntarily* in a situation "where two individuals are joined by legal force in a counseling . . . relationship" (Arcaya, 1973: 58–59). The offender encounters the P/P officer for the first time with a mixture of fear, weariness, and defiance: "Particularly difficult is the non-voluntary nature of the probationer; this individual places a premium on the skills of the PO who must counter resistance with patience, persistence, and good will" (Strong, 1981: 12).

The sizing-up process at the time of the initial interview works both ways. The P/P officer is meeting a stranger who is usually known only through information in the case record and/or presentence investigation report. Although the record may say a great deal about the offender's background, it may not accurately reflect his or her current

Key Fact

The initial interview in P/P practice is considered a crucial time in the supervision process.

attitude toward P/P supervision. How will the client deal with current problems? Will the probationer or parolee follow regulations? Will he or she abscond from supervision if pressured or frustrated? Will the officer be responsible for having a warrant issued and having the offender sent to prison? Will this be, instead, an easy case with a minimum number of problems?

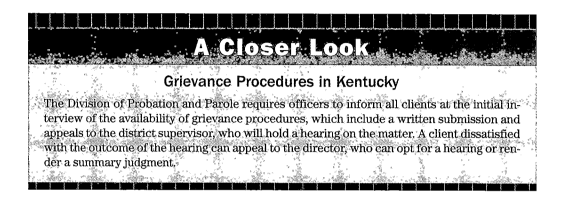

A Closer Look

Grievance Procedures in Kentucky

The Division of Probation and Parole requires officers to inform all clients at the initial interview of the availability of grievance procedures, which include a written submission and appeals to the district supervisor, who will hold a hearing on the matter. A client dissatisfied with the outcome of the hearing can appeal to the director, who can opt for a hearing or render a summary judgment.

The client is asking similar questions: Will the P/P officer give me a difficult time? Will my officer be rigid about every minor rule? Is he or she quick to seek delinquency action? Does the officer have the knowledge and ability to help me secure employment, training, education, and a place to live?

During an initial interview, the officer explains the P/P rules, answering questions while attempting to set realistic standards for a client. Several necessary directives for clients are usually emphasized:

- Make in-person, telephone, or mailed reports.
- Keep the P/P officer informed of current place of residence.
- Seek and maintain lawful employment.
- Avoid unlawful behavior, and report contacts with law enforcement officers.

When a particular problem exists, the officer may set special conditions. For example, an offender with a history of sex offenses against children will be required to keep out of areas where children normally congregate, such as playgrounds; an offender with a history of alcoholism may be directed to refrain from using any intoxicating beverages; a young offender may be required to keep a curfew; and offenders with chemical abuse problems may be required to attend treatment programs. Some agencies require the P/P officer to negotiate a case plan with the client (Figure 10.3).

The P/P officer explains that he or she will be visiting the offender's residence periodically. Officers offer clients assistance with employment or other problems. Some clients need financial assistance because one of the immediate problems encountered by a newly released parolee is finances—the money that an inmate receives on release, *gate money*, is usually inadequate for even immediate housing and food needs. This problem continues, despite research indicating that support payments to just-released prisoners reduce recidivism (Berk, Lenihan, and Rossi, 1980). In Texas, an inmate receives $50 and a bus ticket and an additional $50 upon reporting to the parole office. A parolee may have some funds as a result of prison work, but wages are well below that received on the outside, and some jurisdictions require that any funds possessed by an inmate be used to help pay for his or her incarceration. The P/P officer may refer the client to a public or private agency or a halfway house.

An additional issue in placing parolees is the statute requiring notification of local officials and sometimes neighbors when certain offenders plan to live in their community

ATTACHMENT

CASE PLANNING SHEET

PAGE ___1___

NAME: Jim Donovan _____ CASE NO.____35165____ DATE: July 1, 2007 _____

SUPERVISION LEVEL: Medium _____

NEGOTIATED CASE PLAN

Area of Concern	Objective	Plan of Action	Completion Date–Initial
Criminogenic Needs:			
1. Attitudes	1. To improve his thinking & behavior by participating in & completing the recommended cognitive skills program.	1. Jim will actively participate & complete the cognitive skills program. PO will refer Jim to the PO currently facilitating the group & will determine when the next opening is available. Once Jim begins group, PO will verify attendance with the PO facilitating group a minimum of one time per month.	1. By 7/07
2. Peer Associations	2. To develop relationships with individuals who have no criminal involvements.	2. Jim will return to his health club & will go 3 times per week. Jim will also begin volunteering at the local YMCA 1 time per week for approximately 4 hours. PO will verify this with the director of the YMCA once per month.	2. By 08/31/07
Court-Ordered Conditions:			
3. Employment	3. To improve job skills and obtain employment within one month.	3. PO will refer to DVR to address job skills and training. PO will verify Jim's follow-through. PO will refer to job services for immediate job Jim should have job within four weeks or be able to justify failure.	3. By 8/01/07
4. Drug Usage	4. To remain drug free for three months.	4. PO will refer Jim to mental health for substance abuse evaluation and to follow their recommendations for treatment. PO will verify with mental health periodically to ensure compliance. Jim must arrange first appt. within one week. PO will collect random UA's.	4. By 07/04/07

SIGNATURE: _____   AGENT SIGNATURE: _____

FIGURE 10.3 *Negotiated Case Plan, Wyoming*

(more than 35 states currently have such legislation). In some highly publicized cases, officials have been unable to provide housing for sex offenders, particularly when their crimes involved children or violence.

Initial Parole Interview in New York.   As the name implies, this is the first major interview between the parole officer responsible for the supervision of the case and the newly released parolee. If the arrival report is taken by the officer who will supervise the case, it may be combined with the initial interview. It is at this time that the officer initiates a counseling or casework relationship with the parolee. Because the parole officer is endeavoring to establish this relationship with individuals whose knowledge of and acceptance of parole vary to a great degree, the interview must be planned and handled with casework skills. There are those whose attitudes toward parole are based on prejudice, doubt, and fear brought about by rumors. With this group, only patience and skill will overcome the hostility and resistance to a working relationship.

This is the interview on which the planning for future supervision of the parolee will be based, so it is important that the parole officer prepare for it by studying all the pertinent information contained in the case folder. It is also important that this interview be well planned, unhurried, and without interference, if possible, because it is the key to the future of the case.

The parole officer undertakes the initial interview with four major objectives in mind:

1. Establish a casework relationship with the parolee.
2. Secure the parolee's participation in an analysis of his or her problems.
3. Make constructive suggestions that will give the parolee "something to do" toward beginning the overall parole program.
4. Leave the parolee with some positive assurance of what there is to look forward to as the parole period progresses.

The initial interview will vary with the needs and problems, both immediate and long range, of each individual case. Several areas would have been addressed during the parolee's arrival report, if it was conducted at an earlier time; in that case, the items should now be discussed further to ascertain if there are any continuing or additional problems and to learn whether the parolee's situation has changed. The following items are presented as a general guide to areas that the parole officer might want to cover in conducting his or her initial interview with the parolee:

- *Description of the parolee.* At this time, the parolee's physical appearance should be updated from the time of his arrival report, with any particular changes such as mode of dress and attitude noted. It should be borne in mind that an individual's habit of dress and mannerisms often offer nonverbal communication that can tell much about how a person regards him- or herself. (From time to time during the parolee's period of supervision, the officer should note whether there are any significant changes in the parolee's mode of dress and mannerisms, as these may signal changes in the parolee's self-image or adjustment pattern.)
- *Analysis of any problems and the early casework process.* In conducting an initial interview, the officer is expected to encourage the parolee's participation in discussion of his or her problems and goals. This discussion should be based on information contained in the parolee's folder, other available knowledge about the parolee, and the parolee's input.

There should be a discussion of the parole program. Both the residence and employment aspects of the program should be carefully reviewed to ascertain that they are as approved, and the officer should take pains to fill in any information regarding the residence and employment that may otherwise be missing in the reports. Care should be exercised to make sure any questions or concerns the parolee has regarding the program are addressed. The parole officer should ensure that the parolee understands the employment program; if necessary, arrangements should be made for the parolee to report to the employer. The parolee's prompt reporting to a prospective employer or employment program is, of course, a necessity. The parolee's actual employment or participation in employment program should be verified as soon as possible.

If the parolee has no specific employment or an alternative program, he or she should report promptly to any party or agency that may have offered approved assistance in securing employment. If no such program has been previously established, the officer must assist the parolee during the initial interview to devise a plan for seeking employment. If possible, the parole officer may provide the parolee with referrals to potential employers or parties who might assist the parolee in securing employment. Information should be provided to the parolee concerning the provisions for discharge after 3 years of successful parole supervision as well as possible eligibility for a Certificate of Relief from Disabilities or a Certificate of Good Conduct (discussed later).

Before conducting the initial interview, the officer should make every attempt to determine whether the parolee has any questions, reservations, or misconceptions concerning his or her relationship with parole and the conditions of parole. This should be done in such a manner as to assure the client that the officer is ready and willing to assist him or her in a constructive manner with the problems that might arise during the time on parole. The following are important aspects:

- *Reporting instructions.* Before concluding the initial interview, the parolee should be clearly told why office reports are necessary and helpful and should also understand when, where, and with what frequency to report to his or her parole officer. If the parolee is to report to the officer at a different location, he or she should be given the address of that location and the time to report. The officer should give the parolee an official business card, writing the parolee's name on the front and reporting instructions on the back; the parolee is to be clearly informed that if he or she is unable to make a scheduled report, the officer must be contacted in advance for permission to miss a scheduled report and to obtain an alternative appointment.
- *Attitude toward the officer and the interview.* In noting the parolee's attitude toward the officer and the interview, the officer should include a description of the parolee's attitudes, interpretation of these attitudes, and his or her basis for such interpretation.
- *Recording the interview.* The initial interview is the foundation on which the relationship between the parolee, the parole officer, and the parole system is established. The way it is conducted and its content are highly important to that relationship; it is also important, from both a casework and a legal perspective, that what transpired during the initial interview be clearly and promptly recorded in the parole case folder. Because much of the information discussed during the initial interview is already recorded in the case folder, it is not necessary to repeat that information, except where it relates directly to the problems that were discussed during the initial interview.

In recording the initial interview, the parole officer should bear in mind any immediate problems the parolee has and any long-range problems that are anticipated. In making this assessment, the officer should also indicate what immediate intervention on the parolee's behalf has been undertaken or is contemplated, what immediate and obtainable goals have been established for (or preferably with) the parolee, and what long-range plans for the parolee are being considered.

Supervision Planning Process: U.S. Probation.   The supervision planning process is designed to create a strategy-based plan of action to address specific issues (see Figure 10.3). This process requires that all supervision activities, including personal contacts, be structured to ensure compliance with the conditions of supervision, protect the community, and provide for correctional treatment. The linking of supervision activities to what is necessary to fulfill relevant statutory responsibilities in each case is intended to provide for efficient and effective use of the officer's time.

This process does not de-emphasize the importance of personal contact with the offender but recognizes that the quality of supervision depends on what is accomplished by a particular activity rather than its frequency. The measure of success of the supervision program is the degree to which the offender conforms to the conditions of supervision, identified supervision issues are resolved, and officer intervention is timely and appropriate.

Supervision planning begins with an initial assessment period during which the officer will obtain and evaluate information regarding the conditions of release, the degree and kind of risk the offender poses to the community, and the characteristics and conditions of the offender that indicate the need for correctional treatment. Based on the information gathered, the officer will identify as supervision issues those specific conditions of supervision and case problems that require direct action by the officer during the period and then select the supervision strategies necessary to address those issues.

The plan will be reviewed by a supervisor and, when approved, implemented. The officer is responsible for accomplishing those supervision activities selected as being necessary to enforce the conditions, control risks, and provide the correctional treatment for as long as the supervision issue is relevant.

Initial Interview in Virginia.

1. Background material such as the presentence report and the Institutional Progress Report(s) should be reviewed prior to the initial interview. The initial interview is purposeful and includes a thorough review of the conditions of supervision, the home and employment arrangements, and any situation that the offender may view as a problem that would hinder his or her positive adjustment back into the community.

2. This is the first major interview between the officer and the offender, and at this time the officer initiates his or her counseling and casework relationship. The supervising officer and the offender should jointly develop objectives and the supervision plan. It is important that the initial interview be well planned, unhurried, and without interruption.

3. The major objectives of the initial interview are:
   a. Establish a working relationship with the offender.
   b. Obtain the offender's participation in the analysis of his or her problems, the setting of the objectives, and the establishing of a supervision plan. This should include setting limits and expectations. The supervising officer should make constructive suggestions to assist the offender in making a positive reintegration back into society.
   c. Explain thoroughly the Conditions of Supervision, and have the offender sign them.

Montgomery County (Ohio) Adult Probation Department Probation Orientation Program.

Each probationer is expected to attend one probation orientation program within the first 30 days of placement under supervision (at least two orientation programs are presented each month). Probationers often have a personal view of what probation is all about, as influenced by their own assigned probation officer or fellow probationers. Often they believe there is a difference between officers—the way officers handle their probation cases in terms of service to the client, police tactics, use of special conditions of probation, and so on.

The orientation programs are meant to give each client a clearer understanding of the official probation process and, more important, to introduce them to the services that are available to them through the Community Resource Division of the Adult Probation Department. It is further hoped that the orientation program schedule will allow each client to participate in an orientation session before the formulation of case plans. With the background of the orientation program, the probationer should have more of an opportunity to discuss with the probation officer the types of needs and concerns that he or she personally has that can be addressed by programs within the department or that are directly or indirectly supported by it. It is also an opportunity to convey to the new probationers that they can have an active part in the development of programming within the department.

PRETRIAL SUPERVISION

Many jurisdictions provide for the supervision of persons on bail or released on their own recognizance, that is, without the need to post bail. Contemporary bail reform efforts can be traced back to a Vera Foundation project in New York City in 1961. In response to a jail overcrowding problem, in a 3-year experiment the Vera Foundation proved the feasibility and efficacy of a system of bail, based not on personal assets but on verified social criteria. Programs based on these findings are usually referred to as *pretrial services*. A few years later, the President's Commission on Law Enforcement and Administration of Justice (1972) pointed out that prosecutors often deal with offenders who need treatment or supervision but for whom criminal sanctions would be excessive. Programs implementing this theory are referred to by many names, including *pretrial diversion* and *deferred prosecution*.

These programs use the fact that an arrest has occurred as a means of identifying defendants in need of treatment or, at least, not in need of criminal prosecution. They generally incorporate specific eligibility criteria, a service program, and the opportunity to monitor and control the decision not to prosecute. In eligible cases, the prosecutor agrees not to prosecute for periods ranging from 3 to 12 months, contingent on satisfactory performance during the pretrial period, often under the supervision of a P/P officer or similar worker; at the end of a successful pretrial supervision period, the charges are dismissed. This type of diversion helps to remove minimal-risk cases from crowded court calendars while providing services to those who are in need of such help.

Onondaga (Syracuse) County, New York, has had a program in place for more than 30 years whose goal is to ensure no person arrested for a crime remains in jail solely because of an inability to post bail. The unit is staffed by a probation officer and four probation assistants who screen all detained defendants and, when appropriate, recommend persons for pretrial release (PTR) and community supervision. Every day of the week, a probation assistant screens those defendants who have been arrested in the past 24 hours. The defendant's prior record is reviewed, and those individuals who are selected as possible candidates for PTR are then individually interviewed. Typical of all PTR programs, eligibility is determined by using a risk assessment instrument (Figure 10.4). Referral to and acceptance of appropriate services are often a condition of these individuals' release. Alcohol and drug abuse are the most frequent problems of defendants being considered for PTR. If it is determined that there is an appropriate community treatment program and that the defendant will not present a threat to the community and will likely reappear in court, the defendant is recommended to the court for PTR.

As with probation cases, PTR clients are required to abide by individual conditions that may include weekly contact with a probation assistant, referrals to community agencies, and continuance in school or employment. The PTR unit also provides a liaison function for the probation department and the courts. PTR staff appear at calendar calls to make PTR recommendations, dispense information on people placed on probation, and gather requests for presentence investigations.

The Florida Department of Corrections operates a pretrial intervention program that diverts from prosecution any first-time defendants who are accused of third-degree felonies or misdemeanors; they must volunteer for the program and agree to abide by deferred prosecution conditions of supervision that include restitution and payment of supervision costs. Consent must also be given by the victim, prosecutor, and judge. The subject is placed under the supervision of a correctional probation officer for a period that generally lasts from 90 days to 6 months. Those who complete the program successfully have their charges dismissed; those who fail are subject to prosecution for their original offense(s).

The most extensive program using pretrial supervision is the Pretrial Services of the United States Courts. In 42 districts with large metropolitan areas, pretrial investigation and supervision are provided by pretrial services officers; in the rest, they are

Key Fact

Many jurisdictions provide community supervision of pretrial defendants released on their own recognizance.

1. RESIDENCE
   (a) Length at present address
      - 6 months or less; undomiciled 2
      - Over 6 months to 1 year 1
      - Over 1 year 0
   (b) Location of residency
      - Out of state or out of county 2
      - County resident under 1 year 1
      - County resident over 1 year 0
   (c) Living with at present
      - Nonrelative, friend 2
      - Self 1
      - Relative (including spouse) 0

2. FAMILY IN AREA
   - Family out of state or county 2
   - Family in county 0

3. EMPLOYMENT/SCHOOL
   - Unemployed and/or not attending school 2
   - Inconsistent, sporadic, or part-time employment 1
   - Employed at least 20 hours per week or relatively stable employment
     the last year; homemaker; attends school regularly; disabled 0

4. PRIOR RECORD (past 10 years)
   (a) Felony convictions and delinquent adjudications
      - One or more prior convictions for class X
        or nonprobationable class 1 felony 2
      - One or more prior convictions for a probationable offense 1
      - No prior felony convictions 0
   (b) Prior record of misdemeanor, traffic, or local ordinance convictions
      - 2 or more misdemeanor convictions 2
      - 3 or more local ordinance and/or traffic convictions
        or 1 misdemeanor conviction (add 1 to score if DUI offense) 1
      - No misdemeanor, traffic, or local ordinance convictions 0
   (c) Violent/assaultive convictions
      - One or more prior convictions for violent offenses 2
      - One or more prior misdemeanor or local ordinance
        convictions for violent offenses 1
      - No prior record of violent offenses 0

5. PENDING CHARGES
   - Pending felony 2
   - Pending misdemeanor/traffic/local ordinance 1
   - No pending charges 0

6. PREVIOUS FAILURE TO APPEAR (FTA)
   - One or more felony FTAs 2
   - One or more misdemeanor/traffic/ordinance FTAs 1
   - No prior FTAs 0

7. PROBATION/PAROLE STATUS
   - Currently on probation or parole 2
   - Prior probation or parole 1
   - No prior probation or parole 0

8. SUBSTANCE USE
   - Regular, active use of drugs/alcohol 2
   - Occasional use of drugs/alcohol 1
   - No drug/alcohol use reported 0

TOTAL SCORE ....

RECOMMENDATION

0–9   = Release on recognizance
10–14 = Conditional release
15+   = Cash plus conditional release

FIGURE 10.4 *Illinois Pretrial Services Recommendation Criteria*

provided by U.S. probation officers. The officer submits a Pretrial Services Report, which includes the details of the alleged offense and the history and background of the defendant. Of particular importance is an assessment of the risk the defendant poses for nonappearance and for danger to the community. If the investigator determines that the defendant poses no risk of nonappearance or danger to the community, he or she recommends release without conditions, but if the officer determines that the defendant poses some risk of nonappearance or danger to the community, he or she recommends "the least restrictive conditions that would reasonably ensure the defendant's appearance and the safety of any other persons and the community." Except that the defendant will not commit a crime, there are no general conditions; instead, they are tailored to the individual appearing before the court. Persons posing a reasonable level of risk are placed under supervision, and the officer monitors compliance with court-imposed conditions, such as home confinement with electronic monitoring, urinalysis, surrender of firearms and passports, and any curfew or in-person reports. Home and employment visits are routine; any violations of conditions are reported to the court, which can lead to more restrictive conditions or a revocation of release. The officer may also be called on to conduct diversion investigations for the U.S. Attorney when that office is considering pretrial diversion instead of prosecution. If the person is diverted, the officer will provide supervision, which includes monitoring the conditions of the diversion agreement.

A Closer Look

Typical Day for a Pretrial Services Officer

Routine office activities for a pretrial services officer include meeting with defendants, discussing the release conditions, counseling defendants on drug abuse, encouraging them to maintain or seek employment, monitoring the submission of urine specimens, and reminding defendants of their next court date. Also, officers contact contract agencies to monitor attendance at drug treatment or mental health programs. In addition, officers speak with third-party custodians to ensure that defendants are abiding by release conditions. Another role of the pretrial services officer is to educate defendants on the court process. Sometimes defendants think every time they appear in court, they are going to jail. Pretrial services officers explain the process—which may include a preliminary hearing, grand jury indictment, or arraignment—the role of the officer in preparing the presentence report, the sentencing hearing, and the possibility of self-surrender if a prison sentence is imposed. Knowing the process helps defendants alleviate some of their fears.

While completing routine paperwork, meeting with defendants, and handling phone calls, the pretrial services officer may receive a call that a new arrest has been made and the defendant needs to be interviewed in the marshal's cell block. At that time, the officer stops what he or she is doing and proceeds to the cell block to interview the defendant, conduct an investigation, and prepare a report for the defendant's initial appearance (Wolf, 1997: 23).

Ongoing Supervision

Offenders are usually relieved to be out of the office after their first visit but generally leave with mixed feelings. If the officer has been warm, concerned, and helpful, positive feelings will predominate, but if the officer was not sensitive to the attitude conveyed and did not evince a feeling of acceptance, negative feelings will predominate. Claude Mangrum (1972: 48) notes that "there is nothing necessarily incompatible between warmth and acceptance and firm enforcement of the laws of the land. We must take whatever corrective measures are necessary, but these must not permit us to demean the dignity of the individual."

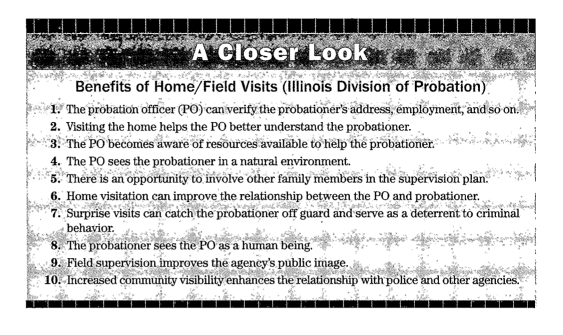

A Closer Look

Benefits of Home/Field Visits (Illinois Division of Probation)

1. The probation officer (PO) can verify the probationer's address, employment, and so on.
2. Visiting the home helps the PO better understand the probationer.
3. The PO becomes aware of resources available to help the probationer.
4. The PO sees the probationer in a natural environment.
5. There is an opportunity to involve other family members in the supervision plan.
6. Home visitation can improve the relationship between the PO and probationer.
7. Surprise visits can catch the probationer off guard and serve as a deterrent to criminal behavior.
8. The probationer sees the PO as a human being.
9. Field supervision improves the agency's public image.
10. Increased community visibility enhances the relationship with police and other agencies.

During periodic visits to the client's residence, the P/P officer should try to spend enough time to be able to relate to the client and the client's family. The home visit provides an opportunity to meet family members and interpret the role of the P/P agency to them, and the worker should leave a business card and invite inquiries for information or help. The home visit also provides an opportunity to ensure spouse or child abuse is not a problem.

When visiting the home, it is incumbent on the officer to try to protect the confidentiality inherent in each case. Officers do not advertise their business or draw unnecessary attention to the visit to a client's home. Florida advises its correctional probation officers: "In order to help maintain the confidentiality of the P/P status of offenders under supervision, unmarked vehicles shall be used by officers. Correspondence shall be sent in envelopes that do not contain references to the Department of Corrections or P/P Services. Notes left at an offender's residence should be done with discretion to avoid broadcasting the status of the offender to others who may have access to the note." In many cases, the client's P/P status is known to neighbors, and the officer may be a familiar figure in the neighborhood. A client or the client's family may escort the

A Closer Look

Home Visits by Colorado Parole Officers (POs)

Home visits are conducted to do the following:

- Confirm parolees' residence locations.
- Identify conditions in which parolees live and potential problems that may exist.
- Acquaint POs with parolees' household relationships.
- Provide POs with opportunities to enforce conditions of supervision, issue lawful directives, advise and counsel parolees.
- Provide POs with opportunities to scrutinize parolees' residence for contraband.
- Provide POs with opportunities to collect urine specimens from parolees.
- Address any other purpose deemed appropriate for case supervision.

A Closer Look

Quarterly Summary

3/9/06 Office report.

3/23/06 Failed to report.

3/30/06 Home visit. Mother and aunt seen.

4/6/06 Failed to report. Notice sent, giving 48 hours to report.

4/9/06 Reported.

4/13/06 Failed to report.

4/20/06 Home visit. Offender and aunt seen.

4/27/06 Reported.

5/1/06 Contact made with Community Settlement.

5/11/06 Reported.

5/25/06 Reported.

During March and April, attempts were made to get the offender to look for work. Early in March, he reported that he had a temporary job as a truck driver and believed that because of this he did not have to report. I corrected this idea and emphasized the importance of keeping his appointments. He had little to say but seemed amenable to conforming. The failure to report in April was excused because of illness.

During home visits, the mother reported that the offender is keeping reasonable hours. She informed me that he spends most of his spare time at the Community Settlement and recently won a trophy for basketball. The aunt, a single woman who lives in the home, takes an active interest in him. She said that the offender is really very shy and needs special attention, which she tries to give him because the mother has little time to spare from the younger children. The aunt has accompanied him to the State Employment Office, where he has been trying to obtain work; however, as he is unskilled, he has few opportunities. Such protectiveness seems inappropriate for a 19-year-old youth.

I called the Community Settlement and talked with the director, Mr. Apt. He is very much interested in the offender but told me confidentially that he is afraid the subject might be getting into a neighborhood gang that is beginning to form. He has noticed that when the offender leaves the settlement, he often joins other young men, some of whom have been in trouble. The settlement has an employment service for members and will try to help the offender obtain employment. When the offender reported, I suggested that he apply at the settlement employment service. The next day, Mr. Apt telephoned. The offender had been referred to a job in a downtown warehouse. He returned to the settlement in tears. He was so frightened that he had been unable to apply. He does not think he could do such work, although it is simple unskilled labor. Mr. Apt thinks that the offender needs psychiatric attention, but this may be the first time the offender has tried to seek work by himself.

At the time of the last report, the offender discussed some of his fears about work. He speaks warmly of the personnel at the settlement but talks somewhat resentfully of his mother and aunt, who "keep nagging" him about work. It is planned to try to encourage this offender by building his self-esteem, giving recognition to his success in settlement activities, and planning visits when he is at home to deal with him directly rather than with relatives. The possibility of psychiatric referral will be explored.

officer back to his or her automobile or public transportation as a gesture of concern in high-delinquency areas.

The accompanying excerpt from a case record shows how increased understanding of an offender caused a change in the direction of treatment and also reveals the value of home visits as a means of gaining new insights into an offender's situation. The second excerpt describes an interview with an offender in jail to indicate how the officer approached a hostile and uncooperative offender. The officer guides the interview to avoid futile and repetitious rationalizations and also explores to find some area in which he or she and the offender can work constructively together.

A Closer Look

Case Notes

Peter, age 18, has been on probation for 2 months. He was accorded youthful offender treatment following indictment for an assault during which he threatened to, but did not use, a knife. During the course of our contact, he has been on a weekly reporting schedule. I have concentrated on trying to help him get work. He has conformed in a rather surly fashion and has never volunteered to discuss any of his problems. He lives at home with his mother, a divorcee, and an older brother, who is a conforming person who did well in school, has regular employment, and generally does everything he should, thereby winning the mother's approval.

Recently, Peter was arrested for drunk and disorderly conduct. He pleaded guilty and received a 30-day jail sentence, which he is just beginning to serve. The arresting officer's report indicated that he was assaultive and that it required three policemen to get him to the station. I visited him at the jail to obtain information for a violation report to be submitted to the court for action regarding his probation status. When I explained this, Peter went into what threatened to be a long harangue against the police and everyone connected with the current offense. He was in jail, he said, only because his girlfriend's father objected to him and was trying to keep him from dating her. I stated briefly and flatly what I knew about his present situation and noted that his own conduct was the reason for his being here. I asked him to tell me something about his girl, but he cut this off by saying that she and her family had moved to get the girl away from him, and he would not be seeing her any more. I asked what he had been assigned to do in jail. He replied that he was just washing dishes and it was a bore, and everyone here was a jerk. Had his family visited him? His mother had, but not his brother. I wondered how he got along with his brother. As if I had turned on a faucet, the story of his resentment toward his brother gushed out. He recalled things that had happened when he was only about 6 years old and revealed that he is conscious of his jealousy over the mother's favoritism.

A Closer Look

Case Notes

JONES, HERBERT L.
CASE # 01-CF-566

10/26/06. Defendant sentenced this date to 3 years' probation; sentenced to credit for time served in jail; fined $300.00 plus costs; ordered to pay $825.00 in restitution to Ace Awning; and ordered to be evaluated by and cooperate with recommended alcohol treatment.

Intake interview conducted by Officer John Miller this date. Conditions read, explained, and signed by defendant in acknowledgment. PSI information reviewed with defendant; no information update. Defendant ordered to contact Sauk River Alcohol Center by 10/31 to obtain an appointment for the evaluation. Defendant to report again to this officer at 10:30 A.M., 11/9, to continue intake process.

SUMMARY OF SUBJECT'S BACKGROUND

Herb is 22, a high school graduate, single, and currently unemployed. His last employer, Rydrox Corp., will consider him for rehire, but there were some attendance problems that may keep him from getting a job there at this time.

Herb was previously on probation in this county for misdemeanor theft and supervised by this officer. He reported regularly and paid all his monies but did not seem motivated to make any change in his life. Besides the prior theft, Herb has also been on unsupervised probation for DUI and on Conditional Discharge for Illegal Possession of Alcohol, and he has had an Illegal Transportation 2, Speeding, and a muffler violation.

Herb has never received any type of counseling. He has no apparent mental health or physical problems. He clearly has a substance abuse problem. He has been drinking since age 14 and using marijuana since 16; he admits to getting drunk twice per week and going to taverns every Friday and Saturday night. He likes to "party" and does not seem to do much else with his leisure time. Herb's father is a recovering alcoholic and attends Alcoholics Anonymous (AA). Both parents had previously been seen by this officer as enablers of Herb's drinking problems. However, with this last arrest, they decided not to bond him out; this is seen as a realization by them that it was time to stop "taking care of him."

10/27/06. Letter sent to Dennis Goodman, Ace Awning re: court order for restitution. It should be noted that Ace Awning has been paid by the insurance company, but because the court order says to pay them, they will have to work out reimbursement with the insurance company (see file).

10/27/06. Referral letter sent to Sauk River Alcohol/Drug Center (see file).

10/28/06. Received statement of costs owed from Circuit Clerk's office: $161.87. Financial sheet updated.

10/29/06. Sauk River Alcohol/Drug Center called. Herb called yesterday for an appointment. He will see Dr. Kim Carter for evaluation on 11/11/06.

11/9/06. Herb failed to keep his appointment as scheduled for this date.

11/10/06. Failure to report letter sent to Herb; rescheduled for 3:30 on 11/16/06.

11/12/06. Herb called to explain that he'd missed his appointment because his grandmother in Oswald, Illinois, fell and broke her hip; he went to visit her at the hospital. Spoke with mother by telephone and she confirmed this.

11/16/06. Herb reported as scheduled. He was advised of the court costs he owed. Herb kept his appointment for alcohol evaluation. Said Dr. Carter was "OK," but her tests and questions were "really stupid." He's to see her again on 11/18/06.

Began discussions with Herb about what changes he believes he needs to make in his life to stay out of trouble. The main thing he wants to do is find a job. His parents say he can continue to live with them, but once he goes to work this time, he will have to pay them for room and board plus pay them back for the car payments they have been making for him. Herb says he'll probably look for his own apartment. He will need to learn some better financial habits if he is going to live on his own, pay the court-ordered monies, and pay back his parents. Herb seems to understand that he will have to cooperate with alcohol treatment if recommended. Right now he doesn't believe it will be, since he does not see his usage as a problem. He does report that he has "only" been out drinking once since his release from jail. He thinks this proves he does not have a drinking problem. Herb is to report again on 11/23/06, after his appointment with Dr. Carter. His case will be assessed by that time, and we will begin the initial case planning.

11/18/06, 7:30 P.M. Unannounced home visit. Herb and both parents were at home. Reminded Herb of his appointment with Dr. Carter and this PO. He has been job hunting, but it doesn't look like Rydrox will rehire him at this time. They flat out asked him if he was still running around with the same people and drinking. He's pretty upset at them for not believing him when he said drinking was not a problem. His parents say it is going better at home. They confirmed that he has been home most nights but were aware of the one night that he did go out drinking. His girlfriend has been coming over to the house frequently, and parents feel she's getting on him about his friends, the drinking, and the partying.

11/19/06. Case assessment. Scored "Max" on RISK and a "High Medium" on NEEDS. Identified problem areas are financial management, employment, alcohol usage, drug usage, companions, and attitude toward supervision. Herb will be supervised at the MAXIMUM level.

11/23/06. Phoned Lynnville Police to conduct a record check. They show no police contact; Sgt. Peters said he hasn't seen Herb out and about lately, but his friends are still doing their share of partying.

11/24/06. Herb reported as scheduled. He said that Dr. Carter had recommended he attend alcohol education classes and that he sees her for individual counseling every other week. He's not happy about this but decided it would be better than going back to jail. Herb starts class next Monday, and the next appointment with Dr. Carter is 12/2/06. Officer will verify information.

Herb continues to reside with his parents and remains unemployed. He has not gone job hunting since he was turned down at Rydrox. He sees employment as the biggest thing to accomplish, while this office, in addition to the need for seeking employment, stressed the need to comply with alcohol treatment and discontinue usage.

OFFENDER EMPLOYMENT

Conventional wisdom—often a poor basis for drawing conclusions—argues that unemployment drives criminal behavior and that unemployment as a negative social experience generates stress-induced aggression against persons and more rational crimes against property. However, research into the connection between unemployment and crime is inconclusive (Carlson and Michalowski, 1997).[1] Definitions of unemployment present further difficulties: Does it include only those who were unemployed and are now looking for full-time or part-time employment? Official unemployment figures cannot include those (usually young inner-city males) who are not part of Labor Department statistics because they fail to qualify for unemployment insurance or sign up for help in finding a job. We know many offenders were, in fact, employed at the time of their arrest, but in what is referred to as the secondary labor market—dead-end jobs having no real advancement potential and paying the minimum or near minimum wage. "A growing body of literature, however, suggests that the quality of the work may be more than the simple existence of a job in the employment-crime relationship" (Henderson, 2004: 84). Under such conditions, explanations of crime may fit the classical model: a rational response to one's financial condition. Criminal involvement by persons in the secondary job market could also be explained by social control theory (discussed in Chapter 8): little stake in conforming behavior. In other words, persons who value their employment would be reluctant to engage in behavior that could jeopardize it. "This would suggest that simply forcing former inmates to obtain a job, particularly low paying unskilled employment, upon release may not be enough to prevent them from coming back to prison" (Henderson, 2004: 92).

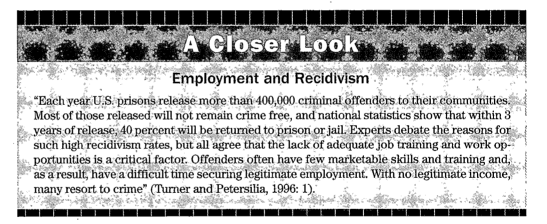

A Closer Look

Employment and Recidivism

"Each year U.S. prisons release more than 400,000 criminal offenders to their communities. Most of those released will not remain crime free, and national statistics show that within 3 years of release, 40 percent will be returned to prison or jail. Experts debate the reasons for such high recidivism rates, but all agree that the lack of adequate job training and work opportunities is a critical factor. Offenders often have few marketable skills and training and, as a result, have a difficult time securing legitimate employment. With no legitimate income, many resort to crime" (Turner and Petersilia, 1996: 1).

There are additional problems with the employment-crime hypothesis:

The observed relationship between criminality and unemployment has been explained in different ways. Some researchers have proposed that there is a *causal relationship* between unemployment and crime, while analysts have agreed that unemployment and recidivism are highly correlated only because each is associated with another factor (e.g., the influence of family members or a decision to "go straight"), which induced widespread behavioral change. Whatever the explanation, unemployment and recidivism are often closely related. (Toborg et al., 1978: 2)

Thus, the variable of *employment* may not be the cause of the variable *go straight*, but both variables may actually be dependent on the (independent) variable *motivation*. In other words, whatever it is that motivates an offender to seek and maintain gainful employment (the P/P officer?) also tends to motivate that offender to avoid criminal behavior.

Nevertheless, the securing and maintaining of employment or training for employment have been considered crucial aspects of P/P supervision: "Perhaps the greatest

---

[1]Indeed, one research effort found that juveniles who were gainfully employed had a *greater* chance of involvement in delinquency (Cullen, Williams, and Wright, 1997).

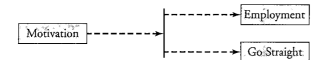

single factor influencing the quality of life of parolees in their communities is the ability to secure and maintain employment" (Davidoff-Kroop, 1983: 1). Many believe that a relationship exists between successful employment and avoidance of further legal difficulties. A study in California revealed that unemployment and underemployment are closely associated with recidivism (Grogger, 1989). Another author stated that "two parolee follow-up studies in New York showed a high rate of unemployment amongst parolees returned to prison" (Davidoff-Kroop, 1983: 1).

A Closer Look

But . . .

The central assumption in the crime-employment argument is that employment is a resiliency factor that would keep individuals from engaging in criminal conduct because of the economic and affective benefits of employment and the high risks of crime and punishment. Some researchers have argued that employment may be, for an undefined percentage of cases, a risk factor—that is, employment increases stress and unhappiness and leads some to abandon employment for illegal pursuits or to add illegal pursuits to legal employment (Krienert and Fleisher, 2004: 40).

In addition to providing economic rewards, employment also enhances the self-worth and image of the client; however, parolees and probationers "who are often undereducated and with few skills learn that finding work is problematical and frustrating" (Davidoff-Kroop, 1983: 1). The employment problem for parolees is often a great deal more difficult than for probationers. The parolee has been separated from employment and community contacts, usually for at least 18 months and often longer. The prison environment offers little help. Three decades ago, the Comptroller General of the United States (1979: 46) reported that federal and state prison systems have been deficient in their approach to training and educating inmates for employment. In view of the punitive shift in corrections, no reason exists to believe that the situation has gotten better since that report was published—20 years after the Comptroller General's report, there were more than 1,231,000 persons in state prisons, but only about 185,000 were receiving job training and job-related education (Shilton, 2000).

In assisting clients with employment, officers make direct referrals to particular employers if they have the necessary contacts, or they may refer clients to other agencies, such as state employment services. Officers may have to provide guidance and counseling concerning some of the basic aspects of securing employment, items that for middle-class persons are taken for granted. For example, officers will emphasize the need to be on time for interviews (in fact, the need to arrive early). They will help to fill out applications or help the client to prepare for this aspect of the job search. Some officers may use role playing to accustom clients to job interview situations and discuss the importance of good grooming and what type of clothes to wear to an interview.

Key Fact

Offender employment is often seen as the key to P/P success, but lack of skills and a criminal record are significant impediments.

Mock Job Fairs

In an effort to deal with the chronic problem of offender unemployment, the state of Texas initiated a prison-based program—Project Re-Enterprise—centering on a mock job fair that enables inmates to hone their job-seeking skills while enabling employers to perform a public service and become familiar with a potential labor pool. The inmates chosen for the program are within 60 days of their return to the community, and the program enlists the

Skills Shop

The Alameda County, California, Probation Department operates a multifaceted approach to aiding client employment efforts. The Probation Center provides computer-based instruction specifically designed so that most participants with 10 hours of applied effort per week can learn enough to pass the various GED tests. The computer lab has online programs available to aid with reading, writing, math, and survival skills, such as reading maps, using phone books, and understanding street signs. Probation staff are available to assist in meeting client employment and educational goals, such as finding job leads or applying for education and vocational training programs. There are Internet service links for employment and employment workshops.

The first week of the workshop has sessions on topics such as application completion, appropriate attire, interview questions, resume writing, money management, and ability to cope with conflict in the workplace. The second week is devoted to an active job search, with participants applying the skills they learned in the workshop. Friday support groups continue after the end of the 2-week program until employment is secured. Newly employed participants are welcome to continue with the support group.

participation of local business leaders whose firms agree to conduct 30-minute practice job interviews at the institution. Program staff help inmates fill out practice job applications and conduct interview practice sessions. Employers who participate are not pressured to hire inmates they agree to interview, nor are they asked to change company personnel policies or make any commitment beyond participation in the job fair. In practice, "some employers have voluntarily altered their policies and practices [and] placed the corporate community in a position to alter social change" (Moses, 1996: 2). This author goes on to state, "At the conclusion of the interview, employers complete a short written evaluation of the applicant's performance that is returned to the inmate on the following day in a classroom setting. Evaluations are used as teaching tools" (1996: 9).

The federal Bureau of Prisons (BOP) requires all its facilities to offer release preparation programs "addressing such life skills as parenting, financial management, problem-solving, stress management, avoiding substance abuse, and related free-world survival skills" (McCollum, 2000: 13). Building on the Texas model, the BOP established the Inmate Placement Program Branch, which uses the **mock job fair**. Staff from the motor vehicles department, social services, and other relevant public and private agencies are invited to send staff who operate information desks during the fair. Participating inmates are required to complete courses whose topics include preparation of job applications,

Job Fair—The Real Thing

Some New Jersey employers are looking to the state prison system to find ways to meet an employee shortfall. They are participating in job fairs sponsored by the Department of Corrections. To qualify, an inmate must be within 18 months of release, write a resume, and undergo educational and vocational training. In 2001, nearly 20 businesses and organizations participated in a job fair at Northern State Prison, where 188 qualified inmates were drawing serious interest. "There's a nationwide shortage of 400,000 drivers. Where are we gonna get them?" asked the owner of a tractor trailer training firm. His company first began interviewing inmates about 3 years ago, and it has trained and found jobs for 18 since then, most of whom have done well on the outside. Many have qualities his trucking clients are looking for. "They're highly regimented. They're used to getting up at a certain time each day, doing a job and being done by a certain time. They take direction well" (Parry, 2001).

importance of good grooming, and proper posture during the job interview. Classes are presented by personnel from local educational and training organizations.

There have been unexpected results, particularly regarding the cooperating company recruiters: "They left impressed not only with the professionalism of the staff and the orderly appearance of the institution, but also with the skilled labor pool they found among the inmates they interviewed" (McCollum, 2000: 15). Inmates gained interview experience that enhanced their self-confidence and learned the importance of preparing a resume and having on hand documents such as a birth certificate and Social Security card. The personal contact between employer and inmate has resulted directly in postprison employment.

STIGMA OF CONVICTION

One critical aspect of employment for ex-offenders is the question of revealing their record. I allowed my clients to decide for themselves; however, I did provide guidance by discussing the experiences of other clients relative to this issue. Many clients reported that their candor resulted in not securing employment, but others reported that some employers were interested in providing them with an opportunity "to make it." Unfortunately, many (if not most) employers will not hire an ex-offender if any alternative exists.

Some offenders are required by law or P/P agency policy to reveal their records when applying for certain jobs. For example, most positions with the government require people having a criminal conviction to reveal this fact; they are frequently fingerprinted for this purpose. Banks, hospitals, and other sensitive areas of employment may also require disclosure. Certainly, allowing an offender with a history of drug abuse to work in a hospital or similar situation would not be advisable, especially if the employer did not know of the person's record. Many states make criminal conviction records available to the public, selling them in digital form to private Internet services, thereby allowing employers to screen prospective hires. The Kansas Bureau of Investigation, for example, has placed all of its criminal history records for the past 65 years on the Internet, which businesses and individuals can access for a fee of $17.50 for each record retrieved, and most of the inquiries come from employers doing background checks. Even records that have been ordered expunged by the courts may remain in commercial databases, affecting a person's employment, housing, and ability to secure loans and mortgages (Liptak, 2006).

The implications are troubling: Access to such records allows employers to deny employment to otherwise qualified ex-offenders, rendering the probationer or parolee virtually unemployable. With respect to public employment, 6 states deny the right to public employment to convicted felons, 10 states leave it to the discretion of the employer, 12 apply a "direct relationship test" to determine suitability, and 17 states permit public employment after completion of the sentence (Olivares et al., 1996).

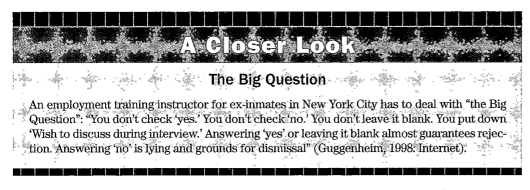

A Closer Look

The Big Question

An employment training instructor for ex-inmates in New York City has to deal with "the Big Question": "You don't check 'yes.' You don't check 'no.' You don't leave it blank. You put down 'Wish to discuss during interview.' Answering 'yes' or leaving it blank almost guarantees rejection. Answering 'no' is lying and grounds for dismissal" (Guggenheim, 1998: Internet).

An expert in the field of ex-offender employment recommends that "the employer should be made aware of an offender's status only when the pattern of the offender's behavior may result in antisocial behavior," such as a former drug addict working in a medical setting (New York State Employment Services Vocational Rehabilitation Service, 1965: 8). The vocational director of the Osborne Association, a prison reform group, goes on to state: "We do not lie about the individual's record, but because of the prejudice that employers may have, we try to postpone complete revelation until the employer has had a chance to try out the offender on the job" (1965: 8).

Richard Schwartz and Jerome Skolnick (1962) studied the effects of a criminal record on the employment opportunities of unskilled workers. Four employment folders were prepared, which were the same in all respects except for the criminal record of the applicant:

1. One of the folders indicated that the applicant had been convicted and sentenced for assault.
2. Another noted that he had been tried for assault and acquitted.
3. The next again showed that he was tried for assault and acquitted, but it contained a letter from the judge certifying the finding of not guilty.
4. One folder made no mention of any criminal record.

The study involved 100 employers who were divided into units of 25, with each group being shown one of the four folders on the mistaken belief that they were actually considering a real job applicant:

- Of the employers shown the "no record" folder, 36 percent gave positive responses.
- Of the employers shown the "acquittal" folder with the judge's letter, 24 percent expressed an interest in the application.
- Of the employers shown the "acquittal" folder without the judge's letter, 12 percent expressed an interest in the applicant.
- Of the employers shown the "conviction" folder, only 4 percent expressed interest in the applicant.

Key Fact

Most employers will not knowingly hire a probationer or parolee whose criminal record is often available on the Internet.

Because most persons on P/P are unskilled, the ramifications of these findings are obvious. In addition, "legal precedent established under 'negligent hiring law' explicitly states that employers must demonstrate 'reasonable care' in the selection of employees or the employer may be held liable for acts of violence or loss of property caused by an employee against a customer or fellow employee." Legal considerations, therefore, exercise a negative incentive to employ ex-offenders (Pager, 2006: 511).

A study (Pager, 2003) to test the effect of a "negative credential" impact of a criminal record on employment opportunity used four 23-year-old college students, two white and two black. They applied for 350 entry-level positions requiring no education greater than high school and no previous experience. The four rotated presenting themselves as having a felony conviction for possession of drugs with intent to sell. The research revealed that race continues to play a dominant role in shaping employment opportunity that is equal to or greater than the impact of a criminal record: 34 percent of white applicants without a criminal record got callbacks, as opposed to 17 percent of whites with a record; among blacks without a criminal record, only 14 percent received callbacks, compared with 5 percent with a record.

One extensive research effort revealed that "in terms of employer willingness to hire ex-offenders, fewer than 40 percent of all employers claim that they would definitely or probably hire ex-offenders into their most recently filled non-college job. This figure stands in sharp contrast to their general willingness to hire other groups of workers that are commonly stigmatized, such as welfare recipients, applicants with a GED instead of high school diploma, or applicants with spotty work histories" (Holzer, Raphael, and Stoll, 2002: 4).

In an effort to minimize the legal harm caused by a criminal record, some states have removed various statutory restrictions on gaining licenses necessary for employment, and a few have even enacted "fair employment" laws for ex-offenders. New York, for example, prohibits the denial of employment or license because of a conviction unless there is a "direct relationship" between the conviction and the specific employment or license or it involves an "unreasonable risk" to persons or property. A direct relationship requires a showing that the nature of the criminal conduct for which the person was convicted has a direct bearing on the fitness or ability to carry out duties or responsibilities related to the employment or license. The statute requires that a public or private employer provide, on request, a written statement setting forth the reasons for a denial of license or employment and provides for enforcement by the New York State Commission on Human Rights. Yet, in New York, a person with a criminal conviction cannot obtain a license for employment as a barber, a trade often learned in prison (New York State Bar Association, 2006). The Federal Bonding Program, which is administered through state employment services agencies, has a long-standing program that provides bonding for probationers and parolees without any cost to either the employee or employer. Devah Pager (2006) recommends an extension of this approach: government offering a cost-free insurance and/or limiting the liability of employers who employ ex-offenders.

A Closer Look

Learning Futility

Abandoned as an infant and raised in foster homes, a New York State inmate spent hundreds of hours learning to be a barber. When he was paroled, however, he was denied a state barber's license because he lacked "good moral character," as evidenced by his robbery conviction. For years he fought unsuccessfully for his license; finally succumbing to AIDS at age 40 (Haberman, 2005).

While this data is anecdotal, while I was a parole officer, I found offenders who were violent (e.g., armed robbers) more aggressive and successful at finding and maintaining satisfactory employment than those who were "sneaks" (e.g., burglars). And there were employers who had such positive experiences with parolees that they sought them out from parole officers. Hiring a parolee meant the employer had someone to complain to if there were problems and the employee had a strong incentive to do a good job. Employers understood that parolees had more to lose—a minor theft by a parolee could cause his or her return to prison, whereas a regular employee has no corresponding concern because prosecution is unlikely. And I remember "Jake," a fearsome-looking and physically imposing parolee who was able to get a service station job for the graveyard (midnight to 8 A.M.) shift. When one of his patrons drew a revolver and demanded money, Jake explained his situation. He couldn't hand over the money without a fight because no one would believe him and there was not enough money in the cash register to risk a murder rap. Then Jake informed the would-be robber that if his first shot did not kill him, Jake would take him apart. The man thought for few seconds and drove off. Jake took down the license plate number and called the police—the car had been stolen.

States vary in the method and extent to which they provide relief from disabilities incurred by probationers and parolees. Some states have adopted automatic restoration procedures on satisfactory completion of P/P supervision; many states also have statutes designed to restore forfeited rights, although they may be subjected to restrictive interpretation in licensing and occupational areas. In Georgia, the right to vote is automatically restored to offenders who have completed their sentences, and the Georgia Board of Pardons and Paroles automatically considers restoring civil and political rights to parolees upon discharge from supervision. Pardon is another method, although its use is generally limited: Some states, such as Missouri, have limited forms of pardon that restore certain rights (discussed in Chapter 7); in New York, the judiciary and parole board have the power to restore certain rights through the granting of a "relief from disabilities."

With respect to voting rights, 48 states deny prisoners the right to vote, whereas 13 states ban some felons either conditionally or permanently from voting. For instance, Arizona and Maryland permanently ban twice-convicted felons from voting, whereas Delaware bans felons from voting until 5 years after they have completed their sentences. There are 7 states that impose lifetime disenfranchisement on anyone convicted of a felony; 22 states permit felons on probation to vote ("Court Orders Trial on Ban of Voting by Felons," 2003; Lewin, 1998; Sengupta, 2000; Zielbauer, 2001).

A Closer Look

New York State Relief from Civil Disabilities

I. Certificates of Relief from Disabilities

a. *Effect of a Certificate of Relief.* A Certificate of Relief removes any legal bar of disability imposed as a result of conviction of the crime or crimes specified in the certificate, although specific disabilities (such as those relating to weapon possession) may be listed as exceptions by the Board of Parole. In addition, by law the Certificate of Relief may not enable an individual to retain or be eligible for public office. Although removing legal bars does restore to the certificate holder the right to apply, it does not compel the granting of employment or license or prevent the potential employer or licensing agency from taking the criminal record into consideration. Possession of a certificate does not authorize an individual to deny that he or she has ever been convicted of a crime.

b. *Eligibility.* A Certificate of Relief may be issued by the Board of Parole to any eligible offender who has been committed to an institution under the jurisdiction of the New York State Department of Correctional Services. The Board of Parole may also issue a Certificate of Relief to an eligible offender who has been convicted in any other jurisdiction and who now resides in New York State. By law an eligible offender is defined as one who has not been convicted more than once of a felony. (Two or more felony convictions stemming from the same indictment count as one conviction. Two or more convictions stemming from two or more separate indictments filed in the same court prior to conviction under any of them count as one conviction.) A plea or a verdict of guilty for which the sentence or the execution of sentence has been suspended or for which a sentence of probation, conditional discharge, or unconditional discharge has been imposed shall be deemed to be a conviction. (It should be noted that juvenile offenders are eligible for Certificates of Relief.) A Certificate of Relief may be issued upon an eligible individual's release from a correctional facility or at any time thereafter.

II. Certificates of Good Conduct

a. *Effect of a Certificate of Good Conduct.* A Certificate of Good Conduct has the same effect as the Certificate of Relief. In addition, the Certificate of Good Conduct may restore the right of an individual to apply for public office. The certificate may be issued to remove all legal bars or disabilities or to remove only specific bars or disabilities. The board may subsequently issue a supplementary certificate removing those bars or disabilities not previously removed.

b. *Eligibility.* The Certificate of Good Conduct is available to those individuals convicted of more than one felony. Such individuals, however, do not become eligible for a Certificate of Good Conduct until a minimum period of time has elapsed from the date of conviction or, if incarcerated, from the date of unrevoked release from custody by parole or termination of sentence. In those cases where the most serious conviction is a misdemeanor, the minimum period of good conduct required is 1 year; in those cases where the most serious conviction is a C, D, or E Felony, the minimum period of good conduct is 3 years; and in those cases where the most serious conviction is an A or B Felony, the minimum period is 5 years.

Lifetime disenfranchisement has an ugly history dating back to the years after the Civil War—it was part of a legal strategy to keep the vote from emancipated African Americans in the states of the Confederacy. When the Reconstruction Congress compelled each confederate state to grant black men the franchise in 1868, Florida responded by denying any individual convicted of a felony or larceny the right to vote, thereby disenfranchising many blacks because such persons were overwhelmingly African American. Throughout the South, poll taxes and literacy tests were also enacted as an attempt to minimize the effect of emancipation. Although the Supreme Court eventually abolished these archaic practices, felon disenfranchisement remains constitutional (Eisenkraft, 2001).

Restorative and Community Justice

Toward the end of the twentieth century, traditional P/P supervision was being challenged by new paradigms, most notably restorative and community justice.

Restorative Justice

In the current system of criminal justice, "an outgrowth of the historical emergence of the state as the dominant power in modern times, crime is perceived as an act against the state. This approach has led to the gross neglect of individual victims, who have been seen as passive entities, have been almost completely locked out from any decision making in the justice proceedings, and often have not been compensated for the harm that occurred to them" (Niemeyer and Shichor, 1996: 3). Emerging during the 1970s as part of the victim's movement, **restorative justice (RJ)** "views crime as a violation of one person by another, rather than against the state" (Maloney and Umbreit, 1995: 43). This approach has proven so popular in some jurisdictions that entire systems are being redesigned (Levrant et al., 1999). Although RJ programs are now quite common at the state and local levels in the United States, they handle mostly property offenses and minor assaults by juveniles (Dzur and Wertheimer, 2002).

RJ is the guiding philosophical framework for a new paradigm that seeks to promote maximum involvement of the victim, the offender, and the community (Bazemore and Maloney, 1994). Instead of simply punishing those who commit crimes—retributive justice—the focus is on allowing the offender an opportunity to make amends to his or her victim (Crowe, 1998; Wright, 1991; Zehr and Mika, 1998). RJ "views crime as a violation of one person by another, rather than a violation against the state" (Umbreit and Carey, 1995: 47). Another author states:

> [T]he depersonalized mechanisms of corrections fail to deliver the message to the offender that by his/her actions s/he has harmed another human being, and that part of the offender's habilitation or rehabilitation should be geared toward making the victim whole again. The evolution of the criminal justice system in this country has resulted in a de-emphasis on the responsibility of the offender toward the victim(s) of his/her wrongful acts. Professionalization and abstract proceduralism . . . hinder the reintegration of offenders into law-abiding society. (Sinclair, 1994: 16)

Punishment (retributive justice) "may have several counterdeterrent effects on offenders, including stigmatization, humiliation, and isolation, that may minimize prospects for regaining self-respect and the respect of the community" (Bazemore and Umbreit, 1995: 300). The treatment response provides little in the way of a message that the offender has harmed someone and should take action to repair damages to the victim. RJ appeals both to liberals, who see it as an alternative to the punishment-oriented practice that has become so popular, and to conservatives, who are attracted to its victim reparation dynamic (Levrant et al., 1999).

RJ offers a new way to look at the response to crime and criminal behavior beyond the traditional debate over treatment and punishment. Instead of advocating more or better treatment or greater punishment, the new model seeks system-wide change, a new philosophical framework in which the victim is at the center: "While P/P place a plethora of educational, counseling and social services at the disposal of the offender, little is done to reach out to crime victims with services they may desperately need" (Sinclair, 1994: 15). RJ argues not only that it is necessary to bring the victim back into the criminal justice system but also that all parties—victim, offender, and community—should be included in the response to crime. P/P agencies are in a unique position to implement RJ because of their long-term relationships with offenders (Sinclair, 1994).

RJ is accomplished by means of victim-offender mediation through which the parties are given a human face:

Key Fact

Restorative justice changes the focus of criminal justice from the perpetrator to the victim.

Facing the person they violated is not easy for most offenders. While it is often an uncomfortable position for offenders, they are given the equally unusual opportunity to display a more human dimension to their character. For many, the opportunity to express remorse in a very direct and personal fashion is important. The mediation process allows victims and offenders to deal with each other as people, oftentimes from the same neighborhood, rather than as stereotypes and objects. (Umbreit, 1994: 9)

This is the basis of the Victim/Offender Reconciliation Program (VORP), a sentencing alternative popular in a number of communities, including Orange County, California, where it is sponsored by the St. Vincent De Paul Center. VORP handles both juvenile and adult criminal cases often referred by the probation department. Mediators are trained volunteers who receive cases from a case manager, make the initial call to the offender, and meet with that person and his or her parents. If the offender is willing to participate, the mediator calls the victim and arranges a joint meeting during which each tells his or her story, expresses feelings, and discusses what might be done to make things right. After an agreement is reached, a contract is drafted and the case returned to the VORP office where a staff person follows up on the execution of the agreed-upon conditions.

A Closer Look

Message to Crime Victims in Montgomery County, Ohio

As the victim of a crime, you have the unique opportunity, if you choose, to become more involved in the justice process as it involves the crime committed against you. The Montgomery County Common Pleas Court makes it possible for victims and offenders to meet in safe and secure settings for the purpose of resolving issues related to the offense.

What if you could meet and talk to the person who committed the crime? What if a neutral third person—a mediator—was in the room to help you talk freely and safely? What if you tell the offender how the crime affected you and others, and what if you worked out an agreement that seemed fair to you and helped make things right? That is possible when victims and offenders meet.

If property has been lost and restitution is owed, a victim has the opportunity to tell the offender how much is owed and then to work out a repayment agreement. Experience has shown that offenders are more likely to complete their obligations when they "put a face on the crime" and are held accountable for their behavior. It is also important to know that offenders who meet with their victims and reach an agreement are less likely to reoffend.

In meetings that last about an hour, victims typically ask, "Why me?" or "Were you watching us?" or "Do you have any idea what this has done to me/us/our family?" This process is believed to hold offenders more directly accountable for their actions—they must listen to the human side of the injuries they have caused and must begin to take some responsibility for repairing the damage they caused. In some cases, that might also include offering genuine expressions of remorse (Gehm, 1998).

Participation rates are high. Victims are most likely to participate in cases involving minor personal crimes and least likely to participate when they are victims of serious personal crime; perpetrators are least likely to agree to participate when convicted of minor personal crimes. Noncompliance with contracts is rare (Niemeyer and Shichor, 1996), and probation and parole officers are in a position to insist on participation and compliance with contracts.

In 1994, the Idaho legislature adopted the restorative justice model for its newly created Department of Juvenile Corrections. In Kootenai County, the juvenile probation department uses a trained professional to mediate sessions between victims and offenders.

"Through mediation, the victims ask their offenders questions they have struggled to understand, such as: 'Why would you want to harm me or my property? What made you target me over others? How can I be sure that you won't do this again? Should I be afraid of you?'" The department also arranges for restitution and/or community service. "Kids are learning that if caught, they can't just show up at juvenile court, pay a fine and call it a day" (Crowley, 1998: 10).

In targeting only offenders for intervention, notes Gordon Bazemore, both the surveillance and the individual treatment models ignore two primary "clients" or constituents of community corrections—victims and the community—and offer weak choices to criminal justice decision makers, placing the victim and offender in passive roles. By holding the offender accountable and responsible, "RJ does not simply seek to punish and reintegrate the offender back into the community" (1994: 19). Some offenders need incarceration, and RJ does not substitute for that need. The offender must take responsibility and perform actions to restore that which he or she destroyed—damage to the victim and loss of a sense of security to the community. Instead of rehabilitation, RJ seeks competency development—beyond simply trying to get the offender to give up crime—by providing life skills so he or she can give back to the victim and the community.

A Closer Look

Life Skills

The Delaware Department of Correction has a 4-month Life Skills Program for inmates to deal with handicaps that range far beyond the ability to read and write: job hunting, uncontrolled anger, inability to form healthy personal relationships, and failure to establish realistic—or any—goals. Offenders often lack the ability or willingness to choose ethical behavior over unethical behavior. Meeting in classes of 12 to 15 inmates for 3 hours per day, the curriculum consists of three components: academics, violence reeducation, and applied life skills. The latter includes such practical matters as credit and banking, job search, motor vehicle registration, legal and family responsibilities, health, cultural differences, government, and law. Initially, the program found it difficult to recruit students, but the opportunity to earn additional "good time" and more favorable consideration at parole hearings provided important incentives that ensure a steady supply of inmates seeking admission (Finn and Kuck, 1998).

Risk management during the time when an offender is under supervision does not enhance community safety in the long range; only offender competence can do this. Providing skills, however, is not enough—the offender must develop empathy for the victim along with skills or else there will be an offender with skills who continues committing crimes (Bazemore and Umbreit, 1994).

Instead of punishment, accountability is the goal. Instead of taking their punishment, RJ seeks to get offenders to take responsibility for the victim and help repair the loss suffered by the community. According to RJ, the most important aspect of crime is the harm caused the victim and the community, so criminal justice should be about repairing the damage caused by crime by helping victims and communities get offenders to undo the damage their crimes caused. Instead of the needs of the offender, the focus is on the needs of the victim. Under RJ, the three clients are the victim and the community (their need to feel safe/secure) and the offender.

Although this approach appears appropriate for less serious crimes and offenders, particularly when a prior relationship exists between victim and offender, with more serious crimes and more hardened criminals, RJ appears difficult. When either victim or offender is unwilling to participate or when the offense is too heinous or the suffering too severe, the offender meets with other victims (often through victim advocate organizations) rather than his or her own victim(s) as a step toward assuming responsibility

(Zehr, 1990). In some programs, victim-offender discussion occurs through video or written dialogue.

Some observers urge caution in adopting the RJ model. They note that liberals and conservatives also supported determinate sentencing:

> The restorative justice movement is reminiscent of the determinate sentencing movement of the 1970s. Both restorative justice and determinate sentencing emerged from contrasting ideologies posited by liberals and conservatives. . . . Liberals sought to limit discretion and create sentencing practices that were more fair while conservatives supported determinate sentencing as a means of controlling crime with harsher sentences that would deter crime and incapacitate criminals. But the conservative view prevailed. RJ, instead of reducing crime through reconciliation, could simply become another variation of the "get tough on crime" approach. This is particularly troubling because RJ programs typically target low-risk offenders. (Levrant et al., 1999: 7)

Crime victims' groups have raised questions about about RJ (Smith, 2001: 5):

- In the hands of community corrections agencies whose habits are offender focused, restorative justice can cast victims as little more than props in a psychodrama focused on the offender to restore him (and thereby render him less likely to offend again).
- A victim . . . while engaged in restorative conferencing and feeling genuinely free to speak directly to the offender may press a blaming rather than restorative agenda. [However, attempts to script victim participation are destructive of the RJ process.]
- Restorative processes depend, case by case, on victims' active participation, in a role more emotionally demanding than that of a complaining witness in a conventional prosecution—which is a role avoided by many, perhaps most, victims.

Community Justice/"Broken Windows"

Community justice refers to a method of crime reduction and prevention based on partnerships within communities. Some refer to the approach as "environmental corrections" (e.g., Cullen, Williams, and Wright, 2002); others use the metaphor of **"broken windows" supervision** to emphasize this linkage between law enforcement and the community (e.g., Reinventing Probation Council [RPC], 2000; Rhine, 2002) that was first applied to policing (Wilson and Kelling, 1982). Whatever the term, the model stresses that P/P "must move well beyond the management of individual caseloads and engage the community in the business of community supervision" (Rhine, 2002: 39). This neighborhood-based supervision abandons the traditional 9 to 5, Monday through Friday, approach typical of many P/P agency operations; instead, offenders who are deemed a potential threat to community safety are subject to surveillance and control by officers who have available a continuum of both sanctions and treatments designed to maintain public safety and to hold offenders accountable for all violating behaviors (Rhine, 2002; RPC, 2000). There is proactive pursuit of absconders as part of a program of offender accountability.

The focus is on crime-fighting policies that "emphasize proactive, problem-solving practices intended to prevent, control, reduce and repair crime's harm" and that "create and contribute to healthy, safe, vibrant and just communities and to improve citizens' quality of life" (RPC, 2000: 16). Regardless of the name, notes Joan Petersilia (2003), the key components of this approach are the same: It is a "full-service" model that stresses "activist supervision" by strengthening linkages with law enforcement and the community. Officers aggressively patrol those neighborhoods of urban America with high concentrations of high-risk offenders. Working out of local offices—community centers, municipal offices, public housing projects, police precincts, mental health centers, and local storefronts—they deliberately maintain a high profile, interacting with the police, human services agencies, community groups, and businesspeople.

Key Fact

Community or "broken windows" justice uses neighborhood-based offices for proactive offender supervision and incorporates close working relationships with the police.

A Closer Look

Vermont Reparative Probation Program

Begun in 1995, reparative probation, which is Vermont's statewide approach to restorative justice, requires probationers convicted of minor crimes to meet with one of 67 Reparative Citizen Boards made up of volunteers. Typically a board is composed of five or six citizens assisted by a department of corrections staff member. Meetings take place in public libraries, community centers, town halls, or police stations; while meetings are open to the public, attendance by uninvolved persons is not common.

After establishing guilt, courts follow a two-track system: "risk management" for violent and other felony offenders thought to be likely recidivists; and the "reparative program" for nonviolent offenders. Reparative probation is part of the reparative program track, and Citizen Reparation Boards (CRBs) typically use sanctions such as community service, victim reparation, and formal and informal apologies. Judges sentence offenders directly to the reparative probation program. If the offender accepts, after sentencing by the court, the reparative services unit (what was previously called a probation agency) conducts an orientation and intake session with the offender to explain the reparative probation program and gathers information about the crime, the offender's history, and the extent of damages or injuries caused. A meeting before a CRB is scheduled, and a reparative team of correctional staff and volunteers prepares an information packet for the CRB that includes the probation order, offense information, criminal record, and any available victim information. This team is also responsible for processing paperwork, identifying and contacting victims, monitoring offender compliance with CRB decisions, and recruiting volunteers for CRB membership.

Offenders are called up, one by one, to answer board members' questions and to determine the requirements for successful completion of the program or to check in with the board. If victims or other affected parties are in attendance—something that happens only in a minority of cases—they are invited to sit in with the board and interact with the offender. An average reparative board session with a single offender lasts between a half-hour and an hour; meetings are usually scheduled at the end of the workday.

At the first meeting, the board deliberates, sometimes in private but frequently with the offender present, on the tasks it will require of the offender, usually allowing the offender 90 days to complete them, but sometimes asking the offender to return after a month or two as a progress check. At the end of the 90-day period, there is a closure meeting where offenders who have successfully completed their tasks are congratulated. The board can return offenders to court for resentencing if they fail to complete their tasks.

In the absence of these RJ programs, many of these low-risk offenders might not have had any contact with a probation worker at all but would have just paid a fine.

One-on-one victim-offender mediation is not a part of the Vermont program, but the program does seek to involve victims at the board meetings. However, Vermont Department of Corrections staff, in contact with victim advocates, have had to do a good deal of work to get victims involved in CRBs—either in dealing with their own case or in serving on a victim impact panel (Dzur and Wertheimer, 2002; Kurki, 1999; Olson and Dzur, 2003).

In Bell and Lampasas Counties in Texas, high-risk offenders are visited by P/Ps wearing official uniform jackets and shirts and driving marked department vehicles (Jermstad, 2002). "By widening the community net, [P/P officers] reduce the anonymity that offenders all too often enjoy while they are under supervision" (RPC, 2000: 21). Supervision officers attend neighborhood meetings and participate in local crime prevention activities. They facilitate the formation of task forces that include representatives from human services and the religious community, in addition to law enforcement, for the purpose of joint staffing and shared accountability for curtailing crime.

The North Carolina Division of Community Corrections implemented community probation partnerships in cities across the state. By working side by side at traffic stops, riding together in police squad cars, and sharing desks at community policing substations in high-crime neighborhoods, P/P officers learn more about each other. In Raleigh, state probation officers have an office in each of the four police substations located in high-crime neighborhoods. On a typical Friday night, six POs don bullet-proof vests and work along with city police setting up roadblocks in neighborhoods known for drug problems. The police officers pass the driver's licenses to the probation officers, who radio back to the probation office where four officers man computers.

One evening probation officers intercepted six probationers: Three were out past curfew, one was on the run, another was carrying a semiautomatic pistol, and one was driving while intoxicated. Another night, they found a deadbeat dad. In the western North Carolina city of Hendersonville, Probation Officer David Oates is dressed in black bike shorts and a black shirt, complete with a badge and the words "PO" emblazoned on the back. Oates is hard to miss as he rides his bicycle along city streets, through neighborhoods, and around parks with a Hendersonville police officer. They are part of the Department of Corrections community policing initiative. By leaving behind their offices and the comforts of their cars in favor of policing by bike, the officers have made themselves more visible and accessible to members of the community, resulting in an increased sense of safety.

On a typical 4-hour ride through town, the probation officer can make 10 to 15 home visits, not to mention the contacts he makes just by running into people on the street or riding through the parks. In fact, Oates said he can make home visits by bike much quicker than he ever could by car because now he can just ride right up to people's front doors without having to park his car and lock it up. Sometimes he does not even have to get off his bike.

Many of Connecticut's towns and cities have adopted community policing as a law enforcement strategy. Partnerships have been formed with several of Connecticut's largest cities to incorporate parole officers into their community policing programs. As a result, many parole-related activities are based in neighborhood substations, where caseloads can be assigned geographically to coincide with these local precincts. In addition, parole officers often team up with local police on routine patrols. These partnerships reaffirm the link between parole and law enforcement and increase the efficiency of parole supervision by enhancing the parole officer's knowledge of neighborhood crime concerns while enhancing the police officer's knowledge of Connecticut's parole system.

For this approach to be feasible, P/P officers need to be sufficiently trained to offer counseling and/or refer clients to appropriate human services agencies. They must be trained and equipped in all aspects of personal protection and law enforcement. Supervising high-risk offenders and operating outside normal business hours in high-crime neighborhoods can be intimidating. During his years as a field parole officer, this writer (at 6 feet 1 inch and 210 pounds), whose recreational activities consisted of weightlifting and boxing, was at times quite uneasy in certain neighborhoods despite carrying a .38 revolver.

Now that the details of P/P supervision have been examined, Chapter 11 looks at special problems and programs in P/P.

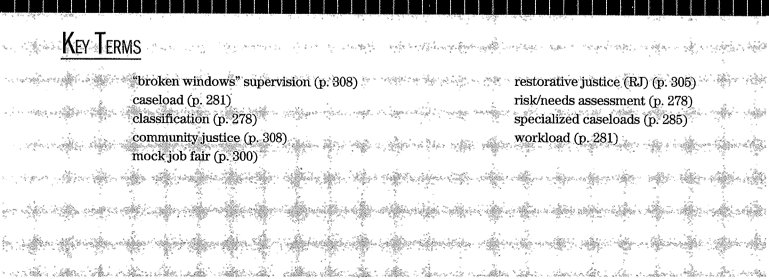

KEY TERMS

"broken windows" supervision (p. 308)
caseload (p. 281)
classification (p. 278)
community justice (p. 308)
mock job fair (p. 300)

restorative justice (RJ) (p. 305)
risk/needs assessment (p. 278)
specialized caseloads (p. 285)
workload (p. 281)

INTERNET CONNECTIONS

American Probation and Parole Association: appa.org

Center for Community Corrections: communitycorrectionsworks.org

Center for Restorative Justice and Peacemaking: www.che.umn.edu/rjp

Criminal justice links: faculty.ncwc.edu/toconnor

International Community Corrections Association: www.iccaweb.org

Officer.Com Corrections Resources: officer.com/correct.htm

Probation and parole links: talkjustice.com/links.asp?453053932

Probation agency links: cppca

REVIEW QUESTIONS

1. How did the advent of the corrections model alter the prison classification process?
2. What led to the widespread use of classification in P/P?
3. What are the two dimensions weighed by a risk/needs assessment instrument?
4. What are the purposes of classifying offenders in P/P?
5. How does a workload differ from a caseload in P/P supervision?
6. Why do parolees often encounter difficulties not experienced by probationers?
7. What are the various methods for assigning cases to P/P officers?
8. What is the purpose of the risk/needs classification system?
9. How does the risk/needs system classify offenders?
10. What are the advantages of incorporating geographic considerations in assigning caseloads?
11. What items are usually emphasized by the P/P officer during the initial interview with a client?
12. Why is the home visit important in P/P supervision?
13. How can the observed relationship between committing crime and being employed be explained in different ways?
14. With respect to prohibiting employment discrimination against ex-offenders, what is meant by a "direct relationship"?
15. What are the purposes of the mock job fair?
16. How does restorative justice differ from retributive justice?
17. What is meant by the community justice or "broken windows" model of supervision?

Special Problems and Programs in Probation and Parole

Offenders are all different so a "one-size-fits-all" approach to supervision will serve neither the probationer nor the community.

—Anonymous chief probation officer

Chapter Outline

- Substance-Abusing Offenders
- Offenders with HIV/AIDS
- Sex Offenders
- Driving While Intoxicated (DWI) Offenders
- Developmentally Challenged Offenders
- Restitution and Community Service
- Supervision Fees
- Halfway Houses
- Work Release
- Interstate Adult and Juvenile Compacts

It has long been recognized that offenders with certain salient characteristics could benefit from the services of a specialist—a probation and parole (P/P) officer who, as a result of education, training, and experience, is in a better position to provide social services and control functions. Many P/P agencies have specialized units or specialists for particular offenders:

- *Substance-abusing offenders*
- *HIV/AIDS offenders*
- *Sex offenders*
- *Driving while intoxicated (DWI) offenders*
- *Developmentally challenged offenders*

We will examine the problems posed by these special problem offenders and the specialized caseloads organized in response. Then we review special issues and programs in P/P supervision.

SUBSTANCE-ABUSING OFFENDERS

Substance abuse is the single most frequently encountered problem across P/P populations,[1] and P/P officers frequently refer clients to substance abuse treatment programs. Substance abuse treatment typically begins with detoxification with or without the assistance of drugs (e.g., the antihypertension drug clonidine, which relieves many of the symptoms of heroin withdrawal). Cocaine detoxification presents serious problems because of the patient's craving for the substance and the extreme depression during the early days of abstinence, which can lead to suicide. Medication (e.g., antidepressants) may be needed by those who are suicide risks during the post–cocaine "crash," characterized by a lack of energy and an inability to feel pleasure. Those who exhibit transient psychotic or severe delusional states and paranoid reactions from excessive cocaine also require medication. Immediate withdrawal from heroin and cocaine can be accomplished without using other chemicals, although the patient may feel quite uncomfortable; detoxification from sedatives can lead to seizures and cardiac arrest and therefore must be accomplished by gradually decreasing dosages.

A Closer Look

Substance-Abusing Inmates

"At least 81 percent of state inmates, 80 percent of federal inmates, and 77 percent of local jail inmates have used an illegal drug regularly (at least weekly for a period of at least one month); have been incarcerated for drug selling or possession, driving under the influence of alcohol (DUI) or another alcohol abuse violation; were under the influence of alcohol or drugs when they committed their crime; committed their offense to get money for drugs; have a history of alcohol abuse; or share some combination of these characteristics" (*Behind Bars*, 1998: 2).

The use of chemicals to facilitate drug withdrawal can serve to attract drug abusers into treatment and increases the probability that they will complete detoxification. However, at least with respect to heroin abusers, the use of chemical aids has some troubling aspects. Addicts typically enter treatment when their habit is too expensive to support and they have to work quite hard simply to prevent the onset of withdrawal symptoms, while a high level of tolerance to heroin reduces the sought-after high. Under such conditions, addiction is no longer fun: "Then he enters a detoxification ward and is comfortably withdrawn from heroin. Detoxification is made so easy, compared to 'cold turkey,' that addicts are not confronted with negatively reinforcing pharmacological and physiological aspects of addiction" (Bellis, 1981: 139). Detoxification reduces the addict's tolerance so that the high can be enjoyed once again at an affordable price. P/P officers should not be surprised "when addicts leave the detoxification ward and inject heroin within a few minutes or hours" (Bellis, 1981: 140).

Some drug programs use chemicals as the primary treatment or as a supplement to (or in conjunction with) some other form of treatment. Scientists have developed a number of heroin **antagonists**, substances that block or counteract the effects of opiates. These substances bind with opiate receptor sites, thereby preventing stimulation, or displace an opiate already at the site (see Abadinsky, 2008, for a discussion). Antagonists, however, often have significant side effects.

---

[1]See, for example, Mumola and Bonczar (1998).

Methadone and Buprenorphine Treatment

Certain synthetic substances—**agonists**—have a chemical makeup similar to that of opioids. The most widely used agonist, **methadone**, which is a wholly synthetic narcotic, produces virtually the same analgesic and sedative effects as heroin and is no less addictive; however, methadone can be administered orally, its effects last longer, and the high it produces is less dramatic (compared to that produced by the shorter-acting opiates such as heroin). Whereas the effects of heroin wear off in 2 to 3 hours, the effects of oral methadone continue for 12 to 24 hours. Methadone can be prepared in a way that makes it difficult to inject, rendering it less likely to be diverted into the black market.

The typical methadone program begins with a period of inpatient care during which low doses of the drug are substituted for heroin (the patient is not informed of the dosage he or she receives). The methadone is usually mixed with orange juice, which helps reduce its bitter taste, and is consumed in front of a nurse. Slow increases in dosage reduce the high, which disappears once significant tolerance develops. Addicts subsequently report daily on an outpatient basis and are given take-home doses for weekends. Patients usually provide a urine specimen before they are given methadone. As they progress, less than daily pickups are permitted. Although methadone impacts the high, which usually lasts several hours, it does not affect the euphoric "rush" (which lasts about 10 seconds). Thus, methadone patients (even those at high daily doses) may continue abusing heroin and other drugs—in fact, cocaine is a major drug of abuse among methadone patients.

Buprenorphine (pronounced byoo-pre-NOR-feen), marketed under the brand name Suboxone, is chemically an opioid but is only mildly addictive. Because buprenorphine is only a partial agonist, it yields the same effects but with less intensity than heroin or methadone. Since it is a partial agonist, buprenorphine exhibits ceiling effects—increasing the dose only has effects to a certain level. Partial agonists usually have greater safety profiles than full agonists because they are less likely to cause respiratory depression, the major toxic effect of opiate drugs (Jones, 2004).

Another benefit of buprenorphine is that the withdrawal syndrome is (at worst) mild to moderate and can often be managed without administration of narcotics. Addicts being maintained on high does of methadone, on the other hand, will go through withdrawal symptoms if suddenly switched to buprenorphine (Pérez-Peña, 2003). However, since it is a partial agonist, "in severely addicted people, it may not provide enough opiate agonist activity to treat them adequately" (Mann, 2004: 8).

In 2002, the Federal Drug Administration announced the approval of buprenorphine and buprenorphine-naloxone (partial opiate agonist with an opiate blocker) under the brand name Subutex. When taken orally, buprenorphine-naloxone does not produce euphoria; if it is injected, it makes the user feel sick—naloxone causes an immediate withdrawal syndrome in opioid addicts. It only needs to be taken over 1 to 3 days. As a result of the Drug Addiction Treatment Act of 2000, these drugs can be dispensed in a doctor's office instead of a clinic and are subject to the same restrictions on quantities as methadone. This has the added benefit of not having addicts associating at clinics while they await their methadone. Legislation enacted in 2005 allows each qualified doctor within a group medical practice to prescribe Suboxone up to the individual physician limit of 30 patients. Group medical practices include large institutions such as hospitals and health maintenance organizations, many of which have numerous doctors certified to treat opioid dependence.

Behavior Modification

Some treatment programs use behavior modification as the primary treatment method. The strength of psychoactive substances as positive reinforcers and the negative reinforcement associated with abstinence provide conditioned responses that can explain the key difficulty in treating drug abusers: finding reinforcers that can successfully compete with these substances. As noted in Chapter 8, according to the principles of operant conditioning, for behavior modification to be effective, reinforcement must follow immediately after the behavior is exhibited; instant gratification is what makes drug use so reinforcing and why it is difficult to use behavior modification techniques with chronic drug users.

Behavior modification can be used with drug antagonists to render opiates or other substances ineffective (i.e., lacking in positive reinforcement). Disulfiram (Antabuse), metronidazole, or chlorpropamide can serve this purpose for alcohol abusers. Antabuse, the best known of these substances, disrupts the liver's metabolism, producing a severe reaction that includes stomach and head pain, extreme nausea, and vomiting. (Milder reactions can be triggered by any number of products that contain alcohol, such as cough medicine, mouthwash, or even skin creams.) In 1990, a patent was granted for a substance that has the appearance and smell of cocaine and that even produces a numbing effect but is not psychoactive. The substance is used in conjunction with an aversive chemical.

In voluntary patients, **aversive stimuli** may be used; for example, electric shocks may be self-administered whenever a craving for the chemical arises. Some researchers report that the use of chemical or electrical stimuli has not proven effective in producing a conditioned aversion in drug abusers, while success has been reported with verbal aversion techniques in which "a patient is asked to *imagine* strongly aversive stimuli (usually vomiting) in association with imaginal drug-related cues, scenes, and/or behavior" (Childress, McLellan, and O'Brien, 1985: 951). Thus, *imagined* aversive stimuli may be superior to *real* aversive stimuli with the drug dependent (although this appears to run contrary to a great deal of research in operant conditioning). In any event, "aversive counterconditioning is not a substitute for support for life-enhancing behavior [but] suppresses the undesirable behavior while other modalities support positive alternatives" (Frawley and Smith, 1990: 21).

Other behavioral therapies use biofeedback and relaxation training, and sometimes assertiveness training, to prepare drug abusers to better cope with the stress and anxiety believed linked to drug use. Researchers have found that certain environmental cues activate drug cravings. These are countered by desensitization treatment: "Patients are usually first relaxed, then given repeated exposure to a graded hierarchy of anxiety-producing stimuli (real or imaginal)" to provide a form of immunity (Childress, McLennan, and O'Brien, 1985: 957).

As noted in Chapter 8, social learning theory, a variant of behaviorism, views people as active participants in their operant conditioning processes who determine what is and what is not reinforcing. The drug abuser is seen as lacking the level of social competence necessary to cope adequately with a variety of situational demands. In using operant conditioning with drug abusers, social learning theory stresses patient analysis to discover the variables that are reinforcing. The therapist attempts to discover the situational demands and their related negative emotions that are related to the patient's drug use. Treatment begins with an assessment of the positive and negative aspects of drug use and a self-report on the type, amount, and frequency of drugs used. The assessment includes a focus on the social, physical, and emotional environments in which drug use occurs. After the assessment, the role of the therapist is to enable the patient to deal with triggering behavior so that it does not lead to drug use, with the patient's own report of the negative aspects of drug use serving as a motivator for adopting more positive coping strategies (Donovan, 1988).

A cognitive approach developed by Anna Rose Childress (1993) first conducts a study to develop a set of cues that trigger drug cravings. Patients are then taught methods of combating the urges, including using a planned delay before acting on a craving, having an alternative behavior planned for this delay period, and using systematic relaxation to counter drug arousal. Other techniques include listening to a recording of positive/negative craving consequences that instructs the addict to list the three most negative consequences of relapsing into drugs and the three most positive consequences of not acting on cravings. Negative imagery is used to encourage patients to remember their worst period of addiction—a type of scare tactic.

Therapeutic Community

The **therapeutic community (TC)** is a generic term for residential, self-help, drug-free treatment programs that have some common characteristics, including concepts adopted from Alcoholics Anonymous (AA):

> There is no such thing as an ex-addict, only an addict who is not using at the moment; the emphasis on mutual support and aid; the distrust of mental-health professionals; and the concept of continual confession and catharsis. However, the TC has extended these notions to include the concept of a live-in community with a rigid structure of day-to-day behavior and a complex system of punishment and rewards. (DeLong, 1972: 190–91)

According to George De Leon, a considerable number of TC clients have "never acquired conventional lifestyles. Vocational and educational deficits are marked; mainstream values either are missing or unpursued. Most often, these clients emerge from a socially disadvantaged sector where drug abuse is more a social response than a psychological disturbance. Their TC experience can be termed *habilitation*—the development of a socially productive, conventional lifestyle for the first time in their lives" (De Leon, 1994: 19).

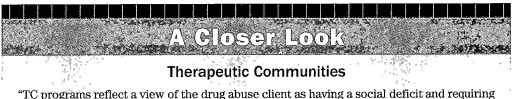

Therapeutic Communities

"TC programs reflect a view of the drug abuse client as having a social deficit and requiring social treatment. This social treatment may be characterized as an organized effort to resocialize the client, with the community as an agent of personal change" (Tims, Jainchill, and De Leon, 1994: 2).

The primary aims of a TC are global changes in lifestyle reflecting abstinence from illicit substances, elimination of antisocial activity, increased employability, and prosocial attitudes and values. The TC becomes a surrogate family and a communal support group for dealing with alienation and the drug abuse that derives from it. Its purpose, notes Mitchell Rosenthal (1973), is to strengthen ego functioning. Therapy, except for the time spent asleep, is total. James DeLong (1972) notes that there is a quasi-evangelistic quality to the "TC movement." The residences are often similar to the communes that were popular during the late 1950s and 1960s counterculture movement, except they generally have a strict hierarchy and insist on rigid adherence to norms even more stringent than those of the proverbial middle class.

A prominent feature of the TC has been the stiff entry requirement: a devastating initial interview that tests an applicant's motivation by focusing on his or her inadequacies and lack of success. Successful applicants must invest completely in the program, which encourages the resident to identify with the former addicts who work in the program and become resocialized into a drug-free existence. The new resident is isolated from all outside contacts, including family and friends. The withdrawal process is accomplished without drugs but with the support of other residents. Once withdrawal has been accomplished, a program of positive and negative reinforcement is implemented. The resident is assigned menial work projects, such as cleaning toilets, but is given an opportunity to earn more prestigious assignments and greater freedom through conformity with the program. Transgressions are punished by public humiliation—reprimands, shaved heads, or signs indicating the nature of the violation. Those who leave, relapse, and return are required to wear a sign announcing their situation. Shame and guilt are constantly exploited to force the addict to conform and to change his or her view of drugs (Platt and Labate, 1976). There is little privacy. Drug use, physical violence, and sexual activity between residents—who are to relate to one another as family—are punished with expulsion.

Residents are kept busy in a highly structured environment that offers little time for idleness or boredom. "A typical day begins at 7 A.M. and ends at 11 P.M."and includes morning and evening house meetings, job assignments, groups, seminars, scheduled personal time, recreation, and individual counseling. As employment is considered an important element of successful participation in society, work is a distinctive component of the TC model. In the TC, all activities and interpersonal and social interactions are considered important opportunities to facilitate individual change (*Therapeutic Community*, 2002: 5).

Residents are expected to be active in all aspects of the TC program. Failing to do so becomes the subject of criticism at the encounter session, a central feature of the therapeutic process. The encounter is a relatively unstructured, leaderless group session in which members focus on a particular resident (who occupies the "hot seat") and bombard him or her with criticisms about attitude and behavior. The target is encouraged to fight back—verbally—although the goal of such sessions is to destroy the rationalizations and defenses that help perpetuate irresponsible thought patterns and behavior—a resocialization process. "The style of the encounter, with its abrasive attacks and its permitted verbal violence, . . . is designed to encourage the spewing out of pent-up hostility and anger, to force the patient to confront his maladaptive emotional response and behavior patterns" (Rosenthal, 1973: 91).

The TC is an exciting, friendly, and highly moral—almost utopian—environment (Waldorf, 1973). However, it is not for all abusers:

> Severe disturbances may be exacerbated by the TC regimen and may have an adverse effect not only on the disturbed client but also on the treatment environment and the progress of others in the treatment population. Also unsuitable for treatment are candidates whose drug involvement is of so limited a nature as to require a less rigorous intervention or who—despite the deleterious effects of drug abuse—are able to function with the help of a positive support network (e.g., family or significant others). (Rosenthal, 1984: 55)

TCs have been established in prisons in New York, California, and a number of other states. These are called "Stay 'N Out" TCs. Inmates selected for the program are recruited at state correctional facilities and housed in units segregated from the general population, although they eat and attend morning activities with other prisoners. The program, which lasts from 6 to 9 months, is staffed by graduates of community TCs and by ex-offenders with prison experience, who act as role models demonstrating successful rehabilitation. Upon release, prison TC graduates are encouraged to become part of the extensive community-based TC network.

Chemical Dependency Programs

During the last several decades, the number of programs to treat substance abusers has increased. Some are profit making and others are nonprofit; many call themselves "therapeutic communities," although they differ dramatically from the TCs already discussed. These programs typically share a number of variables: They do a great deal of outreach—most employ a marketing person—and often advertise for clients likely to have health insurance, such as employed alcohol and cocaine abusers as opposed to heroin addicts, because the costs can run more than $500 per day for inpatient care. Many chemical dependency programs are located in a health care facility, which typically increases the cost of treatment. The treatment approach usually includes individual and group counseling, and the model tends to be eclectic rather than doctrinal. The treatment orientation of these programs is varied but mainly reflects a mix of traditional mental health and 12-step perspectives (discussed in the next section). They offer a variety of services, including education, nutrition, relaxation training, recreation, counseling or psychotherapy, psychopharmacological adjuncts, and self-help groups.

The typical program is a 3- to 6-week intensive and highly structured inpatient regimen. Patient care begins with a psychiatric and psychosocial evaluation and then follows a general education-oriented program track of daily lectures plus two to three meetings per week in small task-oriented groups. The educational component teaches about the disease concept of dependence, focusing on the harmful medical and psychosocial effects of illicit drugs and excessive alcohol consumption. "There is also an individual prescriptive track for each client, meetings about once per week with a 'focal counselor,' and appointments with other professionals if medical, psychiatric, or family services are needed" (Gerstein and Harwood, 1990: 171). Aftercare services are typically meager, so many programs simply refer a patient to an AA or Narcotics Anonymous (NA) group.

Alcoholics and Narcotics Anonymous

AA is a fellowship founded by Robert ("Dr. Bob") Holbrook Smith (1879–1950), a physician and alcoholic, and William ("Bill W.") Wilson (1895–1971), a financial investigator and alcoholic. Bill W. helped Dr. Bob become abstinent, and the two recognized that success in helping alcoholics was not to be found in preaching abstinence but rather in belonging to a fellowship where each alcoholic simply relates his or her story of drunkenness and conversion to a nonalcoholic lifestyle. The "listening" was as important as the "telling." The group became known as Alcoholics Anonymous, after the title of Wilson's 1939 book which AA members often refer to as "The Big Book" (it was quite bulky when originally published). Wilson, who died in 1971, was supported by the substantial royalties the book eventually generated. His wife, who was a nonalcoholic, established Al-Anon, patterned on the AA model, for the family members of alcoholics (Pace, 1988). There are now similar groups for the family and friends of cocaine users—Co-Anon.

AA is the original **12-step program** and requires an act of surrender—an acknowledgment of being an alcoholic and of the destructiveness that results—a bearing of witness, and an acknowledgment of a higher power. While AA is nondenominational, there is a strong repent of your sins–type revivalism—groups begin or end their meetings holding hands in a circle and reciting the Lord's Prayer (Robertson, 1988) or the Serenity Prayer: "God grant me the serenity to accept the things I cannot change; courage to change the things I can; and wisdom to know the difference" (DuPont and McGovern, 1994: 27). As in Protestant revival meetings, the alcoholic/sinner seeks salvation through personal testimony, public contrition, and submission to a higher authority (Delbanco and Delbanco, 1995; Peele, 1985). AA also provides "an important social network through which members learn appropriate behavior and coping skills in drinking situations and become involved in various (nondrinking) leisure activities with other recovering alcoholics" (McElrath, 1995: 314).

AA recognizes the potency of shared honesty and mutual vulnerability openly acknowledged, and the AA group supports each member in his or her effort to remain alcohol free. "Maintenance of sobriety depends on our sharing of our experiences, strength and hope with each other, thus helping to identify and understand the nature of our disease" (AA literature). The AA conceptual model is that alcoholism is a disease, a controllable disability that cannot be cured—thus, there are no ex-alcoholics, merely recovering alcoholics. AA members are encouraged to accept the belief that they are powerless over alcohol, that they cannot control their intake, and that total abstinence is required. New members are advised to obtain a sponsor who has remained abstinent and who will help the initiate work through the 12 steps that are the essence of the AA

AA Alternatives

The "spiritual" dimension of AA and its insistence on a disease model of alcoholism—alcoholics cannot help themselves—have encountered opposition and led to the establishment of alternative groups, such as Rational Recovery (RR) and Secular Organization for Sobriety. Although it is a voluntary self-help group in the AA mode, RR rejects the 12-step approach as fostering dependency and instead argues that alcoholic participants are not powerless but fully capable of overcoming their addiction (Hall, 1990). According to RR, alcoholism is not a disease but an individual shortcoming. Their approach emphasizes taking personal responsibility for behavior ("Clean and Sober—And Agnostic," 1991).

RR uses "The Big Plan," a commitment never to drink again. It focuses on planning to prevent relapses and attempting to gain insight into how self-defeating beliefs encourage drinking behavior. Various strategies are discussed to deal with high-risk situations where temptations may run high (Galaif and Sussman, 1995). There are also groups that reject the total abstinence proviso of AA and instead emphasize sobriety—drinking in moderation—such as Moderation Management (MM) (Marriott, 1995). MM is designed for persons who want to limit, rather than eliminate, their drinking (Foderaro, 1995).

program. Those who are successful, "twelfth steppers," carry the AA message and program to other alcoholics—they become "missionaries" for AA.

> [AA and groups based on the AA approach] attempt to instill the substitution of more adaptive attitudes to replace habitual dysfunctional ones. The extreme use of denial and projection of responsibility for chemical dependency onto other people, circumstances, or conditions outside oneself is an example of a target behavior strongly challenged in the substance abuse self-help group. The familiar opening statement of "I'm an alcoholic and/or drug addict" epitomizes the concrete representation that defense mechanisms of projection and denial run counter to the group culture and norms. (Spitz, 1987: 160)

The basic AA unit is the local group, which is autonomous except in matters affecting other AA groups or the fellowship as a whole: "No group has powers over its members and instead of officers with authority, groups rotate leadership" (AA literature). A secretary chosen by the members plans the meetings and sets the agenda; in most local groups, the position is rotated every 6 months. There are no entry requirements or dues—"the hat is passed" at most meetings to defray costs. Because of their fear of losing employment, recovering alcoholics were often unwilling to admit their problem in front of others, so strict anonymity became part of the AA approach.

Because many AA groups are less than accepting of persons addicted to substances other than alcohol—Bill Wilson was opposed to allowing heroin addicts to become part of AA—there are separate groups for drug abusers based on the 12-step approach, such as NA and Cocaine Anonymous (CA).

The AA approach has been criticized because of its emphasis on total abstinence and its lack of research support: "The erstwhile abstainer who, for whatever reason, takes a drink may in effect be induced to go on a spree by the belief that this is inevitable. Spree drinking could also be induced by the fact that status in A.A. is correlated with length of sobriety. Years of sobriety with their attendant symbols and status can be obliterated by one slip, so the social cost of a single drink is as great as the cost of an all-out binge" (Ogborne and Glaser, 1985: 176). Some 12-step groups "do not consider members 'clean and sober' when they are using any psychoactive medication. Cases of adverse treatment consequences, even suicide, have resulted from well-meaning 12-step members dissuading individuals from taking prescribed medications" (DuPont and McGovern, 1994: 56).

Drug Testing

Primarily because of its low cost, about $5 a test, the enzyme-multiplied immune test is the most frequently used urinalysis. According to Eric Wish (n.d.: 2), "These tests depend on a chemical reaction between the specimen and an antibody designed to react to a specific drug. The chemical reaction causes a change in the specimen's transmission of light, which is measured by a machine. If the reading is higher than a given standard, the specimen is positive for the drug." Wish notes that there have been complaints of relatively high rates of false positives using this test, sometimes as a result of commonly used licit drugs cross-reacting with the test's antibody. "Sloppy recording procedures by laboratory staff and failure to maintain careful controls over the chain of custody of the specimen can also produce serious test errors" (Wish, n.d.: 2).

The most accurate test, gas chromatography/mass spectroscopy, notes Wish (n.d.), is relatively expensive, about $100 per specimen for screening and confirmation. Drug-testing programs often use the enzyme-multiplied immune test for an initial screening and then submit all positives for gas chromatography/mass spectroscopy. But it is not perfect. "The test works by extracting and heating molecules from a sample and using an electric field to separate and identify them" (Hawkins, 2002: 47). At best, however, this is 95 to 99 percent accurate. Some labs, as a cost-saving device, "look for only a few fragments of the drug molecules which raises the risk of mistaking legitimate medicines, herbs, and foods like poppy seeds for illegal drugs" (Hawkins, 2002: 47).

Hair Analysis.   Collecting hair samples is easy and is not subject to evasive actions designed to produce false negatives—shampooing, for example, has no effect (there are shampoos being sold on the Internet claiming to thwart drug testing). Hair analysis has been used for some time to detect exposure to such toxic metals as mercury and lead. In a process similar to urinalysis, dissolved hair shafts reveal whether drugs are in the blood. Because of the unique qualities of hair growth—about one-half inch a month—it may be possible to determine what the amount of drug use is over a period of several months and whether it is increasing or decreasing. There are complications, however: The test can also be positive for those who come in contact with drugs via touching the skin or sweat of a user or by being exposed to air where the substance has been smoked (Baumgartner, Hill, and Blahd, 1989). And these contaminants can be discriminatory in their impact because "drug molecules, whether ingested or picked up from the environment, have an affinity for the pigment melanin and bind more strongly to dark hair than light" (Hawkins, 2002: 48). Hair analysis has been suggested as an initial screening method for drug use, with positives to be corroborated by urinalysis (Hawkins, 2002).

Sweat Patch Tests.   For a sweat patch test, a Band-Aid-like patch is attached to the skin to collect sweat for up to 7 days and subsequently lab-tested for drug residue. If the patch is removed, it cannot be reattached. This test is often used by P/P agencies. However, drug molecules from clothes or other people can penetrate the patch and trigger a false positive (Hawkins, 2002).

Drug Residues.   Portable devices can detect and identify vapors from miniscule particles of heroin, cocaine, and methamphetamines. Samples are gathered at such critical areas as doorknobs or desktops by cloth or vacuum cleaners and analyzed through gas chromatography, a process that separates out compounds according to their boiling points. A readout indicates the type of substance detected.

At best, drug testing can only determine that the subject has used a drug recently; it cannot determine when or how much. Tests cannot discern the casual user from a chronic one. The complications inherent in collecting, storing, and shipping urine samples are revealed by the regulations for testing parolees in Nebraska (Figure 11.1).

The Pennsylvania Board of Probation and Parole operates a drug unit in Philadelphia that utilizes extensive urinalysis. Caseloads are limited to 50, and all offenders

---

DEPARTMENT OF CORRECTIONAL SERVICES STATE OF NEBRASKA

III. DRUG/ALCOHOL TESTING PROCEDURES

A. Testing procedures shall be conducted in private areas/enclosures. Same gender staff will observe parolee's urine samples.

B. The parolee shall be asked if he/she has been taking any medications recently, and the parolee's response shall be noted on the appropriate attachment.

C. The parolee will be pat searched prior to submitting a urine sample and all objects which may adulterate the sample will be removed from his/her person.

D. Staff shall wear protective gloves when collecting and testing urine samples and performing breath tests. *Staff will instruct parolees to wash their hands thoroughly and* will issue and ensure that protective gloves are worn by the parolee being tested. Urine samples will be collected in on-site drug testing device or regular specimen cups. After *on-site* testing is complete on negative samples staff shall dispose of urine samples in a toilet and place cups and protective gloves in a biohazard disposal container.

E. *To the extent possible,* staff shall witness the parolee's urine flow from the parolee's body to the container. Staff shall maintain observation, watching for attempts to adulterate the urine sample. *A minimum of 30 ml (approximately the width of two fingers) of the specimen is required by the lab.* Staff shall immediately obtain the specimen cup upon completion denying the parolee the opportunity to adulterate the specimen with water or other substance.

F. If the parolee cannot provide a urine sample immediately, he/she will be allowed two (2) hours to comply.

  1. The parolee may consume up to eight (8) ounces of water every two (2) hours, to assist in giving a urine sample.

  2. Staff may delegate collection of a urine sample to law enforcement or other DCS personnel during the two (2) hour waiting period as long as Parole Administration procedures or approved law enforcement procedures are followed.

  3. *If a parolee cannot provide a urine specimen immediately under observation in the presence of the parole officer and a dry room with staff in the area are available, the officer will escort the parolee to that dry room. All procedures of the facility where the dry room is located regarding the taking of urine specimens will be followed.*

  4. At the end of two (2) hours, if a urine sample is not obtained, the parolee will be charged with failure to submit to test.

G. If a parolee fails to submit an adequate urine sample or breath test, adulterates a urine specimen *or fails to follow staff or law enforcement instructions for collecting a urine specimen* he/she will be charged with failure to submit a valid test. Additionally, if a parolee avoids submitting a urine sample or breath test by failing to report in as directed, his/her case will be treated as a failure to submit to test.

H. Drug testing will be accomplished in one of the following manners:

  1. Lab testing—Staff (or law enforcement if necessary) will use a regular specimen cup to collect the urine sample from the parolee according to established procedures, and will complete Attachment A entitled, "Statement of Testing Urine for Drugs/Alcohol." After collection, the sample will be forwarded to the appropriate facility for laboratory testing.

  2. On-site Drug Testing—Staff (or law enforcement, if necessary) will use an appropriate on-site drug testing device to collect the urine sample from the parolee according to established procedures and will complete Attachment A. Staff will then test the urine for the presence of drugs as outlined in that attachment. All positive samples will be forwarded to a DCS designated lab for further testing.

  3. Alcohol testing will be conducted via portable breath testing device and in accordance to the checklist technique prescribed by 177NAC 1 of the Department of Health and Human Services Division of Regulation. Parole Officers conducting tests with the AL-COSENSOR III will use HHSR&L Attachment 4 (see Attachment B), and tests with the LION ALCOMETER S-D2, will be done according to HHSR&L Attachment 18 (see Attachment C).

I. Processing the Urine Specimen:

  1. A specimen cup will be labeled with parolee's name, number, date *and time taken.* An "evidence" seal will be placed over the joint of the cup and its lid and placed in an evidence bag. An evidence tag, Attachment D, will be properly filled out and attached to the evidence bag.

  2. All specimens shall be refrigerated after collection. The limit on refrigeration is *TWO* days. After that time, the specimens must be frozen. All specimens will be locked in a refrigerator or *freezer* with limited access until being transported to the appropriate laboratory or storage site.

FIGURE 11.1 *State of Nebraska Drug/Alcohol Testing*

referred for supervision must have been using drugs for at least 3 years. Parole agents assigned to the unit have undergone specialized training and are rotated every 2 to 3 years to regular units "to avoid burnout." All clients assigned to the unit are tested for drug use every 90 days, unless circumstances demand more frequent testing. Offenders who remain drug free for 9 months are reviewed for transfer to general supervision units. Immediately before such a transfer, however, there is a final urinalysis.

Clients whose test results are positive are tested weekly; two positive opiate urinalyses within a 4-month period require that the client be placed in a withdrawal treatment program. If the parole agent believes that a client's pattern of drug abuse is disruptive to the reintegration and treatment process or if the client's behavior constitutes a threat to the community or the client, the agent may place the offender in "protective custody" for 48 hours. If the agent believes that the client should be subjected to violation-of-parole procedures, the detention continues until the hearing is conducted.

The board also has programs for parolees whose technical violations involve substance abuse. Nonviolent offenders are diverted to an inpatient drug and alcohol treatment facility for 90 days, where they receive drug and alcohol education, emotion management, relapse prevention, leisure time management, vocational and educational assessment, and reintegration planning. Released back into the community, the offender will be subjected to electronic monitoring, curfews, and intensive outpatient therapy for 90 days, after which the supervision and therapy levels are reduced. The complete program takes 1 year, after which the offender is placed on regular supervision with frequent urinalysis.

Another program is designed as an alternative to long-term incarceration for technical violations by those with a history of substance abuse. Phase I consists of 6 months in a therapeutic community housed in a correctional facility. Active participation and the development of an approved aftercare plan lead to phase II, a 6-month placement in a community corrections center and intensive outpatient treatment. The offender needs to obtain a sponsor and attend group meetings; vocational and employment training are provided. Success in phase II results in reparole and intensive supervision: weekly contact with a parole agent and frequent urinalysis.

OFFENDERS WITH HIV/AIDS

As noted in Chapter 5, HIV/AIDS is a significant problem in America's prisons. Although some P/P officers may have personal concerns, the manner in which the disease is transmitted places them at low risk. (The primary risk occurs during a search of clients who could have a contaminated hypodermic needle on their person.) Difficult questions concern enforcement of rules and confidentiality. Offenders who are sexually active place their partners in jeopardy. Can the client be required to refrain from unprotected sexual activity? How would this rule be enforced? Should the spouse or sex partner(s) be informed of the client's condition? If so, how is this to be accomplished? These are serious public safety and liability issues with which P/P agencies are struggling.

Probation officers in Kansas are advised that "when staff become aware a specific offender is HIV-positive, disclosure without the subject's informed consent may be a violation of the offender's right to privacy. In special cases where there is evidence suggesting ongoing high-risk behavior that might result in the infection of a third party, the right to privacy may be outweighed by a duty to warn possible victims. In such cases, staff should be encouraged to seek supervisory and legal assistance on a case by case basis." Probation officers and parole agents in California are warned that willful or negligent disclosure of HIV information by a peace officer is a misdemeanor. When it becomes known that a probationer or parolee has tested positive for HIV or AIDS and has not informed his or her spouse, the supervising officer may request that the chief medical officer of the parolee's releasing institution, or the physician treating the spouse or probationer/parolee, inform the spouse. In such cases, the supervising officer shall seek to ensure that counseling is provided to the spouse by the person providing the information to the spouse.

In New York, medical information, including HIV/AIDS, "will not be disclosed within or outside the Division of Parole without written consent of the protected individual." Probation officers in New York are similarly prohibited from disclosing the HIV/AIDS status of clients even to those at risk, such as spouses or sex partners. In Multnomah County, Oregon, confidentiality rules determine how client information is to be recorded.

Key Fact

The rate of HIV/AIDS is higher in the offender population than the general population and presents challenges to prison and community supervision officials.

Offenders who refuse to sign releases will have their HIV-related issues, such as an inability to work, recorded in a manner that does not disclose their status; for example, "This offender is unable to meet the probation condition of obtaining employment for he is under doctor's orders to not work until further notice," and "HIV infected clients who are known to be engaging in activities that put others at risk of HIV infection will be counseled to stop those activities. If such activities continue, the client may be reported to the County Health Officer." The Alabama Board of Pardons and Paroles requires infected inmates to sign a statement of "commitment to a course of personal conduct which maximizes his/her efforts to prevent any risk of transmission of the infection to others." If the board believes the inmate is not prepared to live up to these conditions, it will deny parole. The board also imposes special conditions to protect the parolee's family or coresidents. A failure to abide by these conditions can result in parole being revoked. Some agencies have formed special units or designated officers as HIV/AIDS specialists.

Key Fact

Legal issues concerning confidentiality are serious burdens for P/P officers.

Federal HIV/AIDS Specialists

In the federal system, some districts, such as the Southern District of New York, have officers in specialist positions who handle an HIV/AIDS caseload:

> The officers who supervise this special population frequently excuse offenders who are not able to report to the office for various health-related reasons. Contact is maintained through frequent telephone calls and field visits. And officers often find that their field visits are to the hospital. Sometimes family and friends of these offenders shun them, and the PO is the only visitor they receive. Once a hospital called an officer here to inform her of an offender's death—the offender had named the officer as his next of kin.

Officers who supervise these offenders also serve as HIV/AIDS resources: "They keep abreast of new findings and developments and pass the information along to offenders to help them choose the course of treatment that suits them best. They share their knowledge with their colleagues, presenting training programs to educate their coworkers about HIV and AIDS" (Holmes, 1997: 28).

New York State Division of Parole AIDS Caseloads

The Division of Parole in New York established two specialized AIDS caseloads to develop a working model for providing special assistance to HIV/AIDS parolees; parole officers are volunteers. The need for specialized assistance was increased by a law passed in 1992 that permits the parole board to release certain terminally ill inmates before their parole eligibility date—many of these candidates have AIDS. Parolees often experience difficulties with the community reintegration process, and AIDS is an additional complicating factor. The specialist parole officers participate in ongoing training regarding the illness and its management, and each supervises no more than 20 clients, permitting time to visit clients and arrange contracts with service providers or negotiate with service agencies. About 20 percent of the clients are hospitalized during some point each month, and many others are on nonreport status because of their physical condition; caseload attrition through death is extraordinarily high, which can have a serious impact on officer morale.

Parole officers' activities resemble those typically provided by medical social workers, including aid with securing Social Security, public assistance, and Medicaid. The parole officer works with the client's family, providing support and information under trying circumstances. In many cases, he or she must arrange for housing for clients who lack family resources. Parolees are not required to disclose their condition. With respect to disclosure of the client's HIV/AIDS:

> From a legal perspective, [in New York] disclosure of anyone's HIV-status without consent is against the law. In keeping with this, the Division of Parole's policy is that education, rather than disclosure, is key. While the Division may have knowledge that certain parolees are HIV-positive, there are others that the Division is not aware of. Therefore, even if disclosure were permitted, it would only be marginally effective at reducing transmission. The most effective course of action for the Division to take in response to the risk of transmission is to educate all parolees' families regarding HIV, and appropriate measures to take to reduce potential risks.

Home visits are often accomplished in teams that facilitate working with families and parolees. The visits are considerably longer than those for parole officers with routine caseloads. Some parole officers utilize group methods (discussed in Chapter 8) with their clients. Despite their medical condition, some HIV clients manage to get involved with serious criminal activity and are returned to prison. Because of the problem of HIV-infected clients who also suffer from tuberculosis, parole officers take special precautions to reduce the possibility of infection.

SEX OFFENDERS

The category of sex offender represents a number of different types of offenders, ranging from a 19-year-old who had consensual sex with a 16-year-old to the sexual predator who stalks children in parks and playgrounds (Jenuwine, Simmons, and Swies, 2003). Although child sexual abuse is a serious and widespread problem in the United States, P/P agencies have been slow to respond adequately to this type of offender when he (they are overwhelmingly male) is on a supervision caseload. Indeed, child sexual offenders often end up on probation because of the extreme level of prison overcrowding (Lurigio, Jones, and Smith, 1995),[2] or receive probation as a result of a plea agreement stemming from weakness in evidence or the desire to avoid putting children through the trauma of a trial (Stalans, 2004). Relatively few probation agencies have specialized units—units with intensively trained officers and reduced caseloads—to monitor these offenders.

Sex offenders, particularly those who prey on children, present significant risk factors to the community and supervision problems for the P/P agency. Trauma inflicted on young victims and resulting community outrage pose problems not typically encountered with other types of offenders. This has been highlighted by the passage of registration statutes in virtually every state, a requirement of the federal 1994 Violent Crime Control and Law Enforcement Act. Registration is designed to deter potential offenders while providing law enforcement agencies with a registry to aid their investigations. In addition, most states have enacted notification statutes that either make information about sex offenders available on request to individuals and organizations or authorize or require P/P agencies, law enforcement agencies, or prosecutor offices to disseminate information to the community at large. These laws pose problems for P/P officers who must help offenders deal with potential vigilantism as well as the stigma that presents a significant barrier to housing and employment. In 2007, several Florida post-prison probationers were living under a Miami highway because no facility will provide them with housing and they have been unable to find a residence sufficiently distant from a school

Key Fact

The category of sex offender represents a number of different types of offenders, but those who prey on children present significant risk factors to the community and supervision problems for the P/P officer.

---

[2]Although the U.S. Supreme Court has ruled the practice constitutional (*Seling v. Young*, 531 U.S. 250, 2001), statutes allowing violent sex offenders to be kept in custody beyond their sentence have encountered severe financing problems associated with the cost of providing medical and legal professionals required in such cases (Davey and Goodnough, 2007a, 2007b; Parsons, 1998).

to satisfy state law. Because sex offenders must be prevented from employment where they would have access to potential victims, unnecessary impediments present frustrations that can impact on the offender's behavior. In jurisdictions where community notification is discretionary with the P/P agency, it is sometimes used to motivate offenders to comply with conditions of supervision and treatment efforts (Finn, 1997).

Sexual assault that is most profound in its traumatic implications involves a violation of trust that occurs when, as in most sexual assault victimizations, offenders are known to victims. "Trauma and length and level of recovery seem linked to trust violation more than to many other factors. Thus, what might be regarded by some as a relatively minor type of sexual assault (e.g., 'just fondling') can be extremely traumatic to a victim who trusted the perpetrator" (English, Pullen, and Jones, 1997: 1). Approximately 60 percent of boys and 80 percent of girls who are sexually victimized are abused by someone known to them or their family—relatives, babysitters, persons in authority over the child, or persons who supervise children (Center for Sex Offender Management [CSOM], 2001a).

A Closer Look

Sex Offender Recidivism

Sex offenders are not a homogeneous group, and their rates of reoffending differ. They have a wide variety of racial, ethnic, and socioeconomic backgrounds; the majority of them do not have extensive criminal histories or "traditional" criminal lifestyles; and they differ significantly in age (Gilligan and Talbot, 2000). Studies indicate that for child molesters, the recidivism rate is between 13 and 20 percent, and for rapists, 19 percent. Individual characteristics further distinguish rates of sexual reoffending. One study found that offenders whose female victims were not relatives had a recidivism rate of 18 percent, whereas for male victims the rate was 35 percent. Of course, these statistics can only account for offenders that were convicted—many sex offenses are never even reported (CSOM, 2001a).

An Oregon study also confirmed that unlike other offenders who tend to "age out" of their criminal behavior as they grow older, many sex offenders continue to abuse throughout their lifetimes. Finally, the study revealed that sex offenders frequently score in the low range on traditional correctional risk assessment instruments because these instruments do not address many of the areas that are indicators of risk for sex offenders (Gilligan and Talbot, 2000). A study of sex offenders released in 1994 revealed that 3.5 percent were reconvicted of a sex crime within 3 years. Within the first 3 years following release from prison, 3.3 percent of the released child molesters were rearrested for another sex crime against a child (Langan and Durose, 2003).

There is general agreement in the P/P field that sex offenders need to be treated and supervised differently from other criminals. They typically share certain characteristics (English, Pullen, and Jones, 1997: 2):

- Sex offenders have secretive and manipulative lifestyles, and many of their sexual assaults are so well planned that they appear to occur without forethought. The skills used to manipulate victims have also been employed to manipulate criminal justice officials.
- Many sex offenders are otherwise highly functioning people who use their social skills to commit their crimes.
- Sex offenders typically have developed complicated and persistent psychological and social systems constructed to assist them in denying or minimizing the harm they inflict on others, and often they are very accomplished at presenting to others a facade designed to hide the truth about themselves.
- Many sex offenders commit a wide range and large number of sexually deviant acts during their lives and show a continued propensity to re-offend.

Key Fact

There is general agreement in the P/P field that sex offenders need to be treated and supervised differently from other criminals, and the focus is usually control.

Because of these characteristics, the focus in the supervision of sex offenders is usually on *containment*: Preventing recidivism is the single goal, and the client is the community. As part of this approach, sex offenders may be subjected to periodic polygraph examinations, and the rules of supervision are quite restrictive (Figure 11.2). These can include avoiding places where children can be expected to congregate; not having contact with persons under 18; maintaining a driving log containing mileage, time of departure and arrival, time of return, routes traveled, and passenger names; and

BUCKS COUNTY ADULT PROBATION AND PAROLE DEPARTMENT
SPECIAL OFFENDER CASE PLAN

PROGRAMMING/ TREATMENT

_____ You must successfully enroll, participate in, and complete a program for sex offenders approved by the Court.
Program _____
Telephone Number _____
Contact by _____
_____ You must maintain use of prescribed medications.
_____ Other _____

ALCOHOL AND DRUGS

_____ You may not use alcohol.
_____ You may not frequent bars, taverns, and businesses whose primary function is to serve alcoholic beverages.
_____ You may not associate with alcohol and drug abusers.
_____ You will attend and successfully complete an alcohol and/or drug treatment program.
_____ Other _____

SOCIAL

_____ You may not associate with ex-felons unless they are in treatment with you and your therapist and PO approve of the association.
_____ You must inform all persons with whom you have a significant relationship or close affiliation of your sexual offending history. Therapist and/or PO will determine who shall be informed.
_____ You may not participate in friendships or relationships with women/men who have children.
_____ You may not socialize with individuals under the age of 16 in work or social situations unless accompanied by a responsible adult (approved by your therapist and/or PO) who is aware of your sexual abusive pattern.
_____ You may not engage in activities that will bring you in close contact with children.
_____ Other _____

MONITORING

_____ You are required to meet with your probation/parole officer at least three (3) times per month.
_____ You are required to give your PO search and seizure privileges to confiscate drugs, erotica, and pornography.
_____ You must maintain a daily journal (including such items as daily activities, fantasies, etc.).
_____ You must participate in a plethysmographic examination to determine your sexual arousal to abusive themes. These examinations will be periodic upon the therapist's request.
_____ Other _____

DRIVING

_____ You must maintain a driving log (mileage; time of departure, arrival & return; destination; routes traveled; with whom, etc.).
_____ You may not pick up hitchhikers.
_____ You must comply with specified limitations on driving, i.e., not driving at night, not driving alone, not driving at key times, not driving with female passengers, etc., depending upon your individual criminal history and offense patterns.
_____ You may not drive with a female unless there is a specific reason, for example a prearranged date whose name, address, and phone number you have reported to your PO and/or therapist.
_____ Other _____

VICTIM CONTACT

_____ You may not have any contact with the victim(s) (including letters, phone calls, tapes, videos, visits, or any form of contact through a third party) until approved by your Judge, therapist, the victim (and the victim's parents if the victim is a child), and the victim's therapist.
_____ You (as an incest offender) may not have visitation with the victim unless approved by your Judge, therapist, the victim, the victim's therapist, and the Children and Youth Services agency.
_____ Other _____

FIGURE 11.2 *Bucks County (Pennsylvania) Special Offender Case Plan*

OFFENSE-SPECIFIC CONDITIONS

_____ You may not view videotapes, films, or television shows that are geared towards your modus operandi, act as a stimulus for your abusive cycle, or act as a stimulus to arouse you in an abusive fashion, i.e., pedophiles may not view shows whose primary character is a child.

_____ You may not use pornography, erotica; you may not frequent adult book stores, sex shops, topless bars, massage parlors, etc.

_____ You may not frequent places where children congregate, i.e., parks, playgrounds, schools, etc.

_____ Since you have photographed your victims in the past, you may not possess a camera or video recorder.

_____ Other _____

DAILY LIVING

_____ You must reside in a residence approved by your PO.

_____ You must maintain full-time school and/or employment.

_____ Your employer must be approved by your PO and therapist.

_____ Other _____

GENERAL

_____ You must observe curfew restrictions.

_____ Other _____

Client _____ Date _____

Probation/Parole Officer _____ Date _____

Probation/Parole Supervisor _____ Date _____
☐ Copy to therapist

FIGURE 11.2 *(continued)*

not possessing or viewing any sexually oriented media—printed, video, audio, telephonic, electronic—relevant to the deviant behavior pattern. And these rules are enforced by unannounced home visits and surveillance activities. In Cook County, Illinois, probation officers in their Adult Sex Offender Program report that many offenders "have expressed the view that their POs serve as an external conscience" and that the intensive supervision program "serves to constantly remind each probationer of the consequences for re-offense" (Jenuwine, Simmons, and Swies, 2003: 22).

A Closer Look

Internet Monitoring

Field Search is a free software tool designed to enable P/P officers to efficiently scan an offender's computer. The P/P officer brings the software on a CD or flash drive to the offender's residence and runs it on the suspect computer for about 20 minutes. The software conducts Internet history, image, multimedia file, and keyword searches. Results of the scan include the dates and times each website was visited and images downloaded in any of a variety of formats. The keyword search reveals such things as pornographic materials and stories or the victim's name. The final report can be exported to a flash drive for the officer to review in the office (Russo, 2006).

Research (Gilligan and Talbot, 2000) indicates that specialized sex offender caseloads provide clear advantages for supervision staff:

- The staff gain expertise and training related to sex offender management.
- The specialized caseloads ensure that sex offenders, who might have become "lost" on nonspecialized caseloads because of their seemingly compliant nature, are supervised intensively.
- The staff can establish rapport with sex offenders in order to encourage them to talk openly about their thoughts and activities.

- Feelings of camaraderie and support are promoted among officers who maintain these caseloads, which reduces secondary trauma.
- There is increased agency-wide consistency in sex offender supervision practices.

A Closer Look

Cost of Supervising Sex Offenders

The supervision of sex offenders requires an extraordinary expenditure of P/P agency resources: additional home visits and collateral contacts; aid in locating housing; enhanced surveillance; interacting with law enforcement and the community (Zevitz and Farkas, 2000). Lie-detector testing and electronic monitoring are often additional expenses.

Texas Sex Offender Caseload

In Texas, each district office of the Pardons and Paroles Division has at least one designated sex offender officer. Such officers receive specialized training and attend ongoing seminars to stay current with treatment and supervision issues concerning this special category of client. Offenders classified as exhibitionists, pedophiles, and rapists are referred to a special sex offender officer, whose caseload does not exceed 45. Specialized treatment is provided through contractual arrangement with public and private resources. Place of residence is closely monitored, and a sex offender is not permitted to reside with a past victim or potential victims. Pedophiles are prohibited from any contact with children younger than age 17, unless specific arrangements have been made and permission has been granted by the parole officer after consultation with the therapist; an adult must be present during such contacts. Parole officers also ensure compliance with the state's Sex Offender Registration Program. With the endorsement of his or her therapist, a parolee may be transferred from the Sex Offender Caseload to regular supervision.

Hunt County (Texas) Sex Offender Unit

The Hunt County (Texas) Probation Department's Sex Offender Accountability Program (SOAP) is a specialized caseload monitoring sexual abusers' compliance with conditions of supervision. SOAP uses a team comprising a probation officer, sex offender therapist, and polygraph examiner. The probation officer, accompanied by a peace officer for security reasons, makes random checks of offenders' home environments to discuss special issues and monitor their surroundings for warning signs of risk.

Sex offenders must adhere to the 18 standard conditions of supervision common to all felony offenders, which include refraining from criminal conduct, drug/alcohol use, and association with felons; reporting to the probation officer as directed; and submitting to drug testing. In addition, sex offenders are required to attend and participate in sex offender treatment with a registered treatment provider. These treatment groups typically meet once per week.

The offender must submit to and pay for polygraph testing. These examinations may be required every 6 to 12 months. There is some variation in probation conditions regarding contact with children: Most offenders are initially prohibited from any contact with children, although some offenders are permitted to have supervised contact with their biological children, but as an offender participates and progresses in sex offender treatment, his conditions may be modified gradually to allow more supervised contact with children. An offender cannot reside near a school or daycare center and cannot go to places where children are known to congregate.

SOAP offenders are prohibited from viewing or purchasing pornography or going to sexually oriented businesses. They are typically restricted from accessing the Internet. Texas law allows the judge placing an offender on probation to order him to serve time in the local jail (up to 180 days) as a condition of supervision, an option often used by the Hunt County Courts. Electronic monitoring and home curfews are also options the court may use.

Sex offenders in the program are ordered by the court to submit a blood sample, which is sent to the crime lab in Austin, and a DNA record is made. The DNA database is used to assist in the investigation of unsolved crimes.

Maricopa County (Arizona) Sex Offender Program

In 1987, the Arizona legislature passed a law mandating lifetime probation for sex offenders convicted of crimes against children. The Maricopa County Adult Probation Department's response includes intensive supervision, subsidized treatment and assessment, and services for victims and their families. Maricopa County is a mostly urban jurisdiction, with more than 2.5 million people living in a metropolitan area that includes Phoenix and Scottsdale. Approximately two-thirds of the state's population resides within the county.

Assessment involves the use of psychological testing as well as **plethysmography,** which electronically measures an offender's penile arousal to various audiovisual stimuli. The instrument, similar to a blood pressure gauge, is attached to the offender's penis and measures the arousal, recording changes in penile tumescence, when different types of deviant and nondeviant stimuli are presented. Along with the plethysmograph, a polygraph is used to secure a complete sexual history and to periodically monitor compliance with probation regulations.

Offenders begin their probation terms by participating in 45 classroom hours on sexuality and sexual deviation. They are placed in treatment groups that usually use a cognitive behavior approach and that can last from 18 months to 2 years or (in some cases) longer. Those with the means are expected to pay for the therapy. Offenders are subject to a curfew and may not operate a motor vehicle without the consent of their probation officer.

The supervision units consist of 21 specialized probation officers, whose average caseload is 53 offenders, and 10 surveillance officers, each of whom works with 2 probation officers and thus averages about 100 offenders. Probation officers supervise offenders' progress in dealing with behavioral and life issues and their compliance with program conditions. Surveillance officers make random field visits, particularly evening and weekend visits, and work closely with the other officers.

Jefferson County (Colorado) Juvenile Sex Offender Unit

Jefferson County is a suburban county west of Denver, Colorado, with a growing population of more than a half-million persons. County juvenile officers began to apply the models of specialized treatment and supervision that were being used with adults to the young offenders on their caseloads and developed the first specialized juvenile sex offender unit in the state. There is an average of 160 juveniles on probation in Jefferson County for sexual offenses: About 75 percent of these offenders are adjudicated for felonies, while the remainder are adjudicated for misdemeanors. Most were charged with assaulting younger people; about 10 percent of the juvenile offenders are girls. Two probation officers provide supervision to all juvenile sex offenders in the county. The juvenile unit is coordinated by a unit supervisor, and one officer is responsible for preparing presentence investigations for juvenile sex offenders. Each officer carries approximately 80 cases.

About 98 percent of all juvenile sex offenders in Jefferson County receive a probation sentence, with a maximum statutorily limited to 2 years. Juveniles start supervision at the highest level of supervision. They are classified within 2 months, based on their scores on the Colorado Young Offender Level of Services Inventory (general risk assessment tool) and the Protective Factor Scale (determination of the offender's treatment needs). The unit's probation officers meet up to three times each month to review an offender's supervision plan (see Figure 11.3 for an example from Texas).

PART I – GENERAL INFORMATION

Offender Name: _____

Date of Assessment: _____

Number: _____ Date of Birth: _____

Date of Offense: _____

Current Sex Offense: _____

Penal Code Citation: _____

Evaluator's Name: _____

Title: _____

Location: _____

Anticipated Date of Release: _____

PART II – VARIABLES

SCORE

1. CURRENT SEX OFFENSE
   A. Seriousness of Sex Offense
      Felony 1   ☐
      Misdemeanor 0
   B. Use of Weapon in the Sex Offense
      Firearm/Cutting Instrument 2   ☐
      Other Weapon 1
      None 0

2. AGE AT FIRST REFERRAL
   10 Years of Age 2   ☐
   11–14 Years of Age 1
   15–16 Years of Age 0

3. PRIOR ADJUDICATIONS FOR SEX OFFENSES
   2 or more prior adjudications for sex offenses 2
   1 prior adjudication for sex offense(s) 1   ☐
   No prior adjudications for a sex offense 0

4. PRIOR REFERRALS FOR SEX OFFENSES
   2 or more prior referrals for sex offenses 2
   1 prior referral for sex offense(s) 1   ☐
   No prior referral for a sex offense 0

5. PRIOR ADJUDICATIONS FOR FELONY OFFENSES
   2 or more prior adjudications for felony offenses 2
   1 prior adjudication for felony offense(s) 1   ☐
   No prior adjudication for a felony offense 0

6. PRIOR FELONY REFERRALS
   2 or more prior felony referrals 2
   1 prior felony referral(s) 1   ☐
   No prior felony referral 0

SCORE RANGE		RISK LEVEL	TOTAL SCORE ____	☐
0–5	Moderate Range	2		
6–13	High Range	1	RISK LEVEL ____	☐

FIGURE 11.3 *Texas Juvenile Sex Offender Risk Assessment Instrument*

Juveniles attend weekly group therapy sessions that are cognitively based and focused on learning about their offending behaviors, the abuse cycle, relapse prevention, and victim empathy, and individual and family sessions are held at a minimum of once per month. Probation officers meet frequently with treatment providers and attend treatment sessions and case staff meetings about once a month. Juveniles are also administered polygraph exams and plethysmographs when therapists and officers agree they are needed: Polygraphs are administered to juveniles as young as 12 years old, depending on their level of functioning and the seriousness of their offending behavior, while plethysmographs are used less frequently and are generally administered to older juveniles when there are concerns about deviant arousal patterns.

Juvenile sex offenders are subject to expulsion from the public school system, but in most cases expulsion is counterproductive to a youth's treatment plan. Careful supervision and collaboration between the schools and criminal justice authorities have resulted in the return of the majority of sex offenders to the classroom. Staff are careful not to return any offender who clearly pose a threat to school personnel or other students to a school. Probation staff work closely with school principals to establish structured schedules for offenders, but other school personnel are notified of the offenders' circumstances only on a need-to-know basis.

New Haven (Connecticut) Sex Offender Intensive Supervision Unit

The city of New Haven, Connecticut, has a population of about 150,000. It is a diverse urban area and the home of Yale University but is one of the poorest cities in the nation. The Sex Offender Intensive Supervision Unit is a cooperative effort of the Office of Adult Probation (OAP), a statewide agency housed within the judicial branch, and the Center for the Treatment of Problem Sexual Behavior (CTPSB), a private nonprofit community-based treatment program that operates statewide. The unit supervises high-risk adult sex offenders (age 16 and older) identified through risk assessment by probation and treatment staff. All offenders on the caseload have been convicted of a sex offense and are under the legal supervision of a probation officer.

The team consists of a lead probation officer, four more probation officers, three treatment providers from CTPSB, and a victim advocate from Connecticut Sexual Assault Crisis Services, whose position is funded by OAP and is housed primarily within the New Haven Probation Office. Three probation officers supervise a maximum of 25 high-risk offenders each. These officers are responsible for 24-hour supervision, 7 days per week; are highly mobile and very proactive; are in contact with the offenders on their caseload nearly every day; routinely make unannounced home visits (including evenings, weekends, and holidays); maintain communication with family members, friends, and employers; assess the appropriateness of offenders' residence and employment; search for at-risk behaviors (including evidence of contact or potential contact with children, pornography, illegal substances or alcohol, and Internet use); and collaborate with local law enforcement.

The fourth probation officer is a Relapse Prevention Specialist and has a maximum caseload of 50 offenders. As offenders progress in treatment, they transition from specialized Intensive Supervision to the Relapse Prevention caseload, based on time in treatment, stable behavior, and active engagement in the treatment process. The Relapse Prevention caseload provides heightened but less intense monitoring. Offenders move toward incorporation in nonspecialized "regular" high-risk supervision (maximum caseload of 75). The Relapse Prevention Officer receives specialized training, collaborates with treatment providers, and co-facilitates groups.

The CTPSB treatment staff provide assessment and treatment, and they often accompany probation officers on home visits. Treatment staff use a psychopathy checklist, a psychological survey, and a risk assessment instrument based on current research. Offenders are accepted for treatment if the nature of their offense and their history indicate they would benefit from treatment. Offenders who are assessed as having psychopathic personalities (this is very uncommon) are often refused treatment because such offenders may pose greater risks with treatment. Generally, an offender's evaluation determines the type of treatment received.

Treatment staff are responsible for group therapy provided to offenders. Most offenders begin with an introductory group (the "cognitive lab"), which provides treatment orientation and expectations and lasts about 14 weeks. Treatment draws on cognitive behavior approaches and includes cognitive restructuring, victim empathy training, sexual education, and relapse prevention training. CTPSB offers special bilingual groups and groups for people with developmental disabilities as well as a "family seminar" before family reunification. Whenever possible, rapists, child molesters, and exhibitionists/voyeurs are assigned to separate specialized groups. A portion of the offenders also receive specialized medication to control their impulses and behavior.

Treatment proceeds toward realization of 14 goals, categorized as immediate, intermediate, and extended. The first immediate goal is acceptance of responsibility for the sexual offense. The final goal is to "learn about, and utilize, a Relapse Prevention Strategy and an Offense Prevention Plan." Length of time in treatment depends on the individual's progress because treatment is considered open-ended; it ranges from 1 to 7 years.

A victim advocate supports supervision activities by accompanying probation officers on home and field visits, attending case review meetings, and leading the victim empathy component of treatment groups. He or she initiates contact with the victim and/or the victim's family and maintains that contact as long as necessary. The advocate provides information and raises concerns to probation officers and treatment staff throughout the supervision process, provides referrals for counseling and other services, obtains background information from all probation files on each individual supervised by the unit, and also gathers information from victims or significant others and family members about an offender's behavior as part of supervision.

Notification is provided to victims, victims' parents or guardians (as appropriate), the police, the offender's immediate family members, other occupants of the offender's residence, and treatment providers. For the highest-risk cases, including most unit cases, the team may decide to include notification to neighbors, local schools, employers, and organizations with which the offender is involved. Notification is a probation responsibility but often involves both the probation officer and the victim advocate. Notification is also regarded as an important opportunity for public education about sex offenders. The advocate and/or the officers hold public meetings in advance of notification when possible.

Orange County (California) Probation Department Adult Sex Offender Unit

California's Orange County, with a population of nearly 3 million, is located south of Los Angeles. The Adult Sex Offender Unit (ASOU) has a staff of 11 officers: 1 supervisor, 8 deputy probation officers who supervise approximately 40 high-risk cases each, and 2 deputy probation officers who conduct assessments of incoming cases, classifying each into low-, medium-, and high-risk levels. Risk is reassessed every 6 months, and low-risk cases can be transitioned to regular supervision caseloads. Officers have received specialized training.

Supervision includes at least three in-person contacts per month, plus evening and weekend surveillance activities. All information provided by offenders is verified, and there is ongoing contact with victims to ensure no-contact orders are being obeyed. Specialized sex offender treatment is mandatory, and there is ongoing coordination with treatment providers.

Probationers must provide restitution for victims' medical and/or psychological treatment and reimbursement for the cost incurred by police in gathering forensic evidence. They can be required to submit to AIDS and DNA testing and to undergo periodic polygraph examinations. They are prohibited from viewing or possessing sexually explicit materials or any other exposures that act as a stimulus for their crimes, being in contact with children, and frequenting places where children congregate. Their residence, vehicle, and personal effects are subject to search (Center for Sex Offender Management, 2001b).

DRIVING WHILE INTOXICATED (DWI) OFFENDERS

Increasing public concern (if not outrage) over the fatalities resulting from persons driving while intoxicated (DWI) has led to increased penalties for those convicted of this offense. However, this response has affected correctional officials attempting to deal with jail and prison overcrowding—hence the logic for community-based responses that protect the public without contributing to the jail/prison crisis. As a result, about a

Key Fact

Intoxicated drivers kill many more people than those who commit deliberate homicide.

half-million DWI offenders are on probation, and many states have established diversion programs for DWI cases.

For example, in Nassau County (Long Island), New York, the DWI unit is provided with a list of DWI defendants for whom presentence investigation (PSI) reports have been requested by the court. Each case is computer-checked for a prior criminal record, outstanding warrants, and any motor vehicle record. Cases with multiple DWI arrests are flagged, and their names are entered into a prescreening log, which is used by the unit supervisor to monitor DWI court activity in anticipation of future screening and assignment to probation supervision. This information is then sent to the probation officer assigned to conduct the PSI.

When the case is flagged by the DWI unit, the PSI officer sends it to the mental health unit, where a consultant determines if the defendant is a candidate for the county's drug and alcohol abuse agency and also makes a recommendation regarding therapy that will accompany the final PSI report sent to the sentencing judge. The judge revokes the defendant's motor vehicle license at this time (6 months for misdemeanors and 1 year for felonies), and the case is submitted for DWI unit screening. Any of the following criteria may determine a defendant's eligibility:

- Blood alcohol level of 0.15 or above at the time of arrest or refusal to submit to a chemical test
- Two or more DWI arrests (including the instant offense)
- Not on parole or a defendant in another case
- Alcohol as the primary drug of abuse
- No extensive psychiatric history
- Suitable for therapy based on the evaluation
- Available for evening therapy sessions
- Required to participate because of a concerned family member

Each unit officer maintains a caseload of no more than 30 DWI probationers in a designated area of the county (which is updated periodically in order to conform better to the distribution of DWI clientele). DWI supervision requires the offender to report weekly to a designated agency where he or she completes a 10-week alcohol education program and a 24-week closed group therapy session program; the group sessions are co-led by a probation officer and an alcohol counselor. Individual counseling is made available on an as-needed basis. Clients are subjected to random alcohol testing, and a positive reading can result in a variety of sanctions. On completion of the agency program, the client is encouraged to participate in an AA program. The client is required to report in person to the probation officer, and the officer makes periodic home visits. When an offender successfully completes the program, a letter is sent to the Department of Motor Vehicles indicating that the subject is no longer prohibited from obtaining a driver's license.

DEVELOPMENTALLY CHALLENGED OFFENDERS

The offender who is developmentally challenged presents supervision problems not typically found with other types of cases. Without specialized training and given the myriad of problems caused by rather large caseloads, P/P officers are often unable to meet the needs of these clients—hence the logic of specialized caseloads.

Cuyahoga County (Ohio) Mentally Retarded Offender Unit

Compared with the size of regular caseloads (usually more than 200), the Cuyahoga County (Ohio) Mentally Retarded Offender Unit averages between 55 and 65 probationers. Clients have a tested IQ of 75 or less, and the level of supervision for each offender is determined by a risk/needs classification: extended (mail contact only), low, medium, high, and superhigh. The unit has a clinical director who is a licensed psychologist. Each case is evaluated by a probation officer and the clinical director, and probationers are then referred for appropriate services. An interdisciplinary team—representatives from public and private services and advocacy groups specializing in mental retardation as well as public welfare agencies—aids in case planning for each probationer.

The rules and regulations of probation have been drafted in a form more easily understood by this population, and probation violation hearings are conducted in a manner more likely to be understood by the offender who is mentally retarded. For purposes of evaluation, the unit receives those whom the court believes are mentally retarded. Probation officers spend a great deal of time securing services for their clients (many social services agencies are reluctant to aid retarded offenders, both out of fear and due to the difficulties such clients present due to their disabilities).

Erie County (Pennsylvania) Special Probation Services

Erie County (Pennsylvania) Adult Probation/Parole and Mental Health/Mental Retardation Offices jointly fund a Special Probation Services unit, which provides County Court of Common Pleas judges with alternatives to incarceration for offenders who are mentally retarded—persons with a full-scale IQ score of 74 and below. Special Probation Services is designed to provide individualized and specialized services to developmentally disabled persons who receive an Erie County sentence. The program offers the structure and support of the criminal justice system simultaneously with the expertise of mental retardation services. The P/P officer is responsible for monitoring and enforcing the P/P conditions, while the case manager is responsible for coordinating community services to meet the individual's needs.

In addition, the Special Probation Services unit monitors inmates released under pretrial conditions. The case manager serves on an interdisciplinary evaluation committee, which screens pretrial inmates for program eligibility. A judge can elect to release the qualified offender into the community under the supervision of the Special Probation Services pending disposition. A representative from the unit is on an interdisciplinary team that screens and reviews case histories of newly incarcerated inmates in the Erie County Prison. Persons suspected of being mentally impaired are further evaluated to determine if they are mentally retarded and eligible for services. In addition, referrals are taken from Adult Probation and other agencies. The unit coordinates services with drug and alcohol, mental health, and mental retardation programs.

RESTITUTION AND COMMUNITY SERVICE

Restitution

Restitution—an act of restoring, a condition of being restored, or the act of making good or giving an equivalent for some injury—has become a popular condition of P/P. In addition to paying court costs, fines, and fees, a probationer may be required to make restitution, that is, to pay a percentage of his or her income (as determined by the court or parole board) to the victim of the offense for any property damage or medical expenses sustained as a direct result of the commission of the offense. This concept has an ancient history: The Bible (Exodus 21, 22; Leviticus 5) orders restitution for theft, burglary, or robbery or a form of "community service"—indentured servitude—in the event the criminal has no means of providing restitution. Restitution fell out of favor when monarchs, seeking to centralize power, made crime a public (state) matter and directed payments (fines) away from the victim or his or her kin in favor of the crown. (Personal claims had to be brought in civil court.) Community service emerged as a modern sentencing option in Alameda County, California, in 1966, and the Minnesota Restitution Program was established in 1972. Persons convicted of property offenses were given the opportunity to reduce their jail sentence or avoid incarceration altogether if they secured employment and provided restitution to their victims. The idea soon spread to other states.

Key Fact

While the concept of restitution is appealing, offenders typically have little in the way of resources to compensate victims.

Douglas McDonald (1988: 2) notes that in addition to aiding victims, restitution and community service are animated by the belief that they may contribute to the rehabilitation of offenders: Disciplined work has long been considered reformative. In addition, offenders performing community service may acquire some employable skills, improved work habits, and a record of quasi-employment that may be longer than any job they've held before. Victim restitution, when it brings offenders and victims face-to-face, also forces offenders to see firsthand the consequences of their deeds and thus may encourage the development of greater social responsibility and maturity.

Texas is so committed to the concept of restitution that since 1983, based on models established in Georgia and Mississippi, it has operated restitution centers throughout the state. As a condition of probation, employable nonviolent felony offenders who would have otherwise been imprisoned can be sent to a restitution center for between 6 and 12 months, during which time the restitution center director attempts to secure employment for each new resident. The director also attempts to place each probationer as a worker in a community service project either during off-work hours (if the probationer is employed) or full-time (if the probationer is unable to find employment). The restitution facility, which is operated by probation staff, accommodates between 30 to 60 persons and is usually located in light industrial areas for access to employment.

The probationer's salary is submitted by the employer directly to the director of the restitution center. The director deducts the cost of food, housing, and supervision; support for the probationer's dependents; and restitution to the victim(s)—with the remainder, if any, going to the probationer upon release from the center. If a restitution center director determines that the probationer is knowingly or intentionally failing to seek employment, the director requests that the court having jurisdiction over the case revoke probation and transfer the probationer to the custody of the Texas Department of Corrections. If the judge determines that a resident has demonstrated an acceptance of responsibility, the court may order the resident released from the center. The first 2 months following release, the former resident is on intensive supervision before being transferred to a regular probation caseload.

Community Service

Because relatively few offenders coming into the criminal justice system are in a position to provide meaningful financial restitution, the alternative of **community service** (work in the community to make reparation for the offense) has gained in popularity. In New Jersey, offenders sentenced to community service work without monetary compensation at public or private nonprofit agencies in the community. They usually perform their community service during the evenings and on weekends to complete their sentences: "The punitive aspect of a community service order is reflected in the imposition upon the time and freedom of offenders. While functioning in the traditional role as punishment, a community service order also directly benefits the public through the performance of services that may otherwise not be available" (Administrative Office of the Courts, n.d.: 11).

Key Fact

Community service is an alternative to restitution when the offender has few assets or there is no specific victim.

Community service in Georgia is seen as "an alternative sentencing option which is definitely punitive, yet is not perceived as being as harsh as incarceration, nor as lenient as regular probation." In the state of Washington, compulsory service without compensation performed for the benefit of the community is available as an alternative to incarceration for certain nonviolent crimes. The Department of Corrections Division of Community Services solicits requests for personnel services from nonprofit or governmental agencies, and community service has included chore service, work in food banks, park and street cleanup, industrial oil removal, and recycling. The requesting agency is expected to do the following:

- Refrain from displacing a paid worker with an offender.
- Supply a description of the work site and tasks.
- Assign a supervisor for training and supervision of the offender.
- Provide working conditions for the offender equal to that of paid staff.
- Provide written verification of offender performance.

A. PURPOSE

The purpose of this agreement is to formalize and enhance the working relationship between participating placement agencies and the Bucks County, Pennsylvania, Community Service Program.

B. DEFINITIONS

"Community service" shall be defined as uncompensated labor for an agency whose purpose is to enhance physical or mental stability, environmental quality or the social welfare.

"Agency" means a non-profit organization or public body agreeing to accept community service from offenders and to report on the progress of ordered community service to the court or its delegate.

C. PROGRAM DESCRIPTIONS

Program staff interview and screen convicted offenders who have been sentenced by judges to perform a specific number of hours of community service work. In cooperation with participating placement agencies, program liaisons assign community service clients to placement agencies to perform the required community service work by a specific deadline. These liaisons monitor the progress of the client and assist placement agencies in working with the client. Based on information supplied by placement agencies, program staff make periodic reports to judges, POs, and other members of the justice system.

D. AGENCY RESPONSIBILITIES

1. The placement agency will designate a specific agency staff person who will act as the agency contact. The agency contact will be responsible for accepting or rejecting potential community service volunteers and will provide necessary information to the program liaisons.
2. The placement agency will not discriminate in serving or in selecting clients on the basis of race, sex, age, marital status, religion, handicap, color, political affiliations, national origin, or any other nonmerit factors.
3. The placement agency contact will interview the potential community service volunteer.
   a. If the potential client is accepted by the placement agency, the interviewer and client will establish work schedules and work assignments. The placement agency will provide reasonable training necessary for the successful completion of the work assigned to the client.
   b. If the potential client is not accepted by the placement agency, the agency will notify the liaison and will explain why the client was rejected by the agency.
4. The placement agency will document the hours worked by the client and will record that information on the log sheets. The placement agency will report the hours worked upon the liaison's request. The agency will also notify the liaison upon the completion of hours.
5. The placement agency will report any supervision problems and physical injuries received by the client. When an injury occurs, the placement agency will ensure that proper medical care is provided and will notify the Community Service Program liaison within one working day.
6. The placement agency will advise the liaison of any changes in the agency that would affect future use of the agency as a community service placement site.

E. PROGRAM RESPONSIBILITIES

1. The Program Coordinator will assign a staff liaison to each placement agency. Each agency will be visited at least three times a year by the liaison. The liaison will describe the program to the agency contact and will gather necessary information about the agency.
2. Whenever needed, the program staff will provide assistance to the placement agencies to improve the agencies' utilization of clients and maintenance of information.
3. The program will provide resource information about working with the offenders in a community setting.
4. The liaison will advise agency contacts of any changes in the program that impact placement agencies.
5. Program staff will assist placement agency personnel in resolving specific problems with individual clients.
6. Based on information provided by clients and placement agencies, program staff will assign appropriate clients to the placement agencies.

FIGURE 11.4 *Agreement between Placement Agency and Program*

Similar programs exist in several states, including Georgia, Indiana, Kansas, Louisiana, Maryland, Minnesota, Ohio, Oregon, and Virginia. In Illinois and New Jersey, community service is used as an alternative for persons convicted of DWI. In New Jersey, the community service program is the responsibility of the county probation department; although no offender is automatically disqualified for the community service alternative, the Administrative Office of the Courts recommends that persons suffering from chronic alcohol or drug abuse problems, persons convicted of arson or assaultive offenses, and those with previous convictions for certain sex offenses be excluded. In Georgia, community service is recommended for (but not limited to) persons convicted of traffic and ordinance violations and nonviolent, nondestructive misdemeanors and felonies. In other cases, "The judge may confer with the prosecutor, defense attorney, probation supervisor, community service officer, or other interested persons to determine if the community service program is appropriate for an offender." Typical placements in Georgia have included hospitals, the Red Cross, parks and recreation systems, senior citizen centers, associations for the blind and deaf, and humane societies (Figure 11.4).

The Dauphin County (Pennsylvania) Adult Probation/Parole Department has a Community Resource Program in conjunction with the Harrisburg chapter of the American Red Cross. Clients placed at the Red Cross are regarded as volunteers (even though participation is a mandatory condition of the sentence of probation or county parole) and are provided with the same training, expectations, and benefits that any Red Cross volunteer receives. The Red Cross provides monthly evaluation reports. If work is satisfactory, a completion letter is given to the client and a copy to the P/P officer; unsatisfactory work results in a termination letter. Clients have served as first aid providers and assistants to an instructor of first aid courses and have conducted their own courses in first aid using multimedia systems; others serve in clerical, public relations, custodial, and research positions. Although no restrictions are placed on who may enter the program, clients have been nonviolent offenders.

SUPERVISION FEES

The imposition of **supervision fees**—as distinct from service fees, such as for electronic monitoring and drug testing—has grown in popularity, and most P/P agencies impose them on offenders for supervising services that are rendered. These fees frequently account for a significant portion of an agency's budget; for example, in Texas there is considerable pressure on P/P officers for successful collection of fees. There has been a great deal of success in collecting fees, although a few states scrapped their collection programs because they did not generate enough money to make the effort worthwhile (Finn and Parent, 1992; Mills, 1992). Illinois requires the imposition of a fee of $25 for each month of probation supervision ordered by the court. Instead of collecting monthly fees, Kansas imposes a one-time probation fee: $50 for felonies and $25 for misdemeanors. Alabama charges probationers and parolees a $20 monthly supervision fee, and Kentucky charges not less than $10 per month (with the maximum for a felony set at $2,500 and for a misdemeanor, $500). New York law permits a 5 to 10 percent fee on restitution cases, the higher amount when actual collection costs exceed 5 percent; for example, the Onondaga (Syracuse) Probation Department imposes a variety of fees for different services (e.g., $200 for a custody/visitation investigation and $150 to $500 for an adoption investigation), depending on an offender's adjusted gross income. The department also charges $50 for alcohol/drug testing, while probationers under supervision for DWI pay $30 a month. In Suffolk County, New York, probationers must pay a supervision fee of $30 per month; they are charged an additional $10 for each month they are tested for drug use. In Iowa, the Sixth District Department of Correctional Services requires those on probation or parole to pay a one-time fee of $150 if they were convicted of a felony, $125 for an aggravated misdemeanor, and $100 for a simple misdemeanor, while the state of Washington charges parolees $20 to $40 per year, depending on the nature of their classification level and supervision status. In Arkansas, offenders on intensive supervision pay $10 per month above the basic assessment for regular P/P supervision, and those electronically monitored pay $20 above the basic P/P fee. In Marion County, Indiana, felony probationers pay an intake fee of $100 and a monthly supervision fee of $15; misdemeanants pay an initial $50 fee and $10 for supervision.

Key Fact

Requiring offenders to pay fees for their supervision has proven very popular, although there are questions about its cost-effectiveness.

The use of probation violation as a fee compliance mechanism has been rare, and prison overcrowding makes judges reluctant to revoke probation even for willful failure to pay. Instead, intermediate punishments, such as a short jail stay or several weeks of community service, may be imposed. In 1992, New York enacted legislation requiring parolees to pay a supervision fee of $30 per month, but failure to comply does not result in a violation of parole; instead, interest and late payment fees are assessed through (civil) court action, which can lead to garnishment of wages or attachment of income tax refunds. Parolees falling below economic standards set by the Division of Parole can be given a temporary waiver; those who are disabled or suffering from a terminal medical condition can be given a permanent waiver. A study found that fees and restitution, "if used appropriately and judiciously, can be an effective criminal sanction" (Allen and Treger, 1994: 39). There is a bias by P/P officers against collection efforts: They view themselves more as *helpers* than *collectors*.

Discussion

Steven Chesney (n.d.: 158) studied the use of restitution in Minnesota and reports that "it is clear that the most important determinant of whether an otherwise eligible defendant was to be ordered to make restitution was his supposed 'ability to pay.' " As evident both from interviews with judges and from the cases themselves, this criterion was generally operationalized by choosing offenders who were white and well educated and were from the working and middle classes. This contrasted markedly with what is known about the criminal justice system in general: Those caught up in the system are overwhelmingly the poor, the lower class, and minority group members. Chesney (n.d.) raises some issues with respect to the use of restitution:

- Perhaps the relatively well-educated and well-employed group of offenders that is able to pay restitution is the group of offenders for whom restitution has the least meaning.
- Restitution may be one way that members of the more affluent social classes can avoid incarceration.

Chesney (n.d.: 169) concludes:

[R]estitution is not addressed to a rehabilitative or a victim compensatory need; instead, it answers a moral need. It reflects the way we feel that people should treat other people. As such, the evaluations of the effects of restitution may need to show only that it is no worse than other rehabilitative alternatives and that it does compensate some victims. Any effects beyond these are serendipitous because the primary goal of restitution is the elimination of the contradictions between our systems of morality and our criminal justice system.

Concerns

Although restitution would appear to be a win-win practice, the use of supervision fees raises several serious questions:

1. Will persons who can pay fees be more likely to be granted P/P?
2. Will the need to collect fees change the focus of P/P supervision away from providing services?
3. Will the failure to pay fees result in P/P revocation?
4. Will persons be kept under supervision longer because of their ability to pay fees or a need to collect unpaid fees?
5. Will a person who can pay fees be less likely to be cited for a P/P violation?
6. Will the imposition of fees cause an increase in absconding from supervision?
7. Will fee collection responsibilities detract from the work of already overburdened P/P officers?

Answers to these questions are part of the continuing debate over supervision fees.

In 1983, the Supreme Court (*Beardon v. Georgia*, 461 U.S. 660) ruled that probation cannot be revoked because of an inability to pay a fine and restitution as a condition of probation that is a result of indigence and not a refusal to pay. This point would appear to also apply to supervision fees. Fahy Mullaney (1988: 15) found that failure to pay restitution or fees often results in an extension of time an offender is under supervision: "In fact, some offenders are kept on intensive supervision although they completed all their probation conditions except final payment on a fee." Furthermore, collection-related tasks require 10 percent additional staff time, whereas extending supervision further increases the demands on staff. There are also "subtle value shifts in community corrections agencies, raising the priority of fiscal matters rather than of community safety, community justice, or human restoration" (Mullaney, 1988: 15). Mullaney cautions: "In the early history of incarceration, offenders were required to pay for admission to jail, to pay the jailer for food and bedding while there, and finally to pay upon release. Today we are aghast that such counterproductive, unjust practices could ever exist, [but] across this country, we are swiftly adopting new sanctions, especially fees and special assessments, that have a dramatic financial impact on those who go through our criminal justice system. Without thoughtful development of policy and practice to guide and limit this movement, we may well repeat history rather than learn from it" (1988: 21). In Texas, where about three-fourths of the state's counties collect fees equal to one-half or more of their total expenses, defenders of the system say that rather than detracting from casework, aggressive fee collection actually furthers the goal of helping probationers avoid relapsing into criminal behavior: "They argue that the regularity of fee payments is a good barometer of a probationer's overall adjustment to supervision. . . . Some probation staff believe that the emphasis on fee collections provides an opportunity to help teach offenders how to budget and meet ongoing financial obligations on time" (Finn and Parent, 1992: 11–12).

Halfway Houses

Halfway houses (places where offenders can work and pay rent while they participate in counseling and/or job training) have a long history. "The concept of halfway houses was introduced in 1817 by the Massachusetts Prison Commission. This group recommended the establishment of temporary homes for destitute released offenders as a measure to reduce recidivism" (Rosenblum and Whitcomb, 1978: 9). "It is intended to afford a temporary shelter in this building, if they choose to accept it, to such discharged convicts as may have conducted themselves well in prison at a cheap rate, and have a chance to occupy themselves in their trade, until some opportunity offers a placing of themselves where they can gain an honest livelihood in society. A refuge of this kind, to this destitute class, would be found perhaps humane and politic" (Commonwealth of Massachusetts Legislative Document, Senate No. 2, 1830).

The name *halfway house* itself suggests its position in the corrections world: halfway-in, a more structured environment than P/P; halfway-out, a less structured environment than institutions. As halfway-in houses, they represent a last step before incarceration for probationers and parolees facing or having faced revocation; as halfway-out houses, they provide services to prereleasees and parolees leaving institutions. Halfway houses also offer a residential alternative to jail or outright release for accused offenders awaiting trial or convicted offenders awaiting sentencing (Thalheimer, 1975: 1).

Victor Goetting notes that "it is accepted that these facilities are based on sound correctional theory; in order to ultimately place a person in society successfully that person should not be any further removed from that society than is necessary" (1974: 27). When used in conjunction with prison or training school release programs, the halfway

Key Fact

Halfway houses are an effective means of providing housing and services but often face community opposition.

house provides (1) assistance with obtaining employment, (2) an increased ability to use community resources, and (3) needed support during the difficult initial release period (Griggs and McCune, 1972). The various types of halfway houses operated by public and private agencies and groups can be divided basically into those that provide bed, board, and some help with employment and those that provide a full range of services, including treatment. The latter includes a variety of methods, from guided group interaction to psychotherapy, reality therapy, or behavior modification. A halfway house may be primarily for released inmates, for parolees, or for probationers as an alternative to imprisonment. Halfway houses may also be used for probationers or parolees who violate their conditions of supervision but not seriously enough to cause them to be imprisoned.

The Texas Adult Probation Commission has funded a series of halfway houses (called residential treatment facilities) throughout the state that house felony offenders in need of a brief residency in a structured environment that offers them treatment services rather than placing them in prison or on regular probation. These offenders often need treatment for drug or alcohol abuse, job skills training, and basic education, and the facilities offer a homelike atmosphere with a minimum of security measures. Residents are classified according to their individual needs and assigned to a treatment regimen that usually includes counseling, educational classes, and vocational training; they also share in the housekeeping responsibilities. As residents advance in the program, they are allowed to check in and out of the facility to go to work or training in the community. If unemployed, they may be assigned to do community service work. When residents have advanced to an acceptable level in their treatment plan, they are released from the center and placed under regular probation supervision.

The Georgia Department of Offender Rehabilitation has established more than a dozen halfway houses (called residential diversion centers) to provide judges with an option for sentencing "marginal cases"—an alternative between imprisonment and regular probation. Two centers for female offenders are available. The program requires residents to work, pay for their room and board, and provide restitution to their victims. To qualify for the program, a defendant must meet these criteria:

1. Be one who would otherwise be incarcerated
2. Be a nonviolent property offender
3. Not be regarded as a habitual criminal
4. Be capable of maintaining employment

Each center has room for between 40 and 50 residents, who serve an average of 4 to 5 months before being released to regular probation supervision. The centers provide counseling, basic education, high school equivalency examination preparation, and recreation. Release is based on a satisfactory completion of the treatment contract, which each offender signs to qualify for the program. The centers serve three daily meals, with takeout lunches being furnished to residents who go out to work. Residents are responsible for maintaining the facility and are allowed visitors on the weekends during specified hours; after the fourth week, residents may earn weekend passes. Failing to comply with rules and regulations or absconding from the facility means imprisonment.

The major difficulty with opening and maintaining a halfway house is community reaction. A Lou Harris poll, for example, found that 77 percent of the representative U.S. sample favored the halfway house concept, but 50 percent would not want one in *their* neighborhood, and only 22 percent believed that people in *their* neighborhood would favor a halfway house being located there. Experts stress the importance of getting community support for the project before opening a halfway house. Among some of the strategies used in gaining support is the formation of an advisory board made up of influential community people. Community residents may be placed on the board of directors and hired as staff for the facility.

WORK RELEASE

Many states have prison work release programs, and in some instances these programs involve P/P staff. **Work release** allows people serving sentences to work in the community, returning each evening to the institution. They are still subject to institutional controls (and absconding is considered an escape from confinement), and additional regulations apply to their extrainstitutional status. Under this system, inmates are able to earn a salary and pay taxes, contribute to their families' income, repay debts, make restitution, and even contribute to their keep at the institution; in addition, work release enhances an inmate's self-image.

Legislation authorizing work release programs was enacted in Wisconsin in 1913, but it took more than 40 years before it spread to other states: California and North Carolina enacted work release legislation in 1957. By 1965, 24 states had such legislation, and by 1975 all 50 states and the federal government had legislation authorizing some form of community work and educational release (Rosenblum and Whitcomb, 1978). More recently, however, work release programs have declined, with only about one-third of U.S. prisons now reporting operating such programs and fewer than 3 percent of inmates participating in them: "As the rehabilitation ideal—of which work release was very much a part—started to fade, the public embraced imprisonment as the only sure way to forestall crime" (Turner and Petersilia, 1996: 2).

States vary with respect to the criteria used in selecting inmates for work release programs: Some automatically excuse those who are serving life sentences or inmates who have detainers filed against them. In some states, the court must authorize work release, and in others, the parole board has this responsibility. The final responsibility for selecting candidates, however, is usually under the aegis of the correctional authorities who administer the program. States may have specific restrictions governing who may participate in work release, but more often they use such general expressions as "not a high-security risk" or "not likely to commit a crime of violence." States vary in the number of inmates involved in work release, and in some, the program is combined with furloughs that enable eligible inmates to leave the institution for specific periods of time to seek employment or educational opportunities.

Unfortunately, many (if not most) correctional institutions are isolated from urban areas where employment opportunities are more readily available. Responding to this deficiency, some states operate a variety of facilities for housing work release participants in proximity to areas of employment. These facilities include minimum-security prisons or work release centers, halfway houses, or rented quarters in hotels or Young Men's Christian Associations. Idaho, for example, operates community work release centers that provide 4- to 6-month prerelease programming for inmates within 10 months of their release date (violent offenders and sex offenders are ineligible).

Basic restrictions are typically placed on the employment situations available to inmates:

- Inmates cannot work in a skilled area where a surplus labor force already exists.
- Conditions of employment must be commensurate with those of nonoffenders.
- If a union is involved, it must be consulted, and no work releasee can work while a labor dispute is in progress.

The state of Washington has had a work release program in place since 1970. The Department of Corrections (DOC) has contracts with 15 residential work release facilities that house more than 350 (mostly male) offenders on any single day. According to the 1991 Sentencing Reform Act, eligible inmates must be within 6 months of their release date, have minimum-security status, and not have been convicted of first-degree rape or murder. Those meeting basic criteria will be denied work release if they exhibited assaultive behavior in prison, the offender's victim lives in the area, the offender has

Key Fact

While there is general agreement on the worthiness of work release, finding adequate housing is often a challenge.

made threats against the victim, or the offender has had two or more prior work release failures during the current commitment. "Once DOC judges an offender eligible for work release, the work release facilities' Community Screening Board, consisting of work release staff and local citizens, must agree to accept the inmate for admission" (Turner and Petersilia, 1996: 4).

Offenders are responsible for finding their own employment or employment training, although they receive assistance from facility staff. The residents pay $10 per day for room and board and must support their dependents and make any court-ordered restitution. Community corrections officers are assigned to the facilities to monitor resident behavior and can order them returned to prison for rule violations. A study of the program concluded:

> The program achieved its most important goal: preparing inmates for final release and facilitating their adjustment to the community. The program did not cost the State more than it would have if the releasees had remained in prison. The public safety risks were nearly nonexistent because almost no work releasee committed new crimes [some minor property crime], and when they committed rule violations they were quickly returned to prison. (Turner and Pertersilia, 1996: 2)

INTERSTATE ADULT AND JUVENILE COMPACTS

In the Crime Control Consent Act of 1934, Congress authorized two or more states to enter into **interstate compacts**, agreements for cooperative efforts and mutual assistance in the prevention of crime. Pursuant to this legislation, in 1937 a group of states signed the Interstate Compact for the Supervision of Probationers and Parolees, which enabled them to serve as each other's agents in the supervision of persons on P/P. By 1951, all 48 (and now all 50) states and the District of Columbia, Puerto Rico, and the Virgin Islands were signatories of the compact. In 1998, a revised Interstate Compact for Adult Offender Supervision was established.

The compact provides a system whereby a person under supervision can leave the state of conviction—the **sending state**—and proceed to another state for employment, family, or health reasons, and at the same time it guarantees that the **receiving state** will provide supervision of the offender. The state of original jurisdiction (where the offender was convicted) retains authority over the probationer or parolee and is kept advised of his or her whereabouts and activities by the receiving state. The compact also provides for P/P violators to be returned without the need to resort to time-consuming extradition procedures. Because it is based on a federal statute and governed by the substantive law of contracts, the interstate compact supersedes state law. (The U.S. Supreme Court has never ruled on the constitutionality of the compact, having denied *certiorari* whenever the issue has been raised.) Interestingly, figures on the number of probationers and parolees who are being supervised under the compact are inaccurate: While the National Institute of Corrections has reported approximately 250,000, the 50 states report less than 100,000, but their figures are dubious because the number of offenders supposedly being supervised does not equal the total amount of offenders sent out of state for supervision by several thousand.

Before the establishment of the compact, thousands of convicted felons were permitted to leave the state of conviction with no verified or approved plan of residence and employment in the receiving state. On occasion, dangerous criminals were released by states and permitted (sometimes forced into "internal exile" or "sundown probation or parole") to enter other states without any provision for supervision or even the knowledge of any official body in the receiving state. The compact provides a systematic method for supervision purposes for the receiving state to verify and approve a plan of residence and employment or education before a probationer or parolee is permitted

Key Fact

The interstate compact provides for the orderly visit or transfer of an offender from one state to another.

A Closer Look

Interstate Compact for Adult Offender Supervision

The compacting states to this Interstate Compact for Adult Offender Supervision recognize that each state is responsible for the supervision of adult offenders in the community who are authorized in accordance with the by-laws and rules of this compact to travel across state lines both to and from each compacting state in such a manner as to track the location of offenders, transfer supervision authority in an orderly and efficient manner, and when necessary return offenders to the originating jurisdictions. . . .

It is the purpose of this compact and the Interstate Commission created under this compact, through means of joint and cooperative action among the compacting states, to provide the framework for the promotion of public safety and protect the rights of victims through the control and regulation of the interstate movement of offenders in the community; to provide for the effective tracking, supervision, and rehabilitation of these offenders by the sending and receiving states; and to equitably distribute the costs, benefits, and obligations of the compact among the compacting states.

In addition, this compact will create an Interstate Commission that will establish uniform procedures to manage the movement between states of adults placed under community supervision and released to the community under the jurisdiction of courts, paroling authorities, corrections, or other criminal justice agencies that will adopt rules to achieve the purpose of this compact; ensure an opportunity for input and timely notice to victims and to jurisdictions where defined offenders are authorized to travel or to relocate across state lines; establish a system of uniform data collection, access to information on active cases by authorized criminal justice officials, and regular reporting of compact activities to heads of state councils, state executive, judicial, and legislative branches and criminal justice administrators; monitor compliance with rules governing interstate movement of offenders and initiate interventions to address and correct noncompliance; and coordinate training and education regarding regulations of interstate movement of offenders for officials involved in that activity.

The compacting states recognize that there is no right of any offender to live in another state and that duly accredited officers of a sending state may at all times enter a receiving state and there apprehend and retake any offender under supervision subject to the provisions of this compact and by-laws and rules adopted under the compact.

to enter the state (Figure 11.5). After a probationer or parolee is accepted for supervision by the receiving state, the latter sends quarterly "progress and conduct" reports to the sending state (Figure 11.6).

The compact also regulates interstate travel by probationers and parolees. Each state issues a travel pass, a copy of which is sent to the interstate administrator, who notifies the receiving state of the impending visit. The Association of Administrators of the Interstate Compact formed in 1946, now known as the Interstate Commission for Adult Offender Supervision, has a designated commissioner from each state who is that state's compact administrator and who meets at least once per year, prepares uniform reports and procedures, and attempts to reconcile any difficulties that have arisen with respect to the compact.

Some problems remain.[3] One is the difference in P/P administration. In all states, parole is an executive function with statewide procedures, so interstate activities are centralized through a compact administrator in each state. Probation, however, can be administered on a county basis and may lack statewide coordination. The local autonomy that often exists in the judicial branch can cause difficulties in using and administering the pact in probation cases; in such cases, the probation officer of the sending state may need to make direct contact and arrangements with the court of the receiving jurisdiction.

---

[3]See Clem, Krauth, and Linke (1998) for an evaluation of the interstate compact.

COLORADO DEPARTMENT OF CORRECTIONS
DIVISION OF ADULT PAROLE SUPERVISION
COOPERATIVE CASE REPORT.

To: Texas Interstate
    P.O.Box 13401
    Capitol Station
    Austin,TX 78711

Date: 12-5-06

Name: Smith, Robert
    TX # 574,566
DOC#   CO # X94-1200

SUBJECT MATTER: REPORT OF INVESTIGATION/ACCEPTANCE

The proposed residence at 433 Briar Drive, Woodland Park, Colorado 80863, is verified.
This is the residence of Mr. Richard Smith, the parolee's father. The father is a willing sponsor, and the residence is certainly adequate to house the addition of the parolee in the home. The Woodland Park Police Department was also contacted on December 1, 2006, and they are aware of Mr. Richard Smith's hunting business called the Ace Sports Club and note that the parolee's father has a good reputation in the community.

Regarding employment the placement request from the State of Texas notes that the father has offered employment with his business known as the Ace Sports Club, 1400 W Hwy 24, Woodland Park, Colorado 80866. However, it should be noted that this is a seasonal business and that Richard Smith would not be able to offer his son employment until the hunting season started next year. Therefore, the parolee would, in effect, have to secure his own employment for approximately the next six months until the Colorado hunting season started for the 2007 calendar year. Of primary concern to Colorado authorities is the offense for which the parolee was most recently incarcerated, that being Aggravated Robbery With A Deadly Weapon. For this reason, the Texas Department of Criminal Justice has listed the parolee's supervision level as "L"—highest level. For this reason, Colorado will accept the parolee's supervision with the understanding that he will be on ISP supervision with electronic monitoring for 180 days. The potential sponsors have already agreed to this type of supervision in their home. Also, the parolee will be expected to submit to drug and other substance abuse counseling through our TASC Office and will be held financially responsible for any treatment expenses.

If the parolee is willing to agree to these conditions, please have him report to Parole Officer Tom Peterson immediately upon arrival in the Colorado Springs area at the address listed below.

TOP/js

Direct Correspondence to:

Tom Peterson
Tom Peterson
Parole Officer

Office: Colorado Springs Parole Office
        25 N. Spruce Street, Suite 300
        Colorado Springs, CO 80905
        (719) 635-0800 Fax (719) 473-5152

Larry C. Stuart
Larry C. Stuart
Reviewing Officer

FIGURE 11.5 *Colorado Report of Investigative Acceptance*

Another problem results from different approaches to supervision in various states. One state may exercise close control and require strict enforcement of the conditions of probation or parole, while another state may be more flexible or may simply be incapable of close supervision and control because of the size of its caseloads. When a "strict" state notifies a "permissive" sending state that one of its probationers or parolees is in violation, the sending state may not consider it serious and may leave the offender in the receiving state with a request that it continue supervision. In some cases, the sending state may not want to incur the expense of transporting the violator back to one of its state prisons, which are probably overcrowded anyway (Figure 11.7). The receiving state has two options: continue to supervise an offender it considers in violation, or discontinue supervision and leave the offender without any controls at all. Problems are also associated with the collection of restitution and supervision fees. These types of situations may make a receiving state reluctant to accept future cases from a particular sending state, a situation that needs to be reconciled at the compact administrator's meeting.

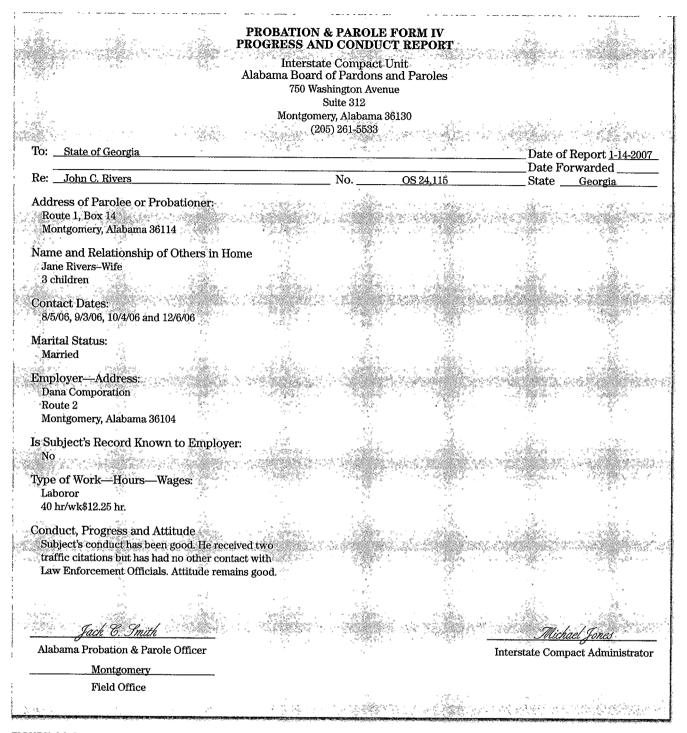

PROBATION & PAROLE FORM IV
PROGRESS AND CONDUCT REPORT

Interstate Compact Unit
Alabama Board of Pardons and Paroles
750 Washington Avenue
Suite 312
Montgomery, Alabama 36130
(205) 261-5533

To: ___State of Georgia___   Date of Report 1-14-2007
                                                                              Date Forwarded _____
Re: ___John C. Rivers___   No. _____OS 24,115_____   State ___Georgia___

Address of Parolee or Probationer:
    Route 1, Box 14
    Montgomery, Alabama 36114

Name and Relationship of Others in Home
    Jane Rivers–Wife
    3 children

Contact Dates:
    8/5/06, 9/3/06, 10/4/06 and 12/6/06

Marital Status:
    Married

Employer—Address:
    Dana Comporation
    Route 2
    Montgomery, Alabama 36104

Is Subject's Record Known to Employer:
    No

Type of Work—Hours—Wages:
    Laboror
    40 hr/wk$12.25 hr.

Conduct, Progress and Attitude
    Subject's conduct has been good. He received two
    traffic citations but has had no other contact with
    Law Enforcement Officials. Attitude remains good.

Jack C. Smith   _Michael Jones_
Alabama Probation & Parole Officer   Interstate Compact Administrator

___Montgomery___
Field Office

FIGURE 11.6 *Alabama Progress Report*

States sometimes allow probationers or parolees to go to a receiving state under the guise of a visit when the offender's intentions are to stay permanently. The receiving state is then contacted by the sending state to investigate "with a view toward accepting supervision." The receiving state is faced with a *fait accompli*.

The Interstate Compact on Juveniles governs the interstate movement of juvenile cases. In the early 1950s, legal and financial problems involving the supervision, transportation, and control of juvenile cases among states reached the point where most of those involved acknowledged the need for some form of interstate compact patterned on

OKLAHOMA DEPARTMENT OF CORRECTIONS

DIVISION OF COMMUNITY SERVICES

CASE REPORT

TO: Interstate Compact Administrator
     State of Florida Probation
NAME: Mitchell Barton, W/M, DOB 11/30/70
NUMBER: 93-1134-CFA DOC #456095
CRIME: False Imprisonment/Aggravated Assault
CONVICTED: 1/14/06; Seminole County; Fifteen (15) years
RECEIVED FOR SUPERVISION: 3/12/06 DISCHARGE DATE: 1/03/2021

VIOLATION REPORT

Subject has violated the following rules of his probation:

RULE 1: Not later than the fifth of each month, you will make a full and truthful report to your probation officer on the form provided for that purpose.

RULE 3: You will not change your residence or employment or leave the county of your residence without first securing the consent of your probation officer.

RULE 17: To immediately leave the State of Florida and reside with your uncle, Jason Barton, until placement in a Veteran's Administration (VA) hospital.

RULE 18: Enter the VA Hospital in Oklahoma City, Oklahoma, within 15 days and actively participate in and successfully complete such programs as are reasonably related to your past and future criminality or to the rehabilitative purpose of probation.

VIOLATION OF RULES AND CONDITIONS

On 4/26/06, subject was transported to and admitted by the VA Hospital in Oklahoma City. On his admittance to the hospital he was diagnosed as having Post Traumatic Stress Syndrome. On 5/27/06, subject's counselor called and advised that he was being released from their hospital due to his refusal to take medication, fighting, disruptive nature, and belligerence. This officer talked to the subject and advised him of the consequences of this behavior. He was released that same day. Subject claimed he would re-enter the VA Hospital on 6/9/06 when he returned for evaluation. On 7/10/06, this officer contacted the VA Hospital and was advised that the subject reported to the hospital on 6/9/06, but was denied admittance due to his attitude. This officer then contacted Mrs. Barton, his aunt, who claims that the last time she heard from the subject was 6/8/06. She claims no knowledge of his whereabouts.
    Subject's last contact with this officer was 6/01/06 by telephone. This officer has no knowledge of the subject's whereabouts.

SUMMARY/RECOMMENDATION

Subject's last known address was Rt. 8, Box 1214, Ponca City, Oklahoma. Subject's employment consisted of sporadic farm work around Perry, Oklahoma. His reporting habits until 5/29/06 were satisfactory. His attitude toward community supervision was ambivalent; one meeting would be positive and the next extremely belligerent. When he would become belligerent, he would complain about the rules that are depriving him of his freedom and that he has no reason to want to continue living. The latter is apparently related to his mother's suicide.
    This officer respectfully recommends that subject's suspended sentence be revoked due to the above violations. It is this officer's opinion that Mitchell Barton is extremely dangerous.
    On issuance of a warrant, the subject should be submitted to the NCIC. Please forward a copy of the warrant and application to revoke.

Harrison McDonnell

Harrison McDonnell
Team Supervisor, District V

FIGURE 11.7 *Violation Report*

the one used for adult cases. In 1954, the National Council on Juvenile Court Judges drafted a preliminary compact on juveniles; later that year, several groups, under the coordination of the Council on State Governments, drafted the Interstate Compact on Juveniles. In 1955, 10 states adopted the compact, and currently all 50 states and the District of Columbia are signatories. In addition to providing for cooperative supervision, the compact provides for the return of juvenile P/P absconders and escapees as well as nondelinquent runaways. The Association of Juvenile Compact Administrators is responsible for developing rules and regulations that govern the administration of the compact.

In contrast to the compact for adults, the juvenile compact has mandatory and discretionary cases. Thus, the receiving state must accept supervision whenever a juvenile will be returning to or has already been placed in the home of his or her legal parents or guardians, and each state must accept its own residents. Other cases are discretionary. When supervision has been arranged, the sending state retains jurisdiction and the receiving state becomes the agent of the sending state. Because of variations in state laws regarding juveniles, a person who is a juvenile in one state may be considered an adult in another. The compact overcomes this problem by applying the law of the state from which the juvenile has run away or from which he or she was sent for supervision: If a person is a juvenile under law in his or her home state, he or she is a juvenile to all member states. Although the compact does not deal with child custody cases, it can provide for the return of a child to wherever a court has determined legal custody is maintained.

In Chapter 12, we examine the intermediate punishment response to the problem of prison overcrowding.

KEY TERMS

12-step program (p. 319)

agonists (p. 315)

antagonists (p. 314)

aversive stimuli (p. 316)

community service (p. 336)

halfway houses (p. 340)

interstate compacts (p. 343)

methadone (p. 315)

plethysmography (p. 330)

receiving state (p. 343)

restitution (p. 335)

sending state (p. 343)

supervision fees (p. 338)

therapeutic community (TC) (p. 317)

work release (p. 342)

INTERNET CONNECTIONS

Addictions page: www.well.com/user/woa

Alcoholics Anonymous: alcoholics-anonymous.org

American Probation and Parole Association: www.appa-net.org

Center for Community Corrections: communitycorrectionsworks.org

Center for Sex Offender Management: csom.org

International Community Corrections Association: iccaweb.org

Interstate Compact guide: www.nicic.org/resources/topics/InterstateCompact.aspx

National Institute on Drug Abuse: www.nida.nih.gov

Parole and Probation Compact Administrators' Association: doc.state.ok.us/PPCAA/index.htm

Smart Recovery: smartrecovery.org

REVIEW QUESTIONS

1. What are the types of specialized units in P/P?
2. How are various chemicals used in substance abuse treatment?
3. Why is behavior modification difficult to use in treating drug-abusing offenders?
4. What is a therapeutic community?
5. What is the Alcoholics Anonymous approach to substance abuse?
6. How have probation/parole agencies responded to the problem of HIV/AIDS?
7. How have P/P agencies responded to the problem of sex offenders?
8. What is controversial about requiring offenders to provide restitution?
9. What are the arguments for and against supervision fees?
10. What has the Supreme Court ruled (*Beardon v. Georgia*) with respect to requiring probationers to pay a fine and/or restitution as a condition of probation?
11. What are the problems encountered in work release programs?
12. What is the major difficulty with opening and maintaining a halfway house?
13. What is the purpose of the Interstate Compact?
14. What are the problems of the Interstate Compact?

Intermediate Punishments

Intermediate punishments can be understood in terms of risk management rather than rehabilitative or correctional aspirations. Rather than instruments of reintegrating offenders into the community, they function as mechanisms to maintain control, often through frequent drug testing, over low-risk offenders for whom the more secure forms of custody are judged too expensive or unnecessary.

—*Malcolm M. Feeley and Jonathan Simon* (1992: 461)

chapter 12

Chapter Outline

PURPOSES OF INTERMEDIATE PUNISHMENTS

The stated explanation for **intermediate punishments** is a classical emphasis on matching the sanction to the offense, while the actual purpose is to reduce incarceration. The trend in favor of classicalism—just deserts and determinate sentencing—has been intertwined with the reality of jail and prison overcrowding. Widespread support for punishment and deterrence through greater use of incarceration—for example, truth in sentencing, "three strikes and you're out"—has encountered serious financial limitations. Judges have been unwilling to permit conditions of incarceration that violate the Eighth Amendment's prohibition against cruel and unusual punishment, thereby increasing the cost of a policy of punishment by way of incarceration. In response, officials have scrambled to create alternative systems that satisfy a public/political appetite for punishment while limiting the financial costs involved.

Intermediate punishments are also used to expand the response to probation and parole (P/P) violators: "In the past, officials had two sanctions for violators—either to continue supervision (perhaps with modest changes in conditions) or to revoke and imprison the violator. Often the choice of options was either too lenient or too harsh for the circumstances of the violation" (Parent et al., 1994: 13).

Key Fact

The stated explanation for intermediate punishments is a classical emphasis matching the sanction to the offense, while the actual purpose is to reduce incarceration.

A Closer Look

Iowa Violation Program

The Iowa Violation Program (IVP) provides an intermediate sanction for P/P violators who would otherwise be admitted to the prison system. They are assigned to the program at revocation hearings on the recommendation of the P/P officer. Those who successfully complete the 60-day residential program are returned to community supervision to complete their probation or parole term. IVP has 60 beds at the Women's Reformatory and 100 beds at the Release Center. At each facility, participants are segregated from the general population and have treatment staff assigned solely to the program.

IVP employs a cognitive approach aimed at changing thinking styles. The major underlying assumption is that offenders typically exhibit cognitive deficiencies such as lack of both self-control and problem-solving skills. Upon admission to the program, participants have a 1- to 5-day orientation period, during which administrative paperwork and some diagnostic procedures are completed. Orientation time varies because inmates are assigned to a group of 3 to 12 offenders who go through the program together, and the administration will wait for all members of a new group to arrive so they can be oriented together. Participants are acquainted with the general rules of the program and the institution. Following orientation, participants settle into a routine of attending classes from 7:30 A.M. to approximately 4:30 P.M. Classes are organized into different modules representing various facets of the program: drug abuse, reasoning, problem solving, values, and group therapy. Each class lasts about 2 hours and employs a variety of techniques, including various exercises and role playing. Physical fitness activities and homework must be completed during free hours.

INTENSIVE SUPERVISION

If one can judge by the amount of agency literature and research efforts, **intensive supervision** has become the most popular program in P/P. Early versions of intensive supervision were based on the premise that increased client contact would enhance rehabilitation while affording greater client control. Current programs are simply a means of easing the burden of prison overcrowding. Thus, the Colorado Department of

Corrections notes that its intensive supervision program "expands prison capacity by requiring participation of selected offenders who would otherwise be incarcerated in departmental facilities." In any event, by 1990, jurisdictions in all 50 states had instituted a community-based sanction called *intensive probation supervision (IPS)* (Petersilia and Turner, 1991).

In probation, IPS is usually viewed as an alternative to incarceration; in other words, persons who are placed on IPS are supposed to be those offenders who, in the absence of intensive supervision, would have been sentenced to imprisonment. In parole, intensive supervision is viewed as risk management—allowing a high-risk inmate to be paroled but under the most restrictive of circumstances. In either case, intensive supervision is a response to prison overcrowding. Thus, although intensive supervision is invariably more costly than regular supervision, the costs "are compared not with the costs of normal supervision but rather with the costs of incarceration" (Bennett, 1988: 298).

IPS can be classified into those types that stress diversion and those that stress enhancement:

- **Diversion** is commonly referred to as a "front door" program because its goal is to limit the number of offenders entering prison. Prison diversion programs generally identify incoming lower-risk inmates to participate in IPS as a substitute for a prison term.

- Enhancement programs generally select already sentenced probationers and parolees and subject them to closer supervision in the community rather than regular P/P. People placed on IPS-enhanced P/P have shown evidence of failure under routine supervision or have committed offenses deemed to be too serious for supervision on routine caseloads (Petersilia and Turner, 1993).

Intensive supervision actually takes many shapes. In Texas, for example, IPS involves an experienced probation officer whose maximum caseload does not exceed 40. In Suffolk County, New York, IPS clients are required to attend a day reporting center (discussed later) where they pass through four program phases before being placed on regular supervision.

Florida Community Control. According to the Florida Department of Corrections, its program of community control "is not intensive probation [but] a distinctively different type of program that is punishment oriented and allows selected offenders to serve their sentences confined to their homes under 'house arrest' instead of prison." Offenders must remain home when not at (or traveling to and from) their place of employment or mandated public service job. They are supervised by special (community control) correctional probation officers who have a maximum caseload of 20. In addition to being armed, the officers are equipped with portable radios for quick access to law enforcement assistance: "Florida's community control initiative represents the single largest intensive supervision prison diversion program in the Nation" (Wagner and Baird, 1993: 1).

Persons may be placed on community control by the sentencing judge if they are found guilty of a noncapital felony but are considered unsuitable for regular probation, or they may be P/P violators. The target population, however, is offenders who have committed nonviolent crimes and would not otherwise be placed on regular probation because of the seriousness of their criminal history (Baird and Wagner, 1990). A correctional probation officer conducting a presentence investigation who plans to recommend that a particular offender be sent to prison because of his or her criminal background or the seriousness of the crime may recommend community control as an alternative.

With community control cases, correctional probation officers are required to make a minimum of seven contacts per week with the offender and others in the community (e.g., employers and law enforcement agencies). Two of these visits must be in person, including at least one in the field. The offender is required to make weekly office visits during which he or she can be subjected to urinalysis. The officer also makes at least 16 personal telephone contacts to ensure the offender is at home as required by curfew restrictions.

Key Fact

Intensive probation supervision (IPS) is an alternative to incarceration—persons who are placed on IPS are supposed to be those offenders who, in the absence of intensive supervision, would have been sentenced to imprisonment.

Key Fact

Intensive parole supervision is risk management that allows high-risk inmates to be paroled but under the most restrictive of circumstances.

Georgia Intensive Probation Supervision. In 1982, faced with the reality of prison overcrowding, the Department of Offender Rehabilitation inaugurated IPS. Although this plan began as a pilot program, IPS has now become a routine method of keeping down prison commitments. In addition to seeking to divert offenders from prison, the program attempts to accomplish the goal of punishment. IPS provides close community supervision to selected offenders who normally would have entered prison if it were not for the existence of the program: "The IPS team, composed of an experienced PO and a Surveillance Officer, supervises a maximum caseload of twenty-five (25) offenders [or two surveillance officers and 40 cases] who present no unacceptable risk to the community in which they are supervised. The caseload consists primarily of nonviolent felony offenders who have been convicted of property offenses."

Program standards include:

- Five face-to-face contacts per week
- Total of 132 hours of mandatory community service
- Mandatory curfew
- Mandatory employment
- Weekly check of local arrest records
- Automatic notification of arrest elsewhere via the state crime information system
- Routine and unannounced alcohol and drug testing

Georgia IPS skims off low-risk offenders—persons who are nonviolent property offenders and drug- and alcohol-related offenders—for the program, although most have been sentenced to imprisonment. An analysis of the program revealed that as a result of IPS, the percentage of offenders sentenced to prison decreased and the number of probationers increased. Furthermore, the "kinds of offenders diverted were more similar to prison inmates than to regular probationers, suggesting that the program selected the most suitable offenders" (Erwin and Bennett, 1987: 2). However, Georgia incarcerates many offenders for nonviolent offenses, including driving with a suspended driver's license, punishable in Georgia by up to 5 years in prison. Thus, the IPS program may indeed be diverting offenders from prison, but there is a serious question of why such persons are being sentenced to imprisonment in the first place. Georgia is in the "top 10" when it comes to rates of incarceration.

Cook County (Chicago, Illinois) Juvenile Intensive Probation Supervision. In operation since 1984, Cook County IPS is funded by the Illinois Supreme Court as a way to decrease juvenile facility overcrowding; whereas it costs about $35,000 per year to keep a juvenile institutionalized, the annual cost of IPS is $3,000. The program was originally intended for nonviolent offenders, but as the number of violent offenders grew, IPS was expanded to include them. Of the county's 300 juvenile probation officers, 18 are assigned to IPS; whereas regular caseloads average 42, each team of 3 IPS officers has a maximum of 45 cases. "IPS officers [who are unarmed but wear bulletproof vests] can drop in on their kids whenever they want, and they shift their schedules from days to nights to weekends to make it harder to predict when they'll come. They also occasionally do 'double backs,' dropping by and then returning later to see if the kids have taken off [in violation of their curfew]" (Krause, 1997: 14).

IPS clients usually range from 13 to 17 years old, are received directly from juvenile court or are releasees from residential care, remain on home confinement for the first 30 days, and are permitted to leave only to go to school, work, or other approved destinations. They do a minimum of 60 hours of community service and must avoid any gang involvement, which includes wearing gang clothing (most of the youngsters are gang members). The probation officers must be familiar with gang territoriality—some youngsters cannot be sent to certain neighborhoods for employment or social services because of gang rivalries. Periodically, there are "roundups" during which the youngsters and their guardians (mostly mothers) are to appear at the juvenile court building auditorium where they are given information about meetings, camp opportunities, and training programs;

many do not show up. The youngsters then break up into small groups for sessions with probation officers while the parents stay behind to ask questions. When the youngsters return from their group sessions, each meets with the three members of their IPS team.

"Robert" is a typical case. At age 16, he was on IPS for armed robbery and firearms possession. He has not completed high school and lives at home with his mother, who is unemployed; he rarely sees his father. His girlfriend has a baby and is pregnant again. Many of the youngsters' parents are drug abusers, and many of the youngsters have been selling drugs for older gang members. If a youngster violates the conditions of supervision in a serious manner, a juvenile warrant is issued and sent to the police for enforcement (juvenile probation officers do not have arrest authority).

New York and Colorado.   Demonstrating through empirical evidence that 80 percent of the parolees who violate their parole conditions do so during their first 15 months under supervision, the critical determinant of what is called *differential supervision* is time under supervision. In both New York and Colorado, those parolees within their first 15 months on the street are designated "intensives." In New York, after 15 months, the offender is placed on "regular" supervision, with less stringent contact standards. Although regular caseloads average 97 parolees, parole officers with intensive cases supervise 38 parolees. In areas where density of parolees is sparse and traveling time between clients poses an obstacle to efficient supervision, officers have mixed caseloads—intensive and regular, with each intensive case counted as 2.55 regular cases.

Colorado also has a time-limited intensive supervision program for parolees, but the time ranges from a minimum of 90 days to a maximum of 180 days, at which time the parolee is transferred to regular supervision. ISP caseloads do not exceed 20, and the focus is clearly on control: weekly face-to-face meetings, daily telephone contacts, electronically monitored curfews, and weekly alcohol and drug testing.

Somerset County (Pennsylvania) Day Report Intensive Probation Program.   With caseloads that do not exceed 18, probation officers supervise offenders who would have been considered for a term of incarceration and are nonviolent or technical probation violators. The offenders are required to pay a supervision fee and report to the probation office or alternative site Monday through Friday. If unemployed, they must attend job readiness classes in addition to any counseling for drugs, alcohol, family, mental, financial, or employment problems. Offenders, who are in this program from 1 to 5 months, must provide a daily schedule of planned activities and are subject to random telephone checks as part of curfew enforcement.

Dauphin County (Pennsylvania) Intensive Juvenile Probation.   The Dauphin County Probation Department has a juvenile IPS program geared to reduce the level of institutional commitments. Each youngster is placed on a suspended commitment to an appropriate juvenile institution with the understanding that he or she would have been committed to this institution if intensive supervision did not exist. Each case is screened to ensure the youngster is not a serious threat to either him- or herself or the community. In addition, sufficient family stability must exist so that the officer can work with the family as a unit, and the family has to be willing to cooperate with the program. If the screening officer determines that the case is appropriate for IPS, the youngster is scheduled for a juvenile court hearing, where the officer recommends that the respondent be sentenced to a suspended commitment to an appropriate institution and placed in the IPS program.

Each caseload (with a maximum of 18 cases) is supervised by one probation officer and one part-time probation officer; the term of IPS is 6 to 9 months. Each juvenile must follow certain regulations, which include a curfew and mandatory school or work attendance, and a treatment plan is based on the needs and interests of each client. Each youngster has three to five weekly meetings, which include counseling sessions in the office and at home, in both individual and family sessions. The IPS officer maintains a high level of visibility with both the client and the community.

Texas Intensive Supervision Program.   Created in 1981 to deal with a prison crisis, the Texas ISP attempts to divert selected felony offenders by offering an alternative to incarceration. For these offenders, intensive supervision is a condition of probation. In most Texas probation departments, ISP caseloads do not exceed 40, and the officers are specially selected and trained for the assignment. In some Texas jurisdictions, however, the officers supervise a mixed ISP and regular caseload. Whenever this occurs, the mixed caseloads may comprise no more than 125 regular probationers before officers receive the first ISP case, and then they must be reduced by 5 regular cases each time a new ISP case is assigned to the caseload. Either cases are received directly from the court after sentencing, or they involve persons facing probation revocation and shock probationers (discussed later in this chapter). To qualify, offenders must meet one or more of the program's criteria:

- One or more prior jail or prison commitments
- One or more convictions
- Chronic unemployment
- Alcohol dependency
- Drug dependency
- Mental retardation or psychological problem
- Seriousness of current offense

Using a risk/needs assessment classification (discussed in Chapter 10), the IPS officer develops a supervision plan that outlines behavioral objectives to be met by the offender within specific time frames. By contracting with various community resources, the IPS officer negotiates for the exact type of services needed for each client. A formal reassessment occurs every 90 days. Typically, an IPS client remains under intensive supervision for 1 year or less and is then transferred to regular supervision. However, the court may amend the terms of probation to continue the offender under intensive supervision for an additional year; in rare or exceptional cases, the period may last beyond 2 years.

Texas also has a superintensive supervision program called *surveillance probation.* It is reserved for offenders whose regular probation has been revoked and those who are sentenced to shock probation; it can also be a special judicially imposed condition pursuant to a grant of probation. Each offender remains in the program for 90 days, although an extension can be granted, during which time two officers (who supervise no more than 20 cases) maintain a minimum of five contacts per week, three of which are in person. A mandatory curfew exists, and frequent drug and alcohol testing are required.

Key Fact

There is an absence of standards for determining if a P/P program of supervision is indeed "intensive."

A Closer Look

North Carolina Probation/Parole Surveillance Officer

In North Carolina, this officer partners with a P/P (intensive case) officer in the supervision and surveillance of high-risk felon and misdemeanor offenders placed under intensive community supervision in lieu of incarceration. The officer prepares investigative and other reports for court use; testifies in court before the parole commission; supervises an absconder caseload of probationers/parolees; conducts in-home visits, drug screenings, employment verifications, and criminal record checks; transports offenders; and deals with crisis intervention, arrest, and search and seizure. This position requires the employee to work various shifts during each 28-day period. The officer may serve on the electronic house arrest team, which includes on-call status, and respond to electronic house arrest violations. Before being issued a firearm, the employee must qualify, according to the Department of Correction, Division of Community Corrections Standards.

Research Findings on Intensive Supervision

Before we begin our examination of the effectiveness of intensive supervision, we should note that the establishment of IPS programming was not based on careful research and evaluation but was simply a response—perhaps ill conceived—to jail and prison overcrowding (Clear, Flynn, and Shapiro, 1987). Indeed, policy implications of evaluative research into IPS may be irrelevant: "If the results are negative . . . then these findings will be viewed as support for both the continued use of incapacitation and the development of even more intrusive, surveillance-oriented community control programs" (Byrne, 1990: 8). In fact, although evidence of the effectiveness of IPS is wanting, the program has been a public relations success (Clear and Hardyman, 1990).

Intensive supervision is usually accomplished by severely reducing caseload size for each officer based on the assumption that this will lead to increased contact between the officer and the client and/or any significant others (such as spouse or parents) and that this increased contact will improve service delivery and control, thus reducing recidivism. Some programs, however, have had difficulty achieving *intensity*: "While it may be inconceivable for intensive supervision to occur in caseloads that exceed some finite number, such as fifty persons, it is certainly conceivable that much smaller caseloads might not result in significant levels of intensity" (Clear and Hardyman, 1990: 44). Two researchers claim that intensive supervision does indeed increase case contacts, often by 50 percent or more, and the amount of time spent in contact also increases significantly. "[However,] the difference between spending one-half hour per month with a client and spending an hour per month is, relatively speaking, an extremely small difference considering the magnitude of the treatment and service provision task which the PO is trying to accomplish" (Carlson and Parks, 1979: 72).

In one Tennessee county, a comparison between a sample of regular and intensively supervised probationers over a 3-year period revealed significant differences in recidivism: 25.8 percent of the regular probationers had new felony arrests, whereas the rate for the IPS sample was 8 percent. The results for technical violations were the reverse: 60 percent of the IPS participants and 34 percent of the regular probationers (Burrow, Joseph, and Whitehead, 2001). Perhaps IPS was successful in screening out—by way of technical violations—those probationers most likely to reoffend. Intensive supervision for drug offenders on probation in seven cities (Atlanta, Georgia; Des Moines, Iowa; Macon, Georgia; Santa Fe, New Mexico; Seattle, Washington; Waycross, Georgia; Winchester, Virginia) did not appear to impact recidivism. Research revealed no significant differences between the arrest rates for IPS participants and a control group receiving regular supervision during a 12-month period (Petersilia, Turner, and Deschenes, 1992). Similar findings were reported in a study of IPS programs in 14 other cities (Petersilia and Turner, 1993). As noted by the researchers, however, drawing conclusions from recidivism statistics can be misleading because recidivism could be a feature of the intensity of the supervision—IPS could increase the probability of new criminal activity being *discovered* (this issue is discussed in the concluding chapter).

> **Key Fact**
>
> Research into intensive supervision has produced mixed results, with no clear indication that the process is successful in meeting its goals.

California.   Research into the effectiveness of intensive supervision dates back to 1953. That was when California conducted "probably the most extensively controlled experiment in American correctional history" (Glaser, 1969: 311).

The California Special Intensive Parole Unit experiment ran from 1953 until 1964, during which time caseload sizes were varied from 15 to 35. In addition, research was conducted into the impact of increased supervision on particular risk classes of offender. A positive outcome occurred only with those parolees classified as "lower-middle risk"—they had significantly fewer violations. In a review of this research, however, Robert Martinson (1974) found that the successful cases were concentrated in northern California, where agents were more apt than agents in southern California to cite both the experimental subjects and the controls for violating parole. The limited success, Martinson argues, was not due to the intensive nature of supervision but was the result of a realistic threat of reimprisonment. A problem also exists with using parole violation as a criterion for success because of what researchers refer to as the "halo effect": a tendency on the part of P/P officers to tolerate greater levels of misbehavior than is usual to prove the experiment is successful.

Later research into California IPS was conducted in three counties. Cases were randomly assigned from a pool of high-risk offenders on probation to IPS caseloads of 40 (Contra Costa), 19 (Ventura), and 33 (Los Angeles) or control caseloads that averaged 150 to 300 offenders. After 6 months, IPS clients received more intensive supervision: two to three times the usual number of contacts. About 30 percent of the IPS cases had a technical violation, a much higher rate than the control caseloads; however, no statistically significant difference existed between new arrest rates for IPS and control cases. The research revealed that intensive supervision in these counties did not affect the rate of new arrests: IPS failed to enhance the rehabilitative or control function of supervision (Petersilia and Turner, 1990). The researchers conclude: "When compared with routine probationers, the ISP participants, with few exceptions, had similar rates of technical violations and new arrests" (Petersilia and Turner, 1991: 9).

Research on a Los Angeles Probation Department IPS program involving gang-member drug offenders also had disappointing results. Although caseloads were small— 33 as opposed to 300—the supervision that resulted was hardly intensive and home visits were infrequent (Agopian, 1990). *Calling* a program "intensive" by reducing caseload size is obviously not the same as *providing* intensive supervision.

Georgia. Research in Georgia has produced mixed results for the concept of intensive supervision. As noted earlier, IPS probationers are under the joint supervision of a probation officer and a surveillance officer in caseloads that do not exceed 25. One comparison of outcomes for 542 IPS probationers and a matched sample of 752 regular probationers revealed that 13.7 percent of the IPS group had their probation revoked for new crimes (none for violent crimes), whereas 10.2 percent was the figure for the control sample. The IPS group had a higher rate of technical violations (11.8 percent) than the control sample (6.5 percent)—which the researchers argue is to be expected considering the intensive supervision—and there was little difference in the absconder rate: 2.2 percent for the IPS participants, 2.4 percent for the control sample. A second study of the program revealed that 18.5 percent of the IPS probationers and 24.0 percent of the regular probationers were convicted of new crimes. However, 42.3 percent of prison releasees during the same period were convicted of new offenses, and "59.4 percent of the IPS cases were more similar to those incarcerated than to those placed on probation" (Erwin and Bennett, 1987: 4; see also Erwin, 1984).

According to Joan Petersilia (1988a), several states have adopted IPS programming based on the apparent success of the Georgia program. However, she cautions, judges in Georgia (like those in many southern states) tend toward the punitive, imposing more sentences of imprisonment and for longer terms than elsewhere. Thus, there is a greater pool of IPS prospects—nonviolent offenders—than would be expected outside of the South in general, and Georgia in particular. In fact, when it comes to the risk of new criminal behavior, IPS clients are not markedly different from the regular probation population in Georgia. The basic claims of IPS in Georgia with respect to cost-effectiveness, diversion of offenders, and improved public safety "are not supported by the available research evidence" (Clear, Flynn, and Shapiro, 1987: 35). In fact, "a convincing argument can be presented that the Georgia evaluation actually demonstrates the opposite" (Byrne, Lurigio, and Baird, 1989: 27).

According to the Georgia plan, the probation officer is supposed to provide typical professional casework services, whereas the probation surveillance officer (with less education, training, and salary) provides "24 hour surveillance capability through day, night, and weekend visits and telephone contacts." Surveillance officers, however, developed greater rapport with clients and their families than did probation officers. The surveillance officer had more direct contact with, and was more easily accessible to, the client and his or her family:

One of the most interesting findings of the IPS evaluation is the near impossibility of separating treatment from enforcement. The Georgia design places the PO in charge of case management, treatment and counseling services, and court-related activities. Surveillance Officers, who usually have law enforcement or correctional backgrounds, have primary responsibility for frequently visiting the home unannounced, checking curfews, performing drug and alcohol tests using portable equipment, and checking arrest records weekly. The Surveillance Officer becomes well acquainted with the family and is often present in critical situations. Both the Probation and Surveillance Officers report a great deal of overlap of functions and even a reversal of their roles. (Erwin and Bennett, 1987: 6)

In practice, the surveillance officer was doing the work of a professional probation officer, while the latter's role was either redundant or reduced to that of a paper-pushing case analyst.

Louisiana.   A study of shock incarceration ("boot camp," to be discussed later) found that positive results were a function of the intensive supervision that offenders received after being paroled: "the more intense the supervision, the better these offenders adjusted during community supervision." In addition, "parolees' performance declined over 6 months of community supervision as the intensity of supervision was reduced" (MacKenzie, Shaw, and Souryal, 1992: 450). The study concludes: "In general, the more intense the supervision the better the offenders performed, probably because this was required of them. There was a threat of revocation if they did not comply" (MacKenzie, Shaw, and Souryal, 1992: 450). Another study of shock incarceration in Louisiana found that boot camp graduates were subjected to more technical violations than regular supervisees; regular P/P supervisees, however, were convicted at higher rates for new crimes. The differences were ascribed to the impact of the intensive supervision given to boot camp graduates (MacKenzie and Shaw, 1993).

Maryland.   A Maryland Division of Parole and Probation pilot project compared "intensive supervision" caseloads of 55 to "normal" caseloads of 100. A matched sample of 274 offenders from the intensive and 274 from the normal were chosen. Both samples were rated "high risk for recidivism" using the division's classification system. The intensive caseload agents were expected to broaden their role from merely monitoring the offender to "facilitating involvement in pro-social activities that focus on building skills to be productive in society" (Taxman, 2007: 99).

After at least 6 months of supervision, research revealed that intensive supervision had no effect on drug consumption patterns for those under a court mandate for urinalysis, but the intensives were less likely to be arrested, 32.1 percent in contrast to 40.9 percent for the normals; and the intensives were 38 percent less likely to be cited for technical violations.

Minnesota.   Intensive supervision has centered mostly on probation: "Relatively few jurisdictions have implemented prison-diversion ISP programs—programs that divert offenders from prison sentences to terms of supervision in the community" (Deschenes, Turner, and Petersilia, 1995: 331). Intensive supervision was tested in Minnesota as a cost-saving device using 300 cases. Experimental and control groups were randomly assigned from a cohort of recently convicted inmates with sentences of 27 months or less and probation violators committed to prison. None had a record of victim harm or weapons use, and they were employable and had a suitable residence—a "boy scout" population. A second set of experimental and control groups consisted of good-time releasees who had served two-thirds of their sentence.

Parole agents in the intensive units supervised caseloads of 12 to 15 offenders (size of control units not indicated). Intensive cases spent the first 6 months on home confinement, during which time they could leave their residence only for employment or with specific permission. Results: There were no statistically significant outcome differences between the experimental and control caseloads, but savings were realized—$5,000 per offender per year—from the early release of inmates (although these persons apparently could have been placed on regular supervision).

New Jersey. Limited to 500 highly select offenders diverted from prison after several months of incarceration, IPS cases in New Jersey were compared with a sample of offenders eligible for the program but who were instead incarcerated and then released on parole. The IPS participants' new conviction rate averaged roughly 10 percentage points lower than that of the comparison group, leading one researcher to conclude that in New Jersey IPS works fairly well with felons who are neither dangerous nor habitual criminals: "The program saves a modest amount of prison space without increasing recidivism; it has been cost-effective compared to ordinary terms of imprisonment and parole; it has been monetarily beneficial (in terms of earnings, taxes, payments to a fund for victims, and so on); and it does provide a level of punishment between probation on the one hand and ordinary imprisonment on the other" (Pearson, 1988: 447).

Three researchers state, "[The] New Jersey program evaluation—by design—should make the IPS program look quite good because it compares IPS cases with a group of class 3 and class 4 felons who represent the poorest risks and who receive the harshest treatment by the New Jersey corrections system" (Byrne, Lurigio, and Baird, 1989: 30). Other researchers find it ironic that the relatively low-risk offenders in the New Jersey program are receiving intensive supervision, whereas the far higher-risk parolee joins a caseload in excess of 100 (Clear, Flynn, and Shapiro, 1987).

New York. Research conducted by the New York State Division of Parole (Collier, 1980) indicates that intensive supervision can have a modest effect on violent felony offenders. In 1978, the legislature provided funding for the supervision of violent felony offenders. In 1979, all released inmates who had been convicted of a violent felony (crimes ranging from robbery to arson, with most being imprisoned for robbery) were placed in intensive units whose officers supervised no more than 35 cases: 97 percent were male; the median age was 27.3; blacks constituted 57.5 percent, whites 23 percent, and Hispanics 19.5 percent; 62 percent completed less than the twelfth grade; and 80 percent were unskilled laborers. Interestingly, two-thirds of this group had little or no prior criminal history.

After 1 year of research (ending March 31, 1980), the 1,905 violent felony offenders released in 1979 and placed under intensive supervision were compared with 1,732 of the same population released in 1978 to regular supervision:

- 12.6 percent of the (1978) controls and 1.8 percent of the (1979) intensives were returned to prison for a new offense.
- 3.3 percent of the controls and 4.0 percent of the intensives were returned to prison for technical violations of parole.
- 5.0 percent of the controls and 3.4 percent of the intensives absconded from supervision.
- 6.5 percent of the controls and 3.9 percent of the intensives had parole violation or court hearings pending.

Ohio. Funded by a state probation subsidy program, the Lucas County Incarceration Diversion Unit (IDU) consists of four probation officers, each with a caseload maximum of 25 (with the exception of the supervisor, who is assigned 15). The IDU probationers were compared with a group of shock probationers under regular supervision. (The study did not indicate the size of regular shock probation caseloads.) The researchers found that the IDU officers recorded almost four times as many client contacts, and more social services were provided to their clients. However, no statistically significant differences with respect to recidivism occurred; the IDU group did have significantly fewer technical violations, which the researchers conclude was the result of a realistic fear of being sent to prison because of the nature of IDU supervision and strict violation practices. (An alternative hypothesis would raise questions about the quality of the supervision.) The researchers conclude that their study "should provide a word of caution to officials seeking ways to limit incarceration rates" by using intensive supervision (Latessa and Vito, 1988: 327).

The Lucas County Intensive Supervision Unit (ISU) was designed to divert nonviolent felony offenders who had already been committed to a Department of Youth Services (DYS) facility because DYS facilities were under pressure from overcrowding. The program excluded youth whose instant offense involved drugs, use of a weapon, or victim injury. Research compared ISU youngsters to similar youth committed to a DYS facility and then paroled. The supervision provided by ISU was indeed intensive, with respect to both control and rehabilitative services, but no significant difference in recidivism occurred: It was rather high for both—almost 50 percent of both groups were reinstitutionalized within the 18-month period of the research. However, there was a potential savings: The annual cost of ISU per client was more than $6,000, as contrasted with more than $32,000 for incarceration (Wiebush, 1993).

A study in Montgomery County (Dayton), Ohio, compared matched samples from IPS units (with 25 cases per officer) and regular units (caseload size not indicated). The research revealed that 11.7 percent of the intensive supervision cases ended with a felony conviction, against 3.8 percent for regular supervision, and that 1.2 percent of the intensive cases were incarcerated for misdemeanors, as opposed to 6.2 percent of the regular cases. Interestingly, the IPS officers, on average, made less than one face-to-face contact per month with their clients in the clients' homes—hardly an *intensive* level of supervision (Noonan and Latessa, 1987).

A study of IPS in the rural Ohio county of Clermont noted that implementing a special supervision program in rural areas is difficult because of long travel times to reach clients, making unannounced visits problematic. The researchers found that persons assigned to IPS were clearly higher risk than those on regular caseloads, but they were unable to determine if these were prison-bound cases. As might be expected, if supervision is indeed intensive, the IPS clients had a higher rate of technical violations: 39 percent (IPS) versus 24 percent (regular). "[However,] there were no significant differences in the number of felony arrests, convictions, or completion rates of probation. A high percentage of both groups were classified as successful" (Haas and Latessa, 1995: 168).

Washington State.   The stated objective of the Washington State Adult Corrections Division was to save tax dollars by removing low-risk offenders from the state's prisons—persons released into the program had on average served less than 3 months in prison. A total of 289 were placed under the intensive supervision of an officer whose caseload did not exceed 20. At the end of 1 year, it was determined whether the individual's behavior warranted a conditional discharge from supervision or supervision by a regular probation officer.

To evaluate the program, a matched historical sample (102) was selected as the control group. Random assignment was ruled out because of "equal treatment under the law considerations." The control group was made up of inmates who were paroled at the same time as those selected for early release and intensive supervision; however, the control group subjects were released after having served normal sentences to a probation officer who supervised an average caseload of 73. A person in the control group was selected on the basis of the same criteria as those in the test group, with the following three results (Fallen et al., 1981):

1. After 1 year of supervision, 19 percent of the test (IPS) group had been arrested or convicted for new (nontraffic) offenses, whereas the figure for control cases was 40 percent.

2. The IPS officers showed a strong tendency to invoke delinquency action. After 1 year, 42 percent of the test group had been cited for technical parole violations as opposed to 24 percent for the control group.

3. The 1-year revocation rate for the IPS group was 17 percent; for the control group, it was 6.1 percent (the average for general supervision in Washington is 15 percent).

Fallon and colleagues (1981) speculate on explanations for their findings:

- Intensive parolees were less likely to commit new offenses because of a fear of detection produced by increased supervision.
- By brief incarceration, intensive parolees received the initial "shock value" of prison but were not in long enough to learn the "skills" or adopt the "values" of the incarcerated criminal population.
- Because many intensive parolees received formal technical violations, these served as effective warnings that undesirable behavior would not be tolerated.
- Because many intensive parolees were revoked for technical violations only, this may have screened out those disposed to commit new offenses.

Wisconsin.   In 1984, the Wisconsin Division of Corrections established an experimental IPS program for high-risk offenders, with 30 offenders (later increased to 40) supervised by two-agent teams in two locations. The research did not indicate the caseload for non-IPS parole agents. Experienced agents screened all new cases in their areas and selected only high-risk offenders (HROs) as clients. To qualify as an HRO, the client requires a history of assaultive behavior; other distinguishing characteristics include a lengthy criminal record, poor prison adjustment record, and poor attitude toward community supervision, as well as an unwillingness to participate in drug and alcohol abuse programs or mental health programs.

As part of intensive supervision, specialized rules were tailored for each offender; these restricted certain associations, use of motor vehicles, and evening hours: "The general tactic is to establish rules which restrict behavior(s) associated with a past criminal pattern" (Wagner, 1989: 23). Offenders were required to provide a weekly schedule indicating where they would be at any given time. Each client registered with the local police, submitting a photograph, fingerprints, handwriting sample, past offense history, and current address. The police were expected to assist in the offender monitoring process. Parole agents made at least four in-person contacts each month, including two visits (scheduled and unscheduled) to the offender's residence. Frequent collateral visits with police, employers, landlords, and associates occurred. In at least one case, school officials and parent association members were informed of the release of a child sex offender so they could aid in the surveillance process.

The HRO group under IPS was compared with a matched sample that received regular supervision. The results were dramatic: After 1 year, only 3 percent of the IPS parolees had been convicted of a felony; it was 27 percent for the control group. The statistics for parole violation provide at least a partial explanation for these differences because only 12 percent of the control group were returned to prison for parole violations, whereas the number was 40 percent for the IPS group. A researcher for the state of Wisconsin concludes that "the IPS program suppresses criminal behavior by preempting it" (Wagner, 1989: 26). The research does not indicate how many of the remaining IPS clients successfully completed their entire supervision period.

Discussion

Despite the modest (at best) results of intensive supervision, the programs remain popular while there has been a dramatic absence of continuing research into IPS. To evaluate IPS, we need to examine the two premises on which it is based.

Premise One. *Intensive probation supervision will divert offenders who would otherwise be incarcerated.* In any number of jurisdictions, this goal is not being accomplished. A study in Tennessee, for example, revealed that even though some offenders were being diverted away from prison, many more IPS clients would have normally been sentenced to regular probation (Whitehead, Miller, and Myers, 1995). Judges continued to send probation-eligible offenders to prison while using IPS for those who would be sentenced to probation in any event. The Florida IPS (Community Control) Program received offenders who were often more serious than those on probation or in jail, but less serious than those sentenced to prison. An undetermined number of these borderline cases (perhaps more than one-half) would have been sent to prison in the absence of IPS (Baird and Wagner, 1990). A study of IPS in Colorado found no significant differences between cases recommended for IPS and those not recommended, leading the researchers to conclude that this program "may not be one of prison-diversion as the state guidelines proclaim" (Reichel and Sudbrack, 1994: 57). Needless to say, this will affect the results of any research on an IPS program.

For the diversion goal to be accomplished, cases need to be assigned to IPS *after* a sentence of imprisonment. Only after conviction, sentence, and remand to jail pending transportation to prison should the IPS screening officer review the case and, if appropriate, submit a recommendation for resentencing. Cases not intercepted should proceed to state prison. With respect to parole, parole boards often assign cases to intensive supervision that would have been granted parole even in the absence of an intensive program. If intensive supervision is to serve the goal of reducing the prison population, it should be reserved for cases that have been denied parole. A screening officer (institutional parole officer) should review the case *after* parole has been denied and, if appropriate, submit a recommendation for reconsideration of parole with intensive supervision.

In sum, many (if not most) intensive supervision programs are not actually diverting offenders—they are simply providing judges and parole boards with an additional supervision option that is not being used in lieu of prison (although this may not have the effect of lowering prison commitments, it certainly has merits of its own). Many IPS programs appear to be accepting those offenders who are not at high risk and who probably should have been on regular probation in the first instance. In some counties, the probation department routinely recommends inappropriate cases for IPS. This serves two intertwined purposes: First, it ensures the IPS program will deliver "good stats"; second, it helps keep down regular caseloads by shifting some cases to probation officers funded by special allocations (and the continuation of these allocations is dependent on "good stats").

However, intensive supervision for inappropriate cases unnecessarily increases the cost of probation and may be harmful to the client: "Behavioral scientists have long speculated that the addition of strains and controls to a human system can, at some time, result in a reaction that is contrary to the direction of the controls" (Clear and Hardyman, 1990: 55). According to the labeling perspective (discussed in Chapter 8), an offender inappropriately identified as "high risk" by virtue of IPS status may indeed assume that role and organize his or her behavior accordingly, so subjecting low-risk offenders to intensive supervision may lead to more—not less—trouble with the law (Altschuler and Armstrong, 1994).

An additional problem involves offenders who believe that intensive supervision is as punitive as imprisonment: "In many states, given the option of serving prison terms or participating in IPS, many offenders have chosen prison" (Petersilia, 1990: 23; emphasis deleted). Petersilia points out that for many/most serious offenders, imprisonment and the stigma that can result are not the frightening phenomena that they are for the community at large: "For many offenders, it may seem preferable to get that short stay in prison over rather than spend five times as long in an IPS" (1990: 25; see also 1994). Under these conditions, in order for intensive supervision to work, it may be necessary to offer it as an option for much more serious offenders than are now being subjected to IPS.

Key Fact

Diversion from prison requires cases to be assigned to IPS after a sentence of imprisonment.

In sum, large amounts of scarce resources are being allocated to less serious offenders, whereas more dangerous offenders are released to the community under parole supervision that is often inadequate because of lack of funding (Clear, Flynn, and Shapiro, 1987). Funding is simply nonexistent in those states that have discontinued postprison community supervision. It is the worst "Alice in Wonderland" situation when armed robbers and other dangerous offenders are released from prison with inadequate or no supervision, while property offenders are placed on IPS. In Florida, for example, less serious offenders are placed on intensive community control, whereas the more serious offenders released from prison are not supervised (Wagner and Baird, 1993).

This irrational approach to crime and justice is exemplified by a 1988 Texas Adult Probation Commission study. IPS cases were compared with offenders eligible for probation but sentenced to imprisonment and offenders not eligible for probation and sentenced to imprisonment using the "risk" part of the Texas Risk/Needs Assessment form. Following are the mean scores:

Intensive probation supervision	20.10
Eligible for probation but incarcerated	18.93
Ineligible for a sentence of probation	26.26

In other words, although the IPS program was apparently diverting offenders from prison (a risk mean of 20.10), there were less serious risks (risk mean of 18.93) who were imprisoned, and the high-risk offenders (risk mean 26.26) who were imprisoned will be released to parole supervision that is not intensive. A similar situation exists in Illinois, where the state has been funding IPS programs while 60 percent of the state's parole agents were laid off.

Alan Schuman (1989: 29) argues that "the new IPS concept actually depicts local communities' original image of how probation services should operate. IPS provides the type of comprehensive surveillance services, restitution payments, drug testing and treatment, employment verification, and networking with other community services that should be expected of all probation agencies that are adequately funded." Gerald Buck (1989: 66) argues that intensive supervision "*is* probation practiced as it was originally intended to be. Other probation programs are a sham that ought not be called probation supervision" (emphasis in original).

Premise Two. *More of whatever it is that the P/P agency does with routine cases will have a salutary effect on cases at greater risk.* Although several research studies have challenged this premise, a strong (if unproven) belief regarding P/P is that *more is better.* I want to dwell on the question *more of what?* The implication of intensive supervision—the bait that hooks funding from elected officials—is that offenders will be closely monitored, be under surveillance, and be made to fear detection for any violations they might be inclined to commit. Arthur Lurigio and Joan Petersilia (1992: 9) note: "[A]n important assumption of IPS programs is that close supervision should increase the probability of detecting and arresting offenders who are not deterred by the program and who continue to commit crimes. Speedy revocation to custody results in incapacitation, and, because IPS participants are encouraged to be employed and to attend counseling sessions, rehabilitation *may* occur. However, newer IPS programs are designed to boost offenders' perceptions of the effectiveness of the system in detecting and punishing their criminal behavior."

P/P officers are portrayed as making unannounced contacts with offenders, whom they are monitoring around the clock, ready to take immediate action to prevent any danger to the community. For agencies whose officers are armed and trained in law enforcement, this approach is a natural extension of the services they are already providing; agencies in which officers do not have adequate law enforcement training or authority, however, cannot live up to the image of *intensive.* Indeed, agencies that adopt a meaningful form of intensive supervision—one that does indeed increase unannounced face-to-face in-field contacts—but fail to equip and train their officers accordingly place these officers in danger. In Vermont, for example, officers expressed a great deal of concern for their safety because intensive supervision meant frequent unannounced visits by unarmed officers. When I worked as a parole officer in New York, my unannounced visits found parolees with firearms left on the dresser, large amounts of heroin and drug paraphernalia on the kitchen table, and other potentially dangerous situations. The neighborhoods in which most clients live are high-crime areas, which can be particularly hazardous at night. Minnesota parole agents providing intensive supervision, for example, "are required to make visits to clientele at all hours in a variety of situations and neighborhoods." However, they carry no firearms, although they are authorized to carry chemical substances to aid in a "safe retreat."

IPS programs are typically set up outside the traditional supervision structure. Clients and officers are handpicked; the latter receive special training and sometimes salary increases, and they report to their own supervisory chain of command. This hierarchy can affect general agency morale because the IPS unit receives a disproportionate share of resources and attention. In some agencies, such as the Cook County (Chicago, Illinois) Adult Probation Department, only IPS officers are authorized to carry firearms, and they are viewed as "elite." These special units experience strong pressure to demonstrate results:

> This is one reason why these programs often seem to be encased in an atmosphere of caution—they are very vulnerable to errors. Based on a rationale of effective offender control, and in contrast to seemingly more lenient traditional probation methods, the idea of intensive probation can be seriously damaged by even one publicized incident of serious client failure, such as a violent crime. Therefore, despite the control rhetoric, program officials seem to bend over backward to avoid the riskiest clients and to resist giving accepted clients many chances to violate probation. (Clear, Flynn, and Shapiro, 1987: 42)

This accounts for the relatively high rate of probation violations in most IPS programs.

When I was a parole officer in New York, each caseload had some cases designated "intensive" by the parole board, and they required at least one face-to-face unannounced home visit and four in-person office visits each month. Cases were subjected to more supervisory review and there was less latitude—in the event of a technical violation of the rules, such offenders were more likely to be taken into custody and returned to prison. New York State parole officers are required to carry firearms while on duty, so this system avoided the elitism that has apparently reared its head in at least some P/P agencies with IPS programs.

There is also a problem inherent in evaluating IPS effectiveness. Random assignment of high-risk cases between the IPS and routine caseloads fails to account for the classification and unofficial intensive supervision typically carried out by P/P officers. When confronted with unmanageable caseloads, P/P officers identify those cases with greatest risks/needs and devote most of their quality working time to these clients (at the expense of most other cases, which receive little more than "paper" attention). Thus, experimental model research is often comparing IPS with quasi-IPS. Recidivism rates may vary according to the ability of the police, the skill of perpetrators, and the cooperation between P/P agencies and law enforcement agencies. Ironically, IPS may "fail" (statistically) by being "successful": While criminals are arrested for relatively few of the crimes they commit, should they recidivate, the greater scrutiny given to those on intensive supervision increases their risk of detection.

ELECTRONIC MONITORING

Electronic monitoring (EM) is used in conjunction with a variety of programs, in particular, home detention instead of jail for defendants awaiting trial and intensive community supervision. Home confinement with EM has proven appealing because it has the potential to satisfy the goals of imprisonment without the social and financial costs normally associated with imprisonment:

- Satisfaction of the demand for punishment
- Deterrent effect
- Community protection

EM can serve to enforce curfews, usually restricting the offender from leaving home at night. It also enforces both detention (a stricter curfew), by requiring the offender to remain at home at all times except for employment, education, or other specified activities, and incarceration, by requiring the offender to be at home at all times except for very limited activities, such as medical treatment (U.S. Bureau of Justice Assistance, 1989).

The first system of EM monitored the location of parolees, mental patients, and volunteers in Massachusetts from 1964 through 1970. Although interest in EM of offenders always existed, until the crisis in prison overcrowding, "market conditions were never attractive enough to make the technology commercially available" (Przybylski, 1988: 1). Reputedly inspired by a "Spiderman" comic strip, Albuquerque District Court Judge Jack Love asked Michael Goss to develop a device suitable to monitor probation curfews. The "Gosslink" was first attached to the ankle of a 30-year-old probation violator for a 1-month period starting in 1983. Judge Love subsequently sentenced four other offenders to monitored home confinement.

Meanwhile, a Monroe County, Florida, judge tried a new EM system with 12 offenders over a 6-month period; they served house confinement sentences ranging from 2 days to 4 months. As a result, the state of Florida incorporated electronic home confinement in the Correctional Reform Act of 1983, and the following year a pilot program was initiated in Palm Beach County for misdemeanants, mostly drunken drivers. By 1988, EM was being used in 33 states for 2,277 offenders: "Most of those monitored were sentenced offenders on probation or parole, participating in a program of intensive supervision in the community" (Schmidt, 1989: 2). That number has now grown to about 75,000.

EM has been associated primarily with probation, and there is little literature on its use in a parole setting. Parole officers in Utah have used continuously signaling EM on a limited scale to supplement curfew restrictions. The New York State Division of Parole and the New Jersey State Division of Parole use EM as an alternative to incarceration for parole violations, for special high-risk cases, and for those who pose a potential danger to spouse or family. Several different types of systems are used for EM.

Continuously Signaling Systems

Two primary types of **continuously signaling systems** are available: those that use telephone or cell phone lines and those that use a radio-like transmitter and receiver. One system that uses the telephone lines or cellular wireless communication involves the offender wearing a battery-powered moisture-, water-, and shock-proof transmitter that is about the size of a pack of cigarettes and weighs about 6 ounces (Figure 12.1). The device is securely fastened by riveted plastic straps just above the ankle; once strapped on, it can only be removed by stretching or cutting the straps in a manner easily detected by visual inspection. Some versions provide an immediate electronic alert if the band is subjected to tampering. A circuit board contained in the transmitter has an individually calibrated unique identification code. The transmitter emits a signal at regular intervals with a range of about 100 to 150 feet. The signal is monitored by a receiver connected to a 110-volt outlet and a standard telephone jack installed in the residence (or a cell phone unit for those not having access to a basic phone line at home or in a halfway house). The receiver automatically dials a central computer and describes the time the person goes beyond the range of the signal or returns within range and automatically dials the computer when it has been subjected to tampering. If the dialer is disconnected or loses its source of power (e.g., by a power outage), the message is stored until such time as power is restored; at that time, a delayed message describing the time of each activity is sent to the computer.

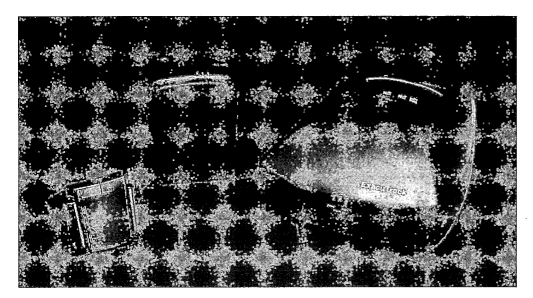

FIGURE 12.1 *Continuously Signaling Ankle Transmitter, Cell Phone, and Monitoring Receiver.*

Source: BI, Incorporated

Simpler continuously signaling systems that do not use a telephone consist of only two basic components: a transmitter and a portable receiver. The transmitter, which is strapped to the offender's ankle or wrist or worn around the neck, emits a radio signal that travels about one city block. By driving past the offender's residence, place of employment, or treatment center, the officer using the handheld portable receiver can verify the offender's presence. This system was used in a pilot program by the New York State Division of Parole to provide enhanced monitoring of parolees whose behavior indicated they were reverting to criminal behavior or were otherwise in violation of parole rules. They were confined to their homes for not less than 60 or more than 120 days. Few hardware failures occurred, and the officer was able to repair them on site. The agency concluded that EM offered a feasible community supervision alternative to incarceration, allowing certain parolees the opportunity to seek treatment while remaining in the community.

Programmed Contact Systems

One **programmed contact system** relies on the telephone and computerized voice identification. The computer records the offender's voice and is then programmed to call him or her at random times and request that a series of words or phrases be repeated; they are then matched with the earlier recording to verify the offender's presence. In the event of a failure to answer the telephone or a voice verification failure, the computer reports a monitoring infraction. Another system requires the offender to wear a pager that is beeped on a random basis, after which he or she is required to call a toll-free number. The caller's voice is verified against an original voiceprint, and the telephone number from which the call is being placed is captured. If the voice does not match or the offender is not where he or she should be, the officer is notified by page within 3 minutes. One programmed contact system uses visual verification through telephone units that transmit black-and-white still pictures of the callers on a 3-inch screen. Another program uses an encoder device attached to a wristband; the band cannot be removed without breaking it. The encoder must be inserted into a verifier box attached to the telephone whenever a computer-generated call is received.

In an effort to address the problem of the repeat drunk-driving offender, Kent County and the Maryland Division of Parole and Probation began a home detention project alternative to incarceration for second- and third-time offenders. These persons, who would normally be incarcerated, are allowed to remain in the community under probation supervision but are restricted to their homes during the evening hours. This latter aspect of supervision is accomplished via a computer that dials the client's home telephone number on random days and times during evening hours. The client answers, and by placing an electronic bracelet attached to his or her wrist to the telephone, he or she sends a code to the computer. The computer then asks several questions of the client. After the call has been processed, a report is sent to the office that confirms that the client's phone number was dialed and verified and gives the date and time. The report is reviewed by the P/P agent the following morning.

Three upstate New York counties, Monroe, Niagara, and Onondaga, used EM with adjudicated juvenile delinquents as a local alternative to out-of-home placement. Participants had been recommended for institutional placement and were instead supervised by a probation officer with a caseload of eight; they were monitored from 3 to 6 months. EM was used primarily to monitor curfew compliance and was supplemented with drug and alcohol tests. Because of caseload size, there was nearly daily contact between the youngster and the probation officer at home, at school, or elsewhere. An evaluation of the program was generally positive but noted a threat to public safety because the probation officer did not have the ability to expeditiously take EM violators into custody— a probation officer is not authorized to make arrests.

Taking advantage of satellite-based technology, some P/P agencies are using a global positioning system (GPS). Orbiting about 12,000 miles above earth, 24 government satellites transmit precise time and position to receivers that pick up signals from multiple satellites simultaneously. A monitoring station determines location by calculating the time it takes the signal to reach the receiver, accurately plotting the receiver's position within a few feet. An active GPS provides constant tracking of an offender's location and is typically used with sex offenders to create customized exclusion zones, such as schools and children's play areas.

A GPS requires the offender to wear a transmitter similar to the EM system's ankle bracelet and to carry, wear, or be near a portable tracking device (PTD). One system allows mobile monitoring on a specially equipped Blackberry handheld device (see Figure 12.2). A GPS cannot track inside buildings or other enclosed areas and is limited to areas with good quality cell phone coverage.

FIGURE 12.2 *Ankle bracelet, GPS tracking device, and Blackberry receiver.*

Source: House Arrest Solution™ is a trademark of ActSoft™, Inc. (c) 2007 Actsoft™, Inc. All Rights Reserved.

The cost is about $15 a day, and it generates large amounts of data that must be processed on a daily basis. It is not unusual for the system to generate a false positive, as when an offender is on a bus that passes through an exclusion zone (Downing, 2006).

Discussion

The appeal of EM is easy to understand when the cost of imprisonment can be in excess of $20,000 per year and the cost of building a new prison can be in excess of $100,000 per bed. Unfortunately, accurate estimates of the cost of imprisonment and the cost of community supervision (intensive or otherwise) do not exist. However, startup costs for EM are high—Albuquerque paid $100,000 for its first 25 devices. To offset these costs, offenders can be required to pay supervision fees or pay for the cost of installing the monitoring telephone, a practice that raises important ethical and legal issues. Should an offender who is otherwise qualified for home confinement be denied access to the program—and thereby face imprisonment—because he or she lacks the ability to pay fees or does not have a residence? If the answer is "no," how far should the county or state go in providing a residence and (in some systems) a telephone? The answers will impact the cost-effectiveness of any electronic home confinement program. Some firms rent and monitor the equipment, but this can be expensive, costing about $25 a day per offender, which does not include personnel costs involved in responding to signal disruptions or checking to see that the equipment has not been tampered with.

Candidates for electronic home confinement are often low-risk offenders who, in most jurisdictions, would be candidates for probation. Thus, the program may actually be adding to the cost of supervision without affecting the problem of jail/prison overcrowding. Conversely, the system is typically used for drunk drivers, and some object that home confinement does not serve as a significant deterrent for a crime that is potentially life-threatening while leaving the offender in a position to repeat his or her criminal act. Home confinement is devoid of any rehabilitative dimension, providing no services to persons who often have extensive social service needs.

Researchers found that the electronic surveillance programs they examined have not affected jail or prison commitments in any noticeable manner. Persons selected for EM are typically from social and economic circumstances that, in any event, would predict a positive outcome. "There is little evaluative evidence to indicate that EM has proved to be a success, however that term is defined" (A. Cohen, 2007: 37). There is also concern over the impact of such programming on P/P officers: "Are these professionals going to see their relationships to offenders change from helping agents to surveillance agents?" (Ball, Huff, and Lilly, 1988: 97).

During 1992, as the popularity of EM grew, news stories began to appear with some frequency detailing the inadequacies of controlling offender behavior through electronic means. The articles highlighted several problems:

- Offenders committed crimes after taking off the device; some even committed crimes while still wearing it.
- Failure to replace older devices with more advanced technology resulted in a failure to monitor offenders adequately.
- Personnel were not always available to respond quickly to tampering or other violations of the conditions of EM.

EM does not prevent crime; it is designed simply to assist in curfew management and location management. However, enforcement is dependent on having sufficient personnel monitoring the equipment and personnel being dispatched to check into reported violations. In New Jersey, for example, the Electronic Monitoring Response Team of parole officers operates 24/7 and is also available to provide emergency backup for field officers.

Key Fact

EM does not prevent crime; it is designed simply to assist in curfew management and location management.

SHOCK PROBATION/PAROLE

In addition to community-based intermediate punishments that have been discussed, some jurisdictions use short-term incarceration that "shocks" the offender while saving prison space. **Shock probation/parole** was pioneered by the state of Ohio, which enacted legislation in 1965 permitting the early release from prison of convicted felons on either probation (within 30 to 120 days of imprisonment) or parole (within 6 months of imprisonment). Since that time, other states (e.g., Idaho, Indiana, Kentucky, Maine, North Carolina, and Texas) have adopted similar statutes. To be eligible for shock probation in Ohio, the offender must be otherwise eligible for a sentence of probation and must file a petition with the court. Those not eligible for probation may file a request with the parole board for shock parole (which excludes those convicted of such crimes as rape, armed robbery, kidnapping, major drug violations, and some burglaries).

Shock probation was authorized by the Texas legislature in 1977 as a rehabilitation technique in which an offender is given a sample of jail/prison and then placed on probation for the remainder of the sentence. Data from Texas indicates that the typical shock probationer is a single white male in his early twenties, a laborer with a tenth- or eleventh-grade education; he was convicted of burglary as a first offense, and the crime is usually drug or alcohol related.

SHOCK INCARCERATION/BOOT CAMPS

In 1983, the states of Georgia and Oklahoma, in an effort to deal with their problems of prison overcrowding, devised shock incarceration often referred to as "boot camp." A **shock incarceration (SI)** program requires short stays of imprisonment—3 to 6 months—combined with shaved heads, marching, close-order drills, exercise, and harassment by corrections officers/drill instructors during 12-hour days. No television, radio, or telephone privileges are available. The **boot camp** resembles its military counterpart—a spartan regimen of rigorous discipline and exercise. (It is of historical interest to note that the use of military discipline was standard in New York's Elmira Reformatory well into the twentieth century—"reinventing the wheel" is symptomatic of American penology.) Georgia has community-based probation boot camps that receive offenders directly from the sentencing court as well as inmate boot camps whose candidates are selected by the Board of Pardons and Paroles. By the end of 1988, 11 states had initiated similar programs; except for New York and Michigan, they are all in the South. By 1992, SI state-operated programs for adult offenders were available in 25 states (MacKenzie and Souryal, 1994).

A Closer Look

Boot Camp for Young Offenders—Historical Antecedent

According to Colonel Vincent M. Masten (1896–1924), a military instructor at Elmira Reformatory, "As part of the institutional regime, they [inmates] are advisedly ordered for supreme military test as to all-around steadiness, which embraces everything a soldier should do, or leave undone; everything from the strictest of undivided attention under command, to execution that exemplifies the highest order of muscular reaction to command, of which constantly improving stature is a component exaction" (Allen, 1926: 378).

Doris MacKenzie et al. (1995: 327) state that "most [boot camps] are designed for young offenders convicted of nonviolent crimes who do not have a prior history of imprisonment." They point out that although "all boot camp prisons use military basic training as a model, they differ considerably in other aspects. For example, some programs select participants from a pool of prisoners sentenced to a traditional sentence of incarceration. Other programs receive inmates directly from the sentencing court" (MacKenzie et al., 1995: 328).

A Closer Look

Women in Shock Incarceration

Rita finishes 50 situps and springs to her feet. At 6 A.M., her platoon begins a 5-mile run, the last portion of the morning's physical training. After 5 months in New York's Lakeview Shock Incarceration Correctional Facility, the morning workout is easy. Rita even enjoys it, taking pride in her physical conditioning.

When Rita graduates and returns to New York City, she will face 6 months of intensive supervision before moving to regular parole. More than two-fifths of Rita's platoon did not make it this far; some withdrew voluntarily, and the rest were removed for misconduct or failure to participate satisfactorily. By completing SI, she will enter parole 11 months before her minimum release date.

The requirements for completing SI are the same for male and female inmates. The women live in a separate housing area of the Lakeview facility. Otherwise, men and women participate in the same education, physical training, drill and ceremony, drug education, and counseling programs. Men and women are assigned to separate work details and attend network group meetings held in inmates' living units (Clark, Aziz, and MacKenzie, 1994).

Varieties of Shock Incarceration/Boot Camps

One program operates in the medium-security prison near Baton Rouge, Louisiana. At dawn there is reveille, and inmates quickly dress in fatigue uniforms and make tight beds; 1 hour later they have formed into four platoons marching to breakfast in step and cadence (Spencer, 1987: 1, 2):

> *Warden, warden can't you see*
> *What this program's done for me.*
> *Sat me down in a barber chair*
> *Turned around and had no hair.*
> *Took away my faded jeans*
> *Now I'm wearing army greens.*

They also spend a considerable portion of their day in counseling and treatment before release to intensive supervision (MacKenzie, Shaw, and Souryal, 1992).

At a prison facility in Beaver Dams (in Schuyler County), New York (Martin, 1988: 15):

A bugle blares at precisely 5:30 A.M., and 32 inmates leap from their bunks.

"Good morning, Sir!" they scream to the scowling corrections officer/drill instructor.

"Are you motivated?" he barks.

"Motivated! Motivated! Motivated! Sir!" the young inmates shout.

In a fury they are dressed, beds made tight, and roaring in unison they are out the door single file. The last man out, a drug dealer from the Bronx, grabs the platoon flag as he runs by.

This regimen lasts 6 months; on successful completion, the inmates are released to parole supervision. The program is limited to persons younger than 26 who have been convicted of nonviolent crimes and are serving their first prison sentence (Bohlen, 1989).

Because of the physical nature of the program, candidates have typically been required to be in good health. In 1998, the Supreme Court ruled that an otherwise eligible candidate could not be denied the boot camp alternative because of a history of hypertension; the plaintiff's rejection was ruled a violation of the 1990 Americans with Disabilities Act (*Pennsylvania Department of Corrections v. Yeskey*, 524 U.S. 206).

A Closer Look

Boot Camp

"Perhaps no other intermediate sanction or prison alternative has captured more attention from the public or policy makers than the boot camp prison. Its combination of punitiveness, visual appeal, and, in the view of some, rehabilitative value seems to offer everything to everyone frustrated with crime committed by young adults, especially males. The idea underlying boot camps is based on simple common sense: give a young rebel a sound three or four month-long thrashing and some firm discipline and that youth will see the evil of his/her way, become an adult, and sin no more" (Jones and Ross, 1997: 147).

Key Fact

Shock incarceration/boot camps stresses brief periods of incarceration under physically and psychologically demanding conditions.

The New York program was authorized by the legislature in 1987 as a way of easing overcrowding—it is the only way inmates (male and female) can be released before reaching their parole eligibility date. Inmates up to the age of 39 can participate if they are within 3 years of release and have not been convicted of a violent felony offense, a sex offense, an escape, or an absconding offense.

Successful SI graduates are typically released 9 months before their eligibility date. The parole division's "Aftershock" program in New York City provides comprehensive services, which are designed to maintain the motivation and discipline the parolee has demonstrated before release, for the parolee's first 6 months on the street. Shock parolees are supervised at a ratio of 25 to 1.

By 1991, New York had the largest SI program in the country and estimated that for every 100 SI inmates released, the state saved $1.94 million that would otherwise be expended for care and custody, plus capital costs associated with the need for greater institutional space. The daily per inmate expense for SI, however, exceeds that of medium-security facilities or camps. The relatively high cost may be linked to the services provided at New York's SI camps—the state rejects the "boot camp" label because that belies the therapeutic environment the program strives to achieve. Although the New York program is considered one of the best, it has a dropout rate of about 25 percent.

The idea behind SI "is to break the prisoners down, strip them of their street identity, and then systematically build them up by providing discipline and self-control" (Spencer, 1987: Sec. 3: 1). Offenders must be young (usually 17 to 25 years old) and in good health and must volunteer for the program—dropouts return to complete their sentences of imprisonment, and many drop out (Parent, 1988). New York SI uses a recycling program for inmates who are removed for disciplinary reasons and for those who are in danger of being removed for unsatisfactory adjustment. It consists of being sent back for refresher training, during which their behavior is closely monitored. Success in recycling leads to being integrated into an existing platoon that will graduate at a date closest to the time owed by the inmate. Inmates who do not perform well after 2 weeks in recycling are removed from the program and returned to prison.

New York, which runs the nation's largest SI program, has a focus on treatment that is absent from most boot camp programs. More than 40 percent of inmate time is spent on treatment and education: 12 hours of academic education, drug and alcohol treatment, prerelease counseling, and decision-making classes (Clark, Aziz, and MacKenzie, 1994; *Seventh Annual Shock Legislative Report*, 1995). The Willard Drug Treatment

Campus is staffed by corrections and parole personnel, and it features a quasi–boot camp environment in which residents participate in daily physical fitness regimens and abide by military standards of bearing, behavior, and dress. Willard is licensed by the Office of Alcoholism and Substance Abuse and must meet standards regarding the number of hours spent in therapy, educational and vocational development, and individual growth activities. The residents are parole violators involved in substance abuse and offenders judicially sanctioned—sent directly to parole supervision by the court for a drug conviction and required to complete the 90-day Willard program. Aftercare includes continuing substance abuse treatment for 6 months through contract agencies.

A Closer Look

Boot Camp, Illinois Style

In Greene County, the Illinois Department of Corrections operates a 200-bed facility where inmates rise at 5:30 A.M. and retire at 9:30 P.M. During that time, they perform 6 hours of manual labor, run two 1.5-mile jogs, and end the day with about 2 hours of basic education and drug treatment. The shaven-headed inmates move double-time everywhere, while corrections officers shout orders and refer to them as "knotheads," "vermin," and "maggots." They are constantly quizzed on the camp's general rules, which include always asking for permission to speak; not "gaping" at visitors; and taking one step back, turning, and waiting for permission to leave after receiving an order. The boot camp term lasts 4 months (Marx, 1994a).

Discussion

Critics of the SI approach argue that it has not proven to have any salutary effect on postincarceration behavior and that even short-term imprisonment exposes the offender to the destructive effects of institutionalization, disrupts his or her life in the community, and further stigmatizes the offender for having been imprisoned (National Advisory Commission on Criminal Justice Standards and Goals, 1975). Furthermore, many SI inmates are released without receiving education or having developed any additional employment skills. No doubt exists that these programs do release strong, healthy, unemployed young men into the community after only a brief term of incarceration. However, in an Oklahoma study, SI graduates returned to prison at a higher rate than did other inmates; in Alabama, boot camp residents, who were first-time nonviolent offenders, had a recidivism rate slightly worse than that of a comparative group of regular inmates (Burns and Vito, 1995). A Georgia study found no difference in return rates between SI and regular inmates (Parent, 1989). In Texas, SI appears to do more harm than good, since within 4 years of release almost 62 percent of boot camp graduates are serving a traditional prison sentence (Anderson, Dyson, and Lee, 1997). Pennsylvania incorporated rehabilitative programming into its six-month boot camp for high-risk adult offenders, but outcome research failed to show any postrelease benefits when compared to similar offenders released from prison (Kempinen and Kurlychek 2003). MacKenzie and her colleagues (2001: 2) conclude that "in general, no significant differences have been found for either adults or juveniles when recidivism rates of boot camp participants have been compared with others receiving more traditional correctional options."

A study of the program in Louisiana found no evidence that SI reduces recidivism. There were no significant differences in recidivism between SI inmates and either parolees from traditional prisons or probationers. All had recidivism rates of approximately 30 percent during their first year of community supervision (MacKenzie, Shaw,

"Tough Love"

At age 14, Gina was in boot camp for a series of petty thefts. The overweight youngster was with 15 other girls on a mandatory 2.6-mile jog at about 6:30 A.M. when she began to lag behind. Two counselors shouted for her to catch up. About 500 feet from the finish, Gina collapsed. Counselors called to her to stop faking. After being examined by a staff nurse, Gina struggled to her feet and began walking to the air-conditioned cottage when she collapsed again. Believing she was faking "again," the staff did nothing. By the time she was transported to a hospital, Gina was dead from heatstroke (Selcraig, 2000). After the death of a 14-year-old boy who was beaten by guards, Florida closed the state's four boot camps (Sexton, 2006).

and Souryal, 1992). A New York in-house research effort revealed that 23 percent of shock parolees were returned to prison within 1 year of their release compared with 28 percent of a comparison group (Office of Policy Analysis and Information, 1989). In a 1992 effort, SI graduates in New York were compared with parolees who matched the SI criteria but who were committed to prison before the establishment of the program (pre-SI) and with parolees who had been removed from the program (removals), as well as with a group who met the SI criteria but did not enter the program (considered). SI graduates were more likely than the comparison groups to be drug offenders with longer maximum sentences. (Those with shorter sentences were less likely to volunteer for SI and more likely to drop out.) After all subjects were out at least 1 year, the following rates of return to prison for violations were recorded:

	Total	Percentage of Violations—Technical	Percentage of Violations—Criminal
SI	1,641	7	7
Pre-SI	1,418	11	8
Removals	1,662	11	9
Considered	366	11	11

After 24 months, SI parolees continued to have lower rates of return to prison for technical and new arrest violations than those of any of the comparison groups (although many of the comparison group members had already been discharged from parole supervision). The New York researchers conclude that SI parolees are more likely to be successful than are comparison group parolees after the completion of 12, 18, and 24 months' time, despite having spent considerably less time in a state prison. A subsequent in-house study (*Seventh Annual Shock Legislative Report*, 1995) revealed that shock parolees are generally more likely, or just as likely, to be successful as a similar comparison group. SI was found particularly effective for young drug offenders.

A boot camp program (IMPACT) was created in North Carolina in 1989. To be eligible, offenders must be ages 16 to 25 and physically fit; they cannot have previously served more than 120 days in an adult correctional facility for convictions of misdemeanors and nonserious felonies. Participants stay for 90 days of drilling, marching, and exercising, which can be extended to 120 days in the event of disciplinary problems, after which they are released to probation supervision. Those without high school diplomas receive educational services, and 70 percent who take the equivalency test receive their general equivalency diploma (GED).

Key Fact

Most research has not revealed benefits for the boot camp approach.

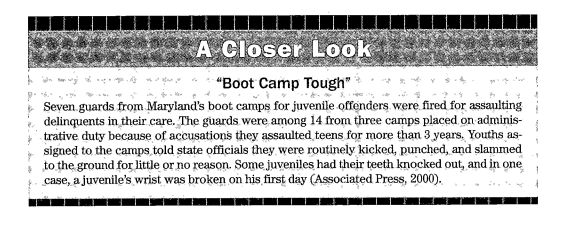

"Boot Camp Tough"

Seven guards from Maryland's boot camps for juvenile offenders were fired for assaulting delinquents in their care. The guards were among 14 from three camps placed on administrative duty because of accusations they assaulted teens for more than 3 years. Youths assigned to the camps told state officials they were routinely kicked, punched, and slammed to the ground for little or no reason. Some juveniles had their teeth knocked out, and in one case, a juvenile's wrist was broken on his first day (Associated Press, 2000).

Researchers compared IMPACT graduates with a similar group on probation who had not gone through boot camp. They found that while other similar studies reported little or no differences, in North Carolina, *boot camp participation was significantly associated with rearrest*. They note that while SI aims to instill pride and responsibility, the boot camp graduates must now bear the stigma of being an "ex-con," a significant barrier to gainful employment (Jones and Ross, 1997). Similar results were found in a Cleveland, Ohio, boot camp program where 72 percent of the graduates recidivated, as opposed to 50 percent of a control group released from Ohio Department of Youth Services facilities (Peters, Thomas, and Zamberlan, 1997).

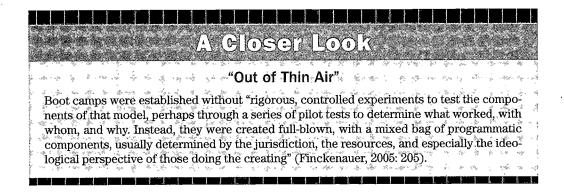

"Out of Thin Air"

Boot camps were established without "rigorous, controlled experiments to test the components of that model, perhaps through a series of pilot tests to determine what worked, with whom, and why. Instead, they were created full-blown, with a mixed bag of programmatic components, usually determined by the jurisdiction, the resources, and especially the ideological perspective of those doing the creating" (Finckenauer, 2005: 205).

Boot camp programs are in place to save prison or juvenile institutional resources; an offender sent to a shock program avoids long-term incarceration. This point assumes that in the absence of such programming, the offender would have been incarcerated and not placed on probation. In Florida, for example, candidates for SI are selected from among those sentenced to traditional incarceration, although one study found that they tended to be those who were less serious offenders (Sechcrest, 1989). In Georgia, however, SI is used by judges as part of probation sentences. In Alabama, boot camp is part of the discretionary sentencing power of a judge and is sometimes the result of a plea bargain agreement (Burns, 1993). In Arizona, which established its program in 1988, research found that only some of the inmates in boot camp were diverted from prison and that "the rest would have been placed on regular probation or intensive probation" (Palumbo and Peterson, 1994: 8).

Although SI might not meet the needs of rehabilitation and community safety, it appears to meet the short-term needs of political officials who can boast of "doing something" about crime and criminals. Dale Parent found that SI was given to "the very offenders who would likely have been given nonconfinement sentences if SI were not available—thus using more, not less, prison space"—referred to as "net widening" (1989: 12). This is not the case in New York, where Department of Corrections (DOC)

A Closer Look

Absurdity

"Based on a vague, if not unstated, theory of crime and an absurd theory of behavioral change ('offenders need to be broken down'—through a good deal of humiliation and threats—and then 'built back up'), boot camps could not possibly have 'worked' " (Latessa, Cullen, and Gendreau, 2002: 44).

personnel, not judges, have charge of the program: "New York law defines SI eligibility criteria. The New York DOC screens prison admissions to identify cases that meet these criteria. If inmates pass their physical examinations, they may volunteer to participate. Judges have no veto power. When inmates complete the program, they are released by the parole board, not by judges. By consulting New York's parole guidelines, the DOC estimates that the average inmate who completes SI will shorten his or her prison term by 12 to 18 months" (Parent, 1989: 15).

An element of absurdity exists in the prison boot-camp approach, particularly in light of the fact that the military has drastically changed the way it trains recruits, no longer using abusive or degrading methods: "While the military has reduced the harshness of its training, boot-camp prisons have embraced an outdated version of military basic training" (Jacoby et al., 1994: 32). Others have stated, "The very idea of using physically and verbally aggressive tactics in an effort to 'train' people to act in a prosocial manner is fraught with contradiction" (Morash and Rucker, 1990: 214). Such programs run the risk of turning out young men who are more aggressive and hostile than they would have been under routine imprisonment: "The irony in emphasizing an aggressive model of masculinity in a correctional setting is that these very characteristics may explain criminality" (Morash and Rucker, 1990: 216). A cynic might argue that the boot camp approach is simply a scam for gaining public acquiescence to the (otherwise politically unacceptable) early discharge of inmates. Two researchers posit a grim possibility—"the effect of boot camp is that it will be effective for those who will subsequently put their lessons of discipline and organization to use in street gangs and drug distribution networks" (Feeley and Simon, 1992: 464).

Others note that after boot camp, military personnel enter a structured, stable environment that provides for their basic needs of food, shelter, clothing, employment, and health care, a situation very different from the environment to which most SI subjects will return (Mathias and Mathews, 1991). MacKenzie (1994: 65) concludes: "If the core components of boot camps (military atmosphere, drill, hard labor, physical training) reduced recidivism, we would have expected that the boot camp releasees in all states would do better than the offenders in the comparison groups. This did not happen. The military atmosphere does not appear to reduce recidivism." The military atmosphere did not increase recidivism among boot camp graduates, whereas postrelease intensive supervision was associated with better adjustment for both boot camp and comparison groups (Cronin, 1994; MacKenzie and Souryal, 1994).

In 1994, Connecticut closed the nation's first boot camp for juveniles run by the National Guard after an investigation revealed gang activity, drug use, and violence (Johnson, 1994). Other states, faced with scandals (e.g., beatings of young inmates) and poor result statistics, have done the same (Blair, 2000).

Conclusions

Based on 10 years of data, boot camp participants reported positive short-term changes in attitudes and behaviors and also had better problem-solving and coping skills, but with few exceptions, these positive changes did not lead to reduced recidivism. Those boot camps that produced lower recidivism rates offered more treatment services, had longer sessions, and included more intensive postrelease supervision. However, not all programs with these features had successful results. The length of stay in boot camps—usually from 90 to 120 days—is too brief to realistically affect recidivism, and there is typically insufficient preparation for reentry into the community. Many boot camps provide little or no postrelease programming to prepare graduates to lead productive lives (Parent, 2003). Based on an analysis of the research, MacKenzie (2006) concludes that there is no evidence that boot camps are effective in reducing the recidivism of juveniles or adults.

Day Reporting Centers

The concept of the day reporting center originated in Great Britain as a response to less serious but chronic offenders who lacked basic skills and were often dependent on drugs or alcohol. The British experience led Connecticut and Massachusetts in 1986 to set up **day reporting centers (DRCs)**, whose purposes are "to heighten control and surveillance of offenders placed on community supervision, to increase offender access to treatment programs and services, to give officials more proportional and certain sanctions to be used for less serious probation or parole violations, or to reduce prison or jail crowding" (Parent, 1990: 9). New Jersey employs the DRC as an alternative to incarceration for technical parole violators, and while offenders are in the program, they are supervised by parole officers assigned to the DRC. "Offenders report to the centers frequently (usually once or even twice a day), and treatment services are usually provided on-site either by the [public or private] agency running the program or by other human services agencies whose staff work at the site" (Parent, 1996: 51).

Typically, offenders must be on the DRC premises 18 hours per week during the program's most intensive phase. An offender usually checks in at the DRC early each morning and briefly talks with a counselor before going to work; after work, offenders often return to the DRC for an evening group counseling session. When not in the DRC, they are monitored by telephone calls to their job sites, homes, or other locations where they are supposed to be. Each offender fills out a daily itinerary, which helps to keep track of their whereabouts in the community: "Itineraries teach offenders the importance of scheduling and planning and of managing one's time to avoid situations that may lead to drug use relapse, to new crimes, or to violations of the conditions of supervision" (Parent, 1996: 52). Most DRCs provide job training and placement services, counseling, and education and also require offenders to provide restitution and perform community service.

In 1990, the Social Services Department of the District of Columbia Superior Court, which administers probation services, established the P/P Resource Center (PPRC) to provide a structured nonresidential program for high-risk offenders with a history of drug abuse. This DRC is located at an independent site, separate from routine P/P operations, in the northeast section of the nation's capitol. The PPRC has P/P officers who are certified addiction counselors (CACs) as full-time staff members. Professional staff includes employees from appropriate federal government agencies assigned to provide on-site direct services or referrals. Staff work on varying shifts to provide comprehensive monitoring of PPRC clients and maintenance of center operations. The project also contracts for additional services from the private sector.

The PPRC program consists of three distinct phases: assessment, treatment, and continuing care. A caseload management approach is employed and coordinated with staff from other participating agencies. The P/P officers/CACs monitor and supervise program participants throughout the treatment and continuing care phases. The assessment phase begins with a series of diagnostic services: intake interviews and medical and psychiatric or psychological screening. In the second phase, drug treatment strategies, education, counseling, support services delivery, and various supervision activities are tailored to meet the identified needs of each client. This includes a range of

Key Fact

Day reporting centers are used as an alternative to incarceration for P/P violators and can provide a variety of services for probationers and parolees.

community sanctions such as curfew, home detention, and electronic surveillance. The continuing care phase carries over into existing P/P supervision programs where participants are assigned to other P/P officers who are CACs. These officers provide long-term treatment and supervision throughout the remainder of the court-imposed sentence.

The Adult Probation Department of Maricopa County, Arizona, has 3 DRCs for nonviolent offenders during the final 60 days of their jail sentence. The participant follows an hour-by-hour schedule of courses offered at the DRC and other community-based agencies and/or participates in a job search program until employed. Participants with employment follow daily schedules; when not participating in work or programs, participants are required to remain at home, where they are monitored by probation and surveillance officers. After completing the program, participants continue under standard supervision or IPS. A failure to complete the program results in reincarceration.

Now that we have examined intermediate punishments, a concluding chapter reviews the research and issues related to the effectiveness of P/P and considers the future of these two approaches to criminal offenders.

Key Terms

boot camp (p. 370)
continuously signaling systems (p. 366)
day reporting centers (DRCs) (p. 377)
diversion (p. 353)
electronic monitoring (EM) (p. 365)

intensive supervision (p. 352)
intermediate punishments (p. 352)
programmed contact system (p. 367)
shock incarceration (SI) (p. 370)
shock probation/parole (p. 370)

Internet Connections

American Correctional Association: corrections.com/aca/index
American Probation and Parole Association: www.appa-net.org
Center for Community Corrections: communitycorrectionsworks.org
International Community Corrections Association: iccaweb.org
National Institute of Corrections: nicic.org

Review Questions

1. What is the real goal of intermediate punishments?
2. What are the different types of programs that come under intermediate punishments?
3. What are the two premises on which intensive supervision is based?
4. Why haven't these two premises been realized?
5. What has research into intensive supervision revealed?
6. What led to the use of electronic monitoring (EM) in P/P?
7. How is EM accomplished?
8. What are the shortcomings of shock incarceration (SI)/boot camp?
9. What has research into the effectiveness of SI found?
10. What are the purposes of a day reporting center (DRC)?

Conclusion: The Future of Probation and Parole

Outline

This concluding chapter examines the question of success or failure of probation and parole and the interrelated issue of recidivism, followed by an exploration of the direction of probation and parole in the second decade of the twenty-first century.

PROBATION AND PAROLE: SUCCESS OR FAILURE?

Is probation/parole (P/P) a success or a failure? In examining the degree to which P/P is successful, the results are often contradictory. The methodology of some research efforts is simply unsound; however, even methodologically sound research has not allowed us to answer the question. For example, one study (Lerner, 1977) found that parole supervision in New York reduced the postrelease criminal activity of a group of (conditional) releasees compared with a group of dischargees released from the same institution without supervision. A similar study in Connecticut (Sachs and Logan, 1979) found that parole supervision resulted in only a modest reduction in recidivism. In California, however, no significant difference was found in the recidivism rates of persons released with or without parole supervision (Jackson, 1983; Star, 1979). A study of prisoners released in 1994 in 15 states (Solomon, Kachnowski, and Bhati, 2005) revealed that parole supervision did not have a significant impact on rearrest rates. But a 2006 study in New Jersey revealed that after 2 years, parole supervision made a significant difference in arrest and conviction rates: 23.6 percent of parolees had been convicted of a new crime while a control group with similar characteristics and offense histories released without supervision had a 2-year conviction rate of 43 percent (Robbins and Ostermann, 2006).

A New Orleans study (Geerken and Hayes, 1993) found that 8 percent of adult arrests for burglary or armed robbery from 1974 to 1986 involved offenders who were on probation; the figure for parolees was less than 2 percent. A study in New York of 22,941 conditional releasees (15 percent) and parolees (85 percent) released in 1991 and supervised by parole officers were tracked for 2 years: Fewer than 13 percent were returned to prison for new felony convictions (New York State Division of Parole, 1994). A 1994–1995 study of more than 2,000 felons placed on probation in Arizona in 1989 and 1990 revealed that 61 percent had completed their term of supervision while 25 percent were convicted of new crimes and sentenced to prison; 4 percent absconded (Administrative Office of the Courts, 1996). The figures for those on probation in Marion County, Indiana, in 2002 revealed that 63 percent successfully completed supervision, 13.2 percent had probation revoked for a new offense, and 23.9 percent had probation revoked for a technical violation. A study of parolees in Hawaii (Kassebaum et al., 1999) who were tracked for 3 years found that 70.7 percent had no criminal convictions, and 11 percent had one or more felony convictions; approximately one-half had their parole revoked, mostly for technical violations. Outcome research in Arkansas revealed that out of a sample of 2,489 probationers, after 3 years, 248 (10 percent) were reincarcerated for new offenses and 170 (7 percent) for technical violations; of 1,741 parolees, after 3 years, 149 (8.5 percent) were reincarcerated for new offenses, and 311 (4.8 percent) for technical violations (Department of Community Corrections, 2006). Do these studies indicate success or failure? In order to appreciate the difficulty of providing a definitive answer, we need to consider two issues:

1. What is meant by the term *success* in P/P?
2. What is meant by the term *adequate supervision* in P/P?

What Is Meant by Success?

A major part of the problem is the word **success**. For example, a researcher for the California Youth Authority candidly portrays his own findings, noting that success depends on which statistics one decides to emphasize:

> Parole behavior in the sample can be made to look quite good, especially considering the high levels of pre–Youth Authority crime, or quite bad. For example, only 13 percent were sent to state prison for parole-period offenses during the 24 months of follow-up, resulting in an 87 percent "success rate" by this criterion. Some correctional jurisdictions who report spectacularly high success

rates in fact use such a restricted measure. Alternatively, regarding the same sample we could accurately report that 77 percent of the sample had been arrested or temporarily detained during the 24 months leaving a "success rate" by this criterion of only 23 percent. (Wiederanders, 1983: 4)

According to the Bureau of Justice Statistics (2001), success rates of those under parole supervision have remained relatively stable for more than a decade. About 4 in every 10 persons discharged from parole successfully complete their term of supervision in the community. As might be expected, the success rates for those released by a parole board are higher (54 percent) than those who released under good-time provisions/mandatory release (33 percent).

The success of a P/P system is usually conceived of in terms of **recidivism** (Maltz, 1984: 54):

[W]hen recidivism is discussed in a correctional context, its meaning seems fairly clear. The word is derived from the Latin *recidere*, to fall back. A recidivist is one who, after release from custody for having committed a crime, is not rehabilitated. Instead, he or she falls back, relapses, into former behavior patterns and commits more crimes. This conceptual definition of recidivism may seem quite straightforward; however, an operational definition, one that permits measurement, is not so simple.

The 1976 edition of the *Dictionary of Criminal Justice Data Terminology* defines the word *recidivism* as "the repetition of criminal behavior; habitual criminality." However, the 1981 edition avoids providing a definition and instead notes:

Efforts to arrive at a single standard statistical definition of recidivism have been hampered by the fact that the correct referent of the term is the actual repeated criminal or delinquent behavior of a given person or group, yet the only available statistical indicators of that behavior are records of such system events as rearrests, reconvictions, and probation or parole violations or revocations. It is recognized that these data reflect agency decisions about events and do not closely correspond with actual criminal behavior.

Jay Albanese and his colleagues (1981: 51) point out that:

- A wide disparity exists in the definition of revocation and recidivism.
- Revocation/recidivism rates without a standardized definition have little comparative value.
- A criterion (or criteria) of "effectiveness" is not well defined.

Gordon Waldo and David Griswold (1979: 230) note that being arrested and convicted for any crime is not sufficient as an operational definition of recidivism. They quote Charles Tittle: "Being arrested for gambling cannot be accepted as evidence of recidivism for a burglar." In addition, the extensive use of plea bargaining means that merely looking at the crime for which a person is convicted does not allow for a determination of whether the person has committed the same crime again, or a less serious or more serious crime. Similarly, with respect to probation recidivism rates, it is necessary to distinguish between those under supervision for misdemeanors and those convicted of felonies because felony probationers have significantly higher rates of recidivism than misdemeanants (Petersilia, 1998b). Then there is the problem of technical violations—do we rate them as recidivism? No consistent definition of recidivism exists, so "one cannot state with any degree of assurance whether a given recidivism rate is high or low; there is no 'normal' recidivism rate as there is a normal body temperature" (Maltz, 1984: 23).

Further complicating efforts to determine success is the issue of *selection*: P/P agencies receiving (via judges and parole boards) a greater number of low-risk offenders are more likely to have higher rates of success. A conservative judge/parole board, or perhaps one fearful of an adverse public reaction, will release fewer offenders to supervision, and those who are placed on probation or parole will tend to be the "boy scouts"—lower-risk offenders who will probably produce impressive (statistical) measurements of success for the agency. Is a comparison of the results of various P/P agencies any more relevant than the one that compares the success rates of doctors treating AIDS patients with those treating less catastrophic ailments?

Research has identified a number of variables that correlate well with success or failure on probation: age (younger offenders have greater difficulty adhering to probation conditions), employment (those who are employed and financially stable do better), marital status (those who are married are less likely to violate probation), and offense (those on probation for drug- and theft-related crimes have higher recidivism rates) (Liberton, Silverman, and Blount, 1990). The reverse is also true: High-risk offenders lessen the chances of success. This is not only so in P/P, but also in education and medicine. Inner-city schools with high rates of both disorganization and impoverished families and the hospitals serving these same populations will have less successful outcomes than their counterparts in middle-class environs. Is crime a symptom, a result, or a causal factor of these conditions? If crime is a dependent variable, what can reasonably be expected of P/P?

Alvin Cohen (2002) points to a policy problem with respect to research on P/P success rates: If an intensive supervision program costs $1,000 a year per offender and has a 55 percent success rate, is it worth spending $1,500 to achieve a 60 percent success rate—assuming that is possible? Suppose it costs $2,000 or $3,000. Is the cost-benefit outcome then worthwhile? Research cannot answer such questions.

The basic mechanism of P/P supervision is client contact. Thus, as noted in Chapter 12, issues of caseload size and increased contacts have been something of a preoccupation in this field. Contacts are easily quantifiable, so little beyond a "numbers game" has been studied. Faye Taxman (2002) notes that the endeavor is essentially atheoretical because other than the contact being seen as some type of control, there has been an absence of interest in the quality of the contact, be it for control or rehabilitation. This issue is of great import because studies of reduced caseload size reveal that "unless the contacts are more than 'check-ins,' it is unlikely that they will impact on offender outcomes" (Taxman, 2002: 17). This is critical because there is research indicating that providing therapy predicts better outcomes and that such provision should follow social services protocols that stress **continuity of care**: "Interventions offered in prison, the community, or community-based facilities should be built on each other" (Taxman, 2002: 20). Because it is likely that clientele will be involved in various interventions during the various phases of the justice process, "it is important for the approaches to be compatible" (Taxman, 2002: 20).

What Is Meant by Adequate Supervision?

Joan Petersilia and her colleagues (1985: v), researchers for the Rand Corporation, noted that "over one-third of California's probation population consists of felons convicted in Superior Court—persons who are often quite different from the less serious offenders probation was originally conceived and structured to handle." They found that 51 percent of a sample of California offenders on **felony probation** who were sentenced in 1980 and tracked for 40 months were reconvicted, 18 percent for violent crimes. They conclude (1985: vi) that "felons granted probation present a serious threat to public safety" and that this threat is not being adequately managed by probation agencies in California and probably elsewhere. In Massachusetts, for example, the number of persons sentenced to probation for crimes against persons increased between 1982 and 1993 by more than 250 percent. As noted in Chapter 1, dramatic increases in probation are often linked to prison overcrowding, which is sometimes exacerbated by abolishing parole (as was the case in Virginia).

Research into felony probation in Missouri and Kentucky revealed a different outcome. Both studies were designed to replicate that of Petersilia and her colleagues in California, that is, to determine whether felony offenders placed on probation in Missouri and Kentucky presented risks similar to those in California. Significant differences were found (McGaha, Fichter, and Hirschburg, 1987):

	California (Percent)	Missouri (Percent)	Kentucky (Percent)
Rearrests	65.0	22.3	22.1
Reconvictions	51.0	12.0	17.7
Violent felonies	18.0	7.1	4.1

The results of research into felony probation in New Jersey fell about midway between the findings in California and those in Kentucky and Missouri—4 years after those convicted of felonies were sentenced to probation, 40 percent had been rearrested and 35 percent were reconvicted (Whitehead, 1989).

Based on their research, Petersilia et al. (1985: 64) argue that "routine probation, by definition, is *inappropriate for most felons.*" What, other than imprisonment, is *appropriate* for most felons? According to Petersilia and her colleagues:

> We believe that the criminal justice system needs an alternative, indeterminate form of punishment for those offenders who are too antisocial for the relative freedom that probation now offers, but not so seriously criminal as to require imprisonment. A sanction is needed that would impose intensive surveillance, coupled with substantial community service and restitution. It should be structured to satisfy public demands that the punishment fit the crime, to show criminals that crime really does not pay, and to control potential recidivists. (1985: ix)

The Rand Corporation researchers recommend a different form of probation supervision:

> In response to changes in the probation population, the system should redefine the role and powers of probation officers. Probation officers cannot deal with felony probationers in the same ways they have dealt with misdemeanants. We certainly do not recommend that they abandon their counseling or rehabilitative roles; however, because the probation population includes a large number of active criminals, we support the growing legal and policy trend toward quasi-policing roles for probation officers, whenever the situation warrants it. Attention should be paid to the recruitment and training of probation officers. Different skills may be required of officers whose primary responsibility is surveillance rather than rehabilitation. (Petersilia et al., 1985: xiii)

This would result in the **combined model**—monitoring/control and social services—discussed in Chapter 10 that involves unannounced home and employment visits; checks for drug use; close working relationships with law enforcement agencies; and attention to client needs, including employment, housing, and counseling, which provides social and psychological support.

Just as there are no recognized standards for P/P success, supervision has no generally accepted levels of quality. Based on this author's experience in parole, any number of jurisdictions included in the research discussed earlier provide little in the way of supervision that offers both monitoring/control and social services.

GOALS OF PROBATION AND PAROLE

What are the goals of P/P? Success can be measured only against anticipated outcomes. If a P/P agency is based on a **social services model**, success is measured by the delivery of or referral to services, including education, training, employment, and counseling, and client-consumer satisfaction with the level of service. This type of agency will often be affected by variables beyond its control, such as variations in the unemployment rate, particularly for low-skilled workers. A relatively low rate of unemployment has apparently made it easier for ex-offenders to secure employment (Meredith, 2000). A jurisdiction with readily available employment will presumably do better at job placement than the same agency in a jurisdiction that has a relatively high rate of unemployment; similarly, an agency located in a community with a variety of available social services will be more likely to show a greater level of success than will one in a community with a paucity of such agencies. The interrelated problems of poverty and the collapse of inner-city families are important issues with which P/P agencies have to contend but are helpless to affect.

If a P/P agency is based on a **control model**, success is measured according to the agency's ability to hold the offender accountable for his or her behavior. The discovery of supervision violations and/or new crimes by close P/P monitoring, however, could statistically increase recidivism rates by uncovering behavior that might not otherwise be discovered. Recidivism may also be related to unemployment—and to the extent that it is, the success of this type of agency will depend in part on the state of the economy. Recidivism is also related to other practical issues. First, one cannot account for undetected criminality; second, arrest and prosecution are often a measure of the law enforcement activity in a given community. Thus, different levels of law enforcement will produce different levels of official (statistical) recidivism, regardless of P/P agency effectiveness. Indeed, a more effective control model agency may enhance the law enforcement function (e.g., through close cooperation with the police) and will thus help to (statistically) *produce* more recidivism—arrests and convictions of agency clientele. David Stanley points out what happens if we use recidivism as a measure: "An offender can be unemployed, ignorant, promiscuous, and drunk but still a success as far as the criminal justice system is concerned if he commits no crime" (1976: 173). Indeed, a cynic (realist?) might suggest encouraging drug abusers to become alcoholics instead.

Further, how are technical violations of P/P rules to be treated (statistically) with respect to agency goals? More vigorous (i.e., intensive) supervision may *produce* more technical violations (although the research is still not clear on this issue), whereas an agency that provides little or no supervision will have few (detected) technical violations—hence, fewer revocations of P/P. The level of individual and agency tolerance for technical violations will also affect the revocation rate, and a higher revocation rate of technical violations may result in a lower number of new convictions—offenders screened out of supervision before they can be arrested for new crimes.

Because neither the social services agency model nor the control model agency need make any claim about rehabilitation, the question of postsupervision arrests and convictions need not be raised. In agencies that include rehabilitation as a (or perhaps *the*) goal, this issue needs to be considered. How long does the agency retain (statistical) responsibility for success or failure of a client who has completed supervision—6 months, 1 year, or life? The implication is that such an agency will succeed in producing a lasting change in client behavior. Is it reasonable to expect a P/P agency—or any other brief intervention—to "correct" a lifetime of problems and problematic behavior? An additional question concerns how to weigh recidivism when the instant offense is a great deal less serious than the original crime. For example, is an armed robber convicted of shoplifting considered a success or a failure?

Perhaps the most difficult agency to evaluate in terms of success or failure is one based on a combined model, and most P/P agencies in the United States fall into this category. In this type of agency, an explicit or implicit claim is usually related to services and rehabilitation *and* control. An agency with such broad purposes—with a plethora of complicated goals—cannot fail, nor can it succeed—it presents no clear-cut basis for measuring anticipated outcome. The claims are too broad, too many, and too dependent on variables beyond agency control (e.g., the economy, the level of law enforcement in the community, the screening of offenders by judges/parole boards, the availability of resources in the community) for a research effort to analyze in any relevant manner. As a result, this type of agency has been subjected to criticism on the basis of research that focuses a "microscope" on one goal and finds it wanting. The goals are literally picked apart, leaving the agency vulnerable to those who would discredit P/P.

Petersilia (1993: 69) argues that P/P agencies need to "customize their mission statement, methods, and performance indicators so that they reflect local resources and priorities." The mission should be one that can reasonably be expected to be fulfilled and clearly related to the unique services provided by the agency, and performance indicators should be specified: "When public agencies fail to define their mission internally, political influences are more apt to define it for them. And when they fail to articulate how they should be evaluated, outcome measurements such as recidivism rates will likely be imposed upon them" (Petersilia, 1993: 76). Petersilia (1998a, 1998b) also notes that responsibilities of P/P agencies include functions that cannot be measured by recidivism rates, including doing presentence and executive clemency investigations; collecting fines and fees; monitoring community service, work release, and furloughs; and providing victim services.

One should consider the very reason that P/P exists. As penological history in the United States indicates (discussed in Chapters 1, 5, and 6), stripped of the humanistic dynamic, P/P exists for *economic reasons*. In terms of budgetary considerations, if P/P were as costly as or even equal in cost to imprisonment, it would be so severely restricted as to no longer constitute an important issue in criminal justice.

A Closer Look

Tough Talk, Weak Policy

"By exercising discretion, parole boards can single out the more violent and dangerous offenders for longer incarceration. When States abolish parole or reduce the discretion of parole authorities, they replace a rational, controlled system of 'earned' release for selected inmates with 'automatic' release for nearly all inmates.

"No-parole systems sound tough but remove a gatekeeping role that can protect victims and communities. Parole boards can demand that released inmates receive drug treatment, and research shows that coerced treatment is as successful as voluntary participation. If parole boards also require a plan for the released offender to secure a job and a place to live in the community, the added benefit is to refocus prison staff and corrections budgets on transition planning" (Petersilia, 2000b: 5).

As noted in Chapter 1, most serious crimes do not result in an arrest. Of those arrested for felonies, well in excess of 50 percent are not prosecuted for felony crimes; most of those prosecuted for felonies plead guilty, usually the result of negotiations (plea bargaining). Thus, when discussing issues of punishment, *residuals* are involved— but these are sufficiently large, so common sense indicates they cannot all be incarcerated. Even if that were a proper response, enough prison space could not be created expeditiously, nor would taxpayers be willing to pay the required taxes and/or allow the shifting of public resources. However, California is spending more money on prisons than on public colleges and universities, and other states are following California's lead (Butterfield, 1995). What options remain viable in the wake of a downturn in the economy and revenue shortfalls in many states?

Probation offers the first line of defense against prison overcrowding, and if no parole system is in operation, probation becomes *the* method by which prison populations are controlled. As a result, serious felony offenders, for whom probation has historically not been intended, become probation clients. At the other end, mandatory prison releasees typically receive inadequate (if any) supervision because little incentive exists for politicians to expend tax dollars on programs for nondiscretionary-released offenders; hence there is complete absence of public officials on whom to lay blame in the event a releasee generates negative publicity. In any event, relatively few offenders

A Closer Look

With Cash Tight, States Reassess Long Jail Terms: Strict Laws Loosened

According to a November 10 *New York Times* article, "After two decades of passing ever tougher sentencing laws promoting a prison building boom, state legislatures facing budget crises are beginning to rethink their costly approaches to crime" (Butterfield, 2003a: 1).

will remain in prison their entire lives—more than 97 percent of all state prison inmates will eventually be released (Schriro, 2000).

In the year 2000, more than half a million persons were released from prison. By way of comparison, in 1980, fewer than 170,000 were released (Travis, 2000). The issue remains: Who will make the release decision—judges, prison officials, or parole boards? Will these decisions involve a careful analysis of the case, comparing it to similar cases (issues of equity and reasonable predictions of future behavior), or involve only risk control? Petersilia (2000a) notes that when states abolish parole or reduce the amount of parole board discretion, they effectively replace a rational controlled system of "earned" release for selected inmates with automatic release for nearly all inmates. And what happens after they are released? "Underfunded parole agencies in many jurisdictions have made parole more a legal status than a systematic process of reintegrating returning prisoners" (Travis, 2000: 1).

"The very existence of discretionary release," notes Peggy Burke (2006: 30), "creates an incentive for inmates to engage in activities that will better prepare them for transition to the community." One of the roles of a parole board is to ensure that an inmate is prepared for release, which includes having a residence and some means of support. In the absence of a parole board, release planning may be inadequate or absent, presenting parole officers with supervision challenges that can translate into more parole violations. But these violations can be without consequences, as is seen in Washington, a state without discretionary release but with an overcrowded prison system.

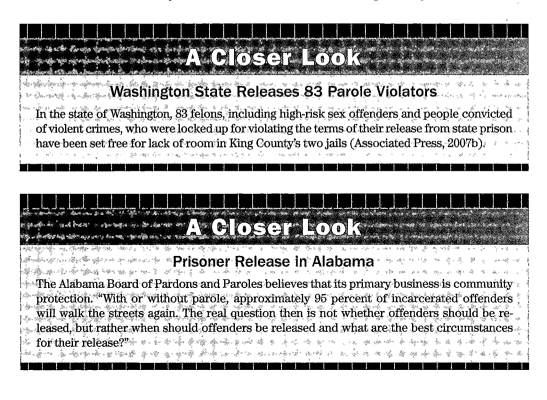

A Closer Look

Washington State Releases 83 Parole Violators

In the state of Washington, 83 felons, including high-risk sex offenders and people convicted of violent crimes, who were locked up for violating the terms of their release from state prison have been set free for lack of room in King County's two jails (Associated Press, 2007b).

A Closer Look

Prisoner Release in Alabama

The Alabama Board of Pardons and Paroles believes that its primary business is community protection. "With or without parole, approximately 95 percent of incarcerated offenders will walk the streets again. The real question then is not whether offenders should be released, but rather when should offenders be released and what are the best circumstances for their release?"

WHERE HAVE WE BEEN, WHERE ARE WE NOW, AND WHERE ARE WE GOING?

When the first edition of this book was published in 1977, the indeterminate sentence and parole were under great scrutiny and pressure, the result of Robert Martinson's article "What Works?" (1974) and publication of the full study (Lipton, Martinson, and Wilks, 1975) the following year (discussed in Chapter 6). In the years that followed, about a dozen states adopted determinate sentencing and abolished parole release. By the twenty-first century, most states had either abolished the indeterminate sentence or severely restricted the categories of offenders eligible for parole release—a turn toward **classicalism**. Although failing to accomplish equal punishment for crimes of equal severity, as per classicalism, determinate sentencing removed a rational vehicle for responding to prison overcrowding. Policy makers and public officials failed to learn the lessons of history reviewed in Chapters 5 and 6. The establishment of parole with the onset of the Great Depression was a means of alleviating prison overcrowding—rehabilitation was not a motivating factor.

A Closer Look

Déjà Vu

The Manhattan grand jury was led to believe that the murders of several policemen were due to an "alleged laxity in the state parole system." According to crime reporter Hickman Powell, "The grand jurors started under the impression, assiduously fostered by J. Edgar Hoover and reactionary policemen, that parole is crooked and incompetent and habitually frees dangerous criminals. They were surprised to discover the murders in question were not to be blamed on parole, and that the parole system was a valuable agency of public protection. In most states, parole continues to be merely a disguise for executive clemency, a means of emptying the prisons and keeping their budgets down. In other states, notably New York, the majority of prisoners continue to be released after a certain time, to live under rigid supervision and to be sent summarily back to prison if they don't behave." Parole judgments are "necessarily fallible, and when the inevitable mistakes are made, the propagandists shout about the inequities of parole" (Powell, 2000 [1939]; footnote 38).

The rightward movement of politics in the United States swept the criminal justice system into overdrive: "Law and order" rhetoric beget a policy leading to more arrests and more convictions, particularly for drug offenses. States began abolishing the **indeterminate sentence** and parole or severely restricting their use. In Georgia, for example, all violent offenders and residential burglars serve a minimum of 90 percent of their sentence; offenders convicted of murder, various sex offenses, and armed robbery serve 100 percent of their prison sentence. In New York, violent offenders are not eligible for parole.

These policies were the driving force behind the corrections overload as prison populations reached record levels and the courts began to intervene. Overcrowding and court intervention led to forced releases, and some states passed "one-in/one-out" legislation. This proved insufficient. As pressure built, criminal justice systems increased their use of probation, particularly in those states without parole release. Offenders who would otherwise have been incarcerated (e.g., serious felons who were not candidates for traditional probation) burdened ill-equipped probation agencies.

In 1994, Congress enacted the Violent Crime Control and Law Enforcement Act providing incentive grants to states that adopted truth-in-sentencing (TIS) laws. TIS requires an offender to serve a fixed portion of his or her sentence before being eligible for release. States that require offenders convicted of a federally defined Part 1 violent crime to serve at least 85 percent of their sentences are eligible for federal TIS grants, which can be used to build or expand prisons to house violent offenders or to construct or enhance correctional facilities for nonviolent offenders in order to free up bed space for violent criminals. The TIS money covers bricks and mortar, but not the staggering operating costs associated with prisons. As noted in Chapter 5, prison systems throughout the United States are struggling with the problem of recruiting and maintaining an adequate number of correction officers.

A hurried scramble for ways to deal with the opposing pressures—arrest and incarcerate offenders versus decrease prison populations—ensued. New terminology resulted, with the term *corrections* being displaced by the buzzword of a new era, **intermediate sanctions**. Under this rubric were regurgitated models: From the late-nineteenth-century Elmira system sprang boot camps reinvented for the 1990s; the California Special Intensive Parole Unit of the early 1950s was reinvented as intensive probation supervision (IPS); and fondness for technology led penology to adopt electronic surveillance.

New "What Works?" research was critical of these schemes because they failed to control recidivism while having little impact on the central problem of prison overcrowding. Despite decreases in the crime rate, prison overcrowding continued with the enactment of more "get tough" legislation. For example, in 1994, when the state ranked sixth in rates of incarceration, Arizona enacted a TIS law eliminating parole and reducing good time to no more than 15 percent of the sentence. "Three strikes and you're out" became a popular metaphor—life without parole on the third (sometimes the second) felony conviction. As a crime policy, it raises important questions, not the least of which is the cost of turning prisons into expensive geriatric facilities for elderly offenders often convicted of nonviolent crimes. In 2003, for example, California imprisoned more than 300 men whose "third strike" was for petty theft (Greenhouse, 2003). Even the terminology began to change; in 1999, for example, Florida turned back the clock, renaming prison superintendents as "wardens."

As the trend toward narrowing or eliminating the discretionary release of prison inmates continues, corrections departments are frequently able to use special good-time provisions (TIS notwithstanding), and new schemes are also being implemented. For example, some jurisdictions are empowering judges to either place offenders directly on parole (New York) or use split sentences. Thus, Connecticut judges are authorized to impose special parole terms on any prison sentence in excess of 2 years; the length of special parole is at the court's discretion but may not exceed 10 years, and in combination with the prison term, it may not exceed the maximum sentence allowable for the crime of conviction. For certain sex offenses, special parole is required. It is easy to see why a governor would find this approach attractive: It accomplishes the early release and supervision of offenders without the need for action by a politically vulnerable parole board. These schemes fail to promote equity, are devoid of accountability, and abandon both classical and positivist approaches in favor of the gross politicization of our system of justice.

What is the public safety cost of this approach? "No one is more dangerous than a criminal who has no incentive to straighten himself out while in prison and who returns to society without a structured and supervised release plan" (Petersilia, 2003: 18). Petersilia notes that "discretionary parole systems provided a means by which inmates who represent continuing public safety risks can be kept in prison [while focusing] prison staff and corrections budgets on planning for release, not just opening the door at release" (2003: 18).

Traditional P/P still bears the major burden, and some states that had used the **determinate sentence** reintroduced parole release. At the same time, the law enforcement role and training of P/P officers increased dramatically as the control model became predominant, while some states with determinate sentencing (e.g., Illinois and Virginia), in an effort to save money, have gone to the opposite extreme by virtually ending supervision of offenders released from prison. Some states (e.g., Oregon and Washington) have refused to allow parolees to be returned to prison for technical violations. Illinois, which does not have a parole board, paid a price for its approach. In 1994, after serving 5 years of a 14-year sentence for torture and rape, Paul Runge was released with a recommendation that he be monitored closely in the community because the prison system was overcrowded. However, there were not enough parole agents to provide monitoring, so

Runge, who had refused to undergo sex offender treatment while in prison, went on a rape and murder spree that did not end until he was arrested in 2001.

In California and other states, there has been a dramatic increase in the number of persons returned to prison for violating the conditions of their release—the result of a form of supervision dominated by control devoid of the social service concerns of an earlier era (Beck, 2000b; Butterfield, 2000b). In the fourth edition of this book, I expressed concern over the movement toward a control model: "This direction brings with it the danger that P/P will become simply offender-monitoring activities devoid of any rehabilitative components" (Abadinsky, 1991: 386). In 1991, I advocated a balanced approach and continue to do so: "A balanced approach to P/P requires that the goal remain protection of the community, but with recognition that this is best accomplished by rehabilitating offenders" (Abadinsky, 1991: 386). I believe that sometime during this new century, a sense of equilibrium, if not a sense of history, will result in a balanced response that combines the needs of offenders and victims with the community's reasonable expectation of safety.

A Closer Look

The Future of Probation?

Several states, such as Colorado, Georgia, Missouri, and Utah, authorize contracts with private probation providers, for-profit companies that supervise misdemeanants and prepare presentence investigation reports. These services are attractive because they are paid for by offender fees rather than tax levy sources.

As we approach the end of the first decade of the twenty-first century, there is an opportunity to advance the supervision process. Research reveals that supervision providing treatment and not just control has significantly greater rates of success (Lowenkamp et al., 2006). A proverbial dollar spent in the community saves many dollars that would otherwise need to be spent on incarceration. P/P officers typically reside far from the neighborhoods where clients reside and "therefore lack an understanding of the situational context that geographically oriented supervision could provide" (Solomon, Kachnowski, and Bhati, 2005: 16). Paralleling the success of community-based policing, P/P agencies can offer field services in their client's neighborhoods. Instead of the more two-dimensional incarceration or continued supervision response to supervision violations, there should be an array of intermediate sanctions ranging from intensive supervision with electronic monitoring to short-term detention.

KEY TERMS

classicalism (p. 389)
combined model (p. 385)
continuity of care (p. 384)
control model (p. 386)
determinate sentence (p. 390)
felony probation (p. 384)

indeterminate sentence (p. 389)
intermediate sanctions (p. 390)
recidivism (p. 383)
social services model (p. 385)
success (p. 382)

INTERNET CONNECTIONS

American Probation and Parole Association: www.appa-net.org

Center for Community Corrections: communitycorrectionsworks.org

Corrections Connection: corrections.com⁻

REVIEW QUESTIONS

1. What has research found with respect to success in P/P?
2. Why is it difficult to provide a definition of recidivism for statistical purposes?
3. What is the "selection" problem with respect to determining success in P/P?
4. What are the variables over which a P/P agency has no control and that can affect case outcomes?
5. What did the felony probation research by Joan Petersilia and her colleagues reveal about probation in California?
6. What did Petersilia and her colleagues recommend in response to their findings?
7. How should the success of a P/P agency based on a *service model* be measured?
8. How should the success of a P/P agency based on a *control model* be measured?
9. What actions of a control model agency could increase the measured rate of recidivism?
10. Why has the movement in P/P been toward a control model?
11. Why would the abolition of parole lead to greater use of probation?

Glossary

abandonment: The most common legal grounds for termination of parental rights, also a form of child abuse in most states. Sporadic visits, a few phone calls, or birthday cards are not sufficient to maintain parental rights. Fathers who manifest indifference toward a pregnant mother are also viewed as abandoning the child when it is born.

absconder: An offender who fails to report for probation or parole supervision, is no longer residing at his or her approved residence, and whose whereabouts are unknown.

abuse: A term for acts or omissions by a legal caregiver. It encompasses a broad range of acts and usually requires proof of intent.

accomplice: A partner in a crime.

acquittal: A term for when a defendant is found not guilty.

addiction: A preoccupation with the use of psychoactive substances characterized by neurochemical and molecular changes in the brain.

adjournment: A delay in trial ordered by the judge, usually at the request of one of the lawyers.

adjudication: A judgment or decision.

adjudicatory hearing: A trial in juvenile court.

administrative law: The body of law created by administrative and regulatory bodies such as a parole board.

adversarial method: A system of fact finding used in American trials in which each side is represented by an attorney who acts as an advocate.

affidavit: A sworn written statement of facts.

affirm: Uphold the decision of a lower court.

affirmative defense: A term for when the defendant, without denying the charge, raises extenuating or mitigating circumstances such as insanity, self-defense, or entrapment.

aftercare: Outpatient support after the intensive phase of drug or alcohol treatment is concluded; also parole for juveniles.

aggravating factors: Elements present in a crime that the judge can take into account at the time of sentencing.

aid and abet: Actively assist another person in the commission of a crime.

anal stage: A term used in psychoanalytic theory to refer to the second stage of psychosexual development.

anomie: A condition characterized by estrangement from society, the result of being unable to achieve financial success through legitimate avenues.

antisocial personality disorder: A disorder characterized by psycho- or sociopathic behavior.

appeal: A legal challenge to a decision by a lower court.

appellate jurisdiction: A court having authority to review and modify the decision of a lower court.

appellate review: The consideration of a case by a court of appeals.

appointment system: Method of hiring P/P officers that provides a great deal of discretion to appointing officials.

arbitration: The submission of a dispute to a nonjudicial third party for binding judgment.

arraignment: The early stage in the judicial process when the defendant is informed of the charges and enters a plea of guilty, *nolo contendere*, or not guilty.

arrest: The physical taking into custody of a suspected law violator or juvenile.

arrest warrant: A document issued by a judicial or administrative officer authorizing the arrest of a specific person.

Ashurst-Sumners Act: A 1939 federal statute that effectively ended the prison contract system.

attorney of record: The attorney whose name appears on the permanent case files.

Auburn system: A fortress-style prison characterized by a factory system exploiting inmate labor.

aversive therapy: Form of behavior modification that uses unpleasant responses.

bail: Money or other security placed in custody of the court in order to ensure the return of a defendant to stand trial.

bailiff: A court officer who keeps order in the courtroom and has custody of the jury.

behavior modification: A psychological approach that emphasizes positive and negative reinforcement.

bench trial: A trial conducted without benefit of a jury.

bench warrant: A court order for a person's arrest for failing to return to court.

best interests of the child: The legal doctrine establishing the court as the determiner of the best environment for raising the child.

beyond a reasonable doubt: The standard of evidence needed for a criminal conviction.

Big House: An Auburn-style prison devoid of a factory system.

bind over: Hold for trial or send to grand jury.

blended sentence: A combination of juvenile and criminal sanctions given to young offenders.

blood-alcohol level (BAL): The amount of alcohol in the blood: .08 or .10 is the legal standard for determining intoxication, usually measured by a Breathalyzer test.

bond: A document signed by a defendant in which he or she agrees to return to court at a subsequent date to stand trial; also personal recognizance or release on recognizance (ROR).

bond hearing: An appearance before a judicial officer who determines the conditions of release—bail—pending trial.

booking: The process of photographing, fingerprinting, and recording of identifying data subsequent to a suspect's arrest.

boot camp: A form of special probation/split sentence that requires offenders, usually between the ages of 16 and 30, to reside in a quasi-military residential program for 90 to 120 days.

brief: A report prepared by an attorney and filed in court that sets forth facts and applicable law in support of a case.

"broken windows" supervision: An approach that emphasizes strengthening linkages with law enforcement and the community.

broker: P/P officer acting to link a client with necessary services.

burden of proof: The need to establish a claim or allegation; in a criminal case, the state has the burden of proof.

calendar: A list of cases to be heard in a trial court on a specific date, containing the title of the case, the lawyers involved, and the case number.

career criminal: A person with a past record of multiple arrests or convictions for serious crimes or with an unusually large number of arrests or convictions for crimes of varying degrees of seriousness.

case law: Previous decisions of appellate courts, particularly the Supreme Court.

caseload: The number of offenders assigned to the officer or agency on a given date or during a specified time period.

case management: Process by which needs and strengths of offenders are matched with selected services and resources in corrections.

casework: A system of counseling.

cause: Any question/action subject to litigation before a court.

cause of action: Facts that give rise to a matter before the court.

certification: The process of transferring a minor's case from juvenile to adult (criminal) court.

change of venue: The act of moving a trial to a county where the crime did not occur in order to avoid an unfair trial due to pretrial publicity.

charge: An accusation against the accused that he or she violated a specific criminal law.

chief judge: A judge who has primary responsibility for court administration.

child in need of supervision (CHINS): A status offender.

child-saving movement: Activities of middle- and upper-class women of the late nineteenth century to establish the juvenile court.

circumstantial evidence: Indirect evidence, such as fingerprints, from which an inference can be drawn.

civil protection order: A court order according to which an adult suspected of abuse must leave and remain away from the home.

classical conditioning: A system of learning in which a primary stimulus that naturally produces a specific response is repeatedly paired with a neutral stimulus. With repeated pairing, the neutral stimulus becomes a conditioned stimulus that can evoke a response similar to that of the primary stimulus.

classicalism: An outgrowth of Enlightenment philosophy that stresses free will and equality before law—"all men are created equal"—and provides a basis for determinate sentencing.

classification: A procedure in which information is gathered about an offender for law enforcement, correctional, or court agencies, including an offender's behavior patterns, needs, skills, and aptitude, as well as factors related to criminal conduct.

clear and convincing evidence: The standard of evidence for certain civil cases that exceeds preponderance of evidence but is lower than beyond a reasonable doubt.

clemency: The granting of mercy, such as a pardon, by a chief executive.

clerk of the court: An official responsible for managing the flow of cases and maintaining court records.

code: A compilation of laws arranged by chapters.

cognitive behavior therapy: A form of treatment that focuses on helping the client learn and use new thinking skills to modify negative behaviors.

cognitive skills training (CST): A rehabilitation approach that emphasizes the importance of problem-solving skills that can be applied to a variety of problem situations.

combined model: P/P supervision that attempts to balance control and rehabilitation.

commit: A court order sending a person to an institution such as a prison, hospital, or reformatory.

community-based corrections: A variety of local, state, or federal activities, in addition to traditional probation and parole, involving punishment and management of offenders within their local communities through such programs as community service, restitution, day reporting centers, drug and alcohol treatment, and electronic monitoring.

community courts: A system of courts pioneered in New York City providing speedy adjudication of minor crimes and misdemeanors, as well as restitution and supervision of offenders.

community service: A sentence requiring an offender to work a certain number of hours as reparation to the community.

commutation: A shortening of sentence provided by a governor or U.S. president as part of the powers of executive clemency.

concurrent jurisdiction: The jurisdiction shared by different courts.

concurrent sentences: Sentences for more than one crime that are served simultaneously.

conditional release: The release from prison based on the accumulation of time off for good behavior and requiring the releasee to abide by certain regulations.

conflict theory: The view that characterizes society by a struggle for power that disadvantages those without financial resources.

consecutive sentence: A sentence beginning at the expiration of another.

consensual crime: An offense that has no complaining victim but has nevertheless been outlawed, such as the possession of heroin or certain sexual activities.

consolidated model: A system in which parole is incorporated into a corrections department.

contempt of court: A summary judgment holding that a person has willfully disobeyed a lawful order of the court.

continuance: A delay in trial granted by the judge at the request of either attorney in a case; an adjournment.

contract system: A method for exploiting inmate labor during the Auburn era.

control model: A type of probation and parole supervision that emphasizes law enforcement.

corroboration: Supplementary evidence that tends to strengthen or confirm other evidence previously introduced.

court of general jurisdiction: A trial court that can adjudicate any type of case.

court of last resort: The highest appellate court in a jurisdiction.

court of limited jurisdiction: A court that can only adjudicate certain minor cases.

court reporter: A skilled stenographer who makes a word-by-word record of what is said in court.

criminal intent: A necessary element to be proved in a criminal trial; *mens rea.*

criminal negligence: A crime based on someone failing to exercise the necessary degree of care.

criminalistics: The science of crime detection, referring to the examination of physical evidence of a crime such as footprints, weapons, and bloodstains.

cross-examination: The questioning of a witness by the attorney who did not call the witness; questions aimed at discrediting the courtroom testimony of an opposition witness.

custody: The detaining of a person by a lawful authority.

custody theory: The obsolete legal view that probationers and parolees are in custody of the courts/prisons and therefore not entitled to due process.

damages: The compensation paid by defendants to successful plaintiffs in civil cases.

day deporting center: An intermediate punishment requiring attendance at a facility on a daily or otherwise regular basis at specified times for a specific length of time in order to participate in activities such as substance abuse counseling, social skills training, or employment training.

death-qualified jury: A jury panel whose members do not oppose the death penalty.

defendant: A person accused of a crime or against whom the plaintiff brings suit.

deferred sentencing: A sentence in which the defendant, after a plea of guilty, is placed under supervision, the successful completion of which can wipe out the conviction.

definite sentence: *See* determinate sentence.

delinquent: A person found to have violated the law, but whose age prevents defining him or her as a criminal.

delinquent subculture: A milieu in which antisocial activity is given high status.

dependent: Anyone under the care of someone else. A child ceases to be a dependent when he or she reaches the age of emancipation, which varies by state law, and even then, some states allow for continued treatment as a dependent.

detainer: A warrant placed against a person incarcerated in a correctional facility, notifying the holding authority of the intention of another jurisdiction to take custody of that individual when he or she is released. Under Inter-State Agreement on Detainers, a detainer is a notification filed with an institution in which a prisoner is serving a sentence, advising that he or she is wanted to face pending criminal charges in another jurisdiction.

determinate sentence: A sentence having a specific number of years and no provision for discretionary release (parole).

determinism: A construct stressing the lack of choice, particularly the belief that one's behavior is "determined" by physiological or environmental variables, devoid of *mens rea.*

differential association: The view of criminal behavior that sees it as being the result of associating with those involved in crime.

direct evidence: Evidence that stands on its own to prove an allegation; usually eyewitness testimony.

direct examination: Questions asked of a friendly witness by counsel at trial.

disposition: The phase of delinquency proceeding similar to "sentencing" phase of adult trial.

diversion: An alternative to trial decided on at intake to refer a child or adult to counseling or other social services, permitting a person charged with an offense to avoid prosecution in exchange for participation in a rehabilitative or restitution program.

docket: The log containing the complete history of each case in the form of a brief chronology.

double jeopardy: The act of trying a defendant a second time for the same offense after he or she has already been found not guilty.

drift: The view that most juvenile delinquents "drift" out of their antisocial behavior.

drug court: A specialized court in which the judge, district attorney, and defense attorney work together in a nonadversarial fashion to help chemically dependent offenders obtain needed treatment and rehabilitation in the hopes of breaking the cycle of crime and addiction.

due process: Those procedural guarantees to which every criminal defendant is entitled under the Constitution and its interpretation by the Supreme Court (e.g., the right to remain silent, to a trial by jury).

due process clause: A judicial requirement, based on the Fifth and Fourteenth Amendments, that prohibits government from taking life, liberty, or property without due process of law.

ego: The psyche's contact with reality that maximizes gratification with a minimum of difficulties.

electronic monitoring (EM): The use of surveillance technology, usually by means of a wrist or ankle bracelet, to monitor an offender's movements from a central location on a 24-hour basis.

emancipation: The independence of a minor from his or her parents before reaching age of majority.

EMIT: A commonly used drug test.

entrapment: The behavior of an agent of government that encourages the committing of a criminal act by a person who was not predisposed to do so. It constitutes an affirmative defense.

equal protection: The Fourteenth Amendment clause requiring government to treat similarly situated people the same or have good reason for treating them differently.

evidence (circumstantial): The evidence from which something can be inferred (e.g., fingerprints).

evidence (direct): Eyewitness testimony.

evidence-guided practice: Probation and parole practices based on research findings.

exclusionary rule: A legal doctrine prohibiting evidence secured in an improper manner from being used at a trial.

executive clemency: A pardon, reprieve, or commutation.

expunge: To seal or purge records of arrests and criminal or juvenile record information.

extradition: The surrender by one jurisdiction to another of a person accused or convicted of an offense committed within the jurisdiction demanding the individual's return.

failure to warn: Legal liability resulting from a failure to inform a reasonably foreseeable victim of a possible danger.

family court: A court having jurisdiction over juvenile cases, as well as issues such as divorce and custody.

felony: The more serious of the two basic types of criminal behavior, usually bearing a possible penalty in excess of 1 year in prison.

finding: The verdict in a juvenile court.

flat sentence: *See* determinate sentence.

foster care: Temporary care funded by government and arranged by a child welfare agency.

free will: A term in classical theory meaning that each person has the opportunity to be law-abiding or criminal (*mens rea*), so the person who opts to commit a crime is deserving of punishment commensurate with the offense.

full faith and credit: The constitutional requirement that the official judicial acts of one state will be respected by every other state.

general jurisdiction: The ability of a trial court to hear any type of case.

genital stage: A term in psychoanalytic theory referring to the third stage of psychosexual development.

good-faith exception: The exception to the exclusionary rule that allows the admission of evidence based on the officer's reasonable, but mistaken, belief that his or her action was proper.

good time: A reduction of the time served in prison as a reward for not violating prison rules; usually one-third to one-half off the maximum sentence.

grand jury: A group of citizens, usually numbering 23, who are assembled in secret to hear or investigate allegations of criminal behavior.

guardian *ad litem*: A Latin term "for the proceeding," referring to adults, often volunteers, appointed by a court to look after the interests of a minor during the course of a judicial proceeding.

guilty but insane: A legal concept according to which a person who is suffering from a mental illness is not relieved of criminal responsibility.

***habeas corpus*:** A legal document challenging custody and designed to force authorities holding a prisoner to produce him or her and justify the custody; often used as an alternate method of appealing a conviction.

halfway house: A place where offenders work and pay rent while undergoing counseling and job training.

hearsay: A statement by a witness who did not hear or see the incident but heard about it from someone else; a statement whose veracity cannot be subjected to cross-examination and is therefore generally not admissible (although there are many exceptions).

high risk: A supervision level for offenders with high risk/high need; close supervision with at least two personal contacts per month.

home visit: Personal contact by a P/P officer in the client's residence.

house arrest: An intermediate punishment that requires an offender to be confined to his or her residence for a period of time unless authorized to leave by the court, parole commission, or supervising officer. House arrest may or may not be accompanied by electronic monitoring.

House of Refuge: A pre–juvenile court facility for children without adult guardians.

id: A term in psychoanalytic theory referring to a primitive human drive.

immunity: An exemption from a civil or criminal action.

independent model: A system in which the parole board is responsible for release decisions and supervision of those released.

indigent: A term referring to someone unable to afford counsel.

infancy: A legal age at which a person cannot be held criminally responsible.

informal probation: Supervision by a juvenile probation officer without court adjudication.

inmate subculture: Customary behavior formed through the prison socialization process.

innovation: A term for sophisticated criminal behavior.

intake: A procedure prior to a preliminary hearing in which a probation officer interviews the police officer or other official, parent, and child in order to determine if the matter is to be handled formally or informally.

intensive supervision: A supervision level that focuses on control characterized by a high amount of contacts and unannounced home visits.

intermediate punishments: Punishments that are more severe than traditional probation but less severe than prison; also called intermediate sanctions. They encompass community corrections measures such as day reporting centers and electronic monitoring.

interstate compact: An agreement between the states that allows travel by probationers and parolees from one state to another and permits them to reside and be supervised in another state.

jail: A local, municipal, or county facility reserved for those awaiting trial, those convicted of a misdemeanor, and those convicted of a felony and awaiting transfer to a prison or another jurisdiction.

judicial conference: A body of judges established to provide uniformity of policy and to consider matters of judicial discipline.

judicial review: The power of the judicial branch to declare acts of the executive and legislative branches unconstitutional.

jurisdiction: The authority to adjudicate a case based on a variety of factors, such as geography, seriousness of the crime, or the value of the amount in dispute.

just deserts: The view that punishment should be based exclusively on the seriousness of the offense.

justice model: An argument in favor of determinate sentencing devoid of any concern for rehabilitation.

juvenile: A person who has not achieved an age set by law.

labeling: The view that a negative identification, a stigma such as ex-convict, can cause a societal reaction that permanently disadvantages the individual and can cause him or her to act in a manner referred to as a "self-fulfilling prophecy."

learning theory: The basis for the psychological concept or view (behaviorism) that all behavior is explained or shaped by its consequences.

lease system: A system used to exploit inmate labor by "renting" it out to private entrepreneurs.

least restrictive alternative: A juvenile court concept for sentencing a youngster to that which restricts liberty the least while meeting the needs of the youngster.

legal aid: Legal services provided by an agency to indigent persons.

liberty interest: The concept that requires due process procedures whenever any type of freedom is at risk from government action.

limited jurisdiction: The jurisdiction of a trial court that can only hear certain types of cases.

magistrate: A judicial officer in a court of limited jurisdiction.

mandatory release: The release of an inmate at the end of his or her sentence minus any good time.

mandatory sentence: A sentence required by law to be imposed for certain crimes.

maximum: The level of offender supervision or the highest range of an indeterminate sentence.

mediation: The submission of a dispute to a nonjudicial third party who attempts to get the parties to agree on an outcome.

medical model: A metaphor for the system of providing rehabilitative services that parallels the way physicians treat patients.

mens rea: A Latin term for "guilty mind," meaning the intent necessary to establish criminal responsibility.

merit system: A method for appointing and promoting public employees that avoids political influence.

methadone: An artificial opiate used to treat heroin addicts.

minimum: The supervision level for low-risk/low-need offenders. It can be a beginning level or a step down from the maximum and is the lowest of the range in an indeterminate sentence.

misdemeanor: An offense less severe than a felony that is normally punished by a fine, a community sanction, or time in a county jail (usually no more than 1 year).

mitigating factors: Elements present in the commission of a crime that may be taken into account by the judge to lower a sentence to prison or jail or to select a more appropriate sentence than incarceration.

mock job fair: A method for preparing offenders for seeking employment.

negative reinforcement: The behaviorist concept that the probability of a behavior goes up after the removal of a stimulus.

neglect: A parental failure to provide a child with basic necessities when able to do so. It encompasses a variety of forms of abuse that do not require the element of intent.

neoclassicalism: The classical approach that encompasses such mitigating factors as age and prior record.

neutralization: The sociological concept that explains how a person can support conventional values while violating the law.

new offense violation: A probation or parole violation that involves an arrest for a new offense.

no true bill: A grand jury decision not to indict.

nolle prosequi: A decision by the prosecutor declining to prosecute a particular defendant.

nolo contendere: The Latin term for a plea of "no contest" to criminal charges. It has the same effect as a plea of guilty but cannot be used as evidence of a criminal conviction at any subsequent civil trial related to the criminal act.

operant conditioning: The application of positive and negative reinforcement.

oral stage: The earliest stage in psychosexual development.

ordinance: A statute enacted by a municipality or county.

organized crime: A term that refers to persons involved in ongoing criminal conspiracies whose goals are personal gain and whose actions may persist indefinitely.

overcharging: A practice of alleging an excessive number of criminal violations when charging a suspect.

pardon: An act of executive clemency that has the effect of releasing an inmate from prison and/or removing certain legal disabilities from persons convicted of crimes.

parens patriae: The Latin term for the legal doctrine that refers to the obligation of the state toward persons who are unable to care for themselves, such as children or the mentally ill.

parole: The release of a prison inmate prior to the expiration of sentence by a board authorized to make such a decision, followed by a period of supervision by a parole officer.

parole board: An administrative body whose members are chosen to review the cases of prisoners eligible for release on parole. The board has the authority to release such persons and to return them to prison for violating the conditions of parole.

parole board guidelines: Formal method for determining if and when an inmate is to be released.

pat-down: The act of frisking, placing the hands about the body of a suspect in order to detect any weapons that he or she may be carrying.

Pennsylvania system: A model used in nineteenth-century prisons and characterized by solitary confinement.

person in need of supervision (PINS): A status offender.

petit jury: A trial jury composed of 6 or 12 persons.

petition: A formal written request or "prayer" for action; form of complaint used in juvenile proceedings.

plaintiff: The person initiating an action in a civil case or on appeal.

plea: A criminal defendant's response to the charges.

plea bargain: A legal transaction in which a defendant pleads guilty in exchange for some form of leniency.

pleading: Written statements of contentions submitted by parties in a legal action, each responding to the other, until the points at issue are sufficiently narrowed to proceed to trial.

plethysmography: A method of testing erectile response to erotic stimuli (usually involving children).

positive reinforcement: The behaviorist concept that behavior is shaped by rewarding consequences.

positivism: The use of the scientific method to study crime and criminals. It denies that crime is simply the result of free will and provides the basis for the indeterminate sentence.

predisposition report: A comprehensive report on a juvenile subsequent to a finding of delinquency or status offense.

preliminary hearing: The bringing of a defendant before a magistrate or judge during which charges are formally presented; also called advisory hearing or initial appearance in some state jurisdictions; sometimes called arraignment.

preponderance of the evidence: The standard used to determine the outcome of a noncriminal action as well as probation and parole revocation.

presentence investigation (PSI) report: A document submitted by a probation department to a judge containing information about the offender on which the judge can base his or her sentencing decision.

presumptive sentence: A model of sentencing that has decreased use of judicial discretion in individual sentencing cases in an effort to make sentencing more equitable overall.

presumptive waiver: A provision according to which certain juvenile offenders must be waived to criminal court unless they can prove they are amenable to rehabilitation, shifting the burden from the prosecutor to the juvenile.

pretrial release: The act of setting free a defendant without requiring bail; also called release on recognizance (ROR).

pretrial services: A system of screening services and investigation that may lead to community supervision, including electronic monitoring, for selected individuals who otherwise would be in jail while awaiting trial.

preventive detention: The act of holding a defendant in custody pending trial on the belief that he or she is likely to commit further criminal acts.

prison: A state-run facility where a person convicted of one or more felonies serves the sentence behind bars. Prisons can vary in security from supermax to maximum to medium to minimum.

prisonization: Being socialized into the prison process and culture.

probable cause: The minimum level of evidence needed to make a lawful arrest or secure certain warrants; a level of information that would lead a prudent person to believe that a crime was being or had been committed by a specific perpetrator.

probable cause hearing: A court hearing to determine if an arrest was justified, that is, whether the officer did have probable cause.

probation: A community punishment that requires the offender to comply with certain court-ordered conditions, such as curfew or attendance at a day reporting center, and may subject him or her to various levels of supervision based on public safety and rehabilitative needs.

probation officer: A public official authorized to accomplish presentence reports and supervise probationers.

probation subsidy: A state grant to encourage the granting of probation.

procedural law: Specific instructions for invoking substantive law.

psychoanalytic theory: The belief that unconscious material controls conscious behavior.

public defender: An attorney employed by government to represent indigent defendants.

public safety exception: An exception to the exclusionary rule on the grounds that the action that resulted in securing evidence that would normally be suppressed was necessary to protect the public from some immediate danger.

reality therapy (RT): A treatment method whose focus is the present and that stresses the need to adopt conventional behavior.

reasonable doubt: Highest standard of evidence necessary for a criminal conviction.

recidivism: The term used to express the return to criminal activity of persons previously convicted of crimes. Recidivism rate refers to the percentage of those who return to crime once a sentence has been served or while on P/P supervision.

recognizance: The obligation to return to court to stand trial.

reformatory: A penal institution for younger offenders.

reinforcement: The behaviorist concept that consequences of a behavior increase the likelihood that it will reoccur.

released on own recognizance (ROR): The release of a defendant without the need to post bail.

remand: Send back, usually for a new trial or sentencing.

reprieve: A temporary stay of the execution of a sentence to allow more time for judicial review.

residential treatment center (RTC): A private facility for juveniles.

restitution: The act of giving money or services to the victim by the offender, often imposed as a condition of probation.

restorative justice (RJ): An approach to criminal justice in which the victim is at the center and that emphasizes the way in which crimes hurt relationships between people who live in a community.

retainer: An advance paid by a client to an attorney in order to engage the attorney's services.

retreatism: The response to anomie that refers to substance abuse.

reverse: An act of an appellate court setting aside the decision of a trial court.

revocation: The administrative or court action that removes a person from either probation or parole status in response to his or her violation of the conditions of probation or parole and that results in imprisonment.

risk/needs assessment: A classification system that uses the degree to which an offender is likely to recidivate and the amount of help required.

rules of evidence: Standards governing the admission of evidence.

self-incrimination: The act of forcing a suspect to provide evidence against him- or herself, which is prohibited by the Fifth Amendment.

sentencing guidelines: The system that directs or guides a sentencing judge.

shelter: A temporary residential facility for children in need of emergency care.

shock incarceration (SI): A facility that duplicates the military environment; also called boot camp.

shock probation/parole: A brief incarceration followed by community supervision.

social casework: A system for providing assistance based on social work concepts.

social contract: The belief that society is tied together by general agreements to conform to law.

social control theory: A theory that assumes a person's ties to conventional society determine his or her behavior.

social investigation: A study prepared by a probation officer in juvenile court to provide the judge with information on which to base a disposition.

social services model: P/P supervision that stresses rehabilitation.

split sentence: A sentence of incarceration followed by a period of probation.

state use system: Prison labor that produces products for government.

status offense: An action that would not constitute a crime if the actor were an adult (e.g., truancy) but, in accord with *parens patriae*, can subject the youngster to the juvenile court process.

strain theories: Sociological theories that explain criminal behavior as the result of gap between aspirations and ability.

street time: The amount of time spent under supervision prior to a finding of a violation.

subpoena *ad testificandum*: A court order requiring a witness to appear and testify.

subpoena *duces tecum*: A term meaning "bring with you," a court order requiring a witness to bring all relevant documents that might affect the outcome of legal proceedings.

superego: A psychoanalytic concept referring to a conscious-like mechanism that exerts a sense of morality.

superior court: A court that can hold felony trials.

supermax prison: A high-security facility that features solitary confinement.

technical violation: A probation or parole violation of rules that does not involve a new crime.

termination hearing: The process for legally severing the parent-child relationship initiated by the filing of a petition in family court and almost always brought forth by a child welfare agency. It requires a finding of "unfitness" and a determination of the best interests of the child.

theory: A building block for scientific knowledge that organizes events, explains past events, and predicts future ones.

therapeutic community (TC): A residential drug treatment program based on Alcoholics Anonymous, emphasizing addicts helping one another to become socially conforming persons.

"three strikes and you're out": A metaphor for life imprisonment upon conviction for a third felony.

token economy: A method for employment of positive reinforcement.

transference: Psychoanalytic term referring to the process by which a therapist is viewed by a patient as a parental figure.

training school: A state facility that houses young offenders.

truth in sentencing: A system that excludes discretionary release and severely limits time off for good behavior.

12-step program: A method for treating substance abuse, such as Alcoholics Anonymous.

unconscious: "A psychoanalytic concept referring to "hidden" psychic phenomena that drive conscious behavior.

victim impact statement (VIS): The part of a presentence report that addresses harm to the victim.

victim services: A range of activities, usually provided by the prosecutor's office, which attends to the needs of victims and witnesses, coordinates their testimony, and supports them until their case is resolved in the criminal justice system.

waiver of jurisdiction: A court action "certifying" the youth as eligible for trial as an adult because it appears rehabilitation is unlikely or the crime was particularly atrocious.

work release: A program that permits select inmates to leave incarceration during the day for employment.

youth authority: A state agency responsible for the incarceration and supervision of young offenders.

References

"A Forecast"
  2007 *Hampton Roads Daily Press* (April 8): Internet.

Abadinsky, Howard
  2008 *Drugs: An Introduction*, 5th ed. Belmont, CA: Wadsworth.
  2007a *Organized Crime*, 8th ed. Belmont, CA: Wadsworth.
  2007b *Law and Justice*, 6th ed. Upper Saddle River, NJ: Prentice Hall.
  1983 *The Criminal Elite: Professional and Organized Crime.* Westport, CT: Greenwood.
  1976 "The Status Offense Dilemma: Coercion and Treatment." *Crime and Delinquency* 2 (October): 456–60.

Abruzzese, George
  1999 "Idaho Youth Ranch: A Seamless Continuum of Care for Today's Youth." *Juvenile Justice Magazine* (January/February): Internet.

Adair, David N., and Toby D. Slawsky
  1991 "Looking at the Law: Fact-Finding in Sentencing." *Federal Probation* 55 (December): 58–72.

Administrative Office of the Courts (AOC)
  1996 *Overview and Summary of the Arizona Probation Outcome Study.* Phoenix: Arizona Supreme Court.

  n.d. *Community Service.* Trenton, NJ: AOC.

Agnew, Robert
  1992 "Foundation for a General Strain Theory of Crime and Delinquency." *Criminology* 30 (February): 47–87.

Agopian, Michael W.
  1990 "The Impact of Intensive Supervision Probation on Gang-Drug Offenders." *Criminal Justice Policy* 4 (3): 214–22.

Aichhorn, August
  1963 *Wayward Youth.* New York: Viking Press.

Albanese, Jay S., Bernadette A. Fiore, Jerie H. Powell, and Janet R. Storti
  1981 *Is Probation Working?* Washington, DC: University Press of America.

Alexander, Franz, and Hugo Staub

1956   *The Criminal, the Judge, and the Public*. Glencoe, IL: Free Press.

Allen, Fred C., ed.

1926   *Extracts from Penological Reports and Lectures Written by Members of the Management and Staff of the New York State Reformatory, Elmira, N.Y.* Elmira, NY: Summary Press.

Allen, G. Frederick, and Harvey Treger

1994   "Fines and Restitution Orders: Probationers' Perceptions." *Federal Probation* 58 (June): 34–40.

Allen, Harry, Eric Carlson, and Evalyn Parks

1979   *Critical Issues in Probation*. Washington, DC: U.S. Government Printing Office.

Altschuler, David M., and Troy L. Armstrong

1994   *Intensive Aftercare for High-Risk Juveniles*. Washington, DC: Office of Juvenile Justice and Delinquency Prevention.

American Bar Association (ABA)

1970   *Standards Relating to Probation*. Chicago: ABA.

American Correctional Association (ACA)

1981   *Standards for Adult Probation and Parole Field Services*. Rockville, MD: ACA.

American Friends Service Committee

1971   *Struggle for Justice*. New York: Hill and Wang.

American Justice Institute

1981   *Presentence Investigation Report Program*. Sacramento, CA: American Justice Institute.

American Probation and Parole Association (APPA)

1995   *Abolishing Parole: Why the Emperor Has No Clothes*. Lexington, KY: APPA.

American Psychiatric Association (APA)

1974   *Behavior Therapy in Psychiatry*. New York: Jason Aronson.

Anderson, Elijah

1994   "The Code of the Streets." *Atlantic Monthly* (May): 80–94.

Anderson, James F., Laronistine Dyson, and Tazinski Lee

1997   "A Four Year Tracking Investigation on Boot Camp Participants: A Study of Recidivism Outcome." *Justice Professional* 10 (September): 199–213.

Anderson, Lisa

1998   "Is 'Supermax' Too Much?" *Chicago Tribune* (August 2): 1, 15.

Andreski, Stanislav, ed.

1971   *Herbert Spencer: Structure, Function and Evolution*. New York: Scribners.

Andrews, D. A., Ivan Zinger, Robert D. Hoge, James Bonta, Paul Gendreau, and Francis T. Cullen

1990   "Does Correctional Treatment Work? Clinically Relevant and Psychologically Informed Meta-Analysis." *Criminology* 28 (August): 369–404.

Andrews, Edmund L.

2003   "Economic Inequality Grew in 90's Boom, Fed Reports." *New York Times* (January 23): C1, 7.

Annual Report of the San Francisco Adult Probation Department

1991   San Francisco, CA: San Francisco Adult Probation Department.

Anspach, Donald F., and S. Henry Monsen
  1989   "Indeterminate Sentencing, Formal Rationality, and Khadi Justice in Maine: An Application of Weber's Typology." *Journal of Criminal Justice* 17: 471–85.

Arcaya, Jose
  1973   "The Multiple Realities Inherent in Probation Counseling." *Federal Probation* 37 (December).

"Arkansas: Early Release for 680 Inmates." *New York Times* (June 2): 14.

Arola, Terryl, and Richard Lawrence
  1998   "Assaults and Threats against Probation Officers and Some Responses to Officers' Safety Concerns." Paper presented at the annual meeting of the Academy of Criminal Justice Sciences, March 12.

Ashford, Jose B., and Craig Winston LeCroy
  1988   "Predicting Recidivism: An Evaluation of the Wisconsin Juvenile Probation and Aftercare Risk Instrument." *Criminal Justice and Behavior* 15 (June): 141–49.

Associated Press
  2007a   "Philadelphia Jails to Return to Court Oversight." *New York Times* (January 27): 13.
  2007b   "State Releases 83 Parole Violators, No Room in King County Jails." (February 27): Internet.
  2001   "Arkansas Corrections Board Agrees to Release Prisoners Early to Ease Overcrowding." *New Jersey Online* (November 27): Internet.
  2000   "Guards Fired over Camp Activities." (January 11): Internet.
  1999   "California Has 2.5 Million Unserved Warrants." (June 23): Internet.
  1998   "12 Convicted in Prison Plot to Control Drug Gangs." *New York Times* (May 31): 8.
  1995   "Sweep of State Prison for Drugs Termed Largest Such Raid Ever." *New York Times* (October 24): 12.

Atherton, Alexine L.
  1987   "Journal Retrospective, 1845–1986: 200 Years of Prison Society History as Reflected in the *Prison Journal.*" *Prison Journal* (Spring–Summer): 1–37.

Attica Commission. *See* New York State Special Commission on Attica.

"Auburn Correctional Facility"
  1998   *Department of Correctional Services Today* (April): Internet.

Auerbach, Barbara J., George E. Sexton, Franklin C. Farrow, and Robert H. Lawson
  1988   *Work in American Prisons: The Private Sector Gets Involved.* Washington, DC: U.S. Government Printing Office.

Augustus, John
  1972   *John Augustus, First Probation Officer.* Montclair, NJ: Patterson Smith.

Austin, James, and Garry Coventry
  2003   "A Second Look at the Private Prison Debate." *The Criminologist* 28 (September/October): 1, 3–9.
  2001   *Emerging Issues on Privatized Prisons.* Washington, DC: Bureau of Justice Assistance.

Austin, James, and John Irwin
  2001   *It's About Time: America's Imprisonment Binge*, 3rd ed. Belmont, CA: Wadsworth.

Baird, S. Christopher, and Dennis Wagner
  1990   "Measuring Diversion: The Florida Community Control Program." *Crime and Delinquency* 36 (January): 112–25.

Baird, S. Christopher, Richard C. Heinz, and Brian J. Bemus
  1982   "The Wisconsin Case Classification/Staff Development Project: A Two-Year Follow-Up Report," in *Classification: American Correctional Association Monographs.* College Park, MD: American Correctional Association.

Bakal, Yitzhak
    1974   *Closing Correctional Institutions*. Lexington, MA: D.C. Heath.

Baldwin, John D., and Janice I. Baldwin
    1998   *Behavior Principles in Everyday Life*, 3rd ed. Upper Saddle River, NJ: Prentice Hall.

Bales, William D., and Linda G. Dees
    1992   "Mandatory Minimum Sentences in Florida: Past Trends and Future Implications." *Crime and Delinquency* 38 (July): 309–29.

Ball, Richard A., C. Ronald Huff, and J. Robert Lilly
    1988   *House Arrest and Correctional Policy: Doing Time at Home*. Beverly Hills, CA: Sage.

Bandura, Albert
    1974   "Behavior Theory and the Models of Man." *American Psychologist* 29 (December): 859–69.

Barnes, Carole Wolff, and Randal S. Franz
    1989   "Questionably Adult: Determinants and Effects of the Juvenile Waiver Decision." *Justice Quarterly* 6 (March): 117–35.

Baumgartner, Werner A., Virginia Hill, and William H. Blahd
    1989   "Hair Analysis for Drugs of Abuse." *Journal of Forensic Sciences* 34 (November): 1433–53.

Bazemore, Gordon
    1994   "Developing a Victim Orientation for Community Corrections: A Restorative Justice Paradigm and a Balanced Mission." *Perspectives* (special issue): 19–24.

Bazemore, Gordon, and Dennis Maloney
    1995   "Rethinking the Sanctioning Function in Juvenile Court: Retributive or Restorative Responses to Youth Crime." *Crime and Delinquency* 41 (July): 296–316.
    1994   "Rehabilitating Community Service: Toward Restorative Service Sanctions in a Balanced Justice System." *Federal Probation* 58 (March): 24–35.

Bazemore, Gordon, and Mark S. Umbreit
    1994   *Balanced and Restorative Justice: Program Summary*. Washington, DC: Office of Juvenile Justice and Delinquency Prevention.

Beaumont, Gustave de, and Alexis de Tocqueville
    1964   *On the Penitentiary System in the United States and Its Application in France.* Carbondale, IL: Southern Illinois University Press. (Originally published in 1833.)

Beck, Allen J.
    2000a   *Prison and Jail Inmates at Midyear 1999*. Washington, DC: Office of Justice Programs.
    2000b   *Prisoners in 1999*. Washington, DC: Office of Justice Programs.

Beck, Allen J., and Jennifer C. Karberg
    2001   *Prison and Jail Inmates at Midyear 2000*. Washington, DC: Office of Justice Programs.

Becker, Gary S.
    1998   *Behind Bars*. Washington, DC: National Institute of Justice.
    1968   *The Economic Approach to Human Behavior*. Chicago: University of Chicago Press.

Bellis, David J.
    1981   *Heroin and Politicians: The Failure of Public Policy to Control Addiction in America*. Westport, CT: Greenwood.

Belluck, Pam

    2001   "Desperate for Prison Guards, Some States Even Rob the Cradle." *New York Times* (April 21): 1, 10.

Bennett, Lawrence A.

    1988   "Practice in Search of a Theory: The Case of Intensive Supervision—An Extension of an Old Practice." *American Journal of Criminal Justice* 12: 293–310.

Berg, Michael H.

    1997   "United States Probation Officers: The Court's Financial Investigators." *Federal Probation* 61 (March): 28–30.

Berk, Richard A., Kenneth J. Lenihan, and Peter Rossi

    1980   "Crime and Poverty: Some Experimental Evidence from Ex-Offenders." *American Sociological Review* 45 (October).

Bersani, Carl A.

    1989   "Reality Therapy: Issues and a Review of Research," in *Correctional Counseling and Treatment*, edited by Peter C. Kratcoski, pages 177–95. Prospect Heights, IL: Waveland Press.

Binder, Arnold, and Gilbert Geis

    1983   *Methods of Research in Criminology and Criminal Justice*. New York: McGraw-Hill.

Bishop, Donna M., Charles F. Frazier, and John C. Henretta

    1989   "Prosecutorial Waiver: Case Study of a Questionable Reform." *Crime and Delinquency* 35 (April): 179–201.

Bisman, Cynthia D.

    2000   "Social Work Assessment: Case Theory Construction." *Families in Society: The Journal of Contemporary Human Services* 80 (May–June): 240–47.

Black, Donald W., with C. Lindon Larson

    1999   *Confronting Antisocial Personality Disorder*. New York: Oxford University Press.

Blair, Jayson

    2000   "Boot Camps: An Idea Whose Time Came and Went." *New York Times* (January 2): WK 3.

Bloom, Barbara, and Anne McDiarmid

    2001   "Gender-Responsive Supervision and Programming for Women Offenders in the Community," in *Responding to Women Offenders in the Community*, pages 11–18. Washington, DC: National Institute of Corrections.

Bloom, Barbara, Barbara Owen, and Stephanie Covington

    2003   *Gender-Responsive Strategies, Research, Practice, and Guiding Principles for Women Offenders*. Washington, DC: National Institute of Corrections.

Blumberg, Abraham

    1970   *Criminal Justice*. Chicago: Quadrangle Books.

Blumenstein, Alfred

    1984   "Sentencing Reforms: Impacts and Implications." *Judicature* 68 (October–November).

Bodapati, Madhava R., James W. Marquardt, and Steven J. Cuvelier

    1993   "Influence of Race and Gender in Parole Decision Making in Texas: 1980–1991." Paper presented at the annual meeting of the Academy of Criminal Justice Sciences, Kansas City, MO, March 16–20.

Bohlen, Celestine

    1989   "Expansion Sought for 'Shock' Prison." *New York Times* (June 8): 14.

Boldt, Richard C.

    1998   "Rehabilitative Punishment and the Drug Treatment Court Movement." *Washington University Law Quarterly* 76: 1205–1306.

Bootzin, Richard R.

    1975   *Behavior Modification and Therapy: An Introduction.* Cambridge, MA: Winthrop.

Borden, William

    2000   "The Relational Paradigm in Contemporary Psychoanalysis: Toward a Psychodynamically Informed Social Work Perspective." *Social Service Review* 74 (September): 352–79.

Boswell, John

    1989   *The Kindness of Strangers: The Abandonment of Children in Western Europe from Antiquity to the Renaissance.* New York: Pantheon.

Bowers, Swithun

    1950   "The Nature and Definition of Social Casework," in *Principles and Techniques in Social Casework: Selected Articles, 1940–1950,* edited by Cora Kasius, pages 97–127. New York: Family Service Association of America.

Bradsher, Keith

    1995a   "Gap in Wealth in U.S. Called Widest in West." *New York Times* (April 17): 1, C4.

    1995b   "Low Ranking for Poor American Children." *New York Times* (August 14): 7.

    1995c   "Widest Gap in Incomes? Research Points to U.S." *New York Times* (October 27): C2.

Breed, Allen F.

    1998   "Corrections: A Victim of Situational Ethics." *Crime and Delinquency* 44 (January): 9–18.

Brennan, Thomas P., Amy E. Gedrich, Susan E. Jacoby, Michael J. Tardy, and Katherine B. Tyson

    1986   "Forensic Social Work: Practice and Vision." *Social Casework* 67: 340–50.

Brockway, Z. R.

    1926   "Character of Reformatory Prisoners," in *Extracts from Penological Reports and Lectures Written by Members of the Management and Staff of the New York State Reformatory, Elmira, N.Y.,* edited by Fred C. Allen, pages 110–18. Elmira, NY: Summary Press.

Broder, John M.

    2004   "Dismal California Prisons Hold Juvenile Offenders." *New York Times* (February 15): 18.

Brooke, James

    1997   "Prisons: A Growth Industry for Some." *New York Times* (November 2): 14.

Brown, Allan G.

    1986   *Group Work,* 2nd ed. Brookfield, VT: Gower.

Brown, Marjorie

    1984   *Executive Summary of Research Findings from the Massachusetts Risk/Need Classification System, Report 5.* Boston: Office of the Commissioner of Probation.

Brown, Waln K., Timothy Miller, Richard L. Jenkins, and Warren A. Rhodes

    1991   "The Human Costs of 'Giving the Kid Another Chance.'" *International Journal of Offender Therapy and Comparative Criminology* 35: 296–302.

Buck, Gerald S.

    1989   "Effectiveness of the New Intensive Supervision Programs." *Research in Corrections* 2 (September): 64–75.

Bureau of Justice Statistics

2001   "Forty-Two Percent of State Parole Discharges Were Successful." Press release (October 3).

Burke, Peggy, ed.

2006   *Topics in Community Corrections: Annual Issue 2006: Effectively Managing Violations and Revocations.* Washington, DC: National Institute of Corrections, Community Corrections Division.

Burns, Jerald C.

1993   "Rediscovering That Rehabilitation Works: The Alabama Boot Camp Experience." Paper presented at the annual meeting of the Academy of Criminal Justice Sciences, Kansas City, MO, March 16–20.

Burns, Jerald C., and Gennaro F. Vito

1995   "An Impact Analysis of the Alabama Boot Camp Program." *Federal Probation* 59 (March): 63–67.

Burrell, William D.

2005   *Trends in Probation and Parole in the States.* American Probation and Parole Association website.

Burrow, Linda, Jennifer Joseph, and John Whitehead

2001   "A Comparison of Recidivism in Intensive Supervision and Regular Probation: Results from a Southern Jurisdiction." Paper presented at the annual meeting of the Academy of Criminal Justice Sciences, Washington, DC, April 3–7.

Butterfield, Fox

2004a   "Study Tracks Boom in Prisons and Notes Impact on Counties." *New York Times* (April 30): 19.

2004b   "Almost 10% of All Prisoners Are Now Serving Life Terms." *New York Times* (May 12): 17.

2003a   "Inmates Go Free to Reduce Deficits." *New York Times* (December 19): 1, 20.

2003b   "Infections in Newly Released Inmates Are Rising Concern." *New York Times* (January 28): 14.

2000a   "Louisiana Settles Suit, Abandoning Private Youth Prisons." *New York Times* (September 8): 12.

2000b   "Often, Parole Is One Stop on the Way Back to Prison." *New York Times* (November 29): 1, 28.

1998a   "Prisons Replace Hospitals for the Nation's Mentally Ill." *New York Times* (March 5): 1, 18.

1998b   "U.S. and Georgia in Deal to Improve Juvenile Prisons." *New York Times* (March 22): 16.

1998c   "Profits at Juvenile Prisons Earned at a Chilling Cost." *New York Times* (July 15): 1, 14.

1998d   "U.S. Suing Louisiana on Prison Ills." *New York Times* (November 6): 14.

1995   "Prison-Building Binge in California Casts Shadow on Higher Education." *New York Times* (April 12): 11.

Butts, Jeffrey A., Howard W. Snyder, Terrence A. Finnegan, Anne L. Aughenbaugh, and Rowen S. Poole

1996   *Juvenile Court Statistics 1994.* Washington, DC: Office of Juvenile Justice and Delinquency Prevention.

Byrne, James M.

1990   "The Future of Intensive Probation Supervision and the New Intermediate Sanction." *Crime and Delinquency* 36 (January): 6–41.

Byrne, James M., Arthur J. Lurigio, and S. Christopher Baird

1989   "The Effectiveness of New Intensive Probation Supervision Programs." *Research in Corrections* 2 (September): 1–48.

Cahalan, Margaret Werner

1986   *Historical Corrections Statistics in the United States, 1850–1984.* Washington, DC: U.S. Government Printing Office.

California Department of Corrections

1981   *Investigation and Surveillance in Parole Supervision: An Evaluation of the High Control Project,* Research Report No. 63. Sacramento: California Department of Corrections.

Campbell, Curtis, Candace McCoy, and Chimezie A. B. Osigweh

1990   "The Influence of Probation Recommendations on Sentencing Decisions and Their Predictive Accuracy." *Federal Probation* 54 (December): 13–21.

Carlson, Eric, and Evalyn Parks

1979   *Critical Issues in Adult Probation: Issues in Probation Management.* Washington, DC: U.S. Government Printing Office.

Carlson, Jill M.

1993   "Restorative Justice: Beyond Crime and Punishment." Master of Science Thesis, Minnesota State University at Mankato.

Carlson, Susan M., and Michael Michalowski

1997   "Crime, Unemployment, and Social Structures of Accumulation: An Inquiry into Historical Contingency." *Justice Quarterly* 14 (June): 209–41.

Carter, Robert M.

1966   "It Is Respectfully Recommended . . ." *Federal Probation* (June).

Casius, Cora, ed.

1954   *New Directions in Social Work.* New York: Harper and Row.

Castellano, Thomas C.

1997   *Illinois' PreStart Program Revisited: A Further Look at Its Impact on Staff, the Prison System, and Offender Rehabilitation.* Chicago: Illinois Criminal Justice Information Authority.

Center for Sex Offender Management (CSOM)

2001a   "Myths and Facts about Sex Offenders." *Perspectives* 25 (Summer): 34–39.

2001b   *Case Studies on the Center for Sex Offender Management's National Resource Sites,* 2nd ed. Silver Spring, MD: CSOM.

Champion, Dean J.

1988a   "Felony Plea Bargaining and Probation: A Growing Judicial and Prosecutorial Dilemma." *Journal of Criminal Justice* 16: 291–301.

1988b   *Felony Probation: Problems and Prospects.* New York: Praeger.

Chapin, Bradley

1983   *Criminal Justice in Colonial America: 1600–1660.* Athens: University of Georgia Press.

Chen, David W.

2000   "Compensation Set on Attica Uprising." *New York Times* (August 29): 1, 25.

Chesney, Steven L.

n.d.   "The Assessment of Restitution in the Minnesota Probation Services," in *Restitution in Criminal Justice,* edited by Joe Hudson. St. Paul: Minnesota Department of Corrections.

Chesney-Lind, Meda

1997   *The Female Offender: Girls, Women, and Crime.* Thousand Oaks, CA: Sage.

1988   "Girls in Jail." *Crime and Delinquency* 34 (April): 150–68.

Childress, Anna Rose

1993 "Medications in Drug Abuse Treatment," in *Second Annual Conference on Drug Abuse Research and Practice: An Alliance for the 21st Century,* pages 73–75. Rockville, MD: National Institute on Drug Abuse.

Childress, Anna Rose, A. Thomas McLellan, and Charles P. O'Brien

1985 "Behavioral Therapies for Substance Abuse." *International Journal of the Addictions* 20: 947–69.

Chira, Susan

1994 "Study Confirms Worst Fears on U.S. Children." *New York Times* (April 12): 1, 11.

Clark, Cherie L., David W. Aziz, and Doris L. MacKenzie

1994 *Shock Incarceration in New York: Focus on Treatment.* Washington, DC: National Institute of Justice.

1991 "Clean and Sober—And Agnostic." *Newsweek* (July 8): 62–63.

Clear, Todd R. and Edward Latessa

1989 "Intensive Supervision: Surveillance vs. Treatment." Paper presented at the annual meeting of the Academy of Criminal Justice Sciences, Washington, DC, March 30.

Clear, Todd, and Ronald P. Corbett

1998 "Community Corrections of Place." *Perspectives* 23 (Winter): 24–32.

Clear, Todd R., and Patricia R. Hardyman

1990 "The New Intensive Supervision Movement." *Crime and Delinquency* 36 (January): 42–60.

Clear, Todd R., Suzanne Flynn, and Carol Shapiro

1987 "Intensive Supervision in Probation: A Comparison of Three Projects," in *Intermediate Punishments: Intensive Supervision, Home Confinement and Electronic Surveillance,* edited by Belinda R. McCarthy, pages 31–50. Monsey, NY: Criminal Justice Press.

Clem, Constance, Barbara Krauth, and Larry Linke

1998 *A Field Evaluation of the Interstate Compact for Probation and Parole: Findings from an NIC Survey.* Washington, DC: National Institute of Corrections.

Clemmer, Donald

1958 *The Prison Community.* New York: Holt, Rinehart and Winston.

Clinard, Marshall B., ed.

1964 *Anomie and Deviant Behavior.* New York: Free Press.

Cloninger, Susan C.

2004 *Theories of Personality: Understanding Persons,* 4th ed. Upper Saddle River, NJ: Prentice Hall.

Cloward, Richard A., and Lloyd E. Ohlin

1960 *Delinquency and Opportunity.* New York: Free Press.

Cohen, Albert K.

1965 *Delinquent Boys.* New York: Free Press.

Cohen, Alvin W.

2007 "Electronic Monitoring: Panacea or Palliative?" *Perspectives* (Summer): 36–41.

2002 "Managing the Correctional Enterprise—The Quest for 'What Works.'" *Federal Probation* 66 (September): 4–9.

Cohen, Lawrence E.

1975 *New Directions in Processing of Juvenile Offenders: The Denver Model.* Washington, DC: U.S. Government Printing Office.

Cohen, Noam S.

1992 "20 Years after Siege Ended in Blood, Attica Is New Prison but Wary Town." *New York Times* (September 1): 15.

Collier, Walter V.

1980 *Summary of First Year Evaluation of the Special Parole Supervision for Violent Felony Offenders.* Albany: New York State Division of Parole.

Comptroller General of the United States

1979 *Correctional Institutions Can Do More to Improve the Employability of Offenders.* Washington, DC: U.S. Government Printing Office.

Conly, Catherine

1998 *The Women's Prison Association: Supporting Women Offenders and Their Families.* Washington, DC: National Institute of Justice. Draft.

Cooper, Irving Ben

1977 *"United States v. Unterman*: The Role of Counsel at Sentencing." *Criminal Law Bulletin* 13.

"Court Orders Trial on Ban of Voting by Felons."

2003 *New York Times* (December 20): 15.

Cox, Stephen M., and Kathleen Bantley

2005 "Evaluation of the Court Support Services Division's Probation Transition Program and Technical Violations Unit: Final Report." Department of Criminology and Criminal Justice, Central Connecticut State University.

Crawford, Cheryl A.

1994 "Health Care Needs in Corrections: NIJ Responds." *National Institute of Justice Journal* (November): 31–38.

Crawford, William B., Jr.

1988 "Inmates Suing over Gangs Lose Case." *Chicago Tribune* (March 8): Sec. 2: 3.

Cripe, Clair

1997 *Legal Aspects of Corrections Management.* Gaithersburg, MD: Aspen.

Cromwell, Paul F., Jr.

1978 "The Halfway House and Offender Reintegration," in *Corrections in the Community,* 2nd ed., edited by George C. Killinger and Paul F. Cromwell, Jr. St. Paul, MN: West.

Cronin, Roberta C., with Mei Han

1994 *Boot Camp for Adult and Juvenile Offenders: Overview and Update.* Washington, DC: National Institute of Justice.

Crowe, Ann H.

1998 "Restorative Justice and Offender Rehabilitation: A Meeting of the Minds." *Perspectives* 22 (Summer): 28–40.

Crowley, Jim

1998 "Victim-Offender Mediation: Paradigm Shift or Old Fashioned Accountability?" *Community Links* (Spring): 10.

Cullen, Francis T., and Karen E. Gilbert

1982 *Reaffirming Rehabilitation.* Cincinnati, OH: Anderson.

Cullen, Francis T., Nicholas Williams, and John Paul Wright

2002 "Environmental Corrections—A New Paradigm for Effective Probation and Parole Supervision." *Federal Probation* 66 (September): 28–37.

1997 "Work Conditions and Juvenile Delinquency: Is Youth Employment Criminogenic?" *Criminal Justice Policy Review* 8 (2–3): 119–43.

Curran, Daniel J.

1988 "Destructuring Privatization and the Promise of Juvenile Diversion: Compromising Community-Based Corrections." *Crime and Delinquency* 34 (October): 363–78.

Czajkoski, Eugene H.

1973 "Exposing the Quasi-Judicial Role of the Probation Officer." *Federal Probation* 37 (September): 9–13.

Darrow, Clarence

1975 *Address to the Prisoners in the Cook County Jail, 1902.* Chicago: Charles H. Kerr.

Davey, Monica, and Abby Goodnough

2007a "Doubts Rise as States Hold Sex Offenders after Prison." *New York Times* (March 4): 1, 20.

2007b "A Record of Failure at a Center for Sex Offenders." *New York Times* (March 5): 1, 16.

Davidoff-Kroop, Joy

1983 *An Initial Assessment of the Division of Parole's Employment Services.* Albany: New York State Division of Parole.

Dedel, Kelly

1998 "National Profile of the Organization of State Juvenile Corrections Systems." *Crime and Delinquency* 44 (October): 507–25.

Degler, Carl N.

1991 *In Search of Human Nature: The Decline and Revival of Darwinism in American Social Thought.* New York: Oxford University Press.

Delbanco, Andrew, and Thomas Delbanco

1995 "At the Crossroads." *New Yorker* (March 20): 50–63.

del Carmen, Rolando V.

1985 "Legal Issues and Liabilities in Community Corrections," in *Probation, Parole, and Community Corrections: A Reader,* edited by Lawrence F. Travis III, pages 47–70. Prospect Heights, IL: Waveland Press.

del Carmen, Rolando V., and Paul T. Louis

1988 *Civil Liabilities of Parole Personnel for Release, Non-Release, Supervision, and Revocation.* Washington, DC: National Institute of Corrections.

del Carmen, Rolando V., Maldine Beth Barnhill, Gene Bonham, Jr., Lance Hignite, and Todd Jermstad

2001 *Civil Liabilities and Other Legal Issues for Probation/Parole Officers and Supervisors.* Washington, DC: National Institute of Corrections.

De Leon, George

1994 "The Therapeutic Community: Toward a General Theory and Model," in *Therapeutic Community: Advances in Research and Application,* pages 16–53. Rockville, MD: National Institute on Drug Abuse.

1986 "The Therapeutic Community for Substance Abuse: Perspective and Approach," in *Therapeutic Communities for Addictions,* edited by George De Leon and James T. Ziegenfuss, Jr., pages 5–18. Springfield, IL: Charles C Thomas.

DeLong, James V.

1972 "Treatment and Rehabilitation," in *Dealing with Drug Abuse: A Report to the Ford Foundation,* pages 173–254. New York: Praeger.

Denzlinger, Jerry D., and David E. Miller

    1991 "The Federal Probation Officer: Life before and after Guideline Sentencing." *Federal Probation* 55 (December): 49–63.

Department of Community Corrections (DCC)

    2006 *Recidivism for Probation and Parole.* Little Rock, AK: DCC.

Deschenes, Elizabeth Piper, Susan Turner, and Joan Petersilia

    1995 "A Dual Experiment in Intensive Community Supervision: Minnesota's Prison Diversion and Enhanced Supervised Release Programs." *The Prison Journal* 75 (September): 330–56.

Dickey, Walter

    1979 "The Lawyer and the Accuracy of the Presentence Report." *Federal Probation* 43 (June): 29–39.

Dietrich, Shelle

    1979 "The Probation Officer as Therapist: Examination of Three Major Problem Areas." *Federal Probation* 43 (June).

Dighton, Daniel

    1997 "States Broaden Scope of Transfer Laws." *The Compiler* 17 (Fall): 11–15.

DiIulio, John J., Jr.

    1993 "Rethinking the Criminal Justice System: Toward a New Paradigm," in *Performance Measures for the Criminal Justice System*, pages 1–16. Washington, DC: Bureau of Justice Statistics.

Division of Probation

    1974 "The Selective Presentence Investigation." *Federal Probation* 38 (December).

Dobrzynski, Judith H.

    1997 "For a Summer Getaway, a Model Prison." *New York Times* (July 11): B1.

Dolan, Edward J., Richard Lunden, and Rosemary Barberet

    1987 "Prison Behavior and Parole Outcome in Massachusetts." Paper presented at the annual meeting of the American Society of Criminology, Montreal, November 11–14.

Dole, Vincent

    1980 "Addictive Behavior." *Scientific American* 243: 138–54.

Donovan, Dennis M.

    1988 "Assessment of Addictive Behaviors: Implications for an Emerging Biopsychosocial Model," in *Assessment of Addictive Behaviors*, edited by Dennis M. Donovan and G. Alan Marrlatt, pages 3–48. New York: Guilford.

Downing, Hugh

    2006 "The Emergence of Global Positioning Satellite (GPS) Systems in Correctional Applications." *Corrections Today* (October): 42–45.

Dressler, David

    1951 *Parole Chief.* New York: Viking Press.

Drug Court Movement

    1995 Washington, DC: National Institute of Justice.

Drumm, Kris

    2006 "The Essential Power of Group Work." *Social Work with Groups* 29 (2/3): 17–31.

Dumm, Thomas L.

    1987 *Democracy and Punishment: Disciplinary Origins of the United States.* Madison: University of Wisconsin Press.

Dunn, Ashley

    1995 "U.S. Inquiry Finds Detention Center Was Poorly Run." *New York Times* (July 22): 1, 8.

DuPont, Robert L., and John P. McGovern

    1994 *A Bridge to Recovery: An Introduction to 12-Step Programs*. Washington, DC: American Psychiatric Press.

Durham, Alexis M., III

    1989a "Origins of Interest in the Privatization of Punishment: The Nineteenth and Twentieth Century American Experience." *Criminology* 27 (February): 107–39.
    1989b "Rehabilitation and Correctional Privatization: Observations on the 19th Century Experience and Implications for Modern Corrections." *Federal Probation* 53 (March): 43–52.
    1989c "Newgate of Connecticut: Origins and Early Days of an Early American Prison." *Justice Quarterly* 6 (March): 89–116.

Dzur, Albert W., and Alan Wertheimer

    2002 "Forgiveness and Public Deliberation: The Practice of Restorative Justice." *Criminal Justice Ethics* 21 (Winter/Spring): 3–21.

Eig, Jonathan

    1998 "Deep Hole." *Chicago* (July): 60–64, 87–89.

Eisenkraft, Noah

    2001 "Taxation without Representation." *Harvard Political Review* (Winter): Internet.

"Elmira"

    1998 *DOC Today* (October): Internet.

Empey, LaMar T., ed.

    1979 *Juvenile Justice: The Progressive Legacy and Current Reforms*. Charlottesville: University Press of Virginia.

English, Kim, Suzanne Pullen, and Linda Jones

    1997 *Managing Adult Sex Offenders in the Community—A Containment Approach*. Washington, DC: National Institute of Justice.

Erez, Edna

    1990 "Victim Participation in Sentencing: Rhetoric and Reality." *Journal of Criminal Justice* 18: 19–31.

Erikkson, Torsten

    1976 *The Reformers: An Historical Survey of Pioneer Experiments in the Treatment of Criminals*. New York: Elsevier.

Erwin, Billie S.

    1984 *Evaluation of Intensive Supervision in Georgia*. Atlanta: Georgia Department of Offender Rehabilitation.

Erwin, Billie S., and Lawrence A. Bennett

    1987 *New Dimensions in Probation: Georgia's Experience with Intensive Probation Supervision*. Washington, DC: National Institute of Justice.

Eskridge, Chris W., and Eric W. Carlson

    1979 "The Use of Volunteers in Probation: A National Synthesis." *Journal of Offender Counseling Services and Rehabilitation* 4 (Winter).

Fabricant, Michael

    1983 *Juveniles in the Family Courts*. Lexington, MA: D.C. Heath.

Falcone, David N.

    2005 *Dictionary of American Criminal Justice, Criminology, and Criminal Law.* Upper Saddle River, NJ: Prentice Hall.

Falk, Gerhard

    1966 "The Psychoanalytic Theories of Crime Causation." *Criminologica* 4 (May).

Fallen, David L., Craig D. Apperson, Joan Hall-Milligan, and Steven Aos

    1981 *Intensive Parole Supervision.* Olympia: Washington Department of Social and Health Services.

Feeley, Malcolm M.

    1979 *The Process Is Punishment: Handling Cases in a Lower Court.* New York: Russell Sage Foundation.

Feeley, Malcolm M., and Jonathan Simon

    1992 "The New Penology: Note on the Emerging Strategy of Corrections and Its Implications." *Criminology* 30 (November): 449–74.

Feld, Barry C.

    2003 "The Politics of Race and Juvenile Justice: The 'Due Process Revolution' and the Conservative Reaction." *Justice Quarterly* 20 (December): 765–800.

    1992 "Criminalizing the Juvenile Court: A Research Agenda for the 1990s," in *Juvenile Justice and Public Policy: Toward a National Agenda,* edited by Ira M. Schwartz, pages 59–88. Lexington, MA: Lexington Books.

    1988 "*In Re Gault* Revisited: A Cross-State Comparison of the Right to Counsel in Juvenile Court." *Crime and Delinquency* 34 (October): 393–424.

Female Offender Resource Center

    1979 *Little Sisters and the Law.* Washington, DC: U.S. Government Printing Office.

Finckenauer, James O.

    2005 "Ruminating about Boot Camps: Panaceas, Paradoxes, and Ideology." *Journal of Offender Rehabilitation* 42: 199–207.

    1984 *Juvenile Delinquency and Corrections: The Gap between Theory and Practice.* New York: Academic Press.

Finder, Alan

    1997 "New York's Chief Judge Moves to Assure Family Courts Are Open to Public." *New York Times* (June 19): 18.

Finn, Peter

    1997 *Sex Offender Community Notification.* Washington, DC: National Institute of Justice.

Finn, Peter, and Sarah Kuck

    2001 *Stress among Probation and Parole Officers and What Can Be Done about It.* Washington, DC: National Institute of Justice.

    1998 *The Delaware Department of Corrections Life Skills Program.* Washington, DC: National Institute of Justice.

Finn, Peter, and Dale Parent

    1992 *Making the Offender Foot the Bill: A Texas Program.* Washington, DC: National Institute of Justice.

Firestone, David

    2001 "Alabama's Packed Jails Draw Ire of Courts, Again." *New York Times* (May 1): 1, 16.

Foderaro, Lisa W.

    1995 "Can Problem Drinkers Really Just Cut Back?" *New York Times* (May 28): 15.

Fogel, David
    1984 "The Emergence of Probation as a Profession in the Service of Public Safety: The Next Ten Years," in *Probation and Justice: Reconsideration of Mission,* edited by Patrick D. McAnany, Doug Thompson, and David Fogel. Cambridge, MA: Oelgeschlager, Gunn and Hain.
    1975 *We Are the Living Proof.* Cincinnati, OH: Anderson.

Ford, Daniel, and Annesley K. Schmidt
    1985 *Electronically Monitored Home Confinement.* Washington, DC: National Institute of Justice.

Fox, Vernon S.
    1977 *Community-Based Corrections.* Upper Saddle River, NJ: Prentice Hall.

France, Anatole
    1927 *The Red Lily,* translated by Winifred Stephens. New York: Dodd, Mead.

Frawley, P. Joseph, and James W. Smith
    1990 "Chemical Aversion Therapy in the Treatment of Cocaine Dependence as Part of a Multimodal Treatment Program." *Journal of Substance Abuse Treatment* 7: 21–29.

Freud, Sigmund
    1933 *New Introductory Lectures on Psychoanalysis.* New York: W. W. Norton.

Fried, Joseph P.
    2006 "Leaving Prison Doors Behind, Some Find New Doors Open." *New York Times* (October 18): B8.

Friedlander, Walter A.
    1958 *Concepts and Methods of Social Work.* Upper Saddle River, NJ: Prentice Hall.

Friedman, Lawrence M.
    1973 *A History of American Law.* New York: Simon and Schuster.

"Full-Employment Prisons"
    2001 *New York Times* editorial (August 23): 20.

Furhling, Larry
    1998 "In Iowa, Some Prisoners Are behind Barns." *Chicago Tribune* (August 7): 10.

Galaif, Elisha, and Steve Sussman
    1995 "For Whom Does Alcoholics Anonymous Work?" *International Journal of the Addictions* 30 (2): 161–84.

Gaylin, Willard
    1974 *Partial Justice: A Study of Bias in Sentencing.* New York: Alfred A. Knopf.

Gebelein, Richard S.
    2000 *The Rebirth of Rehabilitation: Promise and Perils of Drug Courts.* Washington, DC: Office of Justice Programs.

Geerken, Michael R., and Hennessey D. Hayes
    1993 "Probation and Parole: Public Risk and the Future of Incarceration Alternatives." *Criminology* 31 (November): 549–64.

Gehm, John R.
    1998 "Victim-Offender Mediation Programs: An Exploration of Practice and Theoretical Frameworks." *Western Criminology Review* 1 (1): Internet.

Gendreau, Paul, and Robert R. Ross

1987 "Revivification of Rehabilitation: Evidence from the 1980s." *Justice Quarterly* 4 (September): 350–407.

Gerstein, Dean R., and Henrick J. Harwood, eds.

1990 *Treating Drug Problems, Vol. I: A Study of the Evolution, Effectiveness, and Financing of Public and Private Drug Treatment Systems.* Washington, DC: National Academy Press.

Gilligan, Leilah, and Tom Talbot

2000 *Community Supervision of the Sex Offender: An Overview of Current and Promising Practices.* Silver Spring, MD: Center for Sex Offender Management.

Gillin, John T.

1931 *Taming the Criminal.* New York: Macmillan.

Gladding, Samuel T.

1999 *Group Work: A Counseling Specialty.* Upper Saddle River, NJ: Prentice Hall.

Glaser, Daniel

1969 *The Effectiveness of a Prison and Parole System.* Indianapolis, IN: Bobbs-Merrill.

Glasser, William

2000 *Reality Therapy in Action.* New York: HarperCollins.

1998 *Choice Theory: A New Psychology of Personal Freedom.* New York: HarperCollins.

1980 "Reality Therapy: An Explanation of the Steps of Reality Therapy," in *What Are You Doing? How People Are Helped through Reality Therapy,* edited by Naomi Glasser. New York: Harper and Row.

1976 *The Identity Society.* New York: Harper and Row.

1975 *Reality Therapy.* New York: Harper and Row. (Originally published in 1965.)

Glaze, Lauren E.

2003 *Probation and Parole in the United States, 2002.* Washington, DC: Bureau of Justice Statistics.

Glaze, Lauren E., and Thomas P. Bonczar

2006 *Probation and Parole in the United States, 2005.* Washington, DC: Bureau of Justice Statistics.

Glueck, Sheldon, ed.

1933 *Probation and Criminal Justice.* New York: Macmillan.

Goetting, Victor L.

1974 "Some Pragmatic Aspects of Opening a Halfway House." *Federal Probation* 38 (December).

Goffman, Erving

1961 *Asylums: Essays on the Social Situation of Mental Patients and Other Inmates.* Garden City, NY: Doubleday.

Goleman, Daniel

1987 "Embattled Giant of Psychology Speaks His Mind." *New York Times* (August 25): 17, 18.

Goodstein, Lynne, and John Hepburn

1985 *Determinate Sentencing and Imprisonment: A Failure of Reform.* Cincinnati, OH: Anderson.

Gottschalk, Marie

2006 *The Prison and the Gallows: The Politics of Mass Incarceration in America.* New York: Cambridge University Press.

Grann, David

    2004   "The Brand." *New Yorker* (February 16 and 23): 157–71.

Gransky, Laura A., Thomas C. Castellano, and Ernest L. Cowles

    1993   "Is There a 'Next Generation' of Shock Incarceration Facilities? The Evolving Nature of Goals, Program Components, and Drug Treatment Services." Paper presented at the annual meeting of the Academy of Criminal Justice Sciences, Kansas City, MO, March 16–20.

Greenberg, David F.

    1975   "Problems in Community Corrections." *Issues in Criminology* 10 (Spring).

Greenberg, David F., and Drew Humphries

    1980   "The Cooptation of Fixed Sentencing Reform." *Crime and Delinquency* 26 (April).

Greenberg, Jay R., and Stephen A. Mitchell

    1983   *Object Relations in Psychoanalytic Theory.* Cambridge, MA: Harvard University Press.

Greenfeld, Lawrence A., and Tracy L. Snell

    1999   *Women Offenders.* Washington, DC: Office of Justice Programs.

Greenhouse, Linda

    2003   "Justices Uphold Long Prison Terms in Repeat Crimes." *New York Times* (March 6): 1, 26.

    1997   "Immunity from Suits Is Withheld for Guards in Privately Run Jails." *New York Times* (June 24): 12.

Griffin, Patrick

    2005   *Juvenile Court-Controlled Reentry: Three Practice Models.* Pittsburgh, PA: National Center for Juvenile Justice.

Griggs, Bertram S., and Gary R. McCune

    1972   "Community-Based Correctional Programs: A Survey and Analysis." *Federal Probation* 36 (June).

Grissom, Grant R., and William L. Dubnov

    1989   *Without Locks and Bars: Reforming Our Reform Schools.* New York: Praeger.

Grogger, Jeffrey

    1989   *Employment and Crime.* Sacramento, CA: Bureau of Criminal Statistics and Special Services.

Gross, Jane

    1992   "Collapse of Inner-City Families Creates America's New Orphans." *New York Times* (March 29): 1, 15.

Guggenheim, Ken

    1998   "For Ex-Cons, Job Search Tough Obstacle." Associated Press, Nando.net.

Haas, Stephen, and Edward J. Latessa

    1995   "Intensive Supervision in a Rural County: Diversion and Outcome," in *Intermediate Sanctions: Sentencing in the 1990s*, edited by John Ortiz Smykla and William Selke, pages 153–69. Cincinnati, OH: Anderson.

Haberman, Clyde

    2005   "Only at Grave Does a Barber Get a Break." *New York Times* (November 22): B1.

    2000   "In Turbulent Times, a Prison Boiled Over." *New York Times* (January 5): 23.

Hagerty, J. E.

    1934   *Twentieth Century Crime, Eighteenth Century Methods of Control.* Boston: Stratford.

Hahn, Paul H.

   1976   *Community Based Corrections and the Criminal Justice System.* Santa Cruz, CA: Davis.

Hall, Jerome

   1952   *Theft, Law and Society.* Indianapolis, IN: Bobbs-Merrill.

Hall, Trish

   1990   "New Way to Treat Alcoholism Discards Spiritualism of A.A." *New York Times* (December 24): 1, 10.

Hallet, Michael

   2004   "An Introduction to Prison Privatization," in *Visions for Change: Crime and Justice in the Twenty-First Century,* edited by Roslyn Ruskin and Albert R. Roberts, pages 528–52. Saddle River, NJ: Prentice Hall.

Hamilton, Gordon

   1967   *Theory and Practice of Social Work.* New York: Columbia University Press.

Hammett, Theodore M., Lynne Harrold, and Joel Epstein

   1994   *Tuberculosis in Correctional Facilities.* Washington, DC: U.S. Government Printing Office.

Hardman, Dale G.

   1960   "Constructive Use of Authority." *Crime and Delinquency* 6 (July).

Harper, Robert Francis

   1904   *The Code of Hammurabi.* Chicago: University of Chicago Press.

Harris, George A., and David Watkins

   1987   *Counseling the Involuntary and Resistant Client.* College Park, MD: American Correctional Association.

Harris, Patricia M., Raymond Gingerich, and Tiffany A. Whittaker

   2004   "The 'Effectiveness' of Differential Supervision." *Crime and Delinquency* 50 (April): 235–71.

Harris, Patricia M., and Lisa Graff

   1988   "A Critique of Juvenile Sentence Reform." *Federal Probation* 52 (September): 66–71.

Harrison, Mary T.

   2006   "True Grit: An Innovative Program for Elderly Inmates. *Corrections Today* (December): 46–49.

Harrison, Paige M., and Allen J. Beck

   2003   *Prisoners in 2002.* Washington, DC: U.S. Bureau of Justice Statistics.

Harrison, Paige M., and Jennifer C. Karberg

   2004   *Prison and Jail Inmates at Midyear 2003.* Washington, DC: U.S. Bureau of Justice Statistics.

Hartman, Todd

   1994   "Suit Targets Neighbors Who Oppose Group Home." *Miami Herald* (November 11): B1, 3.

Hawkins, Dana

   2002   "Tests on Trial: Jobs and Reputations Ride on Unproven Drug Screens." *U.S. News & World Report* (August 12): 46–48.

Healy, William, Augusta F. Bronner, and Anna Mae Bowers

   1930   *The Structure and Meaning of Psychoanalysis.* New York: Alfred A. Knopf.

Hemmens, Craig, and Rolando del Carmen

1997 "The Exclusionary Rule in Probation and Parole Revocation Proceedings: Does It Apply?" *Federal Probation* 61 (September): 32–39.

Henderson, Marta L.

2004 "Employment and Crime from the Inmate's Perspective," in *Crime and Employment: Critical Issues in Crime Reduction for Corrections*, edited by Jessie L. Krienert and Mark S. Fisher, pages 84–94. Walnut Creek, CA: AltaMira Press.

Hergenhahn, B. R., and Matthew H. Olson

1999 *An Introduction to Theories of Personality*, 5th ed. Upper Saddle River, NJ: Prentice Hall.

Herman, Ellen

1995 *The Romance of American Psychology: Political Culture in the Age of Experts, 1940–1970*. Berkeley: University of California Press.

Hibbert, Christopher

1968 *The Roots of Evil: A Social History of Crime and Punishment*. Boston: Little, Brown.

Hirsch, Adam Jay

1992 *The Rise of the Penitentiary: Prisons and Punishment in Early America*. New Haven, CT: Yale University Press.

Hirschi, Travis

1969 *Causes of Delinquency*. Berkeley: University of California Press.

Hollin, Clive R.

1990 *Cognitive-Behavioral Interventions with Young Offenders*. New York: Pergamon Press.

Hollis, Florence

1950 "The Techniques of Casework," in *Principles and Techniques of Social Casework: Selected Articles, 1940–1950*, edited by Cora Kasius, pages 412–26. New York: Family Service Association of America.

Holloway, Lynette

1995 "Home for Handicapped Still Faces Rough Path." *New York Times* (July 18): 13.

Holmes, Cheryl L.

1997 "AIDS and Supervision." *Federal Probation* 61 (March): 28.

Holsinger, Alexander M., Christopher T. Lowenkamp, and Edward J. Latessa

2006 "Exploring the Validity of the Level Service Inventory-Revised with Native American Offenders." *Journal of Criminal Justice* 34: 331–37.

Holt, Norman

1995 "California's Determinate Sentencing: What Went Wrong?" *Perspectives* (Summer): 19–22.

Holzer, Harry J., Steven Raphael, and Michael A. Stoll

2002 *Prisoner Reentry and the Institutions of Civil Society: Bridges and Barriers to Successful Reintegration*. Washington, DC: The Urban Institute.

Hoover, Kent

2001 "Prison Program May Lose Contracting Monopoly." *BizJournals.com* (June 18): Internet.

Hughes, Robert

1987 *The Fatal Shore: The Epic of Australia's Founding*. New York: Alfred A. Knopf.

Hurl, Lorna F., and David J. Tucker

    1997   "The Michigan County Agents and the Development of Juvenile Probation." *Journal of Social History* (Summer): 905–35.

Hurst, Hunter, IV, and Patricia McFall Torbet

    1993   *Organization and Administration of Juvenile Services: Probation, Aftercare, and State Institutions for Delinquent Youth.* Pittsburgh, PA: National Center for Juvenile Justice.

Hurst, James W.

    1950   *The Growth of American Law: The Law Makers.* Boston: Little, Brown.

Husband, Stephen D., and Jerome J. Platt

    1993   "The Cognitive Skills Component in Substance Abuse Treatment in Correctional Settings: A Brief Review." *Journal of Drug Issues* 23 (Winter): 31–42.

Hutchinson, Elizabeth D.

    1987   "Use of Authority in Direct Social Work Practice with Mandated Clients." *Social Service Review* 61 (December): 581–98.

Ignatieff, Michael

    1978   *A Just Measure of Pain: The Penitentiary in the Industrial Revolution.* New York: Pantheon.

Illinois Criminal Justice Authority

    1999   "Drug Court Provides Treatment Alternative to Incarceration." *On Good Authority* 2 (April): 1–4.

Irwin, John

    2005   *The Warehouse Prison: Disposal of the New Dangerous Class.* Cary, NC: Roxbury.
    1980   *Prisons in Turmoil.* Boston: Little, Brown.

Irwin, John, and James Austin

    1994   *It's about Time: America's Imprisonment Binge.* Belmont, CA: Wadsworth.

Jackson, David, and Cornelia Grumman

    1999   "State Puts Kids' Lives on the Block." *Chicago Tribune* (September 26): 1, 18, 19.

Jackson, Patrick G.

    1983   "Some Effects of Parole Supervision on Recidivism." *British Journal of Criminology* 23 (January): 17–34.

Jacobs, James B.

    1980   "The Prisoners' Rights Movement and Its Impacts, 1960–80," in *Crime and Justice,* Volume 2, edited by Norval Morris and Michael Tonry, pages 429–70. Chicago: University of Chicago Press.

Jacoby, Joseph E., Scott A. Desmond, Edna Gree, Lori I. Kepford, Jacinto F. Mendoza, and Monte D. Staton

    1994   "Why Bootcamps Fail: Historical and Theoretical Analysis." Paper presented at the annual meeting of the American Society of Criminology, Miami, Florida, November.

Jeffrey, C. Ray

    1971   *Crime Prevention through Environmental Design.* Beverly Hills, CA: Sage.

Jenuwine, Michael J., Ronald Simmons, and Edward Swies

    2003   "Community Supervision of Sex Offenders—Integrating Probation and Clinical Treatment." *Federal Probation* 67 (December): 20–27.

Jermstad, Todd

    2002   "*United States v. Knights* and the Diminished Liberty Interests of Probationers." *Executive Exchange* (Spring): 13–17.

Johnson, Kirk
    1994   "Connecticut Closes Boot Camp Built to Assist Troubled Youths." *New York Times* (June 11): 8.
    1989   "U.S. Sues Town over Rights of Retarded." *New York Times* (June 27): 7.

Johnson, Louise C.
    1998   *Social Work Practice: A Generalist Approach.* Boston: Allyn and Bacon.

Johnson, Louise C., and Stephen J. Yanca
    2007   *Social Work Practice: A Generalist Perspective,* 9th ed. Boston: Allyn and Bacon.
    2004   *Social Work Practice: A Generalist Perspective,* 8th ed. Boston: Allyn and Bacon.

Jones, Hendrée E.
    2004   "Practical Considerations for the Clinical Use of Buprenorpine." *Perspectives* 2 (August): 4–24.

Jones, Justin, and Carol Robinson
    1989   "Keeping the Piece: Probation and Parole Officers' Right to Bear Arms." *Corrections Today* (February): 88, 90.

Jones, Mark, and Darrell L. Ross
    1997   "Is Less Better? Boot Camp, Regular Probation and Rearrest in North Carolina." *American Journal of Criminal Justice* 21 (Spring): 147–61.

Johnston, Philip
    2001   "Population of Prisons Hits 66,000 Record." *Electric Telegraph* (June 29): Internet.

Kanfer, Frederick H., and Arnold P. Goldstein
    1975   "Introduction," in *Helping People Change: A Textbook of Methods,* edited by Frederick H. Kanfer and Arnold P. Goldstein, pages 1–14. New York: Pergamon Press.

Kassebaum, Gene, Mel Silverio, Nancy Marker, Paul Perrone, Joseph Allen, and James Richmond
    1999   *Survival on Parole: A Study of Post-Prison Adjustment and the Risk of Returning to Prison in the State of Hawaii.* Honolulu: Hawaii Attorney General.

Kelly, William R., and Sheldon Ekland-Olson
    1991   "The Response of the Criminal Justice System to Prison Overcrowding: Recidivism Patterns Among Four Successive Parolee Cohorts." *Law and Society Review* 25 (3): 601–20.

Kelman, Mark
    1987   *A Guide to Critical Legal Studies.* Cambridge, MA: Harvard University Press.

Kempinen, Cynthia A., and Megan C. Kurlychek
    2003   "An Outcome Evaluation of Pennsylvania's Boot Camp: Does Rehabilitative Programming Within a Disciplinary Setting Reduce Recidivism?" *Crime and Delinquency* 49 (October): 581–602.

Keve, Paul
    1979   "No Farewell to Arms." *Crime and Delinquency* 25 (October).

Kiernan, Louise
    1997   "Trial: At Juvenile Court, an Ongoing Struggle to Mend Broken Lives." *Chicago Tribune Magazine* (January 19): 11–18.

Kilborn, Peter T.
    2001   "Rural Towns Turn to Prisons to Reignite Their Economies." *New York Times* (August 1): Internet.

King, Ryan Scott, Marc Mauer, and Tracy Huling
    2004   "An Analysis of the Economics of Prison Siting in Rural Communities." *Criminology and Public Policy* 3 (July): 453–80.

Kingsnorth, Rodney, and Louis Rizzo

1979 "Decision-Making in the Criminal Court: Continuities and Discontinuities." *Criminology* 17 (May).

Klein, Eric C.

1998 "Dennis the Menace or Billy the Kid: An Analysis of the Role of Transfer to Criminal Court in Juvenile Justice." *American Criminal Law Review* 35 (Winter): 371–401.

Klockars, Carl B., Jr.

1972 "A Theory of Probation Supervision." *Journal of Criminal Law, Criminology and Police Science* 63 (4): 550–57.

Kluger, Jeffrey

2007 "The Paradox of Supermax." *Time* (February 5): 52–53.

Kolbert, Elizabeth

1989 "Court Awards $1.3 Million to Inmates Injured at Attica." *New York Times* (October 26): 14.

Konopka, Gisela

1983 *Social Group Work: A Helping Process*, 3rd ed. Upper Saddle River, NJ: Prentice Hall.

Krajick, Kevin

1978 "Parole: Discretion Is Out, Guidelines Are In." *Corrections Magazine* 4 (December).

Krause, Kitry

1997 "Borrowed Time: Intensive Probation Offers Kids in Trouble One Last Chance to Stay Out of Jail." *Reader* (January 17): 1, 14, 16, 18–25.

Krauth, Barbara

1987 "Parole: Controversial Component of the Criminal Justice System," in *Observations on Parole: A Collection of Readings from Western Europe, Canada and the United States*, edited by Edward E. Rhine and Ronald W. Jackson, pages 51–57. Washington, DC: U.S. Government Printing Office.

Krienert, Jessie L., and Mark S. Fleisher, eds.

2004 *Crime and Employment: Critical Issues in Crime Reduction for Corrections.* Walnut Creek, CA: AltaMira Press.

Krisberg, Barry

1988 *The Juvenile Court: Reclaiming the Vision.* San Francisco, CA: National Council on Crime and Delinquency.

Krisberg, Barry, Orlando Rodriquez, Audrey Bakke, Deborah Newenfeldt, and Patricia Steel

1994 *Juvenile Intensive Supervision: An Assessment.* Washington, DC: Office of Juvenile Justice and Delinquency Prevention.

Kupchik, Aaron

2006 "The Decision to Incarcerate in Juvenile and Criminal Courts." *Criminal Justice Review* 31 (December): 309–36.

Kurki, Leena

1999 *Incorporating Restorative and Community Justice into American Sentencing and Corrections.* Washington, DC: National Institute of Justice.

Kurlychek, Megan C., and Brian D. Johnson

2004 "The Juvenile Penalty: A Comparison of Juvenile and Young Adult Sentencing Outcomes in Criminal Court." *Criminology* 42 (May): 485–517.

Lab, Steven P., and John T. Cullen

1990 "From 'Nothing Works' to 'The Appropriate Works': The Latest Stop on the Search for the Secular Grail." *Criminology* 28 (August): 405–17.

Langan, Patrick A., and Matthew R. Durose

    2003 *Recidivism of Sex Offenders Released from Prison in 1994*. Washington, DC: Bureau of Justice Statistics.

Latessa, Edward J., and Gennaro F. Vito

    1988 "The Effects of Intensive Supervision on Shock Probationers." *Journal of Criminal Justice* 16: 319–30.

Latessa, Edward J., Frank T. Cullen, and Paul Gendreau

    2002 "Beyond Correctional Quakery—Professionalism and the Possibility of Effective Treatment." *Federal Probation* 66 (September): 40–43.

Law Enforcement Assistance Administration

    1973 *Reintegration of the Offender into the Community*. Washington, DC: U.S. Government Printing Office.

Leenhouts, Keith J.

    2003 *Misdemeanors and the Miracle of Mentoring*. Davison, MI: Friede Publications.

Lefcourt, Robert, ed.

    1971 *Law against the People*. New York: Random House.

Lemert, Edwin M.

    1951 *Social Pathology*. New York: McGraw-Hill.

Lemmon, John H.

    2006 "The Effects of Maltreatment Recurrence and Child Welfare Services on Dimensions of Delinquency." *Criminal Justice Review* 31 (March): 5–32.

Lenroot, Katherine F., and Emma O. Lundberg

    1925 *Juvenile Courts at Work*. Washington, DC: U.S. Government Printing Office.

Leonhardt, David

    2000 "As Prison Labor Grows, So Does the Debate." *New York Times* (March 19): 1, 22.

Lerner, Mark Jay

    1977 "The Effectiveness of a Definite Sentence Parole Program." *Criminology* 15 (August).

Levrant, Sharon, Francis T. Cullen, Betsy Fulton, and John F. Wozniak

    1999 "Reconsidering Restorative Justice: The Corruption of Benevolence Revisited?" *Crime and Delinquency* 45 (January): 3–27.

Lewin, Tamar

    2001a "Little Sympathy or Remedy for Inmates Who Are Raped." *New York Times* (April 15): 1, 14.

    2001b "3-Strikes Law Is Overrated in California, Study Finds." *New York Times* (August 24): 10.

    1998 "Crime Costs Many Black Men the Vote, Study Says." *New York Times* (October 23): 12.

Lewis, W. David

    1965 *From Newgate to Dannemora*. Ithaca, NY: Cornell University Press.

Liberton, Michael, Mitchell Silverman, and William R. Blount

    1990 "An Analysis Used to Predict Success of First-Time Offenders While under Probation Supervision." Paper presented at the annual meeting of the Academy of Criminal Justice Sciences, April, Denver, CO; reprinted in 1992 in the *International Journal of Offender Therapy and Comparative Criminology* 36 (4): 335–47.

Lilly, J. Robert, and Richard A. Ball

    1987 "A Brief History of House Arrest and Electronic Monitoring." *Northern Kentucky Law Review* 13: 343–74.

Lindner, Charles, and Margaret R. Savarese

1984   "The Evolution of Probation." *Federal Probation* 48 (December).

Lipsey, Mark W., Gabrielle L. Chapman, and Nana A. Landenberger

2001   "Cognitive-Behavioral Programs for Offenders." *Annals* 578 (November): 144–57.

Liptak, Adam

2006   "Criminal Records Erased by Courts Live to Tell Tales." *New York Times* (October 17): 1, 18.

2004   "Sentencing Decision's Reach Is Far and Wide." *New York Times* (June 27): 16.

Lipton, Douglas, Robert Martinson, and Judith Wilks

1975   *The Effectiveness of Correctional Treatment: A Survey of Treatment Evaluation Studies*. New York: Praeger.

Logan, Charles H.

1990   *Private Prisons: Cons and Pros*. New York: Oxford University Press.

Lombroso, Cesare

1968   *Crime: Its Causes and Remedies*. Montclair, NJ: Patterson Smith. (Originally published in 1911.)

London, Perry

1964   *The Modes and Morals of Psychotherapy*. New York: Holt, Rinehart and Winston.

Lopez, John S.

2007   "Have Perceptions Changed among Staff Regarding Parole Officers' Carrying Firearms? A Description of Changes in Safety Perceptions and Supervisory Styles at the Texas Department of Criminal Justice Parole Division." Masters thesis in Public Administration, Texas State University/San Marcos.

Lou, Herbert H.

1972   *Juvenile Courts in the United States*. New York: Arno Press. (Originally published in 1927.)

Lowenkamp, Christopher T., Jennifer Pealer, Paula Smith, and Edward J. Latessa

2006   "Adhering to the Risk and Need Principles: Does It Matter for Supervision-Based Programs?" *Federal Probation* (December): 3–8.

Lurigio, Arthur J., and Joan Petersilia

1992   "The Emergence of Intensive Probation Supervision Programs in the United States," in *Smart Sentencing: The Emergence of Intermediate Sanctions*, edited by James M. Byrne, Arthur J. Lurigio, and Joan Petersilia, pages 3–17. Newbury Park, CA: Sage.

Lurigio, Arthur J., Marylouise Jones, and Barbara E. Smith

1995   "Child Sexual Abuse: Its Causes, Consequences, and Implications for Probation Practice." *Federal Probation* 69 (September): 69–76.

Luther, Betty

1995   "The Politics of Criminal Justice: A Study of the Impact of Executive Influence on Massachusetts Parole Decisions between 1985 and 1992." Paper presented at the annual meeting of the Academy of Criminal Justice Sciences, Boston, March 7–11.

MacKenzie, Doris Layton

2006   *What Works in Corrections: Reducing the Criminal Activities of Offenders and Delinquents*. New York: Cambridge University Press.

1994   "Results of a Multistate Study of Boot Camp Prisons." *Federal Probation* 58 (June): 60–66.

MacKenzie, Doris Layton, and James W. Shaw

1993   "The Impact of Shock Incarceration on Technical Violations and New Criminal Activities." *Justice Quarterly* 10 (September): 463–87.

MacKenzie, Doris Layton, and Claire Souryal

1994   *Multisite Evaluation of Shock Incarceration*. Washington, DC: National Institute of Justice.

MacKenzie, Doris Layton, Robert Brame, David McDowall, and Claire Souryal

1995   "Boot Camp Prisons in Eight States." *Criminology* 33 (August): 327–57.

MacKenzie, Doris Layton, Angela R. Grover, Gaylene Stywe Armstrong, and Ojmarrh Mitchell

2001   *A National Study Comparing the Environments of Boot Camps with Traditional Facilities for Juvenile Offenders*. Washington, DC: National Institute of Justice.

MacKenzie, Doris Layton, James W. Shaw, and Claire Souryal

1992   "Characteristics Associated with Successful Adjustment to Supervision: A Comparison of Parolees, Probationers, Shock Participants, and Shock Dropouts." *Criminal Justice and Behavior* 19 (December): 437–54.

MacNamara, Donal E. J.

1977   "The Medical Model in Corrections: Requiescat in Pace." *Criminology* 14 (February): 439–48.

Maestro, Marcello

1973   *Cesare Beccaria and the Origins of Penal Reform*. Philadelphia: Temple University Press.

Magura, Stephen, Sung-Yeon Kang, and Janet L. Shapiro

1995   "Measuring Cocaine Use by Hair Analysis among Criminally-Involved Youth." *Journal of Drug Issues* 25 (Fall): 683–701.

Mahoney, Joe

2007   "Short Arm of the Law." *New York Daily News* (May 8): 6.

Malcolm, Andrew H.

1989a   "Florida's Jammed Prisons: More In Means More Out." *New York Times* (July 3): 1, 7.
1989b   "More and More, Prison Is America's Answer to Crime." *New York Times* (November 26): E1, 4.
1989c   "Explosive Drug Use in Prisons Is Creating a New Underworld." *New York Times* (December 30): 1, 10.

Maloney, Dennis M., and Mark S. Umbreit

1995   "Managing Change: Toward a Balanced and Restorative Justice Model." *Perspectives* 19 (Spring): 43–46.

Maltz, Michael D.

1984   *Recidivism*. Orlando, FL: Academic Press.

Mander, Anthony M., Martin E. Atrops, Allan R. Barnes, and Roseanne Munafo

1996   *Sex Offender Treatment Program: Initial Recidivism Study*. Executive Summary. Anchorage: Alaska Department of Corrections.

Mangrum, Claude

1972   "The Humanity of Probation Officers." *Federal Probation* 36 (June).

Mann, Arnold

2004   "Successful Trial Caps 25-Year Buprenorphine Development Effort." *NIDA Notes* 19 (3): 7–9.

Mann, Dale

1976   *Intervening with Convicted Serious Juvenile Offenders*. Washington, DC: U.S. Government Printing Office.

"Manufacturers Complain of Prison Work Programs"

1997   *Chicago Tribune* (November 28): 8.

Marlowe, Douglas

2006   "When 'What Works' Never Did: Dodging the 'Scarlet M' in Correctional Rehabilitation." *Criminology and Public Policy* 5 (May): 339–46.

Marriott, Michael

1995   "Half Steps vs. 12 Steps." *Newsweek* (March 27): 62.

Marshall, Franklin H.

1989   "Diversion and Probation under the New Sentencing Guidelines: One Officer's Observations." Paper presented at the annual meeting of the Academy of Criminal Justice Sciences, Washington, DC, March 30.

Martin, Andrew

1995   "Few Brains behind Bank Heists." *Chicago Tribune* (June 28): Sec. 2: 1, 4.

Martin, Douglas

1988   "New York Tests Inmates' Boot Camp." *New York Times* (March 4): 15.

Martin, Garry, and Joseph Pear

1992   *Behavior Modification: What It Is and How to Do It*, 4th ed. Upper Saddle River, NJ: Prentice Hall.

Martinson, Robert

1974   "What Works? Questions and Answers about Prison Reform." *The Public Interest* 35 (Spring): 22–54.

Martinson, Robert, and Judith Wilks

1975   "A Static-Descriptive Model of Field Supervision." *Criminology* 13 (May).

Maruschak, Laura M.

2006   *HIV in Prisons, 2004*. Washington, DC: Bureau of Justice Statistics.

Marx, Gary

1998   "Panel Uncovers Security Leaks at Juvenile Jail." *Chicago Tribune* (March 2): 1, 12.
1994   "Hard Time." *Chicago Tribune* (October 24): Sec. 5: 1, 6.

Mathias, Rudolf E. S., and James W. Mathews

1991   "The Boot Camp Program for Offenders: Does the Shoe Fit? *International Journal of Offender Therapy and Comparative Criminology* 35: 322–27.

Matza, David

1964   *Delinquency and Drift*. New York: Wiley.

McCarthy, Belinda Rogers, and Bernard J. McCarthy

1984   *Community-Based Corrections*. Monterey, CA: Brooks/Cole.

McCollum, Sylvia G.

2000   "Mock Job Fairs in Prison: Tracking Participants." *Federal Probation* (June): 13–18.

McDonald, Douglas C.

1988   *Restitution and Community Service*. Washington, DC: National Institute of Justice.

McDowell, Edwin

1991   "Inmates Fill the Front Lines for Tourism." *New York Times* (November 24): 1, 15.

McElrath, Karen

1995   "Alcoholics Anonymous," in the *American Drug Scene: An Anthology*, edited by James A. Inciardi and Karen McElrath, pages 314–37. Los Angeles: Roxbury.

McFadden, Robert D.

1997   "Ex-Attica Inmate Wins $4 Million in Suit over Reprisals after 1971 Uprising." *New York Times* (June 6): 20.

McGaha, Johnny, Michael Fichter, and Peter Hirschburg

1987   "Felony Probation: A Re-Examination of Public Risk." *American Journal of Criminal Justice* 11: 1–9.

McKelvey, Blake

1977   *American Prisons: A History of Good Intentions.* Montclair, NJ: Patterson Smith.

1972   *American Prisons: A Study in American Social History Prior to 1815.* Montclair, NJ: Patterson Smith.

McShane, Marilyn D., and Frank P. Williams III

1989   "The Prison Adjustment of Juvenile Offenders." *Crime and Delinquency* 35 (April): 254–69.

McTavish, Thomas H.

1997   *Performance Audit of the Presentence Investigation Process.* Lansing: Michigan Office of the Auditor General.

Melossi, Dario, and Massimo Pavarini

1981   *The Prison and the Factory: Origins of the Penitentiary System.* Totowa, NJ: Barnes and Noble.

Mennel, Robert M.

1973   *Thorns and Thistles: Juvenile Delinquents in the United States, 1825–1940.* Hanover, NH: University Press of New England.

Meredith, Robyn

2000   "Road from Prison to Jobs Gets Smoother." *New York Times* (April 3): 12.

Merlo, Alida V., Peter J. Benekos, and William J. Cook

1997   "Waiver and Juvenile Justice Reform: Widening the Punitive Net." *Criminal Justice Policy Review* 8 (2–3): 145–68.

Merton, Robert K.

1964   "Anomie, Anomia, and Social Interaction," in *Anomie and Deviant Behavior,* edited by Marshall B. Clinard, pages 213–42. New York: Free Press.

1938   "Social Structure and Anomie." *American Sociological Review* 3: 672–82.

Mieczkowski, Thomas

1995   *Hair Analysis as a Drug Detector.* Washington, DC: National Institute of Justice.

Miley, Karla Krogsrud, Michael O'Melia, and Brenda L. DuBois

2004   *Generalist Social Work Practice: An Empowering Approach.* Boston: Allyn and Bacon.

Milkman, Harvey and Kenneth Wanberg

2007   Cognitive-Behavioral Treatment: A Review and Discussion for Corrections Professionals. Washington, DC: National Institute of Corrections.

Miller, Jerome

1992   *Last One over the Wall: The Massachusetts Experiment in Closing Reform Schools.* Columbus: Ohio State University.

Miller, Walter B.

1958   "Lower Class Culture as a Generating Milieu of Gang Delinquency." *Journal of Social Issues* 14: 5–19.

Mills, Jim

1992   "Supervision Fees." *Perspectives* (Fall): 10–12.

Mohler, Henry Calvin

1925   "Convict Labor Policies." *Journal of Criminal Law, Criminology and Police Science* 15: 530–97.

Monti, Crostin
>   1997   "Prison Treatment Program Seeks to Change Sex Offender Behavior." *The Compiler* 17 (Summer): 4–6.

Moore, Kathleen Dean
>   1989   *Pardons: Justice, Mercy, and the Public Interest.* New York: Oxford University Press.

Morash, Merry, and Lila Rucker
>   1990   "A Critical Look at the Idea of Boot Camp as a Correctional Reform." *Crime and Delinquency* 36 (April): 204–22.

Morgan, Robert D., and Carrie L. Winterowd
>   2002   "Interpersonal Process-Oriented Group Psychotherapy." *International Journal of Offender Therapy and Comparative Criminology* 46 (4): 466–82.

Moritz, John
>   2001   "Prison Population in Texas Declines." *Fort Worth Star Telegram* (July 3): Internet.

Morris, Norval, and Michael Tonry
>   1990   *Between Prison and Probation: Intermediate Punishments in a Rational Sentencing System.* New York: Oxford University Press.

Moses, Marilyn C.
>   1996   *Project Re-Enterprise: A Texas Program.* Washington, DC: Office of Justice Programs.

Mullaney, Fahy G.
>   1988   *Economic Sanctions in Community Corrections.* Washington, DC: National Institute of Corrections.

Mullen, Joan
>   1985   "Corrections and the Private Sector." *NIJ Reports* (May).

Mumola, Christopher J., and Thomas P. Bonczar
>   1998   *Substance Abuse and Treatment of Adults on Probation, 1995.,* Washington, DC: Bureau of Justice Statistics.

Murphy, Cait
>   2001   "Crime and Punishment." *Fortune* 143 (April 30): 126–35.

Mydans, Seth
>   1995   "Racial Tensions on the Rise in Los Angeles Jail System." *New York Times* (February 6): 8.

Myers, Linnet
>   1995   "Cultural Divide over Crime and Punishment." *Chicago Tribune* (October 13): 1, 8.

National Advisory Commission on Criminal Justice Standards and Goals
>   1975   *A National Strategy to Reduce Crime.* New York: Avon.
>   1973   *Corrections.* Washington, DC: U.S. Government Printing Office.

National Commission on Law Observance and Law Enforcement
>   1931   *Report on Penal Institutions.* Washington, DC: U.S. Government Printing Office.

National Governors' Association
>   1988   *Guide to Executive Clemency among the American States.* Washington, DC: National Institute of Corrections.

National Institute of Corrections (NIC)
>   n.d.   *Classification in Probation and Parole: A Model Systems Approach. Supplemental Report: The Client Management Classification System.* Longmont, CO: NIC.

Nelson, E. Kim, Howard Ohmart, and Nora Harlow

    1978   *Promising Strategies in Probation and Parole.* Washington, DC: U.S. Government Printing Office.

"Newgate"

    1998   *DOC Today* (February): Internet.

New York State Bar Association

    2006   *The Road to Public Safety.* Albany, NY: Special Committee on Collateral Consequences of Criminal Proceedings.

New York State Division of Parole

    1994   *1993–1994 Report.* Albany: New York State Division of Parole.
    1984   *1982–83 Annual Report.* Albany: New York State Division of Parole
    1953   *Parole Officer's Manual.* Albany: New York State Division of Parole.

New York State Employment Services Vocational Rehabilitation Service

    1965   "Vocational Counseling with the Offender" (mimeo). Albany, NY: Vocational Rehabilitation Service.

New York State Special Commission on Attica

    1972   *Attica.* New York: Praeger.

Niemeyer, Mike, and David Shichor

    1996   "A Preliminary Study of a Large Victim/Offender Reconciliation Program." *Federal Probation* 60 (September): 30–34.

Nietzel, Michael T., Douglas A. Bernstein, Geoffrey P. Kramer, and Richard Milich

    2003   *Introduction to Clinical Psychology,* 6th ed. Upper Saddle River, NJ: Prentice Hall.

Noonan, Susan B., and Edward J. Latessa

    1987   "Intensive Probation: An Examination of Recidivism and Social Adjustment." *American Journal of Criminal Justice* 11: 45–61.

Norman, Michael D., and Robert C. Wadman

    2000   "Probation Department Sentencing Recommendations in Two Utah Counties." *Federal Probation* (December): 47–51.

Northern, Helen

    1988   *Social Work with Groups,* 2nd ed. New York: Columbia University Press.
    1969   *Social Work with Groups.* New York: Columbia University Press.

Office for Victims of Crime

    1998   *New Directions from the Field: Victims' Rights and Services for the 21st Century.* Washington, DC: U.S. Department of Justice.

Office of Policy Analysis and Information

    1989   *Shock Incarceration: One Year Out.* Albany: New York State Division of Parole.

Ogborne, Alan C., and Frederick B. Glaser

    1985   "Evaluating Alcoholics Anonymous," in *Alcoholism and Substance Abuse,* edited by Thomas E. Bratter and Gary G. Forrest, pages 176–92. New York: Free Press.

OJJDP Research 2000

    2001   Washington, DC: Office of Juvenile Justice and Delinquency Prevention.

O'Leary, K. Daniel, and G. Terrance Wilson

    1975   *Behavior Therapy: Application and Outcome.* Upper Saddle River, NJ: Prentice Hall.

Olivares, Kathleen M., Velmer S. Burton, Frances T. Cullen, Debra Oldenettel, and Madeline Wordes

    2000   *The Community Assessment Center Concept.* Washington, DC: Office of Juvenile Justice and Delinquency Prevention.

1996 "The Collateral Consequences of a Felony Conviction: A National Study of State Legal Codes 10 Years Later." *Federal Probation* 60 (September): 10–17.

Olson, Susan M., and Albert W. Dzur

2003 "The Practice of Restorative Justice: Reconstructing Professional Roles in Restorative Justice Programs." *Utah Law Review* 57: Internet.

Oltmanns, Thomas F., and Robert E. Emery

2004 *Abnormal Psychology*, 4th ed. Upper Saddle River, NJ: Prentice Hall.

Omer, Haim, and Perry London

1988 "Metamorphosis in Psychotherapy: End of the Systems Era." *Psychotherapy* 25 (Summer): 171–80.

Pace, Eric

1988 "Lois Burnham Wilson, a Founder of Al-Anon Groups, Is Dead at 97." *New York Times* (October 4): 15.

Pager, Devah

2006 "Evidence-Based Policy for Successful Prisoner Reentry." *Criminology and Public Policy* 5 (August): 505–14.

2003 "The Mark of a Criminal Record." *American Journal of Sociology* 108 (March): 937–75.

Palumbo, Dennis J., and Rebecca D. Peterson

1994 "Shock Incarceration and Intermediate Punishments: Reform or Recycled 'Get Tough' Policy?" Paper presented at the annual meeting of the American Society of Criminology, Miami, FL, November.

Papy, Joseph E.

1997 "Florida's Approach to Probation and Parole Staff Safety," in *Topics in Community Corrections*, pages 23–25. Washington, DC: National Institute of Corrections.

Parent, Dale G.

2003 *Correctional Boot Camps: Lessons from a Decade of Research*. Washington, DC: National Institute of Justice.

1996 "Day Reporting Centers: An Evolving Intermediate Sanction." *Federal Probation* 60 (December): 51–54.

1990 *Day Reporting Centers for Criminal Offenders—A Descriptive Analysis of Existing Programs*. Washington, DC: Office of Justice Programs.

1989 *Shock Incarceration: An Overview of Existing Programs*. Washington, DC: U.S. Government Printing Office.

1988 "Overview: Shock-Incarceration Programs." *Perspectives* 12 (July): 9–15.

Parent, Dale G., Dan Wentworth, Peggy Burke, and Becky Ney

1994 *Responding to Probation and Parole Violations*. Washington, DC: National Institute of Justice.

Parker, William

1975 *Parole*. College Park, MD: American Correctional Association.

Parry, Wayne

2001 "Employers Seeking Workers from Newark Prison Ranks." Associated Press (May 17): Internet.

Parsonage, William H.

1990 *Worker Safety in Probation and Parole*. Longmont, CO: National Institute of Corrections.

Parsonage, William H., and W. Conway Bushey

1989 "The Victimization of Probation and Parole Workers in the Line of Duty: An Exploratory Study." Paper presented at the annual meeting of the Academy of Criminal Justice Sciences, Washington, DC, March.

Parsons, Christi

    1998   "Jury Out on Sex-Offender Law." *Chicago Tribune* (June 28): 1, 12.

Payne, Malcolm

    1997   *Modern Social Work Theory*, 2nd ed. Chicago: Lyceum.

Pearson, Frank S.

    1988   "Evaluation of New Jersey's Intensive Supervision Program." *Crime and Delinquency* 34 (October): 437–48.

Pearson, Frank S., Douglas S. Lipton, Charles M. Cleland, and Dorline S. Yee

    2002   "The Effects of Behavioral/Cognitive-Behavioral Programs on Recidivism." *Crime and Delinquency* 48 (July): 476–96.

Peele, Stanton

    1985   *The Meaning of Addiction: Compulsive Experience and Its Interpretation*. Lexington, MA: D.C. Heath.

Peréz-Peña, Richard

    2003   "New Drug Promises Shift in Treatment." *New York Times* (August 11): 1, B7.

    1998   "Pataki Plan to End Parole Is Tougher Than Others." *New York Times* (January 26): 18.

    1997   "New York's Income Gap Largest in the Nation." *New York Times* (December 17): 14.

Perlman, Helen Harris

    1971   *Perspectives on Social Casework: A Problem Solving Process*. Chicago: University of Chicago Press.

    1957   *Perspectives on Social Casework*. Philadelphia: Temple University Press.

Peters, Michael, David Thomas, and Christopher Zamberlan

    1997   *Boot Camp for Juvenile Offenders: Program Summary*. Washington, DC: Office of Juvenile Justice and Delinquency Prevention.

Petersilia, Joan M.

    2006   *Understanding California Corrections*. Berkeley: California Policy Research Center.

    2005   "Hard Time: Ex-Offenders Returning Home after Prison." *Corrections Today* (April): 66–71, 155.

    2003   *When Prisoners Come Home: Parole and Prisoner Re-Entry*. New York: Oxford University Press.

    2000a "Parole and Prison Reentry in the United States." *Perspectives* 24 (Fall): 38–47.

    2000b *When Prisoners Return to the Community: Political, Economic, and Social Consequences*. Washington, DC: Office of Justice Programs.

    1998a "Probation in the United States, Part I." *Perspectives* 22 (Spring): 30–41.

    1998b "Probation in the United States, Part II." *Perspectives* 22 (Summer): 42–49.

    1995   "A Crime Control Rationale for Reinvesting in Community Corrections." *Spectrum* (Summer): 16–27.

    1993   "Measuring the Performance of Community Corrections," in *Performance Measures for the Criminal Justice System*, pages 61–85. Washington, DC: Bureau of Justice Statistics.

    1990   "When Probation Becomes More Dreaded Than Prison." *Federal Probation* 54 (March): 23–27.

    1988   "Georgia's Intensive Probation: Will the Model Work Elsewhere?" in *Intermediate Punishments: Intensive Supervision, Home Confinement and Electronic Surveillance*, edited by Belinda R. McCarthy, pages 15–30. Monsey, NY: Criminal Justice Press.

Petersilia, Joan, and Susan Turner

    1993   *Evaluating Intensive Supervision Probation/Parole: Results of a Nationwide Experiment*. Washington, DC: National Institute of Justice.

    1991   "Is ISP a Viable Sanction for High Risk Probationers?" *Perspectives* 15 (Summer): 8–11.

1990   "Comparing Intensive and Regular Supervision for High-Risk Probationers: Early Results from an Experiment in California." *Crime and Delinquency* 36 (January): 87–111.

Petersilia, Joan, Elizabeth Piper Deschenes

1994   What Punishes? Inmates Rank the Severity of Prison vs. Intermediate Sanctions." *Federal Probation* 68 (March): 3–8.

Petersilia, Joan, Susan Turner, and Elizabeth Piper Deschenes

1992   "Intensive Supervision Programs for Drug Offenders," in *Smart Sentencing: The Emergence of Intermediate Sanctions*, edited by James M. Byrne, Arthur J. Lurigio, and Joan Petersilia, pages 18–37. Newbury Park, CA: Sage.

Petersilia, Joan, Susan Turner, James Kahan, and Joyce Peterson

1985   *Granting Felons Probation: Public Risks and Alternatives*. Santa Monica, CA: RAND.

Pisciotta, Alexander W.

1994   *Benevolent Repression: Social Control and the American Reformatory-Prison Movement*. New York: New York University Press.

1992   "Doing Parole: The Promise and Practice of the Minnesota and Illinois Reformatories, 1889–1990." Paper presented at the annual meeting of the American Society of Criminology, New Orleans, LA, November.

Platt, Anthony M.

1974   *The Childsavers: The Invention of Delinquency*. Chicago: University of Chicago Press.

Platt, Jerome J., and Christina Labate

1976   *Heroin Addiction: Research and Treatment*. New York: Wiley.

Polakow, Robert L., and Ronald M. Docktor

1974   "A Behavioral Modification Program for Adult Drug Offenders." *Journal of Research in Crime and Delinquency* 11 (January): 63–69.

Porter, Bruce

1995   "Terror on an Eight-Hour Shift." *New York Times Magazine* (November 26): 42–47, 56, 59, 72, 76, 80, 82.

Powell, Hickman

2000   *Lucky Luciano: The Man Who Organized Crime in America*. New York: Barricade Books. (Originally published in 1939.)

President's Commission on Law Enforcement and Administration of Justice

1972   *The Challenge of Crime in a Free Society*. New York: Avon.

President's Commission on Organized Crime

1986   *The Impact: Organized Crime Today*. Washington, DC: U.S. Government Printing Office.

Prison Association of New York

1936   *The Ninety-First Annual Report*. Albany, NY: J. B. Lyon.

Privacy and Juvenile Justice Records: A Mid-Decade Status Report

1997   Washington, DC: Office of Justice Programs.

Proctor, Jon L.

2000   "Parole as Institutional Control: A Test of Specific Deterrence and Offender Misconduct." *The Prison Journal* 80 (1): 39–55.

Program Services Office

1983   *Probation Classification and Service Delivery Approach*. Los Angeles: County Probation Department.

Przybylski, Roger

    1988   *Electronically Monitored Home Confinement in Illinois.* Chicago: Illinois Criminal Justice Information Authority.

Purdy, Matthew

    1997   "As AIDS Increases behind Bars, Costs Dim Promise of New Drugs." *New York Times* (May 26): 1, 12.

    1995   "Bars Don't Stop Flow of Drugs into the Prisons." *New York Times* (July 2): 1, 12, 13.

Puritz, Patricia, and Mary Ann Scali

    1998   *Beyond the Walls: Improving Conditions of Confinement for Youth in Custody.* Washington, DC: Office of Juvenile Justice and Delinquency Prevention.

Puzzanchera, Charles M.

    2001   *Delinquency Cases Waived to Criminal Court, 1989–1998.* Washington, DC: Office of Justice Programs.

Quadagno, Jill S., and Robert J. Antonio

    1975   "Labeling Theory as an Oversocialized Conception of Man: The Case of Mental Illness." *Sociology and Social Research* 60 (October): 33–45.

Rachin, Richard

    1974   "Reality Therapy: Helping People Help Themselves." *Crime and Delinquency* 20 (January).

"Rape Crisis in U.S. Prisons"

    2001   *Human Rights Watch* (April 19): Internet.

Re-Entry Policy Council (REPC)

    2005   *Report of the Re-Entry Policy Council.* New York: REPC.

Reeves, Bob

    2003   "Introduction," in *Misdemeanors and the Miracle of Mentoring,* edited by Keith J. Leenhouts, pages iv–v. Davison, MI: Friede Publications.

Reichel, Phillip L., and Billie D. Sudbrack

    1994   "Differences among Eligibles: Who Gets an ISP Sentence?" *Federal Probation* (58): 51–62.

Reiff, Phillip, ed.

    1963   *Freud, Therapy and Techniques.* New York: Crowell-Collier.

Reiman, Jeffrey

    1998   *The Rich Get Richer and the Poor Get Prison,* 5th ed. New York: Macmillan.

Reinventing Probation Council (RPC)

    2000   *Transforming Probation through Leadership: The "Broken Windows" Model.* New York: Center for Civic Innovation at the Manhattan Institute.

Rhine, Edward E.

    2002   "Why 'What Works' Matters under the 'Broken Windows' Model of Supervision." *Federal Probation* 66 (September): 38–42.

Rhine, Edward E., Tina L. Mawhorr, and Evalyn C. Parks

    2006   "Implementation: The Bane of Effective Correctional Programs." *Criminology and Public Policy* 5 (May): 347–58.

Rhode, David

    2001   "A Health Danger from a Needle Becomes a Scourge behind Bars." *New York Times* (August 6): 1, 14.

Richmond, Mary

    1917   *Social Diagnosis*. New York: Russell Sage Foundation.

Rimer, Sara

    2001   "States Adjust Their Adult Prisons to the Needs of Youth Inmates." *New York Times* (July 25): 1, 13.

Robbins, Ira P.

    1988   *The Legal Dimensions of Private Incarceration*. Washington, DC: American Bar Association.

Robbins, Kelly, and Michael Ostermann

    2006   *2004 Recidivism Study: Executive Summary*. Trenton: New Jersey State Division of Parole.

Robertson, John A.

    1974   *Rough Justice: Perspectives on Lower Courts*. Boston: Little, Brown.

Robertson, Nan

    1988   *Getting Better: Inside Alcoholics Anonymous*. New York: William Morrow.

Robitscher, Jonas

    1980   *The Power of Psychiatry*. Boston: Houghton Mifflin.

Rosenblum, Robert, and Debra Whitcomb

    1978   *Montgomery County Work Release/Pre-Release Program*. Washington, DC: U.S. Government Printing Office.

Rosenthal, Mitchell S.

    1984   "Therapeutic Communities: A Treatment Alternative for Many But Not All." *Journal of Substance Abuse Treatment* 1: 55–58.

    1973   "New York City Phoenix House: A Therapeutic Community for the Treatment of Drug Abusers and Drug Addicts," in *Yearbook of Drug Abuse*, edited by Leon Brill and Earnest Harms, pages 83–102. New York: Behavioral Publications.

Roshier, Bob

    1989   *Controlling Crime: The Classical Perspective in Criminology*. Chicago: Lyceum.

Rothman, David

    1971   *The Discovery of the Asylum*. Boston: Little, Brown.

Rottman, David B., Carol R. Flango, Melissa T. Cantrell, Randall Hansen, and Neil LaFountain

    2000   *State Court Organization 1998*. Washington, DC: National Institute of Justice.

Rousseau, Jean-Jacques

    1954   *The Social Contract*. Chicago: Henry Regnery.

Rubin, H. Ted

    1980   "The Emerging Prosecutor Dominance of the Juvenile Court Intake Process." *Crime and Delinquency* 26 (July).

Russell, Amanda L., Edward J. Latessa, and Lawrence F. Travis III

    2005   "Evidence of Professionalism or Quackery: Measuring Practitioner Awareness of Risk/Need Factors and Effective Treatment Strategies." *Federal Probation* (December): 9–14.

Russo, Joe

    2006   "Emerging Technologies for Community Corrections." *Corrections Today* (October): 26–28.

Sachs, Howard, and Charles Logan

    1979   *Does Parole Make a Difference?* West Hartford: University of Connecticut Law School.

Sagatun, Inger, Loretta McCollum, and Michael Edwards

    1985   "The Effect of Transfers from Juvenile to Criminal Court: A Loglinear Analysis." *Journal of Crime and Justice* 8: 65–92.

Sanborn, Joseph B., Jr.

    1992   "Pleading Guilty in Juvenile Court: Minimal Ado about Something Very Important to Young Defendants." *Justice Quarterly* 9 (March): 127–50.

Schlosser, Eric

    1998   "The Prison-Industrial Complex." *Atlantic Monthly* (December): 51–77.

Schlossman, Steven L.

    1977   *Love and the American Delinquent: The Theory and Practice of "Progressive" Juvenile Justice, 1825–1920.* Chicago: University of Chicago Press.

Schmideberg, Melitta

    1975   "Some Basic Principles of Offender Therapy: Part II." *International Journal of Offender Therapy and Comparative Criminology* 1.

Schmidt, Annesley K.

    1989   "Electronic Monitoring of Offenders Increases." *NIJ Reports* (January–February): 2–5.

Schram, Donna D., Jill G. McKelvy, Anne L. Schneider, and David B. Griswold

    1981   *Preliminary Findings: Assessment of the Juvenile Code* (mimeo). Washington State.

Schram, Paula J., Barbara A. Koons-Witt, Frank P. William III, and Marilyn D. McShane

    2006   "Supervision Strategies and Approaches for Female Parolees: Examining the Link Between Unmet Needs and Parolee Outcome." *Crime and Delinquency* 52 (July): 450–71.

Schriro, Dora

    2000   *Correcting Corrections: Missouri's Parallel Universe.* Washington, DC: National Institute of Justice.

Schultz, J. Lawrence

    1973   "The Cycle of Juvenile Court History." *Crime and Delinquency* 19 (October).

Schuman, Alan M.

    1989   "The Cost of Correctional Services: Exploring a Poorly Charted Terrain." *Research in Corrections* 2 (February): 27–33.

Schur, Edwin M.

    1973   *Radical Non-Intervention: Rethinking the Delinquency Problem.* Englewood Cliffs, NJ: Prentice Hall.

Schwartz, Richard, and Jerome H. Skolnick

    1962   "Two Studies in Legal Stigma." *Social Problems* 10: 133–42.

Scull, Andrew T.

    1977   *Decarceration.* Englewood Cliffs, NJ: Prentice Hall.

Sechcrest, Dale K.

    1989   "Prison 'Boot Camps' Do Not Measure Up." *Federal Probation* 53 (September): 15–20.

Sechrest, Lee, Susan O. White, and Elizabeth D. Brown

    1979   *The Rehabilitation of Criminal Offenders: Problems and Prospects.* Washington, DC: National Academy of Sciences.

Selcraig, Bruce

    2000   "Camp Fear." *Mother Jones* (December): 64–71.

Sellin, Thorston

    1967   "A Look at Prison History." *Federal Probation* 31 (September): 18.

Sengupta, Somini

    2000   "Felony Costs Voting Rights for a Lifetime in 9 States." *New York Times* (November 3): 18.

Seventh Annual Shock Legislative Report

    1995   Albany: State of New York Department of Correctional Services and Division of Parole.

Sever, Brian

    2000   "County Sales Tax, Crime Rate, and Prison Bed Use in Florida: Implications for the Misuse of Prison Space." *Criminal Justice Policy Review* 11 (June): 91–112.

Sexton, Joe

    2006   "After Death of a Boy, Florida Moves to Close Its Boot Camps." *New York Times* (April 27): 18.

    1997   "Opening the Doors on Family Court's Secrets." *New York Times* (September 13): 1, 10.

Shaffer, John and M. David Galinsky

    1987   *Models of Group Therapy*, 2nd ed. Upper Saddle River, NJ: Prentice Hall.

Sheafor, Bradford W., Charles R. Horejsi, and Gloria A. Horejsi

    2000   *Techniques and Guidelines for Social Work Practice*, 5th ed. Boston: Allyn and Bacon.

Shearer, Robert A.

    2003   "Identifying the Special Needs of Female Offenders." *Federal Probation* (June): 46–51.

Sheldon, Randall G., John A. Horvath, and Sharon Tracy

    1989   "Do Status Offenders Get Worse? Some Clarifications on the Question of Escalation." *Crime and Delinquency* 35 (April): 202–16.

Shichor, David, and Clemens Bartollas

    1990   "Private and Public Juvenile Placements: Is There a Difference?" *Crime and Delinquency* 36 (April): 286–99.

Shilton, Mary K.

    2000   *Increasing Offender Employment in the Community*. Washington, DC: Center for Community Corrections.

Short, James R., Jr.

    1968   *Gang Delinquency and Delinquent Subcultures*. New York: Harper and Row.

Sickmund, Melissa, Howard Snyder, and Eileen Poe-Yamagata

    1997   *Juvenile Offenders and Victims: 1997 Update on Violence*. Washington, DC: Office of Juvenile Justice and Delinquency Prevention.

Silverman, Ira J.

    2001   *Corrections: Comprehensive View*, 2nd ed. Belmont, CA: Wadsworth.

Silverman, Mitchell

    1994   "Ethical Issues in the Field of Probation." *International Journal of Offender Therapy and Comparative Criminology* 37 (1): 85–94.

Simon, Jonathan

    1993   *Poor Discipline: Parole and Social Control of the Underclass, 1890–1990*. Chicago: University of Chicago Press.

Sinclair, Jim
    1994 "APPA's Public Hearings Explore Probation and Parole's Response to Victims of Crime: Speakers Call for a New Approach to Victim Issues." *Perspectives* (Special Issue): 15–17.

Skidmore, Rex A., Milton G. Thackeray, and O. William Farley
    1988 *Introduction to Social Work*, 4th ed. Upper Saddle River, NJ: Prentice Hall.

Skinner, B. F.
    1972 *Beyond Freedom and Dignity*. New York: Alfred A. Knopf.

Slevin, Peter
    2001 "Prison Firms Seek Inmates and Profits." *Washington Post* (February 18): 3.

Sluder, Richard D., and Rolando del Carmen
    1990 "Are Probation and Parole Officers Liable for Injuries Caused by Probationers and Parolees?" *Federal Probation* 54 (December): 3–12.

Smart, Frances
    1970 *Neuroses and Crime*. New York: Barnes and Noble.

Smith, Carolyn, and Terence C. Thornberry
    1995 "The Relationship between Childhood Maltreatment and Adolescent Involvement in Delinquency." *Criminology* 33 (November): 451–77.

Smith, Michael E.
    2001 *What Future for "Public Safety" and "Restorative Justice" in Community Corrections?* Washington, DC: National Institute of Justice.

Snyder, Howard N., and Melissa Sickmund
    2006 *Juvenile Offenders and Victims: 2006 National Report*. Washington, DC: Office of Justice Programs.

Solomon, Amy, Vera Kachnowski, and Avinash Bhati
    2005 *Does Parole Work?* Washington, DC: The Urban Institute.

Solomon, Jolie
    1998 "Watching Mike." *Newsweek* (March 2): 54–55.

Specht, Harry
    1990 "Social Work and the Popular Psychotherapies." *Social Service Review* 64 (September): 345–57.

Spencer, Herbert
    1961 *The Study of Sociology*. Ann Arbor: University of Michigan Press. (Originally published in 1871.)

Spencer, Jim
    1987 "Knock 'Em Out, Trainee." *Chicago Tribune* (July 26): Sec. 3: 1, 2.

Spitz, Henry I.
    1987 "Cocaine Abuse: Therapeutic Group Approaches," in *Cocaine Abuse: New Directions in Treatment and Research*, edited by Henry I. Spitz and Jeffrey S. Rosecan, pages 156–201. New York: Brunner/Mazel.

Stalans, Loretta J.
    2004 "Adult Sex Offenders on Community Supervision: A Review of Recent Assessment Strategies and Treatment." *Criminal Justice and Behavior* 31 (October): 564–608.

Stampfl, Thomas G.
    1970 "Comment" [on token economies], in *Learning Approaches to Therapeutic Behavior Change*, edited by Donald H. Levis. Chicago: Aldine.

Stanley, David T.

1976 *Prisoners among Us: The Problem of Parole.* Washington, DC: Brookings Institution.

Star, Deborah

1979 *Summary Parole: A Six and Twelve Month Follow-Up Evaluation.* Sacramento: California Department of Corrections.

State Parole Board Annual Report 2005

2006 Trenton: New Jersey State Parole Board.

Steiner, Benjamin, and Emily Wright

2006 "Assessing the Relative Effects of State Direct File Waiver Laws on Violent Juvenile Crime: Deterrence or Irrelevance." *Journal of Criminal Law and Criminology* 96 (Summer): 1451–1478.

Steinhauer, Jennifer

2007 "California to Address Prison Overcrowding with Giant Building Program." *New York Times* (April 27): 18.

Stephan, James J.

2004 State Prison Expenditures, 2001. Washington, DC: Bureau of Justice Statistics.

Stevenson, Carol S., Carol S. Larson, Lucy S. Carter, Deanna S. Gomby, Donna L. Terman, and Richard E. Behrman

1996 "The Juvenile Court: Analysis and Recommendations." *The Future of Children* 6 (Winter): 4–28.

Stille, Alexander

2001 "Grounded by an Income Gap." *New York Times* (December 15): 15, 17.

Stolberg, Sheryl Gay

2001 "Behind Bars, New Effort to Care for the Dying." *New York Times* (April 1): 1, 20.

Stolz, Stephanie B., Louis A. Wienckowski, and Bertram S. Brown

1975 "Behavior Modification: A Perspective on Critical Issues." *American Psychologist* 30 (November).

Storm, John P.

1997 "What United States Probation Officers Do." *Federal Probation* 61 (March): 13–18.

Strong, Ann

1981 *Case Classification Manual, Module One: Technical Aspects of Interviewing.* Austin: Texas Adult Probation Commission.

Sullivan, John, and Matthew Purdy

1995 "In Corrections Business, Shrewdness Pays." *New York Times* (July 23): 1, 13.

Sulzer, Beth, and G. Roy Mayer

1972 *Behavior Modification Procedures for School Personnel.* Hinsdale, IL: Dryden.

Sutherland, Edwin H.

1973 *Edwin Sutherland: On Analyzing Crime,* edited by Karl Schuessler. Chicago: University of Chicago Press.

1972 *The Professional Thief.* Chicago: University of Chicago Press.

Sutton, John R.

1988 *Stubborn Children: Controlling Delinquency in the United States, 1649–1981.* Berkeley: University of California Press.

Swanger, Harry F.

1988   *"Hendrickson v. Griggs*: A Review of the Legal and Policy Implications for Juvenile Justice Policymakers." *Crime and Delinquency* 34 (April): 209–27.

Sydney, Linda M.

2006a   *Gender-Responsive Strategies for Women Offenders*. Washington, DC: National Institute of Corrections.

2006b   "Supervision of Women Defendants and Offenders in the Community." *Perspectives* 30 (Fall): 26–40.

Sykes, Gresham M., and David Matza

1957   "Techniques of Neutralization: A Theory of Delinquency." *American Sociological Review* 22 (December): 664–70.

Takagi, Paul

1975   "The Walnut Street Jail: A Penal Reform to Centralize the Powers of the State." *Federal Probation* 39 (December): 18–26.

Task Force on Corrections

1966   *Task Force Report: Corrections*. Washington, DC: U.S. Government Printing Office.

Taxman, Faye S.

2007   "Reentry and Supervision: One Is Impossible Without the Other." *Corrections Today* (April): 98–101, 105.

2002   "Supervision—Exploring the Dimensions of Effectiveness." *Federal Probation* 66 (September): 14–27.

Taylor, Ian, Paul Walton, and Jock Young

1973   *The New Criminology*. New York: Harper and Row.

Teeters, Negley K.

1970   "The Passing of Cherry Hill: Most Famous Prison in the World." *Prison Journal* 50 (Spring–Summer): 1–12.

Terry, Don

1993   "Town Builds a Prison and Stores Its Hopes There." *New York Times* (January 3): 9.

Texas Adult Probation Commission

1988   *A Comparison of Special Program Probationers and Prison Inmates*. Austin: Texas Adult Probation Commission.

Thalheimer, Donald J.

1975   *Halfway Houses*, Volume 2. Washington, DC: U.S. Government Printing Office.

Therapeutic Community

2002   National Institute on Drug Abuse Research Report. Washington, DC: U.S. Department of Human Services.

Thorne, Gaylord L., Roland G. Tharp, and Ralph J. Wetzel

1967   "Behavior Modification Techniques: New Tools for Probation Officers." *Federal Probation* 31 (June): 21–27.

Thornton, Robert L.

2003   *New Approaches to Staff Safety*. Washington, DC: National Institute of Corrections.

Tims, Frank M., Nancy Jainchill, and George De Leon

1994   "Therapeutic Communities and Treatment Research," in *Therapeutic Community: Advances in Research and Application*, pages 1–15. Rockville, MD: National Institute on Drug Abuse.

Toborg, Mary A., Lawrence J. Carter, Raymond H. Milkman, and Dennis W. Davis

    1978   *The Transition from Prison to Employment: An Assessment of Community-Based Programs.* Washington, DC: U.S. Government Printing Office.

Tonry, Michael

    2006   "Purposes and Functions of Sentencing." *Crime and Justice* 34 (1): Internet.

Torbet, Patricia, Richard Gable, Hunter Hurst IV, Imogene Montgomery, Linda Szymanski, and Douglas Thomas

    1996   *State Responses to Serious and Violent Juvenile Crime.* Washington, DC: Office of Juvenile Justice and Delinquency Prevention.

Torbet, Patricia, Patrick Griffen, Hunter Hurst, Jr., and Lynn Ryan MacKenzie

    2000   *Juveniles Facing Criminal Sanctions: Three States That Changed the Rules.* Washington, DC: Office of Juvenile Justice and Delinquency Prevention.

Torgerson, Fernando G.

    1962   "Differentiating and Defining Casework and Psychotherapy." *Social Casework* 43 (April).

Torres, Sam

    1999   "Early Termination: Outdated Concept in an Era of Punitiveness." *Federal Probation* 63 (June): 35–41.

Toseland, Robert W., and Robert F. Rivas

    1998   *An Introduction to Group Work Practice,* 4th ed. Boston: Allyn and Bacon.

Travis, Jeremy

    2000   *But They All Come Back: Rethinking Prisoner Reentry.* Washington, DC: National Institute of Justice.

Travis, Jeremy, and Joan Petersilia

    2001   "Reentry Reconsidered: A New Look at an Old Question." *Crime and Delinquency* 47 (July): 291–313.

Treaster, Joseph B.

    1994   "Beyond Probation: Breaking the Cycle of Juvenile Arrests." *New York Times* (December 29): 1, 11.

Turner, Susan, and Terry Fain

    2005   *Accomplishments in Juvenile Probation in California over the Last Decade.* Arlington, VA: RAND.

Turner, Susan, and Joan Petersilia

    1996   *Work Release: Recidivism and Corrections Costs in Washington State.* Washington, DC: Office of Justice Programs.

Twentieth Century Fund Task Force on Sentencing

    1976   *Fair and Certain Punishment.* New York: McGraw-Hill.

Umbreit, Mark S.

    1994   *Victim Meets Offender: The Impact of Restorative Justice and Mediation.* Monsey, NY: Willow Tree Press.

Umbreit, Mark S., and Mark Carey

    1995   "Restorative Justice: Implications for Organizational Change." *Federal Probation* 59 (March): 47–54.

Urbina, Ian

    2003   "New York's Federal Judges Protest Sentencing Procedures." *New York Times* (December 8): B1, 4.

U.S. Attorney General

1939 *Attorney General's Survey of Release Procedures: Pardon.* Washington, DC: U.S. Government Printing Office.

U.S. Bureau of Justice Assistance

1989 *Electronic Monitoring in Intensive Probation and Parole Programs.* Washington, DC: U.S. Government Printing Office.

Visher, Christy A., and Jeremy Travis

2003 "Transitions from Prison to Community: Understanding Individual Pathways." *Annual Review of Sociology* 29: 89–113.

Vold, George B., and Thomas J. Bernard

1986 *Theoretical Criminology,* 3rd ed. New York: Oxford University Press.

Von Hirsch, Andrew

1976 *Doing Justice: The Choice of Punishments.* New York: Hill and Wang.

Von Hirsch, Andrew, and Kathleen J. Hanrahan

1978 *Abolish Parole?* Washington, DC: U.S. Government Printing Office.

Wagner, Dennis

1989 "An Evaluation of the High Risk Offender Intensive Supervision Project." *Perspectives* 13 (Summer): 22–27.

Wagner, Dennis, and Christopher Baird

1993 *Evaluation of the Florida Community Control Program.* Washington, DC: National Institute of Justice.

Waldo, Gordon, and David Griswold

1979 "Issues in the Measurement of Recidivism," in *The Rehabilitation of Criminal Offenders: Problems and Prospects,* edited by Lee Sechrest, Susan O. White, and Elizabeth D. Brown. Washington, DC: National Academy of Sciences.

Waldorf, Dan

1973 *Careers in Dope.* Englewood Cliffs, NJ: Prentice Hall.

Walker, Samuel

1980 *Popular Justice: A History of American Criminal Justice.* New York: Oxford University Press.

Washington State Institute for Public Policy (WSIPP)

2006 *Evidence-Based Public Policy Options to Reduce Future Prison Construction, Criminal Justice Costs, and Crime Rates.* Olympia, WA: WSIPP.

Weber, Max

1958 *Protestant Ethic and the Spirit of Capitalism.* New York: Scribner's.

Weed, William Speed

2001 "Incubating Disease." *Mother Jones* (July 10): Internet.

Weisheit, Ralph H., and Diane M. Alexander

1988 "Juvenile Justice and the Demise of Parens Patriae." *Federal Probation* 52 (December): 56–63.

Weiss, Robert P.

2001 " 'Repatriating' Low-Wage Work: The Political Economy of Prison Labor Reprivatization in the Postindustrial United States." *Criminology* 39 (May): 253–91.

Wellisch, Jean, M. Douglas Anglin, and Michael L. Prendergast

1993 "Numbers and Characteristics of Drug-Using Women in the Criminal Justice System: Implications for Treatment." *Journal of Drug Issues* 23 (Winter): 7–30.

West-Smith, Mary, Mark R. Pogrebin, and Eric D. Poole

2000   "Denial of Parole: An Inmate Perspective." *Federal Probation* (December): 3–10.

Whitehead, John T.

1989   "The Effectiveness of Felony Probation: A Replication and Extension of Three Studies." Paper presented at the annual meeting of the American Society of Criminology, Reno, NV, November; reprinted in *Justice Quarterly* 4 (December 1991): 525–43.

Whitehead, John T., Larry T. Miller, and Laura B. Myers

1995   "The Diversionary Effectiveness of Intensive Supervision and Community Corrections Programs," in *Intermediate Sanctions: Sentencing in the 1990s,* edited by John Ortiz Smykla and William Selke, pages 135–51. Cincinnati, OH: Anderson.

Wicker, Tom

1975   *A Time to Die.* New York: Quadrangle.

Widom, Cathy Spatz

1996   "Childhood Sexual Abuse and Its Criminal Consequences." *Society* 33 (May–June): 47–54.

Widom, Cathy S., and Michael G. Maxfield

2001   *An Update on the "Cycle of Violence."* Washington, DC: National Institute of Justice.

Wiebush, Richard G.

1993   "Juvenile Intensive Supervision: The Impact on Felony Offenders Diverted from Institutional Placement." *Crime and Delinquency* 39 (January): 68–89.

Wiebush, Richard G., and Donna M. Hamparian

1991   "Variations in 'Doing' Juvenile Intensive Supervision: Programmatic Issues in Four Ohio Jurisdictions," in *Intensive Interventions with High-Risk Youths in Juvenile Probation and Parole,* edited by Troy L. Armstrong, pages 153–88. Monsey, NY: Criminal Justice Press.

Wiederanders, Mark R.

1983   *Success on Parole.* Sacramento: California Department of Corrections.

Wiggins, Mike

2007   "Couple Charged with Falsely Accusing Parole Officer of Having Sex with Parolees." *Daily Sentinel* (January 25): Internet.

Wilcock, Katherine, Theodore M. Hammett, and Dale G. Parent

1995   *Controlling Tuberculosis in Community Corrections.* Washington, DC: National Institute of Justice.

Wilensky, Harold L., and Charles N. Lebeaux

1958   *Industrial Society and Social Welfare.* New York: Russell Sage Foundation.

Wilson, David B., Leana Allen Bouffard, and Doris L. MacKenzie

2005   "A Quantitative Review of Structured, Group-Oriented, Cognitive-Behavioral Programs for Offenders." *Criminal Justice and Behavior* 32 (April): 172–204.

Wilson, James A., and Robert C. Davis

2006   "Good Intentions Meet Hard Realities: An Evaluation of the Project Greenlight Reentry." *Criminology and Public Policy* 5 (May): 303–38.

Wilson, James Q., and George Kelling

1982   "Broken Windows: The Police and Neighborhood Safety." *Atlantic Monthly* (March). 29–38.

Wines, Frederick Howard

1975   *Punishment and Reformation: A Study of the Penitentiary System.* New York: Thomas Y. Crowell.

Wish, Eric

n.d. *Drug Testing.* Rockville, MD: National Institute of Justice.

Wolf, Thomas J.

1997 "What United States Pretrial Officers Do." *Federal Probation* 61 (March): 19–24.

Wolpe, Joseph, Andrew Salter, and L. H. Reyna, eds.

1964 *The Conditioning Therapies.* New York: Holt, Rinehart and Winston.

Wren, Christopher S.

1998 "Connecticut Bill Cuts Jail Time for Nonviolent Offenders Who Take Frequent Drug Tests." *New York Times* (May 6): 23.

Wright, Martin

1991 *Justice for Victims and Offenders: A Restorative Response to Crime.* Philadelphia: Open University.

Wright, Ronald F.

1998 *Managing Prison Growth in North Carolina through Structured Sentencing.* Washington, DC: National Institute of Justice.

Wubbolding, Robert E.

2000 *Reality Therapy for the 21st Century.* Philadelphia: Taylor and Francis.

Yelloly, Margaret

1980 *Social Work Theory and Psychoanalysis.* New York: Van Nostrand Reinhold.

Yeoman, Barry

2000 "Steeltown." *Mother Jones* (May/June): 38–47.

"Youth Justice, Separate and Unequal"

2000 *Chicago Tribune* editorial (November 21): 22.

Zawitz, Marianne W., ed.

1988 *Report to the Nation on Crime and Justice.* Washington, DC: U.S. Government Printing Office.

Zehr, Howard

1990 *Changing Lenses: A New Focus for Crime and Justice.* Schottdale, PA: Herald Press.

Zehr, Howard, and Harry Mika

1998 "Fundamental Concepts of Restorative Justice." *Contemporary Justice Review* 1 (1): 47–55.

Zevitz, Richard G., and Mary Ann Farkas

2000 "The Impact of Sex-Offender Community Notification on Probation/Parole in Wisconsin." *International Journal of Offender Therapy and Comparative Criminology* 44 (1): 8–21.

Zevitz, Richard G., and Susan R. Takata

1988 "Paroling Prisoners Sentenced to County Jail: An Analysis of 75 Years of Misdemeanor Parole Legislation." *Journal of Criminal Justice* 11: 61–86.

Zielbauer, Paul

2001 "Felons Gain Voting Rights in Connecticut." *New York Times* (May 15): Internet.

Zimring, Franklin E., and Gordon Hawkins

1995 *Incapacitation: Penal Confinement and the Restraint of Crime.* New York: Oxford University Press.

Author Index

Subject Index